A Textbook of
Biological Feedback

A Textbook of
Biological Feedback

Mariella Fischer-Williams *M.D.,*
F.R.C.P. (Edin.)
St. Mary's Hospital, Milwaukee

Alfred J. Nigl *Ph.D.*
Biofeedback Clinic, Lutheran Hospital, Milwaukee

David L. Sovine *M.D.*
Medical College of Wisconsin, Milwaukee

HUMAN SCIENCES PRESS
72 Fifth Avenue   3 Henrietta Street
NEW YORK, NY 10011 ● LONDON, WC2E 8LU

To Patrick, Marie, and Lydia
who kept the home fires burning
during the pilgrims' progress.

Printed in the United States of America
123456789   987654321

Library of Congress Cataloging in Publication Data

Fischer-Williams, Mariella.
  A textbook of biological feedback.

  Includes bibliographical references and index.
   1. Biofeedback training. 2. Medicine, Psychosomatic.
  I. Nigl, Alfred J., joint author. II. Sovine, David L.,
  joint author. III. Title. [DNLM: 1. Biofeedback
  (Psychology) WL103 F529t]
   BF319.5.B5F57   152.1'88   80-15235
   ISBN 0-89885-014-2

Contents

Foreword

THEORIES about the causality and treatment of mental illness and disability are many and varied. The bodies of knowledge involved include biology, psychology, and the social sciences. They must take into account molecular, cellular, enzymatic, biochemical, physiological, genetic, intrapsychic, interpersonal, and social factors. In most instances, the thoughtful and open-minded student or practitioner reaches the conclusion that causality is multifaceted, and that treatment often must include multiple levels and types of understanding which often consciously, sometimes inadvertently, lead to the simultaneous use of various treatment modalities.

Viewpoints about causality and treatment, which may be modified by new information and experience, should be kept open. We are aware that we will probably modify our scientific views and our belief systems a number of times over a clinical practice or research lifetime. The variability and the changes depend on many factors including the stage of development of the science, the state of the field, the influence of current social factors, and the personal style and orientation of the individual. These circumstances make our fields particularly vulnerable to fads because the disorders with which we deal are of uncertain etiology and are very complex. The treatments that we prescribe and deliver often have both specific and nonspecific effects. As a consequence, we have great difficulty estimating accurately both the elements of causality and the effects of our treatments. The individual professional, whatever the orientation or discipline, usually selects from among several alternatives, ones that are felt to be most effective for this particular patient or client under the existing set of circumstances.

This book represents a balanced view of the state of the science and art of biofeedback. The authors present strongly, but fairly and without prejudice, the current evidence for biofeedback's scientific basis and its usefulness. They provide the psychological disciplines with a long-needed review and synthesis of biofeedback. They use several different approaches to accomplish their objectives. They examine the anatomical and neurophysiological knowledge which forms the biological basis. They place biofeedback in its proper learning and behavioral

13

theory context emphasizing both psychological and social issues. They review relaxation techniques including hypnosis, meditation, and imagery. They approach the theory and the practice comprehensively through organismic, organ system, diagnostic, symptomatic, and treatment approaches. They report and evaluate the literature so that a practitioner may use this text as a guide for further investigation seeking greater understanding about the practices and the extent of the evidence. They make easier the entry and the investigation in depth of a very complex field.

As a consequence of these ambitious and successful efforts, the authors have done much more. They provide a valuable review of important data and experience that will be useful to many practitioners whose interests are not primarily in biofeedback. They place this field in the context of the several scientific fields. This book becomes, therefore, a more general review of many aspects of our fields which are much broader than biofeedback. Thus, at many points the authors strive for a more comprehensive exposition and understanding while maintaining their focus on biofeedback.

The various scientific and practice fields and disciplines need this book to summarize and to direct their attention to and consideration of a very complicated scientific and therapeutic scene. The authors have succeeded in this effort and are to be commended for this valuable contribution.

Robert S. Daniels, M.D.
Professor of Psychiatry and
Dean, College of Medicine
University of Cincinnati
November 1, 1979

Preface

MAN is full of curiosity, particularly in regard to himself.* A technique that enables an individual to receive information about his own physiological responses excites that curiosity. When this information is fed back concurrently ("on-line") to the individual from whom the responses originated so that he appreciates it as his own activity which is being mirrored, then there is heightened interest in the technique. The very nature of the procedure, which opens a "window" into one's own responses to external and internal stimuli, is attractive to many people. Through the method of recording ongoing activity in, for example, the muscles, the heart, or the blood vessels of the skin, and translating this activity into an auditory or visual scale, the subject can be given the opportunity to modify or *alter* (within a certain range) whatever activity is being monitored. As with all techniques, this may be used well or it may be used ill. The various uses are delineated in this book.

Biofeedback, i.e., the feedback of biological data, is, however, more than a technique. It involves a different way for an individual to observe his ongoing processes. It allows him to translate emotionally charged physiological events into an immediate symbol (a number, a tone, or a visual representation). Few physiological processes do not carry an emotional charge to a greater or lesser extent. If man is curious about his physiological functions (e.g., eating, drinking, and motor activity), he is probably even more curious about the emotions that lead him to eat, drink, and behave from a motor point of view in a particular way.

Hence biofeedback offers a fusion of the psyche and soma duality in a way previously not often attained. In medicine throughout the centuries, the study of physical and of psychological events proceeded along parallel lines without significant correlation. It was as though these two sets of data stood parallel to each other but separate; they were like the upright bars of a ladder. Biofeedback supplies the cross bars or rungs of the ladder so that the two types of events can be linked together. There are of course many gaps in our knowledge, but

*For simplicity of style, the male pronoun is used to represent both sexes throughout the book.

15

bridges at strategic points translate information from one part of ourselves to another part more freely than before.

Biofeedback involves the subject in rigorous training, requiring constraints together with motivation to accept change. To teach, guide,
and supervise this training safely and effectively, appropriate medical
and physiological preparation and certification are essential for the
practitioner.

Biofeedback is a tool, not a master. The doctor-patient relationship
is still the primary healing agent. When this relationship is satisfactory,
the training in biofeedback will be valuable to the patient so that he
may choose his own adjustments to a life situation. If the personal
relationship does not bring harmony, then the training through the
intervention of a machine will not have the same potential for content-
ment. While recognizing the ambivalence and the paradoxes of doctor
patient relationships, the practical aspects of treatment are mainly
considered here.

Biofeedback training is not a panacea. It is suitable for only certain
situations. Throughout the book, we have tried to supply background
information upon which proper judgment may be based in deciding
whether or not to offer biofeedback to a particular patient. It has been
used as a clinical tool since the late 1960s, and it can therefore be
considered a "young" procedure as treatment in a clinical situation.
More research is required to consolidate gains.

Although a recent advance, biofeedback has developed from traditional and well-established schools, both in the physical and in the
psychologic domain; it has not originated de novo. The historical
perspective and the sources of the theory of fusion of the psyche and
the soma are outlined throughout the text.

Biofeedback may be regarded as a "mirror" whereby the practitioner enables the patient to view his own responses to internal and
external forces. Like all mirrors, the image may be realistic or distorted, but in either case the viewer risks the advent of a new attitude.

There is always the hope, though it may be in vain, that reading a
book is like writing a book, something of a creation or an experiment
in creation. We trust that in silent dialogue an idea or two is sparked
off on the road. We write, imagining ourselves as the readers, and we
invite readers to imagine themselves as the writers. There is a tendency
for people to "believe" what they see in print. We invite the reader to
ponder the printed word but not to endow it with more than it claims
to be, namely a form of communication. Most people have a need for
both order and disorder, and there is, therefore, a constant desire to

throw facts up in the air and to rearrange them when they fall down like confetti.

There are two types of useful ideas or concepts in science: first, those which are subsequently shown to be "true" and which continue to exist as "facts," like the elucidation of the pulmonary circulation by Michael Servetus (1546), and second, those which subsequently may be shown to be "false" or only "partially true," like the concept of the brain centrencephalic system of Penfield and Jasper (1954). Both types of ideas or concepts act as stepping stones for investigators. Both types generate experimentation because of the challenge to "prove" whether or not they are true. At this juncture, it appears that biofeedback is the treatment of choice in certain disorders and the evidence for this statement is discussed in the text. We respect and recommend, however, the acceptance of transience.

M. F.-W.

REFERENCES

Penfield W, Jasper HH: *Epilepsy and the Functional Anatomy of the Human Brain.* Boston, Little, Brown, 1954.
Servetus, M: *Christianismi Restitutio* (fifth book), 1546.

Acknowledgments

IN the preparation of any book, many more people are involved in its conception and birthing than are listed on the title page. Like others we would like to show our appreciation to those who helped us during this project.

To Stanley Block, M.D., Vice President of the Jewish Hospital, Cincinnati, Ohio, a respected teacher and friend who allowed us to use materials from his course on the history of psychiatry for the background to our historical appendix.

To Stephen Duck, M.D., of Childrens Hospital, Milwaukee, Wisconsin, who spent valuable hours going over and revising our concepts of endocrinology for Chapter 16.

To Thomas Passo, M.D., of Danville, Illinois, a highly respected cardiologist, colleague, and good friend, for his excellent criticisms and helpful comments concerning the material in Chapter 13.

To Joe W. Sovine, M.D., an internist in Indianapolis, Indiana, who carefully, usefully, and untiringly commented on the medical content of our chapters to our benefit.

To Walter McDermott, Ph.D., of the psychology department of the Medical College of Wisconsin, a valued friend and also a practitioner and fellow student in the science of biofeedback, who gave us unflagging support and suggestions for this project from its inception onwards.

To Rick Rubow, Ph.D., President-elect of the Biofeedback Society of Wisconsin, a leading researcher and clinician in the field of biofeedback, who gave us his intellectual support and greatly assisted us in conceptualizing several important issues in biofeedback.

To Stephen F. Emily, Ph.D., of the Milwaukee Developmental Center, of Shorewood, Wisconsin, also a student and practitioner of biofeedback who spent much time reviewing the research sections of several chapters.

To George R. Jacobson, Ph.D., Director of Research, Evaluation and Training, DePaul Rehabilitation Hospital, Milwaukee, Wisconsin, who gave us our first tangible encouragement toward the efforts that follow.

To Patrick Werner who synthesized with unfailing patience American English and "British" into one.

To Ruth B. Russell, Institute of International Affairs, University of California (Berkeley), for her valuable comments regarding the literary style of several of the chapters. Her assistance in making needed modifications in grammar and style was greatly appreciated.

To Cheryl Hagbath (Registered EEG Tech.) and Paul Nuccio, who helped greatly in the compilation of the literature.

To Basil M. Jackson, M.D., Ph.D., and the staff of Jackson Psychiatric Center, Milwaukee, Wisconsin, for their administrative and clerical assistance.

To Evonne Kinowski, our medical artist, for the illustrations in Chapters 13 and 14.

To our tireless and patient assistants, Elaine Cattanach, Marie Nigl, and Audrey Zavodski, all of Milwaukee, Wisconsin, without whose excellent organizational, clerical, and typing skills this book would not have been possible.

1

The Development of Biofeedback

RECENT technological advances in electrophysiology have increased the possibilities for individuals to control events within themselves. The term *biofeedback* is used to describe a technique wherein an individual can learn to control such physiological functioning. It involves the electronic measurement of one or more bodily functions. This information is then instantaneously fed back to the person. Although previously used as a research tool, biofeedback technique after 1969, following the first meeting of the Biofeedback Society of America (BSA) (formerly the Biofeedback Research Society) became recognized as more than an experimental procedure.

Regardless of the nature of the feedback or the clinical application, biofeedback usually involves the same two elements: (1) concomitant monitoring of a specific physiological response, and (2) immediate presentation to the patient of that response. Physiological information is usually transmitted to the patient via a visual or an auditory signal (or both). The creation of this time-bound electrophysiological loop, often referred to as the "biocybernetic loop," (Green and Green, 1979) is the common denominator of a number of seemingly, disparate techniques.

A distinction must be made between biofeedback and other terms which have the prefix "bio," e.g., "biorhythms" and "bioenergetics." Some of these terms have more scientific validity than others. There is no connection between the term *biorhythm* and biofeedback; biorhythm is a faddish belief system which is loosely based on human circadian rhythms. There is no scientific evidence, however, that biorhythms have any validity in predicting or controlling human behavior.

Definition

Because of the variety of techniques and applications that have developed over the last decade, it is difficult to arrive at a single definition of biofeedback. Basmajian (1979) defined biofeedback as:

the technique of using equipment (usually electronic) to reveal to human beings some of their internal physiological events, normal and abnormal, in the form of visual and auditory signals in order to teach them to manipulate these otherwise involuntary or unfelt events by manipulating the displayed signals. This technique inserts a person's volition into the gap of an open feedback loop — hence the artificial name biofeedback, a name that some scientists and clinicians abhor for linguistic and other reasons (p. 1).

Although this statement is a comprehensive description of what occurs during biofeedback training, it does not define the specific processes that underlie an individual's acquisition of physiological control.

Most theorists agree that biofeedback is a special process of learning. An individual, through the experience of receiving sensory information about his own somatic processes, can learn to modify these functions at a conscious level.

Biofeedback is linked to the experimental tradition underlying other types of learning therapy, e.g., behavior modification or systematic desensitization. Biofeedback developed as a result of increased knowledge in the science of human behavior. In order to comprehend how biofeedback originated, it is important to analyze its relationship with other forms of learning therapy, and recent texts have focused on its development in terms of both behavioral medicine and psychology (e.g., Yates, 1980).

This chapter is concerned with the development of biofeedback and its relationship with psychological learning theory. Later chapters discuss biofeedback's relationship to neurology and psychiatry.

Biofeedback and Learning Theory

Several theoretical models of biofeedback have been developed, and many authors have emphasized that biofeedback is a special form of learning.

Although few would deny that learning occurs in biofeedback, it is not clear how this takes place. Conditioning theory has been applied to explain how individuals learn to control physiological events by receiving feedback. The feedback is considered to be positively reinforcing to the individual. McGuigan (1973), however, points out that this hypothesis has no empirical validation; "it has not been established that external feedback . . . has the properties of a reinforcing stimulus" (p. 202).

It appears that patients can learn to control physiological events when strict rules of conditioning are modified or violated (Rubow, 1979). The development of biofeedback treatment, however, is linked closely to the growth of covert conditioning research. According to McGuigan, researchers have attempted to condition nonobservable, or covert, behavior for many years but were hampered by the lack of sensitive recording instruments. With more sophisticated electronic devices, research was done on covert learning and conditioning. Biofeedback developed as a by-product of this research when it became apparent that individuals could learn control of physiological responses.

Although learning theorists are still searching for theoretical explanations of the method, clinicians have concentrated on improving the technique as a treatment method. For better understanding of the biofeedback learning process, a review of learning theory and research is necessary.

Learning and Conditioning

In 1898, with the publication of *Animal Intelligence,* Edward Thorndike (1874–1949) developed a systematic psychological theory of learning. Thorndike's theory emphasized a connection between "stimulus and response," or "S-R." His best known hypothesis is the "Law of Effect," which states that if a response is followed by a reward, the learning of this response is strengthened. Conversely, if a response is followed by punishment, this reduces the tendency to repeat that response. Because Thorndike used terms such as "satisfying" and "annoying" to stand for reward and punishment, he alienated many who found his theory too subjective.

Thorndike's learning theory also included the "Law of Readiness," which concerns the physiological circumstances which help learning to take place. He recognized the neurophysiological basis of learning and viewed the organism as being prepared or having a potential for action prior to the learning of a response. Although Thorndike was unable to specify the neuroanatomical mechanisms involved, he was accurate in his belief that, once a potential for action was created, completion of the act led to a feeling of satisfaction, while noncompletion led to frustration.

The probable electrophysiological accompaniment of this psychological event was described much later by Grey Walter (1964) as the "expectancy wave" or contingent negative variation, (see Chap. 2).

Thorndike observed that the positive effect of a reward tends to generalize to other stimuli which are associated with the reinforcing stimulus. This phenomenon was entitled the "Spread of Effect." Although not always validated by later research, Thorndike's hypotheses stimulated others to investigate the generalization of reinforcement.

The behavioral tradition in the psychology of learning originated with the publication of John B. Watson's (1878–1958) *Behavior: An Introduction to Comparative Psychology* (1914). Watson, and most behaviorally oriented researchers since then, believed that laws of learning should be based only on what can be observed. In his search for a behavioristic model, Watson adopted the "conditioned reflex theory" of the Russian physiologists, Pavlov and Bekhterev (Hilgard and Bower, 1966). In the Pavlovian experiment, salivatory responses in laboratory animals (dogs) were conditioned to a bell and other stimuli. This type of learning or conditioning is referred to as "classical conditioning," in which an unconditional stimulus is presented first, followed by an involuntary response. Stimuli that accompany this unconditioned stimulus can elicit similar responses over time.

Skinner's Operant Conditioning

Following Watson, experimental psychologists, e.g., Guthrie (1935) and Hull (1943), expanded the notion that learning proceeds through a process of classical conditioning. Stimulus-Response (S-R) theory predominated in the behavioristic approach to learning until Skinner proposed a distinction between "respondent" and "operant" behavior. Up to that point, learning research had failed to yield practical methods of modifying human behavior. The development of Skinner's operant conditioning theory, however, stimulated the growth of behavior therapy (Yates, 1970). In many respects, biofeedback is the most recent form of behavior therapy. Skinner, however, was not interested in the therapeutic application of his operant principles; especially techniques that involved nonobserved or covert variables.

Skinner termed the responses elicited by specific stimuli "respondents." Respondents usually occur automatically and reflexly. The animals in Pavlov's experiment, for example, did not have any control over their salivation (respondent) when stimulated by a meat powder.

"Operant" responses, on the other hand, are not automatically linked to one particular stimulus but to a class of similar reinforcing events. The bar-pressing behavior (i.e., reward seeking) of a laboratory animal may be reinforced by many different forms of stimulation, including food, water, and interruption of an aversive electric shock.

These two classes of responses correspond to two types of learning or conditioning. Skinner referred to the conditioning of respondent behavior as "classical" or "Type S" conditioning. In this model, the conditioned stimulus (e.g., a light) occurs coincidentally with the unconditioned stimulus (e.g., meat powder), and together they elicit an unconditioned response (e.g., salivation). After a number of paired stimulus presentations, the light, by itself, can cause the animal to salivate (the conditioned response), although the salivation is less than when meat powder is used. It can be said, therefore, that the animal "learned" to salivate in response to a light; the conditioned stimulus led to a conditioned response.

In contrast, the second type of learning involves the strengthening of a response because it is followed by a reward or reinforcement. Skinner called this type of learning "operant" or "Type R" conditioning. For example, is an infant's chortling is followed by positive parental behavior, e.g., smiling or stroking, the infant is more likely to chortle in the future. In this case, the reinforcement (positive parental behavior) is contingent, or dependent, upon the infant's vocalizations (operant response). One of the basic laws of operant conditioning is similar to Thorndike's "Law of Effect." Skinner (1938) stated that, "if the occurrence of an operant is followed by a presentation of a reinforcing stimulus, the strength is increased" (p. 21). Skinner, however, unlike Thorndike, was not interested in whether or not the reinforcing stimulus *satisfies* the organism nor did he believe in the strengthening of S-R bonds and connections. Operant responses, he felt, stand alone and are not directly linked to any specific stimuli (Hilgard and Bower, 1966).

Skinner, in 1938, suggested a physiological difference between classical and operant conditioning. He proposed that classical conditioning may be limited to responses of the autonomic nervous system (ANS), while operant learning involved only the skeletal muscle responses of the central nervous system (CNS). The later development of autonomic system learning, however, i.e., biofeedback, proved his theory inadequate.

Skinner differentiated between two general types of reinforcers: "positive" and "negative". Positive reinforcers are thought to strengthen the probability of the response they follow, while negative reinforcers are reinforcing because of their absence from a situation; operant responses which result in the removal or elimination of noxious stimuli are said to be reinforced negatively.

In an example of positive reinforcement, social approval is given to a student by his parents for a good report card. In contrast, another student might try hard to receive good grades in order to avoid parental criticism. This student would be achieving because of negative reinforcement. Other examples of these two types of reinforcement are found in Table 1–1.

Schedules of Reinforcement

Ferster and Skinner (1957) delineated the various ways in which reinforcing stimuli can affect the operant responses upon which they are contingent. Outside the laboratory, however, there is no uniformity in the timing of operant behavior. Individuals do not receive a reinforcement every time they produce a response; they are therefore receiving "intermittent reinforcement." Skinner identified two classes of reinforcement: "interval reinforcement" and "ratio reinforcement." Both types of reinforcement can be given under either preset (fixed) conditions or random (variable) conditions. "Fixed-interval reinforcement" is defined as reinforcement which is given periodically at predetermined times, e.g., a reward may be given every five minutes. Feedback from a visual display presents information on a fixed interval schedule; for example, an instrument that measures muscle activity such as the electromyograph (EMG). Certain EMG instruments can be calibrated so that the information is averaged over a range of time intervals, e.g., from 0.5 to 240.0 seconds. The digital display of the interval average is contingent on the activity (muscle relaxation) which is being learned. "Fixed ratio reinforcement" is defined as reinforcement which is presented after a predetermined number of responses have been received, e.g., one reinforcement for every ten responses.

Variable schedules of the fixed or ratio type may be employed in order to stabilize the response rate. For both the ratio and interval schedules, responses tend to lessen following reinforcement once the subject becomes aware of the schedule. The use of "variable-interval" or "variable-ratio" schedules of reinforcement results in a more stable response rate and a smoother learning curve. For information regarding operant conditioning, readers are advised to consult texts of learning theory, e.g., *Theories of Learning* by Hilgard and Bower (1966).

Behavior Therapy

The therapeutic application of theories of learning has been referred to either as "behavior modification" or "behavior therapy" (Yates, 1970).

TABLE 1-1. POSITIVE AND NEGATIVE REINFORCERS

Operant responses	Reinforcing stimulus	Type of reinforcement
1. Putting 20¢ in vending machine	Chocolate bar	Positive
2. Putting on warm gloves	Extreme cold	Negative
3. Turning on lamp switch	Light for reading	Positive
4. Turning down thermostat	Extreme heat	Negative

The term *behavior modification* is used primarily to describe mechanistic, operant conditioning programs, which are carried out under highly structured conditions to modify specific behaviors. An example of this might be an institutional program where schizophrenic patients obtain tokens for appropriate behaviors which they can then exchange for rewards, e.g., weekend passes or other privileges, and is referred to as a "token economy." The term *behavior therapy,* however, is used to describe a variety of psychotherapeutic methods based on theories of learning. Aubrey Yates (1970) attributed the development of behavior therapy to the combined influence of Pavlovian and Skinnerian theories of learning. Although behavior therapy techniques are fairly recent, attempts to modify behavior using learning techniques have existed since at least 1920. Table 1-2 illustrates the wide variety of early therapeutic applications of learning theory which were identified by Yates.

Although behavior therapy originated as a limited method of modifying activity, it soon evolved into a comprehensive system of therapy. Three major advances in learning research and theory have furthered the development of behavior therapy. These developments will be reviewed separately.

Albert Bandura (1969) and his colleagues demonstrated that children and adults could learn vicariously, that is, without receiving direct reinforcement. In their classic study, Bandura and Mischel (1965) presented films to children in which a person (called a "model") received a reward for a specific pattern of behavior. Children who viewed the film reproduced the behavior of the model although they did not receive any reinforcement. This type of learning was called "observational learning" or "modeling." Later experiments with various learning paradigms expanded the "social learning theory" (Miller and Dollard, 1941).

TABLE 1-2. EARLY ATTEMPTS TO MODIFY
BEHAVIOR USING LEARNING PRINCIPLES*

Disorder	Author/year
Sexual perversion	Bekhterev, 1923
Anxiety	Harris, 1934
Tics, stuttering, etc.	Dunlap, 1932
Children's fears	Watson & Raynor, 1920
Homosexuality	Max, 1935
Enuresis	Krasnogorski, 1933
Narcolepsy	Levin, 1934
Hysteria	Marinesco, 1937
Alcoholism	Ichok, 1934
Depression	Ivan-Smolensky, 1928

*Based on Yates (1970), Table 1.1, p. 14. For complete information regarding these references, please consult Yates (1970). Reproduced with permission.

Several behavior therapy techniques have arisen from this observational learning. In the modeling treatment of phobias (Bandura, Grusec and Menlove, 1967), the patient observes a model positively confronting a situation or specific stimulus that triggers the patient's fear response, and modeling approaches to verbal therapy (Marlatt et al., 1966), where patients are exposed to video or audio tapes of "good" therapeutic interaction prior to beginning individual or group therapy.

Kanfer and Phillips (1970) noted that certain well-established therapies are based, in part, on modeling or simulation experiences; for example, "psychodrama" techniques involve "acting-out" of personal problems with feedback from the therapist and patient observers. Kelly's (1955) "fixed role therapy" involves the patients' exploration of new behavioral responses which are practiced with the therapist. "Role playing," "behavioral rehearsal," or "behavioristic psychodrama" are methods developed by behavior therapists (Lazarus, 1966) to help patients assume different behaviors in difficult situations. In behavioral rehearsal, the therapist often acts out the role of a person who stimulates anxiety for the patient, while the patient tries to respond without anxiety. Lazarus (1966) reported that 92 percent of 75 patients treated with behavioral rehearsal noted beneficial changes in their behaviors in anxiety-provoking situations.

In some respects, biofeedback techniques also involve aspects of modeling or observational learning. For example, the patient learns how to react to various physiological events, which are fed back to him, by observing the biofeedback therapist's responses. In other words, the therapist's verbal approval of the patient's ability to reduce physiological arousal informs the patient how to react to a reduction of tension.

Research on self-control, especially in children, led to the second major advance in learning theory. Kanfer (1966) and others observed that children could learn to reinforce themselves rather than rely on external reinforcers to control their behavior.

Various therapeutic techniques have been developed based on self-regulation theories advanced by Kanfer (1966), Homme (1965), and others. Applications of "self-control therapy" have had success with such behavioral disorders as psychogenic morbid obesity, smoking, and sexual disorders. In "contingency management," the patient is taught to exercise self-control through the use of covert verbal responses or *coverants* (Homme, 1965). Other techniques designed to increase self-control include "self-administered shock" to treat fetishes (McGuire and Vallance, 1964), "self-monitoring" (Rutner and Bugle, 1969) and "contract management" (Sulzer, 1962).

Biofeedback methods are often considered to be self-control techniques and therefore are theoretically linked to self-control paradigms developed by behavior therapists over the past two decades.

The third major area of study in this field is "cognitive behavior therapy." Arnold Lazarus (1972) and others expanded Skinner's theory of conditioning and reinforcement to include "nonobserved (covert) events," such as an individual's thoughts, feelings, and images. Joseph Cautela (1972) went one step further and created therapeutic methods based on the concept that thoughts and other internal "responses" could be operantly conditioned. The same learning principles that Skinner used to modify covert responses of laboratory animals were applied in an attempt to refashion an individual's thoughts and cognitive activities. Such methods include "covert positive reinforcement" and "covert sensitization" (see Chap. 19).

In covert positive reinforcement, a subject is taught to imagine something positive after thinking of himself performing a desired behavior. For example, if the patient with limited social skills has high "social anxiety," the desired response may be to approach a stranger and initiate a conversation. The patient imagines this scene with guidance from the therapist who then instructs him to imagine a scene which gives him pleasure, for example, lying on a beach on a summer's day.

Covert sensitization involves the application of negative or noxious imagery. For example, a patient who overeats in response to environmental stimuli is asked to visualize himself vomiting and becoming ill after imagining a meal of desirable, but nonnutritious food. Although these methods supposedly work on the basis of conditioning, several authors have questioned this assumption. For example, Steffen (1974) and Nigl (1975) have both indicated that these techniques may involve the enhancement of memory and improve information processing but have little, or nothing, to do with operant conditioning. (The same point could be made regarding the "conditioning" effect in biofeedback.)

In reviewing covert sensitization research, Lichstein and Hung (1980) indicated that the conditioning model for this technique appears weak. One of the major methodological problems concerns the short duration of physiological effects (ANS arousal) in response to aversive imagery. The authors point out, however, that covert sensitization is relatively easy to administer and 49 of 56 studies surveyed reported that the patients' symptoms had improved. The serious theoretical/methodological problems that Lichstein and Hung identified (e.g., subject expectancy, impotence of aversive imagery and lack of improvement compared to attention-placebo conditions) with respect to covert sensitization, should be considered when evaluating the results of other covert or cognitive therapies.

Joseph Wolpe (1973) also developed a behavioral technique, "systematic desensitization" to treat phobias and other disorders involving fear (response to external threat) and anxiety (response to internal threat). His technique did not originate directly from psychological learning theory, however, but from his own interpretation of conditioning. Wolpe's original contention was that the pairing of images of feared events with deep relaxation led to the reduction of physiological arousal through the process of "counterconditioning." The relaxation response supposedly counterconditioned muscular tension which was originally conditioned by fear. After treatment, the images of feared events would no longer cause physiological tension or arousal. Therefore, the person would then be able to confront his fears directly and eliminate the phobia. Extensive research has failed to support Wolpe's theory, however. There has been no empirical support for the idea that counterconditioning is an important factor in the success of systematic desensitization, which is considered, by many authors, to be one of serveral cognitive techniques that can be used to reduce anxiety and apprehension.

The term *cognitive behavior therapy* has been adopted by many clinicians today to describe a particular form of treatment. The term implies that cortical phenomena can be modified through the application of learning principles. Since biofeedback requires some coordination between peripheral and cortical responses, its development can be viewed as a synthesis of the mechanistic (operant conditioning) and humanistic (cognitive behavior therapy) traditions within the field of applied learning theory.

Biofeedback: A New Therapeutic Technique

From a learning perspective, biofeedback can be viewed as originating from two separate, but parallel, lines of development. First, the intensification of research into the conditioning of covert events and second, the development of covert behavior therapy. Although feedback of physiological responses was first used as a laboratory technique to determine if covert conditioning could be demonstrated empirically, biofeedback's clinical potential gradually became apparent. Therapists who were interested in applying learning principles to modify behavior (especially covert, or nonobservable, responses) adopted biofeedback methods to enhance the effectiveness of their treatment.

Several types of biofeedback are currently used in clinical practice. *Electromyographic* (or EMG) biofeedback involves the measurement of electrical potential from the muscles; usually the forearm extensor or frontalis muscles. *Electrothermal* (or temperature) biofeedback measures skin temperature from the digits (fingers or toes). Skin temperature from the digits is thought to be a reliable indicator of peripheral vasodilatation (or vasoconstriction).

Electrodermal (or EDR) biofeedback involves the measurement of tonic or phasic changes in the electrical activity or responses of the skin, usually of the hands, which is related to anxiety or physiological arousal. The clinical efficacy of other forms of biofeedback which have also been developed has not yet been established. Examples of these include cardiovascular, EEG (electroencephalographic) and blood pressure biofeedback.

Early Research

Edmund Jacobson in 1908 developed the progressive muscle relaxation technique. (1958). Although most of his research on the conditioning of muscle relaxation was conducted 50 years ago, it remains relevant. For example, most therapeutic applications of biofeedback include the use of a systematic relaxation technique. Although Jacobson's system has been modified over time, his ideas and research methods have much to offer clinicians and researchers. Based on an interview reported by McGuigan, he may have been the first researcher to use medical instrumentation to provide feedback about physiological responses (Jacobson and McGuigan, 1978). His procedure, employing a prototype of modern biofeedback instrumentation, involved an individual observing an oscilloscope to determine the level of tension in his forearm extensor muscle. Later, Wolpe (1973) modified Jacobson's technique and popularized it as part of the systematic desensitization procedure.

In 1958, Kamiya (1969) began to study the changes in consciousness that accompanied variations in EEG alpha rhythm of human subjects. He developed a discrimination conditioning task in which a bell was rung periodically and the subject was requested to indicate if he had been generating EEG alpha just prior to the auditory stimulus. Many subjects were able to learn this task and this led to further research of alpha rhythm control. Kamiya and his associates later discovered that subjects could suppress alpha when given auditory feedback concerning its presence or absence. Although the initial claims of alpha wave trainers were found to be exaggerated, research by Kamiya and others continues and may eventually lead to the development of more effective clinical methods. Due to the unpredictability of the results so far, the clinical utility of EEG alpha rhythm training remains problematic (Miller, 1974).

Ancoli and Kamiya (1978) reviewed several areas of controversy surrounding EEG biofeedback. For example, one unresolved issue is whether or not the reported increases in EEG alpha are due to reductions in visual and oculomotor responding. Ancoli and Kamiya reviewed 45 different EEG biofeedback studies from 1968 to 1976 and concluded that a majority of the studies suffered from methodological weaknesses. They believed that many negative results occurred because training times were too short and experimental conditions were not optimum. They suggest that, in the future, researchers should employ at least 4 training sessions, used continuous feedback with quantitative progress scores and use experimental trials which have a duration of at least 10 minutes.

One of the intriguing areas of investigation concerns the search for empirical validation of visceral or smooth-muscle operant conditioning. Since 1938, when Skinner could not demonstrate operant conditioning of the vasoconstrictory responses, researchers have been interested in this area of learning.

Neal Miller and his colleagues (most notably, the late Leo DiCara) have been involved in research on instrumental autonomic conditioning in animals for a number of years. In 1968, DiCara and Miller observed that curarized rats could learn to avoid a shock by lowering their heart rate. Miller's attempts to replicate this finding in subsequent years, however, met with frustration. Nevertheless, during this time other investigators showed that visceral conditioning, through the use of feedback techniques, could be demonstrated in man (Miller and Dworkin, 1974).

Whether or not Miller's original findings were artifactual or due to complex interactions of variables is still undetermined. There is no doubt, however, that the publication of his early research on visceral conditioning in animals did much to stimulate others to investigate similar issues in man, and more sophisticated biofeedback techniques were developed.

Although less well known, H. D. Kimmel (1960) spent years investigating instrumental conditioning of the autonomic nervous system (ANS) in man. Stimulated by results of earlier experiments in conditioning of the galvanic skin response (GSR), Kimmel and his students found that subjects' GSRs could be conditioned using pleasant odors. Kimmel (1974) summarized the research up to 1967, including 16 studies of GSR, five of heart rate, and three of the vasomotor response. Results of all these studies supported the contention that the ANS could be modified through operant conditioning.

These findings were criticized by Katkin and Murray (1968) who argued that such results may be due to skeletal or cognitive mediation of changes in autonomic behavior. However, many studies have controlled for various cognitive and skeletal mediators and have still obtained positive results. For example, Lang and Melamed (1969) were able to condition aversively a 9-month-old child who suffered from ruminative vomiting. In addition, Frezza and Holland (1971) demonstrated that human salivation can be instrumentally conditioned.

Subsequently biofeedback procedures were applied to clinical problems. In 1973, two innovative treatment procedures were developed which are widely used today, with certain technical refinements. Elmer and Alyce Green (1977) developed a clinical protocol for thermal feedback training. They used peripheral skin temperature as a measure of vasodilatation and combined skin temperature feedback with Schultz and Luthe's (1969) "Autogenic Training" (see Chap. 3). Sargent, Green, and Walters (1972) applied temperature biofeedback training to treat migraine. Patients were taught to increase the warmth in their fingers (vasodilatation) while decreasing the temperature of their foreheads (vasoconstriction). They found that almost 75 percent of the subjects were able to decrease both the duration and intensity of migraine attacks. Later studies have confirmed these results (see Chap. 7).

While the Greens were developing their treatment technique for migraine, Thomas Budzynski (1973) and his associates at the University of Colorado developed a feedback technique to treat muscle contraction (tension) headaches. They used EMG training to teach patients to reduce the tension in their frontalis (forehead) muscles. Their results showed that average muscle tension levels dropped from 10 to 3.5 μv (microvolts) and headache intensity was reduced over the 16-week training period. Two control groups of headache patients were employed in the experimental design; one group received "false" or pseudofeedback and the other group received no feedback at all. Neither of these groups improved as much as the EMG treatment group. Since then, the results have been somewhat mixed regarding the effectiveness of EMG biofeedback compared with simple relaxation methods. This will be further discussed in Chapters 7 and 11.

The clinical research which has been reviewed thus far has involved procedures where feedback is used to reduce muscle and blood vessel contraction ("physiological arousal"); however, a technique to increase muscle contraction (a form of EMG biofeedback training) has existed for almost 25 years. John Basmajian's (1979) early research, first published in 1963, indicated that patients can increase the functioning of single motor units through the use of EMG biofeedback. Even earlier, Marinacci and Horande (1960) demonstrated that EMG feedback could be applied to improve neuromuscular functioning in several disorders. Basmajian and his colleagues have designed specially constructed biofeedback instruments for use in rehabilitation, e.g., a miniature EMG feedback device. They have applied such instrumentation to various disorders including paralytic foot-drop. There is significant difference between the EMG units used in rehabilitation and those adapted for use with psychophysiological disorders. The biofeedback units employed in rehabilitation are designed to transmit information about single motor units or the functioning of a specific muscle. Most of the EMG units used to enhance relaxation, however, summate the bioelectrical information of a particular muscle group. The resulting feedback is somewhat less specific.

Prior to 1970, relatively few studies were conducted using biofeedback techniques. Since then, however, hundreds of investigations have been done and the accumulation of data has been impressive. For this reason, BSA task forces were developed to survey the current literature and summarize the current status of biofeedback as a therapeutic technique in a number of areas including: psychophysiological disorders (Fotopoulos and Sunderland, 1978), gastrointestinal disease (Whitehead, 1978), vascoconstrictive disorders (Taub and Stroebel, 1978), muscle tension headache (Budzynski, 1978), and others.

In summary, individuals in certain circumstances can learn to control various physiologic processes as a result of biofeedback training. There is still considerable confusion and controversy regarding how this learning takes place, however. Biofeedback can be viewed as developing from earlier forms of learning therapy. However whether or not biofeedback involves a form of conditioning is still undetermined.

The following chapters will show how biofeedback (though derived from a multiplicity of sources) may be a useful therapeutic procedure which can be successfully applied to a wide variety of human disorders.

REFERENCES

Ancoli S, Kamiya J: Methodological issues in alpha biofeedback training. Biofeedback Self-Reg 3: 159–183, 1978.

Bandura A: *Principles of Behavior Modification.* New York, Holt, 1969.

Bandura A, Mischel W: Modification of self-imposed delay of reward through exposure to live and symbolic models. J Pers Soc Psychol 2: 698, 1965.

Bandura A, Grusec J, Menlove F: Vicarious extinction of avoidance behavior. J Pers Soc Psychol 5: 16 –23, 1967.

Basmajian J: *Biofeedback—Principles and Practice for Clinicians.* Baltimore, Williams and Wilkins, 1979.

Budzynski T, Stoyva J, Adler C, Mullanay D: EMG biofeedback and tension headache: a controlled outcome study. Psychosom Med 35: 484, 1973.

Budzynski T: Biofeedback in the treatment of muscle-contraction (tension) headache. Biofeedback Self-Regul 3: 409, 1978.

Cautela J: Covert processes and behavior modification. J Nerv Mental Dis 157: 27–36, 1972.

DiCara L, Miller N: Changes in heart-rate instrumentally learned by curarized rats as avoidance responses. J Comp Physiol Psychol 65: 8, 1968.

Ferster C, Skinner B: *Schedules of Reinforcement.* New York, Appleton, 1957.

Fotopoulos S, Sunderland W: Biofeedback in the treatment of psychophysiologic disorders. Biofeedback Self-Regul 3: 331, 1978.

Frezza D, Holland J: Operant conditioning of the human salivary response. Psychophysiology 8: 581, 1971.

Green E, Green A: Biofeedback: rationale and applications, in Wolman, B (ed): *International Encyclopedia of Neurology, Psychiatry, Psychoanalysis and Psychology.* New York, Van Nostrand Reinhold, 1977.

Green E, Green A: General and specific applications of thermal biofeedback, in Basmajian, J (ed): *Biofeedback.* Baltimore, Williams and Wilkins, 1979.

Guthrie E: *The Psychology of Learning.* New York, Harper and Row, 1935.

Hilgard E, Bower G: *Theories of Learning.* New York, Appleton, 1966.

Homme L: Control of coverants: the operants of the mind. Psychol Rec 15: 501–511, 1965.

Hull C: *Principles of Behavior.* New York, Appleton, 1943.

Jacobson E: *Progressive Relaxation.* Chicago, University of Chicago Press, 1958.

Jacobson E, McGuigan J: An interview with Edmund Jacobson. Biofeedback Self-Regul 3: 287, 1978.

Kamiya J: Operant control of the EEG alpha rhythm, in Tart, C (ed): *Altered States of Consciousness.* New York, Wiley, 1969, p. 507.

Kanfer F: Influence of age and incentive conditions on children's self-rewards. Psychol Rep 19: 263, 1966.

Kanfer F, Phillips J: *Learning Foundations of Behavior Therapy.* New York, Wiley, 1970, pp. 232–233.

Katker E, Murray E: Instrumental conditioning of autonomically mediated behavior: theretical and methodological issues. Psychol Bull 70: 52, 1968.

Kelly G: *The Psychology of Personal Constructs.* New York, Norton, 1955.

Kimmel H: Instrumental conditioning of autonomically mediated responses in human beings. Am J Psychol 29: 325, 1974.

Kimmel H, Hill F: Operant conditioning of the GSR. Psychol Rep 7: 555, 1960.

Lang P, Melamed B: Avoidance conditioning of an infant with chronic ruminative vomiting. J Abnorm Psychol 74: 1, 1969.

Lazarus A: Behavioral rehearsal vs. non-directive therapy vs. advice in affecting behavior change. Beh Res & Ther 4: 209–212, 1966.

Lazarus A: *Clinical Behavior Therapy.* New York, Brunner/Mazel, 1972.

Lichstein K, Hung J: Covert sensitization: an examination of covert and overt parameters. Behav Engin 6: 1–18, 1980.

McGuigan FJ: Conditioning of covert behavior: some problems and some hopes, in McGuigan FJ, Lumsden DB (eds): *Contemporary Approaches to Conditioning and Learning.* New York, Wiley, 1973, p. 173.

McGuire R, Vallance M: Aversion therapy by electric shock. Brit Med J 1: 151–153, 1964.

Marinacci A, Horande M: Electromyogram in neuromuscular re-education. Bull Los Angeles Neurol Soc 25: 57, 1960.

Marlatt G, Jacobson E, Johnson D and Mourice D: Effect of exposure to a model receiving feedback upon subsequent behavior in an interview. Midwestern Psychological meeting, 1966.

Miller N: Biofeedback; evaluation of a new technic. New Engl J Med 290: 684, 1974.

Miller N, Dollard J: *Social Learning and Imitation.* New Haven, Yale University Press, 1941.

Miller N, Dworkin B: Visceral learning: recent difficulties with curarized rats and significant problems for human research, in Obrist et al. (eds): *Cardiovascular Psychophysiology.* New York, Aldine, 1974, p. 312.

Nigl A: The use of covert reinforcement in the acquisition of dental behavior. Diss Abs Internat 25: 922, 1975.

Rubow R: Personal communication, 1979.

Rutner I, Bugle C: An experimental procedure for the modification of psychotic behavior. J Consult Clin Psychol 33: 651–653, 1969.

Sargent J, Green E, Walters E: The use of autogenic feedback training in a pilot study of migraine and tension headaches. Headache 12: 120, 1972.

Schultz J, Luthe W: *Autogenic Therapy.* New York, Grune and Stratton, 1969.

Skinner B: *The Behavior of Organisms: An Experimental Analysis.* New York, Appleton, 1938.

Steffen J: Covert reinforcement: some facts and fantasies. Paper presented at the Association for the Advancement of Behavior Therapy, Chicago, 1974.

Sulzer E: Reinforcement and therapeutic contract. J Consult Psychol 9: 271–276, 1962.

Taub E, Stroebel C: Biofeedback in the treatment of vasoconstrictive syndromes. Biofeedback Self-Regul 3: 363, 1978.

Thorndike E: Animal intelligence: an experimental study of the associative processes in animals. Psychol Rev Monogr Suppl 2: 1898.

Walter G: Expectancy waves of EEG. EEG Suppl 26: 120, 1964.

Watson J: *Behavior: An Introduction to Comparative Psychology.* New York, Holt, 1914, p. 75.

Whitehead W: Biofeedback in the treatment of gastrointestinal disorders. Biofeedback Self-Regul 3: 375, 1978.

Wolpe J: *The Practice of Behavior Therapy.* New York, Pergamon Press, 1973.

Yates A: *Behavior Therapy.* New York, Wiley, 1970.

2

Neuroanatomical and Physiological Basis of Biofeedback

Introduction

Neurophysiologists and clinical neurologists are aware of the fact that the brain acts as a whole unit, and that the functioning of each and every part of it affects the performance of most of the other parts. Clearly, however, certain areas are more closely allied than others by anatomical or physiological links. Also, there is a localization of function such that the different regions of the brain are specialized for certain activities, and although their role can be substituted to a certain extent, they operate most effectively only when carrying out their particular function. Broadly speaking, the tasks of the brain can be divided into three great categories: (1) *the reception of stimuli* (this is the sensory system); (2) *the association of stimuli* and the analysis or *perception of incoming stimuli;* (3) *the motor response* to those stimuli. These motor responses summate so as to constitute the behavior of the individual.

There is a sequence of neuronal events in the brain, a chain reaction such that one part is called into operation (in the temporal or time sense) and this then leads other parts to go into action which generates further activity. Since, however, all areas of the brain are constantly (and therefore concurrently) active, many elements are carrying out their own intrinsic activities which are not apparent to an outside observer and do not impinge on the consciousness of the individual concerned. It is, therefore, obvious that a good deal of cerebral activity goes unheeded by the originator and all observers. The process of learning consists of excluding from consciousness all stimuli except the one which the individual chooses to focus upon, and to which his attention is directed. The acquisition of new data thus involves a process of selective listening, and consists mainly of rejection or ignoring of stimuli which are nonrelevant at that time.

Biofeedback consists of acquiring a technique for selective "listening" to a particular set of stimuli, which may come from the external environment or from inside the individual's own body (internal environment). Having learned this technique, the student then has the ability to regulate the function himself.

In order to understand how this may be accomplished, we have to study first *the geography or anatomy of specialized functioning*, or localization within the brain, so that we understand behavior, in particular the patient's presentation (Fig. 2–1).

Second, it is important to study *the interconnections* (neuronal connectivity) or microstructural changes in synapses, or linkages, or pathways of the brain, so that we try to understand causation of the *how* of behavior, both that of the patient and of ourselves.

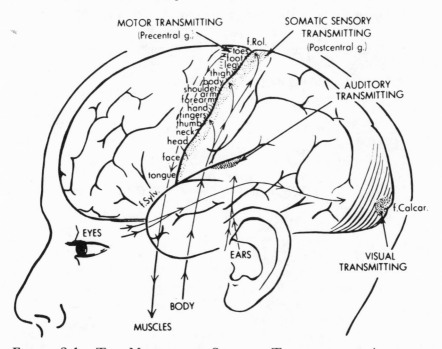

FIGURE 2-1. THE MOTOR AND SENSORY TRANSMITTING AREAS OF THE CEREBRAL CORTEX. THE APPROXIMATE MAP OF THE MOTOR TRANSMITTING AREAS IS SHOWN IN THE PRE-CENTRAL GYRUS, WHILE THE SOMATIC SENSORY RECEIVING AREAS ARE IN A SIMILAR MAP IN THE POSTCENTRAL GYRUS. OTHER PRIMARY SENSORY AREAS SHOWN ARE THE VISUAL AND AUDITORY, BUT THEY ARE LARGELY IN AREAS SCREENED FROM THIS LATERAL VIEW. (Reproduced, with permission, from Eccles, John C.: The Understanding of the Brain, 2nd ed. Copyright 1977, McGraw-Hill Book Company.)

Third, the question of *excitation and inhibition within the nervous system* must be examined. The neurons of the mammalian brain (Figs. 2–17 and 6–12) are either excitatory or inhibitory. When two parts of the brain (two neuronal populations) interact, they may each exert an excitatory or an inhibitory effect. A neuronal impulse may release a neurotransmitter that excites or inhibits. If one part fails to act, there is uncontrolled or deafferented functioning of neurons, because they are lacking their accustomed stimulation or imput.

Constituent Parts of the Central Nervous System (CNS)

The CNS is constituted of the following parts:
1. Spinal cord
2. Medulla oblongata (oblong bulb) and
   Pons (bridge)   The "hind" brain
                             or rhombencephalon
3. Cerebellum
4. Midbrain
5. Diencephalon (the "between" brain)
6. Telencephalon (the "fore" brain)
   a. Cerebral hemispheres (the neopallial "new cloak" brain)
      1. Occipital lobe
      2. Parietal lobe
      3. Temporal lobe
      4. Frontal lobe (Fig. 2–2)
   b. Lateral ventricles (left and right)
   c. Subcortical telencephalic nuclei*
      1. Caudate-Putamen
      2. Globus pallidus complex
      3. Claustrum
      4. Amygdala
   d. White matter of the hemispheres (projection, commissural and association fibers)
   e. Rhinencephalon, limbic lobe (the archipallium, "old cloak," brain)

*These nuclei are collections of gray matter in the interior of the cerebrum. The term *gray matter* indicates nerve cells as opposed to *"white matter"* which indicates nerve fibers with their myelin (insulating) nerve sheaths, so called from its whitish appearance on histological staining.

7. Autonomic nervous system (visceral efferent system)
8. Blood vessels (arteries and veins)
9. Meninges (the coverings of the brain)
10. Cerebrospinal fluid

Organization and Development of the Nervous System: Neuroembryology

The study of neuroembryology provides a framework and background for understanding the anatomy and the functioning of the

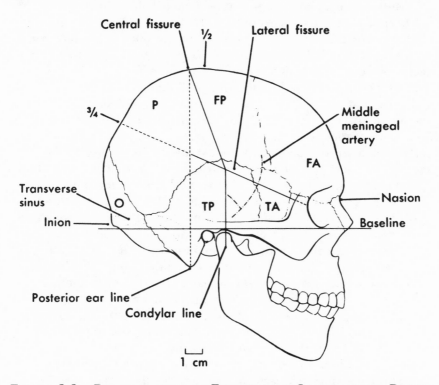

FIGURE 2-2. RELATIONSHIPS OF FISSURES AND LOBES OF THE BRAIN TO MARKINGS OF THE SKULL. ABBREVIATIONS: FA, ANTERIOR FRONTAL LOBE; FP, POSTERIOR FRONTAL LOBE (PRECENTRAL GYRUS); O, OCCIPITAL LOBE; P, PARIETAL LOBE; TA, ANTERIOR TEMPORAL LOBE; TP, POSTERIOR TEMPORAL LOBE. (Reproduced, with permission, from Willis, William D., Jr., and Grossman, Robert G.: Medical Neurobiology, ed. 2, St. Louis, The C. V. Mosby Co., 1977.)

nervous system, and we will therefore review the major points in development briefly.

The nervous system is divided into central and peripheral components. The *central nervous system* is that part located within the spinal column and skull. It is formed from the embryonic neural tube in the human between the 18th and the 25th day of gestation. The *peripheral nervous system* is derived from the embryo's neural crest.*

In the early stages of development of the neural tube, three divisions become differentiated: the prosencephalon, the mesencephalon, and the rhombencephalon. Later the prosencephalon divides into the telencephalon and the diencephalon. The cavities located in the telencephalon are called the lateral ventricles, the one in the right hemisphere and the second in the left (Fig. 2–3). The cavity of the diencephalon is one midline chamber, the third ventricle. The mesencephalon of the embryo becomes the midbrain of the fully developed organism and its cavity is termed the *aqueduct of Sylvius* (named after the anatomist Franciscus de le Boë Sylvius, 1614–1672) (Fig. 2– 4). The cavity of the rhombencephalon ("hind" brain) which includes the metencephalon (cerebellum and pons) and the myelencephalon (the medulla or "bulb") is the fourth ventricle (Fig. 2– 4). The cavity of the spinal cord is the central canal. All these cavities interconnect and are filled with cerebrospinal fluid (CSF). The CSF is elaborated by a process of either secretion or dialysis by the choroid plexuses, which are small tufts of capillary vessels, located within the brain cavities. The CSF is a colorless fluid, with a total quantity ranging from 125 to 150 ml; by a process of osmosis it is emptied into the venous sinuses (large veins) of the dura mater. The dura mater (Latin: "tough mother") is the outer covering of the three coverings of the brain (meninges). The chemical composition of the CSF differs from blood in that it is colorless due to its lack of red blood cells. Disturbances in the pressure or circulation of the CSF may cause headache.

The two columns of cells (the neural crests) which separate from the neural tube during very early development of the embryo form most of the peripheral nervous system. The cells of the neural crest differentiate into the dorsal root ganglia,+ the autonomic ganglia, and Schwann cells (named after the German anatomist Theodor Schwann,

---

*In the early embryo, there are two layers of primitive cells, the ectoderm and the endoderm, and the neural tube is formed from ectodermal cells. As the neural tube separates off from the endoderm, a column of cells splits away laterally on each side of the tube to form the neural crest.

+A ganglion is a collection of nerve cells.

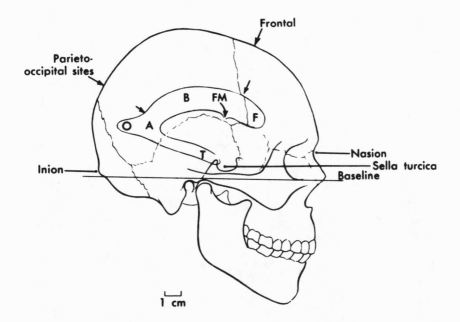

FIGURE 2-3. RELATIONSHIPS OF THE LATERAL VENTRICLES TO MARK-
INGS OF THE SKULL. NOTE FRONTAL AND PARIETO-
OCCIPITAL SITES FOR VENTRICULAR PUNCTURE. AB-
BREVIATIONS: A, ATRIUM; B, BODY OF VENTRICLE; F,
FRONTAL; O, OCCIPITAL; T, TEMPORAL HORNS; FM,
SITE OF FORAMINA OF MONRO. (Reproduced, with per-
mission, from Willis, William D., Jr., and Grossman,
Robert G.: Medical Neurobiology, ed. 2, St. Louis, The
C. V. Mosby Co., 1977.)

1810–1882). Schwann cells carry out an important function in forming
the insulating sheaths called myelin that surround the axons in the
peripheral nervous system. They are located serially along the length
of all peripheral axons and envelop them. Neural crest cells also give
rise to a paired endocrine organ, the adrenal medulla, which sits on
top of each kidney.

Myelin (the insulation on the axons of the neurons) is formed by a
process of wrapping layers of cytoplasm around the axons along their
length. This process is carried out by the oligodendroglia in the CNS
and by Schwann cells in the peripheral nervous system. (Without this
insulation the brain would tend to "short itself in and out"). The

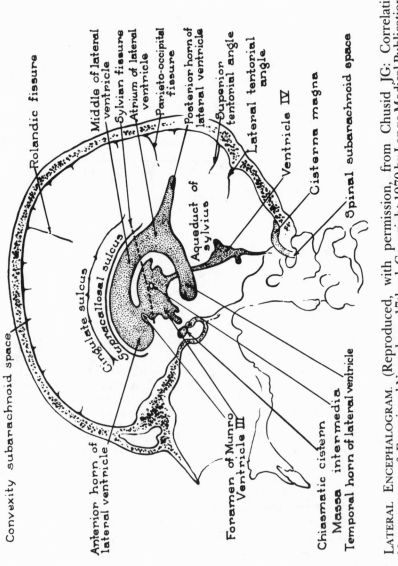

Convexity subarachnoid space

Rolandic fissure

Middle of lateral ventricle

Sylvian fissure

Atrium of lateral ventricle

Parieto-occipital fissure

Posterior horn of lateral ventricle

Superior tentorial angle

Lateral tentorial angle

Ventricle IV

Cisterna magna

Spinal subarachnoid space

Cingulate sulcus

Supracallosal sulcus

Aqueduct of sylvius

Anterior horn of lateral ventricle

Foramen of Munro
Ventricle III

Chiasmatic cistern

Massa intermedia

Temporal horn of lateral ventricle

FIGURE 2-4.   LATERAL ENCEPHALOGRAM. (Reproduced, with permission, from Chusid JG: Correlative Neuroanatomy & Functional Neurology, 17th ed. Copyright 1979 by Lange Medical Publications, Los Altos, California.)

myelin sheath is interrupted at regular intervals by the neurilemma sheath dipping inward to the axis-cylinder to form circular constrictions (Figs. 2–5 and 2–6). These regular constrictions are the nodes of Ranvier.*

The oligodendroglia are part of the supporting cells in the CNS, one class of the glia ("glue") cells, and they are to be differentiated from the neurons that perform the primary function of the nervous system, that is, processing information.

The myelin sheath has been shown by polarization and x-ray diffraction studies to be constructed of alternating lipid and protein layers (Figs. 2–5 and 2–6). The sheath contains three major classes of protein: (1) proteolipid and neurokeratin; (2) basic protein; and (3) acidic protein. The chemistry, ultrastructure (as observed by electron microscopy), and the function of the myelin are complex subjects and beyond the scope of this book. Suffice it to say that the axons which are surrounded by an insulating sheath of myelin transmit the action impulse (the nerve "message") much quicker than the axons which are not sheathed (the nonmyelinated nerve fibers).

Sensory System (see Fig. 5– 4)

The sensory system includes a complex network of structures and pathways at all levels of the nervous system, and it is organized to mediate many types of sensation. These include smell (olfaction), taste (gustation), vision, hearing (audition), vibration, touch, tickle, pain, kinesthesia, joint movement, and awareness of limb position in space (proprioception).

Impulses traveling toward the central nervous system are regarded as sensory and are given the general term *afferent* (Latin: *ferro*, "carry"; *ad*, "towards"). The ability to detect and translate information from the environment is the function of the receptor organs. Many but not all of the sensory pathways have features in common with sensory receptors and consist of three relays or successive orders of neurons.

1. The cell bodies of the first-order neurons (the first relay) lie outside the CNS in a ganglion. The distal axon (distal means nearer the outside or periphery) of each of these cell bodies receives information from the sensory receptor, and the proximal (nearer the brain) axon enters the spinal cord or brain stem via a dorsal (posterior) root or a cranial nerve.

*L. Ranvier, French anatomist, author of *Leçons d'Anatomie Générale sur le Système Musculaire,* Paris, 1880.

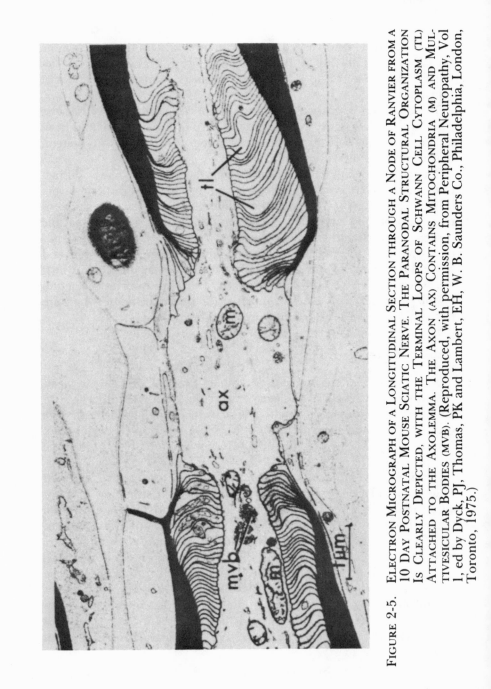

FIGURE 2-5. ELECTRON MICROGRAPH OF A LONGITUDINAL SECTION THROUGH A NODE OF RANVIER FROM A 10 DAY POSTNATAL MOUSE SCIATIC NERVE. THE PARANODAL STRUCTURAL ORGANIZATION IS CLEARLY DEPICTED, WITH THE TERMINAL LOOPS OF SCHWANN CELL CYTOPLASM (TL) ATTACHED TO THE AXOLEMMA. THE AXON (AX) CONTAINS MITOCHONDRIA (M) AND MULTIVESICULAR BODIES (MVB). (Reproduced, with permission, from Peripheral Neuropathy, Vol 1, ed by Dyck, PJ, Thomas, PK and Lambert, EH, W. B. Saunders Co., Philadelphia, London, Toronto, 1975.)

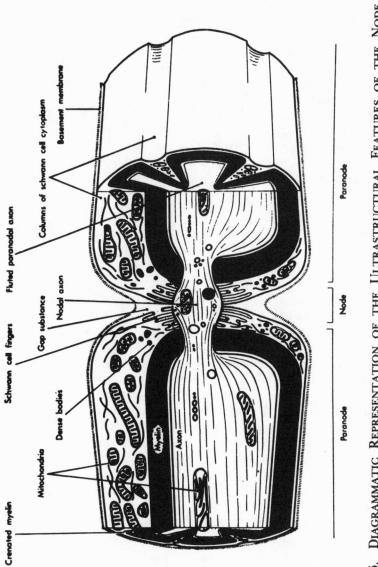

Crenated myelin

Mitochondria

Dense bodies

Schwann cell fingers

Gap substance

Nodal axon

Columns of schwann cell cytoplasm

Fluted paranodal axon

Basement membrane

Myelin

Axon

Paranode

Node

Paranode

FIGURE 2-6. DIAGRAMMATIC REPRESENTATION OF THE ULTRASTRUCTURAL FEATURES OF THE NODE OF RANVIER. (Reproduced, with permission, from Williams, PL and Landon, DN: The energy source of the nerve fibre. New Scientist, 21:166, 1963.)

2.   The cell bodies of the second-order neurons (the second relay) lie within the spinal cord itself. The axons of these second-order neurons decussate (cross the midline) and continue up toward the brain; they reach the thalamus where they terminate in specific sensory nuclei. The thalamus is a massive collection of nerve cells deep to the cerebral cortex, concerned with reception, modification, and transmission of sensation.

3.   The cell bodies of the third-order neurons (the third relay) lie in the thalamus, and their axons proceed to the sensory cortex, which mainly is in the postcentral gyrus* of the parietal lobe. Visual information is relayed to the occipital cortex, while auditory fibers terminate in the temporal lobe.

Motor System

The motor system is likewise a complex network of structures and pathways present at all levels of the nervous system. It is organized to mediate many types of activity to be carried out by striated, somatic muscles or nonstriated, smooth muscles.

Impulses traveling from the CNS (away from the brain) and toward the limb or trunk muscles or the viscera are regarded as "motor," (capable of causing movement) and they are given the general term *efferent*. The ability to initiate movement and transmit the order to carry out a movement is the function of the motor system. There are four major divisions of the motor system involved in the performance of motor activity by somatic and visceral musculature (Daube and Sandok, 1978) and they include:

1.   The final common pathway
2.   The direct activation pathway
3.   The indirect activation pathway
4.   The control circuits

These pathways include the motor cortex, and related cortical areas, the pyramidal tract,† the extrapyramidal system, and the spinocerebellar pathways.

The final common pathway is the peripheral effector mechanism by which all motor activity is mediated. It includes the motor neurons in

---

*The surfaces of the hemispheres are traversed by a large number of grooves called "sulci." The areas and blunt, winding ridges between the sulci are called "gyri."

†The pyramidal cells in the cortex are so-called because of their shape (Fig. 2–17). The pyramidal tracts arise from these cells.

the anterior horn of the spinal cord and their axons extending peripherally via nerves which innervate muscles. These motor neurons are called "alpha" motor neurons or alpha efferents (Fig. 2–17). The skeletal (striated) muscles are all under the direct control of neurons known as the lower motor neurons (LMN) and they contract only in response to activation by these neurons.

Cerebellum

The cerebellum (Fig. 2–7) is part of the hind-brain lying just under and posterior to the cerebrum (Figs. 2–8 and 2–9). It has been called the "arbor vitae" (Tree of Life) because of the way in which its layers of white and grey matter lie close together clearly resembling leaves or "folia." It is not apparently involved in conscious sensations, however.

The neocerebellum is the dominant part of the cerebellum in primates, including humans. It consists of the hemispheres and part of

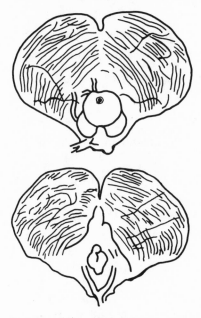

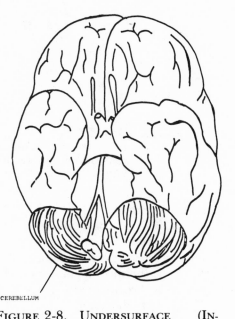

CEREBELLUM

FIGURE 2-7. THE CEREBELLUM. FIGURE 2-8. UNDERSURFACE (INFERIOR SURFACE) OF THE BRAIN SHOWING THE CEREBRAL HEMISPHERES AND THE CEREBELLUM.

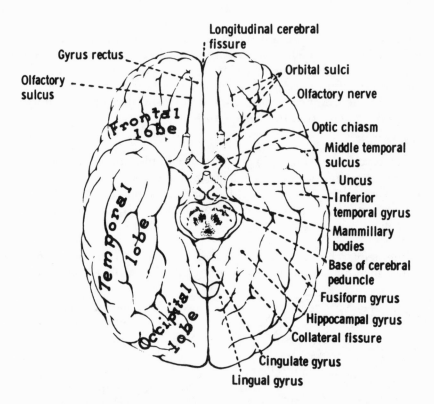

FIGURE 2-9. BASAL VIEW OF CEREBRUM. (Reproduced, with permission, from Chusid JG: Correlative Neuroanatomy & Functional Neurology, 17th ed. Copyright 1979 by Lange Medical Publications, Los Altos, California.)

the intermediate region, as well as some of the middle zone of the vermis. The paleocerebellum is phylogenetically older, and is concerned mainly with balance. The pontocerebellum is so-named because of the large projection to this region from the pontine nuclei. However, the most significant relationship of the cerebellum is with the cerebral cortex, particularly with the motor cortex. From the point of view of biofeedback training, the cerebellum is important for the following four reasons:

1. The function of the neocerebellum appears to include the modulation of the activity of the motor outflow from the cerebral cortex. It accomplishes the coordination and correction of motion errors of muscles during active movements. In addition, experimental

studies show that activity in cells of the deep cerebellar nuclei may precede voluntary movements, suggesting that the influence of the cerebellum on the motor cortex is felt not only in the correction of movement but also in its initiation.

2.   The cerebellum plays an important role in determining postural tone.

3.   The cerebellum is concerned with inhibition within the central nervous system. The complex role of inhibitory mechanisms within the cerebellum has been described in detail by John Eccles (1977).

4.   Through its relationship with the vestibular system, the cerebellum plays a part in the maintenance of equilibrium.

Autonomic Nervous System

Substitution of the term *visceral efferent system* for *autonomic nervous system* will probably lead to a better understanding of this system. It comprises all the efferent nerves through which the visceral organs are innervated.* These include the cardiovascular system, the glands (endocrine and exocrine), and the peripheral involuntary muscles, such as the muscles that regulate the size of the pupil, and those associated with the hair follicles (errector pili muscles).

The tissues that require innervation from this system are widespread throughout the entire body; they include the intracranial blood vessels, the eyes, the lacrimal glands, the salivary glands (the parotid, the sublingual, and the submaxillary glands), the peripheral blood vessels, the larynx, trachea, bronchi and lungs, the heart, the stomach, liver, gallbladder and bile ducts, the pancreas, adrenal glands and kidneys, the intestines, the distal colon, the bladder and the male and female genital systems (Fig. 2–10).

The *autonomic ganglia* are collections of cell bodies of visceral neurons in the trunk and head that send out axons to innervate all the internal organs. They receive connections from outgrowths of visceral neurons in the CNS and from sensory neurons in the internal organs. These ganglia mediate motor and sensory activities of the visceral organs.

Comparison of the Somatic System with the Visceral System

Although the distinction between somatic and visceral portions of the nervous system is arbitrary, it is felt to be useful.

*Innervation means supplying an organ or a tissue with nerves, i.e. the nerve supply.

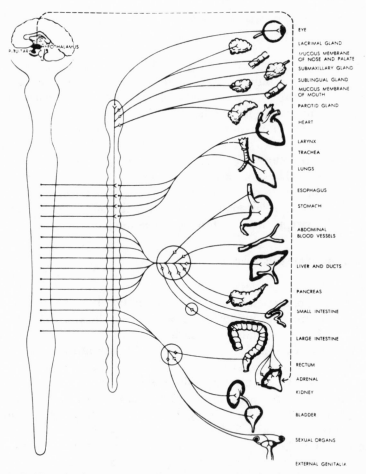

FIGURE 2-10. RESPONSES TO STRESS ARE PARTLY CONTROLLED BY THE PATHWAYS SHOWN IN THIS DIAGRAM OF THE HUMAN SYMPATHETIC NERVOUS SYSTEM. SYMPATHETIC FIBERS (SOLID LINES) ORIGINATING IN THE SPINAL CORD (FAR LEFT) INNERVATE THE INTERNAL ORGANS VIA THE CHAIN GANGLIA (LEFT CENTER) AND THE GANGLIA OF THE CELIAC PLEXUS (RIGHT CENTER). EXTREME STRESS UPSETS THE NORMAL RHYTHM OF THIS SYSTEM, CAUSING DISTURBANCES SUCH AS LOSS OF BLADDER CONTROL AND INCREASED PULSE RATE. STRESS ALSO STIMULATES THE HYPOTHALAMUS AND THE PITUITARY TO PRODUCE ACTH, WHICH REACHES THE ADRENALS VIA THE BLOODSTREAM (BROKEN LINE) AND STIMULATES THEM TO PRODUCE STEROID HORMONES. (Reproduced from Levine, Seymour, "Stimulation in Infancy," May 1960, Scientific American, P. 84. Copyright and approval W. H. Freeman and Company, Scientific American Inc.)

The somatic system (with its sensory and motor parts) establishes contact with the external world through the appreciation of environmental stimuli (the sensory part) and the control of movements that adapt to the environment (the motor part). The visceral system, on the other hand, deals with the internal world by responding to stimuli from the internal (or inner) environment and by regulating the function of the visceral glands and organs.

The visceral system has an organization similar to the somatic, with sensory (afferent) and motor (efferent) components. The visceral efferent structures are referred to as the autonomic nervous system (ANS). It is this part which in some ways is becoming less "autonomic" (self-governing) or automatic because, after the learning of appropriate techniques, it is capable of becoming under more "voluntary," more conscious, control. In classical teaching (Daube and Sandok, 1978), the visceral system has differed from the somatic system in three main respects:

1. *Autonomy of the effector organ.* Unlike somatic striated, or skeletal (outer framework) muscle, many of the organs and glands regulated by the visceral system can function without external control.

2. *Peripheral reflex connection.* Unlike the somatic system where all reflexes are mediated in the CNS, visceral reflexes can occur in the periphery.

3. *Neurohumoral control.* Many viscera are regulated by hormones (chemical messengers, see Chap. 16) secreted into the blood by endocrine glands under neural control.

Muscle Spindle

After the eye and the ear, the muscle spindle is the third most complex sense organ. Some of the early work on muscle spindles was done by Ruffini in the late 19th century and by Charles Sherrington (1857–1952). A great deal of research has been devoted in recent years to the anatomy and physiology of these organs.

Structure

A typical muscle spindle is composed of two types of modified muscle fibers, a capsule and both afferent (sensory) and efferent (motor) innervation (see Fig. 2–11). The muscle fibers are termed *intrafusal fibers* to distinguish them from the ordinary skeletal striated muscle (extrafusal) fibers. The ends of the spindle are attached to extrafusal

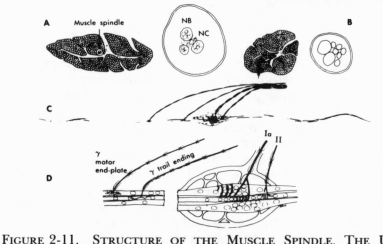

FIGURE 2-11.   STRUCTURE OF THE MUSCLE SPINDLE. THE UPPER
ROW OF DRAWINGS SHOWS THE APPEARANCE OF A
MUSCLE SPINDLE CUT IN CROSS SECTION. IN A THE
SECTION PASSES THROUGH THE LYMPH SPACE NEAR
THE CENTRAL, OR EQUATORIAL, REGION OF THE
SPINDLE. THE NUCLEI OF THE NUCLEAR BAG (NB) AND
NUCLEAR CHAIN (NC) INTRAFUSAL MUSCLE FIBERS
ARE SHOWN IN THE HIGH-POWER VIEW. THE NUCLEAR
BAG FIBERS CONTAIN A CLUSTER OF NUCLEI. THE
NUCLEAR CHAIN FIBERS HAVE A ROW; ONLY ONE
NUCLEUS APPEARS IN A CROSS SECTION. IN B THE
SECTION IS AWAY FROM THE EQUATORIAL REGION OF
THE SPINDLE. C SHOWS THE INNERVATION OF THE
SPINDLE. THE SENSORY ENDINGS ARE IN THE
EQUATORIAL REGION WITHIN THE LYMPH SPACE,
WHICH PRESUMABLY OFFERS SOME PROTECTION
AGAINST INADVERTENT STIMULATION. THE MOTOR
ENDINGS ARE ON THE POLAR REGIONS OF THE SPINDLE.
D IS AN EXPANDED VIEW SHOWING THE INNERVATED
AREAS. AT THE LEFT ARE TWO FORMS OF MOTOR
ENDINGS MADE BY GAMMA MOTOR AXONS. ON THE
RIGHT ARE THE PRIMARY AND SECONDARY ENDINGS
MADE BY GAMMA MOTOR AXONS. ON THE RIGHT
ARE THE PRIMARY AND SECONDARY ENDINGS MADE BY
GROUP IA AND GROUP II FIBERS RESPECTIVELY. NOTE
THAT THE PRIMARY ENDING INCLUDES TERMINALS ON
BOTH NUCLEAR BAG AND NUCLEAR CHAIN FIBERS,
WHEREAS THE SECONDARY ENDING IS CHIEFLY ASSO-
CIATED WITH NUCLEAR CHAIN FIBERS. ALL OF THE
INTRAFUSAL MUSCLE FIBERS RECEIVE INNERVATION,
ALTHOUGH THIS IS NOT SHOWN IN THE DRAWING. (Re-
produced, with permission, from Willis, William D., Jr.,
and Grossman, Robert G.: Medical Neurobiology, ed.
2, St. Louis, The C. V. Mosby Co., 1977.)

muscle; the middle part of the spindle is not. Muscle spindles are arranged in parallel with extrafusal muscle fibers. This means that a stretch (lengthening) of the whole muscle will increase the tension of the muscle spindle, whereas a contraction (shortening) of the whole muscle mass or bundle will decrease the tension of the spindle, unless the spindle itself contracts.

It must be understood that when a joint (for example, the elbow) is bent (flexed) one set of muscles is contracted or shortened (in this case the flexors of the elbow joint including the biceps), while simultaneously the opposite set of muscles is relaxed or lengthened (in this case the extensors of the elbow joint including the triceps). The muscles that contract (shorten) are called the agonists, while the muscles that concurrently relax (lengthen) are called the antagonists.

The mechanism whereby smooth functioning is achieved is termed reciprocal innervation. Reciprocal innervation or reciprocal inhibition was described by Sherrington in 1897. He showed that in a reflex arc where the mechanical action of two muscles is antagonistic, stimulation of the arc activates the one muscle while causing depression of the activity of the other, namely inhibition. This is important in biofeedback in that painful muscle spasm in certain cases is due to the fact that the patients are contracting both sets of muscles that operate a joint. Through training, they relearn the natural way to contract the agonists while relaxing the antagonists.

The muscle spindle is innervated both by sensory and motor fibers. Two kinds of sensory (afferent) fibers end on intrafusal fibers: group Ia and group II (see Table 2–1). Group Ia fibers are the largest of the peripheral myelinated fibers; group II fibers are middle-sized myelinated fibers. The endings of group Ia fibers are called primary endings, formerly referred to as annulospiral endings. The motor innervation of the intrafusal fibers is by gamma motor fibers. Each intrafusal fiber may receive terminals from several gamma axons, and each gamma axon may distribute to several intrafusal fibers. There are at least two functional categories of gamma motor fibers, "dynamic" and "static." The dynamic motor fibers increase the sensitivity of the primary endings to the velocity of stretch; the static fibers increase the discharge of both primary and secondary endings at any given muscle length, while actually reducing the dynamic response of the primary ending.

Operation

When a muscle is stretched, the afferent fibers from muscle spindles show an increased rate of discharge. Thus, the muscle spindle, like the

TABLE 2-1. FIBER TYPES AND THEIR FUNCTIONS

Type	Group	Sub-group	Diameter (μm)	Conduction velocity (m/sec)	Tissue supplied	Function
Sensory (Afferent)						
A	I	Ia	12–20	72–120	Muscle	Afferents from muscle spindle primary endings
		Ib			Muscle	Afferents from Golgi tendon organs
	II Beta		6–12	36–72	Muscle	Afferents from muscle spindle secondary endings
					Skin	Afferents from pacinian corpuscles, touch receptors
	III Delta		1–6	6–36	Muscle	Afferents from pressure-pain endings
					Skin	Afferents from touch, temperature, and pain receptors
C	IV Dorsal root		1	0.5–2	Muscle	Afferents from pain receptors
					Skin	Afferents from touch, pain, and temperature receptors
Motor (Efferent)						
A	Alpha		12–30	72–120	Muscle	Motor supply of extrafusal skeletal muscle fibers
	Gamma		2–8	12–48	Muscle	Motor supply of intrafusal muscle fibers
B			3	3–15	Ganglia	Preganglionic autonomic fibers
C	Sympathetic		1	0.5–2	Cardiac and smooth muscles; glands	Postganglionic autonomic fibers

From Willis, W. D. and Grossman, R. G.: *Medical Neurobiology.* St. Louis, Mosby, 1977, p. 63. Reprinted with permission.

Golgi tendon organ, is a stretch receptor. However, the behavior of muscle spindle afferents is much more complex than is that of the afferent fibers of the Golgi tendon organ. The dynamic responsiveness of group Ia fibers suggests that muscle spindles detect muscle length and its rate of change. The mechanism of gamma motor axons and the unloading effect of muscular contraction on the discharge rates of muscle spindle afferents is beyond the scope of the present text. The ability of the central nervous system to regulate the discharge rate of a receptor organ, however, is a good example of centrifugal control of imput to the CNS. (The term *centrifugal* indicates the direction away from the brain and toward the periphery.)

Feedback System

When the nervous system is perceived as a system of electrical circuits with each and every action impulse leading to a further series of action impulses, it is clear that some of the action impulses increase a particular ongoing neuronal activity whereas others decrease it.

It has already been explained that many activities, such as straightening out a joint, require simultaneous but opposite effects in order to achieve a particular goal. This is a basic principle or tenet of all activity and helps to explain a paradox of human behavior: one cannot do one thing without at the same time ceasing to do another.

In this system of electrical circuits, therefore, it is seen that certain activities feed back a command to go on doing more of the same, and others feed back a command to stop doing more of the same. The principle involved in a negative feedback device is that a part of the output of the system is rechanneled or fed back into the system in such a way as to reduce the activity of the system.

When the output of a system is fed back into the system to increase the output further, a positive feedback mechanism is involved. "Postactivation potentiation" is an example of positive feedback in the CNS, whereby successive impulses are able to trigger the release of further amounts of the synaptic transmitter substance.

Spinal Cord Control Mechanisms

Stretch Reflex as Negative Feedback

The operation of the stretch reflex in maintaining the position of a joint may be regarded as an example of a negative feedback device. Suppose that the extensor and flexor muscles about the knee joint are participating in the maintenance of a particular posture. If one set of muscles contracts too much the opposing muscles are stretched. This will produce an afferent barrage that will tend to inhibit the contraction of the first set of muscles and to produce a further contraction of the second set. An excessive contraction of the second set will result in the reverse process. In this way the opposing muscles will produce a balance of tension that will keep the joint position fairly constant.

Muscle Control Mechanisms

Gamma Loop

Because muscle spindles are located in a parallel arrangement to extrafusal muscle fibers, the contraction of the latter will result in a reduction in the tension of the spindles. This in turn will reduce the afferent discharges of group Ia and II fibers ending in the spindles. The impulses from the Ia fibers help maintain the excitability of the alpha motoneurons (in the anterior horn of the gray matter of the spinal cord) producing the contraction; thus, the decrease in these impulses caused by the contraction serves as a negative feedback mechanism. This is accomplished by the discharge of gamma motoneurons. A muscle contraction may be continued effectively if both alpha and gamma motoneurons discharge during the same period of time.

Group Ib afferents send collaterals to end monosynaptically on the cells of origin of the dorsal and ventral spinocerebellar tracts, which they excite.

Renshaw Cell Systems

As the axons of alpha motoneurons pass through the gray matter of the ventral (anterior) horn towards the point of exit of the ventral (anterior) root, they give off collaterals that innervate a group of interneurons located in lamina VII ("lamina" means layer).* These interneurons are named after their discoverer, Renshaw (1941). Renshaw

*Rexed (1954) introduced a terminology for the various layers of the gray matter of the spinal cord, dividing it into ten laminae (Fig. 2–12). The laminae I through VI occupy the dorsal (posterior) horn. Part of lamina VII corresponds to the intermediate region, and also forms much of the ventral (anterior) horn. The medial aspect of the ventral horn in the cervical and lumbar enlargements includes lamina VIII. The motoneurons are in groups corresponding to functional relations, and they are classed as lamina IX. The zone around the central canal is considered lamina X.

It should be remembered that the dorsal horn consists of sensory nerve cells (receiving sensory imput), whereas the ventral horn consists of motor nerve cells.

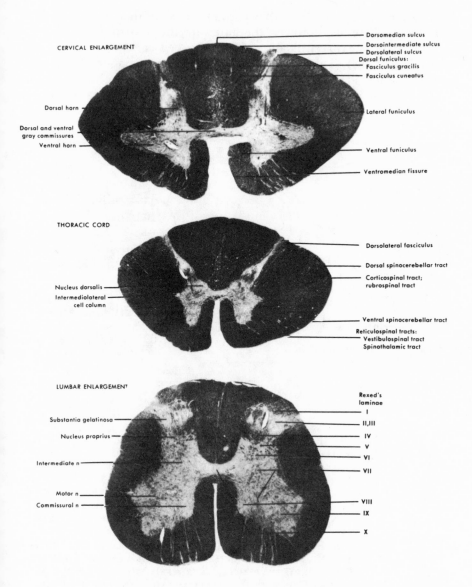

CERVICAL ENLARGEMENT

Dorsomedian sulcus
Dorsointermediate sulcus
Dorsolateral sulcus
Dorsal funiculus:
Fasciculus gracilis
Fasciculus cuneatus

Dorsal horn

Lateral funiculus

Dorsal and ventral gray commissures
Ventral horn

Ventral funiculus

Ventromedian fissure

THORACIC CORD

Dorsolateral fasciculus

Dorsal spinocerebellar tract

Corticospinal tract; rubrospinal tract

Nucleus dorsalis
Intermediolateral cell column

Ventral spinocerebellar tract

Reticulospinal tracts:
Vestibulospinal tract
Spinothalamic tract

LUMBAR ENLARGEMENT

Rexed's laminae
I

Substantia gelatinosa
II,III

Nucleus proprius
IV
V
VI

Intermediate n
VII

Motor n
Commissural n
VIII
IX

X

FIGURE 2-12. TRANSVERSE SECTIONS OF HUMAN SPINAL CORD. (Reproduced, with permission, from Willis, William D., Jr., and Grossman, Robert G.: Medical Neurobiology, ed. 2, St. Louis, The C. V. Mosby Co., 1977.)

cells are excited by several other pathways besides that involving motor axon collaterals; however, the latter are the best studied.

One of the sites of termination of Renshaw cell axons is on motoneurons (Fig. 2–13). These endings produce a postsynaptic inhibition lasting some 50 msec (Renshaw, 1946). Thus the pathways from motoneurons to Renshaw cells to motoneurons constitute a negative

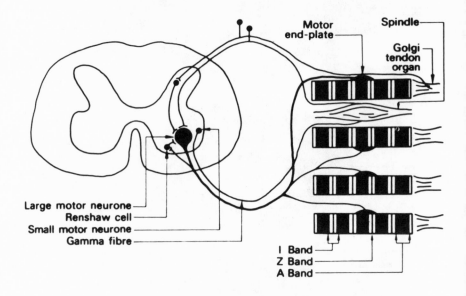

FIGURE 2-13.   DIAGRAM ILLUSTRATING THE INNERVATION OF THE MOTOR UNIT. LARGE ANTERIOR HORN CELLS ARE SHOWN SUPPLYING FOUR STRIATED MUSCLE FIBERS. MUSCLE SPINDLES LIE IN PARALLEL WITH THE MUSCLE FIBERS AND AFFERENTS FROM THE SPINDLES ACT ON THE LARGE MOTOR NEURONS THROUGH A SINGLE SYNAPSE. THE INTRAFUSAL MUSCLE FIBERS WITHIN THE SPINDLES RECEIVE MOTOR INNERVATION FROM THE SMALL NEURONS IN THE SPINAL CORD THROUGH THE GAMMA EFFERENTS. THE GOLGI TENDON ORGANS LIE IN SERIES WITH THE STRIATED MUSCLE FIBERS AND MAKE CONNECTION WITH THE ANTERIOR HORN CELLS THROUGH A SINGLE INTERNUNCIAL NEURON. (Reproduced, with permission, from Lenman, JAR and Ritchie, AE: Clinical Electromyography, 2nd ed., Copyright J. B. Lippincott Company, Philadelphia, 1977.)

feedback. The more actively the motoneurons fire, the more actively Renshaw cells will discharge and inhibit the motoneurons. The situation is, however, more complicated than this. Renshaw cell axons also terminate on interneurons and inhibit them. The particular interneurons inhibited by Renshaw cells are themselves inhibitory to motoneurons. Activation of Renshaw cells, therefore, may decrease the amount of inhibition of some motoneurons resulting in their disinhibition.

The Renshaw cell system is of special interest not only because it is a prototype for the study of the physiological role of recurrent collateral branches of nerve axons, which are quite common in the central nervous system, but also because the pharmacology of the synapses* of the motor axon collaterals on Renshaw cells is to date the best documented pharmacology of the CNS.

Stimulus-Response Mechanisms

In many respects, the central nervous system can be said to be based on stimulus-response mechanisms. Human behavior, however, is so complex that much of what is observed cannot be neatly described in terms of afferent-efferent or stimulus-response systems. It is nevertheless useful to start with this model and the simple anatomy of a stimulus causing a neuronal discharge traveling in afferent pathways (through a variety of excitatory and inhibitory neurons) leading to the neuronal discharges in efferent pathways which cause motor behavior.

In biofeedback, there is a primary concern with two mechanisms: first, when the subject or patient becomes continuously aware of certain physiological activities, such as muscle tone or heart rate; second, when the subject has incentives or rewards for changing or controlling the feedback, and therefore learns to control voluntarily the physiological response associated with the feedback. The continuous information fed back to the subject brings to consciousness something which may not have been previously registered at a conscious level. Consequently, it travels a different neuronal pathway. It is, therefore, important to understand first the pathways known in spinal and cerebral reflexes, second, the principal of divergence and convergence of information, and, third, some of the complex systems that can modify or modulate behavior.

*Sherrington gave the name *synapse* to the functional connections that are made by close contact between nerve cells. The term synapse is now sometimes used to denote the gap (synaptic cleft) between the axon terminal of one cell and the body of the next cell (Fig. 2–14).

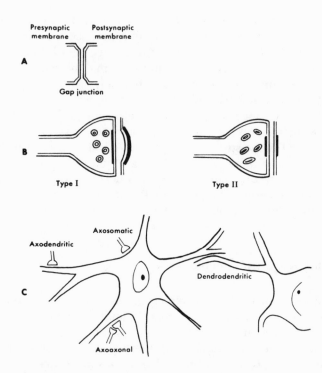

FIGURE 2-14. SCHEMATIC DRAWINGS OF VARIOUS TYPES OF
SYNAPSES. A, ELECTRICAL SYNAPSE. THIS CONSISTS OF
A GAP JUNCTION (2MM) BETWEEN PRE- AND POST-
SYNAPTIC MEMBRANES. B, CHEMICAL SYNAPSES. TYPE I
SYNAPSES HAVE A WIDENED SYNAPTIC CLEFT (30),
ASYMMETRICAL CYTOPLASMIC DENSITIES, AND SPHERI-
CAL VESICLES. TYPE II SYNAPSES HAVE A 20 MM
SYNAPTIC CLEFT, SYMMETRICAL CYTOPLASMIC DENSI-
TIES, AND SOMETIMES OVOID VESICLES. C, SYNAPTIC
ARRANGEMENTS, INCLUDING AXODENDRITIC, AXO-
SOMATIC,   AXOAXONAL,   AND   DENDRODENDRITIC
SYNAPSES. (Reproduced, with permission, from Willis,
William D., Jr., and Grossman, Robert G.: Medical
Neurobiology, ed. 2, St. Louis, The C. V. Mosby Co.,
1977.)

The central nervous system is responsible for the coordination of
much of motor activity. It ensures the smooth performance of movements by causing the proper muscle groups to contract or to relax in
the most efficient sequence. When the needs of the body change, the

nervous system attempts to produce the appropriate alterations in respiratory or digestive systems. Sherrington called this executive role played by the nervous system its "integrative action."

Motor units are the executive units whereby the brain gains expression in movement. All actions are effected by the discharging (firing) of impulses by motoneurons. (An impulse is a message traveling as a brief action potential in nerve or muscle fibers.) When this discharging (firing) is in response to instructions from the brain, the motor unit acts as a perfect servomechanism for the brain.

Spinal and Cerebral Reflexes

Sherrington (1947) in his classic book *The Integrative Action of the Nervous System* analyzed in detail both spinal and cerebral reflexes, and he largely refashioned neurophysiology, describing behavior in neurophysiological terms. He originated the concept that communication from one neuron to another takes place at specialized sites which he termed *synapses* (Greek: *synapto* "to clasp tightly") (Fig. 2–14).

Some of the activities of the nervous system are built in by virtue of the synaptic connections made by particular neurons with other neurons. Excitation of a pathway of this type results in the performance of some relatively stereotyped action.* Such an action is called reflex. Sherrington studied a number of reflexes that can occur through activity in the spinal cord without any connection with the brain.

The simplest reflex arc[†] is the knee jerk (Fig. 2–15). In the extensor muscles of the knee (as in all striated muscles), there are receptors sensitive to stretch located on a special type of muscle fiber called the primary ending (formally the annulospiral ending). In a large muscle, there are, of course, hundreds of muscle spindles with primary endings, each with an afferent fiber of a special type—group Ia. When the muscle is stretched by a brief tap to the tendon at the knee joint, impulses pass up the large Ia afferent fibers at about 100 m/sec into the spinal cord and so directly to motoneurons that are thus excited and send impulses out to the muscles in the leg which are caused to contract (Fig. 2–16). If alternatively the muscle is stretched slowly and then maintained, the primary endings will continue discharging im-

*The term *stereotyped action* indicates an event which typifies or conforms to a fixed unvarying pattern or manner, lacking individuality. (Greek: *stereos* "solid" or "hard.") It has come to be used as firm, three-dimensional.

[†]A reflex arc comprises simple neuronal pathways through the CNS involving afferent input, various interneuronal linkages, and efferent output by motor neuron discharges.

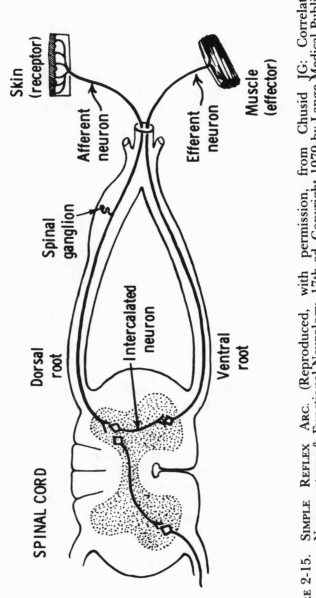

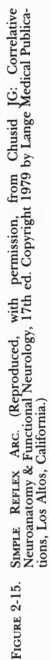

FIGURE 2-15. SIMPLE REFLEX ARC. (Reproduced, with permission, from Chusid JG: Correlative Neuroanatomy & Functional Neurology, 17th ed. Copyright 1979 by Lange Medical Publications, Los Altos, California.)

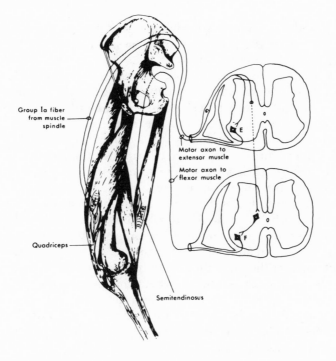

Group Ia fiber
from muscle
spindle

Motor axon to
extensor muscle

Motor axon to
flexor muscle

Quadriceps

Semitendinosus

FIGURE 2-16. PATHWAY OF THE MONOSYNAPTIC REFLEX. THE REFLEX ARC CONSISTS OF AN EXCITATORY AND AN INHIBITORY COMPONENT. THE EXCITATORY PORTION IS MONOSYNAPTIC. GROUP IA AFFERENT FIBERS FROM THE PRIMARY ENDINGS OF MUSCLE SPINDLES ENTER THE CORD THROUGH DORSAL ROOTS, TRAVERSE THE GRAY MATTER, AND END SYNAPTICALLY ON ALPHA MOTONEURONS TO THE SAME MUSCLE AS THAT CONTAINING THE MUSCLE SPINDLES AND TO THE SYNERGISTIC MUSCLES (THE KNEE EXTENSOR, E., QUADRICEPS, IS ILLUSTRATED HERE). THE INHIBITORY COMPONENT IS DISYNAPTIC. GROUP IA FIBERS END ON INTERNEURONS OF THE INTERMEDIATE REGION OF THE SPINAL CORD GRAY MATTER (IN LAMINA VII) TO EXCITE THEM. THE INTER-NEURONS SYNAPSE ON MOTONEURONS OF THE ANTAGONISTIC MUSCLES TO INHIBIT THEM (THE KNEE FLEXOR, F, SEMITENDINOSUS, IS ILLUSTRATED HERE). THIS REFLEX ARC IS THUS CHARACTERIZED BY RECIPROCAL INNERVATION OF MUSCLES OPPOSING EACH OTHER AT A JOINT. (Reproduced, with permission, from Willis, William D., Jr., and Grossman, Robert G.: Medical Neurobiology, ed. 2, St. Louis, The C. V. Mosby Co., 1977.)

pulses and the muscle will give a slow "postural" or "tonic" contraction.* This is an example of a "monosynaptic reflex pathyway" using group Ia afferent fibers.

An example of a more complicated reflex pathway is a flexion withdrawal from a nociceptive stimulus.[†] For example, the skin is stimulated by touch or pressure or by touching something unexpectedly hot. The afferent fiber passes into the spinal cord, but once there, it branches a great deal and the pathway to motoneurons is then always via the interneurons. There are enormous numbers of interneurons, so that the reflex is very widely spread and produces a prolonged response of the muscles. Therefore if a person should touch something unexpectedly hot, he will withdraw his hand before he feels the pain.[‡] Similarly, if he should step on some sharp object, he will withdraw his leg by contracting the flexor muscles acting at all the different joints. This rapid automatic withdrawal is effected by pathways in the spinal cord. At the same time, impulses pass up the spinal cord to the brain (see Fig. 5–6) and report what is happening, but, of course, this information is experienced after the reflex withdrawal has occurred.

In contrast to reflex activity, there is sensory-motor integration in which the motor response depends upon the individual's interpretation of an incoming stimulus.

The Afferent Pathway for Cutaneous Sensation

Any touch on the skin causes a receptor to fire impulses. These impulses then travel directly up the dorsal columns of the spinal cord (the cuneate tract for the hand and arm) and then after passing through a synaptic relay in the cuneate nucleus and another in the thalamus, the pathway reaches the cerebral cortex. At each of the relays (synapses), there is an opportunity for an inhibitory action to clarify the neuronal signals by eliminating all the weaker excitatory actions, such as would occur when the skin contacts an ill-defined

*A tonic contraction is a continuous one. Tonic reflexes are those produced by proprioceptors of the limbs. Thus, in the decerebrate individual, the tonic extensor rigidity of the leg is reflexly maintained by discharges in the afferent neurons reaching the cord from the deep structures of the leg itself. In an epileptic seizure, the body is extended stiffly in the tonic phase with continuous muscle contraction of the extensors.

[†]Nociceptive is a term introduced by Sherrington in 1903. It indicates a stimulus that excites nerve endings adapted to receive a group of excitants which have one feature in common in relation to the organism, namely, a nocuous or noxious character.

[‡]In most multisynaptic reflexes, it is not possible to count the number of interneurons. Suffice it to say that according to Eccles (1977) "there are hundreds and even thousands of synapses for the convergent pathways onto a single neuron. In fact, one type of neuron, the large Purkinje cell in the cerebellum, has about 80,000 of these excitatory synaptic endings, but they are small" (p. 124).

edge. In this way, a much more sharply defined signal with enhanced imagery eventually comes up to the cortex, and again there is the same type or variety of inhibitory sculpturing of the signal. As a consequence, touch stimuli can be more precisely located and evaluated. Because of this inhibition, a strong cutaneous stimulus is often surrounded by an area that has a reduced sensitivity. The concept of inhibition within the nervous system is, of course, intimately linked with excitation phenomena.

Inhibition

The term *inhibition* as applied to synaptic transmission refers to an active process by which excitatory transmission is prevented. Sir John Eccles (1977) defined inhibition as follows:

> nerve impulses exert an inhibitory action when they cause a depression of the generation of impulses by nerve or muscle cell, which is attributable to a specific physiological process and which does not arise as a consequence of its previous activation. Thus, the decrease in excitability of a neuron caused by a large afterhyperpolarization is not attributable to inhibition; it is caused by previous activity of the cell (p. 98).

There are at least two types of central nervous system inhibition, presynaptic and postsynaptic. In a sense, the terms are inadequate because both mechanisms involve synaptic transmission and presumably the release of chemical transmitter substances. The nomenclature was developed, however, because of the different locations of the inhibitor synapses on the membrane of the postsynaptic cell. In "presynaptic" inhibition, the output of the excitatory transmitter is reduced, and the electrical properties of the postsynaptic membrane are unaffected. In "postsynaptic" inhibition, the inhibitory action is exerted solely on the postsynaptic membrane which is hyperpolarized,* and the presynaptic terminals are unaffected.

The presynaptic inhibitory transmitter in humans is gamma-amino butyric-acid (GABA). Presynaptic inhibition has no patterned topography. It is widely dispersed over the afferent fibers of a limb with little tendency to focal application. For example, presynaptic inhibitory action by the afferent fibers of a muscle is effective on the afferent fibers from all

---

*Hyperpolarization indicates the increased potential produced across a cell membrane. In the normal resting state, the cell is polarized in that there is a potential difference between the inside and the outside of the cell, with 70 millivolts (mv) negative charge inside the cell membrane.

muscles of that limb regardless of function. This widespread non-specific character is exactly what would be expected for the general suppressor influence of negative feedback. Nevertheless, there is organization or pattern in the distribution of presynaptic inhibition. It depends on the class or modality of the afferent fiber on which the presynaptic inhibition falls, with the cutaneous afferent fibers being the most strongly affected.

Presynaptic inhibition seems to be mainly operative or effective at the first or primary afferent level (first order neuron, Fig. 5–4) rather than at the higher levels of the brain. It does play an important role, however, in pathways through the thalamus and lateral geniculate body, and this type of inhibitory action is utilized by descending pathways from the cerebrum at synapses made by primary afferent fibers either in the spinal cord or in the dorsal column nuclei. In the thalamus, there is presynaptic as well as postsynaptic inhibition. At higher levels of the brain, including the cerebellar and the cerebral cortices, both the neocortex and the hippocampus, inhibition is mainly carried out by postsynaptic inhibition.

Inhibition Directed from the Cerebral Cortex

Efferent pathways from the sensorimotor cortex excite the thalamo-cortical relay cells and excite both types of inhibitory neurons in the cuneate nucleus in the lower medulla. By exerting inhibition, the cerebral cortex is able to block these synapses and to protect itself from being stimulated by cutaneous stimuli that can be neglected. This happens for example when one is deep in thought, preoccupied with an experience or intensely involved in carrying out an action. Counterirritation to relieve pain acts in this way. Discharges from the cerebral cortex down the pyramidal tract and other pathways will exert an inhibitory blockage at the relays in the spinocortical pathways.

Inhibitory Cells

According to Eccles (1977) inhibitory cells are specific neurons. They act via unique transmitter substances, which in the spinal cord is almost always the amino acid glycine, while at the supraspinal and higher levels of the brain it is nearly always gamma-aminobutyric-acid (GABA). At least ten supraspinal inhibitory pathways are currently known to operate through GABA. Over 30 species of neurons in different parts of the brain function purely as inhibitors. An example of an inhibitory feedback pathway in the spinal cord is the Renshaw cell pathway (Fig. 2–13). Another example of an inhibitory feedback pathway is the basket cell pathway relaying onto a pyramidal cell.

Inhibitory Function of the Cerebellum

The cerebellum is the great "smoother" of all motor activities. The Purkinje cells are large nerve cells, arranged in a one-cell deep layer, located in the cerebellar cortex (Fig. 2–17). The sole output from the cerebellar cortex is by Purkinje cells which inhibit the intracerebellar nuclear cells at the molecular-granular layer junction. In fact, all neurons of the cerebellar cortex are inhibitory except the granule cells, and the unique feature of the cerebellar cortex is that its output is expressed entirely by the inhibitory Purkinje cells. Nowhere else in the brain is the dominance of inhibition so marked. How can information be conveyed effectively in this negative manner? It has to be remembered that this inhibitory action is exerted on nuclear cells that have a strong background discharge and that most of the inputs to the cerebellum give excitatory collaterals to the nuclear cells. Eccles gives the analogy of the sculpture of stone. The sculptor has a block of stone and achieves form by "taking away" stone through chiseling. Similarly, the Purkinje cell output of the cerebellum achieves form in the nuclear cell discharges by taking away from the background discharges through the process of inhibition.

Motor Coordination

In many of the motor disorders for which biofeedback treatment is effective there may be insufficient cerebellar influence. Gordon Holmes (1876– 1962) who studied the effects of cerebellar lesions in man with numerous publications for more than 30 years described disability due to cerebellar abnormality as "decomposition of movement" (1907, 1939). The cerebellum is concerned with the reliable and regulated control of movement. With a cerebellar lesion, the movement which was previously carried out unconsciously has to be consciously thought out at each joint and at each step in the sequence of movement. The cerebellum is the part of the brain which through the process of evolution has come to function as a special computer by handling all the complex inputs from receptors or from other parts of the brain. In the evolutionary scale, it is needed for data computation to accomplish the skilled movements in fish with lateral line organs and in birds for winged flight. The articulation of speech is also subserved by cerebellar mechanisms.

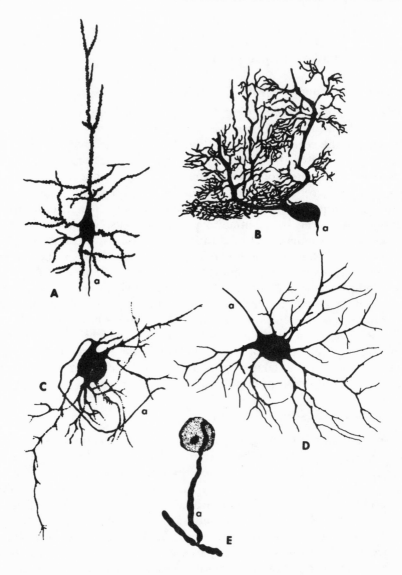

FIGURE 2-17. VARIETY OF FORMS OF NEURONS. THE NEURON IN A IS
CHARACTERIZED BY A CELL BODY THAT HAS A
ROUGHLY PYRAMIDAL SHAPE. THIS TYPE OF NEURON,
CALLED A PYRAMIDAL CELL, IS TYPICAL OF THE CERE-
BRAL CORTEX. NOTE THE MANY SPINOUS PROCESSES
LINING THE SURFACE OF THE DENDRITES. THE AXON
IS LABELED A IN THIS AND THE OTHER DRAWINGS.

THE CELL TYPE IN B WAS FIRST DESCRIBED BY THE CZECHOSLOVAKIAN NEUROANATOMIST PURKINJE, AND IT HAS SINCE BEEN KNOWN AS THE PURKINJE CELL. PURKINJE CELLS ARE CHARACTERISTIC OF THE CERE-BELLAR CORTEX. THE CELL BODY IS PEAR-SHAPED, WITH A RICH DENDRITIC PLEXUS ORIGINATING FROM ONE END AND THE AXON FROM THE OTHER. THE FINE BRANCHES OF THE DENDRITES ARE COVERED WITH SPINES (NOT SHOWN). THE NEURONS IN C AND D ARE MOTOR IN FUNCTION. C SHOWS A SYMPATHETIC POSTGANGLIONIC NEURON; D IS AN ALPHA MOTONEU-RON OF THE SPINAL CORD. BOTH ARE MULTIPOLAR NEURONS WITH RADICALLY ARRANGED DENDRITES. THE CELL IN E IS SENSORY IN FUNCTION. IT IS A DORSAL ROOT GANGLION CELL. THERE ARE NO DENDRITES. THE AXON BRANCHES INTO A CENTRAL AND A PERIPHERAL PROCESS. BECAUSE THE AXON IS THE RESULT OF FUSION OF TWO PROCESSES DURING EMBRYONIC DEVELOPMENT, THESE CELLS ARE DES-CRIBED AS PSEUDOUNIPOLAR NEURONS RATHER THAN UNIPOLAR. (Reproduced, with permission, from Willis, William D., Jr., and Grossman, Robert G.: Medical Neurobiology, ed. 2, St. Louis, The C. V. Mosby Co., 1977.)

Movement Performance

The neural events in the cerebrocerebellar circuits may be visualized during some skilled action; for example, playing the piano or running a machine at work. There will be initially a motor command with a preprogramming of the movements by circuits in the association cor-tex, cerebellum, basal ganglia, and thalamic nuclei. The learned skills are mobilized, and the discharge leads on to the action impulses in the pyramidal tract with the consequent report of the discharge to the pars intermedia, which is that part of the cerebellar cortex receiving and projecting both to the cerebrum and the spinal cord. Cerebral "will-ing" of a muscle movement sets in train neural events that lead to the discharge of pyramidal cells. Some of the electrophysiologic correlates of these events can be recorded on the electroencephalogram (EEG).

If a subject is presented with a warning stimulus followed by a second stimulus to which he is instructed to make a response, then a small electronegative potential can be recorded from the frontocentral region of the brain between the occurrence of the first stimulus and the operant response. This potential change, which is of the order of 20 μv in adults can sometimes be seen in the primary trace but is best displayed by averaging about ten trials. The phenomenon was first described by Grey Walter (1964) who named it the "contingent negative variation" (CNV). It is regarded as a measure of attention and expectancy and for this reason is also known as the "expectancy wave." Only when the two stimuli are associated and the subject is instructed to terminate the second by pressing a button does the CNV occur. Progressive extinction of the CNV occurs when the imperative (second) stimulus is withdrawn and the operant response is no longer performed. The CNV does not depend on the modality or intensity of the stimuli used, but its amplitude is positively related to the subject's degree of attention to the experimental situation. The CNV is thus augmented by incentive and motivation and diminished by distraction and fatigue.

This contingent negative variation or expectancy wave (E wave) appears in normal subjects whenever a warning or conditional stimulus is followed by an event which is expected to involve an action or decision. This event may be a second (imperative) stimulus or a moment when a decision must be taken. Neither external sensory stimuli nor overt motor acts are essential for the appearance of the expectancy wave. The potential difference, which constitutes this wave, arises in the superficial layers of the premotor frontal cortex. It is reduced by equivocation and boredom, and increased by exhortation and on occasion by competition. The E wave can develop in 0.5 sec and may persist for 20 sec if the subject is highly motivated. It is not dependent on stimulus modality or intensity and may be evoked by semantic, pictorial, or verbal signals or imput. Although Walter described it as easily or readily recorded, it requires special direct current (DC) recording and expertise not readily available in most electroencephalographic laboratories. It has therefore remained a research tool rather than a clinical tool with wide application.

The intention wave (**Bereitschaftspotential,** or "I" wave) was described by Kornhuber and Deecke in 1965. It was first noted as a slow increase in negativity at the vertex during a period of about one second before a subject decides to clench the fist. It usually begins about 0.8 sec before the onset of the movement.

As noted earlier the boredom effect was shown by Grey Walter. Responses evoked by monotonous stimuli decline steadily unless the character of the stimulus is changed. When paired stimuli are presented and a normal subject is asked to respond to the second stimulus, the primary responses to the first stimulus are augmented and a new electrical effect (this E wave) appears in the brain in the period between the first ("conditional") or warning stimulus and the second ("imperative") one.

In normal subjects, the CNV is constant but follows variations in mood and attitude. It terminates abruptly when the decision or action is completed. Grey Walter noted that in "conditions of acute or chronic stress, including equivocation in normal subjects, the development of the CNV is correlated with the type and degree of mental disorder."

The potential generated in these experiments with the E wave or the I wave is of very small amplitude, about 20 μv, and can be seen clearly only by averaging from approximately a dozen trials; and they are, therefore, often contaminated by extracerebral potentials, mainly eye movements. The expectancy wave and the readiness or intention wave are probably the same phenomenon. "The properties of these slow potential changes suggest that they may reflect the mechanism whereby cerebral responses to sensory signals are integrated, correlated with internal memory stores, and translated into relevant decisions or actions" (Walter WG, 1967, p. 129).

Conscious Control and "Split-Brain"

The criteria ordinarily adopted in ascribing consciousness to an individual can be equally well-applied to the independent activities of the separated cerebral hemispheres after commissurotomy (section of the corpus callosum and the anterior commissure which are the main tissue bridges connecting the two cerebral hemispheres) resulting in the so-called split-brain. This mental division has been demonstrated in regard to perception, cognition, volition, learning, and memory (Sperry, 1969). We may conceive that during biofeedback training, new linkage pathways are established between perception of the monitor measurements fed back and the unconscious physical changes in whatever modality is being monitored at the time. The patient's body makes physical changes in by-passing the ordinary sequence of volitional motor activity.

The term *co-conscious* was introduced in 1914 by Morton Prince to denote simultaneous but independent conscious events in hysterical patients exhibiting states of dissociation. It is perhaps also appropriate to designate these as split-brain phenomena in the same way. The evidence for attributing consciousness to each of the disconnected cerebral hemispheres is strong (Sperry, 1974).

When lateralized sensory input is fed simultaneously to the two hemispheres, two concurrent yet independent perceptual events will take place. It is not certain how much the findings in split-brain patients can be generalized to persons with intact cerebral commissures. The fact of bilateral sensory representation of certain parts of the body (e.g., the face) at all events, however, raises the possibility of dual perceptual experience in the normal individual (Trevarthen and Sperry, 1973).

Neural Vigilance

"Neural vigilance" (Head, 1926) can be defined as a state of high-grade physiological efficiency of the central nervous system, or of its parts. It is assessed in terms of the perfection, complexity, and adaptiveness of its reaction. At the level of the cerebral cortex, lowered vigilance is expressed in terms of fluctuation of attention, inconstancy of psychophysiological thresholds, and increased variability of response. "Consciousness," wrote Head, "stands in the same relation to the vigilance of the higher centres as adapted and purposive reflexes to those of lower rank in the neural hierarchy." Trevarthen and Sperry (1973) have described the split-brain as "deficient in the production of consciousness." This description can apply to those whose brains are anatomically intact, but functionally split. In biofeedback training, the goal is to restore brain function that links awareness to motor performance, i.e., to resolve the split. For example, in the case of paresis, increased motor activity in the affected limb can lead to improved functioning as the individual learns to attend to physiologic stimuli through receiving biofeedback concerning his motor performance.

Self-Regulation

Before we as individuals can regulate our reaction to events, internal or external, we need to know whether we are reacting in our motor performance (our behavior) in response to a particular stimulus, or to a combination of stimuli. A combination of stimuli may occur when the original stimulus becomes associated with additional stimuli and their concomitant feeling-tone (affect).

Many of the patients for whom biofeedback is useful are those who have at some stage (probably early on in the disease process) "generalized" their symptoms. That is, their symptoms have "spread" beyond the immediate involvement of their specific tissues and have acquired "secondary" qualities or properties. As an example, the symptom of pain as related to a circumscribed tissue injury may be described. Anxiety is added to the pain: anxiety as to what the pain signifies and as to what the consequences of the pain will be for the patient in terms of personal future activities or limitations. Anxiety then acts as a reinforcer of pain. It enlarges the sphere of pain and helps to generalize the symptom. Anxiety multiplies the pain and spreads it beyond the original area of tissue injury. In this way, behavior may be altered. For example, the joint next to the injured one is guarded and is held immobile and so it becomes stiff and painful. Therapeutically, therefore, it is necessary to recircumscribe the pain, and to strip it of its secondary concretions. This is what the patient can learn to do for himself, and it restores to him the power of self-regulation.

Kinesthetic Memory

It may be postulated that body memory, or kinesthetic memory (the reflex action which takes place at the tissue level) is the same as the memory which teaches small children how to walk. This memory may operate through subtle somatic cues. A baby is laying down body patterns which are linked to consciousness at the moment in which they are performed, but he has no memory of them. Thus, we cannot describe how we learned to walk, to ride a bicycle, to pound a nail, or drive a car until we go back and analyze the activity, dissecting it into its component parts. In addition, learning is impeded when the activity is "rewarded" with pain or "responds" with pain leading to withdrawal of the limb or part involved. The process of learning is best served when the subject wishes to repeat the performance.

Learning

One of the important features (or properties) of learning is the ability to make connections between previously separate pieces of information. The connection may be fragile or temporary initially and later become consolidated. These connections are rapid linkages of individual "bits" (in computer terminology), and these separate or disparate pieces of information may occur often at the nonverbal level. We may therefore feel that they occur in or through the right hemisphere pathways, as though by rapid transit of intracortical mechanisms. We often find that one piece of information makes little or no sense until another piece is put into juxtaposition. The temporal (time) element is also crucial for learning, as a finite amount of time is required for a fact to be absorbed. This may be expressed by saying that short-term memory requires a certain specified time to be laid down. In the verbal sphere, the piece of information cannot be retained long enough to adhere to the next, or to make the next piece or "bit" meaningful, unless the thread of logic and grammar is retained. The same is true in the sphere of music: unless the spacing, timing, or rhythm is preserved, the musical meaning does not acquire or take on musical conviction.

A subject may have knowledge of one fact independently. That isolated fact, however, may remain dormant or nonsensical until it is linked to another fact. From this point of view, a "fact" may remain nonmeaningful unless and until it is linked or attached to its biologically related neighbor. A useful analogy is that of an enzyme which is biologically inert until it comes into contact with its appropriate substrate. For example, one may think of the owner of these unrelated facts as someone who is agnostic until the facts acquire meaning. This is the difference between "seeing" and "perceiving"; and in this sense, a fact "known" also becomes a fact that is "felt" to be true.

Very often the acquisition of that piece of knowledge is greeted by the comment or remark: "Ah, of course!" The "of course!" reflects insight or the "rightness" of the feeling that the piece of knowledge gives—as though it were known before, but merely had not been put into words. One may say that it was recognized as a "fact" by the nonverbal right hemisphere but was waiting to be clothed in words before it could become apparent. The quality of insight was added when a feeling could be put into the symbol of words. As a working hypothesis, biofeedback may be considered a technique of fusion which links physiological processes into new chains, so that a movement or a segment of behavior is added to (or taken away from) the organism.

These two elements in learning—the linkage so that an event or a fact previously alone, disconnected, irrelevant, acquires meaning and the time factor, whereby the linkage must be sufficiently rapid for the chemical precipitation to take place—may be considered when transferred to the field of analytic psychology. In this discipline, the "connection" is noted as an "association." The mechanism of using associations (which appear at first meaningless to the originator) to clarify thought processes or behavior patterns to the originator may be the form of learning that takes place, for example, in analysis. Thus, Freud in developing the method of "free association" came to use the mechanism that allows dream and other material to surface to consciousness and fuse with waking and conscious thoughts. This is the form of learning that Arthur Koestler described as the "ah-ha!" of revelation, or insight, or creative thinking.

Language and certain analytic processing are currently thought to be controlled by (represented in) the left hemisphere. This has been termed the "dominant" hemisphere (in the right-handed as well as the majority of left-handed individuals). The term *leading* hemisphere, however, may be more accurate as Zangwill pointed out. It may "lead" or come first in the "willing" or programming of certain events and movements. On the other hand, the "nonlanguage" hemisphere appears to be "dominant" for several cognitive functions such as the ability to generate a concept of the whole from fragmentary spatial information about objects (Desmedt, 1979). The loss of this latter ability is termed *simultagnosia*, meaning that when information is fragmented the subject fails to perceive the picture or the concept as a whole. Cerebral event-related potentials can be recorded, and this may enlighten understanding of the underlying neuronal activities.

Experiments are currently being developed to link biofeedback procedures with cerebral event-related potentials in order to learn more of the neuroanatomical substrates of behavior (Hillyard and Picton, 1979).

The Reward System of the Brain

In this section, the anatomical pathways of the "reward" system will be described, starting with Olds and Milner's (1954) experiments of bar-pressing in the rat and its association with the medial forebrain bundle (MFB). Second, the evidence for similar locations of catecholamine pathways and areas of self-stimulation will be given. Third, it should be noted that certain drugs affect the rate at which the rats will stimulate themselves, and there is a connection between these mood-altering drugs and the catecholamines. Fourth, it should be noted that the anatomical substrate for these self-stimulating experiments overlaps the part of the brain involved in learning and memory functions.

The concept of a reward system in the brain started when Olds and Milner, working at McGill University, first described activity in the rat which seemed related to reward and self-satisfaction (1954, 1958). They demonstrated that a rat with an electrode implanted in the medial forebrain bundle (which is a fiber tract relatively more prominent in the rat than in the human) will press a bar or a treadle which sends an electrical impulse to the electrode in the MFB to stimulate itself. This phenomenon is now referred to as brain reward and can be localized to particular nerve cells and their fibers. The brain reward system can be affected by drugs that interact with the substances secreted by these nerve cells. Stimulation of the MFB (with nerve fibers passing through the hypothalamus) gives rise to the highest rates of treadle-pressing in response to the lowest electric current. Olds and Milner (1954) showed that shocks from electrodes in the MFB produced response rates of more than 100 presses a minute, whereas stimulation in the adjacent septal area caused a response of only about 10 presses a minute. From this discovery that the brain had so-called pleasure centers, research led to a demonstration that these centers belong to a system of pathways that appear to play a role in learning and memory. We shall now trace the sequence of this research and these observations.

Routtenberg (1978) observed that a rat given a choice between two treadles, one delivering a rewarding brain stimulation and the other delivering the only food available to the animal, will forego the food in order to obtain brain stimulation (Routtenberg, 1978). The same self-starvation can be demonstrated in the rhesus moneky, which has a much more developed cortex than the rat (Routtenberg, 1978). Thus, even primates will stop eating in order to obtain rewarding brain stimulation. Since the behavior is so compulsive, one wonders whether the reward system may play a role in drug addiction. For example, there is some evidence that certain regions of the brain, which are sensitive to morphine and contain the morphine-like peptide substance enkephalin (see Chap. 5), are located in the same regions as those supporting brain reward.

The medial forebrain bundle is the projection system of the lateral preoptic and lateral hypothalamic areas. Its fibers arise from limbic structures at the base of the frontal lobe surrounding the termination of the olfactory tract. The bundle passes through the preoptic and hypothalamic nuclei and many fibers ascend, descend, enter, and leave at all levels of the bundle which appears to extend to the midbrain. Some of the descending connections of the lateral hypothalamic area are in the periacqueductal grey matter. Connections are also made with the limbic system, the fornix, mamillothalamic, and mamillotegmental tracts. Certain specific pathways have been found associated with brain reward: in the rat, Routtenberg made lesions at frontal cortex self-stimulation sites and traced a pathway through the caudate nucleus and the internal capsule, and at the level of the hypothalamus, where this pathway is intermingled with the MFB. This system may be only one of several brain-reward systems passing through the MFB.

Self-stimulation points have been observed in the frontal cortex of the squirrel monkey similar to the regions mapped in the rat. Brain reward can be found not only in the frontal cortex and the hypothalamus, but also deep within the brain stem, in the pons and the medulla.

Some of the regions where brain-reward systems are identified seem to overlap the pathways that are associated with catecholamine neurotransmitters. Neurotransmitters are chemicals that allow the nerve impulse to be transmitted across the synapse from one nerve cell to another. Neurotransmitters of this type are suspected of being involved in self-stimulation.

In 1971, Ungerstedt of the Karolinska Institute of Stockholm presented some now classic pictures of monoamine pathways in the rat forebrain, midbrain, and hindbrain. He worked with the technique of histofluorescence in which the location of specific substances in a tissue is revealed by inducing them to emit light of a characteristic color after chemical treatment with fluorescent markers. With this histofluorescence technique, the separate pathways associated with two catecholamines, norepinephrine (noradrenaline) and dopamine, were delineated. This histofluorescent technique is based on histochemical principles; it is chemical in that it reveals brain pathways through a chemical reaction with neurotransmitters, and histological in that the reaction takes place in a thin section of brain tissue on a microscopic slide. Two major noradrenergic systems were discovered; the so-called dorsal and ventral pathways. The dorsal pathway has been implicated in a number of functional states including sleep-wakefulness, water balance, stress and depression. Catecholamine pathways in humans analogous to those observed in the brain of rats and monkeys have now been noted (Hökfelt et al., 1978).

The evidence for similar location of catecholamine pathways and areas of self-stimulation is not the only reason for suggesting a connection between catecholamines and the brain-reward system. The rate at which rats will self-stimulate is affected by certain drugs that are known to interfere with the function of catecholamines. The same drugs are known to affect mood in human beings. Agents that elevate catecholamine levels or mimic the action of catecholamines facilitate self-stimulation. Agents that lower these levels depress self-stimulation. For example, the drug dextroamphetamine potentiates both the action of catecholamines and self-stimulation. The drug chlorpromazine (Thorazine) blocks the action of catecholamines and also blocks self-stimulation.

It is not implied that there is current evidence that the neurochemistry of the brain is altered when biofeedback techniques form a part of the treatment regime of the patient. Since mood changes have been identified concomitantly with biochemical changes (for example, serum cortisol levels are altered during depressive states), however, it is not unreasonable to postulate that functional changes or "spontaneous" fluctuations in endogenous neurochemical substances may accompany behavior changes.

Investigators of brain-reward systems have put forward several hypotheses about the possible differences among the roles played by different catecholamines. They postulate that self-stimulation may be mediated (1) by either norepinephrine or dopamine solely; (2) by both, but independently; or (3) by both in concert. Both the norepinephrine and dopamine systems send their axons into the cerebral cortex. This raises the possibility that the highly complex and intricate patterns of intellectual activity in the cortex are influenced by phylogenetically more primitive catecholamine systems. (Certainly this hypothesis would not have seemed foreign to the thinking of the neurologist Freud.)

A link may be made at this juncture between brain-reward and memory mechanisms. Brain-reward studies have implicated the entorhinal cortex as an area supporting self-stimulation (Routtenberg, 1978). Fibers in this region project to the hippocampus, a brain structure involved in the formation of memory and recently shown to be connected with memory of spatial relations. Routtenberg speculated that the pathways of brain reward may function as the pathways of memory consolidation: "When something is learned, activity in the brain-reward pathways facilitates the formation of memory." Routtenberg and his colleagues found that continuous stimulation of brain-reward regions in the MFB, the substantia nigra, or the frontal cortex applied in the course of learning a simple task disrupted the ability of an experimental animal to remember the task 24 hours later. On the other hand, stimulation of the locus coeruleus (which apparently is not involved in brain reward) had no effect on the retention of the task. Collating experimental results from different laboratories on the findings of "reward" stimulation and memory of learned tasks, Routtenberg postulated that "stimulation must be applied both in the appropriate brain region and at the right moment in the learning process in order to hinder memory." He suggested that the enhancement of memory is to a large extent mediated by the dopamine system of the substantia nigra. However that may be, the evidence shows that the brain-reward pathways play an important role in learning and memory.

"Evidence for the reward effect of localized electrical stimulation, for the control of the brain reward by psychoactive drugs, and for the association of reward pathways with memory formation indicates that the neural substrates of self-stimulation play a vital role in the guidance of behavior" (Routtenberg, 1978, p. 159).

Although several reward systems have been isolated and demonstrated involving all levels of the brain from the medulla oblongata to the cerebral cortex, they all possess pathways leading through the medial forebrain bundle. This suggests that this region of the hypothalamus may be described as the "relay station" or round house through which the brain-reward pathways course.

In addition, a large number of peptide-containing pathways in the brain are now described which are changing our concepts of many neuro-psychiatric states including the experience of pain (Elde and Hökfelt, 1978; Hökfelt et al, 1980).

Response-Reinforcing Stimulus Mechanisms in Biofeedback Training: Operant Behavior

Neurological thinking has been largely governed by Sherringtonian principles of stimulus-response (S-R) mechanisms underlying motor activity and therefore behavior. There now can be added to our neurological thinking the concept that a "response-stimulus" mechanism plays a role in underlying motor activity. This phrase "response-stimulus" may at first sound nonsensical to the classical neurologist. It can, however, be made clearer by adding the qualifying adjective "reinforcing" to the word stimulus and by rephrasing the idea as "activity-reinforcing stimulus." It will be better understood by envisaging an actual situation. For example, a person yawns; the activity of yawning stretches the muscle spindles around the temporomandibular joint and this acts as a reinforcing stimulus for a further yawn. If the subject merely opens the mouth, letting the jaw fall passively with gravity, there is usually insufficient stretch stimulus to cause a second yawn. The subject has to inspire (draw in a breath) as he opens his mouth in order to evoke adequate reinforcing stimulus to produce the next yawn. Such inspiration is termed operative because it leads to or enforces the subsequent activity (the second yawn). In other words, it has operated a piece of motor activity. It is causal behavior. In another example, a person touches a button, and music begins to play; the auditory stimulus of the music acts as the reinforcing stimulus for the subject to push the button again. This, of course, is a more complex or indirect "activity-reinforcing stimulus" situation because there is no choice or latitude in that, if the music does not please the listener, he may not press the button again. In a similar way, however, the subject also has the choice (albeit more limited) of not responding to the reinforcing stimulus of the jaw stretch by a further yawn. Whether or not the initial behavior is repeated after receiving reinforcement by the stimulus depends upon a number of variables. It is with these variables that biofeedback is concerned. It is also concerned with causing motor activity after reinforcing stimuli. Behavior which is followed by a positively reinforcing stimulus or terminates (reduces) a noxious reinforcing stimulus is termed *operant behavior* (see Chap. 1).

Biofeedback sometimes deals with "initial stimulus-response" mechanisms in the Sherringtonian sense, tracing the afferent-efferent pathways through the brain. On the other hand, however, it often deals with the "response-reinforcing stimulus" mechanism (or "activity-reinforcing stimulus" mechanism). In this latter type, the subject performs an action (for example, contracting a weak, partially paralyzed muscle); this causes a sound from the biofeedback instrument and the patient responds by contracting a second time in order to receive the pleasure of hearing the sound (which is sweet music to his ears because it indicates that the muscle is functioning). The fact that the muscle contracts causes summation of action potentials, and with both spatial and temporal summation more muscle fibers contract on the next occasion. This is the kind of "positive" muscle contraction mechanism used for muscle rehabilitation biofeedback when there is insufficient motor activity. Another example of the "response-reinforcing stimulus" situation is when the patient has pain from performing an action (overcontracting the back muscles). This causes a high-pitched grating sound from the biofeedback instrument, and the patient responds by relaxing the muscle so that the intensity of sound goes down and at the same time the pain is less because fewer of the "Type C" fibers which carry pain sensations to the parietal cortex are stimulated. The patient has in fact used his inhibitory mechanisms rather than his excitatory neuronal mechanisms. In the actual practice of motor control, however, the patient does not have to be aware of the exact mechanism whereby the desired effect has been achieved. For example, an individual is not aware of the exact curling movements performed by the tongue when he speaks, until he has a neurological lesion which destroys part of the mechanism of articulation. He then has to become aware of the exact movements of the tongue in order to volitionally direct the operation. Behavior then becomes, in part, operant behavior.

There is a difference between "body-memory" or somatic memory which is not conscious and appears to rely heavily on peripheral mechanisms, and cerebral memory which can be verbalized and is more purely central. This may be illustrated by an example of complex motor movements (complex behavior). The child prodigy violinist produced musical sounds on the violin with greater facility than the "average" child. He is not aware of the exact mechanism whereby the fingers operate on the instrument. Later in life, he may change, and for a number of reasons connected with his "psychological" status, (meaning the internal stimuli which in part caused the original motor behavior of operating the violin), he loses some of the motor skills involved with using his fingers. When he asks himself, "How did I do it?," he is only able to answer partially and incompletely. He then has to use the "response-reinforcing stimulus" mechanisms to relearn. He plays; he watches the fingers both directly and in a mirror; and when the sound is correct to his ears, he "memorizes" both in his consciousness and in his fingers (body-memory, or kinesthetic joint memory) the feeling (meaning the afferent stimulus) which leads to that particular motor response. For all these mechanisms to work, there has to be a "reward" or pleasurable sensation; and clearly the more "conscious" the subject, or in other words, the more aware of the significance of the reward to himself, the quicker will the linkage be established between the reinforcing stimulus and the response. It is in this light that one may look at behavior as a chain reaction composed of an initiating stimulus leading to a response, leading to a reinforcing-stimulus leading to a response, and so on sequentially. In this way, peripheral neuronal activity is linked to cortical neuronal activity, leading to further peripheral activity, and repeated again in sequence.

An analogy may be drawn regarding behavior in an interdisciplinary approach. The psychiatrist and the analyst are examining the factors operating at the "initiating stimulus" end, meaning that they study the patterns of sensation, emotion, and behavior laid down early in the organism's neurological development. The neurologist observes the present ongoing behavior, and in classical tradition the neurologist has frequently regarded the nervous system in terms of exteroceptive or interoceptive stimuli causing responses. There may now be added the dimension of the operant-oriented psychologist who examines a segment of behavior (which the patient finds sufficiently distressing to cause him to seek advice), but who disregards the causes in the distant past for that behavior. By having repetitive reinforcing stimuli linked in the biofeedback technique to the opposite of that particular piece of motor activity, the patient comes to learn a different behavior. This new segment of motor activity is likely to cause new sensations which acquire feeling-tone, and the patient may then view himself or view the world through himself differently.

As a related neuropsychological theme, one may examine the meaning of "control-of-self" being at the basis of, or synonymous with, self-control. From the neurological point of view, it appears that subjects with poor impulse control are in some respects lacking good inhibitory mechanisms in the limbic system and, in particular, in the hypothalamus.

Thorndike (1898), who described the law of readiness (see Chap. 1), also emphasized the mechanisms of stimulus-response activity. This response activity can be termed *respondent activity*. Under specific experimental circumstances, it can be seen as respondent conditioning. It is of interest that with special DC recording of the brain waves, the contingent negative variation or expectancy wave of Grey Walter can be observed to give the electrical component of activity just prior to the operant response in classical conditioning experiments.

The whole field dealing with the role of reinforcement in the explanation of behavior is highly complex and this brief description must be regarded as an introduction to more detailed texts on reinforcement.

REFERENCES

Daube JR, Sandok BA: *Medical Neurosciences*. Boston, Little Brown, 1978, p. 157.

Desmedt JE: Somatosensory evoked potentials in man: Maturation, cognitive parameters and clinical uses in neurological disorders, in Lehmann D, Callaway E (eds): *Human Evoked Potentials*. New York, Plenum Press, 1979, p. 83.

Eccles JC: *The Understanding of the Brain*. New York, McGraw-Hill, 1977.

Elde R and Hökfelt T: Distribution of hypothalamic hormones and other peptides in the brain, in Ganong WF and Martini L (eds): *Frontiers in Neuroendocrinology* (Vol. 5). New York: Oxford University Press, 1978 p. 10.

Head H: *Aphasia and Kindred Disorders of Speech*. 2 Vols. Cambridge University Press, Cambridge, England, 1926, p. 496.

Hillyard SA, Picton TW: Event-related brain potentials and selective information processing in man, in Desmedt JE (ed): *Cognitive Components in Cerebral Event-Related Potentials and Selective Attention*. Progr Clin Neurol Physiol 6: 1979.

Hökfelt T, Elde R, Fuxe K: Aminergic and peptidergic pathways in the nervous system with special reference to the hypothalamus in Reichlin S, Baldessarini RJ and Martin JB (eds): *The Hypothalamus*. New York, Raven Press, 1978, p. 69.

Hökfelt T, et al.: Peptidergic neurons. Nature 284: 515, 1980.

Holmes G: An attempt to classify cerebellar disease. Brain 30: 545, 1907.

Holmes S: The cerebellum of man. Brain 62: 11, 1939.

Kornhuber HH, Deecke L: Hirnpotentialänderungen bei Willkürbewegungen und passiven Bewegungen des Menschen: Bereitschaftspotential und reafferent Potentiale. Pflügers Arch ges Physiol 284: 1, 1965.

Olds J: Self-stimulation of the brain: its use to study local effects of hunger, sex and drugs. Science 127: 315, 1958.

Olds J, Milner P: Positive reinforcement produced by electrical stimulation of septal area and other regions of rat brain. J Comp Physiol Psychol 47: 419, 1954.

Prince M: *The Unconscious*. Macmillan, New York, 1914.

Renshaw B: Influence of discharge of motoneurons upon excitation of neighboring motoneurons. J Neurophysiol 4: 167, 1941.

Renshaw B: Central effects of centripetal impulses in axons of spinal ventral roots. J Neurophysiol 9: 191, 1946.

Rexed B: A cytoarchitectonic atlas of the spinal cord in the cat. J Comp Neurol 100: 297, 1954.

Routtenberg A: Reward system of the brain. Sci Am 239: 154, 1978.

Ruffini A: On the minute anatomy of the neuro-muscular spindles of the cat, and their physiological significance. J Physiol (Lond.) 23: 190, 1898.

Sherrington CS: On reciprocal innervation of antagonistic muscles. Third note. Proc. Roy. Soc. 60: 414, 1897.

Sherrington CS: *The Integrative Action of the Nervous System.* Cambridge, England, Cambridge University Press, 1947.

Sperry RW: A modified concept of consciousness. Psychol Rev 76: 532, 1969.

Sperry RW: Lateral specialization in the surgically separated hemispheres, in Schmitt FO, Worden FG (eds): *The Neurosciences*. Cambridge, MIT Press, 1974, p. 5.

Thorndike E: Animal intelligence: an experimental study of the associative process in animals. Psychol Rev Monogr Suppl 2: 1898.

Trevarthen C and Sperry RW: Perceptual unity of the ambient visual field in human commissurotomy patients. Brain 96: 547, 1973.

Ungerstedt U: Stereotaxic mapping of the mono-amine pathways in the rat brain. Acta Phys Scand Suppl 367: 1, 1971.

Walter WG: Slow potential waves in the human brain associated with expectancy, attention and decision. Arch Psychiat Nervenkr 206: 309, 1964.

Walter WG: Electrical signs of association in the brain. Electroencephalogr Clin Neurophysiol Suppl 25: 258, 1967.

Walter WG: Slow potential changes in the human brain associated with expectancy, decision and intention. Electroencephalogr Clin Neurophysiol Suppl 26: 123, 1967.

Zangwill OL: Consciousness and the cerebral hemispheres, in Dimond SJ, Beaumont JG (eds): *Hemisphere Function in the Human Brain*. New York, Halsted, 1974, p. 272.

3

Relaxation Techniques: Hypnosis, Meditation, and Imagery

ALTHOUGH biofeedback is an effective clinical procedure, it is not used in isolation from other therapeutic techniques. Since many of its clinical applications focus on the reduction of anxiety or physiological arousal, relaxation procedures have been used with biofeedback to maximize this effect. The patient undergoing biofeedback treatment is often introduced to a relaxation technique prior to receiving biofeedback (Fair, 1979). Clinicians using biofeedback frequently develop their own individual relaxation procedures. Most of these modified techniques are based on the progressive relaxation method originally developed by Jacobson (1958) (see Chap. 1).

Standardized relaxation techniques are effective for most patients. If the patient has difficulty, the therapist must be certain that the patient's failure to relax is not due to a misconception or to therapeutic resistance. For example, some patients try too vigorously to relax, which results in increased tension. This may occur with Jacobson's technique because patients spend too much time tensing muscles and too little time relaxing. If a well-motivated patient, however, cannot adjust to the standard relaxation procedure, other methods are available. Biofeedback therapists must be familiar with alternative procedures when a standard technique fails to generate the desired response (i.e., lowered arousal). We define *arousal* as it is commonly used in the field of psychology; i.e., an excess level of muscular tension and hyperreactivity to stress. Current relaxation methods differ in a number of ways. Four major types will be examined: hypnosis, meditation, progressive muscle relaxation, and imagery. Each of these techniques will be discussed.

Hypnosis

Historical Development

The emergence of hypnotic techniques as a recognized form of psychological therapy has paralleled the growth of biofeedback techniques in the last two decades. Although formal hypnosis predates biofeedback by about two hundred years, it has until recently, had a checkered past. The unscientific image of hypnosis has been intensified by the activities of stage hypnotists and the portrayal of hypnosis in fiction and the cinema. However, hypnosis has been extensively and scientifically studied and has become an accepted treatment procedure in certain well-defined therapeutic approaches.

The concept of *animal magnetism* was created by Van Helmont (1577–1644) based on Paracelsus' (1493–1541) theory of magnetic forces. An 18th century Viennese physician, Franz Mesmer, used the concept of animal magnetism to develop a treatment technique based on the idea that illness was caused by an imbalance in an invisible, magnetic fluid. Mesmer and, later, hypnosis came to be regarded as quackery and both were banned in several European countries. However naive and unusual his theory and behavior appears today, Mesmer contributed to the development of modern clinical hypnosis because of his use of trance induction (Boring, 1950; see also Appendix).

Mesmer's controversial theories and practices caused medical practitioners, and others, to form negative opinions about hypnosis. The use of hypnotic techniques, however, by physicians such as Charcot, Liebault, and Bernheim helped maintain its importance in the mainstream of scientific inquiry (Boring, 1950).

Eventually, professional associations (such as the American Society for Clinical Hypnosis and the Society for Clinical and Experimental Hypnosis) established standards for its clinical practice. Professional training programs were developed to insure that hypnosis was used ethically and responsibly. Clinical hypnosis achieved a new level of acceptance in 1956, when an American Medical Association statement described it as a "valuable . . . therapeutic adjunct" (Goleman, 1977).

Theory

There are several theories to account for the clinical effectiveness of hypnosis. Controversy still exists, however, over whether or not hypnosis is a special trance state. For many years it was believed that subjects under hypnosis went into a special state or trance. This is the "state" theory of practitioners such as Milton Erickson (Goleman, 1977).

An alternative, and more recent, concept is referred to as the "non-state" theory (T. X. Barber, 1975). Barber believes that hypnosis is not a specifically different state of consciousness, although consciousness may be somwhat altered in the process. He has demonstrated empirically that anything a subject does under a "hypnotic trance" may be duplicated by those who are not in a trance.

Even theorists who believe that hypnosis produces a special trance state cannot agree on what actually occurs. Measurements of physiological changes in subjects undergoing hypnosis have had mixed results but have generally supported the theory that the neurological status of the subject is not altered qualitatively. There have been no consistent findings of altered EEG rhythms, eye movements, pulse rate, or galvanic skin response (Barber, 1975). Although hypnosis is a well-established clinical technique, basic research is still needed to investigate the process (Kroger and Felzer, 1976).

A thorough review of the therapeutic use of hypnosis, or hypnotherapy, is beyond the scope of this book. Researchers and therapists, who are well-versed in this technique, consider the relaxation which results from hypnosis as only one of many desirable effects of this procedure. In this chapter, only the relaxation effects of hypnosis will be discussed.

Hypnotic Relaxation

A variety of hypnotherapy techniques currently exist. These, however, have in common the induction of a condition (or state) where the subject becomes hypersuggestible. This allows the hypnotherapist to have significant influence over the subject's attitudes and/or behavior.

Kroger and Felzer (1976) summarize the hypnotherapeutic process which they have developed, involving what is described as a "double-bind" induction technique, based on the assumption that the subject will become automatically hypnotized. The term "double-bind" means that the subject cannot easily avoid being hypnotized. The phrase originated in the field of family therapy describing the situation of a child with schizophrenic parents, e.g., the child is given conflicting communication which causes him to be punished no matter what he does. Kroger and Felzer's induction technique involves the presentation of suggestions regarding physical sensations such as "warmth" or "heaviness." The subject is also given the suggestion that he can choose to control these sensations if he wishes. One result of this induction procedure is to make the subject believe that the hypnotherapist is responsible for these sensations, instead of realizing that they are self-produced.

In addition to standard induction techniques, patients are also "placed" into deeper states of relaxation through the use of "scene visualization," which is a technique common to many types of hypnotherapy. A narration is given to the subject describing relaxing scenes with vivid, sensory experiences and colorful, elaborate visual images.

A useful technique developed by Vogt (Kroger and Felzer, 1976) in the last century, is often employed to deepen the hypnotic state of relaxation. This is referred to as "fractionation" and, according to Kroger and Felzer, it involves the hypnotic presentation of sensations and images which the subject reported during previous hypnotic experiences.

After the first few sessions of hypnosis the subject is gradually introduced to "auto-hypnosis" (self-hypnosis). He learns to place himself into a deep state of relaxation through means of a conditioning process. Most therapeutic uses of hypnosis rely heavily on self-hypnosis. Indeed some theorists (e.g., Barber, 1975) argue that all hypnosis is self-hypnosis since the hypnotized subject ultimately can control the situation even though he may be convinced that he cannot.

Hypnotic induction (regardless of how it is accomplished) can result in a deep state of relaxation when employed by an experienced hypnotherapist.

Although biofeedback and hypnosis are frequently applied to treat the same disorders, few studies have been undertaken which compare their relative effectiveness. Some authors suggest that hypnotherapy is more effective than biofeedback but offer little evidence to support their claim (Kroger and Felzer, 1976).

Ian Wickramasekera (1976a) has conducted several experiments exploring the relationship between biofeedback and hypnosis. For example, he found that EMG training resulted in increased hypnotic susceptibility in young college males. Melzack and Perry (1976) combined alpha biofeedback training and hypnosis to teach patients control of chronic pain. They concluded that alpha biofeedback produced a marked reduction in pain only when accompanied with hypnosis and placebo effects (i.e., distraction and suggestion).

Wickramasekera (1976b) also hypothesized that biofeedback, behavior therapy techniques and hypnosis share many common elements. All three techniques arose from experimental laboratory studies, and in all three, various treatment components are specified in order that the therapist can control and predict the specific behavior of each patient. Biofeedback, behavior therapy and hypnosis all tend to focus on specific symptoms, to manipulate cognitive functioning, to focus on physiological consequences of verbal-motor events, emphasize informational feedback and reinforcement and expand the possibility of an individual to regulate his internal environment. Wickramasekera concludes that the important common element among these three types of treatment is that they strengthen the placebo response. In addition, Wickramasekera believes that patients who are good candidates for hypnosis (high hypnotic susceptibility) are also good candidates for biofeedback treatment.

Several biofeedback techniques have qualities similar to standard hypnotherapy, although they are not hypnotic procedures in the strict sense. One of these, "autogenic training," has become associated with biofeedback training. For example, Green and Green (1979) used autogenic training in conjunction with thermal biofeedback in the treatment of migraine (see Chap. 1).

A German physician Johann Schultz developed autogenic training, which he considered a form of self-hypnosis. His student, Wolfgang Luthe, refined the procedure and developed a therapeutic system based on it. The technique is most often used in a simpler form when employed in biofeedback training (Schultz and Luthe, 1969).

The procedure involves the presentation of psychophysiological statements such as: "my hands feel heavy and warm" during a state of passive concentration. Although, at first, the therapist presents these statements to the subject, the latter is to practice the technique after memorizing the appropriate sequence, with frequently repeated sensory statements such as "warm" and "heavy." The repetition of such statements results in deep relaxation which often leads to peripheral vasodilatation. It is, therefore, successful treatment for vasoconstrictive disorders such as migraine and Raynaud's disease (Green and Green, 1979). Many clinicians have developed autogenic feedback techniques based on Green's original study. These can be used in conjunction with thermal training (Green and Green, 1979). After each autogenic statement, the subject's average skin temperature is measured and recorded, so that the effect can be observed immediately. The measurements also allow the therapist to determine which statements best promote vasodilatation. The patient can then use these particular phrases to control vasoconstriction in situations when he cannot go through the entire procedure, for example, when working or engaged in daily activities.

In some ways this procedure is similar to Vogt's fractionation method. In autogenic feedback, however, the subject does not verbalize what he experiences; it is indicated by the electrothermal instrument. Besides being more immediate, such information is more objective and reliable than the subject's verbal report under hypnosis.

For further information, readers are referred to *Hypnosis and Behavior Modification* (Kroger and Felzer, 1976) and *Hypnotic Realities* (Erickson, Rossi, and Rossi, 1976).

Meditation

Meditative techniques have been adopted by many biofeedback therapists to elicit deep states of relaxation.

Meditation, especially that associated with the Eastern religions, such as Zen Buddhism, has been indirectly influential in the development of biofeedback in this country. The physiological effects of various forms of meditation accomplished under empirical conditions, such as Swami Rama's demonstration of bradycardia with cardiac asystole and restitution of heartbeat as reported by Green and Green (1977), stimulated research in the conscious control of physiologic events. It became clear, however, that few people could achieve similar results, though many individuals from diverse populations can be trained in physiologic control of autonomic events (although of a less dramatic nature) through the use of biofeedback.

Historical Development

Although meditation is often associated with the religions of the East, Christian ascetics in the West practiced a form of meditation in the 4th century. These meditation techniques involved the repetition of a single phrase from the Bible. This was later known as "Hesychasm," after a 5th century religious teacher named Hesychius.

The most popular of these techniques was the "Jesus Prayer," consisting of repeating the phrase "Lord Jesus Christ, Son of God, have mercy on us," in the Latin "Kyrie eleison," (as such it is one of the introductory responses of the Latin Mass). Other religions developed their own forms of meditation, including the Moslem "Sufism" and the Judaic "Kabbolah."

"Transcendental Meditation" (TM) was currently popularized by Maharishi Mehesh Yogi (Benson, 1975). As in every form of meditation, TM involves the use of a repetitive thought which leads to a deep state of relaxation and peace of mind. This repeated thought or "mantra" apparently is derived from the Sanskrit of the Hindu religion. Many members of the Western culture have become increasingly aware of other Eastern forms of meditation such as Yoga and Zen meditation or "Zazen".

Zazen has been studied extensively by Japanese researchers, who discovered that Buddhist monks can generate an unusually "high concentration of EEG alpha rhythms" (Kasamatsu and Hirai, 1966). Interest in biofeedback in that country is keen and research on the psychophysiological correlates of Zen meditation is being conducted in Japan. At an international symposium on biofeedback in Kyoto in 1977 the results of numerous investigations of Zazen were presented and an attempt was made to synthesize the Eastern tradition of Zen meditation with the Western technique of biofeedback.

Theory

When examining theoretical explanations for the effectiveness of meditation, it is difficult to separate theory from religious beliefs. Meditation is commonly seen as a method whereby the practitioner can achieve a closer relationship with a being or transcending experience. Altered states of consciousness are also thought to cause the physiological changes which accompany meditation.

Research on the effects of TM demonstrated that it results in "positive" changes in physiological responsiveness; positive in the sense that it lowers arousal. Herbert Benson (1975), a Harvard psychiatrist, reported that TM resulted in 10 to 20 percent lower oxygen consumption than in the normal waking state. (This decrease is greater than usually observed in sleeping subjects). Marked decreases were also observed in serum lactate levels (whereas high concentrations of serum lactate have been reported in chronically anxious subjects). The most significant physiological changes with TM involved reductions in systolic and diastolic blood pressure of individuals who regularly practiced meditation (Benson, 1975).

Meditative Relaxation

Various meditative techniques have been developed but all involve the same factors. Benson delineated four factors: a quiet environment, concentration, a comfortable bodily position, and a passive mental attitude.

Although hypnosis and other forms of relaxation also involve the first three factors, passivity is not stressed. On the contrary, in hypnosis, the subject actively listens to the suggestions of the hypnotist and is very much aware of bodily events. This differs from meditation, where the subject is not supposed to be actively concentrating on anything. The repetition of a certain sound or a single thought prevents the individual from actively engaging in distracting thought or imagery during meditation.

Benson developed a form of meditation (described in his book *The Relaxation Response*) as an efficient and economical alternative to TM. His procedure is straightforward and easy to learn; the subject is given the following six instructions:

1.   Sit quietly in a comfortable position.
2.   Close your eyes.
3.   Deeply relax all your muscles beginning at your feet and progressing up to your face. Keep them relaxed.
4.   Breathe through your nose. Become aware of your breathing. As you breathe out, say the word "ONE," silently to yourself. For example, breath IN . . . OUT, "ONE," IN . . . OUT, "ONE," etc. Breathe easily and naturally.
5.   Continue for 10 to 20 minutes. You may open your eyes to check the time, but do not use an alarm. When you finish sit quietly for several minutes, at first with your eyes closed and later with your eyes opened. Do not stand up for a few minutes.
6.   Do not worry about whether or not you are successful in achieving a deep level of relaxation. Maintain a passive attitude and permit relaxation to occur at its own pace. When distracting thoughts occur, try to ignore them by not dwelling on them and return to repeating "ONE." With practice the response should come with little effort. Practice this technique once or twice daily, but not within two hours after any meal, since the digestive process seems to interfere with the elicitation of the Relaxation Response (Benson, 1975, pp. 113–115).

Patients can learn this technique prior to biofeedback treatment.

Since TM has many adherents it is not unusual that a TM advocate may be referred for biofeedback treatment. It has been the authors' experience that teaching such individuals a different form of meditation or relaxation technique is counterproductive and may alienate them. Although TM may not have been effective in eliminating a specific disorder, therefore, it appears to be an adequate relaxation procedure and can be combined with biofeedback under these circumstances.

The only modification necessary is that concentration on the biofeedback signal may replace the mantra or be combined with it during the biofeedback training. Although TM purists may not favor this suggestion or insist that this is the antithesis of what they are attempting to achieve, many TM patients have been treated successfully using TM and biofeedback in a combined fashion.

Progressive Relaxation

Historical Development

Although both hypnosis and meditation result in states of deep relaxation, that is not their primary function. Relaxation is actually a secondary effect in both techniques. Other methods have been developed specifically to foster a relaxation response, however.

Edmund Jacobson is regarded as the originator of progressive relaxation. In 1908, Jacobson began his research at Harvard on the muscular correlates of anxiety and tension. He observed that tension can be defined, physiologically, as the inappropriate contraction of muscle fibers. From this, he developed the concept that complete relaxation of all muscles may eliminate anxiety. He noted that individuals can learn to relax their muscles deeply through a process of alternately contracting and relaxing major muscle groups. This procedure was termed *progressive muscle relaxation* (Jacobson, 1958).

His procedure consisted of approximately 50 sessions of relaxation training involving 15 muscle groups. These muscles were systematically relaxed; complete relaxation had to be accomplished in one muscle group before the subject was permitted to concentrate on another group.

Jacobson's methods became popular in the 1950s, when a variation of his technique was employed by Joseph Wolpe (1973), a psychiatrist noted for his development of "systematic desensitization" (see Chap. 1).

Wolpe modified Jacobson's technique to make it more practicable; instead of the subject going through the procedure over a long period, Wolpe streamlined the method so that progressive muscle relaxation could be accomplished in one session. All of the major muscle groups were relaxed systematically in less than an hour. Although this modification does not produce all of the physiological changes described by Jacobson, it results in a relatively deep state of relaxation.

Since then, variations of Wolpe's modification have been developed, and therapists have refined the technique to meet specific therapeutic demands. Many biofeedback therapists use a version of Wolpe's method to relax subjects prior to feedback training, and a familiar one was developed by Bernstein and Borkovec (1973).

Theory

The theory of progressive muscle relaxation is that it counteracts the physiological effects of tension. Since a muscle cannot contract and relax simultaneously, total muscle relaxation theoretically results in complete absence of bodily tension. Since bodily tension (i.e., inappropriate excess muscle contraction) and mental states of anxiety are closely related, muscle relaxation should eventually result in the reduction of anxiety. The patient acquires this skill by learning to differentiate between sensations associated with excess muscle contraction and those associated with relaxation. This is accomplished by having the subject carefully observe physiological changes as he alternates between states of contraction and relaxation in each major muscle group.

The efficacy of progressive relaxation was documented by Gordon Paul (1969) a psychologist, at the University of Illinois, with significant decreases in heart rate, respiration rate, muscular tension and reports of anxiety in subjects undergoing relaxation. Similar results were reported earlier for Wolpe's technique and Jacobson's original method (Wolpe, 1973).

Technique

The technique of progressive muscle relaxation involves the systematic contraction and relaxation of major muscle groups (usually 15 groups are used initially). As the subject learns how to relax, these groups can be combined and the entire procedure shortened. Eventually the patient should be able to relax individual muscle groups which do not have to be contracted in order to engage in certain activities.

Through a process of conditioning (see Chap. 1) the patient also learns to associate physiological sensations with various words or phrases used by the therapist. After the patient has gone through the entire procedure, the therapist may ask him to sit quietly and maintain the relaxed state by repeating the word "calm." Eventually, words such as "relax" or "calm" will be associated with a deep state of relaxation and can, therefore, be used to elicit the entire relaxation effect. As was discussed in Chapter 1 with reference to Pavlov's experiment, however, a conditioned response differs in degree from the unconditioned response. Therefore, the relaxation produced by a cue word (conditioned response) would not be as deep as that produced by the entire relaxation procedure (unconditioned response).

Relaxation procedures are further described in recent texts (Basmajian, 1979; Bernstein and Borkovec, 1973).

After the patient has mastered the basic relaxation technique, he can be introduced to the procedure of "differential relaxation." He learns to relax all muscles which do not have to be contracted in order to perform ongoing activity. For example, if he feels tense while driving a car, he can progressively relax all the nonessential muscle groups such as the forehead, neck, chest, and back while allowing essential muscles such as the arms and legs to remain contracted. This procedure takes time to learn and, obviously, may be dangerous if a person cannot maintain necessary tension in task-related muscles (Bernstein and Borkovec, 1973).

Several taped relaxation exercises, currently available, have been developed specifically for use with biofeedback (Budzynski, 1977).

Imagery

Historical Development

Compared with other relaxation methods, imagery techniques have not developed as systematically. The use of imagery for inducing relaxation has co-existed with other techniques such as hypnosis and relaxation training for the last century, however. Before then, imagery experiences (often artificially induced by drugs) played an important role in primitive religious rites. Artists have also used subjective imagery experiences to enhance their expression: e.g., the visual hallucinations experienced by Blake, Milton, and Poe with images of heaven, hell, and the supernatural.

Vivid imagery experiences have been associated with the development of many scientific hypotheses; for example, Kekule, a Belgian chemist, reportedly had a dream concerning the molecular structure of benzene. Similar imagery experiences were reported to have occurred to Descartes and Poincaré (Hilgard and Atkinson, 1967).

Many theorists believe that imagery experiences are influenced by activities of the right cerebral hemisphere, while mathematical and verbal concepts are more dependent on left hemisphere functioning. Highly creative individuals are thought to use imagery more than others, who may be more technically or verbally oriented.

Although most patients are able to produce images, they may have difficulty maintaining them over time. Many patients are unable to produce vivid, life-like images on demand. Individuals differ in their imagery ability; some people have very few imagery experiences or perhaps, none at all. Certain patients may need training in imagery production prior to being presented with imagery therapy.

Singer (1974) recently reviewed and summarized the major therapeutic uses of imagery. Many of these techniques go far beyond the elicitation of relaxation and, therefore, will not be discussed further in this chapter. Imagery techniques have been used to treat a number of disorders although they are rarely used alone. Most often imagery is combined with hypnosis or biofeedback techniques.

Theory

There are several theories concerning how imagery facilitates memory and learning, but the mechanism whereby mental images are produced, and the reason why the production of certain images may result in deep relaxation is little understood. Concentration is a key factor in imagery, however, just as it is in hypnosis and meditation, and restful mental images produce beneficial physiological changes in many individuals.

If a patient is able to picture a tranquil scene, he will become gradually more calm and able to reduce physiological arousal. The physiologically disturbing effect of frightening images, e.g., nightmares, is familiar to everyone. The goal of imagery therapy is to increase production of beneficial mental images to modify emotions and, ultimately, behavior patterns.

Imagery Relaxation: Technique

One technique used to produce relaxation is "scene visualization," a method often employed in hypnosis. Recollection of certain pleasant scenes can elicit relaxation; however, individuals differ in their evaluation of the pleasurable quality of images. Self-report questionnaires assist therapists in selecting the most appropriate scenes.

For example, the Reinforcement Survey Schedule (RSS) created by Tondo and Cautela (1974) contains descriptions of many images which can be developed into pleasing scenes. In taking the RSS, the patient rates those images which are most pleasurable, thereby insuring that the scene narrated by the therapist will actually please the patient.

The following episode illustrates the importance of individual differences in imagery experience during therapy.

A patient undergoing biofeedback treatment was taught to relax.
She was presented with a visual image of herself lying on a beauti-
ful, white beach on a warm, sunny day. Less than two minutes into
this imagery experience, however, the EMG instrument registered
a significant increase in frontalis muscle tension. On questioning
she indicated that the scene had turned into a frightening image
when she suddenly visualized the fin of a great white shark circling
just off shore.

The therapist must be sensitive to changes in the patient's behavior or
physiological responses (if biofeedback is used) so as to prevent distressing imagery experiences.

In scene visualization, the therapist asks the patient to sit back comfortably, close his eyes, and concentrate on imaging the scene narrated
by the therapist. Such narration is a detailed technique which depends
on the style and creativity of the therapist. Colorful references to
sensory experiences are stressed to make the image as life-like as
possible. Whenever possible, all five senses should be involved. For
example, the patient, described above, not only *sees* herself lying on the
sandy beach, but *feels* the spray of the surf and the warmth of the sun,
smells the ocean breeze, *hears* the seagulls and the gentle roar of the
surf, and *tastes* the ocean salt from the spray. Some therapists, however, may feel uncomfortable with narration and, therefore, might
employ a more structured relaxation technique, such as the progressive relaxation procedure presented earlier in this chapter.

Focused Imagery

A relaxation technique, recently developed, combines elements of
all four of the major relaxation procedures discussed in this chapter
(Nigl and Fischer-Williams, 1980). Termed *focused imagery,* it is used in
the treatment of psychophysiological disorders ranging from muscle
contraction (tension) headache to low back strain.

This technique involves the patient's imagining the appearance of
each of the major muscle groups of the body and how they feel. Then
the patient is asked to visualize the site of tension. He is then asked
to visualize each muscle relaxing and to see and feel the tension slowly
disappearing. The process starts with the forehead and systematically
moves down to the feet. In addition, autogenic phrases are incorporated into the suggestions; emphasizing feelings of warmth and heaviness in the limbs. After the progressive relaxation is completed, the
subject is asked to concentrate on the breathing process and allow it
to occur as naturally as possible. Finally, meditation is used to enhance

the relaxation effect using a cue word such as "calm" or "relax"; repeated subvocally with each expiration. The entire technique takes approximately 40 minutes.

In summary, relaxation techniques are important adjuncts which enhance the effect of biofeedback. It is difficult to train an individual to reduce feedback signals without employing one or more of the techniques discussed. Certain authors have criticized biofeedback techniques because they are not often effective when used alone. For example, Orne (1975) states, "This is another instance where a new technique is introduced and found to be wanting, by itself, so it is combined with older, proved therapies." It is not uncommon in medicine and clinical psychology, however, to treat disorders with more than one technique. The fact that the two procedures (relaxation and biofeedback) may be additive increases the probability of successful treatment. Indeed, these two procedures may be synergistic, for example, EMG biofeedback combined with relaxation is more effective in treating muscle contraction headaches than either used alone (Budzynski, 1978).

In summary, many techniques exist which can help individuals learn to relax, and most of these are compatible with biofeedback procedures. It is unusual for biofeedback therapists to treat patients without employing one or more of these relaxation exercises as part of the total treatment procedure. Patients must be able to reduce their physiologic arousal in order to alter the feedback signal, and without the use of one of the techniques outlined in this chapter, this would be difficult. Therefore, biofeedback therapists should be as familiar with relaxation techniques as they are with electronic instrumentation and other aspects of the biofeedback method.

REFERENCES

Barber TX: Responding to "hypnotic" suggestions. Am J Clin Hypn 18: 6, 1975.
Basmajian J: *Biofeedback-Principles and Practice for Clinicians.* Baltimore, Williams and Wilkins, 1979.
Benson H: *The Relaxation Response.* New York, Morrow, 1975.
Bernstein D, Borkovec T: *Progressive Muscle Relaxation Training: A Manual for the Helping Professions.* Champaign, Ill., Research Press, 1973.
Boring E: *A History of Experimental Psychology.* New York, Appleton, 1950.
Budzynski T: *Relaxation Training Program.* New York, Biomonitoring Applications, 1977.
Budzynski T: Biofeedback in the treatment of muscle contraction (tension) headache. Biofeedback Self-Regul 3: 409, 1978.
Erickson M, Rossi E, Rossi R: *Hypnotic Realities.* New York, Wiley, 1976.

Fair P: Biofeedback strategies in psychotherapy, in Basmajian J (ed): *Biofeedback-Principles and Practice for Clinicians.* Baltimore, Williams and Wilkins, 1979, p. 112.

Goleman D: Hypnosis comes of age. Psychol Today, July: 54, 1977.

Green E, Green A: Biofeedback: rationale and applications, in Wolman B (Ed): *International Encyclopedia of Neurology, Psychiatry, Psychoanalysis and Psychology.* New York, Van Nostrand Reinhold, 1977.

Green E, Green A: General and specific applications of thermal biofeedback, in Basmajian J (ed): *Biofeedback—Principles and Practice for Clinicians.* Baltimore, Williams and Wilkins, 1979, p. 153.

Hilgard E, Atkinson A: *Introduction to Psychology.* New York, Harcourt, Brace and World, 1967, p. 386.

Jacobson E: *Progressive Relaxation.* Chicago, University of Chicago Press, 1958.

Kasamatsu A, Hirai T: An electroencephalographic study on the zen meditation (zazen). Folia Psychiatrica Neurolog Jap 20: 315, 1966.

Kroger W, Felzer W: *Hypnosis and Behavior Modification.* Philadelphia, Lippincott, 1976.

Melzack R. Perry C: Self-regulation of pain, in Wickramasekera I (ed): *Biofeedback, Behavior Therapy and Hypnosis.* Chicago, Nelson-Hall, 1976, p. 57.

Nigl A, Fischer-Williams M: Treatment of musculo-ligamentous low back strain with electromyographic biofeedback and relaxation training. Psychosomatics 21:495, 1980.

Orne M: Claims for biofeedback as a therapy method disputed. Clin Psych News 3: 8, 1975.

Paul G: Outcome of systematic desensitization II, in Franks C (ed): *Behavior Therapy: Appraisal and Status.* New York, McGraw-Hill, 1969.

Schultz J, Luthe W: *Autogenic Therapy.* New York, Grune & Stratton, 1969.

Singer J: *Imagery and Daydream Methods in Psychotherapy and Behavior Modification.* New York, Academic Press, 1974.

Tondo T, Cautela J: Assessment of imagery in covert reinforcement. Psychol Rep 34: 131, 1974.

Wickramasekera I: Effects of electromyographic feedback on hypnotic susceptibility, in Wickramasekera I (ed): *Biofeedback, Behavior Therapy and Hypnosis.* Chicago, Nelson-Hall, 1976a, pp. 151–158.

Wickramasekera I (ed): *Biofeedback, Behavior Therapy and Hypnosis.* Chicago, Nelson-Hall, 1976b, pp. 579–588.

Wolpe J: *The Practice of Behavior Therapy.* New York, Pergamon, 1973.

4

Bioelectronics and Instrumentation

ELECTRONIC instrumentation is the key element of the biofeedback method. The use of sophisticated electronic monitoring devices sets biofeedback apart from other forms of psychological therapy. Until recently, psychotherapy was conducted primarily by face-to-face interview. The advent of biofeedback treatment, however, requires the psychotherapist not only to converse with patients but to learn new skills involving the operation and maintenance of various electronic devices. In order to be an effective biofeedback therapist, the clinician must have sufficient knowledge and experience in the use of biofeedback instrumentation as verbal skills, alone, are not enough. Since effective biofeedback treatment depends on the accuracy of the measurements, it is essential that therapists who employ this technique have a basic knowledge of bioelectronics and instrumentation. Before learning how to measure physiological responses, however, there must be an understanding of what is being measured. A review of relevant physiological variables will precede a discussion of the electronic principles involved in biofeedback.

Electronic Recording of Physiological Responses

The application of biofeedback involves the electronic recording of one or more physiological responses. This measurement is either direct (e.g., the EMG measurement of electrical potential in the muscles) or indirect (e.g., the electronic transformation of temperature changes in thermal biofeedback training). Biofeedback instruments measure small (10^{-6} volts) but detectable signals corresponding to relevant physiological variables. In order to obtain quantitative data, specialized sensors measure biochemical, thermal, or mechanical signals. Thus, silver-silver chloride electrodes are used in EMG or EEG recording and an epoxy-tipped thermistor is used in thermal recording.*

*Much of the material in this chapter is based on the review of biofeedback instrumentation contained in the *Handbook of Physiological Feedback* 2: Sec. 4. San Francisco, Pacific Institute, 1979.

It should be noted that sensory neurons in the human interact with external and internal (somatic) stimuli. They do this by transducing energy; for example, sound waves are converted into electrical potentials, and the force of mechanical displacement of hair follicles or skin pressure is changed into action potentials. Biofeedback sensing devices function in much the same way as sensory neurons, transducing force or energy from a less well-recognized form to a more meaningful form.

Because the neurophysiological variables differ markedly from one type of biofeedback to another, the major categories (EMG, thermal, dermal, and EEG) will be examined separately.

Physiological Basis for EMG Feedback

The purpose of EMG biofeedback training is to assist the patient in learning how to gain control over striated skeletal muscles. Patients either learn to relax muscles which are overcontracted as in psychophysiological stress disorders (e.g., muscle tension headaches) or they learn to contract muscles that are partially paralyzed. This paralysis is either of upper motor neuron origin or follows peripheral nerve injury or neuropathy.

The basis for EMG biofeedback is the recording of electrical impulses from muscles which synapse (connect) at the neuromuscular or myoneural junction. Figure 4–1 illustrates the usual placement of EMG sensors to measure activity in the forehead. Action potentials are transmitted from the cerebral cortex down through the spinal cord via a complex series of nerve pathways to individual motor units in the muscles. When a significant number of action potentials is generated in a particular time period over a given area, contraction of the muscle occurs. In other words, contraction occurs as the result of a convergence of temporal and spatial summation of action potentials. Conversely, muscle relaxation represents a decrease in the firing or electrical discharge of motor nerves.

The EMG records spontaneous electrical activity in the "resting" muscle, as well as induced electrical activity during muscle contraction. This activity can be measured either by needle electrodes which penetrate the skin and are placed in the proximity of the muscle fibers, or by skin electrodes which measure electrical activity over a specific muscle or group of muscles. The latter is more often used in EMG biofeedback. This electrical activity is measured in units of "microvolts" (μv), which are millionths of a volt. In the context of EMG

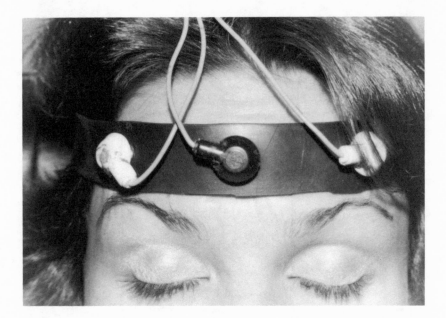

FIGURE 4-1.   USUAL PLACEMENT OF EMG SENSORS IN BIOFEEDBACK
TRAINING - FRONTALIS MUSCLE.

biofeedback, however, the term *microvolt* is incomplete without describing the method by which it was measured. There are at least three methods for microvolt measurement: (1) integral average, (2) root mean square (RMS), and (3) peak to peak. According to some authors, integral average is the preferred method of microvolt measurement (Freeman and Silverberg, 1979).

According to Lenman (1977) "the abundance of electrical activity recorded from a muscle depends not only on the force of contraction but on other factors also, including the characteristics and siting of the recording electrodes, and great caution must be exercised in comparing the integrated electrical activity of one muscle with another" (p. 177) (Figs. 4–2 and 4–3).

Since muscle activity involves mechanical action, the electromyogram is not a direct measure of contraction. However, the amplitude can be used as a measure of both relaxation and tension because the amplitude of the measurement is proportional to the degree of contraction of a particular muscle.

Therefore, EMG measurement may be employed as a general index

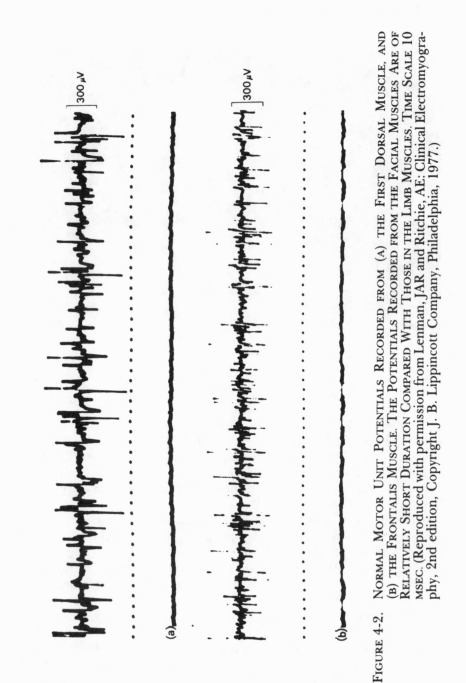

FIGURE 4-2. NORMAL MOTOR UNIT POTENTIALS RECORDED FROM (A) THE FIRST DORSAL MUSCLE, AND (B) THE FRONTALIS MUSCLE. THE POTENTIALS RECORDED FROM THE FACIAL MUSCLES ARE OF RELATIVELY SHORT DURATION COMPARED WITH THOSE IN THE LIMB MUSCLES. TIME SCALE 10 MSEC. (Reproduced with permission from Lenman, JAR and Ritchie, AE: Clinical Electromyography, 2nd edition, Copyright J. B. Lippincott Company, Philadelphia, 1977.)

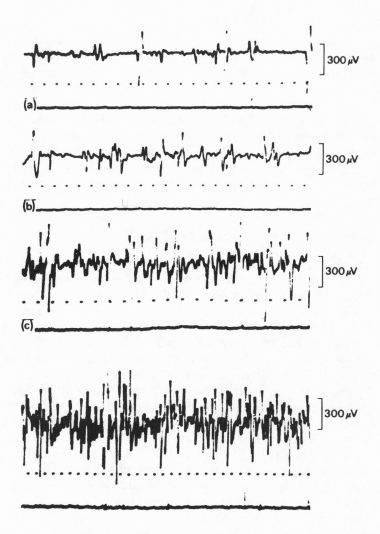

FIGURE 4-3. (ABOVE) MOTOR UNIT ACTION POTENTIALS FROM NORMAL DORSAL INTEROSSEUS MUSCLE DURING PROGRESSIVELY MORE POWERFUL CONTRACTIONS. IN THE INTERFERENCE PATTERN (C) INDIVIDUAL UNITS CAN NO LONGER BE CLEARLY DISTINGUISHED. TIME SCALE 10 MSEC. (BELOW) INTERFERENCE PATTERN DURING STRONG MUSCULAR CONTRACTION. TIME SCALE 10 MSEC. (Reproduced with permission from Lenman, JAR and Ritchie, AE: Clinical Electromyography, 2nd edition, Copyright J. B. Lippincott Company, Philadelphia, 1977.)

of tension; low readings (below $5\mu v$, integral averaged) correlate with low muscle tonus (relaxation) while high readings (above $5\mu v$, integral averaged) indicate high muscle tonus (tension). EMG activity can be an important indicator of psychophysiological arousal or stress.

There is a very close relationship between anxiety and muscle tension. Thus, Goldstein (1964) noted that psychiatric patients have higher than normal levels of muscle tension; in addition they tend to perceive more situations as being stressful than do control subjects. It appears that some individuals respond to stress primarily through the musculoskeletal system as part of the ergotropic ("flight or fight") response.

Physiological Basis for Thermal Feedback

Electrothermal feedback utilizes measurement of skin temperature most often in the distal parts of the body, e.g. hands or feet. Since skin temperature is regulated primarily by the cardiovascular system, it is more closely linked to autonomic nervous system (ANS) activity than to somatic nervous system (SNS) activity. More specifically, the sympathetic branch of the ANS exercises significant control over distal skin temperature through electrochemical changes stimulated by norepinephrine (NE or noradrenalin) and other neurotransmitters.

Sympathetic activation leads to many changes in the body's smooth (nonstriated) musculature preparing the body to react effectively to stress. One of these changes involves the contraction of smooth muscles surrounding the peripheral blood vessels. This contraction (vasoconstriction) eventually results in lowered skin temperature as peripheral blood flow decreases. Parasympathetic activation causes relaxation of the smooth muscles in the vessel wall (vasodilatation).

Other factors also affect distal skin temperature; for example, under low temperature conditions vasoconstriction occurs reflexly, reducing loss of body heat due to transfer of heat from the warm body to the cold exterior. Blood is shunted from the periphery to the core of the body maintaining constant internal body temperature (homeostasis). When environmental temperature increases, vasodilatation leads to an increase in skin temperature, causing heat loss from the body to the environment; however, when the environmental temperature exceeds 37°C elaboration of perspiration causes heat loss—not merely vasodilatation.

Other factors affect peripheral skin temperature, e.g., infection, blood viscosity, skin quality and thickness, skin tonus, and the presence or absence of certain chemicals in the blood. For example, alcohol and nicotine have opposing effects on peripheral vascular functioning. In general, alcohol causes dilatation while nicotine causes constriction. Although such factors usually remain constant during biofeedback therapy, the therapist should be aware of extero- or interoceptive variables which may affect patients' learning of skin temperature control. Evidence suggests that an individual thoroughly trained to dilate the peripheral blood vessels, can continue to do so even under extremely cold environmental conditions (Taub and Stroebel, 1978). Recently, School and Taub (1980) have indicated that individuals have great difficulty shamming vasomotor control, i.e., engaging in other activities during training. Furthermore, warm temperature stimuli directed to the opposite hand from that being measured may increase the difficulty of controlling vasodilatation (raising skin temperature). Nigl (1980) reported that normal subjects who were given a warm temperature stimulus did not increase their skin temperatures as well as subjects who were given a cold stimulus.

There is a finite time lag between vasodilatation and corresponding increases in skin temperature. The rate of blood flow is much slower in the peripheral capillaries than in larger blood vessels. Heat generated by increased blood flow must pass through layers of skin before it reaches the surface where it can then be measured by a thermistor. Figure 4–4 illustrates how skin temperature is measured in biofeedback. Vascular diffusion prevents direct measurement of temporary fluctuations in skin temperature. In skin temperature biofeedback, therefore, the recorded temperature represents an average thermal response over a specific time period.

Physiological Basis for Dermal Feedback

The measurement of electrical discharges in the skin is the basis for electrodermal biofeedback. Although the galvanic skin response (GSR) has been used as a measure of anxiety for more than a century, it has only recently been discovered that skin responses could be modified by conscious effort. Because of variations in measurement, the term GSR has been abandoned in favor of more specific terms such as *skin conductance level* (SCL), *skin conductance response* (SCR) and *skin potential response* (SPR). *Skin activity* is usually measured from sensors placed on the palm or on the tips of the fingers. Figure 4–5 illustrates the usual placement of dermal sensors.

Although skin responses have been studied extensively for years, the

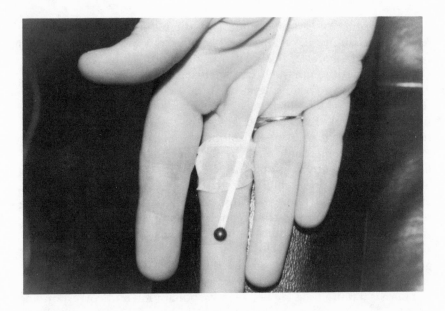

FIGURE 4-4. USUAL PLACEMENT OF THERMAL SENSOR IN SKIN TEM-
PERATURE BIOFEEDBACK TRAINING.

specific chain of events resulting in electric skin events has not been
completely identified or understood. However, the fact that perspiration produces a decrease in electrical resistance, appears to be one of
the important factors in the production of *electrodermal responses* (EDR).
Electrical changes in the skin are directly related to the onset of sympathetic activity. In fact, skin temperature and EDR are closely related in
many individuals. Fearful or anxious individuals often have cold (vaso-
constricted) and moist or "clammy" hands. The EDR is therefore a
physiological expression of various emotional states.

Crider (1979) clarified the difference between specific and nonspecific EDR: the former occurs in response to specific stimuli while
the latter occurs in resting subjects and is not linked to a specifiable
stimulus.

Lacey and Lacey (1958) demonstrated that Skinner's operant conditioning model could be used to account for modification of nonspecific
EDRs. Since the nonspecific EDR is an "emitted" rather than an "elicited" response, it meets Skinner's definition of an operant (see Chap.
1).

Numerous studies have shown that nonspecific EDRs can be oper-

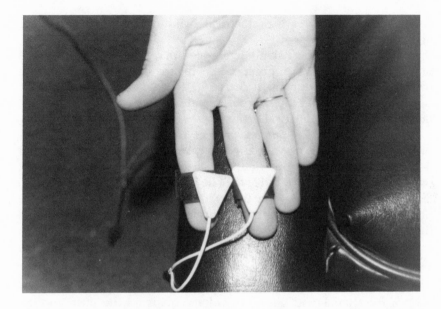

FIGURE 4-5. AN EXAMPLE OF THE PLACEMENT OF SENSORS IN ELEC-
TRODERMAL BIOFEEDBACK TRAINING.

antly conditioned. For example, Shapiro and Crider (1967) found that subjects produced a higher quantity of SPR when they received a monetary reward. Since the magnitude of SPR was signaled to the subjects via a tone, this experimental procedure can be viewed as a type of biofeedback.

Results summarized by Crider (1979) and Kimmel (1974) showed that the nonspecific EDR can be operantly conditioned through a biofeedback procedure. In fact, it may be the only type of biofeedback learning which can be adequately conceptualized based on an operant conditioning model (see Chap. 1). As Crider points out, however, the clinical utility of nonspecific EDR biofeedback has not yet been established.

The basic premise underlying electrodermal feedback is that when a constant voltage is applied to the surface of the skin, the electrical conductivity or "skin conductance" can be used as a measure of anxiety. This factor is measured in micromhos (μmhos) while the reciprocal of skin conductance or "skin resistance" is measured in micro-ohms (μohms). The greater the electrical resistance on the skin's surface, the lower the "physiological arousal" (see Chap. 3);

conversely, the greater the electrical conductance of the skin, the higher the arousal.

Another physiological skin event which may be used as a measure of anxiety is that of "skin potential," which is measured in millivolts (mv). It is defined as the direct current (DC) voltage differential which can be measured from the skin surface; the greater the skin potential, the higher the physiological arousal.

Skin conductance can be measured by passing constant voltage between two electrodes on the skin and evaluating the current (see Fig. 4–5). In contrast to this, skin potential is measured by three electrodes; two active leads and a ground lead. The difference in voltage (potential difference) between the two active electrodes can be demonstrated by placing a lead on a neutral site (back or dorsal surface of the hand) and the other on a physiologically active site (underside or palmar) surface.

Physiological Basis for EEG Feedback

The electroencephalogram (EEG) is a record which provides a measure of the spatial distribution of voltage fields on the scalp and the manner in which they vary as a function of time. Therefore the EEG may be said to have two distinct parameters, namely one of voltage and one characterized by time-dependent variations of that voltage. One may consider first the mechanism whereby current is generated in the extracellular space thereby producing a voltage field within the volume conductor which is the brain, and second, the mechanism whereby such changes in current distribution are regulated to produce rhythmic (or phasic) activity.

Source of Current in Extracellular Space: The Action Potential

The source of current in the extracellular space originates primarily from two sources. One is the action potential, which is the result of a sequence of changes in membrane permeability. The other source of current is due to synaptic activity. This activity may either depolarize or hyperpolarize the membrane. Although the synaptic potentials are of considerably lower voltage than the action potentials, they are apparently "conducted" much further in the extracellular space than the action potentials. The EEG measures the potential within the voltage fields, generated by dipoles within the cortex, which in turn are due to electrical current flowing into and out of cortical neurons. A dipole is an elongated structure with a potential difference across its ends. The pyramidal cell in the cerebral cortex acts as a dipole. The EEG records the sum of electrical events taking place in a population of millions of neurons, including the dendrites which are the fine arborizations arising from the body of the nerve cell. The dendrites are near the surface of the brain, and the electrical current is primarily due to synaptic activity rather than action potentials. The actual generating source(s) of the electrical activity recorded, however, is an extremely complex subject. The electrical signals are of very small voltage, partly because of the intervening layers between the brain and the recording electrodes, namely the meninges, the skull, and the scalp.

Rhythmicity

The source of EEG rhythms is not known. Changes in rhythms recorded can be observed, but a cause-and-effect relationship cannot be definitely stated since many factors may have the same effect. Synaptic potentials generated within the cortex are to a variable degree controled by activity occurring in deeper structures such as the thalamus. The thalamus has therefore been implicated in the generation of certain rhythms. This however does not answer the many questions which primarily interest those doing biofeedback research; at present the correlation between the electrical activity of the brain and psychological events is complex and poorly documented.

The EEG (summation of brain waves) at any given time is composed of many rhythms summed and nonrhythmic activity. A rhythm is composed of regularly recurring component waves. It may be defined in terms of frequency, amplitude, location (localization), persistence, and reactivity. For example, the alpha rhythm is defined not only in terms of frequency (8 through 13 Hz or cycles per second), but also in terms of location and reactivity to alerting procedures (see Chap. 6). Other "rhythms" are defined merely in terms of frequency, for example, theta waves are those of 4 through 7 Hz, and delta waves are those of less than 4 Hz. (see Chap. 6).

The amplitude of theta and delta waves is usually larger than that of alpha waves. Beta waves (14 Hz and over) are usually of low amplitude. Beta activity is present to a variable extent in the EEG of all normal, alert adults, maximal anteriorly. During drowsiness alpha rhythm is replaced by theta activity, and many other changes occur. Mu rhythm is also seen both in normal subjects and in pathological conditions. It consists of runs of 7–11 Hz and it may thus be in the same frequency band as the alpha rhythm but occurs in a different location (the Rolandic region as opposed to the posterior head regions) and in different circumstances, e.g., when the eyes are open (whereas the alpha rhythm is present when the eyes are closed). Also, mu rhythm blocks (disappears) with clenching the fist. Many authors think that mu rhythm in humans is the same as the so-called sensorimotor rhythm in cats.

This brief survey may convey some of the pitfalls in interpreting results, particularly those in EEG biofeedback. As mentioned above, the "raw" EEG is composed of a wide range of frequencies. A frequency analyzer is required to give the percentage amount of any given rhythm or wave band. This information is given for a particular time span (epoch), for example, 1 second or 10 seconds, since the EEG is in constant flux or change. Some of the EEG feedback work therefore requires the output of the EEG to pass through a frequency analyzer in order to state, for example, that alpha rhythm is or is not "dominant" at any given time. By visual inspection, an opinion can be made as to whether alpha rhythm is dominant, and whether it is symmetrical on the two hemispheres. (In normal adults there is symmetry, but this is relative and a percentage of asymmetry is allowed, with higher amplitude usually on the nondominant hemisphere.) For subtle changes and for quantification, however, a frequency analyzer and power spectral analysis is required. Other EEG biofeedback work depends on the conditioning of EEG rhythms, which requires a different technique. Certain rhythms, like the alpha, the mu, and the sensorimotor rhythm can be conditioned.

Synchrony is poorly understood. The term means *beating together* and refers to the fact that the electrical activity of the normal brain is similar recorded from homologous (mirror) areas. Thus the right and left hemispheres seem to be "beating together" to a certain extent. The degree of synchrony can be determined by the eye (a rough guide) or with the aid of sophisticated equipment. The significance of bilateral synchrony or of synchronicity within one hemisphere varies according to the circumstances, such as age, sleep, attention, pathology, and other variables. As a feature of the EEG it cannot be equated with psychological factors.

The EEG is recorded by attaching electrodes to the scalp (usually 20 electrodes monitoring different regions), and passing the electrical activity (which is of extremely low voltage) through a system of amplifiers and filters to the recording pen units. The filters modify the frequency response characteristics of the recording system. The gain or sensitivity of an EEG amplifier has to be such that an input signal of 10 μv results in a pen deflection of at least 1 cm.

Instrumentation and Physiological Recording

Biofeedback therapy is based on the fact that physiological variables can be transformed into electrical signals, amplified and analyzed. For example, the thermistor used to detect changes in skin temperature, converts temperature into electrical resistance which is processed by the feedback instrument.

Two wave forms are electrical by-products of physiological activity; the alternating current (AC) and the direct current (DC). Figure 4–6 illustrates the difference between the AC and DC wave forms. The AC wave form oscillates around a fixed level of voltage, which is usually zero; and produces either negative or positive waves with respect to the reference point. The EEG, the EMG, and the ECG (electrocardiogram) utilize AC signals. Such signals are generated by cellular-membrane depolarization, or firing, of specific neurons.

In contrast to this, the DC wave form does not oscillate around a fixed level of voltage but has a variable polarity (negative or positive). Such indices as skin potential, skin conductance, skin temperature, and blood pressure are measured in DC wave forms. Most of the electrical signals detected by the sensors used in biofeedback training are relatively weak and require significant amplification before being analyzed. For example, the voltage, measured by EEG electrodes, ranges from 1 to 100 μv and must be amplified 100,000 times before further analysis. Once amplified, the signal must be filtered and processed to eliminate artifactual electrical imput. This insures that the measurement will be as accurate as possible. If the signal is in AC wave form, it is generally converted to DC format. The DC voltage is used to power various electrical functions, e.g., meters, lights, and auditory signals. Although a physiological variable (e.g., the EMG) may be measured in AC wave form, it is converted to DC so that meaningful information can be transmitted to the subject.

Criteria for Effective Instrumentation

The effectiveness of biofeedback instruments may be evaluated on several dimensions. One of the most important criteria is the sensitivity of the sensor or transducer used to measure physiological responses. A sensor monitors physiological activity while a transducer converts what is measured to a format which can be electronically recorded. Both sensors and transducers must have a high degree of accuracy and stability for use in effective biofeedback. In order for the

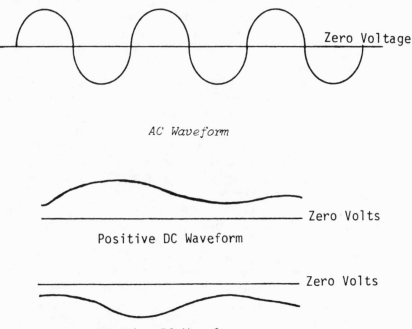

AC Waveform

Positive DC Waveform

Negative DC Waveform

FIGURE 4-6. AC/DC WAVEFORMS. (Reproduced with permission from The Handbook of Physiological Feedback, Berkeley, Autogenic Systems, 1976.)

output of both sensors and transducers to be accurate and reproducible over time, their construction must be durable.

Another criterion for effective instrumentation involves amplification of the electronic signal. A biofeedback instrument must have sufficient sensitivity and amplification of physiological data with maximal fidelity and minimal distortion. The type of amplification appears to vary depending on the nature of the electrical properties of the response monitored.

The filtering capacity of the feedback instrument is another factor which must be considered since artifacts must be reduced. Artifacts can be either physiological or instrumental in origin. Several instrumental artifacts can be identified, including electrical interference (often caused by high-power transmitters), household appliances, and flourescent lighting. Signals emanating from such devices may be detected by the biofeedback sensors, making it difficult to measure true physiological responses (which may have a much lower voltage).

Other artifacts are caused by electrical interference from the instrument itself. Since the biofeedback instrument is an electronic device, it generates a certain level of "noise" (extraneous electrical discharges which may be picked up by the sensors). The use of optically isolated equipment reduces the likelihood of this type of artifact. Artifacts can also be produced by mechanical problems with the machine or the motion of the electrode leads which connect the sensors to the machine. Examples of physiological artifacts include heart sounds (ECG) in EMG feedback, as well as movement of the subject.

The accuracy of the instrumentation is important in determining the measurement. In order for learning to be effective, information the subject receives should be accurate and as instantaneous as possible. Thus, the patient has a greater chance of learning control of physiological responses. Patients may not be able to directly sense certain physiological signals without feedback. Therefore, it is extremely important that the signal fed back to the person actually represents what is physiologically occurring in his body at that time.

"Stability" (the consistency of measurements made by a biofeedback instrument over time) must also be considered an important factor in biofeedback instrumentation. Since the biofeedback patient is given information regarding his performance continuously over the course of treatment, it is important that the data be consistent. In other words, if the calibration of the instrument is not constant, data will vary from session to session. This will cause inaccurate information to be given to the patient which may interfere with the rate of learning. A primary cause of measurement inconsistency is inadequacy of the power source (i.e., batteries) in biofeedback units.

"Resolution" and "sensitivity" refer to variables which determine the quality of the biofeedback instrument. Resolution is defined as the minimal amount of physiological change which can be monitored and fed back by the instrument. For example, an EMG biofeedback instrument with a resolution of 1 μv has a capability of detecting and displaying changes in EMG activity as small as 1 μv. High resolution is an important factor since many of the physiological changes in biofeedback are of extremely small magnitude. If an instrument has low resolution, many of the changes which occur from one session to another, or within a single session will not be measured properly. Sensitivity differs from resolution although the concept is similar, in fact, these two terms are frequently confused. Sensitivity refers to the minimum absolute value of a biological response which can be detected by the instrument. An EMG instrument with a sensitivity of 1 μv can only detect signals which are equal to or greater than 1 μv; it cannot detect signals below 1 μv. The maximum sensitivity of any biofeedback instrument is usually equal to the noise level produced by the unit itself.

Another important criterion of biofeedback instrumentation is baseline capability, i.e., the *accuracy* of the baseline obtained. "Baseline data" refers to the level or range of a physiological response before biofeedback training is initiated (i.e., the pretreatment level). Baseline information is presented in, at least, two ways: one involves the use of a "digital integrator" and the other the "read-out" from a meter.

When monitoring physiological variables that change very slowly (e.g., skin temperature or skin conductance) an instantaneous meter readout is sufficient. However, according to some authors, when using the EMG instrument, it is preferable to transmit information via a meter which has the capability of averaging rapidly shifting variables over time. Some feedback units have exponential averaging systems which provide continuous averaging of physiological activity over preselected time periods. In this case, the electronic circuitry constantly renews the average reading given as an output, by adding "new" information and eliminating "old" information, exponentially. Therefore, "new" information is given more weight is the average output than "old" information.

Another variable which differs from one biofeedback instrument to another is feedback capability. Reliable biofeedback instruments must feed back information so that it can be readily comprehended and incorporated by the patient to enhance the learning process. Several types of feedback exist, employing both audio and visual outputs. The three major types are "analog," "binary," and "derivative" feedback. Analog feedback presents physiological information continuously. For example, this feedback may consist of an audio signal which rises or falls in pitch/tone, proportional to related changes in the monitored response. This type of information is represented by the continuous fluctuation of a needle on a meter. Binary feedback, on the other hand, consists of a signal which is either "on" or "off" depending on a preselected criterion. If for example, a subject's muscle tension rises above a certain threshold level, the audio signal will register; if it stays below the threshold level, the audio signal will not register. The same is true for an array of colored lights which may be used as visual feedback (e.g., on skin temperature feedback, a red light indicates relaxation; a green light, tension). Binary feedback may have special properties which increase learning in certain patients. Nigl (1980) indicated that binary feedback employing a preselected threshold enabled chronic low back patients to learn control of low back muscle tension more than did analog feedback.

Derivative feedback utilizes two separate tones: a high-pitched tone indicates an increase in physiologic response while a low-pitched tone indicates a reduction of the response. In addition, several combinations of these various feedback modalities may be incorporated in one instrument and used simultaneously to facilitate learning. Caution must be exercised, however, especially in the initial phase of treatment, to prevent information overload for the patients, as some patients may be confused or overwhelmed by the complexity of the feedback.

Issues in EMG Instrumentation

The selection of "bandwidth" for the muscle group being monitored in EMG biofeedback is very important. A bandwidth ("bandpass") is created by filtering unwanted and/or artifactual data so only desired frequencies pass through and are recorded. A wide range of bandwidth frequencies can be selected. Some authors suggest that the greatest amount of electrical activity in the muscles falls in the 30 to 100 Hz range. Therefore, frequencies above 200 Hz may be unimportant and need not be measured (Peffer, 1979).

Frequency band passes of 100 to 200 Hz and 400 to 500 Hz appear to have the greatest applicability in EMG biofeedback training. The narrow band width has advantages over a broader band width (e.g., 100 to 300 Hz to 1000 Hz), e.g., because of the greater rejection of artifactual signals and higher signal-to-noise ratio.

Cardiac artifacts (ECG) signals can be a very significant problem in EMG biofeedback, especially when the electrodes are placed on the torso rather than the distal regions of the body. It appears that even a high pass (or lower frequency cut-off) of approximately 100 Hz will not completely eliminate cardiac artifacts. The filter "slope" of the band pass is an important factor here. The higher the number of decibels per octave, the steeper the filter slope. In rejecting ECG signals, a clinical biofeedback instrument should exhibit a slope of at least 30 dB per octave below 100 Hz.

The 100 to 200 Hz band pass is useful in monitoring low EMG levels after initial relaxation training has been completed. For example, in frontalis muscle training 100 Hz is selected because below that level ECG artifacts can contaminate the EMG data.

The 400 to 500 Hz band pass is very useful for EMG biofeedback training involving specific muscle groups. In this band pass, the electrodes appear to pick up EMG activity directly under the placement site. Thus, it appears that the signal measured is isolated from adjacent muscle signals or activity. Therefore, this particular band pass width is useful for muscle training in rehabilitation, whereas the 100 to 200 Hz band pass is more appropriate for muscle relaxation.

Three types of amplitude measurement are currently used: the "integral average," "peak-to-peak," or "root-mean-square" (RMS). Freeman and Silverberg (1976) describe in detail these three amplitude measurements as follows:

1. Peak-to-peak amplitude is the measurement of the highest amplitude of the wave form and as such represents the distance between positive and negative peaks which occur consecutively. (see Fig. 4–7).

2. The integral average amplitude is a constant and represents the transfer of charge in DC voltage which is a characteristic of the electrical wave form.

3. The root-mean-square (RMS) amplitude is the level of voltage which transforms a power equivalent to that of the electrical wave form.

Their conclusion is that the integral average is the best amplitude measurement. One of the important factors they considered is that the wave form measured is merely a representation of the function which is transformed into quantifiable data. They caution biofeedback therapists to take into account the nature of the electrical wave form which is being measured. Although the RMS measurement is desirable in audiophonic applications, it is not as relevant to human electrical functioning. For example, the EMG wave form is not the actual value which is quantified in biofeedback measurement but is representative of a mechanical function, i.e., muscle contraction.

The integral average method is preferred because it provides an average of the voltage directly proportional to the amount of physiological activity actually present. The filtered signals are rectified and converted into DC voltage proportional to the area under the curve of the wave form. Consequently, peak-to-peak amplitude quantification is not advised in biofeedback because it is often unresponsive to momentary changes in muscle activity. Furthermore, it does not quantify low amplitude EMG information occurring between the major peaks (Freeman and Silverberg, 1976).

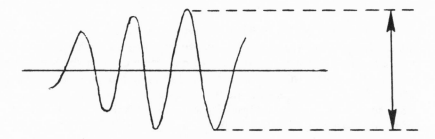

FIGURE 4-7. VISUAL REPRESENTATION OF PEAK-TO-PEAK EEG AMPLI-
TUDE. (Reproduced with permission from The Hand-
book of Physiological Feedback, Berkeley, Autogenic
Systems, 1976.)

Issues in EEG Instrumentation

One of the important factors in EEG instrumentation is the amplification of the EEG signal. Because the voltage of the EEG is very low,
the EEG instrument must be able to isolate the true signals from
artifactual signals. Further, it must amplify them at a level, high
enough, to permit information processing. One of the ways to achieve
this is through the use of a differential EEG amplifier and special
filters.

"Common-mode" signals (the electrical potentials measured concurrently by two electrodes placed on the scalp) are often artifactual
and not due to actual brain activity. A reliable EEG biofeedback instrument, therefore, must be able to reject such signals.

The presence of common-mode signals is one of the reasons why the
use of one active electrode (or monopolar electrode placement) is
favored by many researchers and technicians. In this case, one of the
active electrodes is placed on a neutral site, such as the earlobe, so that
there is less common-mode EEG activity present and more EEG activity can be amplified.

The simplest method of filtering the signal is the use of "analog"
filters. This method consists of passing the EEG signal, which has been
amplified, through a filtering circuit which reduces the amplitude of all
frequency components except those in a preselected band width.
There are several types of analog filters currently available; some have
greater flexibility than others. The least sophisticated are those which
have a fixed frequency band width and do not allow variable feedback
range selection. EEG feedback instruments with analog filters have
drawbacks, however, including lack of discrimination between domi-

nant or subdominant wave form activity. This lack of discrimination can often cause confusion for the patient undergoing EEG training. The patient may associate subjective experiences with the subdominant activity rather than the dominant alpha rhythm. In order to solve this problem, some feedback instruments are currently available with more sophisticated filters. "Power spectrum analysis" may provide the most accurate analysis of EEG frequency data (Peffer, 1979).

Issues in Electrothermal Instrumentation

One of the important factors in electrothermal monitoring is the use of "derivative feedback." In addition to measuring the temperature and processing the feedback, the derivative and acceleration components of the amplified wave form can be analyzed by sophisticated electrothermal instruments. For example, using such instruments, the therapist can make a determination whether the monitored skin temperature is increasing, decreasing, or remaining constant. The rate of the increase can be measured by converting the slope of the wave form to a voltage level proportional to the rate of temperature increase or decrease. This is subsequently fed back to the subject via an array of lights which, through the use of various colors, can indicate whether the patient is relaxing or becoming more tense.

The effects of using "absolute" temperature may be contrasted with "differential" temperatures. It is more effective in some cases to feed back to the patient information regarding the differential temperature from one part of the body to another. For example, Green used one temperature probe on the forehead and the other on the hand to treat migraine. In this procedure, it is desirable that the patient increase the difference between the hand and forehead temperatures so that the forehead temperature decreases (vasoconstriction) while the hand temperature increases (vasodilatation) (Green and Green, 1977).

Many temperature units only allow for single probe monitoring; this is especially true in smaller home units. Often, however, it is desirable to average the sensors (probes) from different sites; some instruments allow as many as six different sensors to be placed on the body. Measurement of skin temperature can then be made over a broad area rather than a localized area, such as the middle phalanx of the third digit (middle finger).

Issues in Electrodermal Instrumentation

The measurement of electrical skin resistance may involve the decision to use either DC or AC current measurement. The simplest technique according to Peffer (1979) is to measure the DC current between two electrodes and detect the drop in voltage. However, DC techniques are more susceptible to artifacts because of electrode polarization; therefore, the measurement should be AC. In addition, it must be remembered that the sensors must make direct contact with the skin and should have no clinical effect on the activity of the sweat glands monitored (Peffer, 1979).

Two methods of currently available feedback combine conductance level and response information. The first method measures two factors: information about the rate of change (derivative) and skin conductance. This type of measurement can cause the patient to become anxious because of the fluctuations of the meter which frequently move in an inverse relationship to the actual response activity. For example, if there is positive conductance or skin potential response, the meter would first go in a positive direction, then reverse to a level below the original baseline as the response fades away. The subject could therefore get an impression that a negative response occurred while in fact there was only a negative rate of change superimposed on a positive response. Such feedback could cause significant difficulties for the subject in distinguishing between negative and positive responses.

The second method consists of superimposing direct response information on the conductance or skin potential level readout and serves to eliminate the disadvantages of the first method described above.

Consumer Variables in Biofeedback Instrumentation

A wide variety of biofeedback instruments have been developed over the last five years. Biofeedback units may range in cost from tens to several thousands of dollars. Such a wide selection often confuses clinicians and researchers.

Girdano (1976) classified biofeedback instruments into three types: "home-trainers," "research equipment," and "clinical trainers." The home-trainers have several drawbacks for clinicians since they are reduced in electrical sophistication to be affordable for the general public. Home-trainers range in price from less than 50 to several hundreds of dollars. A major problem, especially with EMG home-trainers, is that they are not sufficiently sensitive to detect low levels of arousal needed in advanced relaxation training. They may serve to assist individuals in the initial phase of relaxation training, however, and reduce the time required to learn the relaxation response.

Alpha home-trainers were popular when biofeedback first emerged

122 A TEXTBOOK OF BIOLOGICAL FEEDBACK

as a new clinical technique in the late 1960s. These trainers are not applicable to therapy situations because of their improper quantification of signal and their inaccurate feedback.

Recently home units for electrodermal and electrothermal measurement have been developed and are useful for some patients. Small temperature units are within the economic range of most patients. They can assist patients with migraine for example to learn how to warm their hands outside of the clinic setting. Often migraine treatment occurs at a slow rate because patients have difficulty in achieving deep relaxation at home when confronted by stressful daily experiences.

The reader may consult product information from the major biofeedback manufacturers. Figure 4–8 illustrates a typical biofeedback laboratory arrangement with EMG, electrothermal, and electrodermal equipment.

Girdano lists several points which should be considered before purchasing any biofeedback equipment, including:

1. The biofeedback instrument should be appropriate for its intended use.

2. Since a wide variety of instruments are available, an article by Schwitzgebel and Rugh (1975), surveying various manufacturers of equipment, should be consulted.

3. Personal experience and communication with experienced professionals in the field is advisable prior to purchasing equipment.

4. Advertising claims and product literature of various instrument manufacturers should be carefully examined.

In summary, the development of biofeedback instrumentation and methodology requires an appropriate level of knowledge and expertise. Training seminars and workshops can familiarize clinicians with relevant variables in electronics and instrumentation. Responsible biofeedback therapy requires competent professional training and experience. It is unethical to establish a biofeedback practice without training experience in the technique. Biofeedback therapists should receive training from qualified professionals before attempting to treat patients. It is insufficient for clinicians to rely solely upon manufacturers' representatives for their information (although the latter are often technically competent). An understanding of the underlying principles is imperative.

Professional organizations such as the Biofeedback Society of America (BSA) are taking steps to provide guidelines for certification and competency. The American Association of Biofeedback Clinicians (AABC) has already developed certification procedures. Hopefully,

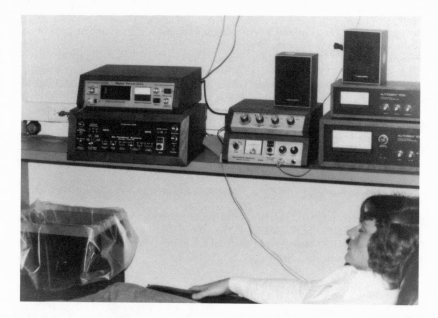

FIGURE 4-8. AN EXAMPLE OF A TYPICAL (CLINICAL) BIOFEEDBACK SETTING WITH AN ARRAY OF DIFFERENT TYPES OF BIOFEEDBACK INSTRUMENTATION.

these issues will be resolved in the near future. Because of the potential harm to consumers, certification or licensing of biofeedback therapists should be instituted as soon as possible to curb potential abuses and to insure professional quality.

REFERENCES

Crider A: The electrodermal response: biofeedback and individual difference studies. Internat Rev Appl Psychol 28: 37, 1979.

Freeman J, Silverberg B: Integral average, RMS and peak-to-peak: a comparison of EMG detection techniques. In *Handbook of Physiological Feedback.* San Francisco, Pacific Institute, 1976, p. 13.

Girdano D: Buying biofeedback, in Barber T, et al. (eds): *Biofeedback and Self-Regulation.* Chicago, Aldine, 1976, p. 573.

Goldstein I: Muscle tension in psychiatric patients. Arch Gen Psychiat 11: 322, 1964.

Green E, Green A: Biofeedback: rationale and applications, in Wolman B (ed): *International Encyclopedia of Neurology, Psychiatry, Psychoanalysis and Psychology.* New York, Van Nostrand Reinhold, 1977.

Kimmel H: Instrumental conditioning of autonomically mediated responses in human beings. Am J Psychol 29: 325, 1974.

Lacey J, Lacey B: The relationship of resting autonomic activity to motor impulsivity. Res Nerv Ment Dis 36: 144, 1958.

Lenman J, Ritchie A: *Clinical Electromyography*. Philadelphia, Lippincott, 1977.

Nigl A: An aversive EMG procedure in the treatment of chronic low back pain. *Proceedings of Kyoto Symposium on Biofeedback*. Tokyo, Sophic University Press (in press), 1980.

Nigl A: External temperature and its effects on thermal biofeedback. Proceedings of 11th Meeting of Biofeedback Society of America, 1980.

Peffer K: Equipment needs for the psychotherapist, in Basmajian J (ed): *Biofeedback—Principles and Practice for Clinicians*. Baltimore, Williams and Wilkins, 1979, p. 257.

School PI, Taub E: Effect on hand temperature of several subject produced behaviors relevant to a thermal biofeedback situation. Proceedings of 11th Meeting of Biofeedback Society of America, 1980.

Schwitzgebel R, Rugh J: Biofeedback apparatus: list of suppliers. Behav Ther 62:38, 1975.

Shapiro D, Crider A: Operant electrodermal conditioning under multiple schedules of reinforcement. Psychophysiology 4: 168, 1967.

Taub C, Stroebel C: Effectiveness of biofeedback in the treatment of vaso-constrictive disorders. Biofeedback Self-Regul. 3:451, 1978.

5

The Symptom of Pain

Introduction

The dual nature of pain as a sensation and pain as an emotion makes it one of the most important and one of the most complex subjects. It is the Janus of neurology, with a double visage which faces both ways.

Pain can be described in anatomical terms, and to a certain extent in chemicophysical and in pharmacological terms. The train of events can be delineated from the individual receiving a potentially noxious stimulus detected by the intero- or exteroceptive receptors, to its transmission via a relay of neurons to the spinal cord, and then a progression up the spinal cord to the thalamus, the central sorting station deep in the brain, and thence to the cortex where it enters into consciousness. This account, however accurate and detailed, would in itself still not explain why one individual feels "pain" and another does not, and why an unvarying, identical stimulus is interpreted differently under different circumstances. The variation in the cortical response depends upon many factors, and it is these factors, both physiological and psychological, which determine the nature of pain experienced as an emotion.

Pain can therefore be described in terms of an emotion, and although this approach mainly emphasizes the state of the receiving ground (the cerebral cortex), it also takes into account the controlling effects of the brain acting on the peripheral organs and at all synapses. This is the so-called "centrifugal effect" (Latin: *fugo,* "I fly"; *centrum,* "from the center"), or feedback control operated by both conscious and unconscious aspects of the brain.

The first part of the chapter, therefore, describes the processes mainly in anatomical and physiological terms from the stimulation of a receptor in the skin, subcutaneous tissues, muscles or viscera, to discharges via the ganglia to the spinal cord, and via the tracts in the spinal cord to the thalamus, and then to the cerebral cortex.

125

The second part of the chapter examines the fact that the state of the receiving ground in the brain is crucial to the nature of the response interpreted as pain or nonpain. The variation in the cortical response depends upon such factors as the level of attention and the nature of expectation; it varies with the state of deprivation of sleep or of oxygen and glucose levels, and it varies according to prior sensitization of the brain by head injury, neoplasm, vascular disease, or other disorder. It also varies with the history of the onset of pain, and with the patient's subsequent experiences. For example, pain from a tibia fractured in a skiing accident may be different from a similar fracture due to an automobile or an industrial accident. For these and many other reasons, the distracting effect of a counterstimulus, and the consoling effect of immediate treatment of an injured part are both important factors. In chronic or long-term pain, secondary gain from psychological or socioeconomic aspects is often relevant, and may play a part in the overall clinical picture. In any description of pain, therefore, the timeframe is important; that is, the length of time that the sensation of pain has been present. The longer the duration of pain as a sensation exists, the greater is the emotional charge invested in this symptom (Fischer-Williams, 1956).

If the state of the receiving cortex appears easier to describe in terms of its emotional flavor than in terms of its anatomical and physiological variables, this is probably because people tend to consider themselves "specialists" in emotional life, sooner than they do in anatomy. Anyone attempting to treat pain should be acquainted with the complexity of the anatomy of pain, so that the sensation of pain is not readily ascribed to factors which seem on the surface easier to understand.

There are, of course, innumerable methods of treating pain, but this textbook of biofeedback is concerned with the pain relief that can come with the demonstration by the patient to himself of the physiological responses associated with pain. It is felt by the authors that those who are directing this demonstration (the practicing clinicians of biofeedback) will be helped in this task by an understanding of the complexities of sensation.

In the treatment of pain, techniques with electromyogram (EMG) or thermal biofeedback can be directed to one of two goals. The aim may be to alter the underlying pathological process (such as muscle spasm or undue vasodilatation) which contributes to the development of pain. Alternatively, biofeedback can actually raise the threshold for pain by adding a stimulus which competes for attention, as a counterstimulus.

Receptor Organs and Sensory Perception

Living organisms make decisions through the CNS utilizing information gathered from the environment, either external or internal (Fig. 5–1). This information is detected by differing receptor organs. Receptors vary in type depending on the kind of stimulus which they sense and include mechanical, thermal, chemical, or photic. Receptor organs transmit this information received to the CNS by means of nerve impulses. Thus, receptor organs act like transducers, devices that convert one form of energy into another.

A variety of sensory modalities are associated with stimuli applied to the skin, to muscle, or to the joints. Those having clinical relevance include awareness of mechanical stimuli (touch, pressure, vibratory sensibility), temperature gradients (cold, warmth), pain, and position in space (proprioception).

The physiology of pain sensation is more complex than any of the other sensory modalities. Even after extensive research, it remains unclear whether or not pain is a specific modality, transmitted by specific pathways.

Pain endings in skin are supplied by both myelinated (insulated fibers, Figs. 5–2, 5–3) and unmyelinated (noninsulated) fibers. The receptors are usually free endings, extending into the epidermis, within the connective tissue of the dermis, and in the close vicinity of blood vessels. Muscle pain is mediated by pressure-pain endings, which have both small myelinated or unmyelinated axons, and by the afferent nerve fibers around blood vessels. Joint pain is presumed to be mediated by free endings in the connective tissue around the joint and also those associated with blood vessels.

Classes of Receptors

Sherrington (1947) divided the receptors into exteroceptive, interoceptive, and proprioceptive according to whether they provide information related to the external environment, the activity of the viscera, or the position of the body in space. There are other classifications, and the following schema prepared by Willis and Grossman (1977) is logical and comprehensive.

Special: Vision (seeing), audition (hearing), gustation (tasting), olfaction (smelling), and balance

Superficial: Touch, pressure, warmth, cold, pain

Deep: Position, vibration, deep pressure, deep pain

Visceral: Hunger, nausea, visceral pain

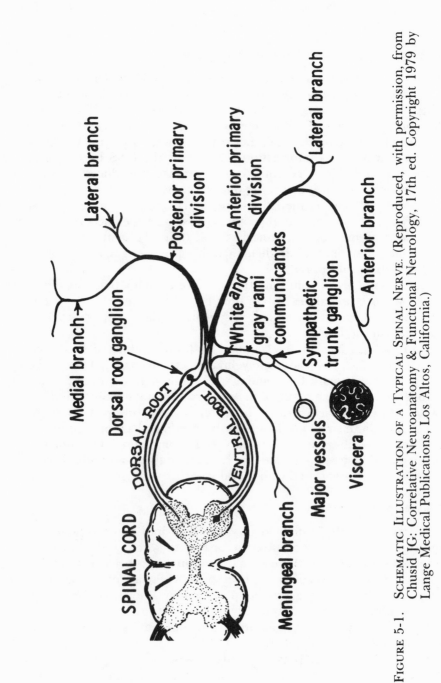

FIGURE 5-1. SCHEMATIC ILLUSTRATION OF A TYPICAL SPINAL NERVE. (Reproduced, with permission, from Chusid JG: Correlative Neuroanatomy & Functional Neurology, 17th ed. Copyright 1979 by Lange Medical Publications, Los Altos, California.)

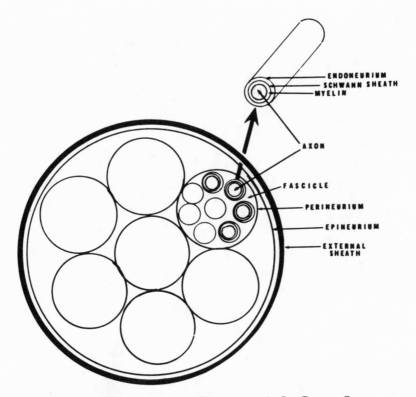

FIGURE 5-2. PERIPHERAL NERVE (SCHEMATIC). IN CROSS SECTION A NERVE IS COMPOSED OF MANY AXONS GROUPED INTO A FASCICLE. EACH AXON IS SURROUNDED BY MYELIN ENCLOSED WITHIN A SHEATH OF SCHWANN. THIS IS IN TURN COATED WITH ENDONEURIUM WHICH IS COMPOSED OF LONGITUDINAL COLLAGEN STRIPS. PERINEURIUM BINDS THE FASCICLES WHICH ARE IN TURN BOUND TOGETHER BY SPINEURIUM. THE ENTIRE NERVE IS COVERED BY AN EXTERNAL SHEATH. (Reproduced by permission of Cailliet, R: Soft Tissue, Pain and Disability, F. A. Davis Company, 1977.)

Since it is not possible to separate entirely one sensory modality from another in an individual's consciousness of total "well-being" (euphoria) or "ill-feeling," (dysphoria) it is important for students of biofeedback to understand the various ramifications of pain as they relate to other sensations. During the course of treatment of pain, the patient undergoes various changes. His sensations are gradually modified so that, for example, what was previously felt as deep pain may become a sensation of deep pressure. Then perhaps by a further change in receptor adaptation, that sense of deep pressure may evolve into superficial pressure, then superficial touch and gradually fade out of conscious awareness.

129

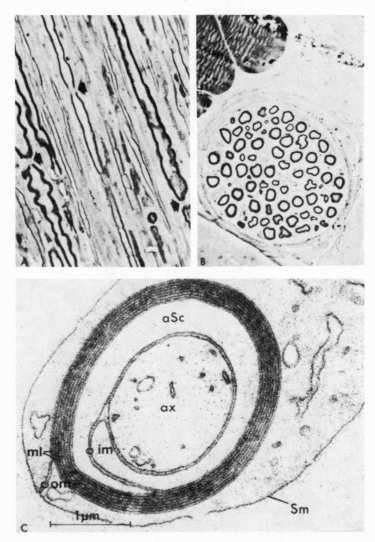

FIGURE 5-3.   A. PHASE CONTRAST MICROGRAPH OF LONGITUDINAL
SECTION THROUGH MOUSE SCIATIC NERVE. THICK AND
THIN MYELINATED FIBERS ARE DISTINGUISHABLE.
THREE NODES OF RANVIER ARE PRESENT (ARROWS). B.
PHASE CONTRAST MICROGRAPH OF TRANSVERSE SEC-
TION THROUGH A FASCICLE FROM MOUSE PERONEAL
NERVE. A POPULATION OF LARGE AND SMALL MYELI-
NATED FIBERS IS EVIDENT. C. ELECTRON MICROGRAPH
OF TRANSVERSE SECTION THROUGH A MYELINATED
NERVE FIBER FROM A FIVE DAY POSTNATAL MOUSE
SCIATIC NERVE. THE OUTER (OM) AND INNER (IM)

Mexaxons Are Easily Visible. The Major Dense Lines (ml) of the Myelin Arise by the Fusion of the Inner Surfaces of the Schwann Cell Surface Membrane (Sm). The Axon (ax) Is Surrounded by a Conspicuous Layer of Adaxonal Schwann Cell Cytoplasm (aSc). (Reproduced by permission of Dyck PJ, Thomas PK, and Lambert EH: Peripheral Neuropathy, Vol. II, W. B. Saunders, Company. Philadelphia, London, Toronto.)

By studying the physiology of the isolated modality, the complexities of these combinations can come to be appreciated. Only by understanding, for example, the close relationship between visceral pain and depression, between loss of position sense and anxiety, or between paralysis and pain from joint immobility, can a therapist truly treat a patient. In the "simple" sensation of a headache or low back pain, there usually underlie a number of different modalities of sensation, each with their specific characteristics and interrelationships. If the biofeedback clinician is not able to steer the patient through the appreciation of his own sensations, then there is considerable danger that other symptoms may supplant the sensation of pain. One symptom in other words may only replace another (symptom substitution).

For these various reasons, students of biofeedback should understand several aspects of receptor mechanisms. These include: (1) receptor potentials, generated by the depolarization that results from effective stimulation, (2) receptor adaptation, (3) stimulus intensity and its relationship to response, (4) receptor fatigue, and (5) the receptor fields. (A receptor field is the area in which the appropriate stimulation causes a discharge in the related afferent fiber. A single afferent fiber supplies one or, more often, several receptor organs.) For further information on receptor mechanisms, readers are referred to textbooks on physiology. Here, three characteristics of the sensory system will be emphasized, because of their importance in relationship to biofeedback mechanisms. These include: (1) spontaneous activity, (2) central control of sensation, and (3) surround inhibition.

Spontaneous Activity

Many afferent fibers will discharge when no *obvious* stimulation of the receptor organ has occurred. This allows a great range of change in the discharge pattern with various kinds of stimuli. Thus, if an ongoing spontaneous background discharge is occurring, both a decrease as well as an increase in stimulation can be signaled and identified.

The fact that spontaneous activity of the nerve cell or nerve fiber exists may be more easily understood by describing intraneuronal recording. When a neurophysiologist impales a large neuron with a microelectrode, the semi-continuous "pop-pop" sound of the neuronal discharges are recorded. These are caused by membrane depolarization. In a neuron at rest, there is an electrical potential difference between the outside and the inside of the cell membrane of approximately 70 μv in magnitude with the inside charged negatively as compared with the outside. Depolarization occurs when the potential difference is reduced to a threshold low enough to cause the propagation of an action potential. The first discharge burst recorded by the neurophysiologist is caused by the microelectrode crossing the membrane, thus causing depolarization (an injury potential). The subsequent discharges constitute the spontaneous neuronal discharges. In the nervous system, there is a constant "cross-talk," or spontaneous discharge activity and it is this spontaneous activity which the microelectrode records. This type of recording is known to neurophysiologists as "listening-in" to the nerve cells. Approximately 30 minutes after placement of the microelectrode, that nerve cell will stop firing (discharging), which indicates that its spontaneous activity ceases. Similar phenomena are recorded when a microelectrode impales a large nerve fiber; for example, the giant axon of a squid ("ink-fish").

It can, therefore, be understood that the CNS is dealing with a "more-or-less" discharge status of the receptor organs in the waking individual. In other words, there is a level of discharge from the receptor organs which can be described as "more-or-less" activity going in to the CNS. Another level of "more-or-less" discharge from the receptor organs into the CNS is presumably operating during sleep, and varies with the stages of sleep.

Central Control of Sensation

Many afferent systems are under the control of the brain and a subject can voluntarily decrease the spontaneous activity in his afferent system. This provides a mechanism for sorting out essential from trivial information. The control system is termed centrifugal (traveling from the brain down towards the periphery). It has been particularly well-demonstrated at the muscle spindle level. In modern life, this central control machine is grossly overworked with hyperstimulation, for example, by constant running of the television when the subject is not watching it, and by other forms of visual and noise pollution. This means that the central control system is flooded, and this overloading is one cause of physiologic fatigue.

Surround Inhibition

Occasionally, an excitatory receptive field of a central neuron is surrounded by an inhibitory receptive field. In this way, a moving stimulus may cross an inhibitory receptive field or zone before entering the excitatory one. This arrangement is of significance for sensory discrimination. It is also likely to be of significance, for example, in epilepsy and for inhibition of seizures.

Dorsal (Posterior) Root Ganglion of the Peripheral Nerve

The first relay (synapse) of the fiber of the peripheral nerve takes place in the posterior (dorsal) root ganglion. (Fig. 5–4).

Since first described by Sir Charles Bell in 1811 and Francois Magendie in 1822, it has generally been accepted that the dorsal root contains sensory axons and the anterior (ventral) root contains motor axons. This concept is usually referred to as the "law of Bell and Magendie," and it was concluded that pain "messages" traveled in the dorsal root from the periphery into the spinal cord. For this reason, it was difficult to understand why dorsal rhyzotomy (surgical section of the dorsal root) often failed to relieve pain in patients suffering from various painful disorders. One possible explanation for this difficulty is that sensation also reaches the spinal cord through the ventral root, and, in fact, receptive fields have been shown to be served by myelinated fibers in the ventral root in the cat (Kato and Tanji, 1971). Human ventral roots examined in the light and electron microscopes (Coggeshall et al., 1975) were noted to contain large numbers of unmyelinated axons. Indeed, these made up 27 percent of the total population of ventral root axons. The function of these unmyelinated axons is not proven, but it is presumed that a significant number are sensory and may be mediating pain.

Spinal Cord

There are at least three important ascending pathways in the spinal cord that mediate somatic sensations arising in the extremities and trunk (Fig. 5–5). These are the dorsal column pathway, the spinocervical tract, and the spinothalamic tract. The spinothalamic tract conveys crude touch, pain, and temperature sensibility. A distinction formerly

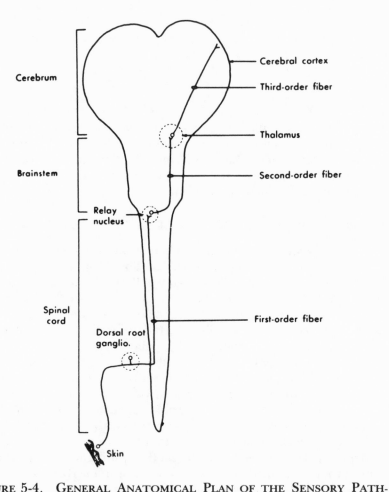

FIGURE 5-4. GENERAL ANATOMICAL PLAN OF THE SENSORY PATH-
WAYS. THE FIRST-ORDER NEURON OF A SENSORY PATH-
WAY IS SHOWN INNERVATING A SENSORY RECEPTOR IN
THE SKIN. ITS CELL BODY IS IN A DORSAL ROOT GANG-
LION, AND THE ASCENDING FIBER ASCENDS IN THE
SPINAL CORD TO END IN THE MEDULLA. IN THIS CASE,
THE SECOND-ORDER NEURON HAS ITS CELL BODY IN
THE LOWER BRAINSTEM. THE DECUSSATION OF ITS
AXON IS SHOWN, AND THE SECOND-ORDER FIBER
ASCENDS TO THE THALAMUS. HERE IT SYNAPSES WITH A
THIRD-ORDER NEURON, WHOSE AXON PROJECTS TO A
SENSORY AREA OF THE CEREBRAL CORTEX. (Repro-
duced by permission from Willis, William D., Jr., and
Grossman, Robert G.: Medical Neurobiology, ed. 2, St.
Louis, The C. V. Mosby Co., 1977.)

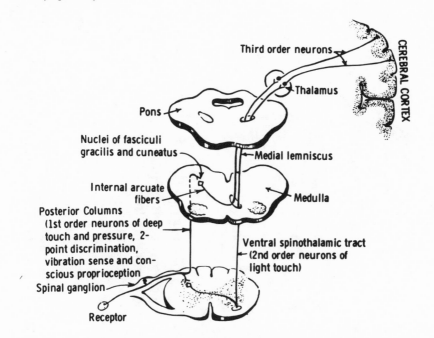

FIGURE 5-5.   TOUCH AND PRESSURE. (Reproduced, with permission, from Chusid JG: Correlative Neuroanatomy & Functional Neurology, 17th ed. Copyright 1979 by Lange Medical Publications, Los Altos, California.)

was made between the lateral and ventral spinothalamic tract, but there now appears to be little anatomic or physiologic basis for such a distinction. The spinocervical tract appears to have functions that overlap those of the dorsal column pathways and the spinothalamic tract. It carries information concerning discriminative touch in addition to pain and temperature sensibility, (Willis and Grossman, 1977).

Spinothalamic Tract (Fig. 5–6)

The afferent fibers supplying information to this pathway enter through the dorsal roots at all levels of the spinal cord. Insensitive mechanoreceptors (mechanical nociceptors or nocireceptors) provide pressure and pain input. Pain information is also provided by thermal nociceptors. The spinothalamic tract fibers arising from neurons of the spinal cord gray matter cross the midline in the commissure just anterior to the spinal canal. The axons then ascend in the contralateral

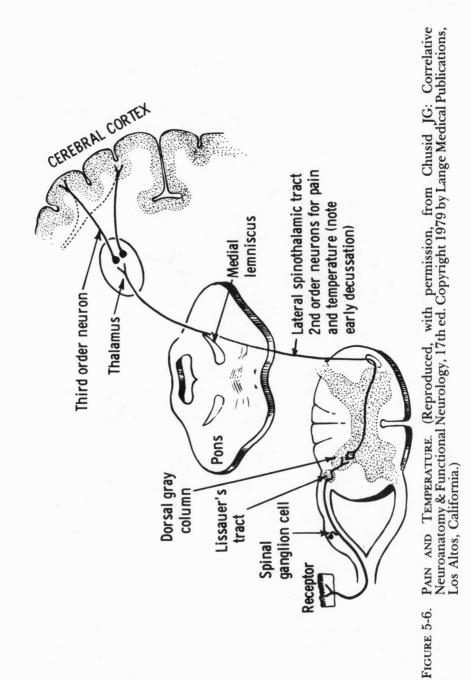

FIGURE 5-6. PAIN AND TEMPERATURE. (Reproduced, with permission, from Chusid JG: Correlative Neuroanatomy & Functional Neurology, 17th ed. Copyright 1979 by Lange Medical Publications, Los Altos, California.)

white matter in the ventral funiculus (column) and the ventral part of the lateral funiculus. The spinothalamic tract has a somatotopic organization in the spinal cord. Fibers representing all levels of the body are found in the cervical cord. Here the tract consists of layers, with the fibers from the lowest levels of the cord located at the periphery of the tract and those from the cervical region located medially in the tract. This arrangement is of importance clinically because it determines the depth necessary for the neurosurgeon to make incisions in the cord (cordotomy) for the relief of chronic pain by sectioning of the spinothalamic tract. Pain arising from the lower part of the body for example can be relieved by a more superficial cordotomy than can pain arising from the chest or upper extremity.

Other Ascending Pathways that May Contribute to Somatic Sensibility

In addition to the three pathways mentioned above, information about somatic sensation may be transmitted by multisynaptic pathways. For instance, pain and temperature sensations are mediated in part by propriospinal and spinoreticular tracts. Because of slight delay at each synapse, action impulses traveling in multisynaptic pathways take longer to be received by the cortex. The message, however, transmitted by these multisynaptic pathways differs slightly from that conveyed by the more direct pathways, because there is an opportunity for modulation at each synapse. This may explain the fact that in many diseases there is a disturbance of sensation such that a "new" sensation is experienced, outside the range of sensation felt in an intact nervous system. For example, in syringomyelia, a patient may describe displacement of localization of pin-prick stimulation which does not correspond with normal anatomy; also unusual sensations may occur with other spinal cord diseases, with thalamic lesions, phantom limbs, or after peripheral nerve injury as with causalgia, probably due to these phenomena.

Thalamus

The spinal cord pathways conveying sensory information travel to the thalamus. The thalamus is the great relay station for sensation before the final transmission to the cortex. Much of the spinothalamic tract ends in the ventral posterior lateral (VPL) nucleus of the thalamus (Fig. 5–6). However, a part of the spinothalamic tract ends in other thalamic nuclei, including a posterior region adjacent to the medial geniculate body and also in some of the intralaminar nuclei. The thalamus (Greek: *thalamus,* "love-seat of the Gods"), phylogeneti- cally, represents the old sensory brain in more primitive organisms in which the cerebral hemispheres are absent or not yet well developed.

Sensations from the face travel in the trigeminal (5th cranial) nerve to the ventral posterior medial (VPM) nucleus of the thalamus. The VPL and VPM nuclei together are often referred to as the ventrobasal (VB) complex. The response characteristics of neurons in the VB complex are well-defined. They include (1) excitation by a single stimulus modality, (2) a small receptive field, and (3) a short latency between stimulus and response. On the other hand, neurons in the posterior nuclear group show the following characteristics: (1) They often respond to several stimulus modalities. (2) Their cutaneous receptive fields are large and frequently bilateral. (3) The latency is longer. These observations are made in experimental animals by in- traneuronal studies with microelectrodes. Most of the neurons of the VB complex respond to a particular stimulus modality such as the bending of hairs or light pressure. Some respond primarily to intense mechanical stimuli, which in humans are associated with a sense of pain. The responsiveness of some of these neurons appears to depend on the state of consciousness of the animal, however. It is not clear whether there are specific pain cells in the VB complex. Furthermore, the neurons that do respond to noxious stimuli seem not to have a somatotopic organization. It is possible that pain localization depends on a separate population of neurons that are responsible for pain recognition.

The neurons of the VB complex can often be inhibited by stimuli applied to areas of skin adjacent to their excitatory receptive fields. In addition to this peripheral inhibition, neurons of the VB complex are subject to recurrent inhibition.

Thalamocortical Projection

Sensory fibers project from the thalamus through the internal cap- sule to the postcentral gyrus of the parietal lobe. Much more elaborate sensory processing occurs within the cerebral cortex. The nature of cortical participation in the mediation of pain sensation is poorly un- derstood. In fact, this is one of the most obscure areas in physiology. Although much is known concerning representation in the cortex of other sensory modalities, *there does not seem to be specific representation of pain as such in the whole of the cortex.* Large areas of parietal cortex may be injured, disturbing two-point discrimination, position sense, and stereognosis without impairment of pain sensation (Russell, 1945). Penfield and Boldrey (1937) explored the somatosensory cortex intensively with electrical stimulation, but only rarely did this stimulation elicit sensation described as painful. In occasional patients with chronic pain, on the other hand, cortical stimulation produced sensations of pain, and cortical excision produced pain relief and analgesia (Lewin and Phillip, 1952).

The Neuropharmacology of Pain

Some light may be thrown on the role of cortical participation in the mediation of pain sensation by recent work on the neuropharmacology of pain. The importance of this subject is emerging, and for proper evaluation it requires a review of neurotransmitters which is outside the scope of this text. A brief description, however, of enkephalins and endorphins is appropriate, because of their presence in the normal brain and gut, and because of their relevance to pain suppression.

In the central nervous system, there are opiatelike peptide molecules: the short chains of amino acids called enkephalins, and the longer chains called endorphins. Enkephalin and another peptide, substance P, have been implicated in pain perception, substance P with the transmission of pain-related impulses and enkephalin with their suppression.

In the last few years, it has become evident that a large number of peptides are produced in specific nerve cells in the brain. At least 17 such peptides have been identified (Hökfelt, 1980). A number of peptides are found in cells in both the gut and the brain, including substance P, enkephalins, and the ACTH family including β-endorphin. The discovery by Hughes and co-workers in 1975 that the probable ligands* (binders) for opiate receptors were peptides (enkephalins) gave support to the transmitter idea for brain peptides. It was subsequently shown that β-endorphin (a derivative of another peptide) also has opiatelike activity. Thus, these two pentapeptides (enkephalin and endorphin) isolated from brain fit opiate receptors and appear to be natural ligands. Enkephalins are concentrated in the spinal cord fibers and cells in the dorsal horns (lamine I, II); they are also found in the substantia gelatinosa of the spinal tract of the trigeminal nerve in the medulla. Enkephalins are widespread in cell bodies and fibers in brain

*A ligand is a substance that binds another to itself.

and spinal cord, including the midbrain periaqueductal grey matter, in the hypothalamus, and in the cell bodies of the arcuate, premammillary, and other nuclei. An enkephalin-containing pathway has been noted from the amygdala to the stria terminalis, and another from the caudate to the globus pallidus (Zimmerman, 1979). There are also nerve fibers in the gut and cells in the sympathetic ganglia which contain enkephalins. Enkephalin-containing cell bodies and fibers appear to be more numerous than those with β-endorphins. The latter are produced in neuronal perikarya in the hypothalamus, in the region of the arcuate nucleus and probably distributed in projections in the hypothalamus, the thalamus, amygdala, and central grey matter. The function of the enkephalins is opiatelike, being analgesic via short neurons; in addition, they mediate presynaptic inhibition in the dorsal horn of the spinal cord. Experimentally, they also play a role in regulating respiration, and in the medulla they cause vomiting. In a similar way, the endorphins are opiatelike and cause experimental analgesia, hyperthermia, and catatonia. They are inhibitory except in the hippocampus. They also cause central release of other brain peptides (Zimmerman, 1979).

The accumulation of evidence that specific nerve cells in the brain are engaged in the production of these pharmacologically-active peptides, together with data on neurohormones, neurotransmitters, and neuromodulators has led to the concept of the brain as a gland.

Place Theory of Neural Coding

Returning to the mechanisms whereby pain is appreciated, it is now appropriate to examine the theories of neural coding or encoding of pain sensation. There is evidence to suggest that pain is mediated by specific receptors, with specific afferent fibers and central pathways. This is the basis for the place theory of neural coding, implying localization in terms of the sensory modality transmitted. It was widely accepted as a working hypothesis until the "gate" theory (see below) challenged some of these established tenets.

Gate Theory of Pain (Fig. 5-7)

This theory maintains that the perception of pain is signaled by an enhanced input traveling in pathways whose activity is normally interpreted as touch or pressure. This is an instance of a "pattern" theory (as opposed to "place"). The recent formulation of a pattern theory is called the gate theory. A number of observations led to the gate theory.

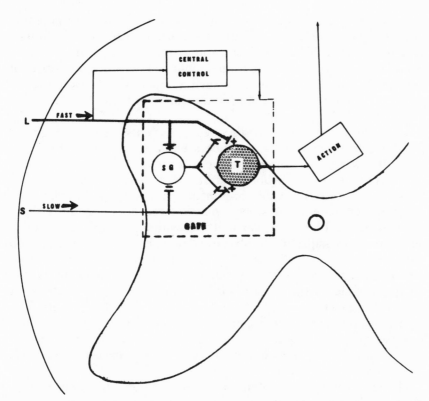

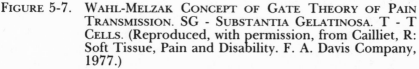

FIGURE 5-7. WAHL-MELZAK CONCEPT OF GATE THEORY OF PAIN
TRANSMISSION. SG - SUBSTANTIA GELATINOSA. T - T
CELLS. (Reproduced, with permission, from Cailliet, R:
Soft Tissue, Pain and Disability. F. A. Davis Company,
1977.)

1. Cutaneous pain can be blocked or reduced by nonnoxious
stimulation of the adjacent skin. The information interpreted as pain
travels to the CNS by small afferent fibers (A - delta myelinated fibers
and C fibers), whereas the touch information travels by large afferent
fibers (A - beta). It is postulated that pain results when the input
traveling in small fibers becomes excessive relative to that carried by
large fibers.

2. Neurons of the dorsal (posterior) horn (laminae IV to VI) (see
Fig. 2–12) were found to respond to all gradations of mechanical
stimulation of the skin; none responded just to noxious stimulation. If
pain is indeed relayed by these cells, the information would have to be
signaled by a patterned input.

3.   Small afferent fibers can evoke a positive dorsal root potential in large fibers. The most likely mechanism for such a positive dorsal root potential is the removal of a tonic depolarization. Inasmuch as presynaptic inhibition results from depolarization of afferent fibers, it may be supposed that removal of such a depolarization would result in a disinhibition, or facilitation, of transmission from the large afferent fibers.

The following substrates and sequence of events has been suggested for the gate mechanism. Large fibers entering the dorsal horn are thought to synapse on and excite two types of cells: large transmission (T) cells in the nucleus proprius, and small substantia gelatinosa (SG) cells. The SG cells then cause presynaptic inhibition of both large and small afferent fibers. Thus, an input of large fibers causes a slight response of the T cells but also interferes with further input. The small afferents also synapse on both types of cells; however, it is suggested that the synapse on the SG cells is inhibitory. Thus, an input over small fibers would activate the T cells but, in addition, would disinhibit the synapses made by the large fibers, making any ongoing input over these fibers much more effective in firing the T cells. In this way, large fiber input results in damping of transmission by a negative feedback, whereas small fiber input opens the gate, a positive feedback mechanism. Pain would result when the T cell discharge exceeds some level monitored by higher centers.

The most convincing evidence in favor of the gate theory is the firm evidence that large fibers inhibit pain transmission. The gate theory, however, is quite controversial. Two points argue against it: First, dorsal horn cells have now been found that respond selectively to intense stimulation of the skin. These are located in lamina I and lamina V in the dorsal (posterior) horn. Thus, there may be a separate central pathway for pain transmission. Second, positive dorsal root potentials were indeed observed when fine afferent fibers were stimulated, but this was with electrical stimulation; with "natural" stimulation, using a noxious level of radiant heat, negative dorsal root potentials were observed.

Types of Pain

Following the above discussion on the theories of coding of pain stimuli in the nervous system, some clinical aspects of pain will be examined. Since pain is an experience, it can only be described subjectively ("by the subject"). It must therefore be understood that the descriptive terms applied by observers and clinicians are purely labels for discussing different properties and factors relevant to the appearance or disappearance of this experience. The description by subjects of their experience of pain does not necessarily differ according to the causes of the pain. Associated factors, such as the context in which pain occurs, however, are likely to vary.

One set of differences was described with plasma cortisol (Shenkin, 1964); a higher mean cortisol value was found in patients with organic lesions causing pain, than in patients with tension headaches. The "organic" lesion group also had a reduced diurnal (daytime) variation in cortisol compared with the other. A good biochemical method to discriminate pain of organic origin from pain of psychogenic origin is the measurement of plasma 11-hydroxy corticosteroids at 6:00 A.M.

Ischemic cold pain caused a rise in plasma cortisol in one study (Black and Friedman, 1968). This rise was distinctly less in those subjects given a hypnotic suggestion of anesthesia. Another study (Lascelles et al., 1974) compared the cortisol level in two groups of patients, 15 with demonstrable organic cause for pain and 10 without. They found a significant difference between the two groups, in that those with organic lesions had higher plasma cortisol levels. However, it should be noted that many factors affect plasma cortisol levels including depression and stress. Both groups in the Lascelles study (1974) showed raised mean plasma cortisol values; thus, the difference is only one of degree. Both groups showed a similar tendency to reduced diurnal variation in the level of plasma cortisol. Depressed patients showed disturbance in the circadian rhythm of adrenocortical activity (Fullerton et al., 1968), which was correlated with the depression. In the depressed patients, a reduced diurnal variation was also noted as compared with the "normal" controls.

Demonstration of pharmacologic fluctuations in patients according to their psychophysiological state is likely to increase with continued neuropsychopharmacological research. Levels of psychologically active substances can currently be measured in the blood, urine, cerebrospinal fluid, and/or the saliva.

It should be reemphasized that when pain arises for psychological reasons, the experience may be qualitatively indistinguishable from pain caused by organic lesions. On the other hand, the subjects themselves are usually aware of the difference because of associated factors.

Referred Pain

In seeking to determine the origin of pain in a given case, whether visceral or somatic, attention must be paid to its distribution, its quality, its time incidence, and to the factors which aggravate or relieve it. Apart from the various types of organic pain which can be explained on the anatomical bases described in the first part of the chapter, there is a type known as "referred pain," mainly because of its distribution.

Not infrequently, impulses set up in the viscera are transferred in part to somatic neuron arcs, and the disagreeable sensations initiated therein are interpreted as pain from the periphery of the body. These sensations constitute so-called referred pain. In such cases, the peripheral area in which the pain is felt is always innervated in part at least from the same sensory ganglia as is the organ involved. Not all the details of these connections are well understood. The following examples of neuron arc illustrates referred pain.

From receptors that are stimulated by distension of the gallbladder, impulses are carried over the splanchnic nerves to their cells of origin in the appropriate thoracic dorsal root ganglia. The visceral gray column neurons then discharge to the intermediolateral cell column neurons in the spinal cord (Crosby et al., 1962). Gallbladder pain is thus referred to the shoulder area. Other visceral impulses may be referred to body wall areas.

There are also instances of somatic pain which are difficult to trace to their source. Kellgren (1939) showed that whereas superficial lesions cause local pain, deeply situated lesions give rise to discomfort which is felt not only at the site of damage but also in the tissues supplied by the spinal segment which innervates the site of the lesion; that is to say, the deeper the lesion from the body surface, the more likely it is that pain will be referred. Pain referred from deep sources is not, as a rule, felt in the skin, e.g., the reference is not in terms of the dermatome but of the deep structures, usually the musculature.

Respondent Pain

Respondent pain is the term used to describe pain that arises in response to a clearly observable and definable factor, which may be in the external environment (exteroceptive) or within the patient's body (interoceptive). Pain in response to such a stimulus (respondent pain) is often of acute onset, as in trauma, or in acute inflammation such as appendicitis. It may, however, be chronic, as in cancer, or in tabes (neurosyphilis), or in spinal cord disease.

Operant Pain

Operant pain is the term used to denote the painful distress which may arise as a result of the psychological experience of the original trauma (Fordyce, 1976).

In the development of pain, the following sequence may take place: an event occurs such as trauma or acute inflammation of an organ which stimulates pain-sensitive endings and the subject feels pain in response ("respondent pain"). This may bring about a change in the subject's status, his behavior and his emotional state such that a further painful distress, associated with anxiety, disease, and a long chain of psychophysiological sensations disturbs the organism. These sensations produce what is called "operant pain" since they cause or operate behavior patterns and further sensations. The term *operant pain* is perhaps more explicit than *psychogenic pain* because it indicates the necessary occurrence of further events, and it is thus operative in shaping a person's behavior and state of mind. It alerts us to the effects of pain, usually chronic pain, rather than merely labeling the cause of the pain as does the use of the adjective "psychogenic" (meaning, "of psychological origin"). The word *psychogenic* was introduced into psychiatry in 1894 by Robert Sommer. "Many attempts have been made to clarify the concept it denotes and apply it to clinical purposes. These attempts have been bedeviled by unsettled philosophical problems. It is suggested that the word should be decently buried" (Lewis, 1979). Almost all pain, when it has been present for a considerable length of time, of necessity becomes "operant" pain, because the subject's attention is drawn to the painful part of the body and thus causes alteration of the normal "body image."

Operant pain can also be described as the pain which arises in response to a reinforcing stimulus, as in operant behavior (see Chap. 1). Just as "respondent pain" tends to be the acute, more short-lived pain, "operant pain" tends to be more long-term and affective. When the original noxious cause is removed, "respondent" pain disappears. "Operant" pain may persist because the pain signals have established a pattern and pathways of reverberating circuits. It is in cases of operant pain that biofeedback treatment is likely to be indicated. This is because many of these reverberating circuits involve responses which the patient can modify, once he has externalized them and observed them for himself.

Therapy for Pain

A general principle in medical therapeutics is that effective treatment may antedate understanding of the pathogenesis (cause of the disease or disorder). For example, syphilis was successfully treated by arsenic and malarial fever long before the causative treponemal organism was discovered. This principle is particularly true with a symptom such as pain. If treatment is effective in reducing pain, then whatever the mechanism, it is an advisable procedure. At the same time, however, as applying this treatment it is necessary to investigate (1) the original cause of the pain and (2) the mechanism whereby the results operate. For example, if by any chance biofeedback should relieve the pain of a cancer, we need (1) to investigate and disclose the cancer in order to treat it appropriately and (2) to understand the anatomo-physiological causes of improvement, whether subjective, objective, or both.

"Sensation" and "Perception"

One of the theoretical problems that haunts the subject of pain and which should be taken into consideration during pain research is that of the distinction between a "sensation" and a "perception." It is still in many ways valid, or at least useful in classification. A "sensation" is a peripheral phenomenon and describes the events up to and including the thalamus, where awareness of crude sensation is usually considered to take place. With projection to the cortex, elaboration occurs, comprising associative factors, further analysis of the neural events, linkage to previous stimuli which evoke memories, affect, and other interpretation according to the individual experience of that particular part of the cortex. With all these added factors, the "sensation" becomes a "perception." Further detail on this very complex subject is to be found in the literature. Until fairly recently, the distinction between a sensation and a perception was considered to hold good for the various modalities of sensation. The modality in which neurophysiological research has been the most detailed is vision; and, therefore, the following example will illustrate the point.

Perceptual discrimination in vision depends upon physiological organization in the receptor organ, the retina, and this in turn depends upon the anatomical fact that a large number of retinal receptors converge upon a single optic nerve fiber, in the ratio according to Granit (1955) "of the order of 100 to 1." As Granit (1955) wrote: "The retinal surfaces are capable of good discrimination on the same basic principle as is the skin, i.e., by using overlapping receptive fields of different sizes, from very large to very small, the latter likely to be multiplied in eyes with a high percentage of cones, which have good visual acuity." He added (p. 54), "on the whole . . . the distinction between sensation and perception has lost its validity . . . a sensation is an exceedingly complex affair." During the past 20 years, intense research on the processing of sensory information in the primary visual cortex (Hubel and Wiesel, 1979), and in other modalities including pain emphasizes the complexity of a sensation. It may, therefore, be concluded that the concept of a sensation requiring conscious appreciation embraces the attributes of a perception.

REFERENCES

Black S, Friedman M: Effects of emotion and pain on adrenocortical function investigated by hypnosis. Br Med J 1: 477, 1968.

Coggeshall RE, Applebaum ML, Fazen M et al.: Unmyelinated axons in human ventral roots, a possible explanation for the failure of dorsal rhizotomy to relieve pain. Brain 98: 157, 1975.

Crosby E, Humphrey T, Lauer, EW: *Correlative Anatomy of the Nervous System.* New York, Macmillan, 1962.

Fischer-Williams M: Treatment of chronic pain. Br Med J 1:533, 1956.

Fordyce WE: *Behavioral Methods for Control of Chronic Pain and Illness.* New York, Mosby, 1976.

Fullerton DT, Wenzel FJ, Lohrenz FN, Fahs H: Circadian rhythm of adrenal cortical activity in depression. 1. A comparison of depressed patients with normal subjects. 2. A comparison of types of depression. Arch Gen Psychiatr 19: 674, 1968.

Granit R: *Receptors and Sensory Perception.* New Haven, Yale University Press, 1955.

Hökfelt T: Brain peptides. Nature 284: 515, 1980.

Hubel DH, Wiesel TN: Brain mechanisms of vision. Sci Am 241: 150, 1979.

Hughes J, Smith T, Morgan B: Purification and properties of enkephalin—the possible endogenous ligand for the morphine receptor. Life Sciences 16(12): 1753, 1975.

Kato M, Tanji J: Physiological properties of sensory fibers in the spinal ventral roots in the cat. Jpn J Physiol 21: 71, 1971.

Kellgren JM: On the distribution of pain arising from deep somatic structures with charts of segmental pain areas. Clin Sci 4: 35, 1939.

Lascelles PT, Evans PR, Merskey H, Sabur MA: Plasma cortisol in psychiatric and neurological patients with pain. Brain 97: 533, 1974.

Lewin W, Phillip CG: Observations on partial removal of post central gyrus for pain. J Neurol Neurosurg Psychiat 15: 143, 1952.

Lewis A: Psychogenic: A word and its mutations. In A Lewis: *The Later Papers of Sir Aubrey Lewis.* Oxford University Press, 1979, p. 185.

Penfield W, Boldrey E: Somatic motor and sensory representation in the cerebral cortex of man as studied by electrical stimulation. Brain 60: 389, 1937.

Russell WR: Transient disturbances following gunshot wounds of the head. Brain 68: 79, 1945.

Shenkin H: The effect of pain on the diurnal pattern of plasma corticoid levels. Neurology (Minneap) 14: 1112, 1964.

Sherrington CS: *The Integrative Action of the Nervous System.* Cambridge, England, University Press, 1947.

Stroebel C: The application of biofeedback techniques in psychiatry and behavioral medicine. Psychiatric Opinion 16: 13, 1979.

Willis WD, Grossman RG: *Medical Neurobiology.* St. Louis, Mosby, 1977, p. 238.

Zimmerman EA: Brain peptides. Neurochemistry course Amer. Academy of Neurol. 1979, p. 16.

6

The Symptom of Seizure

IT is important for students of biofeedback treatment to study the electrical activity of the brain since without this background there cannot be any understanding of epilepsy. There is widespread popular interest in epilepsy and in claims, not all of them fulfilled, about the potential use of EEG biofeedback training to treat this disorder. Since epilepsy is one of the most common neurological disorders, affecting at least 1 in every 200 people in our society, it is a condition frequently encountered. A thorough knowledge of the condition is required, therefore, not only in order to help in the practical management of the attacks, but even more usefully to prevent them.

Epilepsy is synonymous with the word *seizures,* epilepsy being the condition in which recurrent seizures occur. The word *spell* applies to an episode in which there is some alteration in the level of consciousness or awareness, the nature of which is not yet diagnosed; it may or may not be associated with demonstrable changes in the electrical activity of the brain. Thus, it may or may not be due to epilepsy; the causes of alteration in the level of awareness which are not due to epilepsy are legion.

Factors that Affect the Incidence, Occurrence, and Type of Seizure

Epilepsy is a symptom and not a disease. The factors which influence the incidence and occurrence of a seizure (to increase or decrease seizure-proneness) may be considered on several levels or in several perspectives (Table 6–1). The analogy of viewing a field under the microscope can be used in explanation of this concept. In order to get a wide, overall view of the area under discussion, the low-power magnification is used. For greater detail, a higher power magnification is employed, which concentrates down onto a smaller area. Last, for an understanding of the more detailed factors operating in a restricted field, an even higher power magnification is used.

TABLE 6-1. THE MECHANISM OF EPILEPTIC SEIZURES

I. Background factors which predispose to and influence seizures.
    1. Genetics
    2. Phylogenesis*
    3. Age
II. Persisting but intermittently operating factors, related to a focus and usually associated with interictal EEG changes.
    1. Cerebral birth injury
    2. Head injury
    3. Embolism
    4. Intracranial space-occupying lesion
        a. Hematoma
        b. Neoplasm
        c. Abscess
    5. Encephalitides
    6. Degenerative disorders
    7. Experimental focus
    8. Cardiovascular disorders, including impaired cardiac output and cardiac arrhythmias.
    9. Status post episode of acute cerebral anoxia
    10. Metabolic disorders
    11. Edema
III. Proximate or immediately operating factors related to the state of the patient.
    1. Sleep deprivation
    2. Drug intoxication and drug withdrawal including alcohol
    3. Hyperthermia
    4. Hypoglycemia
    5. Sensory precipitation and reflex mechanisms
    6. Excitation and inhibition
    7. Lowering of convulsant threshold by miscellaneous psychophysiological factors.

*Phylogeny or phylogenesis is defined as "the evolutionary development of any species of plant or animal." In the context of epilepsy, it applies to the fact that man is more susceptible to seizures than other animals lower in the evolutionary scale. There is a species gradient in vulnerability to seizures.

With reference to epilepsy (recurrent seizures), the basic factor to be considered is the genetic make-up of the individual. This determines what is called the seizure-threshold or the seizure-proneness. It is well-known that any member of the human species is susceptible to seizures. It is therefore a question of a "more-or-less" chance of whether a clinical seizure occurs. Certain other species are also liable to seizures, but to a much lesser extent than man. It appears that the higher the organism is in the evolutionary scale, the more liable is the organism to seizures. Certain strains of animals (for example, mice) can be bred to be susceptible to seizures. Baboons of the *Papio papio* species, living in Senegal, are susceptible to flicker-light induced seizures. This genetic trait is mainly exhibited by the adolescent baboon. In a similar way, certain types of seizures in man (the classical petit mal with a generalized 3 Hz spike-and-wave EEG accompaniment to the clinical seizure) is an age-associated disorder, with genetic characteristics. This basic make-up of an individual, dependent upon the genetic composition, constitutes the background predisposition to epilepsy. In other words, some individuals have a better developed neuronal inhibitory system than others. What stops or prevents a seizure has been less well studied than what precipitates one; but, in general terms, maintenance of physiological equilibrium prevents seizures, and the body has excellent built-in mechanisms for homeostasis.

The second "level" or middle power of magnification at which epilepsy may be studied refers to the macroscopic state of the brain. Certain brain disorders, such as a mass lesion with a tumor, a blood clot (hematoma), or an abscess can cause seizures. Many other brain diseases are also epileptogenic, namely cerebral arteriosclerosis ("hardening" of the arteries), which causes a narrowing of the arteries and, therefore, insufficient blood supply to the brain, (in particular insufficient oxygen and glucose to the nerve cells). Similarly, impaired cardiac output as with heart disease or partial blockage of the arteries in the neck supplying the brain can cause cerebral anoxia and seizures (Fig. 6–1). Open head injury with cerebral contusion or laceration and subsequent scar tissue formation, or certain closed head injuries are frequent causes of seizures. Cerebral birth injury and intracranial infections such as meningoencephalitis may lead to a large variety of neurological defects with seizures. Degenerative brain diseases such as Alzheimer's disease or latent virus ("slow virus") diseases such as Creutzfeldt-Jakob disease, which cause presenile dementia, are all liable to be manifested by seizures. This large heterogenous group includes what Hughlings Jackson in the 1880s termed a "gross" lesion, and currently this group includes pathology demonstrable under the light microscope and with computed tomography (CT scan) of the brain (or computed axial tomography, CAT scan), and the EEG which usually shows interictal abnormality, meaning that the brain waves are abnormal at a time when there is no seizure.

The third "level" or higher power magnification at which the symptom of epilepsy may be analyzed refers to the proximate or immediately operating factors or causes. These factors determine and finally precipitate the seizure. Some of these factors are detectable, for in-

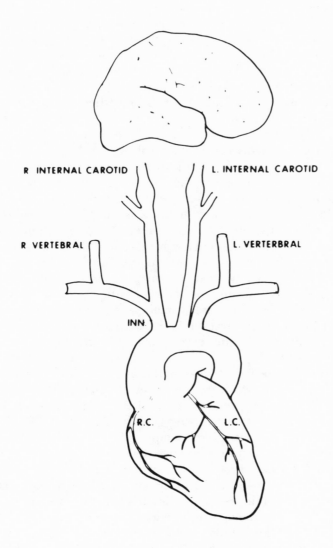

FIGURE 6-1.   DIAGRAM ILLUSTRATING THAT THE BRAIN IS SUPPLIED
BY FOUR ARTERIES, THE RIGHT AND LEFT VERTEBRAL
AND THE RIGHT AND LEFT INTERNAL CAROTID ARTER-
IES. INN. INNOMINATE ARTERY. R.C. RIGHT CORONARY
ARTERY. L.C. LEFT CORONARY ARTERY.

stance sleep deprivation, hypoglycemia (low blood sugar level), excess fluid intake, alcohol and other drug use, excess sensory stimulation, psychological factors—particularly anger—and other factors which can only be surmised. Obviously, when several factors combine, especially when they belong to each of the three classes described above (for example, when there is a genetic predisposition to epilepsy, a severe head injury and sleep deprivation), then the likelihood of a seizure occurring is high.

A further distinction may be made between the three categories of causal factors of seizures as described above. In the first category, the background factors which predispose to epilepsy, affect the brain as a whole. In the second category, there is a focus, meaning there is a part of the brain from which the seizure arises, a part where the seizure-threshold is lowest (Figs. 6–2, 6–3). This can be regarded as a *locus resistensis minoris,* literally "a place of least resistance." This epilepto-genic factor (e.g., formation of a scar following a head injury) persists, but operates only intermittently when other factors intervene. Then it operates locally, causing what is termed a partial, localized, or focal seizure (see below). In the third category, the immediately operating event (or final common cause) usually acts on the brain as a whole. Examples are sleep deprivation, or fluid retention with uremia in end-stage renal disease, or fluid excess combined with alcohol, such as a large intake of beer.

Detection of the factors that determine and finally precipitate a seizure is a task in which many individuals play a role. In order to detect basic genetic predisposition, there is a need for detailed, epidemiological surveys, involving genetic, clinical, and EEG studies not only of patients, but of large samples of their normal relatives with EEGs performed on those who have never had seizures. (This is because the EEG may show features at different ages relevant to the proneness of seizures.) Insofar as the above factors include detection of a macroscopic brain lesion, the patient cooperates with the neurologist in carrying out the appropriate investigations. Insofar as the factors operate at the cellular level, analysis is in the realm of the experimental research worker. It is these factors at the cellular level which some authors regard as the basic mechanisms of the epilepsies.

Detection of a seizure-precipitant (triggering factor) is in the realm of the clinician and the patient. In recent years, it has become more evident that these proximal or immediately operating factors or causes are often under the control of the patient.

It is possible that people can have fewer seizures when they under-

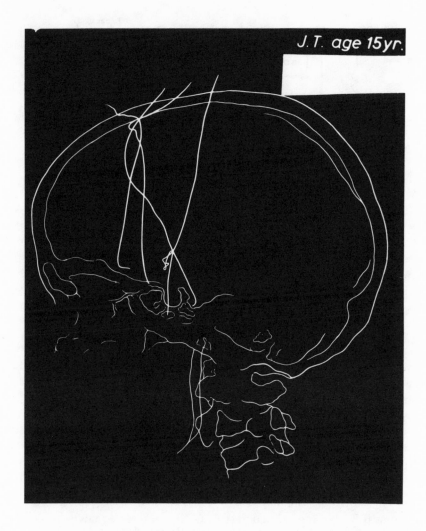

FIGURE 6-2. PLACEMENT OF ELECTRODES RECORDING THE ELECTRI-
CAL ACTIVITY FROM THE DEPTHS OF THE BRAIN. EACH
OF THE FOUR "ELECTRODES" WAS COMPOSED OF A
LEASH OF ELECTRODES, WHICH RECORDED AT 1 TO 2
MM INTERVAL IN THE BRAIN. (Reproduced, with permis-
sion, from Fischer-Williams, M. and Cooper, R. A.:
Depth Recording from the Human Brain in Epilepsy.
Electroenceph. Clin. Neurophysiol 1963, 15: 568–587.)

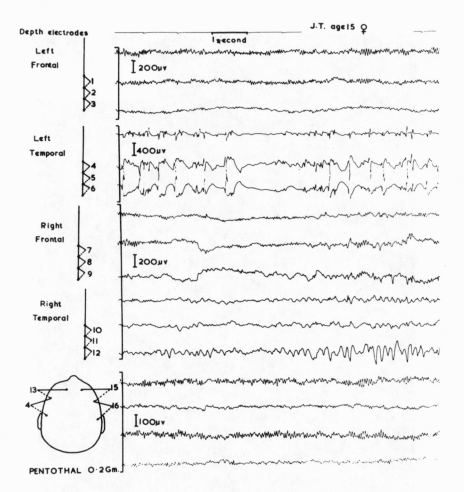

FIGURE 6-3.   SCALP AND DEPTH EEG RECORDING SHOWING A FOCUS
OF ABNORMAL ACTIVITY RESTRICTED TO A VERY SMALL
AREA DEEP IN THE LEFT TEMPORAL LOBE ("LEFT
TEMPORAL DEPTH ELECTRODE"). THE NUMERALS 1 TO
16 INDICATE THE SITE OF THE BRAIN RECORDED ON THE
16 CHANNELS. THE FIGURE ILLUSTRATES INTERICTAL
(BETWEEN SEIZURE) EEG ABNORMALITY. (Reproduced,
with permission, from Fischer-Williams, M. and Cooper,
R. A.: Depth Recording from the Human Brain in Epilepsy. Electroenceph. Clin. Neurophysiol 1963, 15: 568–
587.)

stand what precipitates or triggers their particular seizures. With better education by health professionals to enhance the sophistication of the general public, the number of seizures can be reduced even though the individual's seizure-threshold is not altered.

Seizures amenable to control include those triggered by alcohol, minor tranquilizers such as diazepam (Valium) and other drugs, by excess fluid intake and blood biochemical disturbance, sleep deprivation, hypoglycemia (low blood sugar), excess sensory input, such as television and other flicker stimulation, and by psychological factors.

Biofeedback training and EEG operant conditioning may be useful in reducing the occurrence of certain types of seizures, but EEG conditioning is an extremely costly treatment which so far yields unpredictable results (Wyler et al., 1979).

What Is an Epileptic Fit or Seizure?

An epileptic fit or seizure can be defined as "occasional sudden, excessive, rapid and local discharges of the gray matter of the brain" (Jackson, 1870; reprinted 1939) (Fig. 6–4). This is manifested to the patient and to eye witnesses as a brief episode of a few seconds or minutes with loss or disturbance of consciousness (awareness) and/or abnormal movements and/or abnormal sensation and/or abnormal psychic experience. There may or may not be amnesia (loss of memory) for the seizure. The cause of this brief episode is an abnormal electrical discharge of nerve cells and, therefore, the EEG is abnormal *during* the time of the seizure. The EEG may or may not be abnormal in between clinical seizures.

Classification of Seizures

The reader may consult the International Classification of Seizures (Gastaut, 1969) for a detailed description of the many types of epileptic seizures. A brief summary of the commonly encountered attacks follows. There are three main categories of epilepsy, from both the clinical and the EEG perspective (Figs. 6–5, 6–6, 6–7):

1. Generalized epilepsy, in which the clinical manifestations involve the entire individual and the EEG discharges can be recorded from all over the scalp (Fig. 6–8).

2. Partial epilepsy, in which only a part of the individual is involved clinically and the electrical disturbance can be recorded from a part of the brain only (Figs. 6–5, 6–6, 6–7).

3. Partial epilepsy, becoming secondarily generalized, that is, it spreads in the attack from the initial focus to become a generalized seizure.

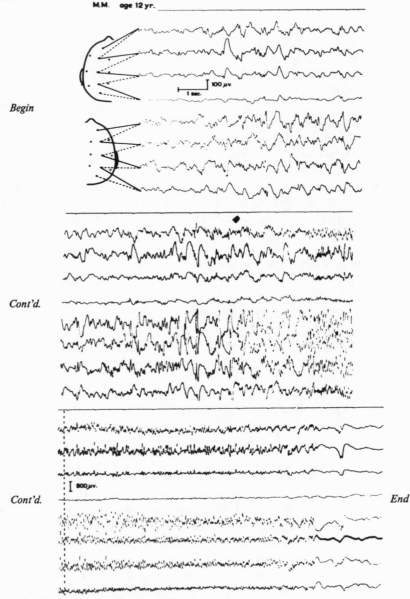

M.M. age 12 yr.

Begin

Cont'd.

Cont'd.   End

Head turned to R. Eyes half open. Slight shaking of head.

FIGURE 6-4.   EEG SCALP RECORDING OF A FOCAL SEIZURE WHICH
LASTED APPROXIMATELY 23 SECONDS, IN WHICH THE
PATIENT'S HEAD TURNED TO THE RIGHT, THE EYES
WERE OPENED, AND THERE WAS SLIGHT SHAKING OF
THE HEAD.

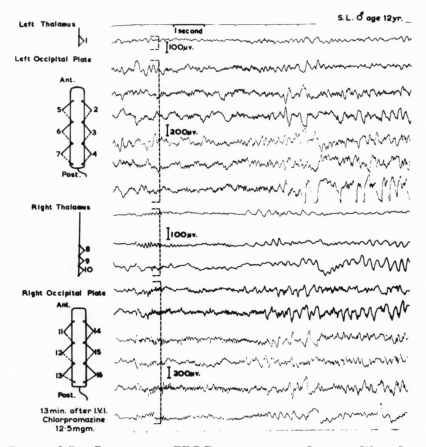

Left Thalamus

S.L. ♂ age 12yr.

Left Occipital Plate

Ant.

Post.

Right Thalamus

Right Occipital Plate

Ant.

Post.

13 min. after I.V.I.
Chlorpromazine
12·5 mgm.

FIGURE 6-5, CONTINUOUS EEG RECORDING OF A SEIZURE, WITH SUB-
FIGURE 6-6, DURAL PLATES RECORDING DIRECTLY FROM THE OCCIP-
FIGURE 6-7. ITAL CORTEX AND DEPTH ELECTRODES IN THE THAL-
AMUS. THE FOCAL SEIZURE ILLUSTRATED LASTED
ABOUT 30 SECONDS, WITH RHYTHMIC SPIKES ON THE
RIGHT (BOTTOM 5 CHANNELS) AND ABNORMAL
SLOW WAVE ACTIVITY ON THE LEFT OCCIPITAL COR-
TEX (TOP CHANNELS 2 THROUGH 7).

Types of Generalized Epilepsy

Grand Mal Seizure

The patient suddenly loses consciousness, with little warning, and
he may fall. He often cries out and there is spasm of the muscles of
the larynx so that he holds his breath and may turn dusky blue or

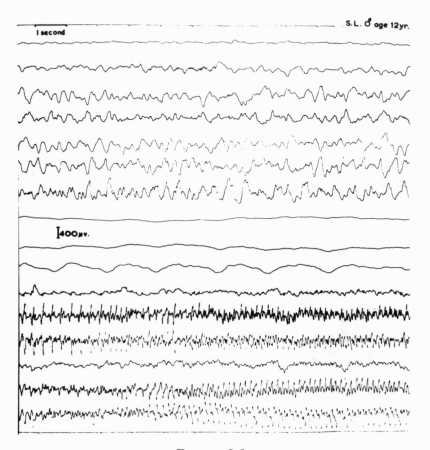

FIGURE 6-6

cyanotic. Respiration then may become loud, and there is excess salivation; he may bite his tongue because the jaw clenches tightly. There
is generalized stiffness with muscle spasm, the limbs stretch out, and
the back arches (tonic phase). This is followed by relaxation of some
of the muscles so that rhythmic jerking of the limbs occurs, usually of
all four limbs, and sometimes of the whole body (clonic phase). There
is usually sweating, dilatation of the pupils, rapid heart rate, and rise
in blood pressure. Urinary incontinence frequently occurs. The seizure lasts a few minutes; and after the rhythmic jerking (clonic movements), the patient lies still and usually sleeps for minutes or hours.
He is amnesic for the whole attack. The EEG during a seizure shows
a sequence of electrical events, with a discharge of rhythmical, bilaterally synchronous and symmetrical spikes (over the two hemispheres)

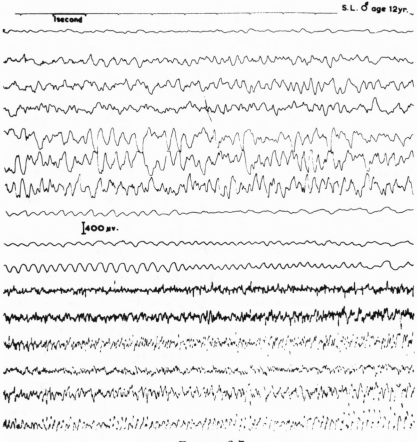

S.L. ♂ age 12yr.

1 second

]400 μv.

FIGURE 6-7.

at 10 ± 2 Hz, the amplitude of which increases while the frequency diminishes and in which the terminal elements, separated by intervals of electrical silence, constitute groups, each corresponding to a jerk in the clonic phase.

Petit Mal Seizure of "Absence" Variety

The patient, usually a child between the ages of 4 and 14 years suddenly stops talking and remains immobile, staring blankly for 5 to 20 seconds. He may drop an object that he happens to be holding. He may blink his eyes rhythmically three times per second or have small twitches of the fingers of both hands, also three times per second. After the seizure is over, he resumes the conversation or the activity he was doing and carries on as if nothing had happened. He may or may not

J.S. æt 5

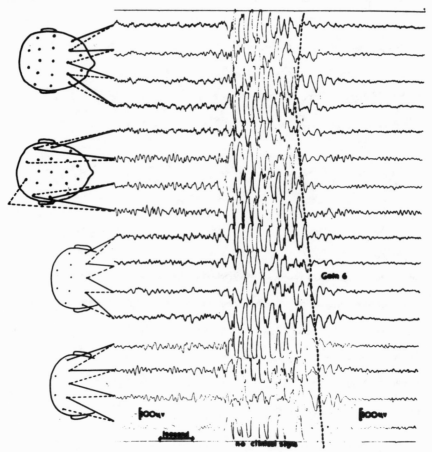

FIGURE 6-8.   PETIT MAL GENERALIZED SEIZURE DISCHARGE IN A
5-YEAR-OLD CHILD LASTING 3 SECONDS AND OCCUR-
RING WITHOUT CLINICAL (OBSERVABLE) MANIFESTA-
TIONS.

know that he had an attack. During the few seconds of the seizure, the
EEG shows a characteristic episodic discharge of high voltage, bilaterally synchronous and symmetrical spike and wave complexes, repeated
rhythmically three times per second, starting and stopping abruptly.
Seizure discharges may occur without clinical (observable) manifestations (Fig. 6–8). Some patients who had petit mal in childhood develop
grand mal seizures following puberty; in other cases, the seizures stop
spontaneously. The genetic incidence of classical petit mal has been
well established (Metrakos and Metrakos, 1960, 1961) and of the many

types of seizures, this is the one in which genetic factors are most clearly demonstrated.

Clinically, in a petit mal seizure, there is cessation of ongoing activity, with transient disturbance of consciousness, staring, slight head nodding, blinking, and bilateral face-twitching at a rate of three per second. Lennox (1960) described the triad of "a stare, a jerk, a fall," in petit mal epilepsy. It should be noted that in many cases, the term *petit mal* is used inappropriately when minor brief seizures occur in children or adults but are not associated with the characteristic, diagnostic EEG pattern. These seizures are more correctly described as "minor seizures" until fully documented. The differential diagnosis lies between classical petit mal seizures of the "absence" type, atypical petit mal epilepsy, or petit mal variant (the Lennox-Gastaut syndrome), minor motor seizures, and complex partial seizures.

Other Types of Generalized Seizure

Other types of generalized seizure may occur in children with organic brain disease including, frequently, some degree of mental retardation. These seizures are more variable. There is arrest of motor activity with transient disturbance of consciousness, but, in addition to this "absence," automatism or vegetative phenomena (pupillary or skin color changes) may occur. Often there is loss of postural tone such that the patient falls suddenly in an akinetic seizure, or there is generalized extensor spasm in a tonic seizure. Concurrently, the EEG shows generalized discharge of very rapid rhythms (the "decremental seizure discharge" of Bickford and Klass); or the EEG shows a generalized discharge of slow spike and wave complexes with rhythmic or pseudorhythmic repetition at 1.5 to 2.5 per second, the so-called petit mal variant, or Lennox-Gastaut syndrome.

Types of Partial Epilepsy

This is a heterogenous group, of which the most common are complex, partial seizures, and simple motor seizures.

Complex, Partial Seizures*

These seizures are manifested by mental, sensory, and/or motor symptoms, and there is great variation in symptomatology. The variation depends upon the site of the discharge in the brain which produces the discharge.

*Formerly known as psychomotor seizures.

Sensory symptoms may be visual, auditory, somesthetic, vertiginous, olfactory, or gustatory. Sometimes the sensation is one of vague "dizziness" without the spinning or rotatory sensation of true vertigo. If there is a hallucination of smell, it is usually unpleasant as, for example, of rotten eggs (uncinate fits), and indicates a lesion of the uncus, which forms part of the anterior temporal lobe. The visual symptoms may be of a formed image, for example a scene, or an unformed perception of phosphorescent light, with bright flashes. The character of the visual symptom is determined by the site of origin in the brain: the unformed shining phosphorescent lights (phosphenes) arise from a discharge in the specific visual cortex of the occipital lobe, area 17 (the striate area), and the formed visions, the scenes, arise from discharges not so far posteriorly, in areas 18 and 19, the so-called associative regions of the parietooccipital lobe (Fig. 6–9).

Mental symptoms include all degrees of clouded consciousness, or a dreamlike state or altered perceptions, ideation, or mood, with or without feelings of anxiety, fear, anger, or rage. Occasionally, there is a pleasurable feeling, but this is less common than the sensation of fear. There may be illusions or hallucinations, a perception of familiarity, of something being "deja vu" (already seen) or "deja vecu" (already lived). There may be "forced thinking" in which a thought comes into the head as if put there from the outside, or there is a blotting out of thought, a blank, an interruption in the train of thought. Often, the patient recognizes the seizure because it brings a recurring thought, which he either remembers or recognizes as his particular recurring thought, although he is amnesic for it. The feeling of fear may be reactive to the content of the mental symptoms, or it may be a nonspecific, unexplained transient sensation of fear. Many of the "mental" symptoms indicate a focus in the temporal lobe or the medial part of the frontal lobe.

Visceral symptoms frequently occur with abnormal epigastric sensations, nausea, smacking of the lips, chewing, and swallowing movements with salivation, borborygmi, tachycardia, and skin color change. Pallor is more frequent than flushing. The insula (Fig. 6–9) is often involved in visceral symptoms.

Somatomotor symptoms are very numerous. The patient's head and eyes may deviate to one or other side; he often turns as if to look at something. He may fidget with the fingers or get up in a purposeless fashion and scan the room with a perplexed look, becoming unresponsive to witnesses. He may make inappropriate "automatic" movements, fiddling with the clothes, tapping with the fingers, mumbling

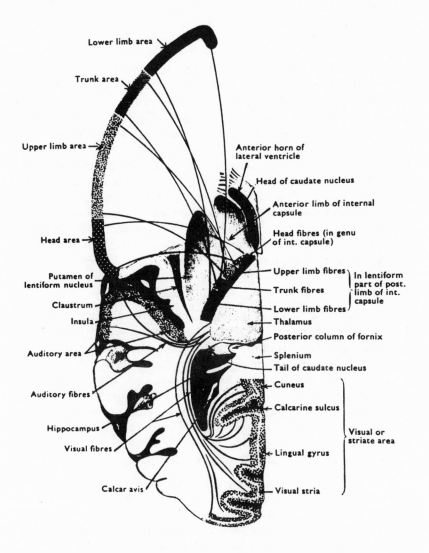

FIGURE 6-9. DIAGRAM OF MOTOR, AUDITORY, AND VISUAL AREAS OF
LEFT HEMISPHERE AND THEIR RELATIONS TO THE
INTERNAL CAPSULE. (Reproduced, with permission,
from Brain's Diseases of the Nervous System. Revised by
John N. Walton, 7th edition, 1969, Oxford University
Press. Oxford, England.)

or repeating short phrases in a confused way. Sometimes, complex gestures and activities, such as cooking, or writing, or driving, may be carried out and the individual may then suddenly "come into focus" (recover consciousness) and be surprised at the situation. There is amnesia for the attack, which usually lasts one to two minutes, but may last 5 to 10 minutes or longer. There is often postictal confusion (the "ictus" being the actual seizure). This postictal clouded state or confusion is frequently associated with speech disturbance and may last much longer than the seizure proper, sometimes 10 to 20 minutes and then gradually clearing. During the seizure, the EEG shows a variety of abnormalities. The only feature in common is the fact that the EEG abnormality is localized or limited to a part of the scalp (and therefore limited to a part of the brain) on one or other side. The seizure discharge characteristically spreads to adjacent areas of the brain and frequently becomes bilateral, but is asymmetrical. Many of the somatomotor symptoms indicate involvement of the hippocampus and other parts of the temporal lobe (Fig. 6–10).

Simple Motor Seizure or Jacksonian Seizures

These are named after Hughlings Jackson, the English neurologist, who described them in about 1880. They start off with rhythmic twitching (clonic movements) of one part of the body, usually the thumb or one side of the face, and then spread up the involved limb and maybe to another limb on the same side. During this time, the patient is conscious. Later, he may lose consciousness and the seizure may become generalized. Jacksonian seizures originate from the motor strip (Rolandic area) of the posterior frontal lobe (Figs. 6–9, 6–10).

Sensory Precipitation and Reflex Mechanisms

The significant difference between this type of seizure and other types may be that in this type the more proximal trigger has been identified either internally within the patient's own body (soma) or in his external environment, whereas in other types the trigger has not been identified. As described by Bickford and Klass (1969), seizures that can be initiated by an appropriate input have been termed *reflex, triggered, stimulus-sensitive, evoked and precipitated.* Forster's book (1977) on reflex epilepsy presents a detailed description of these cases. The term *triggered* is preferred because it is usually not a reflex in the Pavlovian sense of a conditioning or a conditioned stimulus.

Triggered seizures have been noted with the following stimuli:

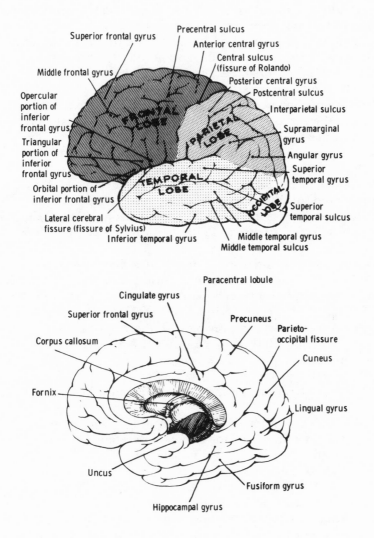

FIGURE 6-10. LATERAL VIEW (CONVEX SURFACE) OF LEFT CEREBRAL HEMISPHERE. MEDIAL VIEW (INNER SURFACE) OF RIGHT CEREBRAL HEMISPHERE. (Reproduced, with permission, from Chusid JG: Correlative Neuroanatomy & Functional Neurology, 17th ed. Copyright 1979 by Lange Medical Publications, Los Altos, California.)

photic, usually with intermittent flash, such as in television epilepsy or self-induced "hand wavers," geometric pattern, auditory (either specific high tone frequencies or music), startle (this may be startle noise such as the telephone), reading, somesthetic, proprioceptive, emotional, or multisensorial. Seizures can also be triggered in bar-pressing, self-stimulating rats.

Sensory-precipitated seizures were previously considered uncommon, but they have attracted considerable attention first, because they provide a means of studying the mechanisms of seizures, and second, because once the subject has identified the precipitating cause he can develop a measure of control over his own seizures.

Certain general features may be mentioned first: A genetic or familial predisposition may be present in some cases, for example (1) in light-sensitive seizures (Davidson and Watson, 1956), (2) in pattern-sensitive seizures (Chatrian, 1970), and (3) in reading epilepsy (Bickford et al., 1956).

In other species, predisposition has also been noted, for example, in rodents (rats, mice, and rabbits) susceptible to auditory seizures, and in the light-sensitive baboon *Papio papio* (Fischer-Williams et al., 1968; Killam, Killam, and Naquet, 1967). It was also noted that once a reflex seizure has been precipitated, there appears to be a relative refractory period which shows individual but characteristic duration.

Seizures can be precipitated by:

1. Sleep deprivation
2. Hypoglycemia, the most common cause being failure to eat breakfast
3. Sudden withdrawal of anticonvulsant medication
4. Excess fluid intake, for example, sweetened carbonated drinks and those that cause metabolic imbalance
5. Excess caffeine in coffee
6. Alcohol abuse; beer drinking adds the factor of excess fluid
7. Excess auditory stimulation
8. Excess flicker stimulation as in television, neon lights, psychodelic lights, movies, fair grounds, bright light with snow or sun.
9. More rarely, seizures can be precipitated with somatosensory stimulation, certain types of pain, and olfactory and gustatory stimuli (certain smells and tastes).
10. Startle, and this is often with noise, sometimes the telephone
11. Unexpected pain, particularly added to fatigue
12. Music and other complex sounds
13. Reading (the rare reading epilepsy)

With multisensorial stimulation, there is a convergence of factors, the most common being sleep deprivation, hypoglycemia, alcohol and excess fluid intake, flicker and auditory stimulation with the television, and psychological states, mainly anger.

Certain Aspects of the Differences in Seizures at Various Ages in Man

The causes of epilepsy, the clinical manifestations, the EEG abnormalities, and the responses to drugs all show age-related differences (Table 6–2).

Seizures Caused by Anoxia or Hypoxia

In many instances, it is artificial to make a distinction between "anoxia," "vascular insufficiency," and "tumor" as causes of seizures, because at the cellular level the seizure in all of these cases may be due to oxygen deficiency. From the clinical point of view, however, the

TABLE 6–2. AGE-RELATED DIFFERENCES IN SEIZURES

Children	Adults
1. Febrile seizures occur	1. Febrile seizures do not occur
2. Seizures associated with cerebral birth injury are frequent	2. Seizures associated with cerebral birth injury are rare
3. Seizures associated with tumor or cerebral vascular disease are rare	3. Seizures associated with tumor or cerebral vascular disease are frequent
4. Seizures associated with alcohol abuse and other drug abuse are rare, except in adolescence	4. Seizures associated with alcohol abuse and other drug abuse are frequent
5. Prolonged focal abnormal EEG discharges may occur	5. Prolonged focal abnormal EEG discharges are less frequent
6. Petit mal seizures occur	6. Petit mal seizures do not occur; complex partial seizures (psychomotor) occur
7. Epileptogenic foci (abnormal EEG foci) may migrate over the years to different parts of the brain	7. Epileptogenic foci do not migrate over the years to different parts of the brain
8. EEG phenomena such as the frequency of the spike-wave complex in children are age-related	8. EEG phenomena such as lower amplitude in adults are age-related
9. Interictal EEG foci are less clearly developed	9. Interictal foci are more clearly developed
10. In the EEG, spike-and-wave complexes are frequent in children	10. In the EEG, spike-and-wave complexes are less frequent in adults

distinction is important, because the treatment of the seizure varies with its cause.

Anoxia is a factor which relates both to the epileptogenic focus in the brain, and to the state of the patient as a whole. In the first, there are certain local changes in the brain (mainly acute impairment) due to alteration of the blood supply (Figs. 8–2, 8–3); and in the second, the operative factor is extracranial, and most often impaired cardiac output (pump failure). There is a third category in which preexisting local brain deficiency causes a *locus resistensis minoris* so that when detrimental hemodynamic changes take place, a seizure may result from acute local ischemic anoxia.

Anoxia in Relation to the Focus

Acute and Subacute Anoxia. Ischemic or stagnant anoxia may be considered the cause of seizures in all conditions in which the brain is locally compressed. Compression may be acute or chronic and may result from head injury with hematoma (epi- or subdural, or intracerebral), from neoplasm (all types), or from abscess. The *site* of compression is an operant factor, related to the difference in the convulsant threshold of various parts of the brain. The *rate* of compression itself operates, the faster rate being, on the whole, associated with a higher incidence of seizures. Seizures are therefore common in metastatic tumors which are associated with considerable local cerebral edema.

Chronic. Anoxia is associated with some forms of cerebral birth injury, but the resultant epileptogenic focus seems more related to the factors such as gliosis, insular sclerosis, porencephaly, atrophy, deafferentation, or other end-stages of anoxia which affect the immature and developing brain.

When anoxia is associated with the development of a focus, the seizure that results is "epileptic" in that it is associated with a demonstrable discharge, and interictal spikes with or without abnormal slow waves are recorded on the EEG (Fig. 6–11). This contrasts with those states discussed in Category II.

Anoxia in Relation to the State of the Patient

In this category, the primary factors causing a critical convulsant degree of hypoxia are extracranial and mostly hemodynamic. These seizures are due to impaired cardiac output (failure of the pump), or to vascular disease (primarily arteriosclerosis) which causes obstruction of blood flow (impaired plumbing). The anoxia may be acute, subacute, or chronic.

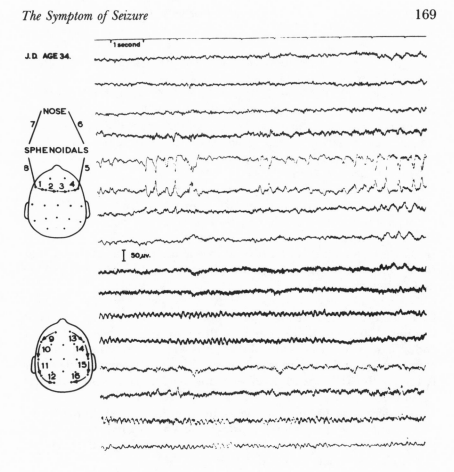

FIGURE 6-11. INTERICTAL (BETWEEN SEIZURE) EEG ABNORMALITY FOCAL AT THE RIGHT SPHENOIDAL ELECTRODE WHICH RECORDS FROM THE INFERIOR MEDIAL ASPECT OF THE RIGHT TEMPORAL LOBE.

Loss of Consciousness due to Acute Anoxia.

VASOVAGAL SYNCOPE. When excess vagal stimulation causes brady-cardia or transient cardiac arrest such that cardiac output falls below a certain critical level, an anoxic seizure may result. A sufficiently severe vasovagal syncope may therefore develop into an anoxic con-vulsion (Gastaut and Fischer-Williams, 1957).

ORTHOSTATIC HYPOTENSION. And other types of sudden hypotension may cause syncope and an anoxic seizure. The resultant seizures are "anoxic seizures" in the sense that they are associated with a lack or loss or acute depression of cortical activity (which may progress through various EEG stages to a few seconds of electrical silence).

Since clinically these seizures may be indistinguishable from those associated with a seizure discharge, they are included here; however, the mechanism of seizure production is fundamentally different, and they are not regarded as true epilepsy because there is no accompanying neuronal discharge. (Fischer-Williams and Cooper, 1963).

Acute or Subacute Anoxia.

CARDIAC ARRHYTHMIAS. Insufficient cardiac output causing subsequent cardiac syncope and eventual seizures may result from: (1) heart block, complete or partial, i.e., Stokes-Adams attack (Regis et al., 1961); (2) atrial fibrillation; (3) premature ventricular contractions (PVC); (4) disorders of an artificial pacemaker; (5) various complications following heart surgery; and (6) congenital heart disease (Shev and Robinson, 1961).

OTHER CARDIAC PATHOLOGY. A variety of transient EEG abnormalities have been recorded during open heart surgery (Fischer-Williams and Cooper, 1964) which are similar to those noted in acute anoxia episodes associated with clinical "seizure" manifestations. Transient compression of the superior vena cava with resultant impaired venous filling of the right heart has been observed during some of these episodes.

Insufficient cardiac output due to impaired right heart filling is presumed during all procedures in which the Valsalva maneuver occurs, such as breath-holding in children, increased intraabdominal pressure, as with bowel evacuation and cough syncope.

Status Post Acute Anoxia. As a result of improved sophistication in the methods of cardiac resuscitation, an increased number of patients now survive after episodes of acute anoxia. There may be: (1) complete neurological recovery, (2) prolonged coma, or (3) persistent neurological deficits with seizures.

Impaired cerebral blood flow can at times be demonstrated during complications of procedures such as coronary angiography (Fischer-Williams et al., 1970), cardiac catheterization (Braunwald and Swan, 1968), carotid or selective vertebral artery angiography, usually associated with preexisting arteriosclerotic disease, embolization ("shower" type) from atherosclerotic plaques, or intracranial vascular spasm associated with intracranial aneurysms or arteriovenous malformations.

Studies of cerebral blood flow throw light on the mechanisms of seizures associated with acute and chronic impairment in blood flow.

Normal cerebral blood flow (CBF) is 54 ml per 100g per minute which constitutes approximately 20 percent of the total body value. CBF in cerebral white matter is only about 20 percent of that in various gray matter areas, although the total volume of white matter in the brain is greater than the volume of gray matter (about 55 and 45 percent, respectively). This is because the neurons in the gray matter have greater oxygen need. In fact, the neurons which comprise only 20 percent or less of the total cerebral cortex cell population account for at least 80 percent of the total cortical oxygen consumption.

Diminished glucose supply to the brain is also a cause of neuronal dysfunction including seizures, because brain metabolism depends not only on oxygen but on glucose.

Self-Regulation of EEG Rhythms

Self- or autoregulation of various specific waves or rhythms of the electroencephalogram by the use of biofeedback training has been described. These observations are important for three reasons:

1. It is theoretically interesting that the electrical activity of the brain can be self-regulated by the individual.

2. The physiological state, mood, or feeling-tone which is concomitant with the induced EEG regulation may be desirable, in which case this form of training could be of practical use as an adjunct to other forms of psychotherapy.

3. If electrical activity can indeed be controlled by the subject, then this ability may possibly be used to prevent epileptogenic activity and thus to reduce the incidence of seizures.

All three of these aspects have been explored, mainly in the 1960s and early 1970s. In order, however, that the reader may be able to assess this work, basic information needs to be summarized first about single cell potentials and secondly about aggregates or populations of nerve cells. The activity of cell populations in the cerebral cortex constitutes the EEG, which is the "print-out" of this electrical activity.

Neurophysiology of Single Cells (Fig. 6–12)

Neurons generate two types of potentials, synaptic potentials and action potentials.

Synaptic Potential (Dendritic Potential). "The synaptic or dendritic potential is a local potential generated in the dendritic portion of the nerve cell as a result of a neurotransmitter interacting with the cell membrane" (Daube and Sandok, 1978, p. 143). These potentials

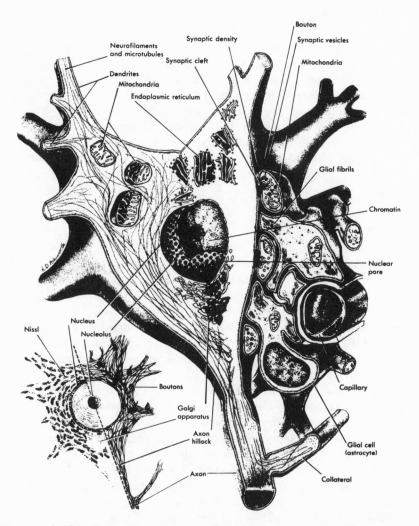

FIGURE 6-12.   DIAGRAM OF THE STRUCTURE OF THE NEURON AS
REVEALED BY THE ELECTRON MICROSCOPE. ORGA-
NELLES OF THE NEURON. THE DRAWING TO THE LOWER
LEFT SHOWS THE ORGANELLES TYPICAL OF A NEURON
AS SEEN WITH THE LIGHT MICROSCOPE. THE PORTION
OF THE DRAWING TO THE LEFT OF THE BROKEN
LINE REPRESENTS STRUCTURES SEEN WITH A NISSL
STAIN. THESE INCLUDE THE NUCLEUS AND NUCLEOLUS.
NISSL BODIES IN THE CYTOPLASM OF THE CELL BODY
AND PROXIMAL DENDRITES, AND, AS A NEGATIVE

IMAGE, THE GOLGI APPARATUS. THE ABSENCE OF
NISSL BODIES IN THE AXON HILLOCK AND AXON
IS ALSO SHOWN. TO THE RIGHT OF THE BROKEN
LINE ARE STRUCTURES SEEN WITH A HEAVY-METAL
STAIN. THESE INCLUDE NEUROFIBRILS. WITH THE
APPROPRIATE HEAVY-METAL STAIN, THE GOLGI
APPARATUS MAY BE DEMONSTRATED (NOT SHOWN.)
ON THE SURFACE OF THE NEURON, A NUMBER OF
SYNAPTIC ENDINGS ARE INDICATED AS STAINED BY THE
HEAVY METAL. THE LARGE DRAWING SHOWS STRUC-
TURES VISIBLE AT THE ELECTRON MICROSCOPIC
LEVEL. THE NUCLEUS, NUCLEOLUS, CHROMATIN, AND
NUCLEAR PORES ARE REPRESENTED. IN THE CYTO-
PLASM ARE MITOCHONDRIA, ROUGH ENDOPLASMIC
RETICULUM, THE GOLGI APPARATUS, NEUROFILA-
MENTS, AND MICROTUBULES. ALONG THE SURFACE
MEMBRANE ARE SUCH ASSOCIATED STRUCTURES AS
SYNAPTIC ENDINGS, ASTROCYTIC PROCESSES, AND A
CAPILLARY CONTAINING A RED BLOOD CORPUSCLE.
(Reproduced, with permission, from Willis, William
D., Jr., and Grossman, Robert G.: Medical Neurobi-
ology, ed. 2, St. Louis, The C. V. Mosby Co., 1977.)

are graded fluctuations of the dendritic membrane and are not propagated. They are excitatory when the neurotransmitter causes a depolarization in the cell membrane (meaning when it reduces the potential
difference between the inside and the outside of the cell), or inhibitory,
when the neurotransmitter causes a hyperpolarization of the cell membrane (meaning it increases the potential difference between the inside
and the outside of the cell membrane).

Action Potential (Axonal Potential). The action potential arises from the
end of the nerve cell near the axon (the hillock) and propagates along
the axon. The action potential occurs only when the neuronal membrane is depolarized beyond a certain critical threshold level. The
resultant spike discharge is an "all-or-none" phenomenon that is
propagated down the axon.

Neurophysiology of Neuronal Aggregates

Neurons function as aggregates and not in isolation. They have
innumerable interconnections, and the electrical activity of the aggregate is the result of the summated effect of all the dendritic potentials
and action potentials occurring within that aggregate.

This activity is recorded as complex wave forms (Fig 6–13); whereas
the activity of a single nerve cell is mainly seen as a single spike.

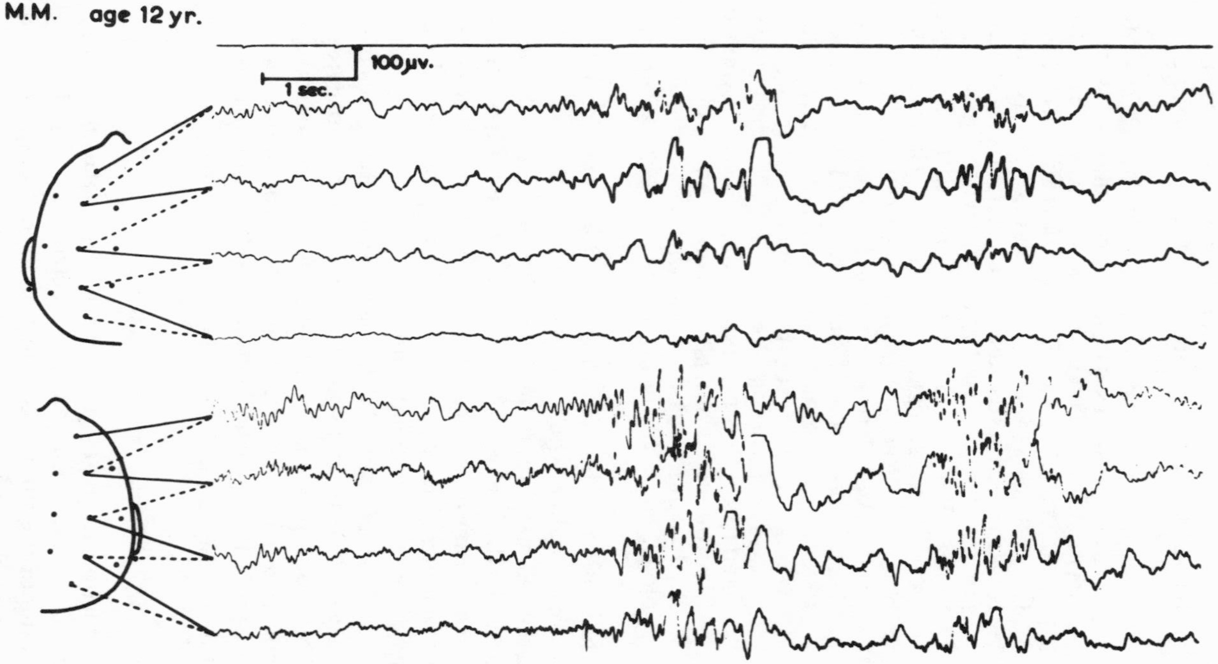

M.M. age 12 yr.

100 μv.

1 sec.

FIGURE 6-13. EEG SCALP RECORDING SHOWING COMPLEX WAVE FORMS IN A PAROXYSMAL DISCHARGE LASTING A FEW SECONDS, WITH BILATERAL BUT ASYMMETRICAL ABNORMALITY.

174

The cortex generates these electrical waves in response to local activity within the neuronal aggregate and in response to input from groups of nerve cells in the depths of the brain, in particular the thalamus.

Origin of the EEG

The electrical activity of the cortex can be detected by the EEG which records cortical activity from electrodes (usually 19 in number) placed on the scalp in various areas. This brain wave activity consists of continuous, rhythmic or nonrhythmic oscillating wave forms that vary in frequency, amplitude, polarity, and shape. The potentials are usually in the range of 20 to 60 microvolts (μv). The activity seen on the EEG reflects the summation of synaptic potentials of many dendrites lying near the surface of the cortex. (Although the EEG records the surface activity, the deeper parts of the brain influence this activity although only indirectly.) Since the EEG is recording the surface activity, the deeper parts of the brain are represented indirectly.

Alpha Rhythm

The alpha rhythm is identified primarily by its location, frequency, and reactivity to visual stimuli. "It is fully developed only when the subject is mentally inactive, particularly in respect to cerebral visual functions, yet alert" (Kooi, 1971). The usual frequency ranges between 9 and 12 Hz (cycles per second), but by convention the frequencies between 8 and 13 are termed within the alpha band. Recording from the scalp, the maximum trough-to-peak amplitude ranges from 10 to 100 μv, but usually falls within a range of 20 to 60 μv. Amplitude tends to wax and wane over periods lasting 1–2 seconds to form "spindles." The alpha rhythm is recorded from the posterior parts of the brain, and the amplitude and abundance may be greatest in either the parietal or occipital region, but it is also present in the posterior temporal region. It is bilaterally synchronous over the two hemispheres and fairly symmetrical but may be more prominent (in abundance and amplitude) over the nondominant hemisphere, particularly in young subjects.

A small proportion of normal subjects—about 10 percent—have little or no detectable alpha rhythm. The frequency of the alpha rhythm is fairly stable in most individuals, during adult life, from the age of about 15 to 60, but there may be an admixture of slower waves in the posterior regions of subjects between the ages of 15 and 25 which can alter results in studies of groups of individuals if not carefully analyzed. Although some authors have reported slowing of the alpha rhythm as if it were a normal variance with age, many workers believe that slowing is a pathologic feature, usually associated with a degree of cerebral arteriosclerosis. Many types of alerting procedures, including mental arithmetic, attenuate or block the alpha rhythm. Eye opening is the usual way of blocking it, and it is patterned light rather than diffuse light that has the suppressant effect. The origin of the alpha rhythm is not known; it has been the object of research for nearly half a century, and many hypotheses have been made for single or multiple generators in the brain, but as yet there is no consensus of opinion.

The Relationship between Psychological Events and EEG Events

There is no known close relationship between the psychological state and the electrical state of the subject. It is well known, of course, that the EEG varies with the state of consciousness, as well as with age, attention, sleep, drugs, metabolic variables, and many organic neurological conditions. But the correlation with more subtle psychological events is poor. This has been a source of disappointment to many generations of researchers, from the "father of EEG," Hans Berger, onwards. (The psychiatrist, Berger (1873–1941) published the first paper on the human EEG in 1929.) It is established that the EEG correlates on the whole well with the neurological state of the individual but not with the psychological (cognitive-emotional) state. For this reason, studies purporting to make these correlations must be examined with great caution, and the design of the experiment has to be carefully appraised. With this proviso, there follows a review of the published work on self-regulation or autoregulation of the EEG: Conditioned suppression of alpha rhythm was studied as early as 1941 (Jasper and Shagass, 1941; Knott and Henry, 1941). The following EEG phenomena have been documented: (1) Alpha rhythm can be suppressed. (2) Alpha rhythm can be increased or enhanced. This means increasing the amount (abundance or percentage time that alpha rhythm is present) or increasing the amplitude. (3) In some cases the frequency of the alpha rhythm can be reduced. (4) Alpha rhythm asymmetry between the two hemispheres can be altered. (5) Theta waves (4 to 7 Hz) can be influenced. (6) A few reports exist that a sensorimotor rhythm (12 to 14 Hz localized activity) can be increased. (7) In another report, the somatomotor rhythm of 6 to 12 Hz was also influenced with reduction in seizure incidence (Sterman and Mac-

Donald 1978). This rhythm may be equated with the "mu" or Rolandic rhythm, which was the object of conditioned suppression studies by Gastaut and Jasper and co-workers in the 1950s.

Decrease or Suppression of the Alpha Rhythm. Of the various ways of influencing the EEG, decreasing, or blocking, or attenuation of the alpha rhythm is the most easily accomplished, since it is indeed one of the criteria of alpha rhythm that it blocks to eye opening. Most subjects can learn within one or two sessions of about 45 minutes each to suppress alpha rhythm significantly whether the eyes are open or closed (Kamiya, 1969). Suggesting to the subject that he concentrate on close-up visual imagery or attend to phosphenes (a luminous visual experience which occurs, e.g., when the eyeballs are pressed—seeing "stars") helps suppress the alpha rhythm.

Increase or Enhancement of the Alpha Rhythm. This is more difficult to learn than blocking, but is still an easily observable phenomenon. It is done daily whenever the EEG recordist induces the subject to relax. It is often seen after the subject has done a standard 3 minutes of deep breathing. With biofeedback training (operant conditioning or instrumental learning), subjects can learn to increase their alpha rhythm in a systematic and reproducible way (Kamiya, 1969). In Kamiya's technique for alpha training with audio feedback, a tone was produced in the subject's room when the amplitude of the alpha rhythm reached a certain threshold. The subject's task was to increase the percent of time the tone was on. He sat with eyes closed in a dark room, (which is an optimum condition for alpha rhythm to be present, unless the subject goes to sleep). Studies of alpha enhancement were also described by Lynch and Paskewitz (1971).

An oversimplistic association was made between alpha rhythm increase and pleasant sensations of being relaxed and calm though alert. The opposite was also presupposed, namely that alpha decrease was associated with more tension, anxiety, and fatigue. These observations led to popular oversimplification and the sale of machines which were advertised with unjustifiable claims, including "alpha-theta brain-wave monitors," EEG biofeedback trainers, "the alpha experience," etc.

In 1975, Travis, Kondo, and Knott published a well-controlled study in 140 subjects of the subjective aspects of occipital alpha enhancement. Under both eyes-open and eyes-closed conditions, approximately 50 percent of the subjects reported that alpha enhancement was "pleasant" and 50 percent "unpleasant/neutral." With eyes-open training conditions, about half the subjects stated that the experience was "relaxing" and the other half "not relaxing." During eyes-closed training, 63 percent of the subjects noted that enhancing alpha was "relaxing," while 37 percent reported that the experience was "not relaxing." In the last case, however, there may be a circular relationship between increased alpha wave production and deep relaxation.

Hart (1968) showed that increased alpha production typically attributed to EEG feedback was due in part merely to sitting quietly in a darkened room.

Another study (Valle and Levine, 1975) reported on the expectation effects in alpha wave control. In a well-designed study, with 40 volunteer college students, they found that whether subjects expected to enhance or suppress alpha rhythm had an important effect on their ability to control alpha. Twenty students actually enhanced the alpha while twenty (the remainder) actually suppressed it in the first task. In each group of 20, 10 were led to believe that they were enhancing and 10 were led to believe that they were suppressing alpha wave activity. They were then crossed over and it was found that the subjects who believed that they were enhancing the alpha rhythm in fact did it significantly better than those who believed that they were suppressing it. Instructions to enhance alpha are therefore assumed to create greater task motivation than instructions to suppress alpha rhythm. This was presumably because of popular treatments of brain wave control that generally extolled subjective states accompanying alpha enhancement.

In another study (Grynol and Jamieson, 1976), 20 women undergraduates were trained to increase their time of alpha rhythm production and two standardized anxiety measures were noted. For 10 subjects a tone was sounded when they had increased alpha rhythm. The other 10 subjects received alternating correct and incorrect feedback. Equally positive psychologic benefits were reported by both groups, and this study therefore did not show unique benefits of increased alpha production beyond those attributable to a placebo effect.

EEG Conditioning for the Control of Seizures

The question of teaching patients to recognize the precipitating trigger that causes their seizures and thus prevents their occurrence is well known, and all epileptologists employ this to a greater or lesser extent with their patients. Forster (1977) worked on this problem for many years and reported a large variety of single or small number case studies, mainly in photogenic or light-sensitive epilepsy, reading epilepsy, musicogenic epilepsy, pattern-sensitive seizures, and other rare or unusual types of seizures in which conditioned methods were designed to reduce seizures. Specific biofeedback training of an EEG rhythm, however, is a time-consuming procedure and therefore costly both for the patient and the staff.

Biofeedback training of the sensorimotor rhythm (SMR) in a 13-year-old boy with seizures was reported (Finley, Smith, and Etherton, 1976). Feedback training was conducted over approximately 6 months, during which time the SMR increased from about 10 percent prior to training to 65 percent after the 34th training session. The rate of clinical seizures decreased to 10 percent and there was a significant reduction in epileptogenic discharges. The nature of this sensorimotor rhythm is uncertain. In 1963 Brazier described a 13 to 14 Hz EEG rhythm recorded from the sensorimotor cortex in cats. When operantly conditioned, this SMR was accompanied by behavioral immobility and correlated with increased resistance to epileptogenic compounds (Roth et al., 1967). Sterman and MacDonald (1978) initially believed that cat SMR was the analog of the human mu rhythm, which is a well-known wave form localized to the Rolandic or sensorimotor region of the brain, present when the eyes are open and which blocks to contralateral clenching of the fist or foot movements. The 12 to 14 Hz activity may exist in humans as a separate rhythm. Kaplan (1975) reported that biofeedback training of 6 to 12 Hz Rolandic activity was carried out in three patients with seizures, of which two were improved. Since, however, no learning of 6 to 12 Hz activity was detected, it was "suggested that the feedback setting provided these two patients with new techniques of relaxation" (Kaplan, 1975). Other work, (Wyler et al., 1974) on the firing patterns of epileptic and normal neurons in the chronic alumina paste focus in undrugged monkeys during different behavioral states may not be relevant in that it deals with the activity of single units rather than cell populations.

EEG operant conditioning for the control of epilepsy was reported by Wyler et al. (1979). They studied 23 severely epileptic patients who were given EEG feedback training. The aim of the study was to reinforce the patients' 18 Hz activity over the scalp approximation of their focus, while suppressing temporalis EMG and low frequency EEG activity. They reported that 43 percent of their patients showed significant changes in seizure occurrence and "a lesser number were felt to have benefitted clinically." None of the neuropsychological test parameters were helpful in identifying (prospectively or retrospectively) patients most likely to respond to this treatment.

Several studies suggested that EEG feedback training may be of variable benefit in controlling medically refractory epilepsy (Kaplan, 1975; Kuhlman, 1978; Sterman and McDonald, 1978; Wyler et al., 1979). Wyler and others note, however, that the results of the treatment have been extremely variable and the potential mode of action of this therapy is not known. In several of the studies, the patients had training only once a week for periods of up to a year. Thus, because the natural history of many patients' epilepsy is unpredictable, it is difficult to determine whether results from long-term training were related to the natural history of the seizure disorder, a change in medication, a change in medication compliance, the extensive attention received, or to a direct effect of feedback training.

The study by Wyler et al. (1979) is a continuation of work started by Wyler et al. in 1974. In the 1979 report, all the 23 patients improved subjectively except one. The patients in this study reported that the conditioning produced the following effects: (1) "They could identify auras more clearly and therefore search for possible ways of aborting seizures; (2) The training decreased the severity of attacks; (3) They could 'think more clearly' after feedback training; (4) The training allowed them to be more relaxed in seizure provoking situations" (Wyler, 1979). In general, the majority of patients who improved related that the seizures per se had become less threatening to them and thus were easier to tolerate. Of these 23 patients, 43 percent (10) demonstrated a statistically significant decrease in ictal events which began within 10 to 16 hours of training regardless of the training schedule. This decrease persisted from 1 week to 6 months after termination of the training.

It should be noted that there are several differences between the methodology of Wyler and that of Sterman and McDonald (1978). First, Sterman's patients were trained to detect two localized cortical (C3–T3) EEG frequency bands (6–9 Hz and either 12–15 or 18–23 Hz) with reward provided for the occurrence of one in the absence of the other; this was regardless of the location of the patient's focus. In contrast, the technique employed by Wyler reinforced 18 Hz activity over the scalp approximation of the focus (excepting generalized epilepsy). Second, the Wyler training schedule was more rigorous but gave less total training time. Third, Wyler postulated that studies which used Sterman's technique provided better results because of the reinforced EEG frequency. However, several authors (Kaplan 1975; Kuhlman, 1978) have questioned whether the SMR exists physiologically in humans (as opposed to cats) and if humans can actually enhance it with feedback training. Wyler et al. (1979) considered that since beneficial results have been obtained by conditioning *various* EEG frequencies both *adjacent* to and *distant* from the focus, it is obvious that no one model is presently available to explain the mechanisms which might account for the results. However, animal studies have shown that operant manipulation of CNS events may directly influence the occurrence of ictal events.

In conclusion, although the principle of self-regulation or control of the electrical activity of the brain is obviously of theoretical importance, and may be of therapeutic value, at present the tools for its widespread application are not yet available. It may be concluded that EEG conditioning is an extremely costly treatment which yields as yet unpredictable results. However, patients likely to benefit may be identified by an intensive period of laboratory training requiring, perhaps, a maximum of 30 hours. Those patients who are benefited could continue training with home feedback units. The study of EEG feedback and operant manipulation of the CNS is clearly a subject of considerable theoretical and practical interest and should be pursued through further research studies.

REFERENCES

Berger, H: On the electroencephalogram of man. Archiv fur Psychiatrie und Nerven Krankheiten 87: 527, 1929. Transl. in Hans Berger on the electroencephalogram of man. Gloor P. Electroencephalogr Clin Neurophysiol Suppl 28, 1969.

Bickford RG and Klass DW: Sensory precipitation and reflex mechanisms, in Jasper HH, Ward AA and Pope A (eds): *The Basic Mechanisms of Epilepsies.* Boston, Little, Brown, 1969, p. 543.

Bickford RG, Whelan JL, Klass DW, and Corbin KB: Reading epilepsy. Trans Am Neurol Assoc 81: 100, 1956.

Braunwald E and Swan HJC: Cooperative studies on cardiac catheterization. Circulation 37 (Suppl 3): 1, 1968.

Brazier MAB: The problem of periodicity in the electroencephalogram: studies in the cat. Electroencephalogr Clin Neurophysiol 15: 287, 1963.

Bridgewater G, Sherry CJ, and Marczynski TJ: Alpha activity: The influence of unpatterned light input and auditory feedback, in Barber TX, DiCara LV, Kamiya J, Miller NE, Shapiro D, and Stoyva J (eds): *Biofeedback and Self-Control.* Chicago, Aldine, 1976.

Chatrian GE, Lettich E, Miller LH, Green JR, Kupter C: Pattern-sensitive epilepsy: clinical changes, tests of responsiveness and motor output, alterations of evoked potentials and therapeutic measures. Epilepsia 11: 151, 1970.

Daube JR and Sandok BA: *Medical Neurosciences.* Boston, Little, Brown, 1978.

Davidson S, Watson CW: Hereditary light sensitive epilepsy. Neurology 6: 235, 1956.

Eccles JC, Ito M, Szentagothai J: *The Cerebellum as a Neuronal Machine.* New York, Springer, 1967, p. 229.

Finley, WW, Smith, HH, Etherton, MD: Reduction of seizures and normalization of the EEG in a severe epileptic following sensorimotor biofeedback training: Preliminary study, in Barber TX, Di Cara LV, Kamiya J, Miller NE, Shapiro D, and Stoyva J (eds.): *Biofeedback and Self-Control.* Chicago, Aldine, 1976, p. 425.

Fischer-Williams M, Cooper RA: Depth recording from the human brain in epilepsy. Electroencephalogr Clin Neurophysiol 15: 568, 1963.

Fischer-Williams M, Cooper RA: Some aspects of electroencephalographic changes during *open-heart surgery. Neurology, 14: 472, 1964.*

Fischer-Williams M, Gottschalk PG, Browell JN: Transient cortical blindness: an unusual complication of coronary angiography. Neurology (Minneap) 20: 353, 1970.

Fischer-Williams M, Poncet M, Riche D, Naquet R: Light-induced epilepsy in the baboon *Papio papio:* cortical and depth recordings. Electroencephalogr Clin Neurophysiol 25: 557, 1968.

Forster F: *Reflex Epilepsy, Behavioral Therapy and Conditional Reflexes.* Springfield, Ill., Thomas, 1977.

Gastaut H: Clinical and electroencephalographical classification of epileptic seizures. 11th International Congress of the International League against Epilepsy. Epilepsia 10 (Suppl): 14, 1969.

Gastaut H, Fischer-Williams M: Electroencephalographic study of syncope: its differentiation from epilepsy. Lancet 2: 1018, 1957.

Gastaut H and Fischer-Williams M: The physiopathology of epileptic seizures, in Field J (ed): *Handbook of Physiology.* Baltimore, Williams and Wilkins, 1: 329, 1959.

Grynol E and Jamieson J: Alpha feedback and relaxation: a cautionary note. *Biofeedback and Self-Control.* Chicago, Aldine, 1976.

Hart J: Autocontrol of EEG alpha. Psychophysiology 4: 506, 1968.

Jackson JH: Epilepsy and epileptiform convulsions. In J Taylor (ed): *Selected Writings of John Hughlings Jackson.* London, Hodder and Stoughton, 1: 8, 1939.

Jasper HH and Shagass C: Conditioning occipital alpha rhythm in man. J Exper Psychol 28: 373, 1941.

Kamiya J: Operant control of the EEG alpha rhythm and some of its reported effects on consciousness, in Tart CT (ed): *Altered States of Consciousness.* Wiley, New York, 1969, p. 507.

Kaplan BJ: Biofeedback in epileptics: equivocal relationship of reinforced EEG frequency to seizure reduction. Epilepsia 16: 477, 1975.

Killam KF, Killam EK and Naquet R: An animal model of light sensitive epilepsy. Electroencephalogr Clin Neurophysiol 22: 497, 1967.

Knott JR and Henry CE: The conditioning of the blocking of the alpha rhythm of the human electroencephalogram. J Exper Psychol 28: 134, 1941.

Kooi KA: *Fundamentals of Electroencephalography.* New York, Harper and Row, 1971.

Kuhlman WN: EEG feedback training of epileptic patients: clinical and electroencephalographic analysis. Electroencephalogr Clin Neurophysiol 45: 699, 1978.

Lennox WG: *Epilepsy and Related Disorders.* Boston, Little, Brown, 1960, p. 66.

Lynch JJ, Paskewitz DA: On the mechanism of feedback control of human brain wave activity. J Nerve Ment Dis 152: 205, 1971.

Metrakos JD, Metrakos K: Genetics of convulsive disorders Part I. Introduction, problems, methods and base-line. Neurology 10: 228, 1960.

Metrakos K, Metrakos JD: Genetics of convulsive disorders, Part II. Genetic and EEG studies in centrencephalic epilepsy. Neurology 11: 464, 1961.

Regis H, Toga M, Righini C: Clinical electroencephalographic and pathological study of a case of Adams-Stokes syndrome, in Meyer JS, Gastaut H (eds): *Cerebral Anoxia and the Electroencephalogram.* Springfield, Ill., Thomas, 1961, p. 259.

Roth SR, Sterman MB, Clemente CD: Comparison of EEG correlates of reinforcement, internal inhibition and sleep. Electroencephalogr Clin Neurophysiol 23: 509, 1967.

Shev EE and Robinson SJ: Electroencephalographic findings associated with congenital heart disease, in Meyer JS, Gastaut H (eds): *Cerebral Anoxia and the Electroencephalogram.* Springfield, Ill., Thomas, 1961, p. 578.

Sterman MB, MacDonald LR: Effects of central cortical EEG feedback training on incidence of poorly controlled seizures. Epilepsia 19: 207, 1978.

Travis TA, Kondo CY, Knott, JR: Subjective aspects of alpha enhancement. Br J Psychiat 127: 122, 1975.

Valle RS, Levine JM: Expectation effects in alpha wave control. Psychophysiol 12(3): 306, 1975.

Wyler AR, Robbins CA, Dodrill CB: EEG operant conditioning for control of epilepsy. Epilepsia 20: 279, 1979.

Wyler AR, Fetz EE, Ward AA: Effects of operantly conditioning epileptic unit activity on seizure frequency and electrophysiology of neocortical experimental foci. Exp Neurol 44: 113, 1974.

7

Disorders of Sensory Function

Introduction

Disorders of sensation can be divided into two large groups, painful and nonpainful. This is a clinically useful classification, although perhaps not a totally logical one from a physiological point of view. Biological feedback is likely to be concerned with those disorders that are painful because of the clamorous nature of the symptom. The patient with pain seeks relief; the patient with numbness or other sensory abnormality may suffer in silence.

One may think that one knows what pain is; but, in fact, this experience is hard to define because it is exclusively personal. The study of pain is beset with pitfalls. Being a sensation and a subjective psychic phenomenon, pain is not open to quantitative analysis. Its nature is as protean as the personality of the sufferer; for, as René Leriche wrote, "Pain is the result of conflict between stimulation and the entire individual." The treatment of painful disorders is helped by the fact that the patients thus afflicted show important similarities to each other however much they may vary because of the diversity of the underlying pathological processes. This is because the mechanisms whereby pain is produced, appreciated, and alleviated as well as the physical and psychological effects of pain are to some extent independent of the underlying disease.

This same fact, however, that people with pain may be suffering from diverse conditions and yet have characteristics in common, may lead to errors in diagnosis. It therefore behooves all those associated with pain relief to identify the neurological basis for the disturbance in sensation.

Disorders of sensation, which can be classified into two general categories, the painful and the nonpainful, may further be subdivided according to the body part involved (Tables 7–1 and 7–2).

Mechanism of Head Pain

The pain-sensitive structures within the cranium include the dural sinuses, part of the basal dura, the dural arteries, the great vessels at

TABLE 7-1. DISORDERS OF SENSATION WITH PAIN

I. Related to the head

  A. Extracranial

    Muscle contraction headache
    Vascular headache
    Migraine
    Temporal arteritis
    Glaucoma
    Trigeminal neuralgia
    Glossopharyngeal neuralgia
    Occipital neuralgia
    Atypical facial pain
    Temporomandibular joint disease
    Sinusitis
    Platybasia or basilar impression

  B. Intracranial

    Mass lesion, including neoplasm, subdural hematoma, cerebral or cerebellar abscess
    Migraine
    Aneurysm
    Subarachnoid hemorrhage
    Arteriovenous malformation
    Hydrocephalus
    Meningitis
    Cyst

  C. Pain of dental origin

II. Pain in the upper limb

    Disease of the cervical cord, including compression from tumor, or abscess, syringomyelia, postirradiation myelitis
    Postherpetic neuralgia
    Degenerative disc and joint disease or cervical spondylosis
    Nerve root compression as from tumor or arthritis or cervical rib
    Brachial plexus neuropathies
    Entrapment neuropathies
    Ulnar or radial neuropathy
    Causalgia and sympathetic reflex dystrophy

III. Pain in the torso (trunk)

    Diabetic neuropathy
    Postherpetic neuralgia
    Syringomyelia
    Osteoporosis
    Tumors of the spinal cord or vertebrae; tumors of the pancreas or posterior abdominal wall

IV. Pain in the low back

    Degenerative osteoarthritis of the lumbosacral spine
    Nerve root compression associated with prolapsed intervertebral disc
    Compression fractures, posttraumatic
    Primary or metastatic tumors of the spinal cord or vertebrae
    Musculoligamentous low back strain
    Fibrositis and myalgia

TABLE 7-1. (CONTINUED)

V. Pain in the lower limb

Degenerative osteoarthritis affecting the lumbosacral spine or the hip joint

Involvement of the cauda equina by compression from tumor or vascular malformations or arachnoiditis

Femoral neuralgia

Phantom limb

Tabes dorsalis (neurosyphilis)

Pervic pathology causing nerve root compression with radiating pain, including gynecological causes, urogenital lesions, tumors, chronic infections, etc.

Peripheral neuropathies

a. Metabolic

b. Toxic

c. Ischemic

d. Carcinomatous

TABLE 7-2. DISORDERS OF SENSATION, USUALLY WITHOUT PAIN

Nonpainful disorders of sensation include numbness, tingling, paresthesiae, itch, loss of sense of temperature or vibration, sensory hallucination, loss of awareness of a limb's situation in space, loss of body-image, and disorders of extrapersonal space.

1. Congenital defects of the spine and spinal cord, such as meningomyelocele
2. Myelitis and myelopathy
3. Spinal cord injury
4. Multiple sclerosis
5. Subacute combined degeneration of the spinal cord
6. Guillain-Barré polyradiculoneuropathy
7. Vascular lesions of the extra- or intracranial arteries
8. Encephalopathies of miscellaneous causes
9. Leprosy

---

the base of the skull, and the trigeminal, glossopharyngeal, and vagus nerves. Most of the stimuli that evoke pain appear to do so through tension on sensitive structures, as for instance the displacement of, and traction upon, such structures by an expanding intracranial mass, or dilatation of dural vessels in migraine, or changes in cerebrospinal pressure. Pain can be referred to the head from upper cervical roots and the vagus (10th cranial) nerve. Irritative lesions involving the first and second cervical roots, or the occipitonuchal region usually cause pain in the posterior half of the scalp and head. Occasionally, however, the pain is referred to the forehead or temple on the affected side from the descending root of the trigeminal nerve lying in the upper part of the cervical cord. Pain can be referred from the throat and esophagus to the head, which is well-illustrated by the occurrence in some people of headache after swallowing a cold substance, e.g., ice cream, as was studied by Henry Head in England approximately 70 years ago. The actual mechanism of headache in many conditions is not well-understood, for example, those associated with certain types of seizures, those produced by allergy to chocolate or other foodstuffs, those caused by oversmoking, or by arterial hypertension. Headaches which follow head injuries are probably associated with changes in intraventricular pressure and are often related to posture. Those which accompany chronic mental fatigue and anxiety are usually associated with excess muscle tension.

The following structures are insensitive to pain: the brain itself, the pia-arachnoid,* the ependyma,† and the choroid plexuses.‡

Benign Causes of Headache Suitable for Biofeedback Treatment

When the patients with a mass lesion or with demonstrable progressive pathology have been excluded by neurological examination and appropriate investigations, there remain a large group of patients with fluctuating pathophysiology as the precipitating cause of recurring headache. These headaches are termed *benign* because although they disturb the quality of life, they do not affect its quantity. The pathogenesis of these may include:

1.   Disturbance of tone in the scalp or neck muscles of extracranial origin, or
2.   Disturbance of tone in the blood vessels of intra- or extracranial origin, or
3.   Posttraumatic, which includes mixed pathology

With such patients, the recurrent head pains are of two main types: excess muscle contraction headache and vascular headache, whether they are associated with initial blood vessel contraction or subsequent blood vessel dilatation. In either case, there is an imbalance in tone in the blood vessel wall (the artery or arteriole more often than the vein). Excess dilatation causes excess pulsation and stretch of the muscle and elastic fibers within the vessel wall. There is often undue contraction

---

*The pia mater and the arachnoid constitute the inner two layers of the meninges which are the coverings of the brain. The pia closely overlies the brain and dips down forming a fold within every sulcus. The arachnoid mater is a thin and delicate membrane like a spider's web, (Greek: *Arachne* - "spider").
†The ependyma is the cellular lining of the ventricles, the cavities within the brain.
‡The choroid plexuses are convoluted vascular networks within the ventricles, which secrete or filter the CSF.

during a crisis or stress period, and pain develops only after the emergency situation or the stress period has passed, when relaxation causes excess stretch within the vessel. Alcohol and other drugs frequently alter the diameter of the cranial or muscular blood vessels. Hunger also affects the tone of the arterial walls. The physiological changes associated with sleep, including lowering of blood pressure and relaxation in vessel tone, are described in Chapter 9. The role of emotional states and anger in particular should be obvious to all, but the ability of headache sufferers to see these causes operating in others and not in themselves is one of the factors that contribute to the persistence of these symptoms.

Biofeedback treatment has been applied successfully to treat headaches of both muscular and vascular types. Reviews of the literature in these areas have recently been published by Budzynski (1979) who studied muscle tension headache, and Dalessio (1979) who studied vascular headache.

Biofeedback in the Treatment of Vascular Headache

Extensive work on biofeedback treatment of vascular headaches was initially done at the Menninger Foundation. It was observed there (almost by chance) that a patient who was reporting her headache while participating in an experiment also noted that her hand temperature increased. This led Sargent, Greene, and Walters (1972) to experiment with autogenic feedback training. They combined thermal feedback with autogenic training involving simultaneous management of mental and somatic functions. In the first pilot study, 63 percent of the 20 migraine sufferers improved and in the second pilot study, 74 percent of the 63 migraine sufferers improved. In these early Menninger studies, information was fed back to the patient of the difference between forehead and finger temperature. It was later found, however, that the same results could be accomplished by using only the finger as the feedback site.

Solbach and Sargent (1977) found that 55 patients (74 percent of those who had completed 270 days of training and follow-up sessions) had a 26 percent or greater reduction of headache lasting for at least two years after conclusion of the study.

Another Menninger Foundation study conducted by Pearse, Walters, and Sargent (1975) involved intensive autogenic biofeedback training for five days. They studied 21 patients, 11 with migraine, and 10 with a combination of migraine and tension headaches. The results showed that a short 5-day program was as beneficial as the longer 6-week program.

Numerous authors have reported similar results. Peper and Gross-man (1974) trained two children with migraine in thermal biofeedback and autogenic techniques and both of them learned very rapidly. Werder (1978) taught four children (between the ages of 10 and 17) to increase hand temperature and to carry out relaxation procedures using body awareness exercises, breathing techniques, and autogenic phrases; they all learned self-regulation of hand temperature easily. Lynch et al. (1976) found that four children were able to acquire instrumental control of skin temperature with visual feedback.

Russ, Hammer, and Adderton (1977) did a follow-up study nine months after termination of treatment with 16 of 50 patients previously treated with biofeedback. These patients had received sessions in autogenic training and also hand temperature feedback. Although they found that headache had not declined (significantly) these patients reported decreased need for medication and subjective improvement of "headache status."

Drury, DeRisi, and Leberman (1975) used a multiple baseline design in four migraine patients. They had combined treatments with cognitive preparation, modified relaxation training, use of autogenic phrases, finger temperature feedback, and self-charting of headaches and medication used. They found a relationship between treatment, the rated headache intensity, and the recorded medication usage; however long-term progress was not reported.

Mitch, McGrady, and Iannone (1975) used a 12-week treatment program with autogenic phrases and continuous temperature feedback. Eleven subjects showed improvement, with eight having "good or excellent results," and three "average improvement."

Other investigators used thermal feedback without the autogenic phrases. Wickramasekera (1973) treated two patients with hand temperature with good results. Turin and Johnson (1976) trained seven patients to use imagery and self-verbalization to increase peripheral temperature. There was a decrease in the number of headaches reported in a week, in medication taken weekly, and in the hours of headache reported each week.

Turin and Johnson (1976) also trained their subjects in thermal cooling. Headache decreased with warming but remained the same or increased with cooling, despite the patient's positive therapeutic expectations.

Taub and Emurian (1971) taught 21 subjects to increase and decrease hand temperature with feedback. After lengthy stabilization periods, the subjects received four sessions of operant shaping of small variations in skin temperature utilizing visual information feedback.

Individuals varied widely in their ability to achieve self-regulatory control of skin temperature. A third of the patients demonstrated considerable magnitude of skin temperature control (8° to 15°F within 15 minutes) and the skill was well-retained over several months. Taub concluded that feedback from a single bodily site may involve a different mechanism from temperature feedback using autogenic phrases.

Taub and Emurian (1976) speculated that the control of skin temperature was due to a direct effect on volume blood flow rather than a result of muscular activity suggesting that:

1.   Their EMG recordings did not correlate with observed temperature changes.

2.   Those who practiced muscular contractions showed only small changes in skin temperature.

3.   Temperature regulation was limited to a precise locus, not a diffuse one.

The same authors, Taub and Emurian (1976) reported that none of the Minnesota Multiphasic Personality Inventory (MMPI) scales correlated with the ability to alter skin temperature.

Roberts, Kewman, and MacDonald (1973) studied six subjects who had received extensive hypnotic training prior to the experiment. They found that some individuals were capable of achieving a high degree of voluntary control over peripheral skin temperature regulation, comparing one hand relative to the other. However, there were significant individual differences in the ability to learn this technique, in the rate of learning particularly, and in the magnitude of control achieved.

Roberts et al. (1975) then went on to compare seven subjects who scored highly in hypnotic susceptibility with seven subjects with low scores. They concluded that some subjects can learn skin temperature control if provided with sufficient training and sufficient motivation, but that hypnotic susceptibility did not seem to have an influence on the learning skills. Maslach, Marshall, and Zimbardo (1972) demonstrated that three hypnotic subjects achieved simultaneous alterations of skin temperature in opposite directions in their two hands, while six awake control subjects could not produce this result.

Keefe (1975) trained eight subjects in either raising or lowering finger temperatures compared with forehead temperature. Leeb, French, and Fahrion (1974) noted a significant effect of instructional sets (positive, negative, or neutral) on 15 subjects' ability to acquire control over peripheral temperature in the hand.

Mathew et al. (1978) randomly assigned 12 normal subjects to either a hand-warming or hand-cooling group to investigate the effect of hand-warming (or cooling) on intracerebral circulation. After the subjects were trained for five weeks, their regional cerebral blood flow (CBF) was measured twice using the Xenon 133 inhalation technique. The mean CBF of both the warming and the cooling groups tended to remain the same or to shift in similar directions even though the subjects were manipulating their skin temperatures in opposite directions. This suggests that the therapeutic gain in migraine is due not to a factor specific to temperature biofeedback but to some more general factor such as relaxation or passive concentration.

Another modality of biofeedback has been used involving the operant conditioning of vasoconstriction on the extracranial arteries. Koppman, McDonald, and Kunzel (1974) encouraged 10 migraine patients to modify the diameter of their temporal artery by feedback. Through the use of a reflectance photo-plethysmo-meter, seven subjects were able to learn dilatation-constriction sequences with considerable proficiency in two to four weeks with two or three sessions per week. Savill and Koppman (1975) trained six nonmigraine subjects to develop control over their blood volume pulse amplitude in either temporal artery or the finger. They found that temporal artery blood volume pulse measures are as easily obtained as finger skin temperature.

Friar and Beatty (1976) investigated operant training in nine experimental subjects taught to vasoconstrict the extracranial arteries, and nine control subjects taught vasoconstriction of the fingers. All the subjects suffered from migraine. The experimental group which demonstrated control of the affected extracranial arteries had less migraine after treatment, while the control group showed no improvement. Zamani (1977) treated 10 migraine patients with (1) operant conditioning of vasoconstriction of the temporal artery or (2) muscle relaxation (number of patients not noted). The biofeedback group improved, whereas the relaxation group showed no significant change.

Feuerstein and Adams (1977) investigated the effect of cephalic vasomotor response (CVMR) and m. frontalis EMG biofeedback on control of temporal artery vasoconstriction and m. frontalis activity in migraine and muscle contraction headache patients (numbers not noted). The greatest reduction in headache occurred when feedback was directed at the relevant pain mechanism.

Price and Tursky (1976) studied 40 migraine patients and 40 controls assigned to one of four treatments: feedback, false (pseudo) feedback, relaxation tape and neutral tape control. Four physiologic measures were monitored while they were trying to increase hand temperature: (1) digital blood volume, (2) digital pulse volume, (3) cephalic blood volume, and (4) cephalic pulse volume. The migraine sufferers differed from the normals in digital vascular responses, with the migraine subjects being less able than normal subjects to produce vasodilatation. Even greater differences between migraine patients and normals were found for temporal artery blood volume changes. Biofeedback technique produced greater digital vasodilatation than did relaxation by listening to an irrelevant tape recording; however, there was no statistically significant advantage of biofeedback over a fourth feedback or relaxation treatment. The authors concluded that the increased blood flow to the hands is probably a component of general relaxation.

EMG feedback was studied in the treatment of vascular headaches. Mitchell (1969) and (1971), in conducting four control studies of migraine compared mixed treatment of "combined desensitization" involving relaxation training, desensitization, and assertive therapy with each form of therapy alone. The combined treatment was the most successful, with an average 67 percent reduction in the number of migraine attacks. They suggested that assertive training may have been the most important variable. In a six-year investigation, Hay and Madders (1971) treated patients with relaxation therapy for migraine. Of these, 69 improved significantly, 25 showed no change, and 4 reported worsening of their symptoms.

Blanchard et al. (1977) studied 30 migraine patients by randomly assigning them to three groups after four weeks baseline. One group used finger temperature biofeedback, autogenic training and home practice; another used progressive relaxation training and home practice and a third was a waiting list control group. Both the relaxation group and the biofeedback group improved significantly, and the waiting list control did not. The biofeedback and relaxation groups gave similar results.

Thermal and EMG Treatments of Vascular Headache

Taub and Emurian (1971) warned against confusing the effects of general relaxation with those of specific training, emphasizing the important part that emotions play on hand temperature. One should therefore not start a training session before the initial relaxation process is completed.

Relaxation clearly facilitates the ability to learn thermal feedback control. Pearse, Walters, and Sargent (1975) showed that good relaxation was vital for learning voluntary control of hand warming. Culver and Hauri (1972) suggested that skin temperature training was most efficiently accomplished when preceded by EMG skeletal muscle training.

Scott and Timmons (1974) showed that a tense subject has low finger temperature and high EMG tension. EMG biofeedback may be useful prior to temperature biofeedback.

Many investigators have used both thermal and EMG feedback in the treatment of vascular headaches. Diamond and Franklin (1975) studied the response of 382 patients to different types of treatment. The patients practiced progressive relaxation exercises followed by EMG training and/or hand temperature control training with autogenic phrases. Training consisted of two office sessions per week for one month, or two-sessions for the 36 out-of-town patients with home practice of relaxation and hand warming techniques. All patients had follow-up training sessions every two months. One hundred and three patients received EMG feedback only, 45 received hand temperature feedback only, and 234 received a combination of hand temperature and EMG feedback. Of 10 migraine patients experiencing EMG feedback alone, two had a good response, and eight a negative one; of the 62 mixed migraine and muscle contraction headaches, 23 had a good response, 2 a moderate, and 37 a negative response. When hand temperature feedback alone was practiced by 20 migraine patients, 17 had a good response, and three a negative response; while of the 25 mixed muscle contraction and migraine headache patients, eight showed good and 17 negative responses. Fifty-three migraine patients with a combination of EMG and temperature feedback showed 38 good responses, four moderate, and 11 negative. Of 167 mixed muscle contraction and migraine patients 75 showed good, 11 moderate, and 81 negative. These results indicate that migraine patients respond well to hand temperature feedback with 85 percent improving, or to the combination of EMG and hand temperature feedback with 79 percent improving. The combination of both temperature and EMG feedback caused improvement in 50 percent of the patients with mixed muscle contraction and migraine headache.

Diamond and Franklin (1974) compared 36 headache patients in an intensive training of two temperature and EMG training sessions per day for 12 days and a one-month follow-up session, with 57 patients participating in the routine two sessions weekly for a four-week period followed by a gradual weaning from the procedure. The differences were not significant between intensive and routine biofeedback therapy.

Medina, Diamond, and Franklin (1976) retrospectively studied 27 patients with migraine or mixed migraine and muscle contraction headache: 64 percent of the patients with migraine had improved, but only four of 13 mixed migraine and muscle contraction headache had improved. Diamond and Franklin (1977) used autogenic training with both EMG and temperature feedback in 32 children with migraine; of these 26 were improved.

Diamond et al. (1978) conducted a five-year retrospective study to examine the long-term effects of biofeedback on headache. They found that the training was significantly more effective, the frequency of headache was reduced and the training effects persisted for a longer time in the younger patients, females, and those with no past drug habituation problem. As time elapsed following training, biofeedback was found to be less effective. The vascular headache patients had improved the most; next came the patients with the mixed vascular and muscle contraction headaches; the least improved were the patients with muscle contraction headaches.

Fried et al. (1977) used a combination of biofeedback, EMG relaxation, and autogenic feedback for 6 patients, and they noted that some patients may lack the necessary motivation for improvement. Hartje and Diver (1978) trained 14 subjects in EMG and thermal feedback. They found that some migraine patients were able to predict the onset or worsening of migraine, by simply monitoring their hand temperature.

Apart from relaxation being an aid to thermal feedback control, it may also help alleviate the vascular headache itself. Pozniak-Patewicz (1975) found that during migraine attacks there was marked muscle spasm in the head and neck muscles. Thus, some investigators will combine temperature feedback, EMG feedback, and various relaxation techniques in the treatment of vascular headaches.

Adler and Adler (1976) carried out a retrospective study 3½ to 5 years after termination of treatment. There were 22 patients with migraine in their study, 12 of whom had mixed migraine and tension headache, and five who had a presenting complaint of cluster headaches, who received temperature feedback after an initial period of EMG feedback. Concomitant psychotherapy was also provided. The success rate for migraine was 81 percent, for mixed headache 60 percent, and for cluster headache 60 percent.

Boller and Flom (1978) found that migraine without the prodromata of the classical migraine attack was less available to modification by a single modality biofeedback training. Their 12-week program combined autogenic training, thermal feedback, and occasional use of EMG feedback, patient education, and counseling. They emphasized cognitive integration of the environmental stressors of trigger headaches. Werbach and Sandweiss (1978) studied 48 patients with migraine. Measurements of digital finger temperature, palmar skin conductance, and frontalis EMG were made before and after each session with biofeedback continuously for one of the three physiologic variables. Of the 37 patients who completed 10 training sessions, 73 percent were improved. There was a lack of correlation between temperature gain across sessions and treatment outcome.

Weinstock (1972) studied seven patients with headaches with self-induced hypnotic relaxation followed by EMG biofeedback and all improved.

Only a few investigators have used alpha feedback in the treatment of vascular headaches. Gannon and Sternbach (1971) reported one patient. Melzack and Perry (1974) used alpha feedback training, but the number of patients was not mentioned.

Andreychuck and Skriver (1974) studied three treatment procedures with 33 migraine patients: biofeedback training for hand warming and alpha enhancement, and training for self-hypnosis. The three different treatment groups all showed significant reduction of headache.

Cohen, Crouch, and Thompson (1976) studied 45 migraine patients with three modalities: temperature feedback, EMG for muscle relaxation, and EEG feedback for an eight-week training period with three sessions a week. Temperature and EMG for self-regulation were reported more therapeutic than EEG alpha feedback.

Biofeedback in the Treatment of Muscle Contraction (Tension) Headache

Budzynski (1979) and with co-workers (1973) studied the application of m. frontalis EMG feedback to muscle contraction headache. They noted: (1) A placebo reduction in headache in 25 percent of the patients studied during the two-week pretraining baseline. These reductions were transitory and most disappeared within two weeks (these people were not continued in the study). (2) Frontal EMG feedback resulted in lower frontal EMG levels than with nonfeedback subjects. (3) Although the feedback and pseudofeedback (noncontingent) groups practiced relaxation twice a day, only the feedback group showed reduction in headache. (4) Headache was reduced in most subjects within a two session per week, 8-week training program. (5)

Analgesics and tranquilizers were reduced in the feedback but not in the no-treatment controls. (6) Regular home practice and relaxation were important.

Wickramasekera (1972) described the reduction in tension headache and frontal EMG levels with biofeedback but not when pseudo-biofeedback (noncontingent) was given. Wickramasekera (1973) studied behavior therapy and verbal relaxation training, but found that these were more effective when frontal EMG feedback was introduced (no numbers given). Epstein and Abel (1977) and Epstein, Hersen, and Hemphill (1974) studied six patients who received music feedback for 16 sessions. They showed improvement that was maintained up to 18 months, but mainly in these patient groups with low initial levels of muscle contraction.

Philips (1977) studied tension headache and mixed migraine tension headaches. Contingent EMG feedback either frontal or temporal was compared with noncontingent feedback. In general, the mixed headache cases did less well than those with pure tension headache.

Frontal EMG was combined with blood volume pulse (BVP) feedback. Sturgis, Tollison, and Adams (1978) found this successful in two cases of mixed headache. The BVP system monitors and feeds back an analogue of the blood flow through the temporal artery to the patient. The patient then attempted to decrease the pulse amplitude of the BVP. Sturgis and Adams (1977) treated 28 headache cases with BVP or frontal EMG or both. They did not state which treatment modality was the most effective, but they noted general improvement.

Chesney and Shelton (1976) compared EMG feedback alone with EMG plus relaxation training, with relaxation alone, with a no-treatment control. In eight sessions, they found that EMG feedback plus relaxation and relaxation alone reduced headache more than the no-treatment control. The EMG feedback plus relaxation was significantly more effective than that in the no-treatment group.

Cox, Freundlich, and Meyer (1975) compared frontal EMG with a placebo capsule and Bernstein and Borkovec's (1973) verbal relaxation. Both the biofeedback and the verbal relaxation were effective in relieving headache, and both of them were significantly better than the placebo. The two treatments were equal in terms of frontal EMG reduction with the biofeedback showing greater, but not statistically significant, percentage improvement in headache, reduction in psychosomatic complaints, and gain in control over the processes by which psychosomatic symptoms are generated.

The question, "Is biofeedback alone more effective than relaxation training?" was answered "yes" by two studies, "no" by one study, "probably" by one study, and "no difference" by one study.

One of the controversies that exists in the application of EMG biofeedback and relaxation training to muscle tension headaches is whether or not nonbiofeedback procedures are more cost effective while just as therapeutically efficacious as biofeedback techniques. Although a study by Haynes, Griffin, Mooney and Parise (1975) indicated that the EMG feedback group did not differ significantly from a group receiving relaxation therapy, other studies have shown that EMG feedback procedures are significantly more effective than placebo treatments or relaxation treatments alone. Positive support for EMG training was found by Haynes et al. (1975) where the use of frontal EMG feedback resulted in a faster decrement of frontal EMG muscle tension than did passive relaxation or no treatment control. This is in contrast to the results of a previous study by Haynes, Griffin, Mooney, and Parise (1975) which found that there was no difference between relaxation methods and EMG feedback training. Other studies by Reinking and Kohl (1975) and Coursey (1975) indicated that EMG frontalis training was more effective in lowering muscle tension than relaxation instructions or a placebo.

Hutchins and Reinking (1976) tested the effectiveness of EMG biofeedback versus an autogenic training program based on work by Jacobsen and Wolpe. Sixty-six percent of the groups receiving EMG feedback training showed a decrease in headache activity while only 20 percent showed positive results with the autogenic training exercises.

It also appears that the combination of EMG biofeedback training and relaxation methods may be more effective than either given by itself. For example, a study by Chesney and Shelton (1976) indicated that a group receiving EMG biofeedback plus relaxation reported significantly reduced headache activity compared with groups receiving relaxation alone or biofeedback alone. In fact, the EMG biofeedback groups did not obtain significantly different results than the no-treatment control on any measure.

The question of placebo effect in biofeedback is a critical one and has been addressed in two excellent publications by Stroebel and Glueck (1973) and Wickramasekera (1976).

Cognitive Skills Training

This involves initial focusing on the subjects' maladaptive thoughts, with the subsequent uncovering of assumptions that may have been inappropriate and from which the thoughts derived. These assumptions can be challenged and modified so that more realistic positive thoughts may develop.

Discrimination Training

The originator of progressive relaxation, Edmund Jacobson, has for many years trained patients first to contract and then to relax the various muscle groups (Jacobson, 1938). Adapting their techniques from Jacobson in 1974, Whatmore and Kohli used EMG feedback to train patients to relax and then to produce small changes in EMG activity voluntarily in various muscles. This fine discrimination training may be effective when used alone. The combination of a progressive relaxation technique followed by a fine discrimination training may prove to be a useful sequence.

Temporomandibular Joint Disease

Pain may be localized to the temporomandibular joint (TMJ) in certain conditions and in these is associated with jaw movements and local tenderness. Frequently, also there is a "clicking" sound perceived and an asymmetry of the two joints. There may be associated rheumatoid arthritis and radiological changes detected as well. Although this disorder has in the past usually been treated mechanically by dentists utilizing splints, EMG biofeedback training has now been applied successfully in many patients to reduce associated muscle tension.

In this approach the electrodes are usually placed on the masseter muscle for EMG feedback. Solberg and Rugh (1972) who used EMG biofeedback for TMJ pain, reported that 10 out of their 15 patients were significantly improved while wearing the device. Dohrmann and Laskin (1976) treated 24 patients with this problem; 16 had auditory EMG biofeedback, and eight received placebo treatment. Twelve of the 16 required no further treatment, and they concluded that EMG biofeedback is useful in this syndrome.

Carlsson and Gale (1972) treated 11 patients with long-term intractable pain related to the TMJ joint. The patients were trained in tension awareness and relaxation using feedback of muscle tension level in the masseter muscle. At follow-up examination, four to 15 months after the end of treatment, eight of the 11 patients were totally symptom-free or significantly better, one was slightly improved, and there was no effect reported in two patients.

Rosenthal (1976) used forehead EMG biofeedback therapy with seven TMJ pain patients. He concluded that biofeedback therapy is effective for patients with short masseter silent periods, since five of the seven patients with this responded well to biofeedback. Fernando (1976) reported two patients who responded to EMG feedback techniques which include general relaxation, targeting on the muscles that were in spasm, and Jacobson's relaxation home training program. Since then, Fernando et al. (personal communication) have treated 10 additional patients with good clinical results.

Clinical Manifestations of Other Common Syndromes Associated with Head Pain

Since patient-selection is the crucial first step for successful treatment, we shall describe the clinical features of entities in which accepted forms of treatment already exist. These conditions should be diagnosed by appropriate neurological examination and investigation, and then treated accordingly. They are described here, because biofeedback is contraindicated as the primary treatment although it may be employed as an adjunct in certain aspects of the treatment of the following disorders.

Trigeminal Neuralgia (Tic Douloureux)

Trigeminal neuralgia is an episodic, intense pain, unilateral in any given attack, and with characteristic time features. The disease usually attacks people in the 6th decade and older. Women are affected more commonly than men in the ratio of 2 to 1. There are six diagnostic criteria:

1. It is a sudden paroxysmal pain, averaging 30 seconds and rarely lasting longer than a minute or two. These brief paroxysms return at irregular intervals, sometimes in a cluster over several hours, days, or a week or two.
2. The pain is intense and excruciating; it is described as sharp, shooting, burning, like "electric shocks," or a "red hot poker." In the intervals between paroxysms, there is usually no pain or at most a mild dull ache.
3. Pain is precipitated by trigger movements such as talking, chewing, yawning, or touch. A draught of air or cold wind on a trigger spot on the face can precipitate the pain.
4. The pain is confined to the trigeminal nerve distribution.
5. In any particular paroxysm, the pain is referred only to one side

of the face. Even in cases of bilateral trigeminal neuralgia, pain occurs on the two sides consecutively rather than concurrently.

6. There is no objective sensory disturbance.

7. In the natural history of the disease, the pain recurs at irregular intervals throughout the patient's life and may continue for 10 to 30 years. Spontaneous remissions may last months or years. The pain commonly starts in the 2nd (maxillary) division of the trigeminal nerve, but it may begin in the 3rd (mandibular) division. In either case, it almost invariably spreads in subsequent attacks to both the maxillary and the mandibular areas and may also involve the 1st (ophthalmic) division. It is rare for the first division to be affected alone or at the onset. The pain is so well-localized that the patient is usually able to trace its course across the face "like a streak of lightning." The pain is rarely in the tongue, but frequently affects the jaw, gums, and buccal mucosa.

Medical treatment is usually effective and, if not, neurosurgical intervention is available. For details regarding these approaches the reader is referred to appropriate medical textbooks. Biofeedback may be used as an adjunct to assist the patient in learning to cope with the pain.

Temporal Arteritis

Temporal arteritis is a chronic inflammatory condition affecting the muscular coat of the temporal artery and is often associated with more widespread arteritis, in particular, the central retinal artery where subsequent blindness may result. For this reason, it is vital to diagnose the condition immediately and initiate anti-inflammatory steroid treatment, e.g., with cortisone (Prednisone) in order to prevent total loss of vision. The pain is felt in the temples and is associated with local tenderness of the artery, which is sometimes visible and palpable as a tender line. The disease usually affects the elderly and causes a low-grade fever, a raised sedimentation rate, and commonly anemia. Biopsy of a small segment of the artery establishes histological proof of the diagnosis and frequently brings curative relief of pain. Biofeedback is contraindicated in this disorder as its implementation might delay the initiation of medical treatment. The differential diagnosis between arteritis and benign forms of head pain may be difficult; and since misdiagnosis can be extremely serious, all biofeedback therapists are cautioned to seek appropriate medical consultation for their patients before beginning treatment for pain in the head.

Glaucoma

Glaucoma which is characterized by elevated intraocular pressure can cause acute or chronic headache or ocular pain and must be excluded from the differential diagnosis by ophthalmologic examination. The disease can be detected by these regular eye examinations; and since it is a common cause of blindness, visual symptoms should always be carefully evaluated by measuring intraocular pressure and performing other appropriate tests prior to the initiation of any biofeedback procedures.

Sinusitis

Pain in the face or forehead is probably often attributed to "sinusitis" on insufficient evidence. Suitable x-rays establish the diagnosis, and appropriate treatment is available. Many patients may be treated (unsuccessfully) with biofeedback techniques only to discover later that they suffered from sinusitis.

Neoplasms

Various types of benign or malignant tumors must be excluded from the differential diagnosis when a patient presents with head pain. The serious consequences of misdiagnosing these disorders should make every biofeedback clinician wary of accepting patients for treatment of pain who have not first undergone a thorough medical examination.

Postherpetic Neuralgia, Following Ophthalmic or Spinal Herpes Zoster

At the onset of infection with the virus of *herpes zoster,* there is severe pain of nerve root (radicular) distribution while the characteristic blister-rash usually appears a day or two later. Herpes zoster virus infection is similar whether it involves the sensory roots of the trigeminal nerve, the posterior root ganglia to the upper limb, or the thoracic nerves of the trunk. The pain of zoster usually resolves as the rash appears or shortly afterwards. However, in a minority of cases it is severe and persistent neuralgia may develop. This is most frequently found in elderly people and though it may occur as a sequel of herpes affecting any of the spinal posterior ganglia, it usually occurs following involvement of the ophthalmic or first division of the trigeminal nerve. This deep, severe pain may persist in the distribution of the affected nerve root and is often associated with slight sensory loss and with unpleasant paraesthesiae in the skin of the dermatones affected. The history of herpetic infection and the scars of the rash will indicate the correct diagnosis. In postherpetic neuralgia, the pain is constant and the patients may commonly say that the area feels raw, or that there is a sensation of formication (feeling as if ants are crawling under the skin). Depression is common because of the persistence of pain. In younger patients, spontaneous improvement is expected gradually during the three months following the acute attack, but in older patients, pain may continue for months or even years. Spinothalamic tractotomy has not infrequently been undertaken if intractable pain has persisted for six months or more from the onset, but even this section of the spinothalamic tract in the spinal cord may be ineffective. To date, there do not seem to have been reports of biofeedback procedures utilized in postherpetic neuralgia, but the opportunities are likely to arise since this is a suitable condition for treatment.

Pain in the Upper Limb

Differential diagnosis here is required, first of all, to distinguish whether the pain arises primarily from involvement of the shoulder joint or other local causes in the bones and joints, or whether it is of neurological origin. The most common causes of neurogenic pain are nerve root compression associated with cervical osteoarthritis (cervical spondylosis), degenerative disc and joint disease, or cervical rib. Other causes include entrapment neuropathy from compression of the median nerve in the carpal tunnel of the wrist. Less frequently, pain is associated with local muscle tenderness and various types of myositis or inflammatory muscle diseases. The anatomical level from which the pain arises must be determined.

Intraspinal Disease

The category of intraspinal disease includes tumors of the cervical cord, syringomyelia, postirradiation myelitis, and postherpetic neuralgia. Of these, the entity for which biofeedback may be indicated is postherpetic neuralgia (see p. 201), since operant pain (see Chapter 5) can be very distressing. Pain may follow an attack with the virus herpes zoster involving the sensory roots to the upper limb. The characteristic scars of the blisters that were present in the acute phase are in the territory of the nerve root distribution. Pain is more likely to persist if there was infection in the acute stage, and if the patient is elderly and in poor general health. Pain is felt as a "deep" sensation and is often associated with unpleasant paresthesias in the skin of the dermatomes affected. The symptoms date from the herpetic rash and may last for months or even years. Biofeedback training may help the patient learn to concentrate on relaxing, thus reducing attention to pain.

Lesions of Vertebrae

Lesions of vertebrae include prolapsed intervertebral disc (often secondary to trauma), osteoarthritis, various types of injury, and neoplasms. The common flexion-extension injury of the cervical spine, usually acquired in automobile accidents typically causes muscle injury with associated pain and muscle spasm and resolves with appropriate rest, local heat, and graduated head and neck exercises. EMG biofeedback may be employed to reduce muscle spasm and concomitant pain.

Lesions of Brachial Plexus (Fig. 7–1)

Lesions of the brachial plexus include the presence of cervical rib and allied pressure syndromes. These disorders have descriptive terms which change with fashion and have included such phrases as the *scalenus syndrome, costoclavicular compression,* and *thoracic outlet* or *inlet syndrome.*

Many of the pain syndromes are attributable to poor posture, occupational activities, undesirable habits, excess weight or loss of weight, and athletic injuries. Traction injuries of the brachial plexus can occur with severe trauma to the upper limb. In any of the above situations, the diagnosis must be clearly delineated. For selected cases, biofeedback may be indicated under appropriate medical supervision.

The rarer neuralgic amyotrophy (paralytic brachial neuralgia) remains a condition of unknown etiology giving rise to pain, paralysis, and minimal sensory changes, and presents as an acute or subacute condition.

Bronchogenic Carcinoma

Bronchogenic carcinoma (Pancoast's tumor) may spread to involve the upper two thoracic roots with pain, paresthesias, and sensory loss along the inner aspects of the arm and forearm. Wasting of the intrinsic muscles of the hand and Horner's syndrome may appear.* Malig-

---

*Horner's syndrome is due to lesions involving the cervical sympathetic chain in the neck or of the roots in which its fibers emerge. It consists of pseudoptosis (drooping of the eyelid), miosis (a small pupil), anhidrosis (loss of sweating), and flushing of the affected side of the face.

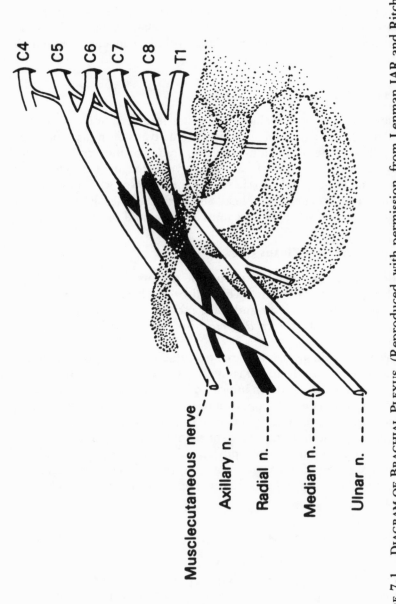

C4
C5
C6
C7
C8
T1

Musclecutaneous nerve

Axillary n. ------

Radial n. ------

Median n. ------

Ulnar n. ------

FIGURE 7-1. DIAGRAM OF BRACHIAL PLEXUS. (Reproduced, with permission, from Lenman JAR and Ritchie AE: Clinical Electromyography, 2nd edition, Copyright J. B. Lippincott Company, Philadelphia, 1977.)

nant metastases in the axillary and supraclavicular glands may cause severe pain which radiates down the arm. After appropriate surgical and/or medical treatment, EMG biofeedback may improve muscle reeducation and functioning by teaching the patient to increase contraction of the affected muscles.

Lesions of Peripheral Nerves

Lesions of peripheral nerves include sympathetic reflex dystrophy (causalgia), entrapment neuropathies, mainly median nerve carpal tunnel syndrome, and ulnar neuropathy in the ulnar groove behind the medial epicondyle. This latter may require surgical transposition of the nerve to the front (anterior aspect) of the elbow. Compression of the median nerve at the wrist can be diagnosed clinically and confirmed by electrodiagnosis and is cured by rest, night splints, injection of an anti-inflammatory steroid, e.g., cortisone at the wrist, or surgical decompression. Carpal tunnel syndrome has been treated by EMG biofeedback procedures. No controlled studies have been reported to determine the effectiveness of using biofeedback in these cases, however.

Causalgia and Sympathetic Reflex Dystrophy

One of the disorders of sensation for which biofeedback may also be indicated is causalgia. Penetrating wounds which injure but do not completely sever mixed peripheral nerves or major plexuses are sometimes followed by an intense burning pain in the sensory distribution of the affected nerve fibers.

Causalgia was first described by Weir Mitchell (1864), mainly affecting the median or sciatic nerves, following nerve injuries in the American Civil War. The term *sympathetic reflex dystrophy* is now frequently applied to include the characteristic pain of causalgia. The pain is a special and a violent one, characterized by a sensation of persistent burning, whence the name of causalgia (Greek: *kausis,* "burning"). In Tinel's classic book of *Nerve Wounds* (1918), he describes causalgia of the median nerve as follows:

Cold, heat, the slightest contact cause the most atrocious pain. What the patients most dread is contact with the air and dryness of the hand; tepid water often relieves them, and we see them wrapping round their hands moist cloths which they constantly renew. It is also to be noted that profuse perspiration of the hand frequently takes place. It is not only cutaneous excitations of the hand that cause painful paroxysms, movement of any kind is painful; simple swinging of the hand when walking causes intolerable recrudescences in these patients. Strong emotion, an approaching carriage, an unexpected sound, the banging of a door, a brilliant light, the dizzy sense of void in a staircase; any of these may bring on a terrible and painful crisis. Thus, we find in these patients special symptoms: emaciated by reason of insomnia and loss of appetite, they are gloomy and peevish; they will neither talk nor go outside; they seek solitude, silence, and obscurity; they walk slowly with short steps, to avoid all shock; if anyone approaches them, they slink away, carefully protecting the hand from all contact by concealing it behind the back, or placing the other arm around it as a shield. There is no paralysis; the hand is simply immobilized as a result of pain. There is hyperaesthesia, with the slightest touch of the skin causing intolerable suffering. Trophic and vaso-motor disturbances are of a special nature. The skin is thin, smooth, and glossy. It is often red and moist. After a few months, there may be atrophy of the extremities of the fingers.

Tinel regarded causalgia as a "sympathetic syndrome. Undoubtedly, vasodilatation or vaso-constriction of the skin, profuse sweats, and the recrudescence of pain through emotion call forth the idea of sympathetic disturbances" (p. 145).

Causalgia occurs in less than 2 percent of peripheral nerve injuries. It may appear hours, days, or weeks following the original trauma. It is accompanied by the motor and sensory signs indicative of the injury, but, in addition, there soon appear excessive local sweating, pallor of the skin, and trophic changes in the skin, nails, and bones of the affected part. As described above, the pain is aggravated by heat, dryness, physical stimuli to the limb or elsewhere, and by emotional disturbances. The limb is carefully guarded against contact with surrounding objects, and relief is sometimes obtained by keeping it covered with cool, moist dressings.

Sympathectomy (cervical, thoracic, or lumbar) is a temporary or a permanent procedure and is often effective. Temporary sympathectomy causes paralysis of function by injection of a local anesthetic agent into the sympathetic nerve chain, and this cervical sympathetic nerve block is anatomically a fairly simple procedure. Injection or surgical section of the cervical sympathetic trunk in the neck below the bifurcation of the common carotid artery causes anidrosis, ptosis, and miosis of the affected side (Horner's syndrome). Causalgia may disappear when the sympathetic chain is injected with a local anesthetic such as procaine, and there may be permanent cure following complete sympathetic denervation of the affected limb by preganglionic sympathectomy. After injection of local anesthetic agents as a temporary procedure, the effect may sometimes last longer than the expected duration of a local anesthetic; this has been explained by the interruption of reverberating circuits within the nervous system. In clinical medicine, a temporary sympathetic nerve block is carried out prior to permanent removal of the chain or interruption of the nerves, in order to observe the clinical therapeutic effect.

Causalgia has been recorded after injuries to the median, ulnar, radial, brachial plexus, sciatic, posterior tibial and common peroneal nerves, of which the median and sciatic are the most common. Many theories have been advanced to explain causalgia, but modern views agree with Tinel (1918). It is usually attributed to altered function in visceral afferent fibers.

A recent personal case (Fischer-Williams and Nigl) demonstrated the efficacy of biofeedback training in sympathetic reflex dystrophy. A professional violist, aged 30, developed right-sided "tennis elbow" in April, 1978, following an athletic injury. Despite treatment with several modalities of physical therapy, analgesics, and numerous local injections over many months, she developed increasing pain with the characteristics of causalgia, blanching of the skin, and the hand and arm became cold. There was hyperaesthesia of the arm and hand, considerable limitation of movement of pronation, supination and extension at the elbow; and she guarded and protected the limb from all contact because of burning pain caused by light touch and jarring. Jolts received while riding as a passenger in a car frequently caused pain such that she had to turn back and go home. For 11 months, she was unable to play the viola because of pain. X-rays performed 10 months after the initial trauma showed slight demineralization from relative immobility. The only treatment which caused transient relief from pain was cervical sympathetic nerve block; but after 11 such blocks, they became less effective. It was at this stage that thermal biofeedback treatment was started.

On first referral to biofeedback, the skin temperature of the right middle finger averaged below 75°F after temperature stabilization. During the course of 15 sessions of thermal feedback training, the patient was able to increase her temperature an average of 4.8°F from the baseline level. In addition, the average initial temperature rose to 83.1°F for the last six treatment sessions. Towards the end of treatment, the patient indicated that her pain had diminished and she was able to play the viola for over an hour at one sitting. Later, she returned to professional symphony playing.

As an additional clinical observation, it may be noted that the return of sweating is a useful early sign of regeneration in peripheral nerve lesion. Hyperidrosis (excess sweating) is a prominent feature of incomplete lesions of peripheral nerves and is especially marked in some cases of causalgia. Furture investigators in biofeedback may monitor sweating as part of the treatment technique. Blanchard (1979) also reported a case where thermal feedback was used successfully to treat a case of reflex sympathetic dystrophy. After one year, the patient still reported a reduction of pain.

Phantom Limb

Sensation of a phantom limb may develop after amputation, or with lesions of the brain stem and thalamus, or with peripheral lesions of the nervous system. A distinction should be made between the perception of the missing limb itself, including its spatial characteristics, and the perception of phantom limb sensations such as paresthesiae, heaviness, cold, cramp, and pain. If the limb phenomenon is to develop, it is usually immediately following the amputation and it is more likely to occur if there had been pain in the limb prior to surgery. Nearly all subjects have a sensation of a phantom limb after amputation, but many do not mention it for fear of an incredulous response from their attendants. The nonpainful phantom limb soon fades from consciousness. The painful one may persist for several months. The phantom limb has a markedly realistic character, can usually be "moved" at will, and may assume a relaxed or a cramped position. In the course of time, it fades and may reappear only sporadically, or it may gradually shorten, telescope, and vanish.

Pain in the phantom limb can be both distressing and intractable. It is typically paroxysmal, burning, or shooting, sometimes occurring with paraesthesiae. The pain may be influenced by changes in the weather, use of a prosthesis, use of the contralateral limb, pain elsewhere in the body, or counterstimulation and mental concentration. Morgenstern (1964) has shown the efficacy of frequently repeating a task of sensory distraction in diminishing awareness of the phantom and lessening pain. Emotional factors play a part in the perception of pain and other sensations. Peripheral factors influence phantom limbs. Some patients (Fischer-Williams, 1956) obtain relief by elevation of skin temperature of the stump by medication. At times, the stump may feel subjectively cold although the skin temperature is within normal limits. Treatment with percussion-vibration utilizing a mechanical vibrator or a hand-operated "hammer" causes relief in selected patients.

Biofeedback treatment for phantom limb is promising and involves both EMG and temperature feedback. EMG feedback is used to increase the patient's concentration skills as a form of distraction to reduce pain. Temperature feedback is supplied to train patients to increase temperature of the stump along with medication or as an alternative approach.

Sherman (1976) reported case results from treating five male patients whose amputations of a lower limb had precipitated phantom limb pain with a combination of EMG biofeedback and verbal relaxation techniques. Patients watched a meter which displayed average EMG and an oscilloscope which displayed "raw" EMG. The relationship between the display and their muscle activity was explained, and they were instructed to attempt to relax the muscles in the stump. Patients were given verbal relaxation instructions similar to the Jacobson technique while they watched the feedback displays. In all cases, EMG levels were sharply reduced and the pain was eliminated at the end of one 50-minute session. One patient's subjective report of feeling in the phantom limb was that it felt as though a blow torch was being applied to it prior to treatment and as though it was pleasantly wrapped in a warm towel afterwards.

The above could also apply to the treatment of the "phantom breast" syndrome, occasionally seen following mastectomy.

Pain in the Torso

Nonneurological lesions within the abdomen which may cause pain have to be excluded first from this grouping. Common disorders causing abdominal pain include peptic ulcer, various types of inflammatory disease of the bowel, neoplasms, and gallbladder disease. Pain in the back, or pain which radiates around the trunk in a girdle fashion is usually of neurological or musculoskeletal origin.

Other more exceptional, nonneurological causes of pain in the back include tumor of the pancreas, tumors of the posterior abdominal wall, enlarged glands from Hodgkin's disease or malignant lymphoma, or rarer processes causing enlargement of lymph glands. Those disorders which are associated with psychophysiological factors such as inflammatory bowel disease may be treated by using biofeedback techniques as an adjunct. Biofeedback and relaxation training may reduce the emotional stress which triggers symptoms in these conditions (see Chap. 14).

Neurological Causes of Back Pain

Tumors of the vertebrae or spinal cord have to be excluded from the etiology of back pain. The types most commonly encountered are meningioma, neurofibroma, and metastatic tumor deposits in the spine. Pain seen in the elderly (particularly in women) is frequently due to nerve root compression of the thoracic nerves associated with osteoporosis. Nerve root compression may also occur with fracture of one or more vertebrae in the thoracic spine. In these cases, there is usually a history of injury. Prolapsed intervertebral disc is rare in the thoracic region, but must also be considered.

Diabetic neuropathy may on rare occasions cause abdominal pain.

Most of the remaining conditions which cause pain in the back are of musculoskeletal origin (see Chap. 11) frequently arising from an initial injury, often exacerbated and perpetuated by anxiety and psychosocial-physiological factors, including "compensation neurosis" (q.v.).

Low back pain is one of the most common complaints and can arise from three major structures: (1) the vertebrae, where tumors and compression fractures can occur; (2) the muscles which can be painful either in protective spasm with underlying pathology or from tension; or (3) the nerve roots which can be compressed, causing much pain. These three major types are discussed below in the section on pain in the lower limb (Fig. 7–2).

Pain in the Lower Limb

The causes of pain in the lower limb fall into two groups. The first includes lesions of the bones, joints, ligaments, muscles, and blood vessels of the limb and pelvic girdle. The nonneurological causes of lower limb pain include lesions of the following structures: bones, joints, ligaments, muscles, blood vessels of the limb and pelvic girdle. The neurological causes of lower limb pain include disease involving

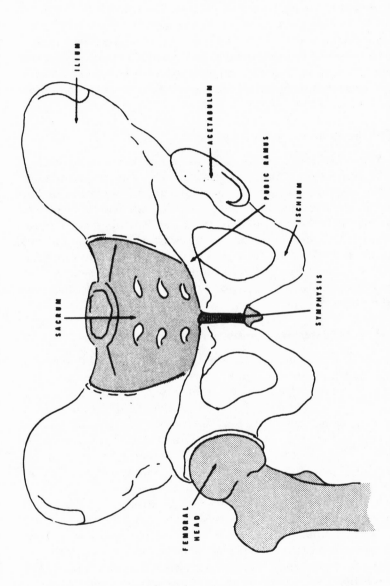

FIGURE 7-2. ANTERIOR VIEW OF BONY PELVIS. THE PELVIS IS PICTURED ANTERIORLY WITH THE LEFT FEMUR OMITTED TO REVEAL THE ACETABULUM. (Reproduced, with permission, from Cailliet, R: Soft Tissue, Pain and Disability. F. A. Davis Company, 1977.)

the sensory pathways in the peripheral nerves, the nerve roots, and the spinal cord. These are conveniently classified according to the site of the lesion.

In the great majority of cases, pain is due to degenerative osteoarthritis of the lumbosacral spine, frequently termed *degenerative disc and joint disease*. Nerve root compression may also be associated with prolapse of a lumbar disc or the lumbosacral disc, the most common interspaces affected being L4–L5 or L5–S1.

Lesions of the Cauda Equina (Fig. 7–3)

Neoplasms of the cauda equina portion of the spinal cord (roots) in the lumbosacral area are rare; but meningiomata, small fibromata of the root sheaths, and giant tumors are the least uncommon. Lumbar pain and pain in the leg may be unilateral or bilateral in these disorders and are commonly of sciatic nerve distribution. Paresthesias are usual in one or more dermatomes. Weakness and wasting are prominent and fasciculations may be seen. Sensory loss is less prominent although impotence and bowel and bladder symptoms may be present. Malignant lymphoma, or hydatid cysts, or other types of tumor may also involve the cauda equina.

Lesions of the Lumbar or Lumbosacral Spine

Osteoarthritis of the lumbar spine is a common cause of nerve root irritation, particularly in the elderly. Posterolateral herniation of the fourth or fifth lumbar discs is a common cause of acute sciatica. A herniation of the fourth lumbar disc will involve the fifth lumbar root as it leaves the spinal canal, whereas the lumbosacral disc herniation implicates the first sacral root. Pain and stiffness of the back, associated with spasm of the paraspinal muscles, is accompanied by pain in the lower limb in the anatomical distribution of the appropriate nerve root. Straight leg raising is prevented by sudden severe pain developing when a certain angle (usually 40 to 50 degrees) is reached because of undue stretching of the nerve roots which make up the sciatic nerve (L4, L5, S1, S2). Numbness, tingling, and the feeling of "pins and needles" with sensory loss and reflex change occur in the appropriate anatomic distribution. There may be weakness of dorsiflexion of the ankle or the big toe, if nerve root compression is severe. Medical treatment is indicated initially for all acute cases of nerve root compression.

Arthritis and subluxation of the sacroiliac joint, various degrees of

⑥

If you are thinking about
ideas or an outside source.
like that, try to tell someone
that something will work when
they hide it, even if it's
not supposed to. Then see if
their mind believes that it
will work.

Saturday, October 7

9:30-11 am ♦ Party for Families to meet Faculty

9:30-11 am ♦ Play Ball! Soccer and kickball in semi-organized games for kids ages 5 and older

11 am-12 noon ♦ President Edwards presents his Vision for the College

11 am-12 noon ♦ Budding Botticellis and Mini Michelangelos: Art projects for kids ages 5 and older

12:20-3:30 pm ♦ College Bowl Campus Tournament

1 pm ♦ Football—St. Olaf vs. Carleton College

1 pm ♦ Women's Soccer—St. Olaf vs. St. Cloud State

1-3 pm ♦ Career Workshop for Parents

3 pm ♦ Men's Soccer—Inter-squad Scrimmage

3:10-3:30 pm ♦ College Bowl Competition
Student Champion Team vs. Faculty Team

4:30-7 pm ♦ Pacific Northwest Theme Dinner

7:30 pm ♦ Family Weekend Concert
(featuring first-year student ensembles)

8 pm ♦ Informal Dance Concert by Student Dancers

Sunday, October 8

10:30 am ♦ Worship Service

11:30 am-1:30 pm ♦ Family Weekend Brunch

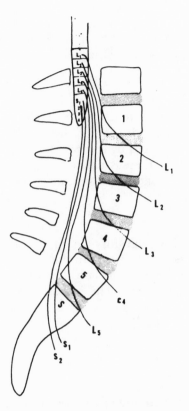

FIGURE 7-3. THE NERVE ROOTS EMERGE FROM THE CONUS OF THE CORD LOCATED AT L 1 LEVEL (1ST LUMBAR LEVEL) AND OBLIQUE DOWNWARD TO EMERGE BELOW THE CORRESPONDENT VERTEBRAL BODY. THE LENGTH OF L 5 AND THE SACRAL ROOTS ARE EVIDENT AND THE OBLIQUITY OF EACH NERVE ROOT IS ALSO DEPICTED. (Reproduced, with permission, from Cailliet, R: Soft Tissue, Pain and Disability. F. A. Davis Company, 1977.)

spondylolisthesis, Paget's disease of the bone, and tumors of all varieties must be excluded, when considering the differential diagnosis of low back pain.

Fracture-Dislocations of the Lumbar Spine

Fracture-dislocations of the lumbar spine give rise to acute lumbar pain and rigidity and can cause pain in the leg if the cauda equina or the emerging roots are irritated by displacement or by callus.* Pelvic conditions are a rare cause of sciatic pain, but should be kept in mind.

Anterior Femoral Pain

Anterior femoral pain is much less common than sciatica. When present it may be due to disease of the hip joint, although in the majority of cases, it is caused by compression of the second, third, or fourth lumbar roots. It is then associated with paresthesias, and sometimes weakness of the quadriceps and diminution of the knee jerk.

Meralgia Paresthetica

Meralgia paresthetica is an uncommon condition characterized by unpleasant numbness and tingling on the anterolateral aspect of the thigh. The symptoms appear for no apparent reason in otherwise healthy adults and may persist. The course is benign, and the patient should be reassured and advised to disregard it. Typically, the sensations involve an area about the size of a hand's breadth and may develop during pregnancy, disappearing after delivery.

Chronic Pain Syndromes

When all of the above etiologies have been excluded, a large number of patients remain who are disturbed by varying degrees of low back pain and stiffness. There is an extensive literature concerning this condition, particularly as it is the basis of much time lost from productive employment. This group of patients constitutes those to whom biofeedback can offer effective treatment. EMG feedback, for example, is effective in the management of chronic pain due to muscle spasm.

Jacobs and Felton (1969) demonstrated the clinical use of relaxation for localized muscle spasm. Both normal and neck-injured subjects were able to relax activity of the trapezius with EMG feedback.

Gottlieb et al. (1977) reported successful use of EMG feedback in patients with low back pain though EMG feedback was only part of a comprehensive pain management program, however. Nigl and Fischer-Williams (1980) reported four cases of relief of low back pain with muscle spasm in a study supported by research.

The indications for treatment of this condition are further discussed in Chapter 11.

*"Callus" denotes hard, bony tissue that surrounds the edges of a fractured bone.

Treatment for Migraine

Case Illustration

Electrothermal biofeedback has been applied in the treatment of migraine. Results of numerous investigations indicate that thermal biofeedback can lead to a reduction in the frequency and intensity of migraine attacks.

A 32-year-old white female, married with three children, was referred for biofeedback treatment by her internist because she was not responding to medication. Migraine attacks had occurred for 12 years and pain medication had been ineffective. In addition, she often developed nausea and other gastrointestinal symptoms, especially during severe migraine attacks. Psychological testing revealed that the patient felt frustrated and trapped in her current life situation. She was trained as a teacher, but not employed as such because her three children below the age of five required her constant supervision. Her husband was required by his occupation to travel frequently, and his many transfers over the past several years had disrupted her life. In addition to feelings of frustration and depression, psychological testing revealed that she had high needs for achievement and set unrealistic goals for herself which she had continuously failed to meet. Such personality characteristics have frequently been noted in individuals with migraine. Furthermore, she was observed to be emotionally constricted and reported having difficulty expressing her feelings.

After an initial diagnostic session it was determined that the average distal temperature of the middle finger of her right hand was consistently less than 70°F. She was then instructed in a relaxation exercise, and given a method of monitoring her finger temperature between sessions. This method involved the use of small, numbered strips of paper which contained a cholesteric substance. (These physiological trend indicators enable the patient to determine approximate distal temperature; when the strip is placed on a finger, a number appears, and the color of the number is interpreted by reference to a temperature chart). The patient was asked to monitor the frequency and intensity of her headaches. After three weeks of relaxation training and home practice, she was introduced to temperature biofeedback training. In the first session, she was not able to increase the temperature, in fact it decreased 2.5°F. However, in subsequent sessions she learned to increase her distal temperature until the tenth biofeedback session, when her temperature increased over an average of 10°F. At that point the migraine attacks became less frequent and instead of averaging three to four times a week, they were occurring less than twice a month. From the 10th to the 15th session (over a 5-week period), the patient reported that no migraine attacks occurred. Treatment was suspended at that point and she was told to continue monitoring herself and to practice the relaxation technique using a cassette tape provided for her. Two months later, she reported that her migraines had not recurred and that she felt well able to control her distal temperature. At that point her daily average distal skin temperature was noted to be approximately 85°F.

This case illustrates a typical treatment program for migraine using relaxation training combined with thermal-biofeedback training. In addition, verbal psychotherapy focused on helping the patient understand her feelings of frustration and enabling her to achieve insight into her life situation. She became more involved in outside activities on a regular basis, which decreased her feelings of frustration. The combination of verbal psychotherapy with biofeedback procedures, contributed to the satisfactory outcome. The personality conflicts were reported reduced as part of the overall treatment process.

Treatment for Posttraumatic Pain

Case Illustration

Physicians are often confronted with patients who complain of sensations not explained by a detectable organic cause. The symptoms frequently date from an incident with trauma, physical and/or emotional, which apparently triggered a disturbance in the somatic and/or the psychologic sphere. A loss of balance or dysequilibrium can lead to clinical distress with somatic and/or operant pain (see Chap. 5). The sensations may be so distressing that the patient is prevented from functioning effectively in employment and in other areas of life.

A 21-year-old white male was referred by his orthopedic surgeon for biofeedback training with a two years' history of burning sensations and other uncomfortable feelings arising from his right testicle. While working in construction he had an accident when he fell through a roof and sustained a penetrating injury of the right leg and thigh. At the time of the injury he complained of severe pain and other sensations in his groin and testicles, but examination failed to reveal the source of his complaints. He was treated with various medications with only slight relief. At the time he was first seen for biofeedback treatment, he complained of a burning feeling, numbness and other distressing sensations in the right testicle, groin and right thigh muscles. He was given relaxation training and taught to monitor the degree of his discomfort on a daily basis. He was introduced to EMG biofeedback training during the third session, and taught to reduce his level of muscle tension using the frontalis muscle. After 10 weeks of treatment he was able to lower the level of muscle tension to below 5 microvolts integral average. By the 15th session the patient reported that his sensations disappeared completely when he went through the relaxation exercises, especially while receiving feedback about his muscle activity. He was also able to eliminate the sensations at home without the biofeedback procedure. After 20 sessions he reported that the daily discomfort had dropped to a very low level and frequently he had no discomfort during the entire day. At this point he was counseled in terms of his vocational future, and he decided to contact the state vocational rehabilitation counselors for job retraining. He was evaluated and given financial assistance to enter a technical school program in mechanics. Prior to being seen for biofeedback, he was poorly motivated and spent the entire day alone in his house, relating the low level of activity to continuous discomfort. At a six-month follow-up visit, the patient reported that the testicular sensations had disappeared completely, and he was actively engaged in technical training to become an automotive mechanic.

This case indicates the value of the nonspecific effects of biofeedback relaxation training as an adjunct in treating patients suffering from sensations of obscure etiology. The central endorphin-mediated placebo effect which biofeedback can bring into play may be beneficial to certain patients who cannot find relief with other forms of treatment.

REFERENCES

Adler CS, Adler SM: Biofeedback-psychotherapy for the treatment of headaches: a 5-year follow-up. Headache 16(4): 189, 1976.
Andreychuk T, Skriver C: Hypnosis and biofeedback in the treatment of migraine headache. Proceedings of the Biofeedback Society of America 5th Annual Meeting, 1974.

Bernstein DA, Borkovec TD: *Progressive Relaxation Training: a Manual for the Helping Professions.* Chicago, Research Press, 1973.

Blanchard EB: The use of temperature biofeedback in the treatment of chronic pain due to causalgia. Biofeedback Self Regul 4: 183, 1979.

Blanchard EB, Theobald DE, Brown DA, Silver BV, Williamson DA: A controlled comparison of temperature biofeedback and autogenic training with progressive relaxation training in the treatment of migraine headaches. Proceedings of the Biofeedback Society of America 8th Annual Meeting 1977.

Boller JD, Flom RP: Treatment of the common migraine: systematic application of biofeedback and autogenic training. Proceedings of the Biofeedback Society of America 9th Annual Meeting, 1978.

Budzynski TH: Biofeedback strategies in headache treatment, in Basmajian JV (ed): *Biofeedback: A Handbook for Clinicians.* Baltimore, Williams and Wilkins, 1979.

Budzynski TH, Stoyva JM, Adler CS, Multaney DJ: EMG biofeedback and tension headache: a controlled study. Psychosom Med 35: 6, 1973.

Carlsson SG, Gale EN: Biofeedback in the treatment of long-term temporo-mandibular joint pain: An outcome study. Biofeedback Self-Regul 2: 161, 1972.

Chesney MA, Shelton JL: A comparison of muscle relaxation and electromyogram biofeedback treatment for muscle contraction headache. J Behav Ther Exp Psychiatr 7: 221, 1976.

Cohen BA, Crouch RH, Thompson SN: Electromyographic biofeedback as a physical therapeutic adjunct in Guillain-Barré syndrome. Arch Phys Med Rehab 58: 582, 1976.

Coursey RD: Electromyographic feedback as a relaxation technique. J Consult Clin Psychol 43: 825, 1975.

Cox DJ, Freundlich A, Meyer RG: Differential effectiveness of electromyograph feedback, verbal relaxation instructions, and medication placebo with tension headache. J Consult Clin Psychol 43: 892, 1975.

Culver CM, Hauri P: Headache clinical proposal. Unpublished manuscript submitted to the National Migraine Foundation, Chicago, June, 1972.

Dalessio DJ: Classification and mechanism of migraine. Headache 19(3): 114, 1979.

Diamond S, Diamond-Falk J, DeVeno T: The value of biofeedback in the treatment of chronic headache: A five-year retrospective study. Proceedings of the Biofeedback Society of America 9th Annual Meeting, 1978.

Diamond S, Franklin M: Indications and contraindications for the use of biofeedback therapy in headache patients. Proceedings of the Biofeedback Society of America 5th Annual Meeting, 1974.

Diamond S, Franklin M: Intensive biofeedback therapy in the treatment of headache. Proceedings of the Biofeedback Society of America 6th Annual Meeting, 1975.

Diamond S, Franklin M: Biofeedback-choice of treatment in childhood migraine, in Luthe W and Antonelli F (eds): *Therapy in Psychosomatic Medicine. Autogenic Therapy,* vol. 4. Rome, Grune & Stratton, 1977.

Dohrmann RJ, Laskin DM: Treatment of myofacial pain dysfunction syndrome with EMG biofeedback. J Dent Res 55 (Special Issue B): B249, 1976.

Drury RL, DeRisi W, Leberman R: Temperature feedback treatment for migraine headache: a controlled study. Proceedings of the Biofeedback Society of America 6th Annual Meeting, 1975.

Epstein LH, Abel GG: An analysis of biofeedback training effects for tension headache patient. Behav Ther 8: 37, 1977.

Epstein LH, Hersen M, Hemphill DP: Music feedback in the treatment of tension headache: an experimental case study. J Behav Ther Exp Psychiatr 5: 59, 1974.

Fernando CK: Audio-visual re-education in neuromuscular disorders. Proceedings of the Biofeedback Society of America 7th Annual Meeting, 1976.

Feuerstein M, Adams H: Cephalic vasomotor feedback in the modification of migraine headache. Biofeedback Self-Regul 2(3): 241, 1977.

Fischer-Williams M: Treatment of chronic pain. Br Med J 1: 533, 1956.

Friar LR, Beatty J: Migraine: management by trained control of vasoconstriction. J Consult Clin Psychol 44: 46, 1976.

Fried FE, Lamberti J, Sneed P: Treatment of tension and migraine headaches with biofeedback techniques. Mo Med 74: 253, 1977.

Gannon L, Sternbach RA: Alpha enhancement as treatment for pain: a case study. J Behav Ther Exp Psychiatr 2: 209, 1971.

Gottlieb H, Strite LC, Koller R: Comprehensive rehabilitation of patients with chronic low back pain. Arch Phys Med Rehab 58: 101, 1977.

Hartje JC, Diver CE: Variation in hand temperature as a correlate to migraine severity. Proceedings of the Biofeedback Society of America 9th Annual Meeting, 1978.

Hay KM, Madders J: Migraine treated by relaxation therapy. J R Coll Gen Pract 21: 644, 1971.

Haynes SN, Griffin P, Mooney D, Parise M: Electromyographic biofeedback and relaxation instructions in the treatment of muscle contraction headache. Behavior Therapy 6: 672, 1975.

Hutchins DF and Reinking RH: Tension headaches: What form of therapy is most effective? Biofeedback Self-Regul 1: 183, 1976.

Jacobs A, Felton GS: Visual feedback for muscle relaxation in normals and patients with neck injuries. Arch Phys Med Rehab, 50: 34, 1969.

Jacobson E: *Progressive Relaxation.* Chicago, University of Chicago Press, 1938.

Keefe FJ: Conditioning changes in differential skin temperature. Percept Motor Skills 40: 283, 1975.

Koppman JW, McDonald RD, Kunzel MG: Voluntary regulation of temporal artery diameter by migraine patients. Headache 14: 133, 1974.

Leeb C, French D, Fahrion S: The effect of instructional set on autogenic biofeedback hand temperature training. Proceedings of the Biofeedback Society of America 5th Annual Meeeting, 1974.

Lynch WC, Hama H, Kohn S, Miller NE: Instrumental control of peripheral vasomotor responses in children. Psychophysiology 13: 219, 1976.

Maslach C, Marshall G, Zimbardo PG: Hypnotic control of peripheral skin temperature: a case report. Psychophysiology 9: 600, 1972.

Mathew RJ, Claghorn JL, Meyer JS, Largen J, Dobbins K: Relationship between volitional alteration in skin temperature and regional cerebral blood flow in normal subjects. Proceedings of the Biofeedback Society of America 9th Annual Meeting, 1978.

Medina JL, Diamond S, Franklin M: Biofeedback therapy for migraine. Headache 16: 418, 1976.

Melzack R, Perry C: Self-regulation of pain: the use of alpha feedback and hypnotic training for the control of chronic pain, in Wickramasekera I (ed): *Biofeedback, Behavior Therapy and Hypnosis: Potentiating the Verbal Control of Behavior for Clinicians.* Chicago, Nelson-Hall, 1976.

Mitch PS, McGrady A, Iannone A: Autogenic feedback training in treatment of migraine:

a clinical report. Proceedings of the Biofeedback Society of America 6th Annual Meeting, 1975.

Mitchell KR: The treatment of migraine: an exploratory application of time-limited behavior therapy. Technology 14: 50, 1969.

Mitchell KR, Mitchell DM: Migraine: exploratory treatment application of programmed behavior therapy techniques. J Psychosom Res 15: 37, 1971.

Mitchell Weir: in *Gunshot Wounds of Nerves,* 1864.

Morgenstern FS: The effects of sensory input and concentration on post-amputation phantom limb pain. J Neurol Neurosurg Psychiat 27: 58, 1964.

Nigl A, Fischer-Williams M: EMG treatment of low back strain. Psychosomatics 21: 495, 1980.

Pearse BA, Walters ED, Sargent JD: Exploratory observations of the use of an intensive autogenic biofeedback training procedure in a follow-up study of out-of-town patients having migraine and/or tension headaches. Proceedings of the Biofeedback Society of America 6th Annual Meeting, 1975.

Peper E, Grossman ER: Preliminary observation of thermal biofeedback training in children with migraine. Proceedings of the Biofeedback Society of America 5th Annual Meeting, 1974.

Philips C: The modification of tension headache pain using EMG biofeedback. Behav Res Ther 15: 119, 1977.

Pozniak-Patewicz E: Cephalgic spasm of head and neck muscles. Sandoz-Information, Proc Bergen Migraine Symposium Suppl 1: 61, 1975.

Price KP, Tursky B: Vascular reactivity of migraineurs and non-migraineurs: a comparison of responses to self-control procedures. Headache 16: 210, 1976.

Reinking RH, Kohl ML: Effects of various forms of relaxation training on physiological and self-report measures of relaxation. J Consult Clin Psychol, 43: 595, 1975.

Roberts AH, Schuler J, Bacon JR, Zimmerman RL, Patterson P: Individual differences and autonomic control: absorption, hypnotic susceptibility, and the unilateral control of skin temperature. J Abnorm Psychol 84: 272, 1975.

Roberts AH, Kewman A, and MacDonald, B: Voluntary control of skin temperature: unilateral changes using hypnosis and feedback. J Abnorm Psychol : 82: 163, 1973.

Rosenthal DA: The effect of EMG biofeedback therapy on MPD patients with long and short masseteric silent periods. Unpublished Master's Thesis. School of Dentistry, State University of New York at Buffalo, 1976.

Russ KL, Hammer RL, Adderton M: Clinical follow-up: treatment outcome of functional headache patients treated with biofeedback. Proceedings of the Biofeedback Society of America 8th Annual Meeting, 1977.

Sargent JD, Green EE, Walters ED: The use of autogenic feedback training in a pilot study of migraine and tension headaches. Headache 12: 120, 1972.

Savill GE, Koppman JW: Voluntary temporal artery regulation compared with finger blood volume and temperature. Proceedings of the Biofeedback Society of America 6th Annual Meeting, 1975.

Scott J, Timmons B: On the relationship between frontalis EMG activity and skin temperature: a preliminary model with very little data. Proceedings of the Biofeedback Society of America 5th Annual Meeting, 1974.

Sherman RA: Case reports of treatment of phantom limb pain with combination of electromyographic biofeedback and verbal relaxation techniques. Biofeedback Self-Regul 1: 353, 1976.

Solbach P, Sargent J: A follow-up evaluation of a five and one-half year migraine headache study using thermal training. Proceedings of the Biofeedback Society of America 8th Annual Meeting, 1977.

Solberg WK, Rugh JD: The use of biofeedback devices in the treatment of bruxism. J South California Dent Assoc 40: 852, 1972.

Stroebel CF, Glueck BC: Biofeedback treatment in medicine and psychiatry: an ultimate placebo? Semin Psychiatr 5: 397, 1973.

Sturgis ET, Adams HE: Use of cephalic vasomotor and electromyogram feedback in treatment of migraine, muscle contraction, and combined headaches. Proc First Internat Meet Biofeedback and Self-Regulation. Tubingen, Germany, Nov, 1977.

Sturgis ET, Tollison CD, Adams HE: Modification of combined migraine-muscle contraction headaches using BVP and EMG feedback. J Applied Behav Anal 11: 215, 1978.

Taub E, Emurian CS: Operant control skin temperature. Proceedings of the Biofeedback Society of America 2nd Annual Meeting, 1971.

Taub E, Emurian CS: Feedback-aided self-regulation of skin temperature with a single feedback locus: 1. Acquisition and reversal training. Biofeedback Self-Regul 1(2): 147, 1976.

Tinel J: *Nerve Wounds*. London, Baillière, Tindall and Cox, 1918, p 187.

Turin A, Johnson WG: Biofeedback therapy for migraine headaches. Arch Gen Psychiatr 33: 517, 1976.

Weinstock SA: A tentative procedure for the control of pain: migraine and tension headaches. Proceedings of the Biofeedback Society of America 3rd Annual Meeting, 1972.

Werbach MR, Sandweiss JH: Finger temperature characteristics of migraineurs undergoing biofeedback assisted relaxation training. Proceedings of the Biofeedback Society of America 9th Annual Meeting, 1978. p. 43.

Werder DS: An exploratory study of childhood migraine using thermal biofeedback as a treatment alternative. Proceedings of the Biofeedback Society of America 9th Annual Meeting, 1978. p. 45.

Whatmore G, Kohli DR: *The Physiopathology and Treatment of Functional Disorders*. New York, Grune and Stratton, 1974.

Wickramasekera I: Electromyographic feedback training and tension headache: preliminary observations. Am J Clin Hypn 15:83, 1972.

Wickramasekera I: Temperature feedback for the control of migraine. J Behav Ther Exp Psychiatr 4: 343, 1973.

Wickramasekera I: *Biofeedback, Behavior Therapy and Hypnosis*. Chicago, Nelson–Hall, 1976, p. 579.

Zamani R: Treatment of migraine, headache: biofeedback versus deep muscle relaxation. Research Report. Minneapolis, University of Minnesota Medical School, PR. 785, 1977.

8

Disorders of Motor Function

Sensory-Motor Integration

Although the focus of this book is on biofeedback as provided by electronic devices, it is interesting to consider the fact that man himself has had sophisticated biofeedback mechanisms built into his anatomy and physiology. These mechanisms are easily demonstrated in motor function. The ability to stand on two feet and to walk requires kinesthetic and proprioceptive feedback signals from the muscles, joints, and tendons that provide instantaneous information about the moment-to-moment position of the limbs and the tension or relaxation of the musculature required to overcome gravitational pull.

Kinesthesia is defined as "the sensation of bodily position, presence or movement resulting chiefly from stimulation of sensory nerve endings in muscles, tendons, and joints" (Greek: *kinesis,* "movement"; *kinema,* "motion"). The way in which movement is regulated by signals that come from within the body was first clearly described by Sherrington, (1906, revised 1947). He stated:

> The deep tissues have receptors specific to themselves. The receptors which lie in the depth of the organism are adapted for excitation consonantly with changes going on in the organism itself, particularly in its muscles and their accessory organs (tendons, joints, blood vessels etc). Since in this field the stimuli to the receptors are given by the organism itself, their field may be called the proprio-ceptive field (p. 283).

Thus, Sherrington introduced the adjective proprioceptive (Fig. 8–1).

During the standard neurological examination, the patient is tested, when the upper limb has been fully extended and the eyes are closed, for the ability to bring the straightened index finger to touch the tip of the nose. A great number of feedback signals are involved in this apparently simple task, which assesses proprioceptive sensation, mo-

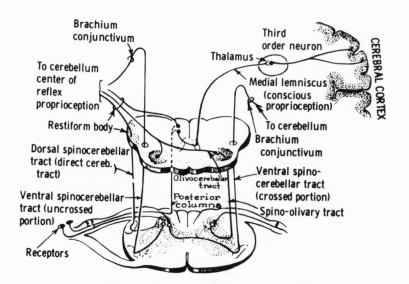

Brachium
conjunctivum

Third
order neuron

Thalamus

To cerebellum
center of
reflex
proprioception

Medial lemniscus
(conscious
proprioception)

CEREBRAL CORTEX

Restiform body

To cerebellum

Dorsal spinocerebellar
tract (direct cereb.
tract)

Brachium
conjunctivum

Olivocerebellar
tract

Ventral spino-
cerebellar tract
(crossed portion)

Ventral spinocerebellar
tract (uncrossed
portion)

Posterior
columns

Spino-olivary tract

Receptors

FIGURE 8-1.   PROPRIOCEPTION. (Reproduced, with permission, from Chusid JG: Correlative Neuroanatomy & Functional Neurology, 17th ed. Copyright 1979 by Lange Medical Publications, Los Altos, California.)

tor power, and cerebellar function in the upper limb.

The cerebellum is the great "smoother out" of movement and when there is cerebellar dysfunction, the movement is decomposed or fragmented into a number of separate segments of movements. Biofeedback mechanisms operate continuously in the learning of coordinated motor skills. The analogy of the basketball player has been used to illustrate this point. The player regulates the force of his next throw of the ball by watching whether his first falls into the basket. If he closes his eyes, he does not have the same amount of feedback whereby he can control the motor activity. Once he becomes extremely skilled he could play with eyes closed, by attending very closely to his proprioceptive stimuli, but it would always be more difficult than under visual control. Any dysfunction of the motor system involves a disruption in the body's own feedback processes.

The motor system will now be discussed in terms of symptoms, with differential diagnosis arising from the localization of pathology. In selected cases, a symptom or a constellation of symptoms will respond to biofeedback therapy.

Disturbances of Movement

Disturbances of movement include:
1. Paralysis
2. Muscular atrophy
3. Disorders of coordination and equilibrium
4. Pathological muscular contractions

Paralysis

Quadriplegia indicates paralysis of all four limbs. It is usually due to trauma of the cervical portion of the spinal cord, but may also result from transverse myelitis, poliomyelitis, Guillain-Barré polyradiculoneuropathy, or less common causes.

Diplegia indicates paralysis of both lower limbs. It is caused by a lesion involving the motor area of both hemispheres in the brain and is usually the result of a birth injury (e.g., Little's disease, cerebral palsy).

Hemiplegia indicates paralysis of one-half (vertical) of the body. It may be flaccid (loss of tone) or spastic (too much tone), and with or without flexion contractures or associated involuntary movements. It may be congenital or acquired in later life. The etiologies of acquired hemiplegia are very numerous, but the common causes include:
1. Cerebral thromboembolism, or cerebral hemorrhage
2. Arteriosclerotic stenosis of the cervical carotid artery with cortical ischemia
3. Head injury
4. Traumatic carotid artery thrombosis
5. Multiple sclerosis
6. Brain tumor
7. Other diseases of the brain or of the cervical cord

Paraplegia indicates paralysis of both lower limbs, similar to diplegia, but by custom it is the term used for lesions acquired in later life, as opposed to diplegia which is mainly reserved for the perinatal birth injuries. Paraplegia is usually due to trauma or neoplasm of the thoracolumbar spinal cord, but may arise from lesions of the peripheral nerves or a tumor involving the motor area of both hemispheres of the brain.

Monoplegia indicates paralysis of one limb, usually of the upper extremities. It may be of cerebral or cervical cord origin, or it may be a conversion-like symptom without demonstrable underlying organic abnormality.

Muscular Atrophy

Muscular atrophy may be due to primary muscle, spinal cord, or brain stem disease, or associated with peripheral neuropathy or genetic abnormality.

Disorders of Coordination and Equilibrium

Disorders of coordination and equilibrium include ataxia from many causes or vertigo.

Pathologic Muscular Contractions and Involuntary Movements

Pathological muscular contractions and involuntary movements include bruxism, spasms, tics, tremors, choreoathetosis, and torticollis.

Clinical Aspects of the Motor System

There are eight clinical aspects of the motor system that require observation and evaluation in each case. These include (1) muscle tone, (2) motor power, (3) tendon reflexes, (4) cerebellar function, (5) involuntary movements, (6) muscle wasting, (7) muscle spasm, and (8) ataxia if present.

1. *Muscle tone* is defined as the resistance to passive movement of a limb.

2. *Motor power* is measured as the strength of a single muscle or more commonly a group of muscles in active, resisted movement, and evaluated in accordance with age, body build, and occupation.

3. *Tendon reflexes* are the mechanical responses to the stretch of a tendon, where the muscle is inserted at its attachment to the bone. Additional pathological reflexes are noted if present.

4. *Cerebellar function* evaluates the coordination of movement in a sequence of movement, for example, running the heel down the opposite shin, or drawing a circle in the air, or touching the examiner's finger and the subject's nose alternatively with the index finger.

5. The presence (or absence) of *involuntary movements*, or movement disorders is noted. These include tremor at rest or during movement, chorea, athetosis, hemiballismus, myoclonus, myokymia, habit spasms or tics, torticollis, or other forms of dyskinesia. These involuntary, abnormal movements can be due to many different types of neurological diseases, and the differential diagnosis is important in clinical neurology, but not in the scope of this book.

6. *Muscle wasting*, if present, indicates disuse atrophy, or lower motor neuron involvement, such as peripheral nerve injury, diabetic

or alcoholic neuropathy, or Guillain-Barré polyradiculoneuropathy; in rare cases, it follows involvement of the parietal cortex.

7. *Muscle spasm* is a form of involuntary movement, but is considered separately in this context, because it frequently occurs in psychophysiological (psychosomatic) syndromes, associated with chronic anxiety. On the other hand, muscle spasm can be reactive to localized pathology, in which case it is a protective mechanism designed to prevent the underlying joint from moving; for example, in an acute posttraumatic condition such as flexion-extension injury of the cervical spine, or in the muscles overlying a prolapsed intervertebral disc. Where there is no significant underlying disease, this muscle spasm is the somatic (bodily) manifestation of anxiety and stress. It is in itself painful because of the excess stimulation of the proprioceptive nerves, and it leads to the formation of a "vicious circle," because the pain causes more anxiety and therefore more spasm. The pain then becomes "operant," (see Chap. 5) causing specific behavior to become associated with muscle spasm and therefore further pain.

8. *Ataxia*. It should be noted that ataxia may be: (1) *of cerebellar origin* (due to a lesion involving the cerebellum or its connections, or spinocerebellar pathways); or (2) *of sensory origin,* due to a lesion involving the posterior columns of the spinal cord and causing impairment in joint and position sensation. *Posture* and *gait* are noted as the composites depending upon the separate components described above.

Pathologic Changes in the Nervous System

Once the observation and evaluation of the patient's motor deficit has been made, and the site of the pathological lesion which is causing the deficit has been determined, the neurologist is in a position to delineate the pathological process that may underlie the symptoms and signs. Pathological reactions in the nervous system can be classified into three broad groups: focal lesions, diffuse disorders, and systemic nervous diseases.

1. *Focal lesions* cause a disturbance in the function of a strictly localized area, for example, monoplegia involving only the foot with a precentral tumor.

2. *Diffuse or generalized disorders* affect nerve cells and supporting tissue throughout the nervous system. They may be of vascular, metabolic, toxic, or other etiology. For example, cerebrovascular disease which may cause cerebral infarction is usually a complication of atherosclerosis or hypertension and is commonly associated with arteriosclerotic heart disease and retinopathy.

3. *In systemic nervous disease*, the pathological process shows a predi-

lection for a particular neuronal structure. For example, the myelin sheath is attacked in multiple sclerosis, while the anterior horn cells are affected in poliomyelitis, and the anterior horn cells together with the corticospinal fibers in amyotrophic lateral sclerosis.

A clear diagnostic distinction should be made between these groups, so that treatment is appropriate. An accurate prognosis should also be attempted based upon what is known of the disease, so that if new factors are introduced into the treatment, there is a reliable baseline for observations. Some of the symptoms in motor abnormality will now be analyzed.

Positive and Negative Elements in Symptomatology

Neurological motor disorder is often better understood if we envisage the cerebrum, the cerebellum, and the spinal cord as contributing different components to the end result. Daube and Sandok (1978) described four major divisions in the motor system: (1) the final common pathway, (2) the direct activation pathway, (3) the indirect activation pathway, and (4) the control circuits. When one component is destroyed or deficient, another component may become overactive (analogous to compensation hypertrophy) in an attempt to replace the missing function, or as a "release" phenomenon.

Hughlings Jackson (1835–1911), neurologist, introduced a concept in the 1870s that has proved useful in clarifying neurological symptomatology. In it he distinguished "positive" from "negative" elements in brain and spinal cord disease. The "negative" elements are the functions that are lost; the "positive" are the new phenomena that appear after the lesion develops. For example, in the case of a vascular lesion, which causes a hemiplegia (the loss of voluntary movement), the functions lost are the negative elements since they were dependent on the integrity of the structures destroyed, namely the corticospinal tract. The new phenomena which appear only after the stroke, such as muscular hypertonus, exaggerated tendon reflexes, and a Babinski response are the positive elements. They are the manifestations of the activity of other intact parts of the nervous system, which are thought to be "released" or wrested from control as a result of damage to the parts destroyed. Some of the negative signs in hemiplegia due to cerebrovascular lesions will now be discussed.

"Negative" Signs in Hemiplegia due to Cerebrovascular Disease

1. *Facial movements.* In many stroke cases, depending upon the anatomy of the lesion, there is weakness of voluntary movements in the

lower part of the face, such as difficulty in showing the teeth and pursing the lips to whistle. Movements of the upper part of the face are preserved, because like other bilaterally synchronous motor activity, movements of each side of the upper part of the face are under the dual control of both cerebral hemispheres. Emotionally-related movements, such as smiling and crying are little affected because the nervous pathways for these movements do not run with the corticospinal fibers.

2. *Movements of the lower jaw and soft palate.* These are mostly bilaterally symmetrical and synchronous, and therefore well preserved. However, slight weakness may be seen with deviation of the jaw on opening the mouth, concomitant with dysarthria (difficulty in the mechanics of speaking).

3. *Movements of the tongue and pharynx.* Dysphagia (difficulty in swallowing) is often marked.

4. *Movements of the limbs.* This is the most prominent disability and is therefore described in detail below. After a slight corticospinal lesion there is clumsiness of fine finger movements and weakness of dorsiflexion of the toes. It is difficult to move the thumb independently of the other digits. Movements are not confined to the appropriate parts, but the limb tends to move as a whole; in the upper limb, movements of flexion are stronger than those of extension, but the reverse is true is the lower limb.

5. *Gait.* The hemiplegic patient circumducts* his leg when he walks, swinging it outward at the hip and round in a semicircular way, because he has difficulty in bending the knee. The foot is plantar flexed, because of weakness of dorsiflexion at the ankle.

"Positive" Signs in Hemiplegia due to Cerebrovascular Disease

1. *Ocular movements.* Immediately after the stroke, there is usually weakness of conjugate deviation of the eyes to the side opposite to the lesion, and therefore unopposed deviation to the side of the cerebral abnormality. These ocular abnormalities usually resolve within a few days of the onset.

2. *Movements of the head.* The unconscious patient usually lies with the head, like the eyes, rotated to the side of the lesion. This is caused by the unantagonized action of the rotating muscles innervated from the "normal" hemisphere.

3. *Muscular hypertonus.* At a variable time following a stroke, spas-

*Latin: *circum,* "around"; *duco,* "I lead."

ticity develops. In spastic ("clasp-knife") hypertonus, there is excess tone mainly in the flexors of the upper limb and in the extensors of the lower limb. The affected muscles are in a state of continuous contraction which can be observed visually and on palpation. It can also be demonstrated by noting the increased resistance to passive movements at the joints. In the upper limb, the adductors and internal rotators of the shoulder; flexors of the elbow, wrist, and fingers; and the pronators of the forearm are usually more spastic than their antagonists. In the lower limb, the hypertonia predominates in the adductors of the hip, the extensors of the hip and knee, and in the plantar flexors of the foot and toes. In time contractures tend to develop in the spastic muscles, if not treated early and adequately.

4. *Tendon reflexes* are exaggerated on the paralyzed side.

5. *Pathological reflexes* appear, such as the Babinski response. In this reflex, there is extension of the big toe and fanning of the other toes when the outer sole of the foot is stimulated by a touch or scratch.

Upper Motor Neuron Lesions

Hemiplegia or Hemiparesis

The cause of the stroke determines the speed of onset and the natural history of the condition. Most cases of hemiplegia that are likely to be candidates for rehabilitation and the use of biofeedback treatment are due to cerebrovascular disease. Cerebral thrombosis or thromboembolism causes a very variable pattern of disability depending upon (1) the site of the vascular lesion (Figs. 8–2, 8–3) and the extent of the infarct; (2) the speed of onset; (3) the degree of collateral circulation established after the acute episode; (4) the association of the other disorders such as hypertension and peripheral vascular disease; (5) the patient's premorbid personality and therefore his degree of motivation towards regaining as much return of function as possible.

The prognosis in cases of acute stroke may be considered to depend upon four major factors: (1) cardiac output, (2) pulmonary ventilation, (3) the prestroke state of the cerebral vascularity (vascular "tree"), and, (4) the site of the lesion in the brain (Fischer-Williams, Telerman-Toppet, and Meyer, 1964).

Stages of Recovery in Stroke Patients

There are several stages of recovery which may be delineated in stroke patients, (Brunnstrom, 1970).

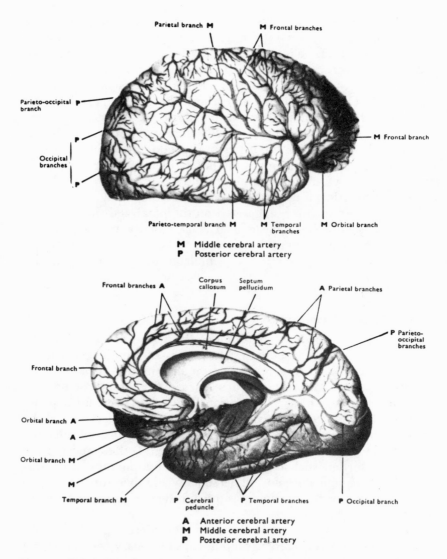

FIGURE 8-2. DISTRIBUTION OF CEREBRAL ARTERIES ON THE SUPERO-LATERAL SURFACE OF THE RIGHT CEREBRAL HEMISPHERE. DISTRIBUTION OF CEREBRAL ARTERIES ON THE MEDIAL AND TENTORIAL SURFACES OF THE RIGHT CEREBRAL HEMISPHERE. (Reproduced, with permission, from Brain's Diseases of the Nervous System. Revised by John N. Walton, 7th edition, 1969, Oxford University Press, Oxford, England.)

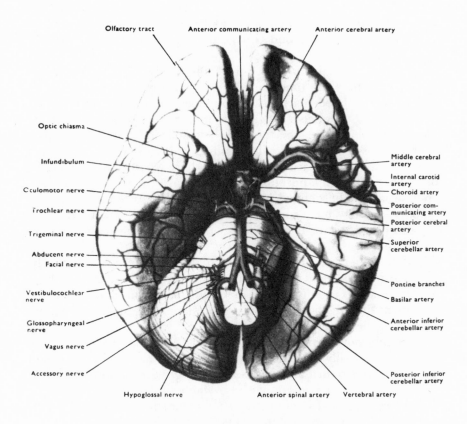

Olfactory tract · Anterior communicating artery · Anterior cerebral artery

Optic chiasma

Infundibulum

Oculomotor nerve

Trochlear nerve

Trigeminal nerve

Abducent nerve
Facial nerve

Vestibulocochlear
nerve

Glossopharyngeal
nerve

Vagus nerve

Accessory nerve

Hypoglossal nerve · Anterior spinal artery · Vertebral artery

Middle cerebral
artery
Internal carotid
artery
Choroid artery
Posterior com-
municating artery
Posterior cerebral
artery
Superior
cerebellar artery

Pontine branches

Basilar artery

Anterior inferior
cerebellar artery

Posterior inferior
cerebellar artery

FIGURE 8-3. ARTERIES OF THE BASE OF THE BRAIN. (Reproduced, with permission, from Brain's Diseases of the Nervous System. Edited by John N. Walton, 7th edition, 1969, Oxford University Press, Oxford, England.)

1. Immediately following the stroke, there is flaccid paralysis, and if complete, no movement can be initiated in the affected limbs or the paralyzed side of the face. The distal part of the limbs is more afflicted than the proximal. The level of consciousness may fluctuate and a variable degree of dysarthria and dysphagia is often present and very troublesome. There may be incomplete bladder control. Sensory loss may add to the motor deficit. Homonymous hemianopia (loss of vision in half of the visual field) or other visual field cuts, neglect of the paralyzed side of the body or of extrapersonal space, and a variety of

cognitive deficits, including loss of awareness or denial of disability, and disturbances of the body image may all add to the picture of a "pure" motor stroke.

2. Spasticity begins to develop usually within a few weeks. At approximately the same time, flexion or extension synergies begin to appear as associated reactions, or minimal voluntary movement responses may be noticed. The lower limb recovers better than the upper, and the proximal better than the distal. Individual digit movement at this stage is not usually possible. Frustration and depression are almost universal reactions, and when there is associated dysphasia, the difficulty in communication adds greatly to the patient's distress. (Dysphasia may be defined by Dejerine as "loss of memory for the symbols whereby men communicate." There are, of course, many varieties of aphasia or dysphasia, but they share, however. this common basis).

3. The patient develops the ability to initiate synergies voluntarily. Spasticity increases and may become severe. The additional neurological abnormalities outlined in the first stage may be more important to the patient than the actual motor deficit, depending upon the type of stroke and the patient's personality.

4. Some movement combinations out of the basic synergies are mastered gradually. Spasticity declines somewhat. Individual digit movement may return and this is always a good prognostic sign.

5. Once the limb stops moving as a whole (in a synergistic pattern), more complex and discrete voluntary movements are relearned. For many years, there was a controversy as to whether movements or muscles are represented in the cortex. It became clear that muscles as such are not represented, but they are dependent on cortical function insofar as they partake in combination-sequence and movement-pattern. In studying the return of voluntary control in stroke patients, the gross movement returns first, and when one joint of a limb is moved, the others move also. Very often the patient can move a limb better if the contralateral one is moved at the same time. Gradually discrete and independent movements may return, to a greater or lesser degree.

6. Discrete movements around individual joints become possible; spasticity disappears and coordination approaches normal. These individuals are relatively rare, however, and many patients never proceed beyond stages 3 or 4.

EMG Biofeedback Techniques in Rehabilitation

EMG rehabilitation techniques were described by Mims (1956) and Marinacci and Horande (1960). Important contributions were also made by research investigators using the EMG to study physiology and single motor unit control (Basmajian, 1963, 1967, 1972; Basmajian and Samson, 1973; Basmajian and Simard, 1967; Harrison and Mortenson, 1962; Johnson, 1976; Simard, 1969); by those exploring cybernetic theories of motor learning and control (Herman, 1973; Smith and Henry 1967); by others extending the principles of operant conditioning to the learning of autonomic responses (Katkin and Murray 1968; Kimmel 1967); and by still others studying involuntary skeletal muscle responses (Lloyd and Shurley 1976; Sachs and Mayhall, 1971).

The types of disorders now treated with EMG feedback techniques include the following: (1) upper motor neuron lesions, (2) lower motor neuron lesions, (3) dyskinesias, (4) orthopedic problems including tendon transfers, (5) muscle spasms causing pain, and (6) paralysis as a conversion symptom.

Biofeedback Treatment for Hemiplegia or Hemiparesis in Vascular Stroke

The value of EMG feedback in muscle reeducation and regulation is generally accepted. Since this is the aspect of biofeedback treatment which has been the longest in use (in excess of 20 years), there is a large literature on its use in various types of paralysis. Marinacci and Horande (1960) reported an improvement of function in the upper extremity by 20 percent. Andrews (1964) studied 20 hemiplegics with improvement in 17. Johnson and Garton (1973) using auditory and visual feedback with 11 hemiparetic patients showed improvement in 7. Brudny et al. (1976) gave good follow-up information, showing improvement using a variety of biofeedback treatment modalities. Some case studies included trials with or without EMG feedback, so that the outcome of treatment demonstrated the efficacy of EMG feedback (Bird, Cataldo, and Cunningham, 1977; Middaugh, 1977; Spearing and Poppen, 1974; Wooldridge et al., 1976).

In the first control study of EMG biofeedback for stroke patients, Basmajian et al. (1975) compared clinical outcome in two randomly assigned groups of hemiplegics; one group received treatment sessions of 40 minutes of therapeutic exercise, the other received 20 minutes of therapeutic exercise plus 20 minutes of exercise with EMG feedback. The EMG feedback group made gains in strength and range of motion that were double those made by the nonfeedback group.

Expanded control studies of the variable that influence the response to EMG feedback were later made by Basmajian, Baker, and Regenos (1977), and Baker et al. (1977). Kleinman and co-workers (1975) started training with EMG feedback after a baseline that involved identical training, but without EMG feedback (Santee et al., 1976). In these studies, half the subjects received EMG feedback training sooner than the other half. This design permitted both within and between groups comparisons. The procedures are well described, the measures quantitative, and the results analyzed statistically. In one of these studies (Kleinman et al., 1975), biceps hyperactivity during EMG feedback training was significant reduced below baseline levels. The second study (Santee et al., 1976) gave equivocal results. EMG activity increased significantly between baseline and follow-up, but the largest increase came with the addition of incentive or motivation (monetary reward or equivalent value in cigarettes) rather than with the addition of EMG feedback.

Two other studies have examined the question of specific EMG feedback effects by comparing short-term performance within subjects during efforts to produce voluntary muscle contractions with and without EMG feedback (Lee et al., 1976; Middaugh, 1977). The rationale was that if the added information provided by EMG feedback contributes to clinical outcome, then practice with EMG feedback must differ in some ways from equivalent practice without EMG feedback. Lee et al. (1976) compared changes across a series of five-second voluntary contractions of the deltoid muscle under different conditions in each of 18 hemiplegic patients. They concluded that there was no specific effect of a brief (five-second) EMG feedback that is dependent on precise cues from peripheral myoelectric signals. It was later considered that this five-second period was too short.

Middaugh (1978) found that EMG feedback significantly improved the ability of normal human subjects to maximize and prolong a voluntary contraction in an unfamiliar and little used muscle. For this reason and others, it is suggested that the five-second contraction in the Lee et al. study was too brief. It takes time to attempt a contraction, to note the information provided by the feedback display, and to make improvements. Middaugh reported 12 subjects, half with a cerebral lesion and half with partial spinal cord injury or a peripheral nerve injury who showed improvement with feedback. Their results suggest that EMG feedback has a substantial positive effect on motor unit recruitment by providing useful information regarding the relatively small, marginally discriminable muscle contractions.

Shahani, Connors, and Mohr (1977) studied 18 hemiparetic patients divided into two groups of nine. One received conventional physical therapy five days a week, and the other group received 45 minutes of EMG feedback three times a week in addition to conventional physical therapy (PT). They concluded that the groups receiving EMG feed-back improved more rapidly in the area of motor power, gait, transfer-ring themselves from lying to sitting to standing positions, and general well-being than those with conventional PT. In addition, they found that those patients with lacunar infarcts showed generally more satis-factory improvement than those with stroke involving the middle cere-bral artery territory. (This is one of the few studies that point out the importance of noting the specific CNS lesion in relation to the treat-ment programs). Brudny et al. (1976) tabulated the effects of feedback treatment on 45 cases of hemiplegia; 39 of their patients were treated for paralysis of the arm; three months to three years later, 20 of them had retained significant functional gains.

Many of these studies are difficult to evaluate. The neurologic status of the patients treated is not always clearly reported: Were the patients hemiplegic or hemiparetic? Were the symptoms treated flaccidity, spasticity, or clonus? Were the EMG feedback techniques designed for the inhibition of spasticity, for the recruitment of motor unit activity, or for general relaxation? What was the pathology? In particular, were there associated defects in sensation, memory, cognition, speech or visual function? It is obviously important to differentiate between con-tributions to treatment outcome due to nonspecific factors and those due to specific EMG feedback information.

Biofeedback Treatment in Cerebral Palsy

In addition to EMG feedback techniques, other feedback techniques are used in treating patients with cerebral palsy (CP), for example the Joint Position Trainer. Halpern et al. (1970) used a mechanical head support on 14 CP patients from the ages of three to 12, noting im-provement in head control in most of the children. Harrison and Connolly (1971) studied four CP patients, aged 18 to 25, with this technique, and noted improvement.

At least a dozen other studies have used feedback in the treatment of CP in both adults and children. Several studies document specific feedback effects (Bird et al., 1977; Spearing and Poppen, 1974; Wool-dridge, Leiper, and Ogsten, 1976). Other studies (Finley et al., 1977) demonstrated reversal of gains upon stopping training and reinstitu-tion of gains when training was resumed. The major problem seems to be the "carry-over" beyond the training. There may be lack of continuation of control once the young patient leaves the experimen-tal session (Wolpert and Wooldridge, 1975; Wooldridge and Russel,

1976). With children, it is usually necessary to combine the feedback procedures with the use of more overt reinforcers. Children may be less likely than adults to practice incorporating their newly acquired control into their everyday life, unless supervised and encouraged to do so.

Harris et al. (1974) developed sensory aids to improve kinesthetic monitoring of the head and limbs. Eighteen athetoid CP children (ages seven to 18 years) were studied. They were treated over a period of two to 12 months, with sessions of 30 minutes of therapy using mainly two devices, namely the limb position monitor and the head control device, which both used visual and auditory feedback. The children improved their postural stability and gained control over voluntary movements. Other reports on the use of the device at several centers in Ontario note similar effects (Walter Johnson, personal communication to Basmajian).

Brudny et al. (1976) used EMG feedback on two patients following tendon transfers, observing that recovery "seemed to be facilitated."

Mechanical Feedback Devices

Force, Position, and Joint Angle Detectors

A number of feedback devices provide information on body movements rather than on muscle contractions. The question as to whether these devices help train movements (assuming the acquisition of control of the individual muscle) rather than training the individual muscles remains unanswered. Studies of feedback in cerebral palsy included use of head position monitors (Wooldridge et al., 1976) and contact switches signaling foot placement (Spearing and Poppen, 1974). One study (Baker et al., 1977) included the use of a joint angle detector as part of a program to train wrist extension in adult hemiplegic patients.

Several studies involve the use of limb load monitors (Moore and Byers, 1976). The clinical objective may be either increasing the percent of body weight put on a limb or decreasing it. Two studies of normal human subjects report success in limiting the percentage of body weight placed on the lower limb when walking. Craik and Wann-stedt (1975) describe improvement in ability to keep weight load within prescribed limits, or to increase loading for patients with orthopedic and neurological conditions. Twelve long-term hemiplegic patients were trained in symmetrical standing. Seven of these twelve made gains. Wannstedt and Herman (1977) studied ambulant hemiplegic subjects. They found that patients with (1) damage to the right hemisphere (left hemiparesis), (2) considerable asymmetry in motor power, and (3) poor immediate response to feedback did not improve even with prolonged training. The degree of neurological improvement was related to the laterality of the lesions and the response to the initial training trial.

Other Aspects of Motor Function

Rigidity is seen in extrapyramidal disorders, the most common disorder being *Parkinson's disease*. In this condition, there is an increase in tone in all muscle groups, the agonists as well as the antagonists. There is also a variable degree of rhythmic tremor present at a rate of approximately five per second. This tremor is present at rest, and is inhibited by action. In addition there is, (1) difficulty in initiating a movement, and, (2) disturbance of balance with a tendency to fall forwards (propulsion) or backwards (retropulsion).

Netsell and Cleeland (1973) reported improvement in lip control in a 64-year-old patient with Parkinson's disease, where they reduced the lip hypertonicity with EMG-biofeedback. Nusselt and Legewie (1975) trained two Parkinson's patients to reduce hand tremors.

Cog-wheel rigidity in extrapyramidal disorder is due to the combination of rigidity and tremor. Here the resistance to passive movement is waxing and waning with the phases of contraction and relaxation of the muscle produced by the tremor. It is characteristically seen in Parkinson's disease, and is a side effect of certain neurotropic drugs, especially the "low-dose, high-potency" antipsychotic preparations such as haloperidol (Haldol).

In *Wilson's disease* (hepatolenticular degeneration), there are both involuntary movements, mainly choreiform, and rigidity in distribution and general character resembling the rigidity of Parkinsonism. The disease occurs in early life, due to an autosomal recessive gene, and is characterized by a disorder of copper metabolism.

In *plastic rigidity*, the lengthening reaction affects one motor unit after another from the beginning of stretch, so that resistance to stretch remains approximately constant. This type of plastic rigidity is seen in some cases of normal pressure hydrocephalus (nonobstructive hydrocephalus) and in cases in which both frontal lobes are pathologically involved.

Involuntary Movements or Dyskinesias

The involuntary movement or dyskinesias may be congenital or acquired. *Congenital* involuntary movements may occur in cases of cerebral birth injury, associated with various degrees of paralysis with cerebral palsy. These movements include chorea, athetosis, or mixtures of the two.

Acquired involuntary movements include *spasmodic torticollis* which is usually described as a type of dyskinesia (for treatment with biofeedback, see below). *Tardive dyskinesias,* which follow Phenothiazine or other neuroleptic* (antipsychotic) medication prescribed for thought disorder, or L-dopa, a medication often used in Parkinson's disease. Treatment of tardive dyskinesia induced by medication with major tranquilizers has been attempted with a variety of drugs including choline, lecithin, lioresal, and reserpine. The results to date remain equivocal (Lishman, 1978).

Blepharospasm is a prolonged spasm of the orbicularis oculi muscle surrounding the orbit resulting in prolonged squinting or actual shutting of the eyelids thus decreasing vision of that eye. It is usually seen in elderly women; and the movements may be bilateral. The involuntary clonic and tonic spasms of the eyelids and surrounding muscles can result in eye closure, facial spasms, and progressive inability to perform activities requiring sight. Ballard, Doerr and Varni (1972) trained a patient with the disorder using both auditory biofeedback of electro-ocular graph eye blink potentials and a conditioned avoidance method using shock as the avoidance stimulus. The patient acquired progressive voluntary control using biofeedback techniques and was reported free of blepharospasm at a 9-month follow-up.

Stephenson (1976) treated a 50-year-old man who had had blepharospasm and facial spasm for two years. He received ten training sessions of 30 minutes deep muscle relaxation, followed by 30 minute EMG biofeedback sessions from the forearm for two sessions and from the frontalis for 50 sessions to achieve generalized relaxation. Toward the end of his biofeedback training, it was reported that the patient had lost the blepharospasm and the facial spasms and was able to return to work. At six-months follow up, the patient was well and had not had any return of spasms. A personal case was cured in 6 sessions.

Clonic facial spasm, also known as *hemifacial spasm*, usually begins in the orbicularis oculi and then spreads very slowly to the muscles of the

*A neuroleptic drug is one which may cause neurological disorder, mainly extrapyramidal motor effects, a Parkinson-like syndrome.

lower part of the face, especially the retractors of the angle of the mouth. Finally strong spasms may involve all the facial muscles on one side almost continuously.

Habit spasm is a brief compulsive movement usually seen in children and young adults. When the face is the site of habit spasm, the movements are bilateral.

Bruxism denotes periodic grinding of the teeth and clenching of the jaw, and is caused by spasm of the jaw muscles chiefly the masseters; it is frequently secondary to tension.

Multiple tics is a distressing but fortunately rare condition described by Gilles de la Tourette in 1885. The syndrome that bears his name usually starts between the ages of five and eight as a simple tic. The tics may be defined as "sudden, quick, involuntary, and frequently repeated movements of circumscribed groups of muscles, serving no apparent purpose" (Kanner, 1957). Vocalization occurs, such as explosive grunts, barks or coughing noises which accompany the motor movements. Coprololia is frequent. Therapeutic approaches utilizing behavior modification have been reported for the multiple tics associated with Gilles de la Tourette's disease although neuroleptic administration of haloperidol (Haldol) is usually the treatment of choice. Thomas, Abrams, and Johnson (1971) used a self-monitoring procedure to treat a patient suffering from Gilles de la Tourette syndrome, and found that the patient had apparently underestimated the frequency of the tics. It may be possible to modify such a treatment technique so as to give the patient accurate feedback about the level of tic activity, and in time this might improve the patient's self-observation. More research is required in this difficult disorder which is often refractory to treatment.

Biofeedback Treatment of Dyskinesias

Torticollis. Of all the conditions with acquired involuntary movements, *spasmodic torticollis* ("wry neck") is the one for which there is probably the best documented treatment with biofeedback. Numerous reports have indicated the efficacy of biofeedback training in this distressing syndrome. While the etiology remains obscure, many authors have emphasized that it is (or represents) a form of organic extrapyramidal disorder (Podivinsky, 1968). It is generally considered, however, to have a strong psychophysiologic ("functional") component. Treatments have ranged from the use of a variety of drugs including the phenothiazines and antihistamines, to surgery (with rhizotomy, or peripheral nerve sectioning) and psychotherapy. At times, the condition is so distressing that psychosurgery has been employed.

Agras and Marshall (1965) reported successfully treating one of two torticollis patients with a "massed negative practice technique." Meares (1973) used a combination of relaxation training and systematic desensitization with improvement in a single case.

Bernhardt, Herson and Barlow (1972) systematically compared the effects of instruction alone, negative feedback without instruction, and negative feedback with instruction. Negative feedback with or without instructions was considerably more effective than instructions alone in the reduction of torticollis. The negative feedback consisted of illumination of a light controlled by an observer whenever torticollis movements were evident. The clinical outcome at follow-up was not, however, noted.

EMG biofeedback has been reported in a number of studies. Russ (1975) used variable click-and-pitch auditory feedback from the frontalis muscle with EMG training for three sessions in one case, and EMG biofeedback to decrease firing in the dominant sternocleidomastoid muscle for 13 sessions in another. The patient's symptoms were alleviated by the 15th session and had not reappeared at an eight-month follow-up.

Brierley (1967) in two cases, reported successful long-term alleviations of symptoms using a shock-avoidance procedure; wrist shock was paired with head position deviations. Cleeland (1973) reported the effects of EMG feedback and contingent electrical cutaneous shock studied in 10 patients with involuntary spasmodic activity of the muscles of the neck (nine with torticollis and one with retrocollis), with follow-up for 14 months. The combination of shock and feedback was associated with reduced spasm frequency in the laboratory in eight of the 10 patients, and sessions using these conditions were of therapeutic benefit in six of the 10 patients. It is suggested that the combination of cutaneous shock treatment and auditory feedback was more effective than either alone.

Cleeland (1979) greatly expanded on his theories and increased his clinical material following his initial paper. He reported the results of treatment in 52 patients who were followed for a mean time of 30 months. Of these patients, 11 showed minimal or no improvement, 18 showed moderate improvement, and eight were described as markedly improved. Fifteen patients were lost to follow-up.

Brudny et al. (1976) reported treatment results in 48 torticollis patients. The goal of this approach was to teach relaxation and simultaneously to increase the muscle strength of the atrophied muscles of the neck. Of the 48 patients trained in this method, 26 showed improvement. Follow-up report showed some regression, but the authors still achieved an approximate 40 percent success rate in patients who had had the condition for periods ranging from three months to many years.

Fernando (1976) reported treatment of 10 patients with torticollis, and since then results with an additional 15 patients have been added. The protocol used was a combination of EMG feedback, psychological evaluation and counseling, and Jacobson's relaxation exercises, which showed a success rate of 20 to 30 percent in alleviation of symptoms. Graffman et al. (1978) (personal communication to Fernando, 1978) also treated spasmodic torticollis with generally satisfactory results, using EMG feedback, and psychotherapy where indicated. Jankel (1978a) using an adaptation of a technique initially described by Booker, Rubow, and Coleman (1969) first trained a patient to match the activity of the two sternocleidomastoid muscles, and then provided feedback contingent upon both muscles producing the appropriate posture. The patient was treated with 20 sessions (lasting 40 minutes each) of EMG biofeedback to modify the EMG levels so that the sternocleidomastoid on the contracted side would more closely reflect the activity of the muscles on the opposite side. This was reported as leading to some clinical relief. In a second phase of the study, the patient was trained with an analogue tone for modification of muscle tension on both sternocleidomastoids in tandem, and his improvement continued.

Other authors (e.g., Brudny et al., 1973; Brudny et al., 1974; Korein and Brudny, 1976; Korein et al., 1976) have reported comprehensive work with a total of 114 torticollis and dystonia patients using sensory feedback therapy. The feedback in these cases consisted of simultaneous visual display of sternocleidomastoid muscle activity on an oscilloscope plus a variety of auditory feedback modalities. The therapy portion consisted of three to five sessions per week each of 45-minute duration: 56 percent of the torticollis patients in this cohort showed significant improvement; 40 percent of the patients maintained improvement over a 3-month followup. Similar improvement was noted in the dystonic patients.

A unique approach to torticollis treatment was developed by Williams (1975) who used feedback of heart rate to train a female patient in relaxation techniques. The patient apparently averaged a substantial slowing of the heart rate after five sessions of such training and a positive correlation was found between the heart rate and EMG measurement of the sternocleidomastoid muscle tension with "significant" clinical improvement noted. It appears, however, that the use of EMG feedback of sternocleidomastoid contraction is the treatment of choice in torticollis.

Brudny and his associates have comprehensively studied over 100 torticollis patients using sensory feedback. Therapy consisted of EMG feedback from the sternocleidomastoid muscles which was presented in both a visual and auditory feedback format. According to their results, 40 percent of the patients maintained improvement at a three-month follow-up (Fotopoulos and Sunderland, 1978).

In addition, the utilization of electroshock treatment which is contingent on muscle spasm activity as measured by the EMG technique developed by Cleeland (1973) would also appear to hold promise for patients who could not benefit from just using EMG activity alone. As Fotopoulos and Sunderland (1978) point out in their comprehensive review, however, there is to date a lack of adequate experimental research to determine the specific factors which result in effective treatment of this disorder.

Tic Syndromes. Individual case studies have been reported in the literature in which a number of behavioral approaches have been used as treatment. Yates (1958) successfully used massed practice training to treat tic. Clark (1963) and Rafi (1962) have used systematic desensitization and negative feedback respectively, with good clinical results.

An operant approach to treatment of tic was developed by Barrett (1962) in which muscle spasms of a patient who had been suffering from multiple tics for 14 years were recorded by measuring the vibrations caused by the patient while sitting in a specially designed chair. The patient was able to reduce the frequency of his muscle spasms when the interruption of music was provided to him contingent upon the incidence of the tics.

Levee, Cohen, and Rickels (1976) used visual display and biofeedback with a flutist suffering from severe throat tics and constrictions. The patient received biofeedback from either the frontalis, orbicularis oris, infrahyoid, or genioglossus muscles for six sessions. After learning to relax these muscles, he was instructed to use the feedback to relax while practicing the flute for four sessions in an acoustically damped chamber, and for ten sessions outside of it. Complete relief of symptoms was reported at a later follow-up visit.

Writer's Cramp. Several case studies have been reported utilizing EMG feedback in treating writer's cramp (Reavley, 1975).

Stuttering. Before a biofeedback approach to the treatment of stuttering was attempted, it was necessary to demonstrate that conditioning of the muscles of the face, throat, or jaw could be accomplished. Budzynski and Stoyva (1973) tested the efficacy of different types of feedback on the activity of the masseter muscles compared with control subjects with no feedback. After a single 20-minute session, the subjects trained with auditory and digital visual EMG biofeedback showed significantly lower EMG values than did the control groups.

Alexander (1974) used EMG feedback from the site of maximum EMG activity with 13 stutterers. There was a significant reduction in nonfluencies and in the physical activity that often accompanies nonfluent speech and stutterers.

Lanyon et al. (1976) employed visual EMG biofeedback (volt meter display) with eight stutterers. They reported a significant decrease in the number of nonfluent words which the patient used in the laboratory, but the extent of transfer of training outside the laboratory was not clearly noted. In the treatment of stuttering, the choice of biofeedback modalities may be critical.

Miscellaneous Disorders. The diagnosis of miscellaneous cases of dysphagia (difficulty in swallowing), dysphonia (voice disorder), or dysarthria (difficulty in articulation) is often difficult, because of the complexity of the nerve supply (Fig. 8–4) among other reasons. As in all clinical situations, the diagnosis should be firmly established prior to start of treatment with biofeedback.

Laryngeal or masseter EMG biofeedback has been successfully used to extinguish subvocalization (Hardyck, Petrinovich, and Ellsworth, 1966), *throat tics* (Levee, Cohen, and Rickles, 1976), *bruxism* (Dowdell, Clarke, and Kardachi, 1976; Kardachi and Clarke, 1977; Solberg and Rugh, 1972) and *chronic dysphagia* (Haynes, 1976). EMG biofeedback has not been successful in the treatment of dysphonia, however (Henschen and Burton, 1978). In a personal case, one of the authors (AJN) also obtained negative results using EMG feedback and other behavior therapy techniques to treat spasmodic dysphonia in a 52-year-old woman. There are some authors (e.g., Levine, 1979) who argue that dysphonia is an organic, not a psychogenic or functional, disorder.

Lower Motor Neuron Lesions

The cell bodies of the lower motor neurons (alpha neurons) are situated in the motor nuclei of the brain stem and the anterior horns of the grey matter of the spinal cord (see Figs. 2–13, 2–17).

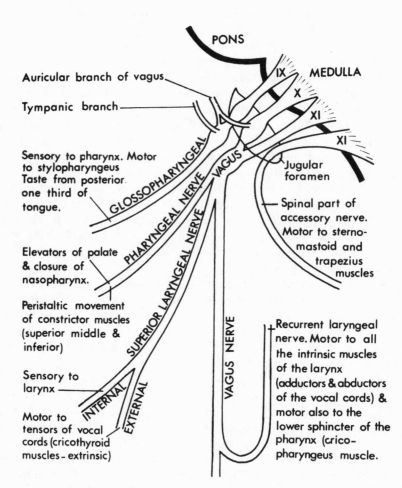

PONS

Auricular branch of vagus

Tympanic branch

IX   MEDULLA

X

XI

XI

Sensory to pharynx. Motor
to stylopharyngeus
Taste from posterior
one third of
tongue.

GLOSSOPHARYNGEAL NERVE

VAGUS

PHARYNGEAL NERVE

Jugular
foramen

Spinal part of
accessory nerve.
Motor to sterno-
mastoid and
trapezius
muscles

Elevators of palate
& closure of
nasopharynx.

SUPERIOR LARYNGEAL

Peristaltic movement
of constrictor muscles
(superior middle &
inferior)

VAGUS NERVE

Recurrent laryngeal
nerve. Motor to all
the intrinsic muscles
of the larynx
(adductors & abductors
of the vocal cords) &
motor also to the
lower sphincter of the
pharynx (crico-
pharyngeus muscle.

Sensory to
larynx

INTERNAL

EXTERNAL

Motor to
tensors of vocal
cords (cricothyroid
muscles - extrinsic)

FIGURE 8-4. THE MOTOR AND SENSORY NERVES SUPPLYING THE
PHARYNX AND LARYNX, EXPLAINING THE VARIOUS
PATTERNS OF PARALYSIS COMMONLY MET WITH.
(REDRAWN FROM AN ORIGINAL DRAWING BY MR.
CHARLES KEOGH.) (Reproduced, with permission, from
Brain's Diseases of the Nervous System. Revised by John
N. Walton, 7th edition, 1969, Oxford University Press,
Oxford, England.)

Symptoms of lesions of the lower motor neuron include:
1. Muscular weakness
2. Muscular wasting

3. Hypotonia (pathologic loss of tone)
4. Diminished or lost tendon stretch reflexes
5. Muscular fasciculation
6. Muscular contractures, in long-term cases
7. Trophic changes
8. Reaction of degeneration
9. Characteristic EMG changes

Muscle weakness involves individual muscles or muscle groups, as opposed to weakness which tends to involve a whole movement, as seen in upper motor neuron lesion. *Muscle wasting* develops after the onset of the causative lesion at a variable rate, according to the pathology of the causative lesion. The degree of *hypotonia* is related to the extent of the musculature involved. *Muscle fasciculation* is particularly prominent as a result of chronic degeneration of the anterior horn cells in progressive muscular atrophy. Spasmodic facial contractions are also seen after incomplete recovery from facial paralysis (Bell's palsy). *Muscle contractures* may occur, for example, in the calf muscles following paralysis of the anterior tibial and peronei muscles in poliomyelitis or Guillain-Barré polyneuropathy. They are also prominent in muscular dystrophy. With *trophic changes*, the affected extremity is cold and cyanosed, the finger and toe nails are brittle, and the bones are smaller and lighter than normal. These changes are probably due to disuse and reflex vascular changes.

Biofeedback Treatment

There are many single case reports in the literature that support the view that EMG feedback techniques could be useful in the management of lower motor neuron lesions. The rehabilitation process can begin as early as when a few motor units are seen. Marinacci and Horande (1960) treated five Bell's palsy patients and a longer series of poliomyelitis patients. Booker, Rubow, and Coleman (1969) had a single case report of the use of EMG feedback with peripheral nerve lesion, and Jankel (1978) reported feedback in Bell's palsy. Case studies were reported with EMG feedback in Guillain-Barré syndrome (Cohen et al., 1977), and in traumatic injury of the hand (Kukulka, Brown, and Basmajian, 1975). Fernando (1976) treated lower motor neuron dysfunction in patients with encouraging results, and Brudny et al. (1976) used EMG feedback in four patients with peripheral nerve injury.

Illustrative Cases

EMG biofeedback can be used to restore motor functioning in cases where there has been impairment due to loss of muscle tissue following surgical procedures. Nigl (1979) reported a case study with EMG training to improve oral cavity functioning in a patient four years after radical surgery to remove a bilateral mucosal skin cancer of the oral cavity. The second case illustrates treatment of neuropathy.

The patient was referred for biofeedback training by her physician because she was unable to masticate and she was still forced to be on a totally liquified diet. This 62-year-old white female had had her teeth extracted and upper and lower gums reconstructed from skin grafts during plastic surgery. In addition, her tongue was sutured down midway limiting its mobility when feeding. During the initial EMG session, the patient was only able to produce 1.34 μv of activity when asked to make chewing movements as if she were eating.

With EMG biofeedback of the masseter muscle the patient significantly increased the level of muscular activity in the oral cavity region and was eventually able to eat semi-solid food. She gradually increased the consistency of her food with coarser grinding setting on her blender. After the last treatment she showed 90% more voluntary muscle activity than during the initial baseline session. She ate more frequent nonliquified meals daily and she reduced the amount of time taken to eat an average size meal. During the last week of treatment, over 92 percent of her meals contained solid or semi-solid foods, and only 8 percent were totally liquified. In addition, her emotional state changed from a state of depression to one of increased self-confidence. As an incidental finding, it was noted that she regained the ability to use her lower lip, which she had not done prior to treatment, reporting it to have "no feeling."

In summary this case indicates that EMG training can be useful in the rehabilitation for mastication of cancer patients who have undergone radical surgery in the oral cavity.

A 29-year-old white female underwent gastric stapling for morbid obesity (weight: 255). Following surgery she developed cardiogenic shock which resulted in severe generalized edema. On recovery, bilateral flaccid paralysis of the quadriceps and the other muscles supplied by the femoral nerves was noted. *Femoral nerve entrapment neuropathy* at the inguinal ligament was confirmed by EMG and nerve conduction velocity studies. The patient was unable to extend either knee for a period of three to four weeks. At that stage, EMG biofeedback treatment was started daily five times a week. Within five weeks, the patient was able to walk with back splints and a month later she was walking unaided. This uncontrolled case may illustrate only the natural history of a compression neuropathy. However, the daily monitoring and the feedback information which provided the patient the "feel" of how to contract her muscles clearly acted as incentive and encouragement to the patient, and facilitated her recovery. Meantime she reduced her weight to 155 pounds.

Spinal Cord Injuries

The prognosis depends upon the site (level) of the lesion in the spinal cord (Fig. 8–5). Biofeedback treatment in a few case reports was noted to be of benefit in the treatment of spinal cord injuries (Dunn, Davis, and Webster, 1978). Four reports (Fernando, 1976; Schneider et al., 1975, Seymour and Bassler, 1977; Toomin, 1976) have described single case studies. Although these patients with spinal cord lesions were receiving other treatment, the authors concluded that the biofeedback techniques had helped the patients and the therapists to locate the target muscles which were all below a "trace" of function.

Brudny et al. (1974) reported on two quadriplegic patients with lesions at the C5 and C6 levels. Both patients improved with EMG feedback, and one even gained the ability to resume activities of daily living, to type, and to drive an electric wheelchair over the subsequent two years.

Visceral and Respiratory Responses with Spinal Cord Injuries

Three studies reported the use of biofeedback in modifying visual and respiratory responses in spinal cord injury patients. Brucker and Ince (1977) reported amelioration of postural hypotension; with biofeedback training the blood pressure increased in one subject. Cheshire and Flack (1977) reported improvements in vital capacity with clinical use of a respiratory monitor during breathing exercises in quadriplegic persons. Szymke and Price (1976) reported using an air cystometrogram to provide feedback on bladder pressure in individuals with neurogenic bladders.

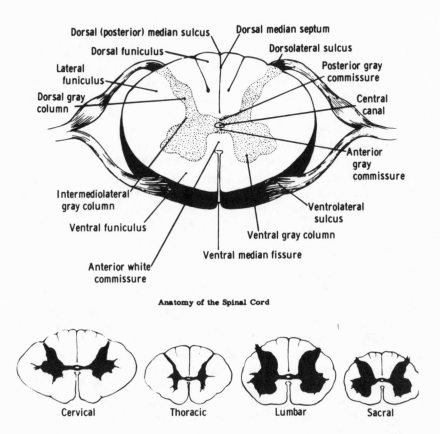

Anatomy of the Spinal Cord

FIGURE 8-5.   (ABOVE) ANATOMY OF THE SPINAL CORD. (BELOW)
               TRANSVERSE SECTIONS OF THE SPINAL CORD AT VARI-
               OUS LEVELS. (Reproduced, with permission, from Chu-
               sid JG: Correlative Neuroanatomy & Functional
               Neurology, 17th ed. Copyright 1979 by Lange Medical
               Publications, Los Altos, California.)

Associated Symptoms of Disorders of Motor Function

In all disorders of motor function, treatment is easier when the
condition is "pure," or in other words an isolated disturbance of motor
function. In many cases, however, particularly in brain disease, motor
disability is associated with defects in perception, memory, cognition,
speech or visual function.

In spinal cord lesions, although the above deficits are not usually
present, there is an associated loss of bladder and bowel control and

of sexual functions. Obviously these additional neurological problems complicate the situation, which therefore requires an even more careful and detailed evaluation.

DeWitt and Palacious (1977) and Fernando (1976) have reported case studies where biofeedback training was useful in conversion reaction involving motor disability.

Summary

It can be seen that biofeedback offers possibilities for treatment in many diverse types of motor system disorders. These include loss of function following upper or lower motor neuron lesions and movement disorders. Systematic, rigorous, and appropriately designed investigations are required, with quantification, uniform procedures, careful determination of suitable patients, and adequate theoretical framework. It is likely that EMG feedback techniques will add to, but not replace, the array of existing clinical tools in treating central and peripheral nervous system disorders.

REFERENCES

Agras S, Marshall C: The application of negative practice to spasmodic torticollis. Am J Psychiatr 112: 579, 1965.

Andrews JM: Neuromuscular re-education of the hemiplegic with the aid of the electromyograph. Arch Phys Med Rehabil 45: 530, 1964.

Baker M, Regenos E, Wolf SL, Basmajian JV: Developing strategies for biofeedback: Applications in neurologically handicapped patients. Phys Ther 57: 402, 1977.

Ballard P, Doerr H, Varni J: Arrest of a disabling eye disorder using biofeedback. Psychophysiology 9: 271, 1972.

Barrett BH: Reduction in rate of multiple tics by free operant conditioning. J Nerv Ment Dis 135: 187, 1962.

Basmajian JV: Control and training of individual motor units. Science 141: 440, 1963.

Basmajian JV: Control of individual motor units. Am J Phys Med 46: 480, 1967.

Basmajian JV: Electromyography comes of age. Science 197: 603, 1972.

Basmajian JV, Samson J: Standarization of methods in single motor unit training. Am J Phys Med 52: 250, 1973.

Basmajian JV, Simard TG: Effects of distracting movements on the control of trained motor units. Am J Phys Med 46: 1427, 1967.

Basmajian JV, Baker MP, and Regenos ER: Rehabilitation stroke patients with biofeedback. Geriatrics 32: 85, 1977.

Basmajian JV, Kukulka CG, Narayan MG, Takebe K: Biofeedback treatment of foot-drop after stroke compared with standard rehabilitation technique: Effects on voluntary control and strength. Arch Phys Med Rehabil 56: 231, 1975.

Bernhardt AJ, Herson M, Barlow DH: Measurement and modification of spasmodic torticollis: An experimental analysis. Behav Ther 3: 294, 1972.

Bird B, Cataldo MF, Cunningham D: Single-subject experimental analysis of EMG biofeedback effects in treatment of cerebral palsied children. Proceedings of the Biofeedback Society of America 8th Annual Meeting, 1977.

Booker HE, Rubow RT, Coleman FJ: Simplified feedback in neuromuscular retraining: An automated approach using electromyographic signals. Arch Phys Med Rehabil 50: 621, 1969.

Brierley H: The treatment of hysterical spasmodic torticollis by behavior therapy. Behav Res Ther 5: 139, 1967.

Brucker BS, Ince LP: Biofeedback as an experimental treatment for postural hypotension in a patient with a spinal cord lesion. Arch Phys Med Rehabil 58: 49, 1977.

Brudny J, Grynbaum BB, Korein J: New therapeutic modality for treatment of spasmodic torticollis. Arch Phys Med Rehabil 54: 575, 1973.

Brudny J, Grynbaum BB, Korein J: Spasmodic torticollis: Treatment by feedback display of the EMG. Arch Phys Med Rehabil 55: 403, 1974.

Brudny J, Korein J, Grynbaum BB, et al.; EMG feedback therapy: Review of treatment of 114 patients. Arch Phys Med Rehabil 57: 55, 1976.

Brudny J, Korein J, Levidow L, et al.: Sensory feedback therapy as a modality of treatment in central nervous system disorders of voluntary movement. Neurology 24: 925, 1974.

Brunnstrom S: Movement Therapy in Hemiplegia. New York, Harper and Row, 1970, p. 34.

Budzynski TH, Stoyva J: An electromyographic feedback technique for teaching voluntary relaxation of the masseter muscle. J Dent Res 52: 116, 1973.

Cheshire DJE, Flack WJ: Operant conditioning techniques in the respiratory rehabilitation of tetraplegic patients. Arch Phys Med Rehabil 58: 532, 1977.

Clark DF: The treatment of hysterical spasm and agoraphobia by behaviour therapy. Behav Res Ther 1: 245, 1963.

Cleeland CS: Behavioral techniques in the modification of spasmodic torticollis. Neurology, 23: 1241, 1973.

Cleeland CS: Biofeedback and other behavioral techniques in the treatment of disorders of voluntary movement, in Basmajian JV (ed): Biofeedback: Principles and Practice for Clinicians. Baltimore, Williams and Wilkins, 1979.

Cohen BA, Crouch RH, Thompson SN: EMG biofeedback as a therapeutic adjunct in Guillain-Barré syndrome. Arch Phys Med Rehab 58(12): 582, 1977.

Craik R, Wannstedt G: The limb load monitor: An augmented sensory feedback device. proc Conference Devices Disabled, 1975, p. 19.

Daube JR, Sandok BA: Medical Neurosciences. Boston, Little, Brown, 1978.

DeWitt DJ, Palacious M: A treatment approach involving EMG feedback of motor disability resulting from conversion reaction. Proceedings of the Biofeedback Society of America 8th Annual Meeting, 1977.

Dowdell LR, Clarke NG, Kardachi BJ: Biofeedback: Control of masticatory muscle spasm. Med Biol Eng 14: 295, 1976.

Dunn M, Davis J, Webster T: Voluntary control of muscle spasticity with EMG biofeedback in three spinal cord injured quadriplegics. Proceedings of the Biofeedback Society of America 9th Annual Meeting, 1978.

Fernando CK: Audio-visual neuromuscular disorders. Proceedings of the Biofeedback Society of America 7th Annual Meeting, 1976.

Finley WW, Niman CA, Standley J, Wansley RA: Electrophysiologic behavior modification of frontal EMG in cerebral palsied children. Biofeedback Self-Regul 2: 59, 1977.

Fischer-Williams M, Telerman-Toppet N, Meyer JS: Clinico-EEG correlation with arterial and jugular venous biochemical studies in acute neurological disorder. Brain Part II 87: 281, 1964.

Fotopoulos SS, Sunderland WP: Biofeedback in the treatment of psychophysiologic disorders. Biofeedback Self-Regul 3(4): 331, 1978.

Halpern D, Kottke FJ, Burrill C, et al.: Training of control of head posture in children with cerebral palsy. Dev Med Child Neurol 12: 290, 1970.

Hardyck CD, Petrinovich LF, Ellsworth DW: Feedback of speech muscle activity during silent reading: rapid extinction. Science 154: 1467, 1966.

Harris F, Spelman F, Hymer J: Electronic sensory aids as treatment for cerebral palsied children. Part II. Physical Therapy: 54: 354, 1974.

Harrison A, Connolly K: The conscious control of neuromuscular firing in spastic and normal subject. Dev Med Child Neurol 13: 762, 1971.

Harrison VF, Mortenson OA: Identification and voluntary control of single motor unit activity in the tibialis anterior muscle. Anat Rec 144: 109, 1962.

Haynes, SN: Electromyographic biofeedback treatment of a woman with chronic dysphagia. Biofeedback Self-Regul 1: 121, 1976.

Henscher TL, Burton NG: Treatment of spastic dysphonia by EMG feedback. Biofeedback Self-Regul 3(1): 91, 1978.

Herman R: Augmented sensory feedback in the control of limb movement, in Fields W (ed): *Neural organization and its relevance to prosthetics.* Miami, Symposia Specialists, 1973, p. 197.

Jankel WR: a) EMG feedback in spasmodic torticollis. Proceedings of the Biofeedback Society of America 9th Annual Meeting, 1978.

Jankel WR: b) Bell's palsy: Muscle re-education by EMG feedback. Arch Phys Med Rehabil 59: 240, 1978.

Johnson CP: Analysis of five tests commonly used in determining the ability to control single motor units. Am J Phys Med 55: 113, 1976.

Johnson HE, Garton WH: Muscle re-education in hemiplegia by use of electromyographic device. Arch Phys Med Rehabil 54: 320, 1973.

Kanner L: Infantile autism, in *Child psychiatry.* Kanner (ed). Springfield, Ill., Thomas, 1957.

Kardachi BJ, Clarke NG: The use of biofeedback to control bruxism. J Peridontol 48: 639, 1977.

Katkin ES, Murray EN: Instrumental conditioning of autonomically mediated behavior: Theoretical and methodological issues. Psychol Bull 70: 52, 1968.

Kimmel HD: Instrumental conditioning of autonomically mediated behavior. Psychol Bull 67: 337, 1967.

Kleinman KM, Keister M, Riggin C, Goldman H, Korol O: Use of EMG feedback to inhibit flexor spasticity and increase active extension in stroke patients. Proceedings Psychophysiological Research Society Meeting, 1975.

Korein J, Brudny J, Grynbaum B, et al.: Sensory feedback therapy of spasmodic torticollis and dystonia: Results in treatment of 55 patients. Adv Neurol 14: 275, 1976.

Korein J, Brudny J: Integrated EMG feedback in the management of spasmodic torticollis and focal dystonia: a prospective study of 80 patients, in Yahr M (ed): *The Basal Ganglia.* New York, Raven Press, 1976, p. 385.

Kukulka CG, Brown DM, Basmajian JV: A preliminary report on biofeedback training for early finger joint mobilization. Am J Occup Ther 29: 469, 1975.

Lanyon RI, Barrington CC, Newman AC: Modification of stuttering through EMG biofeedback. Behav Ther 7: 96, 1976.

Lee KH, Hill E, Johnston R, Smiehorowski T: Myofeedback for muscle retraining in hemiplegic patients. Arch Phys Med Rehabil 57: 588, 1976.

Levee JR, Cohen MJ, Rickles WH: Electromyographic biofeedback for relief of tension in the facial and throat muscles of a woodwind musician. Biofeedback Self-Regul 1: 113, 1976.

Levine HL, Wood BG, Batza E, Rusnov M, Tucker HM: Recurrent laryngeal nerve section for spasmodic dysphonia. Ann Otol Rhinol Laryngol 88: 527, 1979.

Lishman WA: Organic Psychiatry. Oxford, Blackwell Scientific Publications, 1978, p. 783.

Lloyd AJ, Shurley TJ: The effects of sensory perceptual isolation on single motor unit conditioning. Psychophysiology 13: 340, 1976.

Marinacci AA: Applied Electromyography. Philadelphia, Lea and Febiger, 1968.

Marinacci AA, Horande M: Electromyogram in neuromuscular re-education. Bull Los Angeles Neurol Soc 25: 57, 1960.

Meares RA: Behavior therapy and spasmodic torticollis. Arch Gen Psychiatr 28: 104, 1973.

Middaugh S: Comparison of voluntary muscle contractions with and without EMG feedback in persons with neuromuscular dysfunction. Proceedings Psychophysiological Research Society Annual Meeting, 1977.

Middaugh S: EMG feedback as muscle re-education technique: a controlled study. Phys Ther 58: 15, 1978.

Mims WH: Electromyography in clinical practice. South Med J 49: 804, 1956.

Moore AJ, Byers JL: A miniaturized load cell for lower extremity amputees. Arch Phys Med Rehabil 57: 294, 1976.

Netsell R, Cleeland CS: Modification of lip hypertonia in dysarthria using EMG feedback. J. Speech Hear Disord 38: 131, 1973.

Nigl A: Electromyograph training to increase oral cavity functioning in a post-operative cancer patient. Behav Ther 10: 423, 1979.

Nusselt L, Legewie H: Biofeedback and systematische Desensibisierung bei Parkinson-Tremor: Eine Fallstudie. Z Klin Psychol 4: 112, 1975.

Podivinsky F: Torticollis, in Vinken PJ, Bruyn GW: Handbook of Neurology, vol 6, 1968, p. 567.

Rafi AA: Learning theory and the treatment of tics. J Psychosomatic Res 6: 71, 1962.

Reavley W: The use of biofeedback in the treatment of writer's cramp. J Behav. Therapy Exp Psych 6: 335, 1975.

Russ KL.: EMG biofeedback of spasmodic torticollis: a case study. Proceedings Biofeedback Society of America 6th Annual Meeting, 1975.

Sachs DA, Mayhall G: Behavioral control of spasms using aversive conditioning with cerebral palsied adult. J Nerv Ment Dis 152: 362, 1971.

Santee JK, Riggin CS, Kleinman KM, Keister ME: Use of EMG feedback and monetary incentives to increase foot dorsiflexion in stroke patients. Proceedings Psychophysiological Research Society Annual Meeting, 1976.

Schneider C, Scaer R, Groenewald PT, and Atkinson H: EMG techniques in neuromuscular rehabilitation with cord injured patients. Proceedings of the Biofeedback Society of America 6th Annual Meeting, 1975.

Seymour RJ, Bassler CR: Electromyographic biofeedback in treatment of incomplete paraplegia. Phys Ther 57: 1148, 1977.

Shahani BT, Connors L, Mohr JP: Electromyographic audio-visual feedback training effect on the motor performance in patients with lesions of the central nervous system. Arch Phys Med Rehabil 58: 519, 1977.

Sherrington C: *The Integrative Action of the Nervous System.* Cambridge University Press, 1947.

Simard TG: Fine sensorimotor control in healthy children: an electromyographic study. Pediatrics 43: 1035, 1969.

Smith KU, Henry JP: Cybernetic foundations for rehabilitation. Am J Phys Med 46: 379, 1967.

Solberg WK, Rugh JD: The use of biofeedback devices in the treatment of bruxism. J Dent Assoc 40: 852, 1972.

Spearing DL, Poppen R: The use of feedback in the reduction of foot dragging in a cerebral palsied client. J Nerv Ment Dis 159: 148, 1974.

Stephenson NL: Successful treatment of blepharospasm with relaxation and biofeedback. Biofeedback Self-Regul 1: 331, 1976.

Szymke TE, Price M: Use of the air cystometrogram as training aid in a new method of trial off catheter. Arch Phys Med Rehabil 57: 252, 1976.

Thomas EJ, Abrams KS, Johnson JB: Self-monitoring and reciprocal inhibition in the modification of multiple tics of Gilles de la Tourette syndrome. J Behav Ther Exper Psychiatry 2: 159, 1971.

Toomin MK:EMG and GSR feedback in psychotherapy. Biofeedback Self-Regul 1: 361, 1976.

Wannstedt G, Herman R: Use of auditory feedback to achieve symmetrical standing. Proc Amer Phys Ther Assoc 53rd Annu Meet. 1977.

Williams RB: Heart rate feedback in treatment of torticollis. Psychophysiology 12: 237, 1975.

Wolpert R, Wooldridge CP: The use of electromyography as biofeedback therapy in the management of cerebral palsy: a review and case study. Physiotherapy 27: 5, 1975.

Wooldridge CP, Leiper C, Ogsten DG: Biofeedback training of knee joint position of the cerebral palsied child. Physiotherapy 28, 1976.

Wooldridge CP, Russell G: Head positioning training with the cerebral palsied child: An application of biofeedback techniques. Arch Phys Med Rehabil 57: 407, 1976.

Yates AJ: The application of learning theory to the treatment of tics. J Abnorm Soc Psychol 56: 175, 1958.

9

Disorders of Sleep

SLEEP is the great preserver and restorer of body and mind function. Good quality sleep contributes to clarity of thought and well-balanced muscle tone.

The known causes of excess sleep (hypersomnia) and too little sleep (hyposomnia) will first be discussed. The neurophysiological mechanisms of sleep, the EEG and behavioral stages in sleep, the theories of sleep, and the effect of drugs on sleep will next be addressed. The evidence for the anatomical relationship of the hypothalamus to normal sleep and to disorders of sleep will be reviewed. Finally, the effect of the sleep-wake cycle on epilepsy will be analyzed.

Hypersomnia

This is due to a wide variety of causes (Table 9–1). These include withdrawal due to depression and anxiety, and oversedation with many types of drugs, including alcohol, barbiturates, and benzodiazepines, e.g., Valium. An important neurological cause of hypersomnia is increased intracranial pressure. Less frequently, narcolepsy or pathological napping may occur. Various other hypothalamic syndromes need to be considered, including the rare Kleine-Levin syndrome. The so-called Pickwickian syndrome of hypersomnia, with obesity and respiratory insufficiency amounting at times to apnea has recently attracted attention, mainly because of documentation with all-night EEG recordings in laboratories designed for the study of sleep. Encephalitis lethargica is a rare disease causing reversal of sleep rhythms, such that the patient sleeps by day and is restless at night. African trypanosomiasis (sleeping sickness) results in pathological sleep as well.

Hyposomnia or Insomnia

This has to be differentiated into (1) difficulty in falling asleep; (2) poor quality of sleep; (3) early awakening (Table 9–2). The causes of insomnia (hyposomnia) are even more varied than the causes of hyper-

254

TABLE 9-1. CAUSES OF HYPERSOMNIA

Depression and withdrawal	Hypothalamic syndromes
Oversedation with drugs, commonly alcohol, barbiturates, or benzodiazepines (e.g., Valium)	Narcolepsy
	Pathological napping
	Kleine-Levin syndrome
Increased intracranial pressure	Pickwickian syndrome: hypersomnia
Encephalitis lethargica	with obesity and respiratory insuffi-
African trypanosomiasis (sleeping sickness)	ciency

somnia, and systematic differentiation is required before any logical treatment can be suggested. *Sleep may be disturbed by physical pain,* and the most common causes include peptic ulcer or other gastrointestinal disease; nerve compression; bone disease with osteoporosis, osteomalacia, or bone tumor; and muscle spasm.

Sleep Disturbance May Be of Metabolic Origin. This is usually associated with cerebral anoxia, and the most common causes include: (1) low-output cardiac failure; (2) bronchial or cardiac asthma; (3) paralysis or paresis of the muscles of respiration, such as in poliomyelitis, Guillain-Barré polyradiculoneuropathy, transverse myelitis, certain types of muscular dystrophy, and injury to the cervical or upper thoracic spinal cord. All these result in hypoxia and in retention of carbon dioxide. Other metabolic disorders which may be associated with sleep disturbances include hyperthyroidism and uremia. Finally, sleep-related or sleep-induced respiratory disorders need to be recognized (see page 270).

Sleep Disturbance May Be of Psychological Origin. The most common cause is depression. In addition, states of mania and hypomania are characterized by inability to sleep. Insomnia may be due to overstimulation of all kinds, which was described by Pierre Marie in the 1880s as *insomnie des surmenés.* Many forms of anxiety are also associated with insomnia. The patients with chronic anxiety state may consult the physician on account of muscle contraction headache or vascular headache which awakens them at characteristic times.

Sleep Disturbances and Arousal due to Outside Stimuli. These are due to miscellaneous causes, including (1) seizures; (2) urinary frequency or incontinence; (3) dreams, nightmares, night terrors (pavor nocturnus), and somnambulism, either juvenile or adult; (4) noise; (5) bed partner body movements; or (6) benign nocturnal myoclonus.

Altered Sleep Patterns. These are commonly noted in (1) schizophrenia

TABLE 9–2. CAUSES OF INSOMNIA OR HYPOSOMNIA

A. Physical pain	B. Metabolic disturbance (continued)
1. Peptic ulcer, or other gastrointes-tinal disease	4. Hyperthyroidism
2. Nerve compression	5. Uremia
3. Bone disease with osteoporosis, osteomalacia, or bone tumor	C. Psychological disturbance
4. Muscle spasm	1. Depression
B. Metabolic disturbance	2. Mania and hypomanic states
1. Associated with cerebral anoxia, such as:	3. Overstimulation
a. Low-output cardiac failure	4. Anxieties
b. Bronchial or cardiac asthma	5. Periodic nocturnal headache secondary to underlying chronic anxiety
2. Associated with carbon dioxide retention and hypoxia	D. Miscellaneous stimuli
3. Paralysis of the muscles of respiration as in poliomyelitis, Guillain-Barré polyradiculoneuropathy, certain types of muscular dystrophy, and spinal cord injury.	1. Seizures
	2. Urinary frequency or incontinence
	3. Dreams, nightmares, night terrors, somnambulism
	4. Excess noise
	5. Bed-partner body movements
	6. Benign nocturnal myoclonus

and other psychiatric disorders; (2) normal persons under stress; and (3) cervical cord lesions requiring immobilization.

Neurophysiologic Mechanisms and Systemic Correlates of Sleep

"We are somewhat more than ourselves in our sleep, and the slumber of the body seems to be but the waking of the soul. It is the ligation of sense, but the liberty of reason; and our waking conceptions do not match the fancies of our sleep" (Sir Thomas Browne, 1603–1692). Almost one-third of our lives is spent in sleep, and its function may be termed recuperative or consolidatory. Much has been learned about this state during the past 25 years since the observations of cyclic changes during nocturnal sleep, and rapid-eye-movement (REM) sleep in man (Aserinsky and Kleitman, 1953; Dement and Kleitman, 1957). Much, however, remains obscure and later in this chapter certain aspects are pointed out that appear paradoxical and are to date little understood.

The sleep-wake cycle is characterized by alterations in the state of consciousness. Sleep has been defined as "a periodical physiological depression of function of those parts of the brain concerned with consciousness, induced by the appropriate state of the reticulo-hypothalamic system" (Brain and Walton, 1969). Mechanisms of perception are altered, in that the sleeper can be awakened by a sound that is meaningful to him like his own child's cry and yet not react to much louder noises that have no personal significance. The fact that the brain receives stimuli, although perception is altered, is illustrated by the observation that stimuli, particularly of sounds, can be worked into the content of dreams.

Sleep is accompanied by metabolic, biochemical, and physiologic changes that affect the entire body. Like many other functions, sleep is a cyclic or circadian phenomenon (Latin: *circa,* "about," *dies,* "a day"). The length of the period of the cycle is probably related to the 24-hour period of rotation of the earth and the subsequent light-dark cycles. Michel Jouvet et al. (1974), however, published studies of two individuals who lived without any external time cue and had an experimental bicircadian rhythm, with a 48-hour day (34 hours of activity and 14 hours of sleep).

During sleep, the pulse rate, blood pressure, and the respiratory rate fall; the eyes usually deviate upwards; the pupils are contracted but react to light, albeit slowly; the tendon reflexes are abolished and the plantar reflexes may become extensor. There is a diurnal variation in the level of plasma cortisol, as a result of varying function in the adrenal medulla; and during sleep the kidneys secrete a more concentrated urine. Cerebral blood flow increases slightly during sleep and cerebral oxygen consumption falls very slightly compared with values during wakefulness (Kety, 1969).

In humans, the level of cortisol, a steroid secreted by the adrenal cortex, follows circadian rhythm and the maximal secretion occurs in the hours just before and after morning awakening. Peak secretion of growth hormone from the anterior pituitary gland occurs during the first 1 to 2 hours of sleep. Levels of luteinizing hormone fluctuate in complex circadian patterns, and women frequently require more sleep premenstrually than at other times in their cycle. These, and other disparate clinical and laboratory observations, indicate the physiological contrasts between the waking state and sleep, or during what may be termed the basic rest-activity cycle.

Stages in Sleep

Normal sleep is divided into stages, which can be defined in terms of behavior, physiology, and electrical activity of the brain in all animals, varying according to the species.

Dement and Kleitman (1957) on the basis of all-night EEG recording of undisturbed sleep in man defined five EEG stages of sleep: stages 1 through 4 are characterized by a deepening level of sleep without rapid eye movements (REMs) and are referred to as non-rapid eye movement sleep (non-REM); a 5th stage, REM sleep, is also known as "paradoxical" or "activated" sleep because the EEG appears similar to that recorded when the patient is suddenly alerted. Although the EEG during paradoxical sleep resembles the low-voltage EEG pattern of wakefulness when the patient is alerted, the threshold for awakening is higher than during stages 3 and 4, which are also known as "slow wave" or "synchronized" sleep (Jouvet, 1969). Thus, sleep accompanied by rapid eye movements, may be thought of as "deep" sleep in that the thresholds of EEG and behavioral responses to sensory stimuli are elevated. Previous sleep loss, however, modifies responsiveness during all stages of sleep (Williams et al., 1964). EEG responses to afferent stimuli persist during sleep and some components of the responses increase with increasing depths of sleep (Kooi, 1971).

A typical night of sleep in young adults is shown in Figures 9–1 and 9–2. The initial descending stage 1 EEG of sleep onset is usually followed by stages 2, 3, and 4 in that order. Stages 3 and 4 are characterized by high voltage slow waves in the delta frequency range (less than 4 Hz). After approximately 70 minutes of this slow-wave sleep, the first REM period occurs. It is usually heralded by a series of body movements. The cycle described is repeated four to six times throughout the night, depending on the total length of sleep, except that the later cycles do not include the deep sleep of stage 4.

The sleep stages are further described in Figure 9–2. During relaxed wakefulness, the EEG shows alpha activity of 8 to 12 Hz. As the subject falls asleep, his muscles relax and his eyes begin to roll slowly from side to side, while in the EEG, the alpha diminishes and is gradually replaced by low voltage mixed frequencies. Stage 2 is characterized by 12 to 14 Hz sleep spindles, together with K complexes superimposed on a background of relatively low voltage mixed frequencies. K complexes are high amplitude waveforms exceeding 0.5 seconds in duration, composed of a well-defined negative sharp wave followed by a positive component and then by sleep spindles. They occur spontaneously or as a response to an external stimulus. Stages 3 and 4 (slow-wave sleep) are differentiated according to the amount of delta waves present: when the record consists of 20 to 50 percent of this activity, it is classified as stage 3, and when there is more than 50 percent, it is classified as stage 4.

Sleep stages

Stage	Percent of sleep (young adults)	Behavior	EEG
Non-REM			
1	5	Drowsy Rolling eye movements	7 to 10 Hz (theta-alpha) of fluctuating frequency and low voltage
2	50	Light sleep Readily aroused	3 to 7 Hz low-voltage, plus bursts of 12 to 14 Hz sleep spindles K-complexes
3		Moderate-depth sleep Blood pressure reduced Heart slowed Pupils miotic Slightly depressed monosynaptic reflexes	1 to 2 Hz (delta) waves of high voltage, few sleep spindles
4	20	Deep sleep	1 to 2 Hz (delta) waves of high voltage
REM	25	Bursts of eye movement Increased and irregular autonomic activity	Low-voltage fast activity

FIGURE 9-1. SLEEP STAGES. (Reproduced, with permission, from Willis, William D., Jr., and Grossman, Robert G: Medical Neurobiology, ed. 2, St. Louis, The C. V. Mosby Co., 1977.)

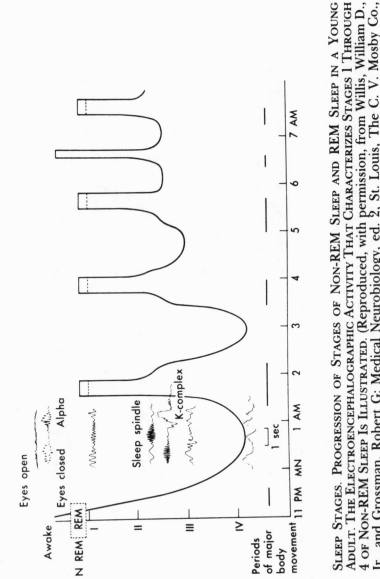

FIGURE 9-2. SLEEP STAGES. PROGRESSION OF STAGES OF NON-REM SLEEP AND REM SLEEP IN A YOUNG ADULT. THE ELECTROENCEPHALOGRAPHIC ACTIVITY THAT CHARACTERIZES STAGES 1 THROUGH 4 OF NON-REM SLEEP IS ILLUSTRATED. (Reproduced, with permission, from Willis, William D., Jr., and Grossman, Robert G: Medical Neurobiology, ed. 2, St. Louis, The C. V. Mosby Co., 1977.)

In non-REM sleep, there is some tone in the postural muscles, such as the antigravity muscles (extensors) of the neck, although tone is less pronounced than in the waking state. The threshold for limb movement evoked by motor cortex stimulation is raised. REM sleep is characterized by a low-voltage high frequency (20 to 30 Hz) EEG pattern that is remarkably similar to that during arousal. In REM sleep, there are bursts of 50 to 60 eye movements per minute. In animals such as the cat, twitchings are not confined to the eye muscles, but also involve the vibrissae (whiskers) and tail; the REM movements are associated with high voltage potentials in the pons, lateral geniculate nucleus and occipital cortex, and they are known therefore as PGO waves, occurring in clusters at a rate of about 60 per minute. REM sleep is also characterized by loss of tone (tension) in the postural (antigravity) muscles, particularly the neck extensors. There is inhibition of brain stem and spinal cord reflexes, irregular respiration, overall reduction in arterial blood pressure interrupted by brief episodes of hypertension during the eye movements, and signs of sexual arousal including frequent penile erection and corresponding clitoral enlargement as well. Dreaming occurs largely during REM sleep periods, but is not confined to REM sleep. Nightmares are associated with REM periods, but night terrors (pavor nocturnus) without specific dream imagery apparently occur in stage 4. For further information, the reader is referred to specialized articles and texts.

Phylogeny of Sleep

Sleep occurs in reptiles, but it is more complex and more developed in birds and mammals. The amount of time spent in REM sleep diminishes the higher the animal stands in the phylogenetic scale, and it is negatively related to the neuronal excitability of the different species. In other words, the more primitive is the animal, the greater is the amount of REM sleep. Also the more REM sleep present, the less excitable is the brain. From these observations, it may be postulated that the susceptibility to seizures (due to excess neuronal excitability) is in some ways related to the total sleep time and/or to the percentage time that the animal species spends in REM sleep. In the phylogenetic scale, it may appear that the more total sleep time and in particular the more REM sleep, the less the neuronal excitability. Man sleeps less than most mammals lower in the phylogenetic scale, and man is more likely to have epilepsy. Also sleep deprivation in man is a potent trigger for seizures. All these observations argue in favor of the therapeutic effect of sleep in preventing seizure activity.

Changes in Sleep with Age

Sleep is also an age-associated phenomenon. The total sleep time, the behavioral manifestations, and the electrical activity of the brain (the EEG) vary considerably over man's life span. In fact, there are few physiologic phenomena that change with age as much as the EEG in sleep. Full-term neonates sleep a mean length of 16.6 hours, with a range of 10.5 to 23.0 hours. Sleep decreases from 14.5 hours during the third week to 13.9 hours during the 26th week, with extensive individual differences. For the age of one through eight years, figures suggest a length of 9.3 hours to 15.0 hours spent in sleep; adolescents vary with social customs but definitely need more sleep than adults; adults function best with about eight hours. People over 65 vary greatly in their sleep patterns, and most of them tend to nap more in the daytime and therefore sleep shorter hours at night; their total sleep time increases if they suffer from cerebral arteriosclerosis or are subjected to major tranquilizer or other psychotropic drug use.

The EEG changes will not be described here, except to alert EEG interpreters as to the effect of age, thus, both frequencies and amplitude change as well as the morphology of the waves; for example, sleep spindles are scanty in the senium.

Theories of Sleep, Including the Pharmacology of Sleep

According to Pavlov, sleep is an active process of "internal inhibition" which radiates widely over the cerebral cortex and subcortical centers. A contrasting point of view attributes sleep to passive deafferentiation (Bremer, 1935) and alertness to ascending influences of the reticular activating system (RAS) in the brain stem (Moruzzi and Magoun, 1949). Later investigators favor neurophysiologic mechanisms involving active processes of stimulation within excitatory and inhibitory systems traversing the brain stem and involving connections with the diencephalon and cerebral cortex. The modern version of the passive theory of sleep is based on these descriptions of the RAS as the neural mechanism that determines the level of arousal. Because the RAS is activated by afferent input from the sense organs as well as from the cerebral cortex, sleep may result from the reduction in sensory input (deafferentiation).

The active theories of sleep invoke a neural triggering mechanism. The RAS may be inhibited, or the triggering system may operate at a higher level of the nervous system in competition with the RAS. Some neurophysiologic evidence exists for increased excitability of the central nervous system during sleep, (Creutzfeldt and Jung, 1961; Verzeano and Negishi, 1961). Cortical excitability, as determined by responses to stimulation of specific thalamic nuclei, is greater during both non-REM and REM sleep than during wakefulness (Pompeiano and Morrison, 1966), and greater during REM sleep than non-REM sleep (Allison, 1965). Inhibitory processes are also evident during sleep, however, spinal neuronal excitability, manifested by reduction of the H reflex, decreases in sleep. The cerebellum appears to contribute to the loss of tone (atonia) of REM sleep.

Sleep and alertness seem to be related to, or actually determined by, various amine transmitter substances active in the central nervous system. Neurochemical substances are involved with initiating, transmitting, and sustaining activities in these hypnogenic systems. "The relationship of specific sleep stages to specific amines has not been shown as direct cause and effect, but amine transmitter substances may modify brain excitability more directly, for example by regulating protein synthesis" (Klass and Fischer-Williams, 1976). "There is now evidence that monoaminergic neurons in the brainstem are involved in the sleep mechanisms. Destruction of the serotoninergic neurons in the raphe nuclei of the brainstem causes almost continuous wakefulness (insomnia) in cats, whereas the administration of drugs that elevate brain serotonin levels causes an increase in the amount of slow-wave sleep and reduces the amount of REM. Changes in brain catecholamines also affect sleep" (Jouvet, 1969). In normal adults, L-dopa (dihydroxyphenyl-alanine) was found to increase both slow-wave and REM sleep.

Effect of Drugs on Sleep

It is well known that a large number of drugs have a profound effect on sleep. Here we can only list some of the psychophysiologic and biochemical changes following the use, abuse, and withdrawal of hypnotics and psychoactive drugs, including CNS excitants and depressants. In the evaluation of drug effects, the following factors should be taken into consideration:

1. The age of the patient.
2. Associated brain disease or circulatory problems. In addition, any liver and/or kidney disease which may alter the metabolic breakdown and excretion of drugs.
3. The time taken to fall asleep.
4. The total sleep time.

5. Selective REM sleep deprivation, in that certain drugs selectively curtail or suppress REM stage. When a subject is deprived of REM sleep by an agent or a set of circumstances for a certain period, there follows a recuperative period on removal of that agent or set of circumstances in which the REM sleep is made up or compensated. This is known as the REM deprivation-compensation phenomenon, and it is well-documented in man and experimental animals. A compensatory REM rebound should follow elimination of REM sleep, but certain drugs prevent this.

6. Shift work alters an individual's circadian rhythm, and drugs may have differing effects under different circumstances.

7. Drug interaction is a widespread phenomenon, and alcohol, caffeine, and nicotine are drugs that should not be overlooked in these interactions.

8. Withdrawal effects are often seen, for example, seizures after withdrawal of alcohol, barbiturates, or minor tranquilizers (e.g., Valium); and the experience of nightmares after withdrawal of alcohol or barbiturates. Chemical dependence is a complex subject being widely studied, and readers are referred to other textbooks for further information on the subject.

REM sleep is calculated from all night EEG recordings, and it may be noted either as an actual duration in minutes or as a percentage of the subject's total sleep time. The effect of drugs on the percentage of REM sleep has been reported for a number of drugs, particularly those that are capable of producing physical or psychological dependence or both. The following potentially addictive drugs suppress REM significantly and after their withdrawal there is REM rebound, or in other words REM compensation: alcohol, amphetamine, barbiturate, diethylpropion, glutethimide (Doriden), meprobamate (Equanil), methyprylon (Noludar), phenmetrazine, and tranylcypromine (Parnate). Three further drugs may be mentioned, which are not reported as producing dependency, but which do suppress REM although there is little or no REM rebound following their withdrawal. These three drugs are amitriptyline (Elavil), diphenylhydantoin (Dilantin), and nialamide (Niamid) (Kales et al., 1969).

Students of biofeedback should be conversant with the basic pharmacology of drugs in cases where chemical dependence arises. The kinetics of drugs, meaning the movement of drugs through the body; the levels in the blood and in the tissues; the absorption, excretion, and protein-binding of drugs; and the intactness or disease of the organs involved in drug elimination are all of importance here. The effects on alertness, attention, memory, appetite, gastric mucosa, platelet function, blood dyscrasias, and sleep may be relevant and interrelated.

The above effects vary with each drug, for example, one dose (650 mg.) of aspirin alters platelet function, and the frequently used analgesic codeine causes constipation. The effects can be readily reviewed in the Physician's Desk Reference, or read in the insert with each drug package. In general, levels of alertness and therefore attention and memory are likely to be slightly diminished, but because of the wide range of effects and because of drug interaction the results of taking drugs will not be summarized here.

Sleep and the Hypothalamus

The Functions of the Hypothalamus

The hypothalamus is involved with sleep regulation, among other functions (see Chap. 16). It is the main control area of the visceral system. It integrates activity for the limbic system with consciousness, and the visceral and endocrine systems. It controls the following functions:

1. Visceral
2. Endocrine
3. Water metabolism
4. Food intake
5. Temperature (through the mechanisms of shivering, sweating, vasoconstriction and vasodilatation)
6. Sleep
7. Cardiovascular functions including effects on the cardiac rate and output, blood pressure, and respiration
8. Emotional functions

It should be noted, however, that localization and representation of function is not established with the same precision in the hypothalamus as in many other parts of the brain. There are many reasons for this, both anatomic (Fig. 9–3) and physiologic. The region extends only about 1 cm by 1.5 cm, and functional representation overlaps; also there are significant species differences, and therefore conclusions drawn from animal experiments cannot always be applied directly to man. In addition, conclusions as to function in man are mainly drawn from pathologic states, since it is physically difficult, if not impossible, to study this area by direct methods in the normal individual. Conclu-

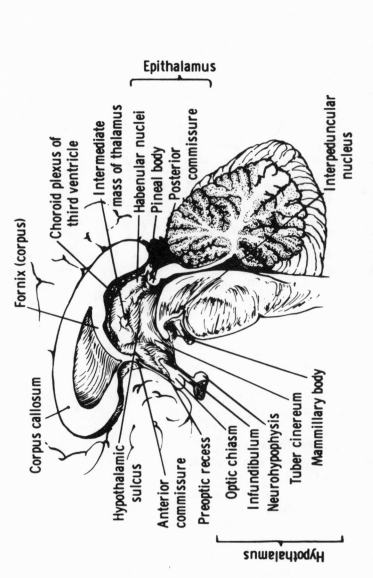

Epithalamus

Fornix (corpus)

Choroid plexus of
third ventricle

Intermediate
mass of thalamus

Habenular nuclei

Pineal body

Posterior
commissure

Corpus callosum

Interpeduncular
nucleus

Hypothalamic
sulcus

Anterior
commissure

Preoptic recess

Optic chiasm

Infundibulum

Neurohypophysis

Tuber cinereum

Mammillary body

Hypothalamus

FIGURE 9-3. SAGITTAL SECTION THROUGH BRAIN SHOWING THE DIENCEPHALON. (Reproduced, with permission, from Chusid JG: Correlative Neuroanatomy & Functional Neurology, 17th ed. Copyright 1979 by Lange Medical Publications, Los Altos, California.)

sions are therefore often based on indirect evidence. Definite physiologic function has been unequivocally shown for only one or two pairs of the nuclei in the hypothalamus. Other localization of function thus far is, at best, regional. There is no evidence of lateralization in the right and left hypothalamus, as there is, for example, in the right and left thalamus and other paired portions of the brain. This is, of course, because the functions controlled by the hypothalamus are not confined to one or other side of the body. Since the goal in many cases of biofeedback training is for the patient to obtain greater self-regulation of functions anatomically related to the hypothalamus, a brief review of some of the physiology of this region seems appropriate.

The functions of the hypothalamus have been investigated by means of stimulation and experimental lesions. The posterior (and lateral) hypothalamus is an important center for the activity of the sympathetic nervous system—referred to as the dynamogenic or ergo-tropic zone of Hess (1954) after W. Rudolph Hess who carried out pioneer hypothalamic studies on cats. Stimulation of the posterior hypothalamus causes an increase of the heart rate, rise of blood pressure, dilatation of the pupil, erection of the hair, and inhibition of movements of the gut and of the tone of the bladder. The nuclei of the posterior hypothalamus are also responsible for the massive reaction known as "sham rage" which occurs in animals when this region has been released from higher control centers. Destruction of this area, on the other hand, causes lethargy and parasomnia (a sleep-like state).

The nuclei of the tuber cinereum (median eminence), on the other hand, appear to be concerned with the functions of the parasympathetic system, and this is the trophotropic zone of Hess (Greek: *trophos,* "growth"; *tropos,* "direction" or "mode"). Hess (1954) considered this area of the hypothalamus to be concerned with growth in the sense of body repair, conservation, and vegetative (visceral) functions. Hess and later workers observed the effects of electrical stimulation of these nuclei.

Stimulation of the Median Eminence (Tuber Cinereum)

The median eminence lies just caudal (posterior) to the infundibulum from which arises the stalk of the pituitary gland (hypophysis). In many respects, the tuber cinereum is the most important part of the hypothalamus; it forms part of the floor of the third ventricle and extends from the optic chiasma anteriorly (in front) to the mammillary bodies behind.

Stimulation of the tuber cinereum causes slowing of the heart rate and increase in the atrioventricular conduction time. There is also an increase in the peristaltic movements of the stomach and of the tone of the bladder. Lesions of this region may cause hemorrhagic erosions of the mucosal lining of the body of the stomach.

The hypothalamus also influences the release of gonadotrophic hormones from the hypophysis (pituitary), and adiposogenital dystrophy which is characterized by great obesity and genital atrophy may be produced by experimental lesions of the tuber cinereum.

Sleep Disorders

Syndromes of the Hypothalamus

Disturbances of sleep may occur with abnormalities of the hypothalamus. Other symptoms associated with hypothalamic dysfunction include (1) adiposity (excess fatty tissue); (2) cachexia (pathologic loss of weight); (3) impairment of sexual functioning, including failure to develop secondary sexual characteristics; and (4) diabetes insipidus.

The role of the hypothalamus in the regulation of normal sleep is still uncertain, but clinical experience shows that lesions in the region of the tuber cinereum may lead either to persistent somnolence or to paroxysmal attacks of sleep similar to those occurring in idiopathic narcolepsy.

Narcolepsy

Russell Brain (1969) defined narcolepsy as "sleep which is abnormal by reason of its onset's being irresistible, although the circumstances may be inappropriate and excessive fatigue is absent. The patient can be roused from the narcoleptic attack as from normal sleep" (p. 966).

The first case of narcolepsy was described in 1877 and the term *narcolepsy* was introduced by Gélineau in 1880. The attacks may be numerous, occurring many times a day. They are most likely to occur in situations conducive to sleep; they are occasionally precipitated by strong emotion such as laughter. The sleep is usually brief, lasting only for seconds or minutes, but if the patient is undisturbed he may sleep for hours. Narcolepsy may be associated with cataplexy (a fall due to sudden loss of muscle tone), sleep paralysis, hallucinatory states associated with sleep, and somnambulism.

The Causes of Narcolepsy. Narcolepsy may be symptomatic or idiopathic, meaning that it may or may not be a symptom of underlying cerebral abnormality. It may be symptomatic following head injury or due to cerebral arteriosclerosis, neurosyphilis, encephalitis lethargica, or intracranial tumor involving the posterior part of the hypothalamus. Far more frequently, no organic cause is found, and the disorder is then termed "idiopathic." Males are more subject to it than females. There are often associated emotional problems.

Cataplexy (Greek: kata, "down"; plesso, "to strike"). Here the patient suddenly loses all power of movement and of maintaining posture, but consciousness is preserved. He sinks limply to the floor with eyes closed and the muscles are hypotonic. Cataplectic attacks usually last less than a minute and recovery is complete. They are commonly precipitated by strong emotion, especially laughter; geloplegia is a condition characterized by falling down with momentary impairment of consciousness as a sequel to laughter.

Sleep Paralysis. This is similar to cataplexy, but occurs during the period of falling asleep or awakening.

Hallucinatory States. These may occur as the patient is falling asleep; they are also termed *hypnagogic* hallucinations and some of these may relate to "autoscopic" hallucinations and disturbances of body image as described by Jean Lhermitte (1951). (This phenomena should not be confused with "twilight sleep" which is a state of anesthesia-induced analgesia given principally to reduce the discomfort of childbirth.) The night terrors of childhood appear to be of a nature similar to hypnagogic hallucination. They occur during stage 4, slow-wave sleep (Gastaut and Broughton, 1964).

Somnambulism. This may be regarded as the reciprocal of cataplexy in that the patient, although partly asleep, is able to stand and walk in an automatic way. This activity occurs in slow-wave sleep, during stages 3 and 4. The sleepwalker will respond to external stimuli and even answer questions, albeit at a lower level of awareness. The patient is always amnesic for the episode.

Kleine-Levin Syndrome

This rare syndrome of periodic hypersomnolence and megaphagia (morbid hunger with overeating) has been described mainly in adolescent males, where it may be of hypothalamic origin, though the exact etiology remains unknown. Kleine (1925) and Levin (1936) first described these attacks of excessive appetite followed by profound somnolence or sleepiness lasting some days, with personality changes and sometimes abnormal sexual behavior occurring during the episode.

Sleep Apnea

This is a rare condition, but it has attracted attention in recent literature because of its dramatic nature. Respiration is reduced during sleep and the individual may stop breathing. It was described as primary alveolar hypoventilation or "Ondine's curse."

These sleep-related or sleep-induced respiratory disorders have now been differentiated into the following three types. The first is "obstructive" sleep apnea, in which there is a cessation of airflow through the nose and mouth because of local obstruction, (for example a mandibular malformation), while respiratory muscle effort remains intact. These patients usually snore. The second is "central" sleep apnea with cessation of nasal and oral airflow for more than 10 seconds presumed due to failure of neural input to the respiratory muscles. The third type is termed "mixed," in that more than one cause appears to operate. Sleep-apnea patients may show hypersomnia with periodic respirations.

Sleep and Epilepsy

Since seizures constitute sudden changes in the level of consciousness, and since in many cases there is a close correlation between the incidence of seizures and the sleep habits of the individual who is subject to seizures, a brief review of some of the relevant aspects follows. Sleep has multiple and highly variable effects on convulsant threshold, or paroxysmal EEG discharges, and on clinical seizures (Klass and Fischer-Williams, 1976). There are also great individual differences. A number of disparate aspects should be considered:

1. The effects of spontaneous sleep have to be differentiated from the pharmacologic effects of drugs that induce sleep, from states of anesthesia, or hypnosis, and from disease states that cause the patient to be obtunded.

2. There is a paradox in that sleep is an activator (with EEG abnormality appearing during drowsiness and light sleep that was not present during the waking state), while sleep deprivation is also an activator, (with people having an increased number of seizures when deprived of sleep).

3. In some stages of sleep, widely synchronized paroxysmal EEG activity tends to be activated preferentially, and focal discharges may be activated during other stages.

4. The terms *synchronized* and *desynchronized* have been used to describe different stages of sleep in animals. Any single stage of sleep

involves both mechanisms to some extent, however, so that descriptive terms are preferable when referring to sleep stages.

5.   Two abnormal epileptogenic electrical foci in the same patient may be differentially activated, one by sleep and one by a pharmacologic agent.

6.   Sleep may "activate" one cerebral system and at the same time "inhibit" another. Sleep may also act by producing disinhibition.

7.   Differences exist among patients with regard to propensity for developing clinical seizures during nocturnal sleep. Some people have characteristic seizure times at night; others, however, rarely have seizures during sleep. Some have seizures just as they fall asleep, or shortly after they have awakened.

Application of EMG Biofeedback in the Treatment of Insomnia

EMG biofeedback and relaxation methods have been employed to treat specific cases of insomnia.

A 55-year-old, white female was referred for EMG biofeedback and relaxation training by her psychiatrist because of chronic insomnia over a five-year period. This coincided with a period of stress in her employment (food service). Having lost her assistant, she was unable to withstand the pressure of working alone and she became so anxious and lacking in sleep that she had to take a leave of absence. Prior to biofeedback treatment, she averaged less than three hours of sleep per night. Her psychiatrist had prescribed a variety of medications, with minimal effect. When first evaluated with the EMG instrument and during the initial sessions, the patient showed very high levels of muscle tension over both the forearm extensors and the frontalis muscle, with readings of 30 to 50 μv integral average.

The patient was trained in deep muscle relaxation and taught to use the relaxation as a means of falling asleep whenever she felt anxious or agitated. The patient was also instructed to play the relaxation tape made for her when she awoke during the early morning hours after two or three hours of sleep. During the treatment session she was trained in EMG biofeedback to relax her muscles, especially the frontalis muscle. Verbal therapy was also employed to improve her self-concept and reduce her obsessive ruminations regarding lack of sleep. Since the patient had not been employed for over a year, her sense of pressure appeared to

be primarily self-induced and related to chronic obsessive ruminations. The patient was unable to control negative thoughts, especially those regarding her insomnia. Cognitive behavior therapy
was employed, with "thought-stopping" which enabled her to
terminate negative thoughts and obsessive worries rather abruptly
and then increase the level of positive thoughts.

After 20 sessions of EMG biofeedback and relaxation training
with home practice, the patient's duration of sleep increased from
an average of 3 hours (the pretreatment level) to 5.3 hours. She
reported feeling less anxious which correlated with recordings of
reduced muscle tension during biofeedback sessions. At the end
of treatment, the patient showed 6 and 9 μv integral average over
the frontalis muscle, which represented a significant reduction
from the levels during the base-line sessions.

This case study, therefore, indicates that EMG training and relaxation methods may be useful in the treatment of insomnia.

Summary

Many of the factors that influence sleep and sleep deprivation have
been reviewed, including the amount of sleep and type of sleep experienced, and the features associated with physiological and pathological
sleep. It is clear that this covers almost as wide a field as that encountered in the waking state, and in addition, there are factors which
operate only during these hours of motor immobility with cerebral
activity. Since the brain directs much of the orchestration of our lives,
there is a need to learn more about sleep. The application of biofeedback techniques to treat sleep disorders requires further study and
documentation.

REFERENCES

Allison T: Cortical and subcortical evoked responses to central stimuli during wakeful-
ness and sleep. Electroencephalogr Clin Neurophysiol 18: 131, 1965.
Aserinsky E, Kleitman N: Regularly occurring periods of eye motility and concomitant
phenomena during sleep. Science 118: 273, 1953.
Brain WR, Walton JN, in Brain WR (ed): *Diseases of the Nervous System,* 7th ed. Oxford
University Press, 1969, p. 966.

Bremer F: Quelques proprietes de l'activite electrique du cortex cerebral "isole." CR Soc Biol 118: 1241, 1935.

Creutzfeldt O, Jung R: Neuronal discharge in the cat's motor cortex during sleep and arousal, in Wolstenholme G (ed): *The Nature of Sleep.* London, Churchill, 1961, p. 131.

Dement WC, Kleitman N: Cyclic variations in EEG during sleep and their relation to eye movement, body motility, and dreaming. Electroencephalogr Clin Neurophysiol 9: 673, 1957.

Gastaut H, Broughton RA: A clinical and polygraphic study of episodic phenomena during sleep. Biol Psychiatr 7: 197, 1964.

Guglielmino S, Strata P: Cerebellum and atonia of the desynchronized phase of sleep. Arch Ital Biol 109: 210–217, 1971.

Hess WR: *Diencephalon, Autonomic and Extrapyramidal Functions.* New York, Grune and Stratton, 1954.

Jouvet M, Mouret J, Chouret G, Siffre M: Towards a 48-hour day: Experimental bicircadian rhythm in man, in Schmitt FO and Worden FG (eds): *The Neurosciences.* Cambridge, MIT Press, 1974, Chap. 41.

Jouvet M: Neurophysiology of the states of sleep. Science 163: 32, 1969.

Kales A, Schart MB, Malmstrom EJ, Rubin RT: Psychophysiological and biochemical changes following use and withdrawal of hypnotics, in Kales A (ed): *Sleep, Physiology and Pathology.* Philadelphia, Lippincott, 1969, p. 326.

Kety SS: Theories and methods for CBF measurement, in Brock M, Fieschi C, Ingvar DH, Lassen NA, and Schurmann K (eds): *Cerebral Blood Flow.* New York, Springer-Verlag, 1969, p. 275.

Klass DW, Fischer-Williams M: Sensory stimulation, sleep and sleep deprivation, in Redmond A (ed): *Handbook of Electroencephalography and Clinical Neurophysiology,* Vol. 3 D, Amsterdam, Elsevier, 1976, p. 5.

Kleine W: Periodische Schalfsucht. Mschr Psychiatr Neurol 57: 285, 1925.

Kooi KA: *Fundamentals of Electroencephalography.* New York, Harper and Row, 1971, p. 60.

Levin M: Periodic somnolence and morbid hunger: a new syndrome. Brain 59: 494, 1936.

Lhermitte J: *Les Hallucinations.* Paris, Masson, 1951.

Moruzzi G, Magoun HW: Brain stem reticular formation and activation of the EEG. Electroencephalogr Clin Neurophysiol 1: 455, 1949.

Pompeiano O, Morrison AR: Vestibular origin of the rapid eye movements during desynchronized sleep. Experientia 22: 60, 1966.

Verzeano M, Negishi K: Neuronal activity in wakefulness and in sleep, in Wolstenholme G (ed): *The Nature of Sleep.* London, Churchill, 1961, p. 108.

Williams HL, Hammack JT, Daly RL, Dement WC, Lubin A: Responses to auditory stimulation, sleep loss and the EEG stages of sleep. Electroenceph Clin Neurophysiol 16: 267, 1964.

Willis WD, Grossman RG: *Medical Neurobiology.* St. Louis, Mosby, 1977, p. 390.

10

Disorders of the Integumental System

THE INTEGUMENTAL system consists primarily of skin (epidermis and dermis), hair (head, body, and pubic), nails and the glandular components (sebaceous, eccrine, and apocrine). The skin is the most important element of this system and is the interface between the body and the environment. In that role it stands as a barrier against the invasion of harmful organisms (e.g., viral, rickettsial, bacterial, protozoan, and more complex parasittical groups). In addition, it serves to prevent dehydration and maintain electrolyte balance, as well as assist in the regulation of body temperature. Also, of equal importance is the skin's role in serving as the most extensive sensory receptor of the organs of the body. Information gathered by the skin in this role includes tactile, thermal, and pain and pleasure imput.

The treatment of most dermatological conditions is either a maintenance approach with treatments given at specific intervals for inhibition of disease processes or as a palliative or curative approach in which the rate of tissue damage is retarded or arrested.

Some categories of dermatological disease exist, however, which do not seem to be acute, distinct, or circumscribed. In these cases, the treatment may not be as well-defined nor is a positive outcome expected to be immediate and limited to brief duration. These categories seem to be more influenced by contributing factors associated with the patient's emotional state and "functional" components may be involved in the etiology of the disorder. This is the area of study Medansky refers to as "dermatopsychosomatics" (1980). These diseases, then, may be expected to be susceptible to psychologic treatment where it is used in conjunction with traditional dermatologic approaches. Medansky (1980) divides these categories into primary emotional disorders (e.g., neurotic excoriations, trichotillomania, factitial dermatitis, and delusional parasitosis), primary organic disorders (e.g., hemangioma, herpes zoster), and organic-emotional disorders (e.g., psoriasis, atopic dermatitis, urticaria, acne vulgaris, alopecia areata, herpes simplex, and verrucae).

In those conditions where the etiologies are discreet, e.g., acute infectious processes, appropriate antibiotic therapy may be sufficient to relieve the disorder and a "cure" may be expected in a relatively short time. In neoplastic process, where surgical, radiation, or chemotherapeutic approaches are the primary treatment of choice, functional factors are less important. With the elimination of those disease states described above, only certain chronic conditions need to be considered as indications for adjunctive biofeedback treatment procedures.

The integumental system is derived primarily from the ectodermal layer of the human embryo. Since the nervous system is also derived from this embryonic layer, those techniques which are used to treat disorders and dysfunctions of the nervous system (e.g., biofeedback) might logically also be useful in approaching disorders and dysfunctions of this system.

Connective Tissue Diseases

An area of current interest in terms of recent findings in this field includes those dermatologic conditions associated with connective tissue diseases. Diseases in this category include the collagen disorders of discoid and systemic lupus erythematosus (SLE), localized and progressive systemic scleroderma, and the dermal diseases such as granuloma annulare, rheumatic nodule, necrobiosis, lipoidaca, acrodermatitis chronica atrophicans, pseudoxanthoma elasticum, cutis hyperelastica (Ehlers-Danlos syndrome), lichen sclerosus et atrophicus, amyloidosis, myxedema, and the subcutaneous diseases such as Weber-Christain disease and sarcoidosis. Thermal biofeedback treatment appears to have some effect on connective tissue disorders (Stroebel, 1979). Training a patient to dilate peripheral vasculature, for example, may help in attaining some amelioration of these diseases.

Inflammatory Disease

Many of the integumental diseases are inflammatory in nature. They are, consequently, more chronic and more benign than those associated with neoplasms or acute infections or infestations. Immunological factors are important in these disorders and thus the potential for the utility of biofeedback may be enhanced.

Rosacea is very often a progressive disease, most common in individuals who blush readily and who are very sensitive to direct sunlight. Historically, emotional factors have been felt to play a part in this disorder, although no clear-cut dynamics have yet been elucidated. Control of blushing is more likely to be achieved through control of blood flow and facial musculature underlying the skin. Electromyographic (EMG) and temperature (thermal) biofeedback could be useful in arresting this chronic and progressive process.

Allergic Cutaneous Diseases and Reactions

This category includes the topical reactions manifested by the body when in contact with some substance when it is either innately sensitized to or has become sensitized through a variety of pathways. These substances may be natural or commercial products, and their number is legion. As with rosacea, efforts directed toward the control of blood flow through thermal biofeedback may assist the patient in lessening his reaction as well as any pain or discomfort associated with the condition. Among these diseases are allergic eczema, contact dermatitis from such agents as plants (poison ivy, poison oak), chemicals, light, and fungal agents. Also included in this category are urticaria, commonly characterized by weals or welts, and atopic dermatitis (generalized neurodermatitis and cystoneurodermatitis). In erythema multiforme, a potentially recurring disorder, psychogenic factors can be important, and therefore biofeedback may be applicable.

Alopecia is often linked with psychogenic causes, particularly in those patients who pull out their hair (trichotillomania) or those who eat their hair (trichophagia). This is likewise the case in the excessively hirsute or glabrous patients where treatment of the disease may be less important than consideration of the patient's conflicted feelings regarding the manifestations of the disease. In a recent personal case (AJN):

> A 32-year-old female who suffered from chronic trichotillomania was treated with relaxation and EMG biofeedback. As long as she continued in therapy she did not engage in the hair-pulling behavior. Although the behavior eventually reappeared after biofeedback training was discontinued, this procedure seems to hold some promise in the condition as a means of helping such patients to relax and thus reduce this variety of symptomatology.

Lichen planus, seborrheic dermatitis, sweat disorders such as hyperhidrosis, pruritis, and psoriasis represent chronic or potentially chronic conditions with frequently undelineated etiologies where psychogenic factors may have a significant importance. The role of biofeedback has not yet been clearly established, with many of the disease states listed above and few published case reports document the use of biofeedback in these disorders. Rickles (1978), however, employed vapor pressure feedback to treat hyperhidrosis in a 16-year-old boy, while Nigl (1979) used electrodermal conductance feedback to treat stress-related hyperhidrosis in two adult males.

Vascular Disorders

Vascular disorders include the purpuras, telangiectasia, acrocyanosis, erythromelalgia, vasculitis, chilblains (pernio), Buerger's disease, venous stasis, Raynaud's phenomenon and Raynaud's disease, and hypo- and hyperthermia, particularly as manifested in the extremities. As indicated by their name, vascular disorders are identified by their color ("red" or "blue") denoting either a localized increase or decrease in blood flow to an area of the skin.

Vascular involvement of the skin, particularly when it is localized, is often easily detected not only visually, but by thermal registration. With the application of thermal sensors direct monitoring by the patient of changes in vascularity is possible. Through the use of thermal or skin temperature feedback patients can become proficient in first detecting, and then moderating the temperature of these areas. Increases in temperature due to vasodilatation are thought to occur because of a relaxation of the smooth muscles surrounding the peripheral blood vessels. Thus, in many cases, not only the symptomatology, but ultimately the disease state itself can be modified, ameliorated, or even resolved through the learning of self-control by the patient. In terms of vascular diseases, Raynaud's disease has been treated very successfully with electrothermal feedback techniques (see Chap. 13).

It is well known that the sweat patterns of exertion, such as in physical labor or athletic competition, and those associated with fear or anxiety, involve different areas of the body. Physical exertion, for example, will stimulate sweat gland activity on the extremities, forehead, and other areas while that of anxiety produces sweat under the arms and on the palms. Chemically sensitive biofeedback equipment, therefore, can be attached to those areas of the body where sweat is associated with anxiety (the origin perhaps of the "smell of fear") as mediated by the sympathetic system ("fight or flight"). The patient could then be given auditory and/or visual feedback regarding the extent and duration of his anxiety response. It might be possible to train the patient not to generate "anxious sweat" when presented with stressful stimuli. The value of this may be that when the patient feels anxious and becomes aware of sweating this may tend to deepen the feeling of anxiety. This can lead to a vicious circle of increasing sweat-anxiety-sweat-anxiety. If the patient can break this circle through biofeedback and relaxation training exercises by eliminating or decreasing consciously one of the symptoms of his anxiety (e.g., the perspiration), then anxiety might be lessened along with the stress response in general. Eventually, "anxious sweat" could actually become a cue for the reduction of response to stress rather than a cue for its production.

In summary, the application of biofeedback to the integumental system is best documented in Raynaud's disease where it is the treatment of choice (see Chap. 13). The potential probably exists for the application of biofeedback techniques as adjunctive procedures to other common dermatologic disorders, however. Further research though is needed before biofeedback develops useful clinical approaches to the majority of these disorders.

Illustrative Case: Hyperhidrosis

A 58-year-old, married white male was referred for electrodermal biofeedback and relaxation training by his physician because of excessive perspiration for many years and palmar sweating especially during times of stress. He was a teacher at a local technical school and had written several books. Excessive palmar sweating occurred during his lectures in class and with anxiety especially when meeting new people. He was extremely embarrassed to shake hands with strangers because of his palmar sweating. He frequently wiped his hands with a handkerchief during class and in a public situation which might involve meeting people.

Electrodermal measurement showed his level of perspiration and the degree of skin conductance was significantly above normal levels for an adult male. In addition to the electrodermal biofeedback training, he was also introduced to a relaxation procedure that was taped for him for practice twice a day. He monitored his sweating response and rated it on a scale that he developed. Cognitive behavior therapy was also employed to assist him in controlling his response utilizing the Premack principle. This principle involves the association of a commonly performed behavior with one which is adaptive but not performed at a very high level. In this case, the patient was instructed to place pieces of red tape at various key places as a cue for him to relax and reduce his level of sweating. For example, since he used his pen frequently during his lectures to emphasize various points, a piece of red tape was placed around his pen to remind him to relax during the lectures.

After 15 sessions of biofeedback treatment, the patient reported significant relief in symptoms and his self-report showed that the frequency and intensity of the sweating diminished. He was able to reduce the level of conductance as measured by the electrodermal instrument, and his average reading during the final session was significantly below the base-line level (Nigl, 1979).

Review of the Literature

Some skin disorders have a significant emotional component, and behavioral therapy has been shown to reduce scratching which often accompanies dermatitis or eczema (Allen and Harris, 1966; Jordan and Whitlock, 1974). For example, aversive conditioning was used by Rutliff and Stein (1968) in combination with relaxation to control the scratching behavior of one patient with neurodermatitis. Very few studies, however, have been published concerning the use of biofeedback techniques.

Miller, Coger, and Dymond (1974) reported that skin conductance biofeedback training led to improvement in eczema. However, only the patients who practiced the feedback procedures regularly at home showed improvement after a month.

In a more controlled study, Miller and Coger (1977) used skin conductance feedback to treat dyshidrotic eczema. Subjects were assigned to two treatment groups, one that received training to decrease skin conductance and one that learned to increase electrodermal activity. The results showed that 73 percent of the patients trained to decrease skin conductance showed clinical improvement in their eczema; only 36 percent of the other group improved.

Schandler (1978) used EMG biofeedback to train five patients with eczema to relax and reduce their itching and scratching behaviors. In addition, five eczemic patients and five normal controls were taught relaxation but did not receive biofeedback training. The results indicated that the patients who received biofeedback were not significantly different from normals following the third session. The eczemic control patients did not show any improvement in their disorder, however.

Biofeedback training has also been used to treat hyperhidrosis but, there has not been correlative experimental data. Several clinical case studies have been reported, however, some of which were discussed earlier in this chapter (Nigl, 1979; Rickles, 1978).

Fuller (1977) used skin temperature and skin conductance biofeedback training to treat successfully a 23-year-old woman with hyperhidrosis.

In a review article of electrodermal biofeedback, Stern and Rogers (1978) indicated that more controlled research is needed to determine the efficacy of electrodermal activity (EDA) feedback to treat skin disorders such as eczema or dermatitis. They state "This (eczema) is one area in which EDA biofeedback may have a direct and important impact on abnormal physiological functioning. This line of research should be vigorously explored" (p. 91).

Haynes et al. (1979) reported that eight patients with atopic dermatitis were given treatment consisting of three phases: no treatment, placebo and EMG biofeedback plus relaxation. The results were mixed, although the entire treatment resulted in a diminution of dermatologic problems for these eight patients, there was no definite relationship between EMG frontalis activity and itching responses. Furthermore, the authors failed to find a relationship between Minnesota Multiphasic Personality Inventory (MMPI) scores and dermatological pathology.

REFERENCES

Allen K, Harris F: Elimination of childs' excessive scratching by training the mother in reinforcement procedures. Behav Res Ther 4: 78, 1966.

Fuller G: *Biofeedback: Methods and Procedures in Clinical Practice.* San Francisco, Biofeedback Press, 1977.

Haynes S, Wilson C, Jaffe P, Britton B: Biofeedback treatment of atopic dermatitis: controlled case studies of eight cases. Biofeedback Self-Regul 4: 193–210, 1979.

Jawetz E, Melnick J, Adelberg E: *Review of Medical Microbiology.* Los Altos, Ca., Lange, 1968.

Jordan J, Whitlock F: Atopic dermatitis: anxiety and conditioned scratch responses. J Psychosom Res 18: 297, 1974.

Medansky R: Dermatopsychosomatics: An overview. Psychosomatics 21: 195, 1980.

Miller R, Coger R: Skin conductance conditioning with dyshidrotic eczema patients. Unpublished manuscript, Los Angeles VA Woodsworth Hospital Center, 1977.

Miller R, Coger R, Dymond A: Biofeedback skin conductance conditioning in dyshidrotic eczema. Arch Dermatol 109: 737, 1974.

Nigl A: Electrodermal feedback in the treatment of stress-induced hyperhidrosis. Unpublished manuscript, 1979.

Rickles W: Treatment of a case of hyperhidrosis with vapor pressure feedback. Proceedings of the Biofeedback Society of America 9th Annual Meeting, 1978.

Rutliff R, Stein N: Treatment of neurodermatitis by behavior therapy: a case study. Behav Res Ther 6: 397, 1968.

Schandler S: Use of muscle biofeedback relaxation in the treatment of eczema. Proceedings of the Biofeedback Society of America 9th Annual Meeting, 1978.

Stern R, Rogers T: Biofeedback of electrodermal activity: origins and applications. Intern Rev Appl Psychol 27: 91, 1978.

Stewart W, Danto L, Maddin S: *Synopsis of Dermatology.* St. Louis, Mosby, 1970.

Stroebel C: The application of biofeedback techniques in psychiatry and behavioral medicine. Psychiatric Opin 16: 13, 1979.

11

Disorders of the Musculoskeletal System

THE MUSCULOSKELETAL system is the system of "action." The most important type of action is locomotion. This system is essentially a mechanical one, composed of levers, blocks, and pulleys. Strains and stresses on this system produce "reaction."

A useful approach to understanding the disorders of the musculoskeletal system is that of "cure" versus amelioration (see Chap. 10). An analogy for this is the differing approach taken for uncomplicated pneumonia ("cure") as opposed to that of diabetes mellitus ("amelioration").

Most treatment modalities also follow this line of thought in their approach to disorders of the musculoskeletal system. With biofeedback, a cure may follow treating muscle spasms associated with stress or tension whereas amelioration may obtain in degenerative disc and joint disease with the use of biofeedback in rehabilitation.

Muscle Contraction

Muscle contraction occurs upon stimulation by nervous tissue. Because the nervous system is involved in both willed (conscious) stimulation of muscles and unwilled (unconscious) stimulation, tension as well as volitional intent are fundamental in the role of the muscle.

Muscle contraction cannot be sustained over indefinite periods of time. There is a finite limit to its efficiency which decays dramatically following the peak or plateau phase. With continual neural stimulation, muscle tissue becomes "exhausted" and can no longer respond physiologically as it did when initially stimulated. This "exhaustion" is the result of the reversible chemical balance involving the contractile properties of the macromolecules peculiar to that tissue. These chemical changes, as in other tissues, involve the consumption of oxygen used in cellular respiration and the oxidation of glucose along with the accumulation of metabolic waste products such as lactic acid, carbon dioxide, and water (Fig. 11–1).

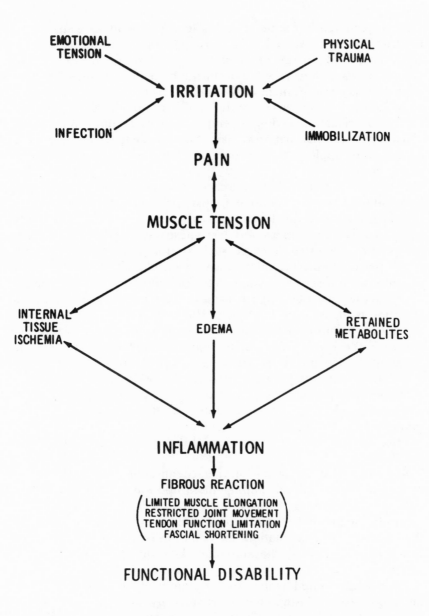

FIGURE 11-1. SCHEMATIC FUNCTIONAL DISABILITY RELATED TO
SOFT TISSUE INVOLVEMENT. (Reproduced, with permission, from Cailliet, R: Soft Tissue, Pain and Disability. F. A. Davis Company, 1977.)

Stress and tension stimulate muscle contraction. Because of the electrical energy involved in the propagation of the excited neural tissue and its discharge upon the muscle, subsequent contractions spread the wave effect (excitation) through the musculature with these contractions. Measurement of the microvolts involved is one method by which the level of tension in the muscle can be observed and is the essence of relaxation techniques employed in biofeedback monitoring. This decreases muscular response; thus, biofeedback is a technique which can be applied to reducing general levels of stress and tension in the body.

When the reversible chemical reaction has gone too far in one direction and the buildup of end-metabolism products has exceeded a certain threshold, the individual notices a dysphoric feeling of exhaustion, ache, and discomfort in his muscles. These feelings are manifested by waves of extended contraction, such as cramping or spasm. Muscle tissue reacts almost instantaneously to cellular damage as with the extravasation of serous exudate. The individual with sudden muscle spasm in the back following such an event knows how immediately his attention is focused on that part of the body (Fig. 11–2).

Another form of muscle injury in addition to strain (torn muscle tissue) is the sprain in which tendons attached to the muscle and ligaments attached to bone are separated or damaged.

Because of the exquisite sensitivity of muscle tissue it takes less stimulation to provoke or initiate painful contractures of this tissue when injured than when it is in a noninjured state. This is why rest with immobility following injury is recommended so that additional contractions leading to further damage of the tissue are minimized (Fig. 11–3).

Reduction of stress or tension (i.e., chemical or electrical) dampens excitation stimuli in their impingement upon muscles. Muscle tissue will then fire (contract) less often and to a lesser degree, thereby reducing the possibility of exhaustion and/or various degrees of further damage. In rehabilitation, the emphasis is reversed and the clinician seeks to stimulate the muscular tissue though it is much more selective.

Currents generated by the process of nerve conduction and muscular response are measurable in microvolts (μv) and can be fed back to the patient with the biofeedback device. Frequently in rehabilitation some conscious slow motor activity has been lost because of the interruption of excitation stimuli by nervous tissue for whatever reason through stroke, trauma, or disease. Attempts are made to stimulate

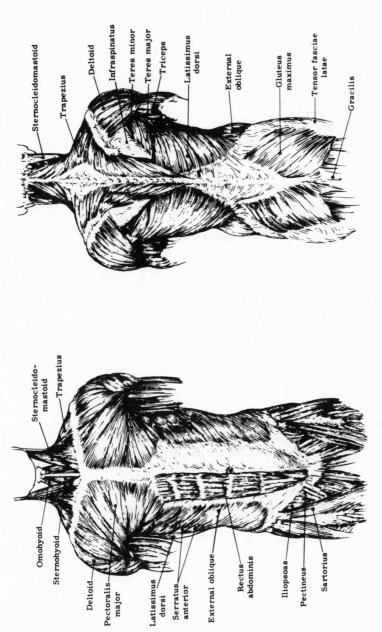

Sternocleidomastoid
Trapezius
Deltoid
Infraspinatus
Teres minor
Teres major
Triceps
Latissimus dorsi
External oblique
Gluteus maximus
Tensor fasciae latae
Gracilis

Sternocleido-mastoid
Trapezius
Omohyoid
Sternohyoid
Deltoid
Pectoralis major
Latissimus dorsi
Serratus anterior
External oblique
Rectus abdominis
Iliopsoas
Pectineus
Sartorius

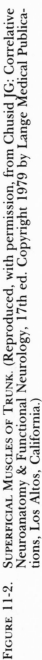

FIGURE 11-2. SUPERFICIAL MUSCLES OF TRUNK. (Reproduced, with permission, from Chusid JG: Correlative Neuroanatomy & Functional Neurology, 17th ed. Copyright 1979 by Lange Medical Publications, Los Altos, California.)

285

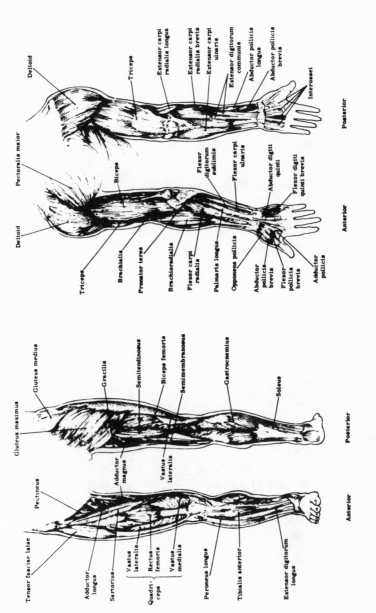

FIGURE 11-3. SUPERFICIAL MUSCLES OF RIGHT EXTREMITIES. (Reproduced, with permission, from Chusid JG: Correlative Neuroanatomy & Functional Neurology, 17th ed. Copyright 1979 by Lange Medical Publications, Los Altos, California.)

alternate neurocircuitry. This has varying success, depending upon the location and extent of the original injury. Rehabilitation is used not only to restore voluntary use of musculature, but also to avoid further damage from disuse (without stimulation muscle tissue atrophies and function may be lost permanently).

Biofeedback techniques are designed to enhance awareness of which muscles the patient needs to contract and which he needs to relax. By placing appropriate sensors (data collection units) over the muscles, the therapist and patient can become almost immediately aware of how successful the patient is in locating, isolating, and then stimulating the appropriate musculature.

Sleep

Muscle relaxation is most complete during sleep. This state of relaxation approaches, though it never achieves, a total "zero" resting point as there is always some neuromuscular tension activity. Evolutionary studies suggest that man's sleep periodicity has emerged as an adaptive pattern due to the rotation of our planet. Other environmental stimuli may also have contributed to various kinds of physiologic adaptations which have become genetically "fixed" through the process of natural selection.

There is still no adequate explanation of why the body requires sleep. The special senses (seeing, hearing, smelling, tasting, and touching) are less sensitive during sleep. Since volition in terms of contraction of specific muscles is often initiated based on input from these sensory data, it is debatable whether these two observations are causally related. That is, does sleep dampen these input stimuli or are these senses dampened so that sleep can occur?

Sleep is cyclical and one of several cycles or rhythms described as "circadian" (see Chap. 9). When these rhythms are disturbed the body and mind's ability to compensate may be unsuccessful and feelings of stress, tension, and dysphoria result, as with "jet lag" or sleep deprivation.

Bony Tissue

Less is known about the factors governing the rate of growth and response to stress of osseous or bony tissue. Certainly, the time frame of muscular response to under- or overstimulation is very different than that of osseous tissue; muscle response being the more rapid.

In disorders of the musculoskeletal system, stressors play an important part in elevating tension levels. Other factors include stimulation or reduction of stimulation in individual muscles, and inherent or innate fluctuations in tension (tone) levels in the muscle mass.

Congenital Abnormalities

Congenital abnormalities usually involve some deformity, deficiency, or supernummerary structure often with resultant impaired function. Such conditions include the varus and valgus positions of the extremities, hypoplastic or pseudoarthritic conditions of the bones, dislocations or subluxations, or hypertrophy of the limbs, along with amputations; also scoliosis, kyphosis, and spina bifida.

Generalized abnormalities of bone include osteogenesis imperfecta, osteopetrosis, achondroplasia, arachnodactyly, enchrondromatosis, and multiple hereditary exostoses.

Generalized abnormalities of the neuromuscular tissue include neurofibromatosis, amyotonia congenita and amyoplasia, and myositis ossificans progressiva. In general, little can be achieved in treating congenital defects with biofeedback training. This is because what is sought is not the restoration of function which was once possessed but is now lost, but rather the initiation of function through structures which are absent, misformed, or undeveloped. Also, individuals with congenital defects may be less able to utilize this process because the emphasis in biofeedback is on "self-help," cooperation, and motivation. These patients may be too young or lack sufficient cognitive resources to understand the procedures.

However, biofeedback may be useful for developing new function following a repair or amelioration of a musculoskeletal defect. For example, awareness of nerve and muscle connections through EMG biofeedback may enable the patient to direct his energy toward developing atrophied musculature. In general, though, biofeedback is likely to remain an adjunct in this group of disorders.

Disorders of the Bone and Joints

The bony tissue serves as "lever and fulcrum" and the medium through which the work of the muscle is performed. Obviously, if the material making up this component is structurally unsound, it is less able to perform its function appropriately.

General Disorders

Several diseases of the bone tend to interfere with its normal functioning. If the muscle tissue cannot pull or contract properly against the bony skeleton, then its stimulation will not be profitable. These diseases include rickets, osteomalacia, scurvy, osteoporosis, hyperparathyroidism, hypo- and hyperpituitarism, hypothyroidism, polyostotic fibrous dysplasia, osteitis deformans (Paget's disease), and skeletal reticulosis. Biofeedback holds little promise as a treatment for these disorders.

Inflammatory Disorders

Inflammatory disorders can be divided into those with specific etiologies and those with nonspecific etiologies. Those with specific etiologies can be traced to either viral, bacterial, or in some cases, fungal infections of the bone and joint tissue leading to loss of function. When cramps, spasms, tears, strains, sprains, or fractures occur, initial immobilization to reduce tension and sensitivity is indicated. With resolution, however, increased tone and tension is helpful not only in terms of stimulating the tissue to recoup losses caused by the disease, but also to enhance mobility and prevent disuse atrophy.

Nonspecific inflammatory disorders are more commonly associated with skeletal joints than bone. These disorders include rheumatic diseases, rheumatoid arthritis, ankylosing spondylitis, chronic and juvenile arthritis (Still's disease) as seen in diffuse connective tissue disease, Reiter's syndrome, psoriasis, rheumatic fever, synovitis, gout, and hemophilic arthritis.

Pain generated through inflammation and the swelling of soft tissues in the joints can be reduced in the appropriate patient with biofeedback. Although still experimental, there is some evidence to suggest that temperature training may improve the inflammation or reaction in rheumatoid arthritis by increasing the blood supply to the affected joints. Tension and stress generally worsen these processes whereas relaxation tends to improve them. Rehabilitation also uses these principles in treating these diseases.

Degenerative Joint Disease

Degenerative disorders of joints limit function as well as lead to changes in tissue structure. Pain, which often accompanies these disorders, is based on inflammation, swelling, or direct tissue destruction and irritation, and frequently plays a significant part in limitation of motion (function). Thus, reduction of pain tends to enhance mobilization. The clinician may find himself walking a thin line between the wish to increase mobilization, function and reduce pain, however, and the fact that increased mobilization contributes to further damage of the tissue. Some compromise is generally indicated with the usual mixed results. Biofeedback in these cases is an adjunct along with more usual treatments such as exercise, medication (antiinflammatory), and sometimes special appliances or prostheses. Recent work with artificial joint replacements, along with new cementing compounds and techniques, has significantly benefited these patients.

Degenerative joint disease in the spine includes segmental (localized) instability, hyperextension, and narrowing, as well as herniation of the intervertebral disc. Other disorders include neuropathic joint disease (Charcot joint), nonarticular rheumatism such as that manifested in myofascial pain syndrome (fibrositis), degenerative tendon and capsule disease including tendonitis and tenosynovitis, tendon rupture, frozen shoulder-hand syndrome, tennis elbow, tenosynovitis, trigger finger, Dupuytren's contracture, popliteal cyst (Baker's cyst), and bursitis.

Neuromuscular Disorders and Injuries

Muscle tissue remains "at rest" until stimulated. Denervation, that is, the interruption of the nervous stimulation of the muscle tissue, leaves it flaccid and/or paralyzed. If the denervation is prolonged, atrophy of the muscle occurs; that is, the muscle mass will shrink due to a reduction of the number of fibers and also the size of each particular muscle fiber. A similar effect is found in astronauts with weightlessness for a long time. Those not exercising regularly will lose muscle mass as well as suffer demineralization of their bones. Mechanical stress, tension, and muscle tone are necessary to a certain degree for optimal functioning. Too little or too much of this stimulation leads to abnormal musculoskeletal function. For further discussion of neuromuscular disorders the reader is referred to Chapter 8.

Just as there is disuse atrophy, there is also "use hypertrophy" of the muscle tissue, for example, with strenuous sports or physically demanding occupations such as in the construction industry.

Since biofeedback involves acquisition of conscious control over specific muscle masses, it depends on the integrity of the nervous pathways which stimulate the muscle mass. Interruptions of these nervous pathways present varying problems for the clinician employing biofeedback. Results partly depend upon what nerve tracts remain intact, the extent of the injury, and what new nerve tracts can be developed or "borrowed" to assume the functions of those lost. As long as neuromuscular connections persist, muscles can be utilized through biofeedback. Without nerve connections, however, function will be lost permanently. It is always possible, of course, that other muscle groups can compensate for the localized loss, but this depends on the extent of the injury. Certain neuromuscular disorders are resistant to mechanisms commonly associated with those found in biofeedback just as are certain other processes such as epiphysial growth. However, the effects of these disorders such as weakness, muscle atrophy, or disuse atrophy may be compensated for to a degree through the application of biofeedback techniques.

Neoplastic Disorders

The next large category of musculoskeletal disorders includes those diseases associated with neoplastic tissue growth. Biofeedback will have little to offer in terms of the disease processes themselves and so it must be reserved for that area defined by the effect of the disease. Rehabilitative stimulation versus relaxation (tension or stress reduction) will be the most useful application in these cases.

Common Disorders

These common disorders include variations due to hypomobility of joints such as "flat feet" (pes planus) and "knock knees" (genu valgum); torsional deformities of the lower limbs include internal and external femoral torsion, internal and external tibial torsion, and bowlegs (genu varum). The last of these is encountered in the normal aging process.

The chronic complaint of low back pain may present difficulty. The subjective nature of the complaint and at times some litiginous or disability-type of determination can further complicate treatment, as for example with secondary gain seen in "compensation neurosis."

Since stress and tension can be generated through both conscious and unconscious mechanisms, elements from these areas raise the general level of tension in various muscles. Psychodynamically oriented theory states that specific organ systems or subgroupings are "targeted," depending upon the factors involved with specific conflicts. This is felt to be no less true in the musculoskeletal area, particularly in the low back region.

Biofeedback can also serve to reduce levels of tension and stress in the targeted system or subsystems and thus tend to alleviate pain and dysfunction. The most important treatment factor, however, is the motivation of the patient. In a compensation-type situation, the motivation for improvement may be compromised at best and lacking in the most difficult cases. Obviously, in such situations biofeedback alone will not necessarily alter the prognosis, but in combination with psychotherapy can serve to present to the patient alternative means of resolving conflicts other than through psychosomatic symptoms. The clinician is limited to offering recommendations to the patient. Whether or not the patient accepts and utilizes these recommendations can only be decided by the patient himself.

Illustrative Case

A 15-year-old male was referred by his psychiatrist for treatment of chronic muscle contraction headaches (Fig. 11–4). He had been taken to a psychiatrist by his parents when he was in the eighth grade because of frequent absences from school due to tension headache. The headaches followed a consistent pattern developing after he had been in school one to two hours and continuing throughout the day, finally ending in the evening just before he went to sleep. He was the eldest son of a man who appeared an "overachiever" with a position usually reserved for college-educated individuals, although he had only a tenth-grade education. The patient's mother was very achievement- and status-oriented, and her husband had difficulty fulfilling her need for material possessions. The patient had learned to be competitive at an early age and was an accomplished sailboat racer, having twice won the class championship at the ages of 12 and 13. However, his grades progressively declined so that he had to take remedial courses in his freshman year in high school.

When first seen his average frontalis muscle tension was greater than $20\,\mu v$ (integral average). His headaches occurred about once per day with an average intensity of 80 on the scale of 0 to 100 where 100 represents extreme or excruciating pain. The patient was taught to relax and given a cassette tape of a relaxation exercise to practice at least twice a day. He was to monitor the frequency and intensity of his headaches.

After approximately 20 sessions the patient reported little relief although during the biofeedback sessions he was able to reduce his frontalis muscle tension to a level significantly below his base-

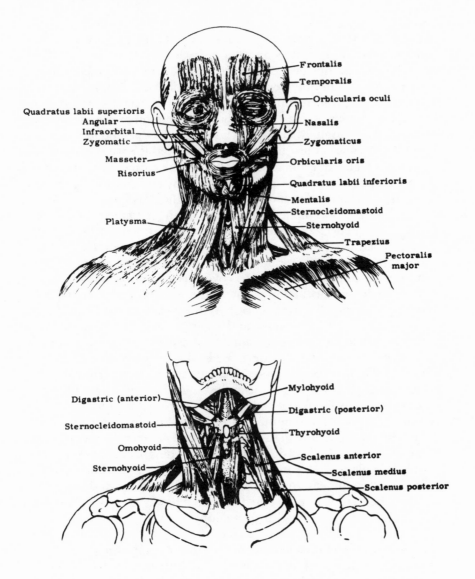

FIGURE 11-4. SUPERFICIAL MUSCLES OF HEAD AND NECK. (Reproduced, with permission, from Chusid JG: Correlative Neuroanatomy & Functional Neurology, 17th ed. Copyright 1979 by Lange Medical Publications, Los Altos, California.)

line prior to treatment. At this point his average EMG reading was below 3 μv measured as an integral average.

The patient, however, appeared very resistant to practicing at home, and his mother reported that he did not comply with the instructions given to him. The self-report sheets seemed to be amended by him so as to meet only the minimum requirements that he bring in the sheet for each session. He seemed to scribble in the information just before his session and the validity of such data was highly questionable. Therefore, the biofeedback sessions were stopped for a time and verbal therapy and counseling given to assess his attitudes and to determine the reasons for his non-compliance. It was immediately clear that the patient was afraid of the consequences of giving up his symptoms, and of losing his special place in the family. Prior to coming in for treatment he was the object of concern for both his parents and his headaches were frequently used as an excuse to cover up for poor schoolwork or to avoid doing work at home. Family therapy sessions were started to improve the effectiveness of parenting skills in terms of their use of positive reinforcement and it was pointed out to the patient that he would have more to gain if he reduced his headaches than if he continued with the pattern. Following six sessions of individual and family therapy, biofeedback treatment was resumed and significant progress was made almost immediately. After 10 additional sessions the patient's headaches were reduced to less than one per week. At a 6-month followup he was functioning well in his sophomore year in high school and had not missed any school. He had stopped all medication and according to his parents, he only complained of a headache once or twice a month. He was more self-confident and less insecure, and he reported that the headaches had very little effect on him. He was more involved in school activities and had begun dating.

This case study illustrates the importance of employing verbal psychotherapy when resistance to biofeedback treatment may reflect an underlying emotional disorder or personality conflict. Noncompliance is frequently due to psychosocial factors operating in the patient's environment which make it difficult to eliminate symptoms. Often parents and other family members reinforce the patient's symptoms in various ways, and they may frequently not be aware of how their behavior relates to the patient's symptoms (see Chap. 19).

Review of the Literature

Biofeedback procedures, primarily electromyograph or EMG feedback, have been applied to treat various musculoskeletal disorders. Two broad areas of dysfunction in the musculoskeletal system have been studied: (1) psychophysiological disorders (e.g., tic) and (2) disorders which involve sensory-motor disability, e.g., paresis. The first of these will be discussed here. The second has been considered in Chapters 7 and 8.

Psychophysiological Musculoskeletal Disorders

According to Fotopoulos and Sunderland (1978), psychophysiological disorders are those characterized by physical symptoms which are caused by emotional factors involving a single organ system which is under the control of the autonomic nervous system (ANS).

Tic. One of the first biofeedback treatments for disorders in the musculoskeletal system involved an "operant" feedback approach by Barrett (1962) for tic. He designed a chair which measured the vibrations a patient experienced secondary to a tic. This information was fed back to the patient in an ingenious manner so that whenever tic activity took place interruption in a musical program occurred. Barrett found that the patient was able to reduce the frequency of muscle spasm activity when the interruption of music was made contingent on the incidence of the tic activity. In a case of severe throat constrictions and tics in a musician, Levee, Cohen, and Rickles (1976) used a visual feedback system. Feedback was obtained from a variety of facial muscles including the m. frontalis and m. genioglossus. According to their results the patient was able to maintain a low level of EMG activity and his symptoms disappeared.

Blepharospasm. Stephenson (1976) used EMG biofeedback from the forearm muscles and m. frontalis to achieve generalized relaxation. After approximately 50 sessions of training, the patient reported that his blepharospasm had ceased and that he was able to return to work. At a 6-month followup he remained symptom-free.

Stuttering. Hanna et al. (1975) used EMG biofeedback from the throat muscles to treat a student with a 10-year history of stuttering. The results indicated that stuttering decreased almost 50 percent from the baseline when the subject was given contingent biofeedback. Alexander (1974) treated 13 stutterers with EMG feedback from the site of maximum muscle activity. Significant reductions were found in nonflu-

ent speech and also in muscular activity in these patients. Positive
results were also obtained by Guitar (1975) and Lanyon, Barrington,
and Newman (1976). Several different placement sites have been used
by researchers to treat stuttering disorders, and at this time there is
insufficient evidence on which to select any particular site. More research is needed to determine specific factors which enhance the possibilities of using EMG feedback to treat stuttering and other nonfluent
speech disorders.

Other Disorders. Other disorders involving the facial muscles have
been treated with masseter EMG biofeedback including subvocalization (Hardyck, Petrinovich, and Ellsworth, 1966), throat tics (Levee,
Cohen, and Rickles, 1976), bruxism (Dowdell, Clarke, and Kardachi,
1976; Kardachi and Clarke, 1977, Solberg and Rugh, 1972), and
chronic dysphagia (Haynes, 1976).

REFERENCES

Alexander P: Effects of EMG feedback conditioning on the severity of stuttering. Diss
    Abst Inter 35: 3653B, 1974.
Barrett B: Reduction in the rate of multiple tics by free operant conditioning methods.
    J Nerv Ment Dis 135: 187, 1962.
Dowdell L, Clarke N, Kardachi B: Biofeedback: control of masticatory muscle spasm.
    Med Biolog Engin 14: 295, 1976.
Fotopoulos S, Sunderland W: Biofeedback in the treatment of psychophysiologic disor-
    ders. Biofeedback Self-Regul 3: 331, 1978.
Guitar B: Reduction of stuttering frequency using analog electromyographic feedback.
    J Speech Hear Res 18: 672, 1975.
Hanna R, et al.: A biofeedback treatment for stuttering. J Speech Hear Dis 40: 270, 1975.
Hardyck C, Petrinovich L, Ellsworth D: Feedback of speech muscle activity during silent
    reading: rapid extinction. Science 154: 1467, 1966.
Haynes S: Electromyographic biofeedback treatment of a woman with chronic dys-
    phagia. Biofeedback Self-Regul 1: 121, 1976.
Kardachi B, Clarke N: The use of biofeedback to control bruxism. J Peridontal 48: 639,
    1977.
Lanyon R, Barrington C, Newman A: Modification of stuttering through EMG biofeed-
    back. Behav Ther 7: 96, 1976.
Levee J, Cohen M, Rickles W: EMG biofeedback for relief of tension in the facial and
    throat muscles of a woodwind musician. Biofeedback Self-Regul 1: 113, 1976.
Solberg W, Rugh J: The use of biofeedback devices in the treatment of bruxism. J So
    Calif Dental Assoc 40: 852, 1972.
Stephenson N: Successful treatment of blepharospasm with relaxation training and
    biofeedback. Biofeedback Self-Regul 1: 331, 1976.

12

Disorders of the Respiratory System

THE RESPIRATORY system has two major functions, each with two phases. One phase consists of the physical transport of gases through a conduit system and the other phase involves metabolic transport of gases across a cell membrane.

The first function is to transport environmental oxygen to the areas (cellular) where actual respiration takes place. Here atmospheric oxygen in the alveoli is converted to metabolic oxygen (electron exchange from O_2) in the capillaries. Oxygenated blood from the capillaries is then distributed throughout the body by the circulatory system.

The second function includes the exchange, in reverse order, of water and carbon dioxide (waste products of glucose metabolism) as well as other substances back across the capillary-alveolar membrane. These metabolites are then exhausted out through the conduit system and back into the environment.

The conducting (conduit) system comprises the nose, pharynx, larynx, trachea, and bronchi. The respiratory division consists of the alveolar sacks located at the bronchial tree termini and the microscopic alveoli. These are essentially chemical transportation laboratories where the transfer of oxygen between the "outer" and "inner" environment occurs. Several of the above organs serve more than one purpose. For example, the nose and nasal passages also have functions connected with the gastrointestinal (GI) system, namely olfaction and gustation. The pharynx also has a dual role with the GI system, serving as a passage connecting the mouth with the esophagus. The larynx is not only part of the conduit system, but also serves as the organ of phonation.

The respiratory or gas exchange function is less available to conscious control, whereas the mechanical function (conduiting system) is susceptible to that control in varying degrees. Disorders of the respiratory system, which affect the respiratory passages (conduit) are therefore more amenable to biofeedback and techniques involving conscious control.

The ANS has been shown to be more responsive to conscious control than previously believed (see Chap. 5). Although the respiratory system is primarily under the direction of the ANS (e.g., at rest), it is otherwise subject to some degree of conscious control. Professions where control of respiration and breathing is important (e.g., athletes, singers, wind instrumentalists, and divers) have long been aware that conscious control can be achieved.

Some diseases of the respiratory system interfere with the chemical respiratory component thus leading to states where there may be too little oxygen (hypoxia), too much oxygen (hyperoxia as in special cases seen in hyperbaric chambers as with deep sea divers or astronauts), insufficient carbon dioxide (hypocapnea), or excess carbon dioxide (hypercapnea). Other respiratory disorders involve the respiratory passages themselves and are usually manifested by some form of chronic obstructive pulmonary disease (COPD).

Psychogenic factors such as anxiety can play an important role in respiratory rate and function. For various disorders of the respiratory system, treatment effective in dealing with the psychogenic components will be a helpful adjunct and perhaps the treatment of choice. Biofeedback offers a potentially useful technique in certain of these disorders.

Neurorespiratory Disorders

Although the conduit and chemical components of the respiratory system serve as the major foci of this system, they are ineffective without the musculature to drive them. The muscles of respiration are the diaphragm, the intercostal muscles, and the accessory muscles of respiration (e.g., sternocleidomastoid). These muscles, particularly the diaphragm, act as a bellows to pull air into and push air out of the lungs. Therefore, the regulation of the action of these muscles is extremely important. Respiration is largely innervated by the cervical sections of the spinal cord (C_3–C_5) for the diaphragm and the thoracic sections (T_1–T_{12}) for the intercostal muscles, while laryngeal musculature is controlled in the brain stem. Diseases that affect these regions will affect respiration. Trauma to these areas, hemorrhage, or neoplasm (tumor) may also have an effect as well as the ingestion of toxic drugs and other CNS depressants (e.g., barbiturates, opiates, and alcohol). Neurologic disorders such as Guillain-Barré-Strohl syndrome, polyneuropathy, poliomyelitis, diphtheria, and porphyria may also interfere with respiration.

Musculorespiratory Disorders

Diseases or disorders of the respiratory muscles may cause dyspnea (difficulty in respiration). If the "bellows," even though adequately innervated, cannot pump in oxygen because they are inflamed or non-functioning, then respiration cannot take place. Thus, disorders of the muscles and the myoneural junction such as muscular dystrophy, myotonia, curare poisoning, tetanus, and myasthenia gravis can cause dyspnea. Often respirators and other mechanical aids are required for varying periods of time.

General Disorders

Other conditions that compromise pulmonary function and are unlikely to utilize biofeedback are many. Infections (viral, bacterial, fungal, or parasitic) require specific medication management.

Neoplastic diseases may be treated by surgical procedures, poisoning of the tumor by toxic medications, the use of immunological-stimulating agents (e.g., interferon), or radiation therapy. Toxic and traumatic causes of respiratory disease are also unlikely to benefit from biofeedback. Generally, the less acute the process, the more time available there is for psychogenic components to operate and manifest themselves. It is at this stage that biofeedback may play a role.

Spirometry

Because the respiratory system uses a bellows and given volumes of air, its measurement can be well-documented. The process of ascertaining the volume of air inspired or expired is known as spirometry. These measurements are made by a tube running from the mouth to another bellows which activates a monitoring system providing a read-out (the spirometer) of the air exhaled. A system, therefore, which can be physiologically monitored and which demonstrates susceptibility to psychogenic factors lends itself to techniques such as biofeedback.

There are many indices of air movement that are used in these measurements. These include timed vital capacity, forced expiratory volume (FEV), maximal midexpiratory flow rate (MMF), and peak expiratory flow rate (PEFR). Most respiratory diseases have an adverse effect on the capacity to handle air volume, and thus these measurements tend to decrease during illness.

Disorders of the respiratory passages include obstruction which can be mechanical (neoplastic or inflammatory), traumatic due to damage of the conduit system, or metabolic. The result is often a decrease in the amount of oxygen reaching the chemical-perfusion (gas exchange) portion of the respiratory system, with resultant hypoxia.

Instrumentation for biofeedback therapy based on the spirometer, however, has yet to be developed. If patients are presented with data in a biofeedback setting, they can be taught "normal" values and thus compare their own values with these. By adapting different techniques of relaxation or augmentation of various muscle groups, respiratory function (e.g., volumetric oxygen) may be enhanced. If the patient's efforts are successful, the feedback of the data system will show values nearer to normal.

It may be possible to construct a biofeedback mechanism which operates not only on the volume transported through the respiratory passages, but also on the chemical saturation level of either oxygen or carbon dioxide. Development of this might offer an advantage as factors associated with continual blood gas monitoring (analysis) in biofeedback training are very complex, and the level of control the patient might be able to exercise remains undetermined.

Hiccups

Hiccups may occur with a posterior fossa lesion or factors producing phrenic nerve spasm (e.g., cardiac pacemaker insertion). There may though be a psychological component to hiccups. With prolonged hiccupping, however, tension generally increases and relaxation therapy could therefore be useful, and acquisition control of the hiccup through biofeedback may thus be possible. This symptom of involuntary spasm of the diaphragm tends to be unique in that the distinctive sound produced by the hiccup brought about by the abrupt closure of the glottis produces its own auditory feedback component to the patient.

Pickwickian Syndrome

The Pickwickian syndrome derives its name from the description of the obese child Joe in the *Pickwick Papers* by Charles Dickens. One of the characteristic symptoms of the disease, periodic hypersomnia (which differs from sleep apnea or "Ondine's curse" as described in Chapter 9), is linked to poor ventilation, perfusion, and gas exchange associated with significant obesity and diminished respiratory capacity. In this syndrome, mechanical factors such as nasal obstruction and extreme obesity may prevent optimal function of the system although there is no identifiable disease of the tissue per se. Biofeedback could be involved with treatment of this condition, and lead to an overall increase in alertness, decrease in weight, and increase in oxygen utilization.

Chronic Obstructive Pulmonary Disease (COPD)

Emphysema and Chronic Bronchitis

Two disorders characteristic of COPD, encountered in an increasingly urbanized society, are chronic bronchitis and emphysema. Both diseases are a result of recurring airway obstruction. Patients with COPD show symptoms of both disorders more often than a "pure" form of either one. These diseases have been characterized euphemistically as "pink puffer" for the emphysematous type and "blue bloater" for the bronchitic type of disease. In the emphysematous type of COPD, elasticity of the airway is diminished so that the chest wall cavity expands to compensate for the resulting loss of air volume. Short puffing breaths are required because deep inspirations are not possible. Exertion results in peripheral vasodilatation so that a ruddy or "pink" appearance develops.

The bronchitic type of disease is also in part due to environmental pollution. Increased inhaled chemical debris, particularly from smoking, leads to chronic inflammation and increased mucous production of the lungs. Over time chronic inflammation causes progressive destruction of the lung tissue itself so that reduced oxygenation is the result. The patient assumes a bluish hue and his chest becomes hyperinflated (barrel chest) causing him to appear "bloated."

Direct treatment with biofeedback may result in reduced overall tension and anxiety which contribute to decreased dysphoria. Biofeedback, however, may have more intrinsic value as an indirect procedure in terms of eliminating some of the factors responsible for progression of these diseases (e.g., increased or chronic cigarette use).

Asthma

One of the best known respiratory disorders often connected with psychogenic elements (e.g., anxiety and depression) is asthma. It is a serious disease which can be fatal and is characterized by a hyperreactivity of the intrinsic musculature of the lung bronchi. When the hyperreactive bronchi are exposed to various stressful stimuli they tend to constrict and lead to pulmonary obstruction. Often mucous production is overstimulated so that it also becomes a factor which prevents adequate oxygenation as well as a blocking of some of the smaller terminals of the bronchial tree.

Some of the stimuli which can lead to asthma in allergic patients include histamine, dusts, cold air, pollens, irritants (e.g., tobacco smoke), mold spores, fungi, animal dander, house dust, grain dust, and flour. Some food allergies that may lead to asthma include sensitivity to eggs, shellfish, and chocolate.

From the psychological point of view the dynamics of families studied with asthmatic members reveal a sensitivity to rejection and abandonment developing early (first two years of life) in the patients, and leading to overdependence. When this dependence is threatened by loss of the individual (frequently a parent-figure), this dysphoric psychological stimulus can produce a psychosomatic reaction resulting in an asthmatic attack. The attack serves to focus attention on the patient as well as often to forestall the loss of the parent-figure, or causes his hasty return due to the physiological distress brought on by the attack.

The more psychological factors play a part in the patient's asthmatic attacks the more susceptible his condition should be to psychophysiological approaches, including biofeedback. The goal of treatment is the reduction of tension and anxiety associated with loss. Tension can be measured with traditional biofeedback methods rather than with a spirometer. Biofeedback techniques in this disorder could be combined with established treatment procedures.

Chemical and Physical Irritants (Environmental and Occupational Diseases)

These diseases are frequently lumped together under the title of "the pneumoconioses." Generally, pneumoconiosis refers to a pulmonary process in which the lung reacts to foreign particles usually connected with chronic exposure to industrial sources (i.e., not found concentrated in nature). The greater the exposure to the particulate matter over time the more tissue destruction occurs in the alveoli. Two types of pneumoconiosis are described, the first a discreet nodular kind, the second a more diffuse variety. The first is generally associated with insoluble dust particulates, the second with soluble dust particulates. Particle size is also a factor in the disease.

Those nodular pneumoconioses resulting from dust particles which contain more dust and less fiber include coal workers' pneumoconiosis (black lung), siderosis (iron dust) and welder's disease in hematite and magnetite miners, stannosis in tin miners, baritosis in barium miners, pneumoconiosis in chromite (china clay) miners, and in those who work with Fuller's earth. Nodular inorganic dust pneumoconioses resulting from particulate matter that contain more fiber and less dust include silicosis (from silica) of hard rock miners (e.g., granite), silicosis in iron and steel workers, sand blasters, and in the pottery industry and other industries using silica flour. Examples of diffuse organic pneumoconioses include asbestosis, (asbestos workers), aluminosis as in Shaver's disease, talcosis found in talc miners and millers, and chronic beryllium disease of the lung from those who handle beryllium.

The organic dust pneumoconioses are illustrated by farmer's lung, bagassosis, mushroom worker's lung, maple bark stripper's lung, superosis of cork workers, and malt worker's lung. Another dust pneumoconiosis is byssinosis which may occur with cotton and its dust. Chemical irritants can produce lung damage in workers exposed to sulphurous acid, sulphur dioxide, pulp and paper industry products, ammonia, refrigeration processes using chlorine, oxides of nitrogen, or phosgene. Chemical irritants which produce sensitization are found in lacquers, resins, plastic films and allied material as in the upholstery, toy, and insulation industries.

Because of the organic change induced by occupational-environmental lung diseases, psychogenic factors are usually confined to anxiety and tension generated by the knowledge of the potential for acquiring the disease. Thus, there may be little effect on the course of the disease other than in terms of the patient's reaction to it.

Ventilation and Atmospheric Disorders

Biofeedback may be useful in the respiratory system in the weaning of a patient from a respirator. This is frequently a difficult task and motivation and patience are requisite. The same qualities are necessary for biofeedback therapy.

Biofeedback instrumentation could be coupled with those respirators which notify the patient when he is breathing on his own versus when he is breathing through the aid of the machine. The data gathered would record positive results as the patient became increasingly in command of his own respiration. Initial steps would be signaled when the patient is able to trigger the respirator by his own attempts at initiating breathing or possibly even before that with the ability to halt the respirator's automatic action by breath-holding. The patient could then learn through direct feedback to increase these periods of control until eventually he is weaned from the apparatus.

A similar technique could be applied to psychophysiological acclimatization for oxygen-poor environments. Repeated treatments over time, allowing for adjustment and gradual adaptation seem to fall within the realm of what biofeedback could accomplish. Examples of patients who might benefit from such a process are those who live in areas of considerable elevation and who cannot otherwise adapt to these areas. Athletes in sporting events held at high elevations are another example. The reverse process for acclimating to oxygen-rich atmospheres could follow the same technique, going from an oxygen-rich environment to one less so. An example of the latter could occur when hyperbaric treatments over time are used by the patient to become acclimated to an atmosphere with a richer oxygen content. (Such cases, however, are likely to be quite rare.)

Psychophysiologic Respiratory Disorders

Psychogenic factors may operate in hyperventilation, breath-holding attacks, yawning, sighing, aerophagy (air swallowing), and tobacco use.

Hyperventilation

Hyperventilation is often a symptom of anxiety and it is most commonly seen during the course of acute anxiety or "anxiety attack." The patient who hyperventilates experiences an "air hunger" and feels he cannot get enough of a breath. His respiratory rate is increased significantly and consequently excess carbon dioxide is "blown off " leading to respiratory alkalosis, tingling of the fingers, and even loss of consciousness. Whatever psychological stimuli encourage anxiety can provoke hyperventilation.

Biofeedback treatment of anxiety can be approached by either monitoring the patient's respiratory rate or his oxygen/carbon dioxide concentration ratio. The latter is the more sophisticated technique and could be accomplished by chemoreceptors within the feedback instrumentation or through continuous monitoring of the gases dissolved in the bloodstream (invasive technique). The respiratory rate is measured by a masklike device fitting snugly over the face (mouth and nose). The patient is signaled per respiration so that control is easier to moderate. It is also possible that the mask itself will serve a purpose similar to that of the "brown bag," so that carbon dioxide levels return to normal as the mask "traps" the gas.

Breath-holding

Breath-holding attacks which usually occur in small children are self-limited and the treatment is directed toward the underlying psychological factors. The anxiety component can be treated with biofeedback.

Yawning, Sighing, Aerophagy

Yawning and sighing, particularly when the attention-getting behavior occurs repetitively and without control, may often be psychologically determined. Yawning and sighing are generally symptomatic of underlying anxiety, and individuals with this symptom often have emotional concerns. The lessening of tension and the proper feedback of the yawning or sighing respiration allow the patient to be aware of the behavior perhaps even as or just before it is performed, by noting the increase in tension which anticipates the point of general discharge through the behavior. Biofeedback could then play a part in the elimination of this behavior. Patients with aerophagy, which is even more of a tension or anxiety-linked trait, usually present with psychological factors.

Smoking

One of the most important concerns in society today is "self-pollution." Research indicates that multimodal approaches to the cessation of smoking are usually more successful in long-range remission rate than using only one or two techniques in isolation. Biofeedback could be utilized by noting the increased tension levels that often precede the initiation of smoking, and thus signal the individual over a specific period of time, to divert this tension through therapy or other measures. This assumes, of course, that a correlation between increased tension and smoking exists.

The diversity of biofeedback allows it to be adapted for use as a procedure in both divisions of the respiratory system; ventilation-conduit-mechanical and perfusion-gas exchange aspects. Mechanical monitoring can be accomplished through measurement of inspiration through either tidal air volume or change in chest diameter. Chemical respiration can be measured through chemoreceptors or detectors. It may be that some respiratory disorders will require a combination of these two modes to be maximally effective.

The first step in the treatment of chronic respiratory dysfunction is to educate the patient in the mechanics of normal respiration.

Illustrative Case

A 64-year-old, white male was referred for biofeedback treatment by his family physician. He lived in a nursing home because COPD made him unable to breathe independently without the use of supplemental oxygen. He was referred for biofeedback treatment because his physician felt that he was "abusing" the oxygen and was causing himself further damage by breathing air with a higher than normal oxygen content. Furthermore, he seemed afraid of the possibility of using his lungs and would not participate in physical therapy to increase his lung capacity. Psychological testing indicated that he was chronically depressed and extremely fearful of dying. He had a brother-in-law with the same illness who had recently died and the patient feared the same fate.

A portable EMG unit was brought to the nursing home for the treatment sessions. The patient was seen three times a week in the initial phase and taught to relax using a standardized relaxation procedure. Frontalis EMG feedback was used to teach deep muscle relaxation and to help the patient learn to control anxiety symptoms. His initial EMG readings averaged 15 to 20 μv (integral average) over the frontalis muscle. Although his attitude was extremely negative, it intrigued him to learn to control the feedback, and he also indicated that when he was deeply relaxed he did not feel as anxious or fearful. After approximately 30 treatment sessions, the patient had reduced his daily oxygen consumption by over 75 percent and had become more active. Instead of having his meals in bed, he came down to the dining room to eat with the other patients. Staff reports indicated that his personality changed remarkably and he was less hostile and negative and less depressed overall.

At the end of the biofeedback treatment, he was able to relax the frontalis muscle to well below 2 μv (integral average). Approximately five months after the treatment, the patient contracted pneumonia and was transferred to a general hospital where he died shortly thereafter.

The results of biofeedback treatment would suggest that relaxation and biofeedback procedures may be of some benefit to individuals who suffer from respiratory disorders. More research should be done in this area, however, to determine the factors that lead to effective treatment and also to determine whether or not information that is directly related to the patient's respiratory disorder is more meaningful or relevant than the information about other physiological responses such as frontalis muscle contraction.

Review of the Literature

In one of the early studies involving biofeedback training, Davis et al. (1973) reported that asthmatic children receiving EMG biofeedback training significantly reduced airway resistance as measured by a Wright Peak Meter. The group of children receiving only relaxation instructions did not do as well but did reduce airway resistance more than the "no-treatment" control group. The biofeedback procedures appeared to have an effect on children with mild or moderate asthmatic conditions; however, those with severe asthma did not change significantly.

Khan, Staerk, and Bonk (1973) found that the use of biofeedback and other operant conditioning techniques led to successful reductions in experimentally produced bronchospasm. A 1-year followup indicated that the patients sustained their clinical improvement.

Feldman (1976) developed a unique respiratory feedback system, employing total respiratory resistance (TRR) as the dependent variable. The patients (four asthmatic children) wore earphones through which simulated breathing sounds were presented. They were asked to match their breathing with the sounds they heard. Simultaneously, they were given TRR feedback by means of an auditory tone and were told that a lower tone meant they were breathing better. The results indicated that all of the asthmatic patients showed improvement on three measures of airway obstruction. However, Feldman cautioned that these results were only preliminary and that more controlled research was needed.

Vachon and Rich (1976) employed a respiratory resistance unit (which measures TRR) and visual feedback system that enabled subjects to learn when they had reduced airway resistance. In addition, the patients were operantly rewarded with small amounts of money given in proportion to their success. Forty-six adult asthmatics were recruited for the study, and the results indicated that subjects given contingent feedback significantly reduced their TRR readings. Patients given noncontingent feedback, however, did not show significant improvement in TRR.

Feedback techniques have also been used to train patients to breathe more effectively. Cheshire and Flack (1977) reported that chest expansion feedback improved the vital capacity of quadriplegic patients. EMG feedback was used by Johnston and Lee (1976) to improve the breathing function in emphysematous patients.

Fuller (1977) described a case of childhood asthma treated with electrodermal biofeedback. The 5-year-old patient learned to relax and subsequently was able to reduce her asthma to the point that she did not require hospitalization. She maintained her improvement over a 1½-year followup period. However, the use of electrodermal biofeedback to treat asthma has not been well-studied experimentally.

A feedback device to monitor the wheezing breath sounds of asthmatic patients was developed by Tiep (1979). Patients suffering from asthma apparently learned to control the frequency of their bronchospasm through this method.

In summary, the area of respiratory feedback has not received as much attention as it deserves, especially in view of the fact that millions of people suffer from respiratory disease. The wide variety of feedback techniques developed makes it difficult to identify a single method as the treatment of choice. Further research is needed to determine the extent to which biofeedback can be used in a total treatment program for disorders of the respiratory system.

REFERENCES

Beeson P, McDermott W, Wyngaarden J: *Textbook of Medicine*. Philadelphia, Saunders, 1979.

Cheshire D, Flack W: Operant conditioning techniques in the respiratory rehabilitation of tetraplegic patients. Arc Phys Med Rehab 58: 532, 1977.

Davis M, Saunders D, Creer T, Chai H: Relaxation training facilitated by biofeedback apparatus as a supplemental treatment in bronchial asthma. J Psychosom Res 17: 121, 1973.

Feldman G: Effect of biofeedback training on respiratory resistance of asthmatic children. Psychosom Med 38: 27, 1976.

Fuller G: *Biofeedback: Methods and Procedures in Clinical Practice.* San Francisco, Biofeedback Press, 1977.

Johnston R, Lee K: Myofeedback: a new method of teaching breathing exercises in emphysematous patients. Phys Ther 56: 826, 1976.

Khan A, Staerk M, Bonk C: Role of counter-conditioning in the treatment of asthma. J Asthma Res 11: 57, 1973.

Tiep B: Respiratory biofeedback table clinic. Proceedings of the Biofeedback Society of America 10th Annual Meeting, 1979.

Vachon L, Rich E: Visceral learning in asthma. Psychosom Med 38: 122, 1976.

13

Disorders of the Cardiovascular System

THE CARDIOVASCULAR system is a closed hydraulic system, that is, it consists of a central pump mechanism which serves to distribute blood forcibly from the central part of the body to the periphery and back again. This system consists of not only the pump (the heart, Fig. 13–1) but also two systems of tubing: the arteries and the veins. The arteries carry blood away from the heart, and veins return the blood to the heart. From the heart on its trip outward, the blood first enters the large arteries, then small arteries, then even smaller arteries called arterioles, and finally the capillaries which are thin-walled (one cell in thickness) vessels which join the venules (very small veins), then the small veins, and finally the large veins which drain and conduct the blood back to the heart. Although the perfusion of the body described does not always precisely follow this pattern, it is a closed system such that blood does not freely extravasate into the tissues (except, perhaps, in the spleen), rather there is a controlled permeability existing throughout.

The purpose of this system is twofold. The first is to deliver needed chemical nutrients to the cells of the tissues in each organ system and second, to return unwanted chemical "waste" away from the tissues and cells. Those substances which are sent to the periphery include oxygen, nutrients (e.g., glucose), and chemical messengers (e.g., hormones), which have to do with the operation of specific tissues. The unwanted "waste products" that can also serve as chemical messengers in a feedback sense include carbon dioxide and other products of the metabolism of the cells of the tissue. These so-called waste products are delivered variously to the liver and the kidneys for final processing and excretion or elimination.

Disorders of the cardiovascular system can be thought of as occurring in two broad categories. Either there is a disorder or problem with the heart itself or there is a defect or difficulty with the tubes or delivery system, or both. In either of these cases the potential exists for individual cells and tissues not to receive the necessary nutrients or be unable

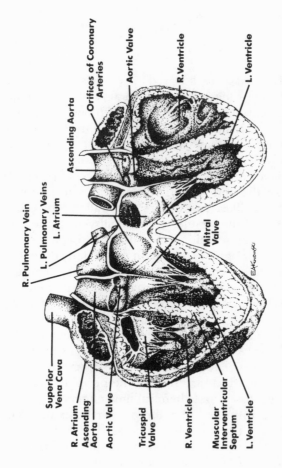

R. Pulmonary Vein

L. Pulmonary Veins

L. Atrium

Ascending Aorta

Orifices of Coronary Arteries

Aortic Valve

R. Ventricle

L. Ventricle

Superior Vena Cava

R. Atrium

Ascending Aorta

Aortic Valve

Tricuspid Valve

R. Ventricle

Muscular Interventricular Septum

L. Ventricle

Mitral Valve

E. Kunowski

FIGURE 13-1. ILLUSTRATION OF THE HEART SHOWN IN SECTION AND DIAGRAMMED TO SHOW THE FOUR CHAMBERS (COMPARTMENTS): THE RIGHT (R) AND THE LEFT (L) VENTRICLES AND THE R. AND L. ATRIA. THE BLOOD ENTERS THE HEART FROM THE SUPERIOR VENA CAVA, AND FLOWS INTO THE R. ATRIUM; THENCE IT GOES TO THE R. VENTRICLE. THE R. VENTRICLE PUMPS THE BLOOD TO THE LUNGS FOR OXYGENATION THROUGH THE PULMONARY ARTERIES. THE BLOOD RETURNS FROM THE LUNGS TO THE HEART VIA THE PULMONARY VEINS AND INTO THE L. ATRIUM; FROM THERE IT GOES TO THE L. VENTRICLE, AND IS PUMPED THROUGH THE ASCENDING AORTA TO THE REMAINDER OF THE BODY. THE MUSCULAR WALLS OF THE HEART ITSELF ARE SUPPLIED BY THE CORONARY ARTERIES.

to get rid of unwanted ones. In the first case, cells may "starve" and in the second case they may become poisoned by their own "waste."

Formerly, it was felt that control of this highly complex system rested with the ANS so that conscious volition or control, therefore, was not possible. With the development of the technique of biofeedback, however, evidence has accumulated that demonstrates that some degree of volition can be achieved, even over such important functions as one's own heart rate or blood pressure.

One of the first practical applications of biofeedback came with the discovery that through this process a patient could "learn" to alter the force with which his heart pumped. That is, control over blood pressure was, to some degree, possible. Prior to this time the only well-known demonstration of this had occurred with a few individuals from the Indian subcontinent, who practiced techniques which came to be called meditation. The disadvantage of this process was that it required years of practice and the acquisition of a certain mental attitude to achieve this control. The goal of this practice, however, was generally not control of physiological processes as much as a search for some higher philosophical "truths."

The advent of the "electronic age" allowed a doorway to be opened to many more individuals than had previously been possible to establish similar control over bodily function with much less effort than was required by the "ascetics."

The importance of being able to modify one's blood pressure lies in the fact that there is a certain range of force with which the blood is pumped which is both desirable and adequate. If the pressure of this system goes either below or above this range for a prolonged period of time, serious disorder or death can result. For example, if the force which propels the blood through the system falls too far below this optimal range (hypotension), then nutrients needed by the brain are not able to be delivered to their destination and so unconsciousness, coma, and eventually death will result if it remains uncorrected. The brain is the most sensitive tissue in the body to lowered oxygen and glucose levels. Other tissues also are sensitive to this but because of the brain's extrasensitivity it is more noticeable here. If hypotension were sustained, however, it would equally affect these other tissues as well.

When the blood pressure exceeds optimal levels (hypertension), the brain is again affected. Cerebral hemorrhage, a condition in which the arteries and arterioles supplying the cerebrum rupture due to the increased pressure and their inability to withstand the stress, is per-

increased pressure and their inability to withstand the stress, is perhaps the most dramatic end result of hypertension. (Chronic hypertension more often results in the disease of the heart itself, however.)

The unique sensitivity of neural tissue lies not only in the fact that it is easily susceptible to damage under such conditions, but also that when the brain cells die, they are not replaced.

Hypertension

There are many causes for both hypo- and hypertension. The etiologies range from the mechanical, such as too much or too little resistance along the length of the blood vessels, to obstruction and dilatation and to more complex disorders involving congenital, metabolic, inflammatory, and degenerative disorders. No organ system functions entirely independently, and a very complex interrelationship exists. Factors that affect one system can affect them all. For example, in essential hypertension, changes in biochemical pathways in the angiotension-renin system of the kidneys can markedly affect the force with which the heart pumps. Thus, many systemic disease states as well as many external or environmental factors can produce harmful effects on the hemodynamic system, leaving the brain and other vital organs in a precarious state.

In considering vasomotor responses, it is well known that a patient who is anxious about his blood pressure (BP) can become even more anxious when told it is too high, thus elevating it further (Fig. 13–2). Measurements of BP taken with a sphygmomanometer have traditionally been available only to the examiner. Recent lay interest in health care has made available to the general public the instrumentation which allows self-measurement. From here it is a short, but crucial, step to the more immediate feedback made possible through biofeedback techniques and instrumentation. The patient then has a chance to receive instruction and learn what effect his feelings, tension, and various activities have upon his BP. He then is able to select out those factors which result in a more favorable change and selectively apply them.

Biofeedback can thus assist individuals in changing their BP. The controversy, however, now centers around the duration of this effect. Can there be permanent changes in the BP through biofeedback techniques? As with most other medical interventions, the response varies with the individual circumstances. Such factors as the doctor-patient relationship, the patient's motivation for change, the medications and treatment procedures, the etiology and severity of the disease all play

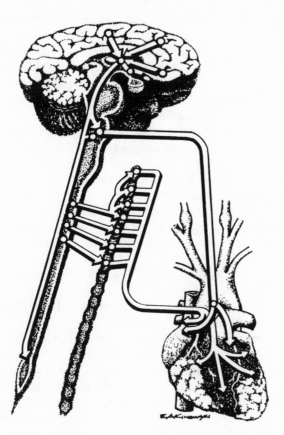

FIGURE 13-2.   CEREBRAL CONTROL OF THE HEART. NOTE THAT THE
FRONTAL CORTEX INTERCONNECTS WITH THE HYPO-
THALAMUS AND THE BRAINSTEM. THE TENTH CRANIAL
OR VAGUS NERVE (PARASYMPATHETIC) WITH ITS
NUCLEUS IN THE BRAINSTEM INNERVATES THE HEART
DIRECTLY. NERVES FROM THE THORACIC REGION OF
THE SPINAL CORD VIA THE SYMPATHETIC TRUNK,
ALSO CONTROL THE HEART. IN ADDITION, HEART
FUNCTION RESPONDS TO CIRCULATING EPINEPHRINE
(NORADRENALINE) ELABORATED BY THE ADRENAL
MEDULLA, WHICH IS ITSELF INNERVATED BY THE
SACRAL NERVES.

a part. Most people with hypertension who are motivated for change, however, can usually be successful in bringing this change about with biofeedback. Whether it is used as the primary treatment or as an adjunct will depend upon the type and degree of the patient's disease.

Increased striated muscular tension is a common finding in hypertensive patients. Since this tension can be reduced by biofeedback, hypertension, which involves musculature with some striated properties should be able to be modified. The exact mechanism as to how this occurs is not known. Whether this involves a neuromuscular reflex pathway or whether metabolic factors are involved (or both) is uncertain.

Many medications can affect the course of essential hypertension, and each has its own advantages and disadvantages, particularly in its side effects. Biofeedback offers some advantage in that it has no undesirable side effects and tends to be target specific. Medication, on the other hand, does not always affect the specific site desired and may affect undesired sites.

The aggressive individual, often described as a "hard-driver" or a "Type A" personality, is an example of one who can benefit from biofeedback in order to reduce his overall level of tension, and as a consequence, lower his blood pressure. This will diminish his risk of cerebral hemorrhage or vascular accident and thus lower the chance for significant loss of function or death. The same reasoning applies to other "at risk" populations (e.g., diabetics, the obese, and smokers).

The decrease in the muscular tone and tension levels in the body which tends to reduce hypertension, can be central, peripheral, or combined. The central mechanism seems to represent an increase in the force of the pumping, though perhaps not an increase in its efficiency, due mainly to stimulation as through anxiety. The resistance of the peripheral vasculature can increase through the narrowing of the diameter of the blood vessels due to a "clamping down," or to some accumulative process such as atherosclerosis with plaque deposition. This can be lowered to some extent, particularly where tension is involved. Thus, the peripheral vessels will tend to relax and dilate, resistance will decrease, and the blood flow will require less force behind it to deliver an equivalent volume. Although the central versus peripheral model is useful, not all the target systems are peripheral. This is found, for example, in the lungs where hypertension can result in interference with absorption of oxygen and discharge of carbon dioxide.

The clamping down or spasm of the vessels in the periphery is not common to them alone, but can occur in any vessel, even those vessels which supply the heart itself with blood. When this occurs the flow of necessary oxygen and nutrients and the elimination of waste products is obviously impaired. This makes any target organ function less well. When this target organ is the heart, it becomes doubly important since this is the pump and the *sine qua non* for the entire system. These spasms or "narrowing" of the coronary vessels result in a "starvation" of certain areas of the heart served by these vessels that is called ischemia. When ischemia lasts beyond a certain threshold point, a myocardial infarction ("heart attack") results. The tissue mass served by the vessels which have become occluded will die in this case. Biofeedback, with its ability to reduce tension, may play a part in alleviating this to some extent. Also, rehabilitation and prevention are areas in which this technique could be valuable.

Heart Failure

Heart failure may be of three varieties: that of the "right" side of the heart which pumps blood to the lungs, as described above, and encounters less resistance and therefore is generally the lesser developed of the two sides of the heart in terms of the musculature; the left side of the heart which pumps blood to the remainder of the body, and is therefore the more thickly walled structure because of the greater resistance encountered in this task. Both sides of the heart can "fail" in terms of becoming weaker and not performing the job efficiently. The third variety occurs when both are affected. The last is the most usual case and it then becomes a matter of degree as to which of the two sides is the more affected. The causes of heart failure are numerous, and if their compensatory mechanisms are not sufficient, serious effects result in the hampering of health and daily life functions. As in other areas, those conditions which are more chronic, tend to be more susceptible to adjunctive procedures, such as biofeedback. Not only can one address the issue of the primary disorder, i.e., the heart failure, with, for example, reduction of tension, but also the secondary effect, i.e., the attendant anxiety and other dysphoric and psychogenic ramifications which are found in those with this condition. Thus not only may the course of the primary disease be affected, but the "quality of life" or feeling state of those people who have the disease may be enhanced through the use of biofeedback therapy.

As indicated, biofeedback training is an adjunct in the treatment of heart failure except perhaps where medication management has not proved entirely successful, the patient is refractory to the medication, or toxic side effects supervene. In such cases, biofeedback may have more of a primary role to play in the treatment.

Congenital Heart Disease

Congenital heart disease, i.e., malformations of the heart present at birth, falls within a spectrum of function ranging from minimal effect to incompatibility with life. In general, the less acute the condition, the milder it tends to be. It is these chronic conditions which are more amenable to biofeedback approaches. A two-pronged approach directed toward not only the primary disease but also the secondary reaction to this disease will fall within this province. Since these primary disorders are more often due to structural dysfunction, biofeedback treatment is likely to be geared more toward the secondary effects of the disorder in the patient.

Cardiac Valvular Disease

The heart rests periodically while opening and closing its valves (inlets and outlets). Without this characteristic, the pump would become just another segment of the tubing. There are four major valves within the heart which serve this purpose. These valves can become damaged in a multitude of ways and when this happens those chambers affected assume more of the characteristics of a conduit rather than a pump and varying degrees of disease and discomfort result from this state (including regurgitation and stenosis). Stress and tension play a role here as with the other processes indicated previously, and the primary and secondary roles of biofeedback can be utilized to improve the quality of the remaining cardiac function in these patients.

Conduction Defects, Dysrhythmias

As the cardiac muscle contracts intrinsically, the nervous tissue found in the heart functions as a regulator of the inherent rate of contraction. When this electrical circuitry is damaged, however, portions of the heart affected may revert to their own intrinsic rhythm or to no rhythm at all (asystole). Thus, the heart is affected and the remainder of the body also to varying degrees. These conduction defects or dysrhythmias are not uncommon. "Pacemaker" devices, external or internal (implanted), serve in the place of the damaged nervous tissue. They do this by electronically regulating the cardiac impulses.

In patients with conduction defects, anxiety, stress, and tension may play a key role. These factors may cause the firing of the nervous impulses in the heart to be either premature or delayed so that dysfunction results. They may at times initiate attacks or spasms of diffused or ineffectual firing of excitatory neurons. Also, they may either cause firing to occur in an erratic fashion or to cease entirely. Through the use of the electrocardiogram (ECG) or cardiac monitor, the patient is provided (after training) with means of recognizing this kind of functioning as it occurs. Through the same mechanism the patient can learn what effects certain feelings, states, and tensions have in terms of his conduction pathways. It is not unreasonable to think that with appropriate training, patients may come to recognize at least general changes in their ECG tracings and distinguish normal from abnormal. Sharing the responsibility of the disease state and its treatment with the patient should tend to enhance the investment of the patient in the regaining of his own improved cardiac status and health. The sense of mastery derived from participating in such changes should reinforce future similar behavior.

Peripheral Vascular Disease

The effect of biofeedback upon peripheral vascular disease such as Raynaud's disease and Raynaud's phenomenon is discussed at the end of the chapter. The strategy is the same with whatever disease state of the peripheral vasculature is involved. Varying degrees of resistance to hemodynamic flow maintain hemeostasis unless disease intervenes. Some degree of resistance in the vasculature is necessary so as to maintain tone and avoid malnutrition of the tissues served by the peripheral vessels. If blood flowed as quickly in the capillary bed region as it does in other areas, there would be insufficient time for the exchange of nutrients and metabolic waste products to occur. On the other hand, if resistance to the peripheral vasculature is excessive, then these tissues are "starved" and metabolic nutrient and waste exchange is impaired.

Biofeedback can affect tension and tone of the smooth as well as the striated musculature and can cause dilatation and constriction of the peripheral vascular bed. Examples of thermal biofeedback equipment are well known and cited elsewhere (see Chap. 4). Since tension can be induced from a wide variety of sources, including psychogenic, it is susceptible to such external monitoring procedures as biofeedback. The patient who suffers from stress and is able to see the results of this in the format of a "readout" of an increase in temperature of his fingers, or who can see the results of decreased tension when certain psychological difficulties are resolved, will gain a sense of mastery over himself and his body and thus increase his independence and at the same time his investment in his state of health.

It is not accidental that the heart has been often seen as the "seat of the emotions" from earliest times. It has been obvious to many generations that there is a strong and binding connection between the emotional state and cardiac functioning. The techniques which have been developed over the last 10 years through the development of biofeedback now allow the clinician to take advantage of this fact and add a pragmatism to something which before had been only in the province of the behavioral theorist or the philosopher.

Hematopoietic System

It is noted that reduction of stress via hypnotherapy can lead to a reduction in the number of hemorrhagic episodes in certain of the hemophilias. It should follow then that biofeedback could be applied to this same condition with similar results. The hematopoietic system may, therefore, prove just as amenable to biofeedback as has the cardiovascular system.

Illustrative Case

A 48-year-old married white male (with three children in elementary school) was referred for biofeedback treatment by his internist. He was an automobile mechanic in a small shop. He had once worked as a supervisory mechanic but his doctor had advised a job with less pressure because of hypertension. His average BP without medication was 170/100; with medication this was reduced to 150/90. The patient was prone to explosive temper outbursts which caused him great discomfort and family difficulties. Psychological testing showed him to be extremely rigid and overcontrolled, with great trouble expressing emotions. He tended to set difficult objectives for himself, and he was somewhat of an "overachiever."

He was treated with electromyograph (EMG) biofeedback and

deep muscle relaxation. He was also taught to monitor stressful incidents on a daily basis and to rate his physiological response to these events. An attempt was made to have him become acutely aware of physiological responses which might be related to increases in BP as a function of stress. Furthermore, pre- and post-blood pressure readings were taken during the course of the biofeedback treatment to determine the effects of relaxation on the patient's hypertension.

During 12 treatment sessions the patient learned to reduce the level of frontalis muscle tension significantly. The frequency of stressful incidents decreased significantly from the baseline period to the final treatment session. His average BP reading following the biofeedback and relaxation training was 130/84. In fact, on one occasion he developed hypotension and almost lost consciousness due to his level of relaxation. At that point his physician was contacted and his medication was adjusted downward but he was admonished to continue practicing the relaxation response while on the lower dosage of medication. Although his treatment stopped prematurely due to financial constraints, he reported that he was pleased with the progress, and at 1-year followup he was still on a lower dosage of medication and was practicing the relaxation response regularly. This case points out the importance of collaboration between the biofeedback therapist and the referring physician.

Review of the Literature

According to Engel (1979), the rationale for using biofeedback to treat cardiovascular disorders is related to the fact that cardiovascular functioning is mediated to some extent by the cognitive-emotional system. Therefore, biofeedback procedures may permit an individual to control these cardiovascular responses through a conditioning process. Engel notes that the patient can also learn to identify abnormal cardiac responses in order to control them using the relaxation and concentration techniques of biofeedback. Engel cautions clinicians that, although there is some evidence that biofeedback can lead to control of certain cardiovascular responses, no large-scale clinical experiments have been conducted to test these procedures rigorously. Three main areas of cardiovascular dysfunction have been examined: hypertension, vasconstrictive disorders, and heart disease. Relevant research findings will be discussed for each of these areas separately.

Hypertension

Although research with normal subjects has indicated that individuals can learn to control their BP (Taub and Blanchard, 1979), there is controversy regarding the effectiveness of biofeedback as a primary treatment for essential hypertension (Williamson and Blanchard, 1979).

Frankel (1978) found that hypertensive patients did not learn how to control their BP as a result of undergoing biofeedback treatment. In a critical review of the literature, Franklin et al. (1978) concluded that there was no evidence that biofeedback procedures could effectively reduce hypertension over time. In addition, they reported that relaxation procedures seemed to be superior to biofeedback overall.

In contrast to this, positive results have been found by many researchers including Kristt and Engel (1975). They found that patients who learned to control their BP in the laboratory maintained this skill over a 3-month followup period. Kleinman et al. (1977) found that patients who learned to reduce their BP also showed improved performance on cognitive tasks.

Patel (1973, 1975, 1977) conducted a series of experiments with hypertensive patients using relaxation methods and indirect feedback training. (In other words, biofeedback was used to enhance the relaxation effect but did not feedback cardiovascular information to the patient.) In the first study, she discovered that 80 percent of the subjects significantly reduced their arterial pressure and also reduced their need for antihypertensive medication. Patel (1975) reported an average reduction in arterial pressure of 16 mm Hg following a 1-year treatment program. There was no significant change in a control group, however.

In 1977, Patel reported that the results of another study demonstrated that control subjects displayed the same degree of arterial pressure reduction as the experimental group when given training in relaxation and biofeedback.

Engel (1979) also reviewed the literature and came to a conclusion different from that of Franklin et al. (1978). He indicated that biofeedback and relaxation methods are complementary approaches rather than representing different methods to treat hypertension. He also cautioned that the research to date has not clearly established the efficacy of using biofeedback to treat hypertension. One advantage to using biofeedback however, according to Engel is that it may enhance the compliance of patients and reduce the dosage level of antihypertensive medication required to maintain normal BP levels.

Huffer (1979) pointed out the necessity of using biofeedback in a therapeutic manner rather than as strictly a laboratory procedure. She further states that the negative findings reported by Frankel (1978) may have been due to the biofeedback procedure. In fact, Frankel also speculated that in trying to be rigorous and objective in their approach they may have hampered the clinical effectiveness of the biofeedback procedure itself.

In summary, it appears that it is too early to tell whether or not cardiovascular biofeedback can effectively reduce hypertension over time. Engel (1979) sounded a warning in his review chapter, regarding the prematurity of making conclusive statements in this area: "I cannot emphasize strongly enough that the biofeedback and relaxation procedures that I have reviewed . . . are subjects of intense investigation at the time of writing."

Vasoconstrictive Disorders

Taub and Stroebel (1978) reviewed the literature and concluded that the experimental data collected at the time of their writing indicate that biofeedback can be an effective treatment for vasconstrictive disorders. Most of the research has been focused on Raynaud's disease. According to Taub and Stroebel (1978), Raynaud's disease is "a functional disorder of the cardiovascular system involving interruption of local blood flow usually in the fingers due to proxysmal spasm." The etiology of this disorder is still unclear, however. There is also debate as to whether or not two types of Raynaud's disease exist; one which involves vascular obstruction and one which does not (Mendlowitz, 1954; Peacock, 1958).

Research on the self-regulation of peripheral temperature (usually the hands) has progressed since Lisina (1965) and Green, Green, and Walters (1970) first investigated this phenomena. Taub (1977) summarized the major findings of research with normal subjects (i.e., subjects who were not suffering from vasoconstrictive disorders). According to his analysis, normal subjects have been found to be able to do the following: (1) maintain self-control of increases in hand temperature for almost an hour; (2) retain the self-control up to one year; and (3) increase hand temperature even after being exposed to cold temperatures which had caused vasoconstriction.

Research has also been conducted with patients suffering from Raynaud's disease. Shapiro and Schwartz (1972) studied two individuals with this syndrome and found that thermal biofeedback training led to significant clinical improvement. Other successful case studies were reported by Peper (1972) and Surwit (1973). In 1977, Taub used thermal biofeedback training to treat seven patients with Raynaud's disease. The results indicated that these patients learned self-control of peripheral temperature as well as normal subjects.

Freedman et al. (1978) studied six patients with Raynaud's disease as well as four individuals with Raynaud's phenomena which was reported to be secondary to other causes. They found that all 10 patients showed a significant reduction in the frequency of vasospastic attacks following thermal biofeedback training.

Stroebel (1979) reported treatment of 80 patients with Raynaud's disease. Vasospastic attacks in the majority of these patients were virtually absent 18 months after biofeedback treatment was terminated. In addition to electrothermal training, these patients were given cold stressor tests and taught how to monitor and record their vasospastic attacks.

Sedlacek (1979) reported that 70 percent of the 20 patients with Raynaud's disease succeeded in regulating their symptomatology with biofeedback training; biofeedback treatment ranged from 12 to 36 sessions for each patient and many of the patients were followed over three years. This rate of treatment success is very similar to that reported by Stroebel and Glueck (1973) who followed more than 50 patients with Raynaud's disease for 2 years.

Gerber (1979) studied 20 patients who were given three months of either thermal biofeedback training or relaxation training. All but one of these patients were able to abort a vasospastic attack when exposed to environmental temperature as low as 3.3°C. The patients were also able to control the rate of descent of the skin temperature which before training fell an average of 6°C when exposed to cold temperatures. Following training, the average temperature drop was only 4°C. Gerber suggested that the patients controlled the rate of descent by not allowing severe vasoconstriction to set in. There was no difference between the two types of self-regulation procedures that were used; thermal biofeedback and the autogenic relaxation exercises (see Chap. 3) were equally effective.

Jacobsen, Manschreck, and Silverberg (1979) indicated that relaxation exercises were even more effective than thermal biofeedback. The group of patients that received relaxation averaged a 1.4°C increase in finger temperature compared with the 0.5°C increase for the group receiving thermal biofeedback.

Reviewing the literature, Sappington, Fiorito, and Brehony (1979) indicated that research evidence was still "sketchy" as to the efficacy of biofeedback treatment of Raynaud's disease. Although biofeedback training demands a significant commitment on the part of both therapist and patients, these researchers state that biofeedback may be preferable because it has the least undesirable side effects compared with pharmacological and/or surgical methods. In addition to Raynaud's disease other vasoconstrictive disorders have been found to be potentially amenable to biofeedback treatment (see Chaps. 7 and 10). These include acrocyanosis, scleroderma, and other collagen-related vasospastic diseases, causalgia, and posttraumatic reflex sympathetic dystrophy (Taub and Stroebel, 1978). Blanchard (1979) described a case in which reflex sympathetic dystrophy (causalgia) was treated by electrothermal biofeedback. After the seventh treatment session, the patient began to demonstrate control of his hand temperature and following that was able to increase temperature from 1.2 to 2.6°C. Pain ratings also decreased to the zero level after 12 sessions. A 1-year followup indicated that clinical improvement was maintained.

Cardiac Dysrhythmias

According to Engel (1979), supraventricular arhythmias have been controlled through biofeedback procedures. Engel and Bleecker (1974) and Scott et al. (1973) reported success in teaching patients suffering from sinus tachycardia to lower their heart rate. In these studies, the feedback consisted of direct beat-to-beat data concerning heart rate.

Engel and Bleecker (1974) have also successfully treated two patients with paroxysmal atrial tachycardia and one patient with Wolff-Parkinson-White syndrome.

Patients with fixed atrial fibrillation have also been treated by using feedback involving their ventricular rates (Bleecker and Engel, 1973).

REFERENCES

Blanchard E: The use of temperature biofeedback in the treatment of chronic pain due to causalgia. Biofeedback Self-Regul 4: 183, 1979.

Beeson P, McDermott W, Wyngaarden J: *Textbook of Medicine.* Philadelphia, Saunders, 1979.

Bleecker E, Engel B: Learned control of ventricular rate in patients with atrial fibrillation. Psychosom Med 35: 161, 1973.

Engel B: Behavioral applications in the treatment of patients with cardiovascular disorders. In Basmajian J (ed): *Biofeedback-Principles and Practice for Clinicians.* Baltimore, Williams and Wilkins, 1979, p 170.

Engel B, Bleecker E: Applications of operant conditioning techniques to the control of cardiac arrhythmias. In Obrist P et al. (eds): *Cardiovascular Psychophysiology: Current Issues in Response Mechanisms, Biofeedback and Methodology.* Chicago, Aldine, 1974, p 456.

Frankel B: Biofeedback may not control most mild hypertension. Psychosom Med 40: 296, 1978.

Franklin K, Nathan R, Prout M: Nonpharmacologic control of essential hypertension in man: a critical review of the experimental literature. Psychosom Med 40: 296, 1978.

Freedman R, Lynn S, Ianni P, Hale P: Biofeedback treatment of Raynauds' phenomenon. Proceedings of the Biofeedback Society of America 9th Annual Meeting, 1978.

Gerber L: Biofeedback for patients with Raynauds' phenomenon. JAMA 242: 509, 1979.

Green E, Green A, Walters E: Voluntary control of internal states: psychophysiological and physiological. J Transpersonal Psychol 2: 1, 1970.

Huffer V: Biofeedback: the need for a flexible approach. Psychosom Med 20: 413, 1979.

Jacobsen A, Manschreck T, Silverberg E: Behavioral treatment for Raynauds' disease: a comparative study with long-term follow-up. Am J Psychiatr 136: 844, 1979.

Kleinman K, Goldman H, Snow M, Korol B: Relationship between essential hypertension and cognitive functioning. Psychophysiology 14: 192, 1977.

Kristt D, Engel B: Learned control of blood pressure in patients with high blood pressure. Circulation 51: 370, 1975.

Lisina M: Role of orientation in the transformation of involuntary ones. In Voronin L et al. (eds): *Orienting Reflex and Exploratory Behavior.* Washington D.C., American Institute of Biological Sciences, 1965.

Mendlowitz M: *The Digital Circulation.* New York, Grune and Stratton, 1954.

Patel C: Yoga and biofeedback in the management of hypertension. Lancet Nov: 1053, 1973.

Patel C: 12 month follow-up of yoga and biofeedback in the management of hypertension. Lancet Jan: 62, 1975.

Patel C: Biofeedback-aided relaxation and meditation in the management of hypertension. Biofeedback Self-Regul 2: 1, 1977.

Peacock J: Vasodilatation in the human hand: observations on primary Raynauds' disease and acrocyanosis of the upper extremities. Clin Sci 17: 575, 1958.

Peckering T, Miller N: Learned voluntary control of heart rate and rhythm in two subjects with premature ventricular contraction. Br Heart J 39: 152, 1977.

Peper E: Case report. Paper presented to Biofeedback Research Society, Boston, 1972.

Sappington J, Fiorito E, Brehony K: Biofeedback as therapy in Raynauds' disease. Biofeedback Self-Regul 4: 155, 1979.

Scott R, Blanchard E, Edmundson E, Young L: A shaping procedure for heartrate control in chronic tachycardia. Percept Mot Skills 37: 327, 1973.

Sedlacek KW: Biofeedback for Raynaud's disease. Psychosom Med 20: 535, 1979.

Shapiro D, Schwartz G: Biofeedback and visceral learning: clinical applications. Semin Psychiatr 4: 171, 1972.

Stroebel C: The application of biofeedback techniques in psychiatry and behavioral medicine. Psychiatric Opin 16: 13, 1979.

Stroebel C, Glueck B: Biofeedback in medicine and psychiatry. In Birk L (ed): *Biofeedback, Behavioral Medicine.* New York, Grune and Stratton, 1973.

Surwit R: Biofeedback: a possible treatment for Raynauds' disease, in Birk L (ed): *Biofeedback: Behavioral Medicine.* New York, Grune and Stratton, 1973.

Taub E: Self-regulation of human tissue temperature, in Schwartz G, Beatty J (eds): *Biofeedback: Theory and Research.* New York, Academic Press, 1977, p. 265.

Taub E, Stroebel C: Biofeedback in the treatment of vasoconstrictive syndromes. Biofeedback Self-Regul 3: 363, 1978.

Weiss T, Engel B: Operant conditioning of heart rate in patients with premature ventricular contractions. Psychosom Med 33: 301, 1971.

Williamson D, Blanchard E: Heart rate and blood pressure control I and II. Biofeedback Self-Regul 4: 1, 1979.

14

Disorders of the Gastrointestinal System

THE PURPOSE of the gastrointestinal (GI) or alimentary tract is to transport food from the environment to specialized areas within its "tubing system," and there modify it to a form which can be utilized by the body for its nutritional needs. That part of the food not useful for this purpose is then expelled back into the environment.

The intake end of this tract begins with the lips, which constitute the first "sphincter." Only when this sphincter is relaxed may the food gain access where it then goes into the mouth cavity followed by the oral pharynx, esophagus, and stomach. From there food travels to the small intestines made up of the duodenum, the jejunum, and ileum. From this point, food passes to the large intestine made up of the cecum; appendix; ascending, transverse, and descending colon; rectum; and the anus (Fig. 14–1). The anus is also a sphincter, only here the direction of flow is outward. The function, however, remains the same, i.e., material does not pass unless the sphincter is relaxed. Occasionally, the directionality of either sphincter may be reversed under certain circumstances. Violation of undirectionality will generally exact a price, however.

Various accessory organs support and enhance the functioning of this tract. These include the teeth, salivary glands, tongue, gallbladder, liver, and pancreas.

There are several functions of the alimentary tract, the first of which is a mechanical function, in other words, delivering the food (fuel) to the place where it is to be absorbed in a form suitable for absorption. The food, as it comes from the outside environment, is not immediately useful to the molecular absorption centers in the lower tracts. To transform it from macromolecular to molecular size requires macerating it into bits. The larger pieces are separated into macromolecular complexes which can then be further reduced and transported across the gut membrane. The teeth are first in this process and do most of the primary shredding, tearing, and grinding. In the stomach, the bits received from the mouth begin to be dissolved and put "into solu-

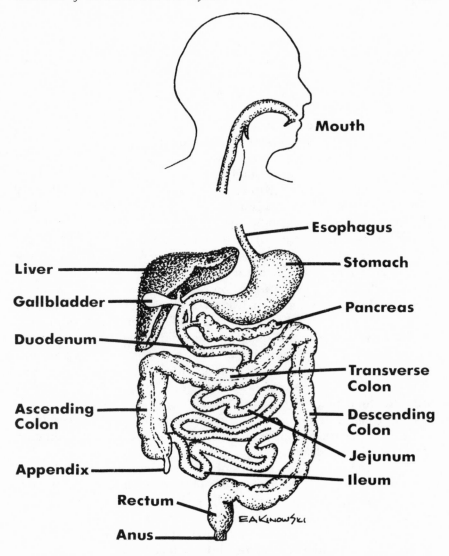

Mouth

Esophagus

Stomach

Liver

Gallbladder

Pancreas

Duodenum

Transverse Colon

Ascending Colon

Descending Colon

Jejunum

Appendix

Ileum

Rectum

EAKINOWSKI

Anus

FIGURE 14-1. DIAGRAM OF THE GASTROINTESTINAL (DIGESTIVE) TRACT. FOOD FROM THE MOUTH PASSES TO THE PHARYNX (12–14 CM. LONG, NOT ILLUSTRATED) AND THENCE TO THE ESOPHAGUS (23–25 CM. LONG). THE SMALL INTESTINE, APPROXIMATELY 6.5 METERS IN LENGTH, CONSISTS OF THE DUODENUM, THE JEJUNUM AND THE ILEUM. THE LARGE INTESTINE IS APPROX. 1.5 METERS LONG, AND CONSISTS OF THE ASCENDING, TRANVERSE AND DESCENDING COLON. THE RECTUM IS APPROX. 12 CM. LONG, AND TERMINATES IN THE ANUS.

tion." As this process nears completion, it is passed into the next chamber, the duodenum, where more basic digestion occurs and so on.

Another element in the mechanical process is that of locomotion. The food is propelled through the tract by the alternating contraction and relaxation of the smooth musculature of specific areas of the gut. This process is known as peristalsis. It, too, is by and large unidirectional, although the direction and rate of propulsion can be altered.

A second function of the alimentary tract, digestion, is a chemical rather than a mechanical process. Once the nutrients are of molecular size they can be absorbed through the walls of the intestine and then through the membranes of the intestinal capillaries. The nutrients are further metabolized, and carried throughout the body via the bloodstream. Although this process is fairly selective, in terms of accepting useful molecules and rejecting nonuseful or toxic ones, it is not 100 percent effective; thus the ingestion of some substances can cause a number of disorders and even death. For this reason, secretions of the auxillary or accessory GI organs such as gallbladder, pancreas, and the walls of the stomach and small intestine aid in the transport of the digested substances. Absorption of digested materials takes place primarily in the small intestine. The large intestine, although it participates in this process, is more a conservator of water, which it absorbs from the foodstuff and digestive secretions.

Fluid balance in the bowel becomes important when the results of imbalance—severe constipation or diarrhea—have led to debilitating disease and even death.

The movements and secretions of the digestive tract generally work in concert. This coordination is accomplished by a fine neural network running throughout the length of the system. This network responds to stimulation primarily from the vagus (10th cranial) nerve which controls over two-thirds of the alimentary tract (Fig. 14-2). The innervation of the vagus nerve carries both sympathetic and parasympathetic components (see Chap. 2) so that factors affecting those components will naturally affect the gut. Thus, a dysphoric mood can be reflected in dysphoric feelings perceived from the GI tract and vice versa. Local hormones are also important.

Other influences from the CNS upon the GI tract is less direct, but of equal importance. It includes that of the hypothalamus and part of the limbic system which is thought to be closely related with appetite satiation, "food approach," intake, and digestion. The close connec-

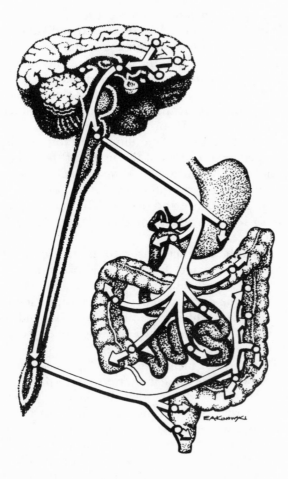

FIGURE 14-2.   CEREBRAL CONTROL OF THE GASTROINTESTINAL
(DIGESTIVE) TRACT. NOTE THAT THE FRONTAL COR-
TEX INTERCONNECTS WITH THE HYPOTHALAMUS AND
THE BRAINSTEM. THE TENTH CRANIAL OR VAGUS
NERVE (PARASYMPATHETIC), WITH ITS NUCLEUS IN THE
BRAINSTEM, INNERVATES THE STOMACH, DUODENUM,
JEJUNUM, ILEUM AND THE FIRST TWO-THIRDS OF THE
COLON. FROM THE SACRAL REGION OF THE SPINAL
CORD, THE PARASYMPATHETIC NERVES EXERT CON-
TROL OVER THE LAST ONE-THIRD OF THE COLON, THE
RECTUM AND THE ANUS.

tion between the satiation center and pleasure centers of this tract is more than likely not coincidental and is discussed later.

The GI tract itself is coated with an absorbing substance (mucous) secreted from specialized cells of the gut lining. The mucous assists in transportation of nutrients across cell membranes throughout its length. The walls of the tract, however, contain smooth muscle and so have the power of contraction and relaxation, without which the peristalsis could not take place. Disorders of the GI tract may therefore include disorders of ingestion, motility, secretion, absorption, and elimination, as well as disorders of the tissue of the tract itself or its attendant supporting structures. Thus, disturbance of any portion of the tract which is affected can influence the rest of the length of the tract depending on its nature and degree. The various regions of the gut have more or less individual functions, but it is a "unitized" and interdependent system.

Those regions of the GI tract nearest to the environment are, naturally, more easily investigated. Conversely, those innermost portions of the GI tract are less accessible to exploration and sampling of their contents. However, the development of the fiberoptic scope, a flexible tube with a lens system which can follow the twists and turns of the tract, now allows visualization of the entire digestive system, including auxillary organs, usually without resorting to surgical intervention. Refinement of biofeedback measurement techniques is finite, however, and its usefulness will cease when it interferes by its presence with what is being measured, to the degree that the data are significantly distorted. In other words the act of measurement distorts the measurement. Technology has not as yet developed innocuous, benign, and reliable data-gathering instruments which can be positioned at any point desired in the GI tract and maintained there until its purpose is complete. If direct measurement and feedback techniques are not practical due to the limitations of present technology, however, some indirect evidence of contraction rate and chemical composition of this GI tract may be obtained. Psychological factors including general body tension as well as spasm, motility, mucosal reactions, evacuation, and other disturbances will frequently reflect an increase in distress of the tract. The effect of such qualitative and quantitative factors as food selection (i.e., pleasurable versus nonpleasurable foods) and intake (i.e., insufficient or excessive amount of food) is well known.

Volition also plays a factor in terms of GI functioning. Conscious decisions are made in terms of when to eat, what amount to eat, and when to eliminate. Volition is often tempered by other factors, however; for example, although a person may choose when to eliminate, the time for this choice may physiologically fall within certain boundaries, limits or time constraints.

The importance of psychological factors in the giving of food is evident from birth. The nourishing of the neonate, whether by breast or by bottle, occupies a major portion of the infant's life during the early weeks and months. A nursing mother and suckling infant rapidly establish a bond which becomes the first and primary relationship involving communication to which the newborn individual is exposed. The tone and vagaries of that relationship have often been felt to have an astounding influence on the development of almost all subsequent relationships. For example, too little or too much of this nurturing, both physiological and psychological, can lead to significant emotional difficulties. Patterns are established which can later be changed only with great effort or as a result of emotional trauma.

Individuals who demonstrate significant psychophysiological responses involving the digestive tract may be amenable to biofeedback techniques through the reduction of tension. This is demonstrated by the fact that when an individual does not ingest food, the psychological need is neglected and tension in the form of anxiety can result. This tension can be reflected by a general increase in muscle tone in the body which can be measured by EMG biofeedback instrumentation. Such information, once the patient is made aware of it, can then be explored by the therapist through psychotherapy.

Anorexia

Disorders involving lack of food ingestion as with anorexia or inanition are hardly amenable to treatment with biofeedback. Since anxiety plays an integral role in the maintenance of these disorders, however, relaxation and biofeedback training can be applied to assist the patient in learning to reduce tension. The relaxation response can be induced in conjunction with eating and through a process of conditioning (see Chap. 19).

Dysphagia

Difficulty in swallowing (dysphagia) may be due to emotional factors and is multidetermined. Important elements include the patient's reaction to the consistency, color, texture, or odor of the food. Following mastication, these factors generally have little importance in terms of the functioning of the digestive tract. Such factors, therefore, are more likely to have psychologic components. The tension demonstrated by, for example, the patient who has a lump in the throat and "can't swallow" (e.g., globus hystericus) can be measured and desensitization procedures involving the use of EMG biofeedback can be employed to resolve this. Psychogenic vomiting may be approached in a similar fashion.

General Disorders

Diseases of the gastrointestinal tract where the etiology is infectious, congenital, toxic, metabolic, or neoplastic are less likely to respond to biofeedback techniques. However, the general principle that the more chronic the condition, the more likely psychogenic factors are involved is applicable. Consequently, biofeedback can be effective in these chronic states.

Peptic Ulcer Disease

One of the most important secretory disturbances of the gastrointestinal tract is peptic ulcer disease. This disorder is characterized by hypersecretion of acid from portions of the stomach lining (Fig. 14–3) when there is either no food or insufficient food there to neutralize it. Following its passage through the pyloric valve, this hypersecretion damages the wall of the duodenum. The acid, if of sufficient quantity and concentration, over time can actually digest portions of the duodenum itself. If the body's ability to generate the protecting mucosal secretions falls behind the acid's ability to digest the duodenum, the underlying lining and muscle layers are exposed and may eventually perforate. This can be a life-threatening situation as the contents of the gastrointestinal system include highly toxic substances. In addition to the duodenum, the stomach is also a frequent site of ulceration. Stress ulcers can affect this area as well as inflammatory processes such as are seen in alcoholic gastritis and the Zollinger-Ellison syndrome.

Reduction in tension is beneficial to patients with these disorders and can be accomplished through biofeedback techniques. With development of effective chemical biofeedback monitoring devices located in the stomach, its level of acidity could periodically be determined or sampled. These chemical monitors, e.g., could be implanted on the gastric or duodenal wall via a fiberoptic scope. Information from the device could be monitored with electronic transmissions. Through training the patient should be able to change the acidity by relaxation

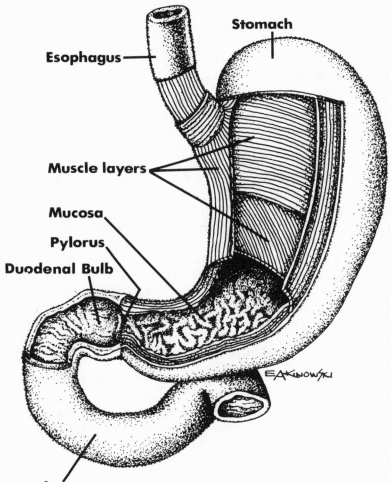

Esophagus

Stomach

Muscle layers

Mucosa

Pylorus

Duodenal Bulb

E.A.KINOWSKI

Duodenum

FIGURE 14-3.   DIAGRAM OF THE STOMACH. THE SHAPE AND POSITION OF THE STOMACH ARE SO GREATLY MODIFIED BY CHANGES WITHIN ITSELF AND IN THE SURROUNDING VISCERA THAT NO ONE FORM CAN BE DESCRIBED AS TYPICAL. THIS REPRESENTATIVE DRAWING, HOWEVER, ILLUSTRATES (1) THE WALL WITH THE THREE LAYERS OF MUSCULAR FIBERS: LONGITUDINAL, CIRCULAR AND OBLIQUE; AND (2) THE STOMACH LINING WITH MUCOUS MEMBRANE (MUCOSA) IN WHICH GLANDS SECRETE THE VARIOUS DIGESTIVE JUICES.

techniques.* Bile secretion from the gallbladder and other secretory activity might also be controlled consciously through similar feedback techniques.

Disorders of Motility

The disorders of motility include ileitis, irritable colon, colitis, spastic colon, megacolon, and diarrhea. Measurement of general body tension in these disorders, especially with hypermotility, would be useful. With the development of specialized biofeedback devices, direct measurement and control of this tension and flow rate of the contents of the alimentary canal could be possible as with a balloon catheter transducer, for example. Thus an individual could monitor his rate of flow and by concentration learn to control the contractions which cause this flow rate. The constipated or megacolonic individual could learn to modify the movement of the bowel contents by not only regulating fluid concentration to assist in bowel lubrication, but also by increasing the efficiency of peristalsis through biofeedback training.

Disorders of motility are often indicative of a general increase in body tension which can be documented and biofeedback treatment applied. This approach is likely to be more effective with disorders that cause hypermotility rather than hypomotility because excessive activity is more easily detectable than decreased activity.

Fecal Incontinence

The exquisite innervation and rich blood supply of the anus suggests that volitional control over this sphincter's operation could be enhanced. This would have importance in such disorders as diarrhea and fecal incontinence and some forms of sphincter dysgenesis. The control achieved in the use of the anal sphincter could be broadened through biofeedback techniques to include those artificial or de novo sphincters which result from surgical procedures such as ileostomies where parts of the bowel are brought to the surface of the skin, and an "os" is formed. These procedures are performed because of cancer or some other disease preventing the normal functioning of the lower bowel. Usually control is not "automatic" with these sphincters and so an ostomy bag is worn over the os to collect the drainage. The ostomy bag must be changed periodically and, especially in the initial phases, it is often psychologically unpleasant both to the patient, family, and

*Current biofeedback methods involving gastric sampling through traditional means have not, however, met with lasting alteration in acid secretion (Whitehead, 1978).

associates. If this sphincter control could operate "on demand" then the need for the ostomy bag and other apparatus would be obviated. Biofeedback techniques could be developed to measure the tension, degree of closure, and ability to withstand peristaltic pressure of the os and thus affect this control. Again, balloon catheter transducers or similar instruments could be employed.

Another factor influencing ostomy bag use is their tendency to become dislodged because of increased skin perspiration. Biofeedback devices may be created to help patients realize that adjustments are needed in order to prevent accidental spillage of the waste material.

Hemorrhoids

Hemorrhoids are varicosities of the anal, rectal, and perianal region. They are often accompanied by pain, inflammation, pruritis, and hemorrhage, occasionally of severe proportions. Among the factors which enhance exacerbation of hemorrhoids are prolonged maintenance of sedentary positions, increased intra-abdominal pressure, and contraction of rectal musculature. Increased general body tension (e.g., with anxiety) may also be contributory.

Treatment approaches to hemorrhoids include "rubber band" ligature, cryosurgery, cautery, application of stringents, antiinflammatory agents, and excision. Biofeedback techniques may also have application in this disorder. Since hemorrhoids are vascular, thermal feedback could be employed. The patient could learn to reduce the temperature in hemorrhoidal tags, thus reducing hemorrhoidal blood flow and therefore hemorrhoidal size and ultimately the symptoms. It is even possible to conceive of a dual biofeedback strategy where strain gauge, muscle tension transducers, or EMG biofeedback sensors are employed in the rectal/anal area to reduce tension locally in combination with the external thermal biofeedback. The patient might then concentrate on both inputs simultaneously; decreasing both muscle tension and peripheral vascular temperature for symptom relief. There are, however, no case studies reported in the literature on either approach.

Again, one cannot overemphasize the emotional coloration and symbolism of the alimentary tract. The close association of the GI system with psychological elements should be clear to anyone aware of such cultural phrases as "biting sarcasm," "tongue lashing," "quit your bellyaching," "butterflies in the stomach," "intestinal fortitude," and similar word groupings. Wherever, therefore, significant emotional content may lie, biofeedback has an excellent chance of probability in participation in the cure. Since anxiety is closely related not only to muscle contraction and tone but also to psychological factors, volitional control of these components through biofeedback may lead to improved GI functioning for many patients.

Illustrative Case

A 63-year-old white female was referred by her internist for biofeedback treatment of chronic abdominal pain and gastritis. She had received medication for over 5 years without relief. In addition, exploratory surgery was performed but no discrete lesion was found. Her pain occurred following ingestion of even small amounts of food. She did not have stomach pain when she did not eat. She lost weight because she refused food due to fear of the pain which would follow a meal. She was depressed and unhappy and despondent regarding the future. Psychological testing failed to reveal any psychological factors which could be related to the pain symptom. Secondary gain did not appear to be a primary factor in this case.

The therapy for this patient consisted of EMG biofeedback treatment with relaxation training. The patient was instructed to practice relaxation responses prior to eating a meal in order to prepare her body for digestion and to enhance overall GI functioning. Treatment sessions were conducted for 5 weeks after which time the patient's pain completely disappeared. She relaxed before each meal and reported that the pain at first was diminished and eventually ceased. A 7-month followup interview revealed no recurrence of symptoms. It is not known exactly what the effective component in this treatment was; however, it appeared that the relaxation enhanced the digestive process and enabled her to prevent anticipating pain if there was no reason for it to occur. Therefore EMG biofeedback training and relaxation methods may be valuable in the treatment of similar disorders.

Review of the Literature

According to Whitehead (1978), biofeedback techniques have been used successfully to treat various GI disorders including rumination, reflex esophogitis, hyperacidity, irritable bowel syndrome, and fecal incontinence.

Rumination

Lang and Melamed (1969) reported a case of a 9-month-old infant with severe chronic rumination. Aversive electric shock to the leg was given whenever nuchal EMG activity indicated that he was about to regurgitate. After six sessons, the rumination was eliminated and the child made a complete recovery. A 1-year followup indicated that he was developing normally.

Successful treatment of rumination by applying contingent electric shock was also reported by Toister et al. (1975), Cunningham and Linscheid (1976), and Linscheid and Cunningham (1977). White and Taylor (1976) suppressed rumination in two mentally retarded patients and similar results were reported by Luckey, Watson, and Musick (1968) and Kohlenberg (1970). Sajwaj, Libet, and Agras (1974) suggested that injecting lemon juice into the patient's mouth can be substituted for the electric shock in the treatment of infant rumination.

Esophageal Motility Disorders

Achalasia, diffuse esophageal spasm, and reflux esophagitis may be treated by biofeedback. Schuster, Nikoomanesh, and Wells (1973) employed feedback of lower esophageal sphincter pressure to treat three normal subjects and six patients with esophageal reflux. Both groups of subjects learned to increase lower esophageal sphincter pressure voluntarily in a relatively short period of time. In a later study, Schuster (1977) replicated these results.

Peptic Ulcer

Several researchers have attempted to use biofeedback procedures to train patients to modify excessive gastric acid secretions. For example, Welgan (1974) conducted two studies in which duodenal ulcer patients were provided with feedback of the pH of gastric contents which were continuously aspirated from the stomach. Subjects were trained to increase gastric pH and decrease acid concentration. Although the acid concentration decreased from the initial baseline level, no consistent differences between feedback and no-feedback treatment conditions were found. Although this experimental design contrasted "true" feedback with "false" feedback, no significant differences in acid concentration were found.

In a single subject case study, Moore and Schenkenberg (1974) reported that feedback enabled the subject to modify acid secretion.

When no feedback was given, however, the subject could not produce significant changes.

Whitehead, Renault, and Goldiamond (1975) reported an experiment with four normal subjects. Three of the four learned to increase acid secretion to several times the normal level and then reduced the rate of secretion back to the baseline. The subjects were operantly conditioned with money in the reinforcement, and acid secretion was measured indirectly by successive titration of gastric contents pH to 7.

Similar results were reported by Gorman (1976). He studied three normal subjects who learned to reduce acid secretion after receiving reward and feedback.

Beaty (1976) reported on three patients whith nonspecific biofeedback for treatment of peptic ulcer. They were given 6 weeks of forehead (m. frontalis) EMG biofeedback training plus instructions to relax at home. In two of the three, stomach pain ratings declined after they were instructed to begin skeletal muscle relaxation; however, there was no objective evidence of ulcer healing.

Aleo and Nicassio (1978) reported that EMG frontalis biofeedback alone was not effective in reducing ulcer pain. The pain ratings of four patients with active duodenal ulcers were reduced only when cognitive behavior therapy was employed along with the biofeedback technique.

Researchers have also used electrogastrogram (EGG) biofeedback. The EGG uses an indirect measure of gastric motility with which it is correlated (Russell and Stern, 1967). Four normal subjects demonstrated control either by increasing or by decreasing EGG in four sessions (Deckner, Hill, and Bourne, 1972). Although Walker, Lawton, and Sandman (1977) replicated these findings, no clinical utility for feedback of EGG has so far been determined. As Whitehead (1978) stated in his review, none of the results to date have shown that peptic ulcer can be treated effectively by biofeedback, and further research is needed to determine whether gastric pH is a useful variable to help patients learn self-control and reduce ulcer symptoms.

Irritable Bowel Syndrome

Irritable bowel syndrome or spastic colon may be suitable for biofeedback treatment. Several studies have investigated the possibility of using biofeedback procedures in treating this disorder. Bueno-Miranda, Cerulli, and Schuster (1976) used balloons which were placed in the sigmoid colon. Patients were instructed to increase distension in the walls of the colon by inflating the balloon. Two-thirds of the patients were successful in learning to reduce spasticity, and their improvement was maintained over an 8-week followup period.

Furman (1973) used an electronic stethoscope which amplified abdominal sounds. Five patients with functional diarrhea learned to modify these sounds. These results have yet to be duplicated, however. For example, Weinstock (1976) studied 12 patients who were unable to achieve the success reported by Furman.

In a similar study, O'Connell and Russ (1978) reported that feedback of abdominal activity did not result in reduction of abdominal pain; however, m. frontalis EMG training did produce positive results.

Further research is needed to determine whether or not feedback of abdominal sounds is an effective procedure compared with generalized relaxation resulting from m. frontalis EMG biofeedback training.

Inflammatory bowel syndrome has been treated with biofeedback techniques. In 1978, Gregory reported that five patients had remission of symptoms after electrothermal and electrodermal biofeedback training; three of the patients suffered from ulcerative colitis and two had Crohn's disease.

Fecal Incontinence

Engel, Nikoomanesh, and Schuster (1974) reported a biofeedback procedure for retaining appropriate sphincter control in patients with fecal incontinence. Balloons were used to measure the response of the internal and external sphincters, and a third balloon was inflated in the rectum to stimulate internal sphincter relaxation and external sphincter contraction. Out of six patients, four became continent after treatment and two were much improved. Cerulli et al. (1976) studied 50 patients of whom 72 percent were either completely continent or at least 90 percent improved following treatment.

Kohlenberg (1970) reported a single case study of a 13-year-old boy with fecal incontinence secondary to the removal of a segment of colon. After extensive training he was able to reduce the frequency of soiling. Schuster, Nikoomanesh, and Wells (1973) indicated that patients can also learn to control spastic colonic response.

New techniques are being developed to train patients with gastroesophageal reflux. These patients are given feedback regarding the resting pressure of the lower esophageal sphincter muscles and trained to increase this pressure to reduce reflux.

Schuster (1977) listed four factors that led to positive results in the treatment of fecal incontinence with biofeedback: (1) the patient must be motivated to change; (2) the patient must respond cooperatively;

(3) the response must be under the control of the CNS; and (4) a cue must be identified that signals the patient to initiate a response. Schuster (1977) also reported that successful results were frequently seen in one or two sessions. The self-control which is learned apparently lasts over a long period of time. Hopefully, other researchers will attempt to replicate these findings. Available data suggest that biofeedback training is a useful technique in the treatment of fecal incontinence and spastic colonic responses.

REFERENCES

Aleo S, Nicassio P: Auto-regulation of duodenal ulcer disease: a preliminary report of four cases. Proceedings of the Biofeedback Society of America 9th Annual Meeting, 1978.

Beaty, E: Feedback assisted relaxation training as a treatment for peptic ulcers. Biofeedback Self-Regul 1: 323, 1976.

Bueno-Miranda F, Cerulli M. Schuster M: Operant conditioning of colonic motility in irritable bowel syndrome. Gastroenterology 70: 867, 1976.

Cerulli M, Nikoomanesh P, Schuster M: Progress in biofeedback conditioning for fecal incontinence. Gastroenterology 70: 869, 1976.

Cunningham C, Linscheid T: Elimination of chronic ruminating by electric shock. Behav Ther 7: 231, 1976.

Deckner, C, Hill J, Bourne J: Shaping of human gastric motility. Proceedings of American Psychological Association 80th Annual Meeting, 1972.

Engel B, Nikoomanesh, P, Schuster M: Operant conditioning of rectosphincteric responses in the treatment of fecal incontinence. N Engl J Med 290: 646, 1974.

Furman S: Intestinal biofeedback in functional diarrhea: a preliminary report. J Behav Ther Exper Psychiatr 4: 317, 1973.

Gorman P: Cephalic influences on human gastric acid secretion and their voluntary control through feedback training. Dissertation Abstracts International 36, 1976.

Gregory C: Personal communication. In Whitehead, W: Biofeedback in the treatment of G-I disorders. Biofeedback Self-Regul 3: 375, 1978.

Kohlenberg R: The punishment of persistent vomiting: a case study. J Appl Behav Anal 3: 241, 1970.

Kohlenberg R: Operant conditioning of human anal sphincter pressure. J Appl Behav Anal 6: 201, 1973.

Lang P, Melamed B: Case report: avoidance conditioning therapy of an infant with chronic ruminative vomiting. J Abnorm Psychol 74: 1, 1969.

Linscheid, T, Cunningham C: A controlled demonstration of the effectiveness of electric shock in the elimination of chronic infant rumination. J Appl Behav Anal 10: 500, 1977.

Luckey R, Watson C, Musick J: Aversive conditioning as a means of inhibiting vomiting and rumination. J Ment Defic Res 73: 139, 1968.

Moore J, Schenkenberg T: Psychic control of gastric acid: response to anticipated feeding and biofeedback training in man. Gastroenterology 66: 954, 1974.

O'Connell M, Russ K: A case report comparing two types of biofeedback in the treatment of irritable bowel syndrome. Proceedings of the Biofeedback Society of America 9th Annual Meeting, 1978.

Russell R, Stern R: Gastric motility: the electrogastrogram, in Venables P, Martin I (eds): *A Manual of Psychophysiological Methods.* Amsterdam, 1967, p. 219.

Sajwaj T, Libet J, Agras S: Lemon-juice therapy: the control of life-threatening rumination in a six-month-old infant. J Appl Behav Anal 7: 557, 1974.

Sarris I, Stone R, Berman D: Biofeedback therapy in the treatment of irritable colon, in *Handbook of Physiological Feedback.* Berkeley, Autogenic Systems, 1976.

Schuster M, Nikoomanesh P, Wells D: Biofeedback control of lower esophageal sphincter contraction in men. Proc Intern Symp Gastroint Mot 4 Annu Meet, Alberta, Canada, 1973, p. 138.

Schuster M: Biofeedback treatment of gastrointestinal disorders. Med Clin North Am 61: 907, 1977.

Toister R, Colin J, Worley L, Arthur D: Faradic therapy of chronic vomiting in infancy: a case study. J Behav Ther Exper Psychiatr 6: 55, 1975.

Walker B, Lawton S, Sandman C: Discriminative control of electrogastrographic activity. Proc Soc Psychophysiology Res 17 Annu Meet, Philadelphia, 1977.

Weinstock S: The reestablishment of intestinal control in functional colitis. Biofeedback Self-Regul 1: 324, 1976.

Welgan P: Learned control of gastric acid secretion in ulcer patients. Psychosom Med 36: 411, 1974.

White J, Taylor D: Noxious conditioning as a treatment for rumination. Ment Retard 5: 30, 1976.

Whitehead W: Biofeedback as treatment of G-I disorders. Biofeedback Self-Regul 3: 375, 1978.

Whitehead W, Renault P, Goldiamond I: Modification of human gastric acid secretion with operant-conditioning procedures. J Appl Behav Anal 8: 147, 1975.

15

Disorders of the Genitourinary System

THE GENITOURINARY system is comprised of two separate systems: the urological (excretory or urinary) system and the reproductive (genital) system.

The Excretory System

The main functions of the excretory system involve filtering the blood of the waste products of metabolism and regulating bodily fluids and electrolyte concentrations by the excretion of water into the outer environment.

This system is comprised of the kidneys, ureters, urinary bladder, and urethra. The primary difference between the sexes in regards to the components of this system is in the length of the urethra. In women, it averages 2.5 to 3.0 cm and in men from 18 to 20 cm, the major or distal portion being found in the shaft of the penis and serving a dual purpose, both excretory and ejaculatory.

The kidneys play the major role in filtering the blood of waste products and maintaining homeostatic fluid concentrations. Although the remainder of the portions of the excretory system are important their function is mainly concerned with the collection and elimination of urine.

In addition to its filtering and concentration functions, the kidneys also play a significant role in regulation of other body processes through the elaboration of angiotensin-renin. Angiotensin assists in controlling peripheral vasodilatation and constriction and plays a significant role in the pathogenesis of hypertension. Therefore, disorders or diseases which affect the kidneys can also have far-ranging effects on other organ functions in the body as mediated through renal metabolism and other renal hormone systems.

Renal Disease

The kidneys are complex organs and are subject to a wide variety of disorders and disease states. Disorders involving the kidneys' excretory function can be diagnosed by noting abnormal changes in either the urine concentration and/or volume. Disorders which potentially may be approached through biofeedback training are those which involve elimination (volume) as opposed to those involving metabolism or excretion (concentration). The following diseases are unlikely to fall under the conscious control of the patient: glomerular nephritis, glomerular sclerosis, cystic disease of the kidney, chronic renal insufficiency, pyelonephritis, analgesic nephropathy, papillary necrosis, chronic renal failure, glomerular disease, obstructive nephropathy, toxic nephropathy (as with analgesics), renal calculi, renal cysts, oliguria, acute tubular necrosis, and uremia. However, diseases such as nephrotic syndrome and disorders associated with sphincter control, obstruction, vesical ureteral reflux, nephrocalcinosis, neurogenic bladder, acquired ureteral stricture, dialysis, and factors involved in toxemia of pregnancy may be more likely to respond to psychological therapy including biofeedback.

Neurogenic Bladder

Neurogenic bladder spasm may lend itself to a certain extent to biofeedback therapy. The neurogenic bladder arises following denervation of the bladder at various neural levels. When the bladder is spastic it is due to upper motor neuron disease, whereas when it is flaccid, lower motor neuron disease is usually the cause. A related disorder is known as uninhibited neurogenic bladder. The focus in biofeedback strategy is the same as that found in other rehabilitative efforts, particularly those following cerebrovascular damage, spinal injury, and peripheral nerve injury (see Chap. 8).

Enuresis, Involuntary Micturition, Public Bladder

The problem of the neurogenic bladder involves *how much* (quantitative) urine will be eliminated from the bladder. There are disorders more susceptible to biofeedback control which have to do with *when* (time-sense) urination will take place. These include enuresis, involuntary micturition, and "public bladder."

One of the earliest attempts at biofeedback (Mowrer and Mowrer, 1938) involved the treatment of enuresis where a patient was aroused by a stimulus sufficiently early so that he could then micturate in the toilet. The term "primary enuresis" indicates that the patient has never been "dry" throughout the night, whereas secondary enuresis is diagnosed when there has been an initial "dry" period before the onset of enuresis. Biofeedback mechanisms continue to be refined through conscious effort (i.e., the waking state) although disorders of "timing" of micturition are more effective when treatment occurs with the conscious ("wakeful") patient than the sleeping individual. Bladder control exercises are also helpful in psychogenic enuresis, particularly secondary enuresis which is often accompanied by tension. Dissolution of the tension through biofeedback training may lessen the degree of enuresis. Antidepressants (Tofranil) have also been useful.

"Public bladder" is a condition in which individuals, particularly males, have difficulty initiating a stream of urine in a public place or when others are present. Dynamic elements such as competition and castration anxiety may play a significant part in the generation of this symptom. Tension is often a common component in this disorder, and bladder training exercises combined with relaxation and biofeedback training could be useful in treatment.

Obstructive Disorders

Blockage of micturition secondary to stricture and in certain cases of calculi ("stone") or foreign object may be approached through utilization of relaxation of the smooth musculature of the "conduit" walls by tension reduction. As a result, the urine may flow freely around the blockage, or alternatively, the blockage or obstruction may be diminished or the stone expelled with less discomfort than otherwise. Ureteral and bladder (vesicular) stones have individual characteristics based on their specific chemical composition, size, and location, and each may respond differently.

A biofeedback procedure could be developed employing a volumetric apparatus. Bladder tension might also be measured indirectly through the abdominal wall, however. Direct bladder tension measurement offers the same problem as direct gastrointestinal tract measurement. In other words, it would be an intrusive process, potentially painful, and certainly uncomfortable, leading to increased tension itself, and therefore inaccurate readings. In the case of the neurogenic bladder, such a direct measurement might also stimulate infectious processes. As with ulcer disease in the GI system (see Chap. 14), it is possible to conceive that a micro pH, volumetric, tension-sensitive device might be developed which could be implanted on the bladder wall cystoscopically to transmit these data to the biofeedback displays.

Nephrotic Syndrome

Biofeedback techniques could come to play a part in the nephrotic syndromes and other diseases involving renal damage. In this disorder, salt balance is commonly critical to the point that it is titrated by the physician to maintain the patient in a slightly edematous state. Edema is used to signal the patient's response to the salt concentration and intake. Slight edema, therefore, could be measured chemically, mechanically, or with appreciation of the degree of skin turgor using biofeedback training.

End-Stage Renal Disease

Dialysis and renal transplantation are important in the treatment of renal disease. Anxiety surrounding the dialysis process and the development of the so-called dialysis neurosis could be obviated through the application of biofeedback. Since relaxation training is essentially a psychological process, it could be speculated that biofeedback procedures might be developed to assist in modifying immunological processes, and thus reduce the rejection risk inherent in renal transplantation. Dialysis days can be used for biofeedback training.

Although research is lacking, biofeedback procedures may hold some promise in the treatment of genitourinary disorders. One of the major difficulties has been the absence of sophisticated direct monitoring devices to provide instantaneous feedback concerning genitourinary functioning.

Illustrative Case

A 28-year-old, white male married with two small children was referred for biofeedback treatment by his neurologist. The patient had suffered severe low back strain 8 months prior while working in a meat-packing plant. No disc injury was identified diagnostically. However, he did seem to be suffering from significant strain. In addition, he had developed enuresis which coincided with the back injury. An extensive evaluation by a urologist failed to reveal significant organic dysfunction of the genitourinary system. It would appear that there was a relationship between his low back strain and enuresis.

The patient's parents were divorced when he was very young and he was forced to live with each parent at various times of his childhood, which was described as stormy and traumatic. He developed enuresis when he was a child, and it continued on a daily basis until he married. At that point, it resolved and he had not been troubled with it until the present time. Not only did it occur when he slept, but also during the day when he was engaged in a variety of activities. The quantity of urine, however, was not as great in the daytime as it was at night.

Initial biofeedback treatment focused on how to relax his lower back muscles and concentrate in order to eliminate the pain. After 10 biofeedback and relaxation sessions, he was able to return to work without any restrictions. He still reported pain but felt he could cope with it. His primary concern at that time, however, was that the enuresis had not disappeared and was occurring at work, which caused him great embarrassment.

Since it appeared that there was a relationship between his low back strain and the elimination of urine, a unique biofeedback treatment procedure was developed to train him in urinary control. He was to take a calibrated flask with him to the bathroom after having consumed large quantities of fluids and deliberately attempt to hold back the urine while concomitantly straining the lower back muscles. The quantity of urine passed during these periods was measured and recorded.

During the first week the average amount of urine eliminated was approximately 3.0 ml. During the second week it dropped below 1.0 ml and during the third week no enuresis occurred.

At this point the patient reported that his daytime urinary incontinence became less frequent and eventually stopped as he became more conscious of controlling the passage of urine. Within 2 weeks nocturnal enuresis also stopped. After two weeks enuresis reoccurred and the patient became quite agitated and depressed. At this point, further exploration in therapy revealed that he resented the fact that he had to work while experiencing pain and wished that he could stay home and not have to suffer just to earn a living. Enuresis was seen as a means of avoiding responsibility and of providing him with an excuse so that he could stay home from work and be dependent upon others for support. After he realized his own conflicts, he made a commitment to return to work without the enuresis and within 2 weeks it again stopped. The nocturnal enuresis continued for another month but was gradually reduced until it no longer occurred either. The patient remained symptom-free over a 6-month followup period.

This case illustrates that biofeedback may be of value in certain types of genitourinary disorders but especially illustrates the need to explore psychological variables which may be playing a causative role in the maintenance of symptoms.

Review of the Literature

One of the earliest feedback techniques involved the genitourinary system, with the symptom of urinary incontinence. Mowrer and Mowrer (1938) used the bell and pad technique of classical conditioning to treat nocturnal enuresis. Since that time, numerous studies have been reported which have successfully used this technique.

Suhel and Satler (1977) developed a biophysics model of urinary incontinence in terms of the differential pressure between intraurethral and intravesical systems. Pearne et al. (1977) explained, however, urinary incontinence in terms of the relationship of high muscle tension levels of the general musculature to the relatively small distension signals from the bladder. They used EMG biofeedback from the frontalis muscle to train relaxation in a female patient with chronic urinary incontinence. An air cystometrogram can provide feedback on bladder pressure in individuals with neurogenic bladders.

Dosa et al. (1971) developed a micturition feedback system for use with disabled or confused patients. This device gives audible and/or visual signals denoting the exact time of micturition. Although developed specifically to alert nursing staff for observational-diagnostic purposes, it might be applicable as a self-control device for patients suffering from enuresis.

The Genital System

The genital system has reproduction as its main function. The purpose of this system is to propagate the species via paired reproducing units. Evolutionary principles (e.g., natural selection) have played a part in establishing the pleasurable feelings, both physical and emotional, generated during procreation, thus insuring the attainment of the purpose of this system.

Although, embryologically, the genital system and reproductive system share a common origin, it is only in the male that this dual function persists, and then only in a relatively minor capacity. In the male, the reproductive system includes the testicles which elaborate the sperm, the epididymis, ejaculatory ducts, the efferent ductuals, the scrotal sac containing these organs, vas (ductus) deferens, urethra, and the penis. The engorgement of the spongy tissue in the penis to the erect state (tumescence) allows for deposition of the sperm in the vagina and then disengorgement (detumescence) when not in use for this purpose. Auxiliary glands in the male include seminal vesicles and the prostate gland.

In the female, the ovaries contain the ova which, when discharged, travel through the oviducts, fallopian tubes, and then to the uterus, where if not fertilized, they are discarded (the menses) down through the cervix and the vagina. The external outlet of the vagina includes the labium major, the labium minor, and vulva as well as the clitoris, which is the homologue of the male penis and is the organ of primary sexual stimulation. Auxiliary glands in the female include the breasts which serve as areas of arousal (erogenous) in sexual behavior, and are the organs of lactation (nursing, breastfeeding) following pregnancy.

Congenital Disorders

Disorders or dysfunctions can arise from either congenital absence or dysgenesis of any segment of a patient's reproductive system, or they may be affected by emotional (functional) factors. Dysfunctions are inherent not only in the actual end organs themselves, but can also be present at higher centers from the periphery back to the spine and the remainder of the central nervous system. Since emotional and physiological functions both play important roles, this system is particularly vulnerable to a wide variety of stressors.

Pathological factors affecting the reproductive system include dysgenesis or dysfunction of the reproductive organs or of the brain and spinal cord (e.g., meningomyelocele), particularly motor portions of sacral nerves S2 to S4, and the sensory component in the lumbar and sacral nerves. Sterilization through bilateral oophorectomies, tubal ligations, complete or partial hysterectomies, and castration (orchiectomy) or vasectomy represent other examples of altered function.

In infectious, neoplastic, traumatic, or toxic conditions, biofeedback is less important than in more functional disorders.

General Dysfunction

Pathological dysfunctions unlikely to respond to biofeedback include in the female neoplastic or dysplastic conditions such as uterine hypoplasia, polycystic ovarian disease, adrenal hyperplasia, leukoplakia, granulomatous disorders, uterine myomas, endometriosis, fibroids, polyps, and ovarian tumors. Infectious processes that interfere with sexual functioning include venereal diseases such as chancroid, lymphogranuloma venereum, granuloma inguinale, gonococcal disease, and syphilis. These can induce pelvic inflammatory disease resulting in vaginitis and cervicitis in the female, and orchitis and prostatitis in the male.

In the male, neoplastic or dysplastic diseases in any of the organs including benign prostatic hypertrophy are also significant. Glandular dysfunction in the hormonal system from pituitary failure, hypo- or hyperthyroid conditions, or adrenal dysfunction are important in both sexes. Congenital absence or anomalies including undescended testicles in the male will lead to various degrees of dysfunction. In the male, disorders such as absent or retrograde ejaculation as well as blockage or strictures in the female will often prevent successful reproduction. Biofeedback may play a limited role in these disorders through tension reduction and "retraining."

Gynecologic disorders that potentially affect sexual behavior include a variety of conditions often believed to possess a psychosomatic overlay. Such categories include orgasmic dysfunction ("frigidity"), anorgasmia, vaginismus, and "abnormal" coitus such as coitus interruptus. Other conditions where biofeedback may be useful are precocious puberty, ovulation, premenstrual tension, menstruation, dysmenorrhea, difficulties with abnormal uterine bleeding, amenorrhea such as that seen in premenarche, uterine displacement (anterior, lateral, or posterior downward), dyspareunia, and pseudocyesis.

It is important to determine in these patients what emotional or psychogenic factors exist in their symptoms or complaints. A careful medical and psychosocial history (including a formulation of the dynamics), is required, together with physical examination and appropriate laboratory studies. The physician will then be in a position to decide what role biofeedback may play in treatment.

Through biofeedback a greater degree of control over bodily function with tension reduction and function monitoring may be achieved than has been considered previously. Ovulation "on demand" through functions extrapolated from those presently used may be postulated using biofeedback approaches. Recording of morning basal temperatures as presently used in the "rhythm method" of birth control and infertility studies offers one avenue for further research.

With increasing sophistication of techniques, it may be that certain breast disorders including engorgement, suppression of lactation, and inflammation as well as cystic activity may be treated with biofeedback, but further study is necessary. Certain authors propose that psychological factors play a role in mammary size. For example, some studies have suggested that hypnosis can lead to temporary augmentation of breast mass.

Pregnancy generates its own characteristic changes in physiology, and psychosomatic elements may play a part in these changes. Pathological conditions such as hyperemesis gravidarum, habitual abortion, preeclamptic toxemia, prolonged labor, spontaneous abortion, premature labor, precipitate labor, obstetric paralysis, and postpartum reactions may be modified by the learning of greater control through biofeedback techniques. It may be speculated that biofeedback can come to play a part in the selection of the day upon which conception (other than through artificial insemination) occurs, parturition commences, and induction or Caesarian section takes place.

Infertility has a number of general causes such as obesity, severe anemia, anxiety, fear, sexual problems such as marital maladjustment, ignorance, timing, douching, sperm leakage, low fertility indices, absent, infrequent or excess frequency of coitus, fatigue, excessive smoking, impotence, and possible immunological incompatabilities. Other causes include those of neoplastic, infectious, metabolic, toxic, or congenital disorders. The correction of a number of these disorders may be aided through application of biofeedback principles. It is suggested that infertility "on demand" may also be a worthy goal to pursue, and biofeedback may have a role to play here as well.

Intersexuality

In approaching the reproductive system, the concept of a spectrum will be useful. On this spectrum, there exists a pole at either end with a gradual shading toward each pole. For example, if a physiological male is placed at one end of the spectrum and a physiological female at the other, the area in between can be referred to as representing intersexuality. This zone is comprised of a relatively small number of individuals and is marked by mixing, overlap, or absence of certain combinations of characteristics of both the male or female. Individuals in this area may be represented by such syndromes as Klinefelter's (XXY chromosome characteristic), Turner's (XO chromosome characteristic), adrenogenital syndrome, pseudohermaphroditism, true hermaphroditism, male hermaphroditism, and female hermaphroditism without fertility. The role of biofeedback in these individuals is directed toward the reduction of tension and in coping with their current life situation and adjustment to their "habitus" in a world of individuals from whom they are set apart.

Psychosexual Disorders*

In studying psychosexual disorders, the concept of a spectrum may again be helpful. Such a spectrum can range from sexual variations

*The following classification is based on *Diagnostic and Statistical Manual of Mental Disorders,* 3rd ed.

through sexual disorders, dysfunctions, deviations, and sexual orientation disorders, as well as gender dysphoria. The four basic components of sexuality which are parameters on this continuum are biological sex, sexual identity, sexual gender, and sexual role behavior. These elements are strong determinants in observed sexual behavior and contribute to a greater or lesser extent toward the manifestation and eventual resolution of conflicts generated in the above.

Gender Identity Disorder. Gender identity disorder (transsexualism, or gender dysphoria) is described as the feeling that the patient from earliest youth (for example a male) is "trapped" within a female habitus (for a male), or vice versa. These patients are often characterized by early cross-dressing, a preference for the company of the opposite anatomical sex with a feeling of greater comfort in their society, and a general disinclination toward overt homosexual activity. Many of these patients express a desire to have their anatomical sexual presentation made consistent with their internal feeling and gender sense, hoping eventually to form lasting relationships (including sexual activity) with a member of their original anatomical designation.

Ideally, current treatment procedures involve a gradual process. The patient is likely to feel the need for treatment after having become aware of strong feelings regarding a wish for sex change (sexual reassignment). The decision to seek this treatment is usually made following adolescence. Cross-dressing is often a first step. These patients present with a lack of concordant feeling between body and "self" in terms of gender sense. Contacts with professionals and specialists, principally in mental health, neurology, surgery, and endocrinology are established, although the chronological order of these contacts may vary. In the case of the phenotypic male who wishes to change to a phenotypic female the sequence of events may occur as follows: A series of appointments with a cosmetologist is made to facilitate cross-dressing, makeup application, and the learning of gender-appropriate body movement. Concurrently, there may be visits to a speech therapist for the purpose of altering voice pitch, learning sex-appropriate word choice, and other female gender-appropriate speech behavioral patterns. Dermatologists or cosmetologists may be contacted for electrolysis in terms of removal of facial and other bodily hair and otolaryngologists or other surgeons may be consulted for "tracheal shaves" to reduce the prominence of the tracheal cartilage ("Adams apple"). Endocrinologists may be consulted for estrogen and other hormone supplements to suppress androgen levels and encourage estrogenlike effects to simulate female secondary sexual characteristics. These changes include development of breast mass tissue, widening of the pelvis, and alteration in fatty tissue distribution to resemble a more closely typical female phenotype. Usually after a period of 2 or more years, this process is culminated by the actual castration of the testes, removal of the penis, and the inversion of the scrotal sac or outer covering of the penis into an "artificial" vagina. This tissue is often plastic enough to begin to assume glandular function and cellular patterns closely resembling that of a "true" vagina. The fact that such tissue changes can occur suggests the magnitude of the dynamic potential the body possesses in terms of physiological adaptation and response. This, of course, underscores the potential that biofeedback offers in assisting this change. At least 1 year of intensive psychotherapy is recommended for these patients, during this process, to assist them in working through what is perhaps one of the most significant and basic life changes an individual can experience.

Overview of Sexual Deviation. The effects of sexual deviations (variants) which are not considered to be secondary to intrapsychic conflict, will be contrasted to those perversions (sexual neuroses) which *are* thought to be secondary to intrapsychic conflict.

There are a wide variety of sexual behaviors that are termed *dysfunctional* under certain conditions, but when circumstances change the behavior may be less inappropriate. Much of what determines which category these behaviors fall into depends upon how the participants and/or their society view the behavior. Examples of these activities may include premarital and extramarital sexual relationships, and unconsummated marriages. Certain sexual techniques or behaviors are also grouped in this category and include fellatio, cunnilingus, anallingus, and anal intercourse (sodomy). Also noted are those physiological events which may affect sexual function, feelings, and behavior, such as imperforate hymen, menarche, menopause, climacteric, abortion, miscarriage, contraception, and masturbation.

Each of the above physiological events and sexual behaviors often involve some feelings of increased tension in their performance or being and may indicate the presence of underlying conflicts. The decision as to whether or not treatment is indicated depends upon the following three factors: (1) the degree to which distress is felt by the individual; (2) the degree of exclusiveness to which the sexual behavior or state is practiced or exists; and (3) the intensity of the patient's motivation for change. Symptoms indicative of distress associated with these behaviors or states include disinterest, perceived physical incapacity, overt anxiety, or persistent excuse (Masters and Johnson, 1966, 1970).

Reduction of tension can be sought through applications of biofeedback training which may help reduce tension in conjunction with psychotherapy in the treatment of these sexual behaviors. Using biofeedback instrumentation, anxiety/tension can be signaled at the moment it emerges through changes in the patient's physiological function. The therapist can then help the patient to pinpoint those conflict-laden areas for further exploration. The patient can therefore begin to resolve and gain mastery over both their emotional feelings, conflicts, and physiological response to the stimuli provided by these conditions.

Sexual Dysfunctions. Sexual dysfunctions include primary and secondary impotence. Primary impotence is diagnosed when a patient has never been able to obtain an erection, which often indicates physiological dysfunction. Secondary impotence is diagnosed when the patient has experienced the ability to gain and/or maintain an erection at some time in the past but since then has lost this function. Emotionally colored factors often play a more important role in secondary impotence.

Another dysfunctional category in the male includes retarded, inhibited, or premature ejaculation. These disorders are sometimes seen in connection with coitus interruptus and can be viewed psychodynamically as a manifestation of castration anxiety—the fear that unless early ejaculation and withdrawal is achieved, dismemberment may result. Alternate theories suggest performance anxiety may be prominent. Dyspareunia also falls within a category sometimes associated with these dynamics and an example of this is the fear of pain on ejaculation.

Analogous conditions have been described in the female. Examples of these include vaginismus where tenseness of the vaginal musculature precludes penetration, and orgasmic dysfunction ("frigidity") where anorgasmia or "sexual anesthesia" is the presenting complaint. Dyspareunia (pain on intercourse) also falls within this category.

Hypersexuality includes nymphomania in the female and satyriasis in the male. Priapism (the state of perpetual tumescence) is a rare disorder and has a pathophysiological basis.

Tension and anxiety are connected with many of the disorders mentioned above. The physiological state in these disorders can be a representation or manifestation of underlying psychological conflicts.

Biofeedback may be useful in the reduction of tension in these states. Plethysmography or the ability to measure muscle tension caused by swelling of tissue and muscle contraction and tension is a primary example of physiological phenomena which can be measured by biofeedback instrumentation. Although the attachment of leads from the biofeedback instrument directly to the patient's genitalia could provide the patient with data as to current levels of tension, this approach is fraught with multiple problems and perhaps should best be reserved for the research laboratory.

Psychotherapy in combination with biofeedback techniques can result in a diminution or resolution of the psychosomatic symptomatology. With biofeedback techniques, self-awareness and learning may be stimulated and may lead to success and mastery over disturbing symptoms; this enhances the potential for continuing success.

The Paraphilias. Paraphilias (sexual deviations or perversions) are approached as to how they affect the participant. Many of them combine sexual and aggressive drives in their attainment. Paraphilias range in varying degrees from anonymous ("victimless") situations to more hostile and aggressive, other-directed behaviors.

The anonymous deviations include voyeurism in which sexual stimulation and satisfaction are achieved by viewing others involved in sexual behavior ("peeping toms") and exhibitionism, in which an individual, usually a male, will expose his genitalia to selected others. In psychodynamic terms, exhibitionism in males is considered as a search for the "phallic woman" in which the exhibitionist tries to impress the viewer with his genitalia; he hopes in return to be not only admired but to view the fantasied female penis. This behavior is believed to be a defense against castration anxiety.

Fetishism is a category in which a sexual object usually having some connection with the female body is used for sexual, often masturbatory purposes. The fetishistic object may be clothing, (e.g., underwear) or footwear, such as high spiked heels. The condition is labeled fetishism when it is either used exclusively or when sexual arousal or ejaculation cannot occur without the presence of the object. Partialism, a rarer form of fetishism, occurs when some part of the female body is used for the same purpose as the fetishistic object. Examples of partialistic objects include hair, a foot, or a breast. This diagnosis is made only when the object is used exclusively for sexual gratification or when orgasm cannot occur without it. Both fetishism and partialism are thought to represent the fantasied female penis and are traditionally viewed as defenses against castration anxiety. Fetishism in the female is more rarely reported and may be manifested by shoplifting behavior.

Transvestitism is another form of anonymous deviation in which an individual attains gratification from sex role cross-dressing, and where the point of the cross-dressing is in order to provide sexual gratification. This is distinct from transsexualism (q.v.).

Obscene telephone calls and letters (scatographia) also fall in this category. In these disorders, as with exhibitionism, the fantasy is that the individual whom the patient addresses will respond positively and will admire and become sexually aroused by the person who initiated the communication.

Disorders involving physical contact form a subgrouping of the anonymous deviations and include not only fetishism but also zoophilia (beastiality) and frottage. In zoophilia, fondling, masturbation or intercourse primarily involving an animal is the main symptom. This behavior is often, but not exclusively, seen in rural settings, perhaps because of either the enhanced isolation or the increased availability of the desired or substitute sexual objects (animals). The diagnosis is made when it becomes a primary or exclusive behavior for sexual stimulation or gratification.

Frottage is described as the rubbing of the genitalia, usually momentarily, against another individual. This brief contact may be sufficient of itself to cause orgasm. The behavior often occurs in a crowded or public area such as on the subway or in an elevator. Only transient contact is sought by the frotteur and the establishment of a relationship does not play a part in this behavior.

Anonymous deviations are often forbidden by so-called blue or morality laws. Usually, however, prosecution is withheld pending referral for psychotherapy. This is generally not the case, however, in the "aggressive" sexual disorders or perversions, which include incest, pedophilia or pederasty, rape, sadism, masochism, lust murder, and necrophilia (copulation with a cadaver). It is easier in these categories to define a perversion in the traditional sense and to view the difficulty as one of major importance in sexual functioning. The degree to which the behavior is necessary for sexual gratification designates the degree of psychopathology in these disorders. Biofeedback involving not only psychotherapy but perhaps even aversive techniques may be indicated here (see Chaps. 3 and 19).

Incest and pedophilia share similar dynamics and are viewed as containing elements of castration fears. For example, a child is selected over an adult partner because the child is seen as less threatening. The act of incest may not be possible unless there has been, at least at some level, agreement among the parties concerned that the behavior is at least temporarily acceptable and/or can be ignored. At some point, however, the behavior is usually detected and brought to the attention of law enforcement agencies. With incest, the behavior almost always ceases after the exposure of the activity.

In sadism and masochism (S&M), the sexual behavior involving the infliction of pain is usually clearly defined beforehand, and the pain is gratifying only under these conditions. Pain inflicted outside of the sexual experience has the same noxious quality to these individuals as to the population at large. Masochists outnumber sadists; consequently true sadists who practice commercially are much sought after by highly motivated masochists. "Bondage and discipline" (B&D) involving, for example, black leather paraphernalia (e.g., boots and whips) is often a trademark of these practices.

Necrophilia is an extreme example of sexual gratification obtained with a passive sexual object. Some argument can be given as to its inclusion here versus its inclusion in anonymous deviations, however. Typically so much anxiety is raised in the necrophiliac by the confrontation with a living partner that sexual performance is either seriously hampered or precluded.

Another group of paraphilias includes that of the "excretory perversions." In this category, the excretory product, i.e., the feces or the urine can often be interpreted psychologically as representing a phallus. Coprophilia and urolagnia are the two major examples of this category. In coprophilia the feces may be smelled, tasted, touched, fondled, and used for masturbatory purposes. In urolagnia, the urine is swallowed, smelled, touched, or directed onto some portion of the patient's or his partner's body. Elements of castration anxiety are present, although this behavior usually signifies a more primary dysfunction and conflict at an earlier developmental stage. The degree to which the behavior is practiced will give the therapist a clearer indication of whether or not to designate it as a perversion ("sexual neurosis"). As in the examples cited above, it is classified as a disorder if the behavior is absolutely or primarily necessary for sexual stimulation or gratification.

Sexual disorders involving interaction of a group include *ménage à trois,* spouse ("wife") swapping, and group rape. Latent homosexual elements are felt to be common to these three examples where the sharing of the same "receptacle" (vagina) may be psychodynamically equivalent to direct interaction.

It is unusual for a patient to seek therapy because of involvement with this type of group action, unless the patient is the victim of a group rape. Although biofeedback therapy would be applicable here to reduce anxiety, the search for underlying conflicts should be very intense since the acting-out behavior is usually an indication of a significant underlying conflict.

Homosexuality

Noncompliance with what is defined as "normal" by society can lead to an increase in tension and dysphoria to the extent that sexual dysfunction can occur in varying degrees. Resolution of this tension centering around underlying psychological conflicts can lead to heightened sexual function and heightened pleasure derived from that function. Motivation plays a key role in biofeedback therapy of these individuals and is particularly important in a discussion of homosexuality (Masters and Johnson, 1979).

Homosexuality has run the gamut of classification ranging from sexual perversion to normal sexual variant, and all stages in between. If the existence of significant tension, dysphoria, or diminished function is experienced in an individual's drive toward sexual gratification then he has the potential for change. This is the role that motivation plays. Change can be accomplished from homosexual to heterosexual functioning and vice versa, as well as the stages in between (bisexuality) with sufficient motivation.

Role of Brain Opiates in Orgasm

In recent years, the brain opiates (endorphins, enkephalins) have created much excitement in the field of neurobiochemical research (Miller, 1979; Snyder, 1977). If it is assumed that these endogenous opiate peptides share some of the properties of the exogenous opiates, then one can extrapolate their possible role in the neurophysiology of the genitourinary system. It is interesting to speculate, for example, regarding the similarities of the "rush" experienced by heroin users and the euphoria described for the release of the sexual tension during orgasm. Apparently opiate antagonists (e.g., Nalorphine HC1) do not block orgasmic responses (Goldstein and Hansteen 1977), however, other "pleasure center" receptors may be involved.

If biofeedback techniques can reach the stage of refinement where they can influence brain opiate levels as is proposed in terms of placebo therapy (see Chap. 21), then some interesting possibilities suggest themselves. For example, such a technique could be useful in the treatment of orgasmic dysfunction; however, other questions must be asked. Will those who master this skill find themselves being "addicted" over time to a form of "mental masturbation"? Further research will be necessary before these and other questions in this area can be successfully approached.

Case Study for Sexual Deviation

A 26-year-old man, married with one child, was referred for biofeedback treatment by his psychiatrist. He had a history of transvestitism since he was 13 years old. Recently his transvestite episodes had increased in frequency and he was beginning to go out in public dressed as a woman. He also was concerned because masturbation while dressed in women's clothing had increased significantly over the past few years. He was referred for biofeedback treatment when, after several months of verbal psychotherapy, there was no significant improvement.

He was first taught muscle relaxation and given EMG biofeedback training. He was then instructed to masturbate only while considering heterosexual fantasies and never while wearing women's clothing. After 4 weeks, the patient demonstrated the ability to relax during the biofeedback session and had eliminated masturbatory activities involving either fantasies about himself being a woman or wearing or touching women's clothing. He was then asked to bring in the woman's clothing that he had used in the past. After the therapist left the biofeedback room the patient changed into the woman's clothing (including underclothing, a wig, and cosmetics). When the therapist reentered he instructed the patient to consciously tense his muscles while the EMG instrument was attached to his forearm extensor muscles. The patient attempted to change the auditory feedback in the direction indicative of increased muscle tension. While engaged in this activity the patient was asked to imagine that his wife, child, and parents were observing him dressed as a woman (a scene which the patient had previously indicated to be very disturbing to him).

After 20 minutes, the patient was asked to remove the woman's clothing and to dress in gender-appropriate clothing while the therapist again left the room. Following this, the patient was instructed to relax and to imagine how good it felt to be his own sex while listening to the auditory feedback from the EMG instrument and trying to relax very deeply. After six treatment sessions the patient reported that he no longer felt the urge to engage in transvestite behavior. (A total of 10 treatment sessions was given to the patient.)

A 1-year followup indicated that the patient had continued to be symptom-free and his heterosexual adjustment appeared to be normal according to both his own report and that of his wife.

Review of the Literature

Behavior therapy has contributed significantly to the treatment of sexual disorders. Aversive therapy techniques, faradic shock or aversive imagery, which "punish"positive physiological response to either heterosexual or homosexual stimulation, can contribute to a change in the individual's sexual functioning. However, biofeedback training using information obtained from measurements of penile tumescence has "not been particularly successful to date" in homosexual disorders (Barlow et al., 1975). Those individuals who feel "comfortable" with their sexual behavior orientation and are not "distressed" (ego dystonic) by it to any great degree are unlikely to seek change or to be affected by attempts at being "changed." It is well to remember this as studies which show high percentages of successful change in sexual orientation have traditionally been based on a population which is already prescreened and thus "selected" to have the highest potential or desire for change. It is likely that these statistics may be quite different if the general population were considered without the benefit of a prescreening phase.

The role of biofeedback is not yet fully explored but could represent an important adjunct to this process in terms of working through these changes. This is a challenging field and a continuing refinement of biofeedback application seems promising in the future.

Biofeedback treatment may also be used to treat dysmenorrhea experiences.

Another type of biofeedback procedure was developed by Gregg (1979) to train pregnant women in relaxation for labor. Gregg and his colleagues developed a unique EMG feedback system and in controlled study compared the labor of 30 women who received biofeedback training with 30 control subjects. The women who received training spent less time in the first stage of labor (4.1 hours versus 6.7 hours) as contrasted with the untrained group.

Gregg also reported that the training may be effective in reducing the chances of premature labor and delivery in high-risk women. Ten patients who had a history of premature delivery were given biofeed-back training and all delivered at 38 weeks or later. Further research is needed, however, especially under controlled conditions, to determine if this technique is more widely applicable because the disorder is complex with multiple causes.

Tubbs and Carnahan (1976) investigated the use of frontalis EMG and skin temperature (hand warming) feedback in eight patients. Four of the eight reported dramatic decrease in menstrual cramping, within the first months following treatment and two showed moderate improvement.

A controlled study with 40 subjects who were classified as having "regular" menstrual cycles was reported by Clayman and Simkins (1975). The authors cautioned that although some symptoms may have decreased during treatment of the biofeedback (hand warming) group, the lack of evidence of differential skin temperature learning between groups prevented drawing a conclusion that the biofeedback was responsible for clinical change.

Sedlacek and Heczey (1977) reported improvement in three cases given treatment that included training subjects in the EMG frontalis, hand temperature warming, and vaginal temperature warming.

Biofeedback techniques have recently been developed to enhance sexual functioning, especially in females. Goren (1977) examined the relationship between physiological and perceived sexual arousal in women. Thirty-six normally responsive (orgasmic) women were instructed to attempt to increase or decrease vaginal blood volume (VBV) on instruction in response to the viewing of erotic videotapes or sexual fantasy under one of three conditions: auditory biofeedback, monitoring of perceived VBV, or instruction only. The biofeedback and monitoring groups showed better control than the group receiving instructions only. Demand characteristics affected perceived and physiological arousal similarly. When no performance expectations were given subjects perceived themselves as unaroused even during high physiological arousal; in states with high arousal expectations, subjects perceived themselves as aroused even under low physiological arousal. Further, results indicated that voluntary suppression was more difficult than enhancement, and that the higher the physiological arousal, the more difficult was suppression and the easier was enhancement. The author concluded that with female oriented stimuli, sexually "normal" women reported arousal to erotic material, and were able to subjectively discriminate and voluntarily control physiological response (VBV). This may mean that VBV biofeedback procedures could be employed to treat cases of orgasmic dysfunction ("frigidity") or lowered sexual arousal.

Zingheim and Sandman (1978) observed that women could learn to control their vasomotor responses when given feedback about their vaginal pulse amplitude. A specially designed vaginal plethysmograph was utilized in this study.

Biofeedback training has also been employed to treat disorders of sexual function in the male, such as chronic penile detumescence (impotence). A variety of devices have been developed to measure penile erection that have effectively been used in voluntary control and biofeedback experiments or treatment modalities. The most commonly used device is a mercury strain gauge for recording penile circumference (Bancroft, Jones, and Pullan, 1966; Laws and Bow, 1976). Rosen (1973) and Rosen, Shapiro, and Schwartz (1975) demonstrated that normal subjects could suppress or increase penile tumescence through biofeedback training. A penile plethysmograph biofeedback technique was also developed by Laws and Powlowski (1973).

Csillag (1976) studied the efficacy of using a device similar to that used by Laws and Powlowski to treat patients suffering from psychogenic impotence. Of a total of six patients, three improved sufficiently to participate in successful intercourse with their partners. The other three patients, however, although demonstrating the ability to achieve an erection during biofeedback training were unable to generalize this response successfully to their actual life experiences. More controlled studies are needed to determine if penile tumescent feedback can be an effective treatment of psychogenic impotence.

REFERENCES

Bancroft J, Jones H, Pullan B: A simple transducer for measuring penile erection, with comments on its use in the treatment of sexual disorders. Behav Res Ther 4: 239, 1966.

Barlow D, Agras W, Abel G, Blanchard E, Young L: Biofeedback and reinforcement to increase sexual arousal in homosexuals. Behav Res Ther 13: 43, 1975.

Clayman K, Simkins L: The relationship of temperature control to menstrual distress. Proceedings of the 6th Meeting of Biofeedback Society of America, 1975.

Csillag E: Modification of penile erectile response. J Behav Ther Exper Psychiatr 7: 27, 1976.

Diagnostic and Statistical Manual of Mental Disorders (3rd ed). Washington, D.C.: American Psychiatric Association, 1980.

Dosa S, Bojtos A, Houston IB: The pee-peeper: micturition alert device. Lancet: 2: 530, 1971.

Goldstein A, Hansteen R: Evidence against involvement of endorphins in sexual arousal and orgasm in man. Arch Gen Psychiatr 34: 1179, 1977.

Goren E: A psychophysiological analysis of female sexual arousal. Dis Abst Intern 77 - 24982, 1977.

Gregg R: Biofeedback and biophysical monitoring during pregnancy and labor, in Basmajian J (ed): *Biofeedback—Principles and Practice for Clinicians.* Baltimore, Williams and Wilkins, 1979, p 238.

Laws D, Bow R: An improved mechanical strain gauge for recording penile circumference change. Psychophysiology 13: 596, 1976.

Laws D, Pawlowski A: A multipurpose biofeedback device for penile plethysmography. J Behav Ther Exp Psychiatr 4: 339, 1973.

Masters W, Johnson V: *Human Sexual Response.* Boston, Little, Brown, 1966.

Masters W, Johnson V: *Human Sexual Inadequacy.* Boston, Little, Brown, 1970.

Masters W, Johnson V: *Homosexuality in Perspective.* Boston, Little, Brown, 1979.

Miller R: From analgesia to schizophrenia: the potential of endorphins. Behav Med: 30, 1979.

Mowrer OH, Mowrer WM: Enuresis: method for its study and treatment. Am J Orthopsychiat 8: 436, 1938.

Pearne DH, Zigelbaum SD, and Peyser WP: Biofeedback assisted EMG relaxation for urinary retention and incontinence: a case report. Biofeedback Self Regul: 2 (2): 213, 1977.

Rosen R: Suppression of penile tumescence by instrumental conditioning. Psychosom Med 35: 509, 1973.

Rosen R, Shapiro D, Schwartz G: Voluntary control of penile tumescence. Psychosom Med 37: 479, 1975.

Sedlacek K, Heczey M: A specific biofeedback treatment for dysmenorrhea. Biofeedback Self-Regul 2: 294, 1977.

Snyder S: Opiate receptors in the brain. N Eng J Med: 266, 1977.

Suhel P, Satler J: Use of biological feedback in correction of urinary incontinence. Urol Int: 32, (2-3): 238, 1977.

Tubbs, W, Carnahan C: Clinical biofeedback for primary dysmenorrhea—a pilot study. Biofeedback Self-Regul 1: 323, 1976.

Zingheim P, Sandman C: Discriminative control of the vaginal vasomotor response. Biofeedback Self-Regul 3: 29, 1978.

16

Disorders of the Endocrine System

THE ENDOCRINE system is basically a servomechanistic system of which the most important component is feedback. End-organ response is detected by the sensing elements of the endocrine system and adjustments are made, both quantitatively and qualitatively. The components of the endocrinological system are called glands and their function is to alter the rate of their secretions in response to the information received.

Secretions of the endocrine glands are called hormones. Hormones are released into the blood rather than through ducts (hence "ductless glands") and travel via the bloodstream to certain target organs. These target organs are often at a distance from the gland itself.

Upon reaching the target organ, polypeptide hormones act on (and perhaps within) cell membranes once internalized by the process of pinocytosis. Steroid hormones, however, act only when internalized. All hormones affect the rate at which that cell functions or the rate at which enzymes are produced and elaborated in that cell. The latter process binds the hormone onto a receptor site which then stimulates a second chemical which may act directly or stimulate a third chemical, and so on, in what is referred to as the "cascade system." Since it is the genetic (nuclear) material which is often affected, hormones can be said to have a genetic as well as an enzymatic effect. Hormones in general do not initiate or terminate bodily processes but rather are rate-limiting. They are usually either stimulatory or inhibitory in regards to this rate.

Hormonal action accounts for a wide variety of bodily activity including, but not limited to, growth, fluid and electrolyte concentration and regulation, reaction to stress, control of glucose metabolism, fluctuation in heart rate, sense of well-being and other important functions.

Many of the endocrine organs are strongly influenced and "coordinated" by the pituitary gland located in the sella turcica at the base of the skull, just inferior to the optic chiasm. The pituitary gland has in the past been referred to as the master gland or the "conductor of the endocrine orchestra." It has been found, however, that the pituitary in its turn is subject to the influence of hormonal substances released from the hypothalamus, which in their turn may be subject to the influence of higher brain centers, perhaps even reaching cortical levels.

There are a plethora of short- and long-loop feedback pathways which indicates that the endocrine system is highly complex and diverse. The purpose of this intricate system is the maintenance of physiological homeostasis. The endocrine system has both vegetative (slow) and adaptive (rapid) responses to changes in this homeostasis. Since CNS control is involved, this system allows the organism to adapt to change in the environment. Thus the endocrine system acts in a liaison capacity between the organism's internal and external environments.

While the CNS has often been viewed as a computer-like complex, with electrical connections and discharges, the endocrine system can be viewed as a "thermostat" using chemical communication and stimuli. Each endocrine gland possesses adrenergic input stemming from the CNS, however, so that the two systems work in concert to achieve orderly homeostasis.

There are a bewildering array of hormones acting to effect various levels of physiologic control. Those hormones which act in the "periphery" are referred to simply as "hormones" with an adjective prefix which describes their site of origin. The pituitary hormones, (often seen as regulating the peripheral hormones), bear the adjective "stimulating" or the suffix "-tropin." The hypothalamic hormones, which in turn affect the pituitary hormones, are generally given the descriptor "releasing hormone." (If a hypothalamic hormone is hypothesized, but not proved, it is referred to as a "factor" and abbreviated "F"). The following describes by level the various well-known hormones and their functions.

Peripheral Endocrine Organs

Not all endocrine functions are "new" in the evolutionary sense. Some have developed and functioned much longer in phylogenetic time than others proceeding up the evolutionary scale. Thus, in man, some endocrine functions have become what could be described as "vestigial." The best example of this concept in man is the pineal gland. The pineal gland, which is situated in the roof of the third ventricle of the brain, elaborates the hormone, melatonin. Melatonin has a maturational rate effect on puberty in lower animals though no effect is yet known in man which is felt to be essential or exclusive to the pineal. In animals maturation can be delayed, retarded, or over-stimulated (in which case, precocity results) by this hormone.

The paired lobes of the thyroid glands are located in the neck. The thyroid gland requires iodine because the primary hormone it elaborates (thyroxine) is a molecule bearing four iodine atoms. In the body following its release, thyroxine ("T-4") is converted to tri-iodothyro-nine, a three-iodine atom containing molecule ("T-3") which is approximately ten times more potent than thyroxine. The thyroid gland also produces tri-iodothyronine itself, though usually in smaller quantities than thyroxine.

The effects of thyroid hormone are protean and it has been described as a "general body toner." For example, thyroid hormones have an impact upon the body's basal metabolic rate (BMR), as well as the kidney, heart, and bone.

The thyroid gland also elaborates the hormone calcitonin (CT). This hormone decreases the body's concentration of serum calcium ions which (most likely) increase the body's concentration of phosphate ions. The electrolytic balance of these ions is important in terms of both muscle contraction and tone as well as bone density. Calcitonin might also be considered a vestigial hormone, however; this is because situated behind the thyroid gland itself is another endocrine organ system, that of the parathyroids. One each of the four parathyroid glands are located behind each of the poles (lobes) of the thyroid gland. The primary function of parathyroid hormone (PTH) is to regulate calcium and phosphate ion concentrations. This it does more effectively than calcitonin. Parathyroid function may also be affected by vitamin D levels.

The pancreas, located in the abdomen posterior and caudal to the liver, produces among other substances insulin (from the islets of Langerhans) and glucagon. The pancreas is described as a "pituitary-independent" endocrine organ in that its feedback loop is very short involving essentially bloodstream concentrations of glucose. Glucagon stimulates the breakdown of more complex carbohydrates into the "sugar" glucose while insulin depletes blood levels of glucose and favors a synthesis of complex carbohydrates. The feedback mechanism used is that of the blood level of glucose.

Since glucose is the fuel which the body, particularly the brain, metabolizes, it must be replenished when depleted. When glucose levels are decreased, therefore, glucagon levels are increased. The glucose level can be increased to meet demand, but when this level is exceeded insulin is produced in greater quantities, thus tending to reverse the process. This interaction can serve as an outstanding model of how feedback is used to maintain homeostasis.

The kidneys are situated just dorsal to the pancreas in the retroperitoneal space. Atop the pole of each kidney sits an adrenal gland, which has both a cortex (outer shell) and medulla (inner portion). The cortex of the adrenal gland elaborates two main varieties of hormones, corticosteroids (corticoids) and androgens (gonadic hormones). The corticosteroids are divided into two groups, the glucocorticoids and the mineralocorticoids. The main glucocorticoid is cortisol, while the most important mineralocorticoid is aldosterone. The major androgens are androsteredione and dehydroepiandrosterone (17-keto-steroids). All of the adrenocortical hormones are derived biochemically from cholesterol.

As is true of the thyroid hormones, the adrenocortical or cortical hormones have very wide-ranging effects, a significant portion of them relating to stress. The medullary hormones are even more directly and immediately involved with stress in terms of the "fight or flight" reaction mediated by the hormone epinephrine (adrenalin).

Glucocorticoids can affect various metabolic rates and bodily functions such as glucose homeostasis, linear growth, fat deposition, and the general state of health and sense of well-being, including regulation of the inflammatory and healing process. Mineralocorticoids are closely involved with regulating electrolyte balance, and particularly salt (sodium) and bicarbonate retention, as well as potassium and hydrogen-ion excretion.

The androgens or sex steroids assist in the growth and development of secondary sex characteristics, and are present, though in differing quantities, in both females and males.

In the female, the ovaries elaborate sex steroids: estrogens and progesterone. Estrogens are important in oocyte maturation, secondary sexual characteristics, and fertility. Progesterone is essential in the maturation of the uterine endometrium and in ovulation. Estrogen and progesterone tend to be mutually inhibitory so that estrogen favors periodic cycling and release of the ova while progesterone favors inhibition of this process and the retention and growth of the fetus. During each menstrual cycle the levels of these steroids vary depending on the stage of the cycle.

Secondary sexual characteristics are influenced strongly by these sex steroids and include the distribution of head, facial and bodily hair, fat deposition, sweat patterns, and exocrine functions.

Although in the male, the adrenal gland produces testosterone (the major male sex hormone) its primary elaboration occurs in the testicles. The role played by this steroid includes the growth and viability of the sperm, elaboration of seminal fluid, contribution to the sexual drive, and development of secondary sexual characteristics. Also, sex steroids inhibit long bone growth in both sexes by bringing epiphyseal growth to closure so that further lengthening is retarded. Obviously, if sexual reproduction is connected with maturity and the individual can never mature, there can never be reproduction. Maturation via sex steroids can contribute, therefore, to a dampening down of the growth process with the focus now being shifted to reproductive processes.

Between the neck of the bladder and the external urethra in the male lies the prostate gland circumscribing the urethra. This chestnut-sized lobulated organ has become the center of a heightened degree of interest because of the discovery of the prostaglandins, so named because they were first identified in the prostate gland. Since their discovery many varieties of prostaglandins have been identified, and they are now known to be present in every major organ system of the body. Prostaglandins have been referred to as "non-hormone hormones," though they are not hormonal in the traditional sense but are local inducer substances.

Pituitary Gland

The pituitary gland itself, while serving in the role of "administrator" of peripheral endocrine function, has not only stimulating effects on the peripheral endocrine glands, but it also manufactures primary effector hormones in its own right. The posterior pituitary (neurohypophysis) is not a gland but is a direct extension of the hypothalamus which apparently elaborates several hormones, two of which have well-known effects. The first of these, vasopressin, (antidiuretic hormone or ADH), is connected strongly with the regulation of free water and the concentration of the sodium ion in body fluid levels. It requires the permissive role of certain adrenal hormones, and together acts mainly on the kidneys, where sodium is either retained or excreted due to its influence. Vasopressin conserves free water in order to prevent diuresis, hence its alternate name, antidiuretic hormone. Several substances such as diphenylhydantoin (Dilantin) tend to inhibit vasopressin which then leads to water loss via the urine.

The second important hormone of the posterior pituitary gland is oxytocin, the principal function of which is to assist in the stimulation of uterine contraction during labor. During labor if endogenous oxyto-cin levels are insufficiently high exogenous oxytocin preparations may be administered to further the process of parturition.

A third posterior pituitary hormone, neurophysin, has been de-scribed though its function has not yet been as clearly delineated.

The remainder of the principal pituitary hormones are elaborated from the anterior pituitary gland (adenohypophysis). This portion of the pituitary gland has a different embryonic origin than that of the posterior pituitary. There are seven anterior pituitary hormones of importance. Two of these hormones are primary effector hormones: prolactin (PRL) or lactogenic hormone, and somatotropin (STH). PRL, principally important in the female, assists in breast develop-ment, maturation, and milk production. The fact that prolactin release is inhibited by dopamine or dopaminergic compounds has led to the interesting observation that some dopaminergic agonists such as ma-jor tranquilizers, like promazine (Sparine) and chlorpromazine (Thorazine), can stimulate breast development in males, a condition known as gynecomastia.

The other primary hormone, somatotropin or human growth hor-mone (HGH), regulates linear growth in the individual. This is accom-plished by its action on the liver to stimulate the release of somatomedin which will promote, for example, linear growth in the adolescent. Human growth hormone also has effects on glucose me-tabolism as well as other aspects of growth, maturation, and mainte-nance.

The remaining five anterior pituitary hormones are mainly effective in stimulating peripheral hormones. Among these is thyrotropin or thyroid-stimulating hormone (TSH) which stimulates the release of thyroxine.

A second "administrative" hormone is adrenocorticotropic hor-mone (ACTH). This hormone serves to stimulate the adrenal cortex to release cortisol. Melanocyte-stimulating hormone (MSH) has previ-ously been identified as another stimulating type hormone. Recently, however, there has been some question as to whether both MSH and ACTH are actually independent and separately elaborated hormones. This question has arisen due to their possible connection with a much larger macromolecule (see below).

The two gonadotropins are follicle-stimulating hormone (FSH) and lutenizing hormone (LH). The latter hormone is also called interstitial cell-stimulating hormone (ICSH) in males though it is the same mole-cule.

Lutenizing hormone is important in ovarian hormone production and ovulation and in the male it stimulates testosterone production, while FSH supports the growth and maintenance of the sperm.

Hypothalamic Hormones

The hypothalamus is found just dorsal to the infundibular process and stalk of the pituitary gland. The releasing factors for the pituitary stimulating hormones are elaborated in the hypothalamus although it is possible that releasing factors or hormones are found in other parts of the brain as well.

Corticotropin releasing factor (CRF) is presumed to act on ACTH through stimulation by the anterior pituitary. The question raised earlier, however, lies in the fact that both ACTH and MSH may be part of a larger molecule, β-lipotropin hormone (β-LPH). Other components of this same large molecule which have stimulated interest currently are the endorphins and the enkephalins, the endogenous brain opiates (see Chap. 5).

If this macromolecule elaborates all of these factors, then a problem arises as to what the stimulation of ACTH may involve, since if only ACTH is elaborated, other parts of the molecule, including the brain opiates, MSH, and others would be elaborated too, all originating from the one large macromolecule. Further research is expected to resolve these questions.

Traditionally, however, corticotropin-releasing factor is thought to stimulate ACTH, which in turn stimulates the adrenals to release the corticosteroids.

Thyrotropin-releasing hormone (TRH) stimulates the pituitary to release TSH which then stimulates the thyroid gland to produce and release thyroxine. However, hormone releasing factors are not the only releasing substances which can stimulate hormone elaboration in the peripheral glands. It is noted that some of the thyroid-stimulating immunoglobins or TSI (e.g., long-acting thyroid substances or LATS) which are clearly not hormonal have similar effects.

Another substance, growth hormone releasing factor or somatotropin releasing factor, is presumed although not yet clearly identified. There is also a somatotropin-releasing-inhibiting factor (SRIF) or somatostatin. It is a very potent inhibitor of growth hormone and several other peripheral hormones such as insulin and glucagon.

Gonadotropin-releasing hormone (GnRH), also known as lutenizing hormone releasing hormone (LHRH), stimulates the release of gonadotropin substances. Prolactin-releasing factor (PRF) and prolactin-inhibiting factor (PIF) are proposed but not identified absolutely. The question of an intermediate lobe inhibiting factor (MIF) is connected with the MSH "problem," and its status is not clearly defined.

Many other releasing factors in the hypothalamus have been postulated though none of these are yet "proved." Their exact identification must await further research.

Cortical Hormones

The "cascade effect" mentioned earlier has application in this hierarchical endocrine system in that higher centers of the brain are suspected of contributing to the release or stimulation of the hypothalamic releasing factors themselves. Areas such as the amygdala, limbic system, mamillary bodies, and hippocampus are primary suspects. To a fifth level are added still higher cortical control centers which might stimulate the above areas of the brain. Of course, higher cortical control centers could then be acted upon by the external environment as mediated by the special sense organs (visual, auditory, olfactory, gustatory, and tactile). When these higher centers are also considered, the total complexity of the endocrine system with the elaboration of thousands of potential combinations of feedback loops (ultra-short, short, intermediate, and long), all neurochemically modulated, is an awesome proposal. Added to this complexity is the fact that the quantity of the various chemicals elaborated is in the range of picoliters (one trillionth or 10^{-12}). It is therefore understandable why the model of the brain as a "gland," as opposed to the model of a "telephone switchboard" is currently gathering more support.

Several organs in addition to the above secrete substances which could be considered as hormones under certain conditions. Among these are the thymus (thymin, thymosin); the kidney (erythropoietin, renin); the alimentary tract (APUD cell subsystem); stomach (gastrin somatostatin, substance P); duodenum and small intestine (secretin, motilin, CCK, GIP, VIP, Bombesin); large intestine (enteroglucagon); and the lung (prostaglandin-related compounds). The concept of the endocrine system as a rigid structure seems misleading. Further research is needed before more definitive statements can be made as to the "all-inclusiveness" of this system.

Common Glandular Disorders

Disorders of endocrine function primarily involve either primary hyperfunction, primary hypofunction, or secondary hyper- or hypofunction, based upon activity of the stimulating glands, which in turn are subject to the same conditions and so on up the pyramid of hierarchical control levels. Also, deficiencies of one substance in a gland may lead to excessive stimulation of that gland, causing hyperrelease of other glandular hormones, while the one deficient hormone remains in a hypoconcentration state.

Though rare, tumors of the various peripheral glands, pituitary gland and hypothalamus, often cause hypersecretion and at times, in more dysplastic states, secretion of related (or even nonrelated) chemicals in abnormal amounts. These disorders can serve as "minilaboratories" in terms of observing the effects of the dynamics of the endocrine system. Although it is possible that tumors are also hyposecreting, the reverse is more usually the case.

Hypothyroidism (Gull's disease, myxedema) usually presents with goiter and is associated with a "slowing down" of many physiologic processes. In neonates and infants, such a deficiency leads to the disorder of cretinism. Hyperthyroidism (Graves' disease) stimulates basal metabolic rate and is usually manifested with exopthalmos and goiter. Hypoparathyroidism causes the disorder of hypocalcemic tetany. In a hypoparathyroidal state, calcium is not mobilized from bone and serum calcium levels fall, while phosphate levels increase due to failure of renal excretion. Bone becomes denser, and the muscle tissue without its normal supply of calcium becomes highly irritable. Prolonged and dramatic muscle spasms can involve the whole body and may occur upon the application of the slightest stimulus. Hyperparathyroidism increases serum calcium levels and decreases phosphate levels.

Hyperadrenalism, especially oversecretion of the adrenal cortex glucocorticoids produces Cushing's disease. A similar clinical state is also seen in individuals who have been on prolonged and excessive treatment with exogenous steroids. Hypoadrenalism (Addison's disease or adrenal insufficiency), is usually characterized by hyperpigmentation, lethargy, anorexia, and hypotension. The adrenogenital syndrome, an autosomal recessive disorder caused by selective enzyme deficiencies in the synthesis of cortisol. Hallmarks of this disorder are usually virilization and female sexual ambiguity. The most important syndrome associated with the adrenal medulla is that of pheochromocytoma. Overproduction of catecholamines (dopamine, norepinephrine, or epinephrine) in this tumor produce hypertension, headache, sweating, and palpitations in most adults.

Hyperstimulation of the gonadal-dependent steroids can lead to isosexual or heterosexual development or a spectrum of the two. Overproduction of the androgens in the male produces virilism manifested by increased beard growth and coarsening of features. Increased production of estrogens in a male will lead to feminization.

It is interesting to speculate upon hypothetical hypo- or hyperfunction of higher cortical control centers in terms of releasing factors. This applies particularly to the case of the brain opiates and their possible regulation of hypo- or hypersensitivity to pain. A genetically determined factor could also be postulated in such cases.

Pituitary hypo- and hyperfunction generally have more far-reaching effects since the pituitary gland possesses such a great number of hormonal agents confined within one space. Thus panhypopituitarism causes a whole host of deficiency states manifested by such symptoms as small stature, inappropriate sexual development and function, and a wide variety of other symptoms. Hyperpituitarism could produce the opposite effects but the more dramatic symptomatologies are seen in hypersomatotropinism where, if it occurs before puberty, gigantism may result and after puberty, acromegaly results with its characteristic subcutaneous thickening, striking facies, and bodily habitus. Selective hyposomatotropinism leads to the opposite condition, the "true" midget.

Application of Biofeedback to Endocrine System Feedback

The current model for biofeedback treatment and for endocrine disorders presupposes an ability to measure these hormonal effects to bring them into the individual patient's awareness and thereby lead to the potential for alteration of the source of the activity being measured. Currently no procedure exists to directly measure hormonal concentrations, at least in the office setting. And even if such existed, it is difficult to see how change could be effected through "dealing directly" with the thyroid gland, for example. However, the symptoms of these conditions such as high or low blood pressure, bradycardia versus tachycardia, muscle tonus, and similar manifestations could be measured. Again, though, how these measurements might thus be "modified" even though they were taken directly, certainly poses a formidable challenge to biofeedback technique. Since both endocrine function and biofeedback depend on the principle of feedback, it is tempting to speculate how such treatment could be developed.

With the continuing delineation of mechanisms and sophistication in technology, however, one might suppose that proven tract connections leading to higher cerebral centers might be identified and a biofeedback "cascade-effect" utilized by this means. If, for example, a deficient thyroid state exists, a route tracing the stimulating hormone for the thyroid function back through the releasing factor to higher stimulating and/or releasing factors in cerebral centers could potentially serve as the mechanism through which control by conscious motivation might be achieved. Though this is obviously speculative the development of such potential mechanisms for change would be very exciting.

Selective manipulation of homeostatic mechanisms without undue disruption of hormone function is certainly a goal worth striving toward, though the goal is at best "long term." Currently, traditional replacement and/or suppression techniques utilizing the more direct biomedical applications remain the surest form of treatment. The circuitry and pathways may be presumed to exist and when structure is delineated then change of structure becomes a possibility.

Another area of speculation involves the possible role of biofeedback and relaxation methods in the production of brain opiates, i.e., endorphins and enkephalins. It has been shown that placebo administration can stimulate (and is perhaps mediated by) production of endorphins and result in pain relief. It is possible, therefore, that the patient could learn to control the production of his endorphins through various cognitive techniques. It seems logical that the effectiveness of biofeedback (and perhaps hypnosis) in providing relief of pain may be due, in part, to the measured production of brain opiates while the patient is in an altered state of awareness.

Review of the Literature

Fotopoulos and Sunderland (1978) found only one published report of the application of biofeedback training in the treatment of endocrinological disorders. Fowler, Budzynski, and Vandenburgh (1976) used EMG biofeedback training to treat a diabetic patient who had experienced difficulty in controlling her condition. The goal of the biofeedback training was to decrease her insulin requirement, as well as to reduce episodes of ketoacidosis. The patient's average daily insulin requirement dropped from 85 units to 59 units, following a 9-week training program. As this is an uncontrolled case study, however, the results must be interpreted cautiously.

Prospective researchers should be aware of the inherent danger of using insulin intake as a dependent variable of treatment effectiveness. Patients may feel better subjectively as a result of being more relaxed but their physiological need for insulin may not have changed (Fotopoulos and Sunderland 1978). Research in this area should always be done under strict medical supervision with frequent and appropriate laboratory analyses of blood and urine (Williams, 1968).

In summary, the use of biofeedback techniques to treat endocrinological disorders has not yet been tested. Biofeedback techniques may be useful in treating endocrinological disorders with known emotional and psychological components (Beeson, McDermott and Wyngaarden, 1979).

REFERENCES

Beeson P, McDermott W, Wyngaarden J: *Textbook of Medicine.* Philadelphia, Saunders, 1979.

Fotopoulos S, Sunderland W: Biofeedback in the treatment of psychophysiologic disorders. Biofeedback Self-Regul 3: 331, 1978.

Fowler J, Budzynski T, Vandenburgh R: Effects of EMG biofeedback relaxation program on the control of diabetes. Biofeedback Self-Regul 1: 105, 1976.

Williams R: *Textbook of Endocrinology.* Philadelphia, Saunders, 1968.

17

Disorders of the Cognitive-Emotional System

THE TERM *cognitive-emotional* reflects what the brain does in terms of two of its most important functions: cognition, which includes thinking, reasoning, and judging; and emotion, as in feeling, experiencing, and affect. Further, cognitive-emotional phenomena seem to function along the same continuum of brain activity as neurologic phenomena.

Human behavior must ultimately have as its basis cellular, nuclear, molecular, and submolecular interaction. Outside of the brain the remainder of the body is essentially a life support system which serves to sustain us while we gather information about our environment in order that we may subsequently act upon it in idiosyncratic ways.

Freud, in his paper, *Project for a Scientific Psychology,* attempted to explain this function through physiological and mathematical symbolism, but lacking the appropriate sophistication had to abandon this in favor of a more philosophical representation. Though these concepts (symbols) are yet lacking, we may anticipate the time when human behavior will be understood through physiologic, biochemical, and ultimately mathematical formulae (Freud, 1966).

From this we can conceive of the function of the human brain as a logical process. The brain attempts to arrange events for itself which are as stress-free as possible, as well as to see to its own "immortalization" through a variety of means including reproduction.

To accomplish this formidable task in an efficient fashion many "executive-type" decisions must be made. Not every drive or impulse can or should be gratified instantaneously; the outside environment must be taken into account. The task of the executive, as with any administration, is to arrange for a series of compromises that will satisfy this basic goal, yet still allow itself to remain "in office." To accomplish this, it employs data-gathering mechanisms including special sensory and other informational modalities. This information becomes part of the "input" which is processed in the "through-put" in the main computer functioning portion of the brain, with resulting amended thought-responses constituting the "output" which is manifested in human behavior.

The factors that can cause difficulties in this process are multideter-mined. Data, for example, can be gathered inaccurately; also, if gath-ered accurately and presented incorrectly, or if data are gathered correctly but interpreted inefficiently, or gathered correctly and inter-preted appropriately, but processed and acted upon incorrectly, con-flict can occur with the environment or an attainment of what the "self wants."

According to Stone (1979), four ways of approaching how to deal with cognitive-emotional deficiencies or conflicts exist and are desig-nated the biological, psychological, behavioral, and social schools of thought. There are doubtless others less often used that represent either combinations of the above or different approaches entirely.

Unfortunately scholars have spent a great deal of energy and re-sources in deciding which approach is more "correct" in dealing with the disorders of this system. One might even speculate that more energy has been devoted to the comparison of intellectual systems than in the actual treatment of these disorders. Perhaps we can con-clude that all systems contribute both to the etiology of the disorders and their resolution.

Because of the relative lack of "hard data" regarding the functioning of this system and its disorders, conceptualization and treatment are less precise and uniform than for disorders in other systems. It is in the cognitive-emotional system that medicine most clearly remains an "art" and not entirely yet a science.

Disorders of Infancy, Childhood, and Adolescence*

The young patient manifests disorders which, although they overlap at times with those of adults, often have their own characteristics and unique symptom constellations.

Mental Retardation

Among the disorders most frequently found in the young is mental retardation. In mental retardation there is a relative inefficiency of the cognitive portion of brain function. Ranges for mental retardation have been described and defined by psychological testing instruments. Although this approach is controversial, a scale with numerical values has been assigned to measure cognitive function. Individuals with test

*The following classification is based on the *Diagnostic and Statistical Manual of Mental Disorders,* 3rd ed.

scores falling within certain ranges are then assigned a number to indicate their degree of mental retardation. Those ranges below the "normal" range in terms of standard deviation (SD) of I.Q. scores have used the following descriptors: Borderline mental retardation (between 1 and 2 SD: 83–68); mild mental retardation (between 2 and 3 SD: 67–52); moderate mental retardation (between 3 and 4 SD: 51–36); severe mental retardation (between 4 and 5 SD: 35–20); and profound mental retardation (greater than 5 SD: 20–0). Other ranges of descriptors have been used including "educable" to "noneducable" to represent various functional categories. Discreet causes of mental retardation vary and include (1) genetic, (2) metabolic, (3) traumatic, (4) birth or perinatal cerebral injury, and (5) intrauterine infection or meningoencephalitis in infancy or childhood. Unfortunately, detection of mental retardation is easier than the elucidation of its etiology. The clinician is too often left with the unsatisfactory conclusion that the retardation is due to "cerebral dysgenesis, etiology unknown." Though the etiologies may vary in this condition, the resulting behaviors are remarkably similar.

Treatment of these disorders is difficult and often frustrating. Structure (anatomy) is necessary in order to expect appropriate function. Those patients with relatively greater resources, however, are able to take relatively greater advantage of available therapies. Biofeedback applied in conjunction with psychotherapy may have a role to play in assisting the patient to gain some degree of mastery over himself and eventually his environment. Whether the conflict lies with self or environment, there is frequently tension and/or anxiety present. Where tension or anxiety exists, biofeedback may have utility in assisting the individual. Gaining some degree of control over self, whether physiological or cognitive and emotional, may enhance the helpfulness of those resources and increase their "efficiency" as well as limiting dysphoria. The goal in treatment of these patients should be to maximize their potential so as to make them as contributory as possible to themselves, their families, and society.

Attention Deficit Disorders

Attention deficit disorders include states with hyperkinesis ("hyperactivity"), states without, and residual type. Treatment of the disorders with hyperactivity is complicated by the fact that in order to profit from therapy the patient must be willing to pay attention and respond to what is being offered to him. When the span of attention is limited the difficulty in treatment is obvious. Those objects in the patient's environment, however, which can hold his attention, are often those which are novel and utilize mutliple major sensory inputs. Thus the therapist who uses biofeedback devices may have an advantage over the therapist working alone. Concentration and motivation, which are often lacking in these patients, however, are still required. With persistence, physiological feedback can assist in helping the individual learn how to gain some control over himself to lessen the ever-expanding vicious "circle" of stimulus-overresponse, overstimulus-overresponse. In conjunction with appropriate medication (e.g., Ritalin, Cylert), the role played by biofeedback can be additive or even synergistic. Certainly, hyperkinesis and the tension disorders in general manifest significant degrees of stress and anxiety in the patient, and reduction of these is one of paramount importance.

Conduct Disorders

Conduct disorders include both aggressive and unaggressive presentations, each either socialized or unsocialized. Disorders in conduct refer to behavior that is different from that of the majority of those who surround the individual. Often this is either a response to anxiety (internalized or otherwise) or productive of it, once the behavior is manifested. Biofeedback in conjunction with psychotherapy may assist in the patient in learning how these stimuli affect him, how he can understand and resolve these conflicts, and then begin to gain a greater measure of control over the behavior with the sense of choice developing rather than the quality of "driven-ness."

Anxiety Disorders

Children and adolescents manifest anxiety disorders as a reaction to separation or with avoidance or overanxious behavior. Children and adolescents may be more distrustful of biofeedback devices through lack of understanding or fear of the machine, but more often there is fascination as with a new toy. The machine is also on occasion endowed with magical powers by many, particularly children. Time spent in responding to questions and explanations regarding the instrumentation will be beneficial. This is why biofeedback in conjunction with psychotherapy may permit a more useful approach to identifying and dealing with anxiety. Any initial discovery that the patient makes that demonstrates a gain of control over self or reduction in tension and anxiety will markedly increase interest and investment in the therapy process for that patient. Frequently, children and adolescents are more apt to be open in the expression of positive feelings generated by this kind of gain in mastery over their bodies and feelings.

Other Disorders of the Preadult

Other disorders of this age group include separation anxiety disorder, attachment disorder, schizoid disorder, elective mutism,* oppositional disorder, and identity disorder. These descriptive disorders represent significant underlying difficulties though the degree of distress felt with each may vary from patient to patient and disorder to disorder. Such difficulties as attachment disorders and schizoidal disturbances indicate a more basic problem in terms of ability to form relationships. Elective mutism represents a refusal to communicate whereas oppositional disorders indicate that the communication is adverse or hostile.

Biofeedback techniques in these conditions will be of more use to the less severely disturbed patients. Biofeedback offers a way in which communication can be established, whether the patient initially wishes it consciously or not. The hypothesis followed is that the patient will be in rapprochement with the machine and that his physiological responses will be monitored accurately and instantaneously. If he is asked certain questions, for example, or if certain areas are explored, and he elects to remain mute regarding them or is more withdrawn into his own thoughts, there may be no verbal response but there will be a physiological response, particularly if the material covered is of significant importance. This can then be brought to the patient's attention and can lead to the establishment of more verbal lines of communication.

Eating Disorders

Anorexia nervosa, bulimia (overeating), pica, and rumination constitute a class of eating disorders and offer an interesting variety of dynamics as well as significant degrees of frustration in terms of effective treatment. Biofeedback used in the context of psychotherapy can come to play an important part in the treatment of some of these conditions. In the adolescent who is anorectic, significant degrees of internal tension, rage, or anxiety are often acted out through the refusal to eat. Exploration of psychological areas touching on some of

*Elective mutism is a disorder where a patient elects not to verbalize, or even refuses to talk, yet has the physiological capacity for speech.

these underlying concerns during biofeedback treatment will register immediately to the patient and therapist and will serve as "red flags" to be pursued in an empathic manner. The use of behavioral models may provide more treatment success with these patients. Aversion techniques ("punishments") administered via machine-linkage through dysphoric stimuli are not felt to be helpful and are contraindicated.

Stereotyped Movement Disorders

The treatment of stereotyped movement disorders, such as transient tic, chronic motor tic, Gilles de la Tourette's syndrome, and other tic disorders, with biofeedback techniques is seen as having much potential for useful application. These difficulties share some overlap with torticollis ("wryneck") discussed earlier in Chapter 8. Some control over these spasms may be gained by using biofeedback with muscle tension sensors and videotape resources. With the readout on the machine adjusted so that initial success in control will signal a large imprint on the sensitivity of the machine, the patient could be encouraged to redouble his efforts. As the patient acquires more sophistication with his biofeedback skills, the electronic gain can be returned to more typical use levels.

Other Physical Disorders

Other distressing conditions such as stuttering, functional enuresis, encopresis, somnambulism, and pavor nocturnus (night terrors) could also be approached in the same way as the stereotyped movement disorders, i.e., with a combination of biofeedback incorporating an audio and videotape format. It is noted that individuals with stuttering often do not "hear" how they actually sound until they are able to review their own activity through the use of the recording equipment.

Enuresis was one of the first disorders approached through biofeedback techniques (see Chap. 15). A strategy similar to that described above is recommended for this disorder as well as encopresis. Childhood somnambulism and night terrors are indicative of severe underlying anxiety. Biofeedback can assist in uncovering and then resolving this tension, through "channel exploration" where identification of sensitive (emotionally charged) areas can be made. These are the areas which stimulate a high arousal effect from the biofeedback device. Sleep laboratory studies using electroencephalogram (EEG) monitoring are also helpful both diagnostically and therapeutically in these

PROZAC®
fluoxetine hydrochloride

- VITAMINS?
- CALCIUM ENTRY BLOCKER?
    - FOUND NATURALLY?
- FOOD?

DISTA

conditions. By following rapid eye movements (REM), dream activity can be identified, the patient awakened, and the distressing material obtained directly. Pavor nocturnus, however, differs from childhood somnambulism in that REM sleep is not observed prior to the onset of the night terror (see Chap. 9). A generalized tensing of the musculature signals the approach of this experience and the instrumentation can alert the therapist to its onset. Medication combined with psychotherapy may be useful then as a treatment along with the inclusion of biofeedback.

Specific Developmental Disorders

Autism is one of the most disturbing of the childhood syndromes. In the severe case, verbal interaction or communication is absent. Biofeedback, however, may provide some basis for more communication than would otherwise be possible.

Some allowances will be necessary for the young patient's lack of understanding, which may lead him to tear off leads, attempt to injure the machine, or simply ignore its readings. Those professionals experienced in taking EEG tracings of children, however, know well the techniques of obtaining the cooperation of resistant young patients. Biofeedback equipment can provide video displays which are colorful and the electronic components themselves can be less ominous and more intriguing through console and cabinet design. Also, a wide variety of auditory responses are available which are either more soothing or more strident, depending on the goal of therapy. Any gain in communication with the autistic preadult, however small, is a therapeutic victory and worth the investment of time.

Learning disorders include dyslexia (developmental reading disorders), acalculia (developmental arithmetic disorder), dysphasia (developmental language disorder), and dysarthria (developmental articulation disorder). Although these conditions may exist in isolation these are often accompanied by other preadult disorders. Anxiety not only accompanies but is often the result of poor performance in learning. This anxiety can be monitored. As the patient reads, calculates, or speaks, difficulty with these tasks will be instantly signaled through biofeedback. Those associations made at the time of the appearance of the anxiety can be identified and the material generated can then be used in the therapy. Even in severe organic neurological disabilities, the patient may be assisted in developing coping skills while reducing his anxiety around the performance of these tasks.

Disorders of the Adult

Organic Mental Disorders

Though all disorders are ultimately "organic" those with discreet etiologies are more easily identified by specific causative agents and are referred to as organic brain syndromes. In the classification of disorders of the sensorium, the causes range from infectious, neoplastic, toxic, metabolic, and traumatic to "unknown."

These conditions include delirium which is transient or self-limited, dementia which is of longer duration, or permanent residual amnesia, delusions, hallucinations, or affective personality changes (e.g., depression) where those components constitute the presenting complaint, or the most noticeable change in behavior.

In the management of organic mental disorders, the first task of the clinician is to identify the cause and to eradicate and modify any etiological agent. The second task is to assist in the recovery of the patient, and to reevaluate and note the remaining function. Rehabilitation may be indicated. Biofeedback techniques can play a role by assisting in the latter phase of treatment.

Anxiety may often be present and the patient may be satisfied in gaining coping strength, enhancing appropriate alternate pathways, or strengthening those which are only partially functioning. The potential recovery of function will depend upon the surviving cerebral tissue ultimately defined by number, type (neuronal versus glial), and location of surviving brain cells, as well as the extent and localization of the neural "drop-out" due to tissue injury. Where the tissue has been irrevocably compromised or destroyed, then the help available is limited unless alternate pathways can be developed. The brain shows some plasticity and certain functions can be subsumed by associated tracts. The younger the organism, the greater is this plasticity and the potential for recovery by compensating for injury through "substitution." EMG biofeedback training has been used to restore muscle functioning in cases of paralysis of other organic disorders. It may also increase overall functioning in organic brain syndrome by strengthening neural pathways through conscious exercise.

Substance Use Disorders

The important parameters here are first the determination of whether the substance use disorder can be diagnosed as either an abuse, dependence, or combination of the two. The therapist must then decide whether the misuse is continuous, occasional (episodic) or "in remission."

Although almost any substance is potentially "addictive" (e.g., food abuse), the majority of chemical substances misused fall into one of the following categories: alcohol, barbiturates, opioids, cocaine, amphetamines (or other sympathomimetic drugs), phencyclidine (or other arylcycloalkylamines), hallucinogens, cannibis (marijuana), and tobacco (nicotine).

It is common for patients to initially misuse these substances for the momentary relief of dysphoria or "psychic pain." With continued use of these substances, a form of psychological or physiological dependence (or both) develops. This misuse is usually pursued without regard to subsequent consequences, and these patients often show an inability to tolerate even minimal delays in gratification. Over time the habituation and addiction itself produces a progressively increasing amount of dysphoria with tolerance so that a vicious circle is formed. The consequences resulting from this behavior cut across all major areas of life activity and include marriage, family, occupation and social experiences, and relationships.

Alcohol clearly predominates in this group due to the numbers of patients involved and calculated loss to the individual and society as a whole in terms of life expectancy, work hours, dollar amounts, or by any other standard measure.

Typically these conditions, particularly alcoholism, are under- or nondiagnosed (denied or unrecognized) until the disorder is far advanced. Social and professional discomfort with making these diagnoses is one important factor affecting this observation. The patient's denial is typical, characteristic, and significant. Any delay in making the diagnosis and in initiating appropriate treatment is a disservice to the patient and those close to him.

Evidence now accumulating suggests a possible genetic predisposition toward substance abuse (especially alcohol). The authors therefore believe that total abstinence from the abused substance is indicated when treatment planning is considered.

It is unusual for substance abuse to occur in isolation. These patients handle stress poorly and often have significant degrees of unmet dependency needs which feed into this process. These elements can often be traced back to early family conflict or trauma. However, the elucidation of elaborate dynamics while perhaps intellectually stimulating for the therapist is rarely helpful in bringing about the patient's recovery in isolation. "Self-help" programs including such organizations as Alcoholics Anonymous or other appropriate support-oriented groups continue to maintain the highest success rate when matched against other approaches to treatment of this population.

Substance use disorders are best attacked by a multimodal approach. For example, in the case of alcoholism, following detoxification, Alcoholics Anonymous, should be combined with group and individual therapy, educational programs, and alcohol metabolite enzymatic blocking agents such as disulfiram (Antabuse) to maximize recovery. In the case of opiate addiction, comparable modalities include Narcotics Anonymous and naloxone (for detection). The use of heroin itself as in Britain or methadone (an opiate derivative which successfully competes for the same receptor sites) remains controversial in the treatment of opiate dependency. The brain opiates (endorphins, enkephalons) may come to play a role in the treatment of an addicted patient, though further research must be awaited as to their efficacy.

Biofeedback is another modality which may be introduced into this eclectic ("holistic") approach. When dependency is frustrated in a patient suffering from substance abuse through interaction with his environment, psychogenic pain may often result. The failure of alleviation of this pain and the delay in gratification of these needs can bring about a dramatic increase in general tension or anxiety levels. Biofeedback can be helpful in lowering general body tension levels. If the patient can "learn" that he has some control over decreasing his tension, then the felt "need" to return to the substance of abuse may be lessened. It is important to keep in mind, however, that a match must be made between the therapy approach, the patient's needs and his particular substance of abuse. Withdrawal phases require appropriate medical management and the usual precautions should be observed in dealing with each of these specific substances of abuse. When more than one substance of abuse is involved, the need for a comprehensive treatment plan is even more important.

Psychosis

Patients suffering from organic mental disorders may at times be "psychotic" (i.e., experience difficulties in terms of reality-testing and appropriateness to situation). This may be due to discreet pathology. Psychotic disorders are often referred to as "functional," a term, which though vague, has traditionally been used to distinguish them from "organic" disorders.

The diagnosis of psychosis in a patient necessitates a further elaboration into one of the following categories: (1) schizophrenic disorders (disorganized "hebephrenic," catatonic, paranoid, undifferentiated and residual), (2) paranoid disorders, and (3) major affective disorders. This classification is necessary because appropriate treatment will vary depending upon the precise diagnosis.

As with the substance use disorders, genetic factors seem to be important in the psychoses. A patient may possess, for example, a genetic predisposition for a psychosis which is then "triggered" by a series of as yet imprecisely defined external (environmental) phenomena; this brings the underlying psychosis into expression often in proportion to the degree of stress experienced. This hypothesis is not proven and is not even proposed for all of the psychotic disorders, but it is a tempting one, particularly in the schizophrenic and major affective disorders.

Schizophrenic Disorders

Although the diagnosis borderline schizophrenia or borderline psychosis remains controversial, this does not lessen its utility in certain cases. The continuum extending from mildly neurotic to frankly psychotic is useful in conceptualizing the borderline condition. On this continuum, the borderline diagnosis may lie closer to the premorbid psychotic state than other disorders. Since borderline is also a term applied to personality disorders, however, its use remains confusing. Patients who seem to demonstrate what is referred to as a "psychotic core" but who do not typically demonstrate bizarre behavioral manifestations are sometimes described as "borderline."

The clinical indication for biofeedback therapy of schizophrenic disorders is not yet clear and may even be contraindicated in all but a few specific situations. The problem is that in achieving the relaxation states which are associated with biofeedback technique, the treatment might actually promote deterioration of reality contact. Yet, schizophrenic patients also suffer from tension and anxiety as a result of their condition. It is possible, therefore, that under a controlled and structured therapeutic setting biofeedback could be a useful adjunct to appropriate psychopharmacotherapeutic and supportive intervention. To use biofeedback techniques with schizophrenic patients without appropriate medication or other recognized treatment approaches, however, is contraindicated until further clarified. The psychotic patient's ego boundaries are more porous in schizophrenia, and projection, especially of the paranoid variety, is more apt to occur. For example, the biofeedback machine itself may be imbued with a variety of unrealistic properties and a psychotic transference could be stimulated. However, the reported successes of direct analysis and other more recent techniques of treating psychotic states seem to indicate that experienced and highly skilled therapists can work with the delusions and hallucinations of their patients to bring about significant therapeutic gains. Absolute contraindications therefore may well be modified to become situational contraindications. Of the schizophrenic diagnoses, it may be the patient with residual schizophrenia who could derive use from biofeedback, although this will necessitate treatment decisions on a case-by-case basis.

Paranoid Disorders

Paranoid disorders have proven almost uniformly frustrating in terms of effective treatment by most currently recognized therapeutic approaches. The degree to which the patient's delusional system is encapsulated is important, as those with discreet delusions have more emotional resources available to examine their intrapsychic conflicts. Those patients with expanding paranoid delusional systems are less likely to be able to take advantage of this process.

Affective Disorders

In the major affective disorders (manic-depressive illness) psychopharmacotherapeutic intervention (Lithium) remains the treatment of choice. In conjunction with this, however, biofeedback may play a part in relieving the tension and anxiety generated by the patient's awareness of the differences between his perception of his environment when matched against external reality. These same principles can be applied to other psychotic disorders such as schizophreniform disorder, the brief reactive psychoses, and schizoaffective disorders.

Minor affective disorders such as the hypomanic, depressive, or cyclothymic type may respond to biofeedback. Depression has been classified in a number of different ways: primary versus secondary, masked versus typical, endogenous versus reactive, and unipolar versus bipolar. Depression is a manifestation of loss, or the threat of loss, of an individual or object where the conscious experiencing of feelings typically associated with loss such as grief, rage, resentment, bitterness, and ambivalence are unable to be consciously utilized.

According to the biogenic amine theory of depression, neurotransmitters such as norepinephrine and serotonin play an important role in this condition though the details of how the perception of a loss results in a failure of propagation of appropriate levels of neurotransmitter across the synaptic cleft are yet unclear.

Treatment of depression with biofeedback therapy is problematic in that the deep relaxation which often accompanies biofeedback training may exacerbate the depression. Therefore, biofeedback treatment might better be reserved until a change in the patient's affect has been achieved through traditional psychotherapy and antidepressant medication when appropriate (see Chaps. 19 and 21).

Anxiety Disorders

Anxiety disorders include many of the symptom constellations referred to as neuroses. The term *neurosis* emphasizes the etiological rather than the descriptive factors of the patient's symptoms. Phobic disorders, obsessive-compulsive disorders, generalized anxiety disorders, conversion disorders, and depressive disorders have been included under the category of neurosis in the past. This concept continues to demonstrate utility in the understanding of the dynamics of the patient's intrapsychic conflicts. The most important concept, however, is the understanding of both the quantitative and qualitative presence of anxiety and how it affects the patient's symptoms. It is this which holds the most meaning for biofeedback techniques.

Phobic disorders have not responded as anticipated to traditional psychotherapeutic approaches. Behavior modification approaches utilizing covert sensitization, desensitization, and implosion methods have a history of greater success in this diagnosis. Biofeedback techniques can be useful in giving immediate information regarding the patient's degree of tension or anxiety when presented with the phobic object or its representation. Using this model, the patient can learn to gradually tolerate the presence of the phobic object. Dynamically, phobias have been considered as situations where anxieties are fixed to certain objects in the environment as opposed to "free-floating" or generalized anxiety where such a focus is not seen.

Panic disorders and generalized anxiety disorders are disorders of degree. These disorders respond well to treatment with biofeedback where reduction of anxiety is primarily emphasized.

Obsessive-compulsive disorders present a problem in working with the patient's emotions. Feelings in obsessive-compulsive patients are often so threatening that they are repressed and controlled because of the fear that if allowed conscious expression they would become overwhelming. Because of this, intellectualization is a prominent defense mechanism, among others, used by the obsessive-compulsive patient. Compulsive rituals over which the patient has little control are also used to defend against the unwanted feelings. Relief from obsessive thinking and ritualistic behavior must be achieved through a gradual process. The obsessive-compulsive patient will often focus on "doing well" with the biofeedback techniques to the exclusion of working through underlying conflicts. In the course of treatment, however, the therapist can begin to assist the patient in understanding that his efforts to do well with the machine constitute a wish to avoid looking at other material. With the working through of these conflicts dealing with feelings will become a less frightening prospect. Tension registered by the biofeedback unit will indicate which material is most conflicted for the patient and which then will need to be approached more rigorously in the therapy.

Somatoform Disorders

Somatoform disorders include somatization disorders, conversion disorders, psychogenic pain disorders, hypochondriasis, and atypical somatoform disorders. These categories were previously described under the neuroses (psychosomatic, hysterical neurosis-conversion type, hypochondriacal, and neuresthenic). In these conditions, psychological distress is converted into a physical manifestation expressed through the ANS. The physical symptom usually retains some psychological meaning. Psychosomatic and psychogenic pain disorders are discussed elsewhere (see Chap. 9).

Conversion disorders frequently develop rather suddenly after an event considered by the patient to be traumatic (conflict-laden). Usually the disorder is manifested by loss of sensation, special sense, or motor function. Loss of vision, paresthesias, anesthesias, and atypical pain are observed frequently in these patients. The symptoms described are generally not consistent with anatomical distribution, but rather are "conceptual," e.g., stocking/glove anesthesia. Removal of the symptoms can often be effected through hypnotherapy; however, the symptom will either return with time or another symptom of equal intensity will take its place (symptom substitution). The severity of impairment is usually proportional to the degree of stress (psychic conflict) suffered by the patient.

In a personal case of one of the authors (DLS), a 34-year-old farmer who felt that his wife was having an affair, followed her one afternoon in his pickup truck. He was subsequently involved in a minor vehicle accident which was not disabling to himself and in which no serious injury was sustained. He suddenly found, however, that he was "blind." Subsequent ophthalmological evaluation was within normal limits. His symptom remitted after a period of several weeks of intensive psychotherapy.

This patient did not want to "see" that his wife was on her way to meet a lover. The anxiety generated by this conflict was bound up in the symptom of hysterical blindness. Since the anxiety was thus bound and not expressed, the patient demonstrated the classical *la belle indifférence* regarding his loss of vision. However, these symptoms caused some concern for the patient and his family, and so resulted in a visit to the physician's office.

Biofeedback techniques, as in the other somatoform disorders can assist the patient in dealing with the anxiety that is present even though it may be bound up in somatic expression. Physiological responses, particularly of the affected part of the body or the symptom itself, can be demonstrated to the patient to be emotionally derived. As long as this symptom is dealt with concomitantly in the course of psychotherapy, the patient can begin to work through the conflict and expect a degree of symptom resolution.

Dissociative Disorders

The dissociative disorders include psychogenic amnesia and psychogenic fugue, multiple personality (rare), and depersonalization disorder. These disorders were also previously listed as neuroses (hysterical neurosis-dissociative type and depersonalization neurosis). The symptoms of these disorders are distressful for the patient and thus are more amenable to biofeedback since anxiety is more consciously experienced. The patient's transference to the biofeedback equipment in these cases can aid in the detection of areas of emotional pain, distress, and conflict. The patient, in discussing certain aspects of current or childhood history, may suddenly trigger the machine, indicating a physiological response. This can serve as a "red flag" to both the therapist and the patient that some anxiety is connected with this material. The areas of conflict thus identified can then be pursued so that the patient is assisted in uncovering, working through, and resolving more conflict. This may be applied more broadly to the other disorders in this category although the therapist must be aware that stimuli other than emotional arousal can affect GSR or EMG recordings (see Chap. 3).

Psychosexual Disorders

Psychosexual disorders include egodystonic homosexuality, gender identity disorders (transsexualism, asexuality, homosexuality, or heterosexuality), the paraphilias (fetishism, transvestitism, zoophilia, pedophilia, voyeurism, exhibitionism, sexual masochism, and sexual sadism), and the psychosexual dysfunctions (inhibited sexual desire and excitement, inhibited female or male orgasm, premature ejaculation, functional dyspareunia, and functional vaginismus). These disorders are discussed in more detail in the chapter on genitourinary disorders (see Chap. 15).

Factitious Disorders

The factitious disorders include those conditions where the patient has acquired physical or psychological symptoms that are due to secondary gain. The most dramatic of these is the Münchausen ("hospital hobo") syndrome, in which a patient presents himself at various treating facilities with a variety of complaints, including self-injury, so as to gain or maintain hospital stay. The array of symptoms often "baffle" his clinicians and the patient may take pleasure herein. Typically, once the "pretender" is uncovered, he quickly exits in search of another facility to begin the process over again. These patients frequently undergo repeated extensive and expensive physical and laboratory evaluation in an attempt to elucidate the confusing and often changing symptoms. The object of his symptoms is to gain attention and remain "cared for" in a sheltered environment. The patient has little thought beyond that though apart from gaining attention he also delights in maintaining the concern of his doctors as well as perhaps furthering their frustration and confusion.

Tension is generated in these cases with frustrations or failure to achieve these ends and it is at that point where biofeedback might be employed. Final discovery of the patient's diagnosis is, unfortunately, often made toward the end of the patient's stay or serves to precipitate his flight to another institution. If identified early enough, however, such treatment procedures as biofeedback used as an adjunct to psychotherapy might be interposed in an attempt to assist the patient in beginning to examine his behavior. These patients, however, remain fairly treatment-resistant.

Disorders of Impulse Control

Disorders of impulse control include pathological gambling, the manias (kleptomania, pyromania, etc.), and explosive disorders. The dynamics of pathological gambling (risk-taking and compulsion towards the behavior) are similar to those dynamics described in substance abuse disorders. As with the latter, abstinence from the gambling behavior leads to frustration which can be discharged only through the act of gambling itself. Interruption to this cycle increases anxiety levels, so that biofeedback may be a useful treatment approach. The gambling behavior and what it means to the patient may be explored simultaneously while noting his associations during biofeedback treatment. This allows both the therapist and the patient to recognize immediately when issues regarding deeper conflicts are touched upon through the signaling of the machine. These "loaded" areas should then be explored carefully since confronting the patient in his conflict-laden areas too directly will only heighten the patient's anxiety and erode the therapist–patient relationship.

Kleptomania and pyromania are clearly impulse control disorders where the "driven-ness" toward the object or act forms as much of a compulsion as does the gambling behavior. The dynamics underlying these disorders are similar and therefore the same type of biofeedback treatment strategy is indicated.

Explosive disorders are likewise indications of general tension discharge as the result of increasing degrees of anxiety. Most patients with these patterns of behavior have less stress tolerance than control subjects. There is usually a long history of problems with impulse control, often including "temper tantrums" in childhood. Parents of the patients were often similarly "afflicted," though this behavior is more likely learned than genetic.

These patients require assistance in both unlearning this behavior and learning to broaden their base of control over the acting-out of impulses. Stressful areas uncovered by psychotherapy will be quickly noted through the biofeedback responses and can be dealt with at the time. These patients often do not seek help directly and typically it is the family, or some civil institution, which brings the patient to treatment. The patient should learn to avoid circumstances and situations which lessen impulse controls such as alcohol ingestion or other drug use. Presenting the patient with effective means to control impulses and reduce anxiety, such as is possible through biofeedback will decrease his felt need to search for this through artificial means or through inappropriate tension discharge.

Adjustment Disorders

There are times when patients who are otherwise reasonably "well-adjusted" face certain environmental stresses which cause acute and usually time-limited overreaction(s). The degrees and kinds of stress which can be tolerated vary from individual to individual, depending upon their coping threshold. When these overreactions produce psychological symptoms they are designated as adjustment disorders. Patients may have adjustment disorders due to problems with coping with stress involving loss where depression is predominant, "threats" where anxiety is predominant, or mixtures of the two. Other stresses such as those found in family relationships and employment situations can also frequently combine to produce adjustment disorders. The hallmark of these disorders is that they are characteristically stress-related and time-limited. Removal of the stress and passage of time are usually "curative," until or unless, another stress of a similar or greater magnitude supervenes. If no treatment is offered, the patient will typically recover often after several weeks to months following the "triggering" event. The rationale for treatment, however, is to limit both the intensity and duration of the adjustment reaction. Care must be taken in diagnosing this category so that it does not become a "wastebasket" designation. Appropriate clinical history and evaluation must be provided in order to establish this diagnosis.

Anxiety, as noted, often plays a part in adjustment reactions and is sometimes the primary presenting complaint. Biofeedback in conjunction with psychotherapy offers the patient means to identify, work through, and resolve the conflicts and thus control his symptoms. This serves to diminish the patient's inner sense of dysphoria and helplessness concerning his emotional state. These patients frequently find the symptoms disconcerting and egodystonic and are often well-motivated to pursue therapy.

Personality Disorders

Personality disorders describe those characteristic patterns of behavior that are habitually manifested by a patient which are maladaptive to his environment and subsequently cause an increased sense of personal discomfort. These patterns serve as a "compromise," though an inappropriate one, in dealing with life events and life stressors. A distinction should be made between the diagnosis of a personality trait and a personality disorder. Any of the personality descriptions, including paranoid, schizoid, schizotypal, histrionic, narcissistic, antisocial (sociopathic, psychopathic), borderline, avoidant, dependent, compulsive, passive-aggressive or mixed can be observed in many nondysfunctional control subjects. It is only when the personality mechanism is so obtrusive that it interferes significantly with areas of daily living that the personality diagnosis should include the designation "disorder."

One significant difference between the personality disorders and the adjustment disorders (or "neurotic" syndromes) is that personality disorders are not "egodystonic" but rather "egosyntonic." That is, the patient does not view his personality traits as abnormal but feels they are an integral and acceptable part of himself. It is only when his manner of behavior interfaces poorly with society or his living situation that difficulty ensues. At these times, the patient sees society at fault rather than himself. These patients are usually brought to, or referred for, therapy by others rather than coming of their own accord, as they experience little sense of inner distress regarding their behavior. Since the patient finds little wrong with his own behavior, but is frustrated at others' reactions to his behavior, there is often little or no motivation for change. Personality disorders especially illustrative of this point are the paranoid, compulsive, and antisocial ones.

Personality disorders as a group represent a great challenge for biofeedback treatment. Anxiety the patient experiences concerning his symptoms often serves to propel the therapy forward. When this anxiety is at a low level as in personality disorders, little internal motivation remains to assist the patient in overcoming his resistance to the therapeutic process. Great patience, therefore, is required on the part of the therapist to assist these individuals in working through the difficulties caused by their personality disorders. Such signs of anxiety as are present, however, should be monitored closely and taken advantage of in the therapy. In some situations direct or confrontational therapeutic strategies as opposed to reflective or passive approaches on the part of the clinician will lead to more work on the patient's part toward a better therapy outcome. Biofeedback therapy can demonstrate to these patients that they are able to exercise control over themselves which will move them away from the view that "Oh, that's just the way I am." Once the patient can realize that change is possible, then the idea of responsibility for self and behavior in terms of therapeutic gain can be introduced in order to facilitate the therapy process.

The psychological conflicts in those patients with personality disorders are thought to be generated early in life, perhaps in the first 1 to 3 years. This indicates the establishment of early and very primitive conflictual structures. During later middle life, the personality disorders may change as if maturation which had been arrested years before may suddenly begin to take place. A number of contributing factors have been postulated to account for this late maturation phenomenon. These include such factors as the loss (usually through death) of parents or important supporting figures. Whatever its origin, the effect is that until such time as the maturational lag is corrected, treatment is more problematic.

Conditions Not Attributable to a Mental Disorder

Conditions that are the focus of psychological attention or treatment but are not attributable to a specific mental disorder include malingering, borderline intellectual functioning, preadult or adult antisocial behavior, marital problems, parent–child problems, interpersonal problems, academic problems, occupational problems, uncomplicated bereavement, noncompliance with medical treatment, phase-of-life problems, or other life circumstance problems.

Malingering is a term describing those individuals who purposefully and consciously strive to appear ill, either physically or mentally, in order to achieve some clear-cut purpose (e.g., a soldier who may "play sick" in order to miss a troop movement). Since the behavior is not in conflict with the patient's mental functioning or feelings, it resembles to a degree that described for the personality disorders. The condition is infrequently amenable to treatment, including biofeedback. These individuals generally do not present themselves for treatment but may come to the therapist's attention because they are incarcerated or otherwise in difficulty. Motivation is an important factor in these disorders as a predictor of successful therapy outcome. Those individuals with low motivation levels have the least chance for success in therapy. However, biofeedback may be used diagnostically to identify malingerers who simulate chronic pain symptoms (e.g., low back pain). Since there is a strong relationship between muscle contraction and pain, the absence of significant muscle tension with subjective report of high pain levels may indicate malingering.

Borderline intellectual functioning is discussed under the category of mental retardation (see p. 376).

Antisocial behavior, which has also been referred to as dyssocial behavior, includes those kinds of activities manifested by vandalism, prostitution, robbery, and other social deviance. The individual exhibiting this behavior is generally concerned only with some specific gain, revenge, or some "thrill," all of which is contrary to societal interests. These individuals regret their acts when apprehended only because they are apprehended, not because they feel remorse for what they have done. The role of biofeedback in the treatment of these individuals is very limited. Little anxiety in regard to behavior is apparent and little motivation for change usually exists.

Difficulties in "essential" communication underlie most marital, parent–child, and other interpersonal problems. Nonverbal communication or messages given by one individual are often at variance with the verbal messages received by another thus creating confusion and leading to a significant potential for frustration, disharmony, and resentment. Individuals with these conditions also demonstrate difficulties with caring and consistency.

Therapies involving marital, family, or other interpersonal problems form special subgroups of group psychotherapy while exhibiting traditional group dynamics. Group therapy using biofeedback as an adjunct creates some special complications, however. Stress on the patients in this type of subgroup therapy is greater than in traditional individual therapy. This is particularly true if there is a dysfunctional group and group behaviors such as "scapegoating" occur.

The use of biofeedback techniques in group therapy has not yet been fully explored. In such a treatment format, each group member may be monitored by his own biofeedback instrument and audio and/or visual output of each machine would be in common group view. The therapeutic advantage of this arrangement lies in the potential for the group to be immediately aware of individual member's physiological responses to group material. The responses may represent tension or anxiety and may be due to conflicted psychological material, prevarication, ambivalence, and the like. Such intimate and automatic revelations of an individual in a group setting may prove quite stressful for the patient, particularly if the group is composed of people with whom he has very close personal ties, e.g., family. Another concern with this method centers around those therapists who choose to be viewed as group members rather than group leaders. The therapist must then decide whether or not he too will be monitored by biofeedback and what impact his physiological responses will have upon his own role and function in the group. This and other complications inherent in group dynamics, particularly groups made up of family, marital, and other network systems indicate the need for a cautious approach in using this modality for group work. At the same time, however, this method suggests some interesting and intriguing possibilities.

Occupational (industrial, academic) problems often arise as a result of stress associated with the particular conditions of employment and the patient's own stress or frustration tolerance level. These problems may also reflect the individual's inner turmoil which allow less attention and energy to be invested in the work setting. The setting or co-workers may in themselves be stressors and prevent optimal adjustment to the work setting. Biofeedback may be useful in dealing with these reactions to stress from employment since stress generates anxiety and the latter can be diminished with biofeedback. This approach would not be applicable where individuals are working above their level of competence; however, this could occur in educational or employment related environments. Where the focus of the treatment is directed toward the stress felt by the patient in the educational/employment situation, the therapy is similar to that used in the case of an adjustment disorder.

Uncomplicated bereavement which follows the loss of a spouse, family member, or close friend will generally not require the intervention of psychotherapy or biofeedback. In fact, it may be a necessary and helpful life task in working through feelings associated with individual loss, so that final and appropriate introjection of the person lost can take place. If the bereavement becomes difficult, complicated, or incomplete, then it is more likely to be connected with depression and should not be diagnosed in the bereavement category, but approached in the same way as other depressions.

Noncompliance with medical treatment can represent multidetermined behavior. The exact reason or cause for the behavior must be delineated by the therapist. If it involves significant conflictual material, it is better diagnosed in one of the adjustment reaction categories. Individuals who exhibit simple noncompliance, however, are not likely to present themselves for treatment.

Phase-of-life or other life circumstance problems include such categories as physiological changes induced through puberty, pregnancy, bearing children, educational involvement, marriage, moving, parenting, the seeking and maintaining of employment, loss of parents, loss of children with maturation, grandparenting, retirement, loss of life partners, entering a retirement community or extended care facility, and one's approaching death. These changes and life stressors resemble the category of uncomplicated bereavement in the sense that if the reaction to the life problem is inappropriate or symptom producing, it is better diagnosed as an adjustment problem necessitating different treatment approaches. The goal of treatment with phase-of-life problems is to offer assistance and understanding to the patient through supportive measures. The patient should be allowed to work through these difficulties independently with psychotherapy and biofeedback reserved for the occasional complicated situation.

Review of the Literature

Glueck and Stroebel (1975) investigated the use of biofeedback and meditation in the treatment of psychiatric illness. They found that psychiatric patients could not learn alpha EEG control and, in fact, became more anxious because of the lack of specific task requirements. They concluded that the use of biofeedback with psychiatric patients should be considered very carefully to correctly match the type of biofeedback with the type of disorder. They believed that EEG biofeedback training is often inappropriate in general relaxation training for psychiatric patients. Other investigators have studied the application of biofeedback to specific psychiatric disorders such as neurosis or behavior problems.

Mills and Solyom (1974) used EEG biofeedback to treat patients suffering from obsessive rumination. The treatment technique was based on the fact that mental relaxation might inhibit rumination in individuals suffering from obsessive neurosis. Five patients were treated for 7 to 20 sessions, and the results were quite encouraging. These patients learned control of alpha wave rhythm; however, rumination continued outside of the treatment environment. Weber and Fehmi (1974) also reported using EEG alpha biofeedback with patients suffering from psychoneurosis. Positive results were documented in 6 of 10 patients, with some improvement in one. The treatment program included verbal psychotherapy, so that the role played by biofeedback was not entirely clear.

Other researchers have treated anxiety neurosis with EMG biofeedback training. Raskin, Johnson, and Rondestuedt (1973) found that relaxation EMG biofeedback training resulted in the lowering of anxiety levels in psychoneurotic patients. No control group was observed, however. Townsend, House, and Addario (1975) reported on 10 patients with chronic anxiety who were given relaxation training with EMG biofeedback, while eight patients were given group therapy alone. EMG measurements were taken on both experimental and control subjects throughout the study. The results indicated that the group receiving biofeedback training significantly decreased their anxiety test scores and their disturbances of mood as measured by the Profile of Mood States (POMS). Followup data were collected for only two patients six months after the study ended. Both of these patients had continued the self-control relaxation practices and were able to maintain (upon retesting) their EMG levels at or below the level they achieved after 14 days of biofeedback training. Canter, Kondo, and Knott (1975) studied 28 patients with anxiety neurosis aged 19 to 48 years drawn from a hospital's inpatient and outpatient pool. Patients were assigned to either an EMG biofeedback group or a progressive relaxation training group. The biofeedback group displayed significantly lower muscle tension levels than the progressive relaxation group upon completion of treatment. The authors concluded that "highly anxious" psychiatric patients were able to reduce muscle tension by either the EMG feedback technique or progressive relaxation, although the EMG technique was felt superior over time. In addition, the patients who received biofeedback training were rated by themselves and their therapists as having improved significantly greater than the relaxation group.

Transient emotional states have been treated with biofeedback. Gatchel and Hatch (1977) compared the effectiveness of two types of biofeedback in treating speech anxiety. Of four groups, one group received feedback of their pulse rate, another group received muscle relaxation training, a third group received combined pulse rate and muscle biofeedback training, while a fourth group received false biofeedback. All four groups reported a decrease in anxiety, when tested by public speaking. However, heart rate and skin conductance levels indicated that the three treatment groups had less physiologic tension than the false feedback control group. The relaxation biofeedback combination group demonstrated a lower level of physiologic arousal at the end of treatment. Lally (1976) reported that EEG biofeedback training and relaxation therapy had a significant effect on college students who displayed high anxiety while taking a reading test. The subjects who received biofeedback and relaxation training significantly lowered their anxiety levels and increased their total reading and vocabulary scores. Subjects receiving only relaxation therapy lowered their anxiety but did not increase their reading scores. Romano (1976) employed EMG biofeedback training to reduce anxiety among college students combined with a desensitization program.

The EMG biofeedback training reduced test anxiety but it was not more effective than systematic desensitization alone. In a related study, Bridges (1977) found that electrothermal biofeedback training led to lower test scores on an anxiety scale. Groups which received biofeedback on skin temperature levels or biofeedback and desensitization did significantly better than groups receiving only autogenic training and desensitization or autogenic training alone. Overall, all groups showed improvement from the pretest treatment, but the author attributed this change to increases in study skills and training, and the autogenic phrasing which enhanced their ability to take tests in a relaxed manner.

In a study on dental phobia, Miller et al. (1976) found that EMG biofeedback training and progressive relaxation reduced tension levels when patients were seen by their dentist. In addition, both groups showed significant changes on the State-Trait Anxiety Inventory and the Mental Anxiety Scale. Both progressive relaxation and EMG biofeedback were effective in reducing stress reactions in dental patients, but the decline in trait anxiety which was demonstrated by the biofeedback group suggested that greater generalization occurred as a result of feedback training.

Biofeedback has also been used in conjunction with systematic desensitization to treat specific phobias. Lowenstein (1977) reported on a 24-year-old female with apiphobia (fear of bees) who was treated with feedback from the EMG, skin temperature, and left occipital EEG. This multimodal feedback approach was combined with desensitization and the patient's anxiety attacks stopped after 6 weeks of training. Pre- and posttreatment psychologic testing showed clinical improvement. Delk (1977) treated a 25-year-old woman who suffered with phobic thoughts regarding animal abuse or neglect. She was treated with systematic desensitization and EMG biofeedback. The EMG responses were used to aid the therapist and the patient in the correct pairing of imagery and muscle relaxation during the desensitization procedure. The EMG responses helped to pinpoint the patient's muscular tension reaction to phobic imagery. The patient successfully eliminated her phobic thoughts and resultant depression, and this improvement was maintained over a 6-month followup period.

Performance anxiety and phobia were treated by Dorsey (1977) with EMG biofeedback and systematic desensitization. College age gymnasts were given the EMG relaxation training followed by desensitization training. Biofeedback training was effective in reducing m. frontalis muscle tension but neither the EMG training nor the relaxation reduced the level of state anxiety in these individuals. Performance in gymnastics was not enhanced by the relaxation training experience. No difference between the experimental group and the control group was found. Benjamin (1976) used EEG alpha feedback training and muscle relaxation with systematic desensitization of college students who reported ophidiophobia (fear of snakes). Both the systematic desensitization and EMG biofeedback training resulted in phobic reduction compared with the control group. However, the biofeedback group decreased their level of trait anxiety significantly more than either of the other two groups. Alpha feedback training resulted in a more significant effect on overall anxiety than the desensitization and relaxation training alone.

Although most of the research has been concentrated on anxiety neurosis, one case study of biofeedback treatment for obsessive-compulsive neurosis was reported by Wargin and Fahrion (1977). Alpha EEG training combined with thermal and EMG biofeedback may be more effective than either thermal or EMG training alone in obsessive patients. This particular patient with headaches had not been relieved by single modality biofeedback training (thermal or EMG). She did report, however, improvement when alpha EEG training was combined with the two other types of feedback. Nigl and Jackson (1979) reported on 2 groups of 10 psychiatric patients each and a group of 10 control subjects. One group diagnosed as suffering from neurotic anxiety were given diazepam (Valium) alone. They did not learn to relax their physiologic tension through EMG biofeedback as well as a group of control subjects or a group of schizophrenics. These results corroborated the results of Kazarian, Tekatch, and Ifangumyl (1978) who reported that the combination of relaxation training and mild tranquilizers resulted in increased tension rather than relaxation. Subjects receiving relaxation training alone did better than subjects receiving relaxation training and mild antianxiety agents. La Vallee et al. (1977) reported that patients given diazepam and relaxation training did not relax as well as subjects who received relaxation training alone. Further research is needed to determine whether the efficacy of biofeedback training and relaxation methods is more effective than mild tranquilizers in the treatment of chronic anxiety.

Biofeedback training has been applied to treat various characterological or behavioral problems such as alcoholism and drug dependency. Eno (1975) studied the effectiveness of biofeedback training in reducing tension levels of institutionalized alcoholics. This procedure was compared with a relaxation procedure and with a combination of biofeedback and relaxation. The subjects receiving the combination of

EMG biofeedback and relaxation showed a greater reduction in the state of anxiety than did other groups. All three treatment groups, however, showed significant EMG reduction from the baselines taken on admission and those taken following treatment. Valle and Degood (1976) studied the effectiveness of EEG biofeedback in the treatment of drug dependency. Patients who learned to control their alpha rhythms reported using significantly more barbiturates but less alcohol, and more marijuana though less tobacco than patients who did not learn this control. Since drug use corresponds to the level of the subject's anxiety, the authors concluded that anxiety appeared to mediate the relationship between drug users and the ability to control EEG alpha.

Jones and Holmes (1976) indicated that alpha wave feedback did not result in significant increases in alpha rhythm in a group of 20 alcoholics. They also reported that alcoholics produced less alpha wave activity (and more low voltage fast activity) than nonalcoholics prior to receiving biofeedback training.

Bowman and Faust (1977) used EMG biofeedback training and autogenic training to treat alcoholics. They found no difference between the reported positive results and reduction of anxiety for alcoholics given biofeedback training and those given cognitive behavior modification. The authors observed that the greatest reduction of tension occurred among alcoholics with concomitant personality disorders.

Few studies have investigated the use of biofeedback in the treatment of cigarette addiction; however, Havelick (1977) used EMG and temperature biofeedback to treat one patient suffering from combined Valium dependency and cigarette smoking. Cigarette smoking behavior was eliminated by use of twilight learning suggestions when the patient produced EEG alpha activity. In addition, the patient's Valium dependency was reduced through the relaxation and biofeedback treatment.

Several authors have indicated that biofeedback procedures should not be used with psychotic patients. Adler and Adler (1979) stated that the use of feedback and relaxation procedures could exacerbate psychotic behavior and might tend to intensify hallucinatory experiences.

This was also suggested by Stroebel (1979) who reviewed the experimental evidence collected by Glueck and Stroebel (1975) and Weber (1977). He concluded that psychotic patients display a tendency to become increasingly confused and disorganized when given biofeedback and that this confusion was most noticeable in patients' paranoid delusions. Marcus and Levin (1977) reported that biofeedback training enabled one psychotic patient to reduce paranoid hypersensitivity through learning to reduce physiological arousal.

However, it appears that in those patients with psychosis who have been stabilized with appropriate psychotropic medication, biofeedback procedures may be helpful in reducing muscle tension and anxiety and may therefore serve as a useful adjunct to psychiatric treatment. In support of this, Nigl and Jackson (1979) indicated that schizophrenic patients who received Sparine (promazine hydrochloride) were able to reduce their muscular tension almost as well as a group of control subjects who received no medication. In addition, followup data indicated that this group had a very low rate of hospital readmission and that their average length of stay was much shorter than that of other schizophrenic patients. Later, Nigl, Jackson and Murphy (1980) contrasted the effectiveness of EMG biofeedback training and an attention-placebo procedure with acute schizophrenic inpatients. EMG feedback resulted in greater reduction of muscle tension than occurred in the group receiving placebos. It appears that biofeedback procedures should not be routinely applied to psychotic populations but may be helpful in selected patients who are free from active delusional or hallucinatory experiences. There is currently no evidence that would indicate that biofeedback training is more effective than other types of psychiatric treatment. Biofeedback therapy should not be used alone in the treatment of psychosis.

An intriguing application of biofeedback is in the treatment of tardive dyskinesia resulting from iatrogenic psychotropic medication administration. Tardive dyskinesia is a disorder characterized by stereotyped, involuntary movements. Albanese and Gaardner (1977) reported on two patients who were treated with EMG biofeedback training to reduce tardive dyskinesia. Both patients improved after training and showed a general reduction of tension levels. Since spontaneous remission can occur in tardive dyskinesia, biofeedback may not have been entirely responsible for the results. However, the improvement was noted in such a short time that it is strongly suggested that EMG training might be useful for this disorder. Recently, Sherman (1979) reported that both EMG frontalis biofeedback and masseter feedback were used to treat a patient with tardive dyskinesia. Although frontalis training resulted in a reduction of chronic headache, the patient's orofacial dyskinesia was not diminished. Treatment involving masseter EMG feedback, however, did result in a significant reduction of jaw movements. This improvement was sustained over 15 months.

REFERENCES

Adler C, Alder S: Strategies in general psychiatry, in Basmajian J (ed): *Biofeedback-Principles and Practice for Clinicians.* Baltimore, Williams & Wilkins, 1979.

Albanese H, Gaardner K: Biofeedback treatment of tardive dyskinesia: two case reports. Am J Psychiatr 134: 1149, 1977.

Benjamin J: The effectiveness of alpha feedback training and muscle relaxation procedures in systematic desensitization. Biofeedback Self-Regul 1: 352, 1976.

Bowman B, Faust D: EMG-autogenic training and cognitive behavior modification for alcoholics. Biofeedback Self-Regul 2: 312, 1977.

Bridges W: Biofeedback and desensitization: an assessment of their functions in reducing test anxiety. Dis Abs Internat 77 – 20636, 1977.

Canter A, Kondo C, Knott J: A comparison of EMG feedback and progressive muscle relaxation training in anxiety neurosis. Br J Psychiatr 127: 470, 1975.

Delk J: Use of EMG biofeedback in behavioral treatment of an obsessive-compulsive phobic depressive syndrome. Dis Nerv Sys 38: 938, 1977.

Diagnostic and Statistical Manual of Mental Disorders, 3rd ed. Washington, D.C., American Psychiatric Association, 1980.

Dorsey J: The effects of biofeedback-assisted desensitization on state anxiety and performance of college age male gymnast. Dis Abs Internat 77 – 6158, 1977.

Eno E: A comparison study of the level of state-trait anxiety and muscle tension of alcoholics. Dis Abs Internat, 75 – 22496, 1975.

Freud S: *The Standard Edition of the Complete Psychological Works of Sigmund Freud, Vol I – Pre-psycho-analytic Publications and Unpublished Drafts – "Projects for a Scientific Psychology."* London, Hogarth, 1966.

Gatchel R, Hatch J, Watson P, Smith D, Gaas E: Comparative effectiveness of voluntary heart rate control and muscular relaxation as active coping skills for reducing speech anxiety. J Consult Clin Psychol 45: 1093, 1977.

Glueck B, Stroebel C: Biofeedback and meditation in the treatment of psychiatric illness. Comp Psychiatry 16: 303, 1975.

Havelick R: The use of biofeedback and twilight learning in the treatment of migraine headache, valium dependency and cigarette smoking. Biofeedback Self-Regul 2: 297, 1977.

Jones F, Holmes D: Alcoholism, alpha production and biofeedback. J Consult Clin Psychol 44: 224, 1976.

Kazarian S, Tekatch G, Ifangumyl O: Effects of antianxiety agents in relaxation training. Can Psychiatr Assoc J 89, 1978.

Lally M: Biofeedback auditory alpha EEG training and its effect upon anxiety and reading achievement. Dissert Abst Internat 76 – 20650, 1976.

La Vallee Y-J, La Montagne Y, Pinard G, Annable L, Tetreault L: Effects of EMG feedback, diazepam and their combination on chronic anxiety. J Psychosom Res 21: 65, 1977.

Lowenstein T: Multimodality feedback and relaxation training in desensitization of one client. Biofeedback Self-Regul 2: 314, 1977.

Marcus N, Levin G: Clinical applications of biofeedback: implications for psychiatry. Hosp Community Psychiatry 28: 21, 1977.

Miller M, Miller T, Murphy P, Smouse A: The effects of EMG feedback and progressive relaxation training on stress reactions in dental patients. Biofeedback Self-Regul 1: 329, 1976.

Mills G, Solyom L: Biofeedback of EEG alph in treatment of obsessive ruminations. J Behav Ther Exp Psychiatr 5: 37, 1974.

Nigl A, Jackson B: Electromyograph biofeedback as an adjunct to standard psychiatric treatment. J Clin Psychiatr 40: 433, 1979.

Nigl A, Jackson B, Murphy G: EMG biofeedback and relaxation as adjunctive treatment modalities for acute schizophrenia. Proceedings of the 11th meeting of Biofeedback Society of America, 1980.

Raskin M, Johnson G, Rondestuedt J: Chronic anxiety treated by feedback induced muscle relaxation. Arch Gen Psychiatr 28: 263, 1973.

Romano J: Effects of EMG biofeedback training and systematic desensitization of test anxiety. Dis Abs Internat 76 – 29801, 1976.

Sherman R: Successful treatment of one case of tardive dyskinesia with EMG feedback from masseter muscle. Biofeedback Self-Reg 4, 367–370, 1979.

Stone A: Response to the presidential address. Am J Psychiatr 136: 1020, 1979.

Stroebel C: The application of biofeedback techniques in psychiatry and behavioral medicine. Psychiatr Opin 16: 13, 1979.

Townsend R, House J, Addario D: A comparison of biofeedback-mediated relaxation and group therapy in the treatment of chronic anxiety. Am J Psychiatr 132: 598, 1975.

Valle R, Degood D: Alpha control and self-rep drug use. Biofeedback Self-Regul 1: 356, 1976.

Wargin M, Fahrion S: A case study – synchronized alpha training for the obsessive compulsive headache patient. Biofeedback Self-Regul 3: 299, 1977.

Weber E: The use of relaxation and biofeedback techniques in psychiatric practice. Carrier Clinic Letter 39, 1977.

Weber E, Fehmi L: The therapeutic use of EEG biofeedback. Proceedings of the 5th Biofeedback Society of America, 1974.

18

Clinical Indications and Contraindications for Biofeedback

BIOFEEDBACK is the treatment of choice for certain conditions. These include: (1) vasoconstrictive syndromes, in particular Raynaud's disease; (2) spasmodic torticollis; (3) causalgia, or as it is now more often termed reflex sympathetic dystrophy; (4) certain cases of rehabilitation for paralysis following stroke or a lower motor lesion as an adjunct to other forms of therapy; and (5) intractable tension headache.

The following types of patients may also be suitable for biofeedback training:

1. Those with psychophysiological disorders, including some cases of migraine or vascular headache who have not responded to simpler measures.

2. Many patients with chronic pain syndromes, who have not responded to other forms of treatment, are suitable for biofeedback training, in particular those with low back pain and muscle spasm.

3. Some patients who because of their own interests or background are attracted to instrumentation and instrumental demonstration of their physical state. These people are likely to respond better to instrumental methods of data presentation than to taking drugs or receiving other therapeutic intervention.

4. Certain patients may require biofeedback because they cannot take medication for one of two reasons: their physical condition may preclude the use of specific drugs, or they are already taking a particular medicine and another class of drugs would be contraindicated because of undesirable interaction. For example, a person on medication for narrow-angle glaucoma cannot take many types of antipsychotic medications.

5. Not infrequently, individuals show a high degree of resistance with strong defense mechanisms to psychological interpretation of their symptoms. These persons can often accept biofeedback training more readily and obtain relief of symptoms.

6. Certain individuals are less comfortable with physicians than

with allied health professionals. Those who harbor fear, resentment, or hostility towards the medical profession may accept biofeedback therapy, finding it less threatening.

7.   Finally, biofeedback is a research tool in many clinical situations to elucidate the pathophysiology of biological responses. Other less well-documented indications, for example, in the field of gastrointestinal disorders, are mentioned in the relevant chapters.

Before discussing each of the above categories, some of the general principles of selection of patients for biofeedback treatment will be reviewed. Since the biofeedback technique is essentially one in which the subject takes responsibility for his sensations and behavior, in other words, in which he learns self-regulation, motivation is of primary importance. Motivation to get well is not always easy to gauge, in that the more subtle indications of secondary gain are sometimes well-hidden from the patient himself. It may be a truism to say that certain psychophysiological disorders would not have arisen in the first place if motivation to remain well had been a prime mover. The genesis of psychophysiological states is outside the scope of this text, however. By whatever mechanism the condition came about, it is important to allow the patient sufficient time to be introduced to the method. It usually takes several sessions for the patient to begin to "get the feel" of the technique as described in Chapter 19. Patients often need careful encouragement to persist for the first few sessions, and motivation is of vital importance at this early stage. Once individuals can express an interest in learning the technique, they are likely to persist in the effort.

Patients suitable for treatment are those with a particular symptom which can be approached directly or indirectly by existing modes of physiological feedback. In some cases, the symptom is an isolated one, or if there are multiple symptoms they can be treated in sequence. In either case at any given session or course of therapy some particular manifestation of disease or discomfort receives concentrated attention. On the other hand, multimodal biofeedback may lead to greater improvement, and it may be more suitable for those with multiple symptoms. Pattern biofeedback training as described by Schwartz (1975) has yielded interesting results. It is likely that a basic sufficient level of understanding of body processes should be sought for; a patient with significant defects in perception is not a suitable candidate. On the other hand, different treatment modalities are available for individuals with varying levels of understanding of their body processes and disorders, and it may be sufficient to require a willingness to learn and motivation to change patterns of response, rather than to expect accurate knowledge of physiology. The indications for treatment are likely to increase as more sophisticated instrumentation and techniques become available.

Disorders for Which Biofeedback Is the Treatment of Choice*

Vasoconstrictive syndromes, in particular Raynaud's disease, respond to thermal biofeedback control, and are described in Chapter 13. Spasmodic torticollis responds to various forms of EMG biofeedback training and is described in Chapter 8. In both of these conditions, significant numbers of patients have been reported to be benefited. Causalgia or reflex sympathetic dystrophy responds to thermal biofeedback regulation, and is described in Chapter 7. There are only few cases in the literature because the disorder is fortunately rare, but characteristically it is difficult to treat, and the results with biofeedback are far superior to those treated with other methods (Blanchard, 1979). Paralysis from upper or lower motor neuron lesions is in a different category in that the patient's psychological state is relatively less complex, and they are less likely to be ambivalent towards making a recovery. Serial demonstration of improvement in muscular recovery acts as a strong positive reinforcement to increasing function and activities, and over the past 10 years reports from many centers have indicated that this is an adjunctive therapy which has taken a standard place in the armamentarium of rehabilitation (see Chap. 8). The sensory-motor integration that takes place with EMG biofeedback used in cases of paralysis has a well-founded basis in physiology.

Disorders for Which Biofeedback May Be Indicated†

Psychophysiologic Disorders

It is clear that whenever there is a somatic symptom, there is anxiety which is engendered by the symptom. This anxiety may go unrecognized, but is present nonetheless. It is also clear that underlying psychological conflict itself generates anxiety which may then be bound into (manifested by) a somatic symptom. This "psycho"-somatic symptom may then itself produce an anxiety reaction. For that reason, every

*A "treatment of choice" is one that is indicated above all other methods. It is therefore the one that is preferably applied first.

†In these "indicated" disorders, biofeedback has proved its worth, but it may not be the treatment of first choice.

clinician knows that psychophysiologic symptoms are the most common type encountered, and it is usually estimated that 85 to 90 percent of the patients who walk into a medical waiting room are suffering in this way (Feinstein, 1967).

People have been classified as follows:
1. The unworried well
2. The worried well
3. The unworried ill (sick)
4. The worried ill (sick)

Well-documented biofeedback treatment has been reported for muscular contraction or vascular headache, as described in Chapter 7. Physicians treating tension headache (whether it is manifested as muscle contraction or vascular changes) adopt an individual attitude to treatment appropriate to the patient. The following steps are described as a basis or guide for discussion and the reader will form a personal approach according to experience.

Tension Headache

Once the diagnosis of tension headache has been made, the first step is to discuss with the patient the mechanism whereby the symptoms arose. This procedure may, in itself, be curative. The next step is to teach the patient relaxation exercises. A whole range of progressive relaxation exercises can be devised to suit appropriate groups of patients, and these are described in Chapter 3. Clinics are widely available for these treatments, which shows their usefulness. Progressive exercises include head and neck exercises, breathing exercises, and whole body relaxation exercises. Those customarily employed are based on Jacobson's deep relaxation method, which involves systematic and controlled contraction prior to relaxation.

Discussion in depth with the patient as to how he perceives his illness and the symptoms is imperative (see Chap. 23). Appropriate medical, pharmacological, physical, and other modes of therapy may be used in an on-going way.

When symptoms persist despite these measures, then the question of the use of biofeedback arises. It is here that the physician's attitude is important. When the physician understands the possibilities of the patient gaining greater independence, he can recommend it in such a way that the patient's expectations are appropriate. Because of the nature of the symptoms, however, there is likely to be resistance in losing those very symptoms. Therefore, however much there is verbal acceptance of treatment there is likely to be psychophysiologic resistance (see Chap. 19).

Resistance may also lie with the referring physician. Although (it is hoped) physicians rarely say to the patient: "it is all in your head," this sentiment is transmitted to him, or the patient feels it before consulting (and for this reason often does not consult and remains symptomatic, e.g., depressed). The sentiment arises probably because there is still difficulty in accepting the close linkage of physical and psychologic events, which are yet believed to be separate (that is, mind-body dualism, see Appendix). The physician who recommends biofeedback treatment will do well to explain to the patient the principles of therapy and outline to him the steps that will be required of him in the beginning. The patient will then learn more quickly and will have a more realistic approach to the subject.

The colloquial use of the term *headache* in the phrase "what a headache" implies a tedium and a nuisance. This sometimes colors the approach to a patient with a headache. The first step therefore in the prevention of headache is an attitude of realistic empathy towards what underlies the complaint of headache.

In a personal series of one of the authors (MF-W, unpublished), the followup treatment results of 470 consecutive patients over a five-year period with the presenting symptom of "headache" were analyzed. The cases with a mass lesion or with demonstrable progressive pathology were excluded; the patients studied showed fluctuating pathophysiology as the precipitating cause of recurring headache. The patients were treated with the following: (1) an explanation of the mechanism of symptoms, following neurologic examination and appropriate investigations which gave normal results; (2) training in relaxation exercises, with an individually tailored home program; and (3) the patient was encouraged to suggest methods of avoiding his particular headache. Of the 370 patients who completed a detailed questionnaire on followup (carried out a year after the last of the series had been treated over the 5-year period), 49 percent reported that they "felt better," 45 percent reported that they felt "neither better nor worse," and 6 percent stated that they "felt worse." Biofeedback training was not at that time available. From our followup study, it would appear that in this series of unselected cases of vascular and/or muscle contraction tension headache, approximately 20 percent of the patients would have been potential candidates for biofeedback training.

Chronic Pain Syndromes

When patients have not responded to a variety of appropriate methods of pain relief, and when the diagnosis is firmly established as to the underlying condition causing pain, biofeedback is often indicated. Appropriate candidates may suffer from a wide variety of pain syndromes, but probably the patients most likely to profit are those who have demonstrable muscle spasm. This will respond to EMG biofeedback and the progressive lessening of EMG readings with concomitant pain relief is a good measure of an improving situation. Whether or not the two facts are causally related and interdependent, or whether the reduction of EMG reading with lessening of muscle spasm is merely a so-called epiphenomenon is probably unimportant to the sufferer, so long as he gets well. Many cases of low back pain, post-traumatic or associated with degenerative osteoarthritis, will respond to EMG biofeedback. All candidates probably are best taught Jacobson's deep exercises prior to beginning biofeedback sessions. These practices teach the patients to contract before relaxing each individual muscle or muscle group, and the subjects learn a measure of anatomy and brain-muscle control* which makes the achievement of biofeedback training more facile.

Jacobs and Felton (1976) demonstrated the clinical use of relaxation for localized muscle spasm. Both normal and neck-injured subjects were better able to relax activity of the trapezius with EMG feedback.

Gottlieb et al. (1977) reported successful use of EMG feedback in patients with low back pain. EMG biofeedback was only part of a comprehensive pain management program, however. Nigl and Fischer-Williams (1980) reported four cases of relief of low back pain with muscle spasm. Many clinics are reported to be actively exploring biofeedback and general relaxation therapy for patients with chronic back problems (Medical World News, 1976). Nouwen and Solinger (1979) reported that EMG levels of low back pain patients returned to pretreatment levels at follow-up but pain was reduced significantly.

Many other types of chronic pain may respond to biofeedback treatment including temporomandibular joint pain (see Chap. 7). Atypical facial pain may respond to biofeedback training; this group of patients is often very resistive to many other forms of therapy including psychotherapy.

*Control implies linkage between thinking about a movement and carrying it out, the ideation and the performance of movement.

Individuals Interested in Instrumental Demonstration

Symptomatic patients with a strong interest in instrumentation may be attracted to biological demonstration of their responses as a method of understanding their own bodily functions, and thereby gaining greater control over their reactions and activities.

Individuals Resistive to Psychological Interpretation of Their Symptoms

It has been repeatedly noted that biofeedback is an aid and adjunct to psychotherapy, particularly for those who may have difficulties in personal relationships or in giving verbal expression to their feelings. Also, it is useful for those who do not readily accept the relationship between psyche and soma in the production of their symptoms. Biofeedback can also be beneficial for those who feel that the environment is malevolent. When they learn by machine demonstration that they themselves have the power to control their own reactions, they acquire satisfaction in regaining lost power, or in gaining it for the first time.

Individuals Who Are Less Comfortable with Physicians than with Allied Health Professionals

There is probably a sizeable section of the population who for various reasons wish to avoid consulting with a physician. These individuals may be interested, however, in learning a technique that offers them control over their biological functioning. This is, perhaps, the public that was drawn towards biofeedback by the enthusiastic and not very well informed advertisements of the "alpha machines," and "sleep machines," of the 1960s. It is likely that if this particular public reaches a medical professional who understands the potential for biofeedback treatment, symptoms will be relieved more quickly than they are at present.

Clinical Research

Finally, biofeedback is a research tool in many clinical situations and can be used to elucidate the mechanism of biological responses. It is probably in the field of gastrointestinal activities both normal and abnormal that this type of research will prove fruitful, because the tools for measurement of motility are now available, including esophageal, gastric, and duodenal motility, and the secretions from nearly all parts of the gastrointestinal tract can be obtained for analysis. The cardiovascular system also offers many avenues for research, again because of the available methods of measuring normal and abnormal function.

Psychiatric Contraindications and Nonindications

Since biofeedback therapy is most successful in treating disorders where tension and anxiety are major elements, conditions lacking these symptoms are less likely to respond to this mode of therapy.

Biofeedback treatment is not a primary indication in those psychiatric disorders where it is unlikely to effect a change in the level of anxiety, for example, in personality disorders. It is also usually not indicated in conditions where anxiety is not accessible or available to be worked with because the patient is unable to follow or respond to the treatment procedure, even though the anxiety exists; this applies to patients with profound mental retardation, congenital disorders, or chronic organic brain disease.

Biofeedback is contraindicated in those disorders in which the treatment itself generates, rather than alleviates, anxiety. In depression, psychic energy is diverted by sense of loss and "turned inward" and thus not available to be manifested as anxiety, unless the depression is stressful to the patient himself as in agitated depression. For those patients demonstrating psychomotor retardation as an expression of their depressed state, the relaxation portion of the treatment is not useful, since muscle tension is reduced here already. This is also the case in disorders manifested by hypersomnic states (e.g., narcolepsy).

As with other approaches to substance-abuse disorders, no utility can be expected from biofeedback treatment during the actual period of intoxication. The patient must first be detoxified before integration of the biofeedback process will have impact. In other categories of illness where the sensorium is affected by some external agent, biofeedback is also not indicated, e.g., delirium as from CNS infection (e.g., meningitis, malaria), trauma (e.g., head injury, due to ruptured cerebral aneurysm, hematoma), other toxic states (e.g., poisoning, ingestion of intoxicants), neoplasm (brain tumor), and metabolic disease (e.g., uncontrolled diabetes, hypothyroidism).

The major contraindication for biofeedback therapy at this time appears to lie with the psychoses, such as schizophrenia, manic-depressive illness, and paranoia, except under certain circumstances (see Chap. 17).

In the manic phase, the patient is unable to attend to the biofeedback due to increased sensitivity to a myriad of other stimuli. This inability of discrimination in focusing attention is a major factor.

The main concern with biofeedback in schizophrenia is the risk of dissolving already "porous" ego boundaries so that differentiation by the patient of self from biofeedback device, for instance, may become impossible. Psychotic episodes may increase and a psychotic transference may develop, particularly in the paranoid patient.

The same caution applies in the patient suffering from nonschizophrenic paranoia. If the patient's primary treatment form (usually neuroleptic medication in the psychoses) is sufficient to ensure strengthened ego boundaries, however, then biofeedback may be considered as an adjunctive procedure in certain selected cases.

For a more detailed description of indications for biofeedback treatment in the patient with emotional disorders see Chapter 17 on disorders of the cognitive-emotional system and Chapter 19 on biofeedback in psychotherapy.

Lack of motivation towards the enjoyment of health is a contraindication to biofeedback training. There are many reasons why people are not motivated towards getting well or remaining well, and a discussion in depth on motivation is outside the scope of this book. Suffice it to say that the individual who "enjoys ill-health" or has secondary gain in preserving his symptom(s) (e.g., disability or compensation neurosis) should not be referred for biofeedback training.

It may be clearly contraindicated to break down an individual's ego defenses. On the other hand, many patients may be ambivalent, and with a slow and careful therapeutic approach, they may find themselves willing to shed the load of their psychosomatic symptoms. Exploration of their sensations through instrumental demonstration (rather than verbally) may lead to a more satisfying body image.

As with all forms of therapy, the attitude of the patient's family or close associates plays an important part in the patient's progress. It is therefore important that cooperation with the family is sought from the beginning. A critical or negative attitude on the part of the close relatives may hinder the patient's improvement.

The single most important aspect to consider when evaluating the indications for biofeedback training is the motivation to change and, therefore, the ability to change. Those with rigid personality structure or sociopathic individuals who have no desire to alter their status quo do not profit from biofeedback. This attitude may be detected from the initial psychological screening, or it may become obvious after the first few sessions. On the other hand, patients who will risk change and wish to explore new body-mind fusion or sensory-motor integration should be encouraged to become acquainted with biofeedback techniques.

REFERENCES

Blanchard E: The use of temperature biofeedback in the treatment of chronic pain due to causalgia. Biofeedback Self-Regul 4: 183, 1979.

Editorial: Management of chronic pain: medicine's new growth industry. Med World News, Oct. 16, 1976, p. 54.

Feinstein A: *Clinical Judgement.* Baltimore, Williams and Wilkins, 1967, p. 147.

Gottlieb H, Strite L, Kohler R: Comprehensive rehabilitation of patients having chronic back pain. Arch Phy Med Rehab. 58:101, 1977.

Jacobs A, Felton GS: Visual feedback of myoelectric output to facilitate muscle relaxation in normal persons and patients with neck injuries. Arch Phys Med Rehabil 50: 34, 1976.

Nigl A, Fischer-Williams M: EMG biofeedback in the treatment of chronic low back strain. Psychosomatics 21: 495, 1980.

Nouwen A, Solinger J: The effectiveness of electromyographic biofeedback training in low back pain. Biofeedback Self-Regul 4: 103, 1979.

Schwartz G: Biofeedback, self-regulation and the patterning of physiological processes. Am Sci 63: 314, 1975.

19

Biofeedback and Psychotherapy

MANY clinicians view biofeedback therapy as more complex than verbal psychotherapy (Stroebel, 1979). Although psychotherapy involves a two-way interaction between therapist and patient, biofeedback therapy consists of several two-way interactions (e.g., therapist–patient, therapist–instrument, and patient–instrument) and one complicated three-way relationship between patient, therapist, and instrument. All of these relationships are more important in certain applications than in others. For example, the patient–instrument interaction is more important in biofeedback training for muscle rehabilitation than the others. In fact, a distinction can be made between biofeedback therapy and biofeedback training. Biofeedback therapy involves the application of feedback techniques to treat stress-induced psychophysiological disorders. Biofeedback training, on the other hand, is concerned primarily with the retraining of specific motor and muscle functions; significant modification of the patient's emotional and/or mental functioning is not usually the primary goal. There are exceptions, however, and often the patient's attitudes or behavior must be first treated with therapy before muscle training is effective.

Therapeutic Use of Biofeedback

Biofeedback therapy may be viewed as a form of psychotherapy involving the use of electronic instrumentation. As such, it is essential that a biofeedback therapist have the necessary personal qualities and training that have been identified as necessary for effective psychotherapy (Truax and Carkhuff, 1967). Biofeedback therapists must be warm, empathic, understanding and have positive regard for their patients.

Novice biofeedback therapists may overemphasize instrumentation and other unique elements of the biofeedback technique. It is important for all biofeedback therapists to understand that the quality of the therapeutic relationship and the personal qualities of the therapist are just as essential in biofeedback therapy as in verbal psychotherapy. Biofeedback consists of a system of techniques and operations having no inherent healing properties in, and of, themselves. The way in which a biofeedback therapist uses the equipment and presents it to the patient has significant bearing on the outcome of treatment.

Transference in Biofeedback Therapy

As stated previously, the interactions between the patient, therapist, and instrument make biofeedback a complex form of therapy. In fact, Stroebel (1979) stated that biofeedback is too complex to be considered a type of *psycho*therapy. He advocates the use of the term *psychophysiologic therapy*. Other authors believe that a transference reaction may develop between the patient and the biofeedback instrument (Adler and Adler, 1979). That is, patients may attribute magical qualities to the instrument to which they are "attached." Just as transference in verbal psychotherapy develops because of the patient's past experiences with other important individuals (especially parents), a patient undergoing biofeedback treatment may have preconceived notions about the power or the infallibility of electronic instrumentation; we have become a nation of "knob-twirlers," "button-pushers," and "light-emitting diode watchers." This transference can be either positive or negative just as in verbal psychotherapy. The biofeedback therapist must be aware of how the patient is reacting to his attachment to various biofeedback instruments.

Two common positive transference reactions can be identified involving either complete faith and trust (and, perhaps, unrelenting optimism that the machine will "cure" the patient's problem) or an attitude of childlike awe and fascination.

A common negative transference reaction occurs when the patient becomes anxious at the very thought of being attached to something which may appear to him as a cleverly disguised electroshock unit or "mind-control" device.

In order to eliminate the patient's apprehension concerning the biofeedback instrument or to reduce his extreme optimism, the therapist should explain thoroughly the functioning of the biofeedback instrument prior to attaching the electrodes or sensors to the patient. Many therapists supply informational pamphlets in order that patients are introduced to the theory and technique of biofeedback prior to their first appointment. In addition, it may help to use a brief questionnaire after each session to give the patient an opportunity to state his reactions and feelings regarding the experience; these can then be explored and discussed.

Although it is recognized that distinct types of psychotherapy exist, representing diverse schools of thought, only the relationships between biofeedback and psychodynamic and behavior therapy will be examined in this chapter.

Biofeedback and Psychodynamic Therapy

Biofeedback techniques can be used in conjunction with other forms of therapy including psychodynamic therapy. Green (1979) reported that EEG alpha or theta wave training could assist psychiatric patients in integrating unconscious conflicts. According to preliminary results a significant increase in hypnagogic imagery occurs when a patient is producing theta waves (i.e., when theta activity predominates in the EEG; see Chap. 4). There has also been much discussion about the creative possibilities of hypnagogic imagery in other areas outside of therapy. Individuals may learn to solve interpersonal as well as job-related problems through use of imagery experiences. EEG biofeedback training, specifically theta wave training, may have the potential for enhancing creative processes.

In Green's (1979) study, patients were randomly assigned to different experimental groups. One group was given training in beta-wave feedback (beta waves are usually associated with cortical activity in the normal waking state) and another theta-wave activity (theta waves are associated with drowsiness and states of deep relaxation). The results indicated that patients given theta feedback reported more frequent imagery experiences, including "integrative" imagery experiences. This term is used when a patient sees himself as being improved in personal and social function, and also able to solve interpersonal problems which may be related to his disorder. Green hypothesized that the patient's ability to become more aware of his unconscious feelings and drives in the theta state enhances his ability to benefit from dynamic and other insight-oriented therapy experiences.

Another use of biofeedback techniques with psychiatric patients was reported by Adler and Adler (1979). In their technique, there is no particular emphasis on the use of EEG training; what is important is a state of deep relaxation. They report that feedback and deep relaxation allow a patient to explore various images and problems. Thus, the patient may discover which thoughts or images lead to increased tension as indicated by the feedback. This can be done either through a free association method in which the patient relaxes and allows his mind to wander or in a more direct fashion where the therapist narrates scenes involving family members or other areas of conflict.

Some insight-oriented psychotherapists employ electrodermal or EMG units for enhancing the initial psychiatric interview. The patient is monitored by the instrument, and the therapist observes the electrophysiological information while the patient responds to various questions. Given the potentially intrusive nature of such procedures, however, it is important that the patient give his appropriate consent prior to undergoing this process.

For those patients who might deny or repress discrepancies between their verbal statements and physiological responses, biofeedback may be helpful. When biofeedback is used to develop insight, it functions as a desensitization process where patients are gradually presented with information regarding their internal physiological state (which may be discrepant with their conscious and/or verbalized opinion of self). The biofeedback therapist can guide the patient to explore areas of potential conflict correlated with fluctuations in the biofeedback signal. In addition, the continual process of relaxation which is inherent in the biofeedback technique insures that that patient will not experience "traumatic" anxiety that could increase repression.

Adler and Adler (1979) describe derivative temperature feedback as a method of monitoring an individual's conflict states in psychoanalytic psychotherapy. They suggest a relationship between the use of biofeedback to foster insight and the development of empathy. According to their hypothesis, biofeedback techniques enable individuals to achieve greater self awareness. Often patients are not aware of how their external and internal states differ and especially how they may vary from one stressful situation to another. Therefore, the patient is sensitized to these discrepancies within himself. He then becomes more sensitive to the internal/external dichotomy in other individuals. Once the patient is more aware of his own internal state, he may be more sensitive to the needs of others, plus he will develop empathy through the psychophysiologic insights gained in biofeedback treatment.

Biofeedback should not be applied "routinely" to psychiatric patients, however. For example, the indiscriminate elimination of anxiety could foster impulsive acting-out in vulnerable patients. Anxiety often serves a protective function. Therefore, the biofeedback therapist should be acutely aware of the defensive nature of anxiety in patients referred for biofeedback and relaxation treatment. That is why it is important that medical-psychiatric and psychological evaluations be conducted prior to engaging in such therapy. It is one thing to eliminate physiological responses that are primary symptoms, and it is quite another to remove physiological responses that are a useful and necessary part of the person's defense mechanisms (Adler and Adler, 1979). The consequences are more serious in the latter case and great care should be exercised when working with individuals who have developed physiological defense mechanisms. When eliminating such defenses, the therapist must be prepared to deal effectively with the patient's predictable emotional anger and grief reaction. The biofeedback therapist should also be aware of the possibility of "symptom substitution" developing after physiological defenses are eliminated (Greenspan, 1979).

In a personal case of one of the authors (AJN) a female patient developed severe depression following a significant reduction in chronic muscle tension headache through EMG biofeedback. At that point, the biofeedback treatment was terminated and verbal therapy was initiated.

Patient Resistance

Regardless of the type of biofeedback employed, the patient's attitudes and personality can have a significant effect on treatment outcome. *Resistance* is a term used by dynamic therapists to describe a defense mechanism involving the patients' attempts to subvert or negate therapists' efforts to promote change. Resistance can also occur in biofeedback therapy and should be dealt with as soon as possible by the therapist. At least three major categories of patient resistance can be identified and will be summarized in what follows. (Fromm-Reichmann F, 1950, Castelnuvo-Tedescu, 1965, and Nigl, 1975).

Noncompliant Passive-Aggressive Type

Patients who have difficulty following through with the therapist's directions for self-monitoring and/or home practice may be demonstrating psychologic resistance. As previously discussed, self-monitoring is an extremely important procedure; the lack of it can be frustrating to the therapist because it slows the rate of progress. Patients who show this form of resistance often have difficulty accepting responsibility for their physiological symptoms.

Chronic lateness for appointments, frequent "no-shows," or cancelling of appointments can be manifestations of resistance in the passive-aggressive patient. The biofeedback therapist must act swiftly and firmly to counteract such defensiveness; in some cases, the treatment may have to be terminated prematurely if noncompliance continues. Alternatively, a biofeedback therapist can help the patient interpret such acting-out behavior and increase the patient's insight regarding his defensiveness.

Denial of Physiological Control

Some patients emphatically deny that they have any control over their physiological symptoms. Even though the biofeedback instruments show significant reductions in physiological arousal, such patients cannot accept these data and continue to make statements to the therapist such as "I don't think it's working on me" or "How long do I have to go through this?"

Such patients probably employ defenses as "projection" and "rationalization" in an attempt to deny personal responsibility and attribute their disorder to external causes outside of their control. It may be difficult for the biofeedback therapist to separate the resistive patient from those who actually may have little control over their symptoms (e.g., a headache patient suffering from an allergic reaction). Adequate pretreatment medical, psychiatric, and psychological screening will assist the therapist in making this determination. Diagnosing "resistance" should never be a substitute for a thorough medical and/or psychological evaluation.

Obsessive-Compulsive Type

Patients may be resistant to change when they develop an obsessive and/or compulsive attitude toward treatment. Certain patients may not be able to relax because of their need to be "perfect." Such perfectionistic tendencies cause them to be overly critical of their relaxation response and may interfere with treatment.

Certain headache patients respond in this way, especially at the beginning of treatment. Headache often occurs as a result of obsessively motivated strivings and overachievement. Since it is not possible to relax completely, such patients are constantly frustrated during the biofeedback session and at home while practicing. Frequently, such patients not only criticize themselves but also the therapist's technique or equipment.

A patient who was referred for biofeedback treatment by his psychiatrist had learned Jacobson's progressive muscle relaxation program as an undergraduate. He was continually upset because he could not relax each and every muscle, and he criticized the biofeedback therapist for not having sensitive enough equipment to detect the tension he believed was present (even though the EMG registered a very low reading). Consultation with the referring psychiatrist indicated that such perfectionistic needs and overly critical attitudes were part of this patient's defense mechanisms. By ignoring his complaint and concentrating instead on positively reinforcing the improvement which was occurring, the patient came to realize that significant changes had occurred.

In summary, the following criteria may be used to detect therapeutic resistance after a reasonable time (e.g., 6 to 8 weeks of treatment).

1. Little or no progress in attaining physiological control in the absence of significant organic dysfunction.

2. Noncompliance in self-monitoring or home practice exercises.

3. Discrepancy between the patient's level of physiological control (as measured by the biofeedback instrument) and the patient's verbal statements and attitudes.

4. Chronic criticism of self, therapist, and instrumentation.

5. Patient's attribution of external causes for symptoms; inability to take responsibility for his disorder.

Biofeedback and Behavior Therapy

The close relationship between biofeedback and therapies based on psychological learning theory has been previously discussed (see Chap. 1). It is obvious that biofeedback could be used effectively in conjunction with such treatment modalities. Many biofeedback clinicians are well versed in behavior therapy and practice biofeedback as a consequence of their training and exposure to behavior therapy techniques.

The basis for all techniques grouped under the term *behavior therapy* is that every response an individual makes can be seen as a consequence of learning, either directly conditioned through classical or operant procedures or indirectly developed by vicarious or observational learning. Although the importance of genetic and constitutional factors is recognized, the behavior therapist believes that there is a learned sequence to the development of symptoms. Therefore, symptoms can be treated by establishing a new sequence of learning (relearning). In other situations, desirable responses or behaviors which a particular individual does not show can be instituted through behavioral learning. Techniques, therefore, exist for the treatment of behavior *excesses* (i.e., the elimination of undesirable responses) or the treatment of behavioral *deficits* (i.e., the learning of desirable responses).

Many behavior therapy techniques employ relaxation as part of the method. Biofeedback can be used to assist the patient by enhancing the strength and effectiveness of relaxation learning. The relaxation effect of biofeedback may be used in conjunction with behavior therapy techniques which employ operant conditioning procedures. Several behavior therapy methods have been based on Skinner's operant theory and use operant conditioning to modify undesirable behaviors or increase the expression of desirable responses. Biofeedback's inherent reinforcement system may be employed in conjunction with an operant-based program such as a token economy or a program of self-reinforcement. EMG biofeedback training has been used for children with hyperactivity or excessive negative behavior at home, at school, or both. In such cases, parents and/or teachers may be instructed to reinforce desirable behaviors (e.g., quiet play or cooperativeness) and extinguish undesirable responses through the use of "time-out" procedures. In time-out, a child is placed in a particular part of his environment (which has a low level of stimuli) for a short time so that reinforcement is highly unlikely or improbable. In this way, positive or negative reinforcement of undesirable behaviors will be eliminated through the process of extinction; undesirable behavior will be extinguished over time.

Biofeedback training can be useful by teaching children to relax and inhibit their tendencies to respond negatively or excessively. Children appear particularly eager to learn the biofeedback techniques and are able to achieve significant levels of relaxation because of their fascination with electronic gadgetry.

Illustrative Case

An 8-year-old white male was referred to biofeedback treatment by his psychiatrist on account of a hyperkinetic syndrome. The boy had a long history of severe behavioral problems with aggressive acts, fire-setting, cruelty to animals and disturbing other children in the classroom.

The EMG instrument showed that the patient was extremely tense; his frontalis activity was very high averaging above $20\mu v$ (integral average). He was trained in a relaxation method which was taped for his use at home. Following six EMG biofeedback sessions, his average frontalis tension decreased to below $5\mu v$. His mother reported that his behavior had markedly improved both at home and at school, based on teachers' reports.

This case indicates that children can benefit from EMG biofeedback training. Shouse and Lubar (1979) reported that EEG biofeedback training enhanced the therapeutic effectiveness of Ritalin in controlling hyperkinetic behavior in four children.

Parents can also learn to reinforce their children by observing the biofeedback session. They can see for themselves how important positive reinforcement can be in maintaining appropriate behavior.

Another use of biofeedback training is in conjunction with operant methods in institutional settings with individuals of limited intelligence or diminished cognitive resources due to organic disorders. For example, EMG biofeedback can be employed successfully with retarded individuals as part of a total program of self-control and self-care. Many EMG instruments have the capability of being connected to audiovisual devices such as phonographs or slide projectors which may enhance the reinforcement effect. This is especially important with younger children or retarded individuals who may not understand the digital output but may be interested in music or animated cartoon slides.

An area of successful operant conditioning treatment is the use of positive reinforcement procedures in bowel and bladder training with normal or retarded individuals. Since many children consciously withhold elimination through continual contraction of sphincter musculature, EMG biofeedback and relaxation may enhance the training process by causing specific relaxation of the sphincter muscles as a result of general relaxation.

Biofeedback techniques may be employed to enhance the efficacy of systematic desensitization. In this technique, developed by Wolpe (1973), the patient is presented with a hierarchical series of scenes related to an anxiety-provoking object or event. After the patient learns relaxation, he is asked to imagine these scenes vividly. He must be able to imagine the scene comfortably without feeling any tension before the next one is presented. After the entire series has been presented, he is encouraged to encounter the scenes in real-life situations to enhance "generalization" of the effect. The treatment may not be effective if the patient does not want to appear uncooperative (or perhaps unintelligent) and, therefore, will not tell the therapist of his discomfort or anxiety while imagining certain scenes. This lack of self-disclosure (due to social desirability) may cause treatment to stop prematurely and the patients may not practice the desired responses. Therefore they may be unable to encounter the real-life stimuli which maintain their phobia.

Biofeedback monitoring enhances the therapist's perception of the patient's internal physiological state. EMG or electrothermal instruments may be useful in this regard once threshold levels have been established. The therapist can interrupt the desensitization procedure whenever responses occur above the threshold. The auditory stimulus may not have to be on continuously for it may interfere with the patient's relaxation and imagination experiences. The therapist can monitor the visual output while the patient is imagining the scenes in the desensitization hierarchy.

Although these biofeedback procedures are promising, only a few clinical cases have been reported. Wickramasekera (1972) reported a successful treatment of test-taking phobia using desensitization combined with relaxation and biofeedback training. In a similar study, Reeves and Mealiea (1977) treated several individuals who had phobias with fear of flying. Mathews and Gelder (1969), however, reported that relaxation training and EMG biofeedback may only decrease muscle activity and not lower autonomic states of anxiety during desensitization therapy. This merits further research; it may be that skin temperature biofeedback (which is a good measure of autonomic functioning) would be more desirable in desensitization therapy than EMG biofeedback.

Other areas of behavior therapy for which biofeedback procedures may be valuable adjuncts include the cognitive (covert) therapies, such as cognitive relabeling or covert reinforcement. Such therapeutic techniques are based on the hypothesis that thoughts and images (covert behavior) can be conditioned or learned just as for overt responses. Cautela (1971) developed several techniques based on the concept of covert conditioning. However the theory that covert responses can be conditioned has not been empirically supported. Covert therapy techniques do appear to be effective in changing behavior, however (Nigl, 1975).

Biofeedback may enhance the effectiveness of these techniques by enabling the patient to realize how certain thoughts or images are related to physiological tension. Biofeedback may also be used by the behavior therapist to monitor patients' physiological arousal as an indicator of treatment success. Thus, if covert sensitization is used to eliminate undesirable sexual responses, the biofeedback instrument (e.g., EMG) may indicate that the aversive images have a pronounced negative effect on the patient, an effect necessary for treatment success. On the other hand, if covert conditioning (e.g., covert positive reinforcement) is used to enhance desirable behaviors, the biofeedback instrument may indicate the time when imagination of previously anxiety-arousing behavior becomes less threatening to the patient. Similar uses of biofeedback can be combined with other types of cognitive behavior therapy such as cognitive relabeling (see Chap. 21).

In conclusion, biofeedback techniques may be used in conjunction with diverse forms of therapy. For any form of therapy, the penultimate goal is the patient's development of greater self-awareness with respect to his disorder. Eventually, the patient can separate from the therapy having gained greater independence. The danger in employing biofeedback techniques in therapy is that the patient may have difficulty gaining independence because of the stimulation he received through the sophisticated, electronic instrumentation.

The stimulating effect of some of the newer techniques (e.g., television monitors and other captivating multisensorial displays) may unintentionally "seduce" the patient to become more dependent on the technique than is appropriate. This can be true not only for the patient but also for the therapist. If the therapist relies solely on sophisticated instrumentation, the patient may develop an overly passive attitude toward the resolution of his disorder. This may be analogous to the difference between an individual who passively watches a film depicting a shoreline and an individual who actively imagines it. Although the individual who watches passively relaxes during the film, he may have difficulty relaxing in the same way when not exposed to the visual stimulation. On the other hand, the individual who actively creates a relaxing state, through imagery, has developed a technique that can be employed in a variety of situations.

Therefore, biofeedback therapists must be aware of the inherent problems in becoming overly preoccupied with techniques and instrumentation. Biofeedback should only be a tool to promote self-control and the identification of internal feedback systems, not an end to itself. Biofeedback is a good servant but a poor master.

REFERENCES

Adler C, Adler S: Strategies in general psychiatry, in Basmajian J (ed): *Biofeedback-Principles and Practice for Clinicians.* Baltimore, Williams and Wilkins, 1979, p. 180.
Castelnuvo-Tedescu P: *The Twenty Minute Hour.* London, Churchill, 1965.

Cautela J: Covert conditioning, in Jacobs A, Sachs L (eds): *The Psychology of Private Events.* New York, Academic Press, 1971, p. 112.

Fromm-Reichmann F: *Principles of Intensive Psychotherapy.* Chicago, University of Chicago Press, 1950.

Green E: Biofeedback-adjunct to psychotherapy. Psych News Feb 2, 1979.

Greenspan K: Biological feedback: some conceptual bridges with analytically oriented psychotherapy. Psychiatr Opin 16: 17, 1979.

Mathews A, Gelder M: Psychophysiological investigations of brief relaxation training. J Psychosom Res 13: 1, 1969.

Nigl A: Use of covert reinforcement in the acquisition of dental behavior. Diss Abs Internat 25: 922, 1975.

Reeves J, Mealiea W: Biofeedback-assisted cue-controlled relaxation for treatment of flight phobias. J Exp Psych Behav Ther 1977.

Shouse M, Lubar J: Operant conditioning of EEG rhythms and Ritalin in the treatment of hyperkinesis. Biofeedback and Self-Regul 4: 299–312, 1979.

Stroebel C: The application of biofeedback techniques in psychiatry and behavioral medicine. Psychiatric Opin 16: 13, 1979.

Truax C, Carkhuff R: *Toward Effective Counseling and Psychotherapy.* Chicago, Aldine, 1967.

Wickramasekera I: Instructions and EMG feedback in systematic desensitization: A case report. Behav Res Ther 3: 460, 1972.

Wolpe J: *The Practice of Behavior Therapy.* New York, Pergamon, 1973.

20

Biofeedback in Perspective—Current Trends

BIOFEEDBACK began as a laboratory technique for use in animal and human research, undertaken to discover processes involved in visceral conditioning and conscious control over biological functions. Its clinical utility became obvious, however, and it has developed also as a widely used clinical technique in the treatment of many disorders. As such, it is being used in a number of fields and at a number of levels of professional experience. Some ten years after the emergence of biofeedback, it is appropriate to examine its present status as well as its probable future trends. There is danger in trying to put things in perspective, in a rapidly growing field, because the subject matter may soon be outdated. The rapid growth of biofeedback has created problems of communication however; therefore, some synthesis is needed to integrate the varied approaches.

Current Clinical Applications of Biofeedback

A review of clinical applications of biofeedback serves as a starting point. As may be expected, there is great diversity among such applications. Bird et al. (1979) reported that EMG biofeedback benefited choreoathetoid cerebral palsy (CP) patients. In other studies of children with CP, Mandel and Sharp (1979) indicated that biofeedback was superior to traditional physiotherapy in teaching head control. A similar finding was reported by Leiper et al. (1979) in the use of augmented sensory feedback for head position control.

There are reports of biofeedback success in treating ocular disorders. Yolton and Hirons (1979) described a biofeedback paradigm for strabismic patients whose eyes deviated outward or inward. Improvement in the control of strabismus was noted in several weeks of treatment and complete cures for two patients with no further medical treatment or surgery needed; this also applies to children.

Primary dysmenorrhea or menstrual discomfort can be treated successfully by using thermal feedback and relaxation training. Dietvorst and Osborne (1978) reported a patient with an 18-year history of dysmenorrhea who was treated successfully.

Few studies have applied biofeedback procedures to cancer patients; however Nigl (1979) reported EMG biofeedback to be of value as part of a behavioral program of rehabilitation for individuals recovering from radiation treatment and surgical procedures. In this case, a 62-year-old woman was given EMG biofeedback training involving the masseter muscles to improve her ability to chew and swallow whole food. She had been on a liquid diet because of the after effects of radical surgery to treat lymph node cancer. After 6 weeks of treatment, she learned to chew and swallow whole food.

Motor speech disorders are being treated by biofeedback techniques involving intraoral air pressure and static lip force. Rubow and Flynn (1980) presented a case with closed head injury from an auto accident. They found that visual feedback of oral pressure (P_o) increased the patient's ability to increase P_o. They concluded that biofeedback training "can improve physiologic parameters of speech even in patients with severe dysarthria."

Redington et al. (1980) reported that algorhythm EEG biofeedback training increased sleep latency in a 43-year-old narcoleptic patient. They cautioned, however, that more research is needed before this can be considered effective treatment of narcolepsy.

EMG biofeedback may be useful for heterotropia (a deviation of the eyes which is uncorrected by fusion). Jackson and Cain (1980) employed EMG training of muscles in getting the patient to maintain visual fusion while attempting to lower the EMG auditory feedback. The visual problems improved markedly.

These cases represent only a sample of the diverse and innovative applications of biofeedback reported. A trend appears in the emergence of new forms of biofeedback to treat disorders that formerly were treated only by standard clinical approaches. Since there are insufficient controlled studies, it is not yet possible to compare the efficacy of biofeedback techniques with the results obtained by traditional methods.

Feedback Systems

Another trend is the application of sophisticated and complex systems to biofeedback therapy. The concept of multiple modality (multimodal) biofeedback has existed for several years, but has only recently been utilized widely in hospitals, outpatient clinics, and in the offices of private practitioners. Multimodal matrix video systems are available and may improve the effectiveness of biofeedback therapy and training. The development of multimodal feedback systems has been somewhat hampered by the lack of sophisticated electronic instrumentation. Prior to the new matrix feedback systems, clinicians either had to monitor simultaneously several biofeedback instruments or to use a simple binary matrix system. Now, however, multiple matrix systems are available. Such systems, though costly, evaluate and feedback information for four or more physiological variables at one time. This information is not only presented through auditory signals, but can be fed into a television monitor where colored bars (in a histogram format) are used to indicate visually to the subject how he is doing with respect to the physiological variables measured.

Another major development has been the creation of microcomputer systems for data acquisition. Such systems greatly enhance the collection of clinical data and allow clinicians to obtain more meaningful information. Heretofore, clinicians were limited by a lack of access to computer systems and/or a lack of necessary training or background in microelectronics to construct their own systems. The level of hardware and instrumentation now available increases the ability of the clinician to accurately monitor and record physiological data.

Biofeedback Centers

Biofeedback centers are being developed associated with various hospital and university clinics. Such centers also exist independently but are not generally as multifaceted or comprehensive in terms of the treatment available. By now, there has been an increased concentration of biofeedback clinicians in various health centers. Therapists are beginning to specialize in various aspects of treatment, and collaboration is increasing among professionals.

Biofeedback technique is rapidly being adopted by existing clinical programs, especially in pain clinics, and it is now recognized as an effective clinical tool that can be used adjunctively with other techniques. Nigl and Fischer-Williams (1980) demonstrated how biofeedback can be used in conjunction with other types of medical and physical therapies, as well as with social counseling and activity therapy, to rehabilitate individuals suffering from chronic low back pain. Most urban hospitals now have the capability of using biofeedback as one of the available treatments for patients.

Current Status of Biofeedback

The status of several biofeedback techniques was evaluated by researchers commissioned by the Biofeedback Society of America (BSA). These BSA Task Force reports reviewed the literature up to 1978; some of their conclusions will be summarized below.

Fotopoulos and Sunderland (1978) reviewed the application of biofeedback for the treatment of psychophysiological disorders. They concluded that the majority of studies were relatively uncontrolled; many of these were case reports. However, EMG treatment of torticollis seems to have been both clinically and empirically established. Over 100 cases of successful treatment of this disorder have been reported (Brundy, Grynbaum, and Friedman, 1974; Korein et al., 1976).

Fotopoulos and Sunderland also concluded that case studies support the use of biofeedback for treatment of blepharospasm and some tic syndromes but few controlled studies have yet been done.

Biofeedback may be a potentially useful technique in treating dysmenorrhea, stuttering, and sexual dysfunction in males.

Few studies, however, have investigated biofeedback treatment of other psychophysiologic disorders such as urinary incontinence, skin disorders, and endocrine dysfunctions.

Taub and Stroebel (1978) reviewed the use of thermal (or skin temperature) feedback to treat vasoconstrictive disorders. They concluded that skin temperature feedback is a promising method of treating Raynaud's disease and related vasoconstrictive syndromes. In fact, biofeedback may be advantageous to the patient because of the lack of negative side effects and because it can be applied when necessary (i.e., only when vasoconstrictive attacks occur). They note that traditional treatment for Raynaud's disease may have unpleasant side effects or long-term negative consequences (e.g., radical surgical procedures).

In summary, Taub and Stroebel state that several areas need improvement including more long-term followup studies, greater numbers of patients, more objective recording of vasoconstrictive symptoms, and control for placebo and other nonspecific effects.

Biofeedback treatment of gastrointestinal disorders was reviewed by Whitehead (1978). Techniques for treating rumination, esophageal motility disorders, peptic ulcer, irritable bowel syndrome, inflammatory bowel disease, and fecal incontinence were discussed. The author concluded that the method used by Engel, Nikoomanesh, and Schuster (1974) for treating fecal incontinence is the treatment of choice in this disorder. Although only case reports are available, treating chronic rumination with electric shock appears to be effective, especially for patients who do not respond to other forms of medical treatment.

However, Whitehead concludes that using gastric pH feedback is not effective for peptic ulcer treatment. EMG biofeedback may be of value in this disorder but control studies are lacking.

Whitehead urged future researchers to investigate the possibility of using biofeedback to treat esphogeal dysfunction. This appears promising because motor responses of the upper tract can be modified and otherwise the only available treatment for some patients is surgery.

In summary, Whitehead indicated that nonspecific (or indirect) biofeedback training (e.g., EMG) and relaxation methods may be more effective in reducing stress-related GI disorders than specific (direct) feedback procedures using GI responses (e.g., colonic motility).

Diamond, Diamond-Falk, and DeVeno (1978) surveyed the literature of biofeedback treatment of vascular headache. They concluded that thermal biofeedback, when used alone or with autogenic training, is effective in treating migraine and other vascular headaches. There are problems with the research to date, however; critiques have been offered by Blanchard and Young (1974) and Price (1974). These critiques focus on empirical inadequacies such as lack of placebo, "no-treatment" methods, or inadequate data analyses.

Precautions in interpreting available data should be taken according to Diamond and his co-workers. Many factors are involved in causing vascular headaches and some of these may interfere with successful biofeedback treatment. For example, the classical migraine patients' personality (which is manifested by perfectionistic strivings, obsessive worries, and sexual maladjustment) may make it difficult for these patients to learn physiological self-control.

Sargent, Green, and Walters (1973) stated that psychological factors can have an important effect on migraine treatment success. Other factors which must be considered prior to beginning biofeedback treatment were listed by Diamond and co-workers, including accurate diagnosis, depression, and drug dependency. They also concluded that children are good candidates for biofeedback and may respond more quickly than adults to this type of treatment.

Although clinical reports are encouraging, they conclude that several major issues need further investigation under carefully controlled conditions. Individual differences in learning control of vascular headaches should be explored; also, it would be beneficial to determine whether certain personality factors can be used to predict treatment success. Other factors needing further clarification include placebo effects, symptom substitution, and the use of particular combinations of different biofeedback techniques to treat various types of vascular headaches. Although not included in the 1978 report, Diamond's research group recently observed that certain migraine patients may develop neurotic disorders following relief of their headache symptoms (Szajnberg, 1979). Negative consequences of thermal biofeedback should be carefully researched before this method can be applied routinely to vascular headaches.

Thomas Budzynski (1978), who has been credited with developing the EMG feedback technique for tension headache, was asked to review this specific area of research. He stated that EMG treatment has been shown to be effective for over 70 percent of the headache cases evaluated. Individuals suffering from other than simple muscle contraction headaches do not receive as much benefit, however. Combining thermal or blood volume pulse feedback may add to the effectiveness of EMG treatment according to Budzynski. He also concluded that frontalis EMG training is more efficient than relaxation methods used alone, and that the quality of the feedback signal appears to be an important factor.

Budzynski (1978) stressed the importance of helping the patient to relax through effective biofeedback procedures. However, he suggested that biofeedback may not be any more effective than relaxation training or other methods over a long period of time. Conclusive longitudinal research has not yet been reported and long-term follow-up studies are needed.

In summary, Budzynski emphasizes the importance of assessing the efficacy of home practice, transfer of skill training and psychotherapy as adjuncts to the EMG treatment of tension headache.

Fernando and Basmajian (1978) evaluated the status of biofeedback techniques in rehabilitation. They concluded that the efficacy of biofeedback in treating disorders of upper and lower motor neuron lesions has primarily been shown in clinical studies. Few well-controlled investigations have been conducted. They point out, however, that more research has been done recently on EMG feedback than physical therapy techniques which have been in use for many years. They predict, therefore, that EMG training will eventually become one of the standard procedures in physical therapy. They state that EMG feedback will not replace existing methods but will supplement them and enhance the efficacy of rehabilitation. They recommend that EMG training be an adjunct to routine treatment of hemiplegic patients, and that EMG feedback should be used in upper motor neuron lesions

following regeneration. They also advise it in treating spasmodic torticollis. Other recommendations were also made regarding clinical
application and practice, and the reader is referred to this Task Force
report.

Biofeedback and Education

There has been renewed interest among educators in teaching children about themselves. Courses have been designed to prepare children for making better adjustments to life as adults. Biofeedback
techniques hold promise as methods of illustrating to children how
they can consciously control biological processes and, possibly, improve their overall health. Although this is innovative in our educational system, it is not unprecedented. Many experts in the field of
biofeedback have emphasized the differences between the educational
experience given to children in our Western culture and that in Eastern societies such as India or Japan. Those societies have traditionally
emphasized the learning of internal control, while Western societies
stress control over external events. Biofeedback training might be
utilized in our school systems to help children understand and control
the internal functioning of their own bodies. Such experiences would
help balance the traditional Western educational curriculum, so that
control of one's internal world is learned coincidentally with learning
to control the external environment.

Tradional educational practices in this country have been criticized
for stressing the type of learning assumed to take place in the left
hemisphere (verbal and mathematical skills), while neglecting those
activities assumed to be part of right-hemisphere functioning (art,
imagery, and creative expression). Since biofeedback procedures are
thought to involve the right hemisphere (Brown, 1977), inclusion of
biofeedback training might increase the involvement of right hemi-
spheric learning in traditional, verbally-dominant educational curricula. EMG and thermal biofeedback could be employed in
conjunction with deep-muscle relaxation training on a regular basis,
just as physical exercise is usually interspersed with academic activities
as part of the daily school routine (Engelhardt, 1978). Given awareness
of the stresses of modern life and the high incidence of stress-related
disease (Brown, 1977), it seems desirable to have children learn relaxation skills, as well as reading, writing, and arithmetic. Relaxation skills
may be even more useful and beneficial to them later in life by increasing their chances of physical and mental survival in a world of constant

"future shocks." Even young children may derive physiological benefit from such training. Hughes and Collins (1978) presented data that indicate that numerous school children can learn to reduce physiological tension when presented with a standard relaxation training.

Beyond the obvious benefits of biofeedback training as part of the regular elementary and high school curricula, such procedures appear to have potential as adjuncts to special educational treatment of specific learning disorders (LD). For example, hyperactivity (a behavioral condition commonly seen in children with learning disabilities) has been treated successfully with EMG biofeedback (see Chap. 19). Braud, Lupin, and Braud (1975) used EMG biofeedback training and relaxation on a 6-year-old boy who was "extremely hyperactive." After 12 sessions of EMG training, the boy showed improvement in his control over muscle tension as well as his behavior. His performance in school also improved dramatically. In more recent studies, significant improvement was found in children's performances on psychological tests (Braud, 1978; Lupin et al., 1976).

Research with learning disabled (LD) children who were not necessarily hyperkinetic also suggests that EMG feedback improves school performance. Russell and Carter (1979) studied groups of LD children given relaxation training and EMG biofeedback. They were also given achievement tests, such as the Wide Range Achievement Test, the Gray Oral Reading Test and others commonly used to diagnose LD. The results suggested that EMG biofeedback and relaxation training improves daily classroom performance of children with LD as measured on various routine cognitive academic tasks. Similar improvement was found on Wide Range Achievement Arithmetic Test scores for LD adolescents by Cunningham and Murphy (1978).

Another educational area in which biofeedback may have potential value is the treatment of common disorders that prevent children from learning in school, childhood migraine and "school phobia." The treatment of childhood migraine was reported by Diamond (1979), showing 26 of 32 children responding with positive results; i.e., by a decrease in both frequency and severity of migraine headaches through EMG and temperature biofeedback training.

Werder (1978) treated four children aged 10 to 17 with hand temperature biofeedback and relaxation methods. Drug usage in the group dropped by almost 50 percent after the 3rd week of training and after 4 months all subjects were free of headaches and had stopped all medications. According to Werder, children are excellent candidates for such treatment because they are not as skeptical and biased as adults about the possibility of learning self-control and self-regulation. One drawback is that they do not keep as precise records as adults, however, although the use of reinforcement techniques may improve the recordings obtainable.

In their review of biofeedback treatment of vascular headaches Diamond et al. (1978) concluded that children make excellent subjects for biofeedback. The initiation of biofeedback in schoolage children may help reduce their chances of suffering from migraine under the stress of adult life. In addition, parents and teachers can participate in a behavioral program to enhance the effectiveness of self-control training. For example, biofeedback training can be used to reduce physiological stress resulting from performance anxiety (test-taking anxiety).

Another childhood disorder that prevents adequate performance is school phobia. In this, children exhibit extreme fear or anxiety regarding school-related activities and may eventually drop out altogether. Although there is not as much research here, it appears that the use of biofeedback training combined with systematic desensitization and other relaxation techniques may be effective. In a personal case, a 15-year-old girl was referred for treatment of school phobia. In addition to being afraid of school-related activities, this adolescent showed severe phobic reactions to males and also appeared to be agoraphobic, having great difficulty leaving the house by herself. She had been treated with verbal psychotherapy with little success and was referred for biofeedback treatment. After 10 sessions of EMG biofeedback training and relaxation, she was able to feel comfortable in the presence of a male tutor and earned credits following an 18-month absence. She joined a special educational program in the public school system. As is true with many conditions involving anxiety (see Chap. 17), this particular patient showed more severe behavioral abnormalities than might be seen in other children with a more circumscribed phobia. According to the psychological test results, she also had severe withdrawal, was schizoidal with a high potential for development of schizophrenic thought disturbance. Therefore, treatment consisted not only of biofeedback training but also verbal psychotherapy and the use of a psychotropic medication. This case illustrates why the biofeedback therapist must be aware of the possibility that a more serious condition may underlie the symptoms for which the patient is referred. Successful treatment of such cases requires more than just biofeedback techniques; for example, appropriate psychiatric consultation may be needed (AJN).

Biofeedback techniques can also be used in a program of general

education as valuable adjuncts to other learning experiences, especially concerning the effect of external agents on the body. The effects
of smoking and alcohol can be graphically demonstrated by making
students aware of the corresponding changes in vasodilatation and
increased skin conductance through the use of thermal biofeedback
and electrodermal feedback instruments. Moreover, EMG biofeedback
and relaxation can be used to provide students with an alternative to
using drugs and alcohol in combating stress and anxiety. In a group
setting, these may be employed to modify attitudes and change behavior patterns in impressionable individuals.

In summary, biofeedback as applied in education (although still at
a rudimentary level) may serve to help improve children's understanding of themselves and their bodies.

Biofeedback in Business and Industry

Attention has recently been turned to the use of biofeedback in
business and industry. One such application is the development of
stress management programs for executives. Research indicates that
certain occupational groups are more prone to stress-related disorders
than others, e.g., nurses, medical technologists, and waitresses. Industrial psychologists and other consultants have been increasingly aware
of the potential of group relaxation and self-control training to teach
executives how to prevent psychophysiological disorders in response
to stress.

Biofeedback techniques appear useful in creating a safer and more
productive industrial environment. In combination with other environmental approaches, they help to increase workers' productivity and
to reduce absenteeism. Biofeedback training could become part of
ordinary health screening and other related programs normally carried out in business and industrial settings. These techniques could be
used with workers predisposed to develop stress-related disorders,
e.g., low back pain or ulcerative colitis. Such individuals could be
identified and given regular training on the job to reduce stress.

Biofeedback may also be beneficial to industry in the treatment of
work-related injuries (i.e., low back pain). It is often of value in chronic
pain disorders, and it appears that such techniques may improve the
rate of return to work, and reduce compensation claims as well as
absenteeism. Current information indicates that low back pain accounts for the largest number of compensation claims. In the authors'
experience, individuals with chronic low back pain return to work

much sooner than expected when so treated even though their compensation has not expired (Nigl and Fischer-Williams, 1980). Biofeedback might be included as part of comprehensive medical treatment available to workers in company clinics.

Since biofeedback techniques are new in this area, business and industrial leaders should be educated about the value of such techniques. Carefully controlled evaluative studies are needed to determine parameters within which biofeedback techniques can be applied in industry and business. Allen and Blanchard (1980) reported that a biofeedback-assisted stress management program for executives effectively reduced specific psychophysiological symptoms but was not more effective in general stress reduction than group discussion.

Biofeedback and the Legal Profession

Biofeedback has recently been applied in the legal system, primarily in the treatment of various offenders referred by the court following trial. One of the important areas of application is that of sexual deviancy and disorders, such as transvestism, exhibitionism, child molestation, and related disturbances (see Chap. 15). There is evidence that biofeedback techniques may be useful in ameliorating sexual behavior disturbances when standard psychotherapy proves ineffective (Nigl, 1980).

Illustrative Case

A 40-year-old white male married patient with 2 children was self-referred for behavior therapy of pedophilia. He had sexually molested approximately 20 children over a 15-year period and was apprehended once and charged with three counts of felony. He was released on probation with the condition that he must receive psychotherapy.

Following extensive psychological testing and behavioral analysis, it was determined that the patient's primary source of gratification came via masturbation. He was attracted to girls aged 6–10 because he found them to be easily manipulated and naturally curious about male genitalia. He felt too embarrassed and reserved to ask his wife to masturbate him.

Treatment consisted of using the EMG biofeedback instrument to recondition this patient's physiological responses to pedophiliac imagery. A similar technique is described in Nigl (1980).

He completed ten sessions where he was asked to tense muscles using EMG feedback in response to pedophiliac imagery and fantasy and relax muscles through EMG biofeedback when imagining sexual experiences with adult females. Following this, the patient reported feeling an intense headache every time he began to think about young girls (even nonsexual thoughts). Furthermore, he reported that sexual activities with his wife gave him greater pleasure and increased his feeling of satisfaction.

A 9-month followup found that he had not continued masturbation involving pedophiliac fantasies and had not attempted to approach a child although he had had numerous opportunities.

Biofeedback treatment may be of value in reducing criminal behavior in antisocial (psychopathic or sociopathic) individuals. Such individuals tend to be poor candidates for verbal psychotherapy, and therefore biofeedback treatment may be applicable because of the use of instruments rather than verbal techniques. Research is still needed to determine the efficacy of such biofeedback approaches, however.

In legal cases where objective evidence is needed of subjective experiences, such as pain disorders, biofeedback may be useful. It is often difficult to obtain objective findings through standard medical procedures, because experiences such as pain are subjective. On the other hand, since EMG biofeedback measurements are correlated with muscle contraction (tension) and they in turn are often related directly to pain experiences, biofeedback measurements may be introduced as evidence to either support or refute claims of pain (especially in low back injuries). One of the authors (AJN) has provided such testimony in a few selected cases. No controlled studies exist in this area, however, and the use of biofeedback must be conducted with appropriate caution at this stage.

Finally, there has been increased interest in using biofeedback in rehabilitation settings, such as penal institutions. Biofeedback would appear to offer some benefits to incarcerated individuals, especially those suffering from poor impulse control. Biofeedback training could be made part of regular psychotherapeutic treatment where indicated. Group relaxation and biofeedback techniques might also be used to improve the level of self-control and self-esteem among prisoners in general. Such techniques could be used educationally to improve self-understanding.

Summary

The objective of this chapter has been to give the reader a sense of the current diversity in the field of biofeedback and its potential for both clinical and nonclinical application.

REFERENCES

Allen J, Blanchard E: Biofeedback-based stress management training with a population of business managers. Proceedings of 11th Meeting of Biofeedback Society of America, 1980.

Bird B, Cataldo M, Parker L, Baker T, Francis D: Generalization of EMG biofeedback in choroathetoid cerebral palsy. Proceedings of the Biofeedback Society of America 10th Annual Meeting, 1979.

Blanchard E, Young L: Clinical applications of biofeedback training. Arch Gen Psychiatr 30: 573, 1974.

Braud L: Effects of frontal EMG biofeedback and progressive relaxation upon hyperactivity and its behavioral concomitants. Biofeedback Self-Regul 3: 69, 1978.

Braud L, Lupin M, Braud W: The use of EMG biofeedback in the control of hyperactivity. J Learn Dis 8: 21, 1975.

Brown B: *Stress and the Art of Biofeedback.* New York, Harper and Row, 1977.

Brundy J, Grynbaum B, Friedman L: Electromyography in the practice of rehabilitation medicine: therapeutic application. Arch Phys Med Rehab 55: 564, 1974.

Budzynski T: Biofeedback in the treatment of muscle-contraction (tension) headache. Biofeedback Self-Regul 3: 409, 1978.

Cunningham M, Murphy P: Effects of bilateral EEG biofeedback on verbal, visual-spatial, and creative skills in learning-disabled male adolescents. Proceedings of the Biofeedback Society of America 9th Annual Meeting, 1978.

Diamond S, Diamond-Falk J, DeVeno T: Biofeedback in the treatment of vascular headache. Biofeedback Self-Regul 3: 385, 1978.

Diamond S: Biofeedback and Headache. Headache 19: 180, 179.

Dietvorst T, Osborne D: Biofeedback assisted relaxation training for primary dysmenorrhea: a case study. Biofeedback Self-Regul 3: 301, 1978.

Engel B, Nikoomanesh P, Schuster M: Operant conditioning of rectosphincteric responses in treatment of fecal incontinence. N Engl J Med 290: 646, 1974.

Engelhardt L: Awareness and relaxation through biofeedback in public schools. Proceedings of the Biofeedback Society of America 9th Annual Meeting, 1978.

Fernando C, Basmajian J: Biofeedback in physical medicine and rehabilitation. Biofeedback Self-Regul 3: 435, 1978.

Fotopoulos S, Sunderland W: Biofeedback in the treatment of psychophysiological disorders. Biofeedback Self-Regul 3: 331, 1978.

Hughes R, Collins N: Group instruction in relaxation training with nursery school children. Proceedings of the Biofeedback Society of America 9th Annual Meeting, 1978.

Jackson S, Cain R: Use of EMG biofeedback in the treatment of heterotropia. Proceedings of 11th Meeting of Biofeedback Society of America, 1980.

Korein J, Brudny J, Grynbaum B, Sachs-Frankel G: Sensory feedback therapy of spasmodic torticollis and dystonia. Adv Neurol 14: 375, 1976.

Leiper C, Miller A, Lang J, Herman R: Influence of augmented sensory feedback on head position control in the cerebral palsied child. Proceedings of the Biofeedback Society of America 10th Annual Meeting, 1979.

Lupin M, Braud L, Braud W, Duer W: Children, parents and relaxation tapes. Acad Ther 12: 105, 1976.

Mandel A, Sharp E: Biofeedback versus traditional physiotherapy as means of improving head control in children with cerebral palsy. Proceedings of the Biofeedback Society of America 10th Annual Meeting, 1979.

Nigl A: Effects of imagery ability and covert reinforcement on the acquisition of oral hygiene behavior. Diss Abs 25: 922, 1975.

Nigl A: Electromyograph training to increase oral cavity functioning in a post-operative cancer patient. Behav Ther 10: 423, 1979.

Nigl A: EMG feedback in the treatment of sexual deviation. Behavioral Engineering, in press 1980.

Nigl A, Fischer-Williams M: EMG biofeedback in treatment of chronic low back strain. Psychosomatics, 21: 495, 1980.

Price K: Application of behavior therapy to the treatment of psychosomatic disorders: retrospect and prospect. Psychother Theor Res Prac 2, 1974.

Redington D, Hoed J, Dement W: Computer algorithm EEG biofeedback training of sleep onset in a narcoleptic patient. Proceedings of 11th Meeting of Biofeedback Society of America, 1980.

Rubow R, Flynn M: Physiologic feedback techniques in the treatment of motor speech disorders. Proceedings of 11th Meeting of Biofeedback Society of America, 1980.

Russell H, Carter R: Academic gains in learning disabled children after biofeedback-relaxation training. Proceedings of the Biofeedback Society of America 10th Annual Meeting, 1979.

Sargent J, Green E, Walters E: Use of autogenic feedback training in a pilot study of migraine and tension headache. Headache 12: 120, 1972.

Sargent J, Green E, Walters E: Preliminary report on the use of autogenic feedback training in the treatment of migraine and tension headaches. Psychosom Med 25: 129, 1973.

Stroebel C: The application of biofeedback techniques in psychiatry and behavioral medicine. Psychiatric Opinion 16: 13, 1979.

Szajnberg N: Migraine relief may trigger psychoneurosis. Clin Psychiatr News, October, 1979.

Taub E, Emurian C: Operant control of skin temperature. Proceedings of the Biofeedback Society of America 3rd Annual Meeting, 1971.

Taub E, Stroebel C: Biofeedback in treatment of vasoconstrictive disorders. Biofeedback Self-Regul 3: 451, 1978.

Werder D: An exploratory study of childhood migraine using thermal biofeedback as a treatment alternative. Proceedings of the Biofeedback Society of America 9th Annual Meeting, 1978.

Whitehead W: Biofeedback in the treatment of gastrointestinal disorders. Biofeedback Self-Regul 3: 375, 1978.

Yolton R, Hirons R: Biofeedback treatment of ocular disorders. Proceedings of the Biofeedback Society of America 10th Annual Meeting, 1979.

21

Adjuncts to Treatment with Biofeedback

BIOFEEDBACK treatment is never, strictly speaking, conducted in isolation without other forms of treatment for the simple reason that it is initiated on a one-to-one basis between the patient and the therapist. There is, therefore, an initial interpersonal relationship established, which is continued, although perhaps intermittently, throughout the period of observation, and colors the results, however objective the design of the therapeutic study. Thus, biofeedback cannot be applied in isolation from other treatment modalities. In previous chapters, biofeedback was presented as an adjunct to a variety of approaches. There are, however, situations where biofeedback is the treatment of choice. In these cases, it is important to identify other treatment modalities which interface with biofeedback training. These adjuncts are presented below.

1. Jacobson's Deep Relaxation Exercises (Skeletal Muscle Relaxation)*
2. Physical Therapy (multimodal)
3. Occupational Therapy
4. Medical Devices
   a. Joint position trainer
   b. Head position monitor
   c. Joint angle detector
   d. "Talking" pen
5. Transcutaneous Electrical Nerve Stimulator (TENS)
6. Acupuncture
7. Surgical Procedures
8. Psychotropic Drugs
   a. Minor tranquilizers (antianxiety agents; anxiolytics)
   b. Sedative-hypnotics
   c. Antidepressants (mood elevators)
   d. Major tranquilizers (neuroleptics; antipsychotics)

*This approach is discussed in detail in Chapter 3.

    e. Stimulants

    f. Analgesics

    g. Specific drugs, antihypertension, anticonvulsants, and antiinflammatory agents

9. Placebo Treatment (pills or physical measures)

10. Psychotherapy

11. Behavior Therapy

    a. Systematic desensitization

    b. Behavior modification (incentives with monetary reward or other tangible reward)

    c. Aversive (contingent) electric cutaneous shock (shock avoidance)

    d. Assertive therapy

    e. Cognitive techniques

    f. Visual imagery, autogenic training, self-suggestive phrases, self-verbalization

    g. Hypnosis (self-induced hypnotic relaxation)

Physical Therapy

There are many modalities of physical therapy and these can only be summarized briefly here. The most important include:

1. Hot packs and other types of local heat therapy

2. Massage

3. Relaxation exercises

4. Strengthening exercises of which Williams' exercises in the treatment of low back pain are the most commonly employed

5. Ultrasound for a variety of disorders including synovitis, bursitis, fibrositis, and myalgia

6. Cervical or pelvic traction, intermittent or semicontinuous with graduated increases in the weights applied to the traction

7. Hydrotherapy, including Hubbard's tank and whirlpool therapy

Reeducation of Body Posture

Patients with musculoskeletal pain and discomfort and a combination of spasm, musculoligamentous strain, motor weakness, and resultant injuries constitute a large population. Many of these disabilities result from poor posture and a lack of exercise in adolescence, or from posture at work with inadequate attention paid to normal body mechanics and the quality of sleep. The problem is frequently compounded with psychological factors, namely, a reluctance to accept responsibility for physical well-being. In all these situations, initial diagnosis with identification of the posture component resulting in musculoligamentous stresses and strains is imperative. With education of body posture, body mechanics and corrective physical therapy, biofeedback training will prevent recurrence of the disorder.

Occupational Therapy

This form of therapy may be more accurately described as functional neurologic therapy. Prior to therapy, diagnosis and analysis of the particular patient's disability are required in terms of perception, sensory impairment, tonus, motor weakness, involuntary movements, gainful employment, leisure skills, and emotional components. Individual procedures and techniques will not be described in this text. It should be emphasized, however, that functional neurological therapy, or occupational therapy, is an imperative adjunct with many patients who are receiving biofeedback training.

Mechanical Devices

A number of devices provide information on body movements, and they should therefore be regarded as forms of biofeedback and thus part of the procedure rather than adjuncts to biofeedback training, (see Chap. 8). Insofar as they may be combined with the EMG, providing feedback on muscle contraction, these mechanical devices added to the EMG constitute a multimodal biofeedback approach in rehabilitation. When they are secondary to EMG biofeedback, they may be considered as "adjuncts."

A joint position trainer may be valuable, particularly in cerebral palsy (CP) due to cerebral birth injuries or various dystonias. A mechanical head support, monitoring the position of the head, may also be helpful. Various types of joint angle detectors have been developed for wrist extension or ankle movements. Contact switches may signal foot placement. In several studies, limb load is monitored where the clinical objective may be either to increase or to decrease the percentage of body weight placed on a limb (Moore and Byers, 1976). Other mechanical devices include a "talking" pen that emits sound as a patient attempts to write. This device can aid in the rehabilitation of cases of dysphasia and dysgraphia or various types of paralysis.

When electronic engineers collaborate with therapists, a wide variety of mechanical devices can utilize the principles of biofeedback training. In some situations, these devices will constitute adjuncts.

Transcutaneous Electrical Nerve Stimulation (TENS)

This clinical approach in the treatment of chronic and acute pain is usually given in the physical therapy department. TENS is, actually, a process of sensory modulation and therefore the techniques and responses differ markedly from motor nerve stimulation. TENS involves the use of low voltage or low amperage current to produce analgesia by a process of differential sensory nerve excitation, stimulating the large A-delta myelinated nerve fibers rather than the small unmyelinated C fibers (see section on acupuncture).

Although there are a number of different units available, the characteristics are reasonably similar and consistent. TENS devices are usually solid-state generators that produce pulsed direct current. Primarily the units produce either an asymmetrical, biphasic wave with a positive rectangular wave component combined with a negative spike component or, a monophasic wave form with a positive rectangular component only. The larger units frequently utilize disposable or rechargeable batteries (Lampe, 1977). There are many styles of electrodes used on the skin although carbon impregnated silicone is the most common. Most TENS units have adjustable rate, width, and amplitude controls. After suitable electrode application on the skin, one suggested sequence of control adjustment is as follows:

1. Turn the machine on and increase the amplitude until the patient reports a subjectively comfortable stimulation.

2. Increase the width until he reports a mildly unpleasant stimulation. (Machines that produce the monophasic wave form have a width range of 0 to 100 μsec.)

3. Decrease the amplitude until the patient again reports a subjectively comfortable stimulation.

4. Increase or decrease the rate control to the level that produces the most comfortable sensation of stimulation.

Units are available to the patient for home use under supervision. The electrodes are placed according to the site of the pain, usually over the painful area. Disorders suitable for this treatment include low back syndromes, shoulder-hand syndromes, certain cases of headache, phantom limb, intercostal neuralgia, and back pain following compression fracture of the vertebrae. Contraindications for TENS are as follows:

1. Cardiac pacemaker
2. Adverse skin reactions
3. The use of this modality over the pregnant uterus

4. Exacerbation of the original pain during stimulation

It appears that TENS is more likely to be effective the more the pain is of purely "organic" origin. When psychological factors predominate, biofeedback alone may be more effective. Little research has been done to support these clinical observations, however. In addition, the biofeedback clinician should be aware of the fact that particular patients may have TENS units. This is especially important during EMG feedback treatment because the electrical discharge of the TENS unit may affect the measurement and cause, artifactually, high readings.

The Chemistry of Acupuncture

Acupuncture, the ancient Chinese art of relieving pain by inserting fine needles at specific points and depths on the surface of the body, has been reviewed in the light of the physiology of pain by Chang Hsiang-tung (1979) of the Shanghai Institute of Physiology. In traditional Chinese medicine, the pain-suppressing effects of acupuncture were explained by the fact that needles were inserted in accordance with 12 hypothetical meridian channels. These meridians do not correspond with anatomy, and therefore the site of insertions in the ancient system is not likely to be of significance. However, there are physiological mechanisms associated with the insertion of fine needles into the skin that may explain the salutory effects of acupuncture. Needles inserted at various points of the body can activate the nervous system to yield analgesia (inability to feel pain) in distant parts of the body. The analgesic effect takes about 20 minutes to develop and persists for some time after the needles have been withdrawn. There are two major classes of nerve fibers that carry pain information from the peripheral receptors to the spinal cord: the low-threshold A-delta fibers, which give rise to sharp, mild pain, and the high-threshold C fibers which give rise to severe, burning pain. Chang suggested that mild stimulation of the acupuncture needles selectively activates the low-threshold A-delta fibers in the deep tissues underlying the acupuncture points. The resulting impulses are transmitted to relays in the spinal cord and the brain where they interfere with the transmission of messages from the high-threshold C fibers so that severe pain is kept from reaching consciousness. Furthermore, the large myelinated A-delta fibers transmit more quickly than the smaller nonmyelinated C fibers (see Chap. 2). This "gate" hypothesis is supported by a number of experimental findings. For example, if a local anesthetic is injected into the tissues under an acupuncture point, it completely abolishes both the characteristic mild discomfort caused by the needle and the remote analgesic effect. The specificity of acupuncture points seems to lie in the segmental organization of the spinal cord: each segment of the cord innervates a particular region of the trunk and the limbs. This suggests that the low threshold pain impulses generated by acupuncture needling travel to the spinal cord and block the transmission of severe pain messages entering the same segment of the cord or adjacent segments. It is likely that the endogenous opiates are involved in the mediation of the pain centrally in the brain, perhaps through the placebo response.

Surgical Procedures

Surgical procedures for symptomatic relief of pain may include implantation of a dorsal column stimulator, rhizotomy (section of the dorsal roots entering the spinal cord), spinothalamic tractotomy, and implantation of a cerebral "pacemaker." These procedures together with the indications and contraindications will not be further described. In all patients with chronic pain associated with severe behavioral manifestations, who do not respond to medical treatment with biofeedback training, more extensive measures such as the well-proven spinothalamic tractotomy or some of the above procedures may be considered. At this point, these treatments cannot be considered as adjuncts to biofeedback training.

Psychotropic Drugs

The synergistic or additive model of applying entirely different treatment modalities in approaching a single disease entity is well known. A case in point is the conjunction of psychotherapy with biofeedback as noted in Chapter 19.

The combination of psychotropic medication and biofeedback, however, has not proved as useful though not all classifications of drugs when paired with this modality have been fully investigated as yet. A list of psychotropic drugs is presented in Table 21–1.

Minor Tranquilizers (Anxiolytics), Sedatives-Hypnotics

Anxiety and tension are the keystones on which biofeedback treatment is built. As in psychotherapy, where anxiety serves to propel the course of treatment, the measurement of physiological tension fulfills a similar purpose in biofeedback.

TABLE 21-1. PSYCHOTROPIC DRUGS

Minor tranquilizers	Antidepressants
Benzodiazepines derivatives: Clordiazepoxide (Librium) Diazepam (Valium) Oxazepam (Serax) Clorazepate Dipotassium (Tranxene) Clorazepate Monopotassium (Azene) Lorazepam (Ativan) Prazepam (Verstran, Centrax) *Thiazanone derivatives:* Chlormezanone (Trancopal) *Glycerol derivatives:* Meprobamate (Equinil, Miltown, Deprol) Tybamate (Solacen, Tybatran) *Diphenylmethane derivatives:* Hydroxyzine (Atarax, Vistaril)	*Monoamine oxidase inhibitors:* Hydrazines: Nialamide (Niamid) Isocarboxazid (Marplan) Phenelzine sulfate (Nardil) Tranylcypromine (Parnate) *Tricyclics:* Dibenzazepines: Amitriptyline (Elavil, Endep) Desipramine (Norpramin, Pertofrane) Imipramine (Tofranil, Presamine, Janimine, Imavate) Nortriptyline (Pamelar, Aventyl) Protriptyline (Vivactil) Dibenzoxepine derivatives: Doxepin (Sinequan, Adapin) Amoxapine (Asendin) *Tetracyclics:* Maprotiline (Ludiomil) *Lithium:* Lithium Carbonate (Eskalith, Ethane, Lithane, Lithonate)

Sedatives and hypnotics	Major tranquilizers
Chloral Hydrate Ethchlorvynol (Placidyl) *Barbiturates:* Pentobarbital (Nembutal) Secobarbital (Seconal) Amobarbital (Amytal) Butabarbital (Butisol) Barbital (Veronal) Phenobarbital (Luminal) Butalbital (Fiorinal) *Glutarimide derivatives:* Glutethimide (Doriden) Methyprylon (Noludar) *Quinazolones:* Methaqualone (Qualude) *Antihistamines:* Orphenadrine (Norgesic) Promethazine (Phenergan) *Clordiazepoxide derivatives:* Flurazepam (Dalmane) Temazepam (Reftoril)	*Phenothiazines:* 1. Aliphatic Clorpromazine (Thorazine) Promazine (Sparine) Triflupromazine (Vesprin) *Piperazine derivatives:* Carphenazine (Probetazine) Acetophenazine Maleate (Tindal) Butaperazine Maleate (Repoise) Fluphenazine (Prolixin) Perphenazine (Trilafon) Trifluoperazine HCl (Stelazine) 2. Piperidine Mesoridazine (Serentil) Piperacetazine (Quide) Thioridazine (Mellaril) *Thioxanthines:* Chlorprothixine (Taractan) Thiothixine (Navane) *Dibenzoxazepine derivatives:* Loxapine (Loxitane, Daxolin) *Rauwolfia derivatives:* Reserpine (Serpasil) *Butyrophenone derivatives:* Haloperidol (Haldol) Indolics Molindone (Moban, Lidone)

447

TABLE 21-1 CONTINUED

Stimulants	Analgesics
Sympathomimetic amines:	*Nonnarcotic Analgesics:*
Amphetamine (Benzedrine)	Salicylates:
Dextroamphetamine (Dexedrine)	Acetylsalicylic acid
Methamphetamine (Desoxyn)	Meprobamate (Equagesic)
Phenmetrazine (Preludin)	Aniline derivatives:
	Phenacetin
Diphenylmethane derivatives:	Acetaminophen (Tylenol)
Methylphenidate (Ritalin)	Phenylubutazone (Butazolidin)
Pemoline (Cylert)	Zomepirac (Zomax)
	Narcotic Analgesics:
	Morphine sulfate
	Hydromorphone (Dilaudid)
	Pentazocine (Talwin)
	Codeine sulfate
	Methadone (Dolophine)
	Propoxyphene (Darvon)
	Meperidine (Demerol)
	Oxycodone (Percodan)

Minor tranquilizers and sedative-hypnotics eliminate tension and thus decrease that which can be measured and fed back to the patient. They also, in eliminating the dysphoria of stress, decrease motivation for treatment. (Ayd, 1975; Baldessarini, 1977.)

Townsend, House, and Addario (1975) conducted a study comparing biofeedback-mediated relaxation and group therapy in the treatment of chronic anxiety. Of 10 patients completing the study in the feedback group, only two were found to have the dosage decreased, the remaining eight patients had no change in dosage. Stroebel (1979) has indicated that patients who receive minor tranquilizers, e.g., diazepam, concurrently with biofeedback do not learn how to relax as easily as other patients. There is some evidence that patients on such medication may not learn to relax at all and may not benefit from biofeedback (Nigl and Jackson, 1979).

Antidepressants (Mood Elevators)

No studies have yet addressed the concurrent use of antidepressants (monoamine oxidase inhibiters or trycyclics) and biofeedback (see Chap. 18). Likewise, there is as yet no evidence that biofeedback enhances the effect of lithium or electroconvulsive therapy.

Major Tranquilizers (Neuroleptics, Antipsychotics)

Although Adler and Adler (1979) believed that biofeedback is contraindicated in the treatment of psychotic individuals, another recent study (Nigl and Jackson, 1979) seems to indicate otherwise. As yet, however, no conclusive findings have demonstrated any significant synergistic effect of this combination.

Stimulants

The use of stimulants, e.g., amphetamine preparations and appetite depressants such as Ritalin and Pandomin, have few clinical indications at this time. Since stimulants are tension-producing and biofeedback is tension-reducing, it is difficult to see how this combination could work successfully. The rapid development of tolerance, production of dependence and appearance of toxic psychosis would militate against their application in any event. No specific studies are known in which biofeedback and stimulants are used concomitantly.

Analgesics and Specific Drugs

Many patients referred for biofeedback treatment of chronic pain and other disorders may also be receiving medication for suppression of pain. These analgesics ("pain-killers") include morphine and its derivatives (e.g., Percodan), codeine and its derivatives (e.g., Empirin #3 and #4, Tylenol #3 and #4), Demerol, Talwin, Darvon, Fiorinal, and Aspirin.

Biofeedback is designed to treat the manifestations and certain causes of pain, thus obviating the need for analgesics. The gradual reduction in analgesic use can be a measure of the success of biofeedback training.

In the initial stages of biofeedback training, analgesics serve an adjunctive role by reducing pain levels sufficiently so that the patient may focus his attention on the biofeedback process. It is important to recognize that too abrupt a withdrawal of pain medication ("cold turkey") may have adverse effects on the patient's physiological status and the biofeedback treatment. In fact, premature cessation of analgesics may precipitate "withdrawal" symptoms necessitating medical intervention. The interaction between biofeedback and the use of analgesics has not been adequately researched to date. This is an important area for future research.

Placebo Treatment

Biofeedback treatment in all likelihood possesses a placebo component. The use of other placebo (pills or physical measures) may thus be unnecessary. It is important to remember, however, that placebo treatment can be effective in selected patients. The potential mechanism of action of placebo (e.g., the speculated action of endogenous endorphin stimulation) is an interesting subject for future research. It is possible that biofeedback, placebo activity, and acupuncture all share in some measure the ability to stimulate the body's own release of natural analgesics. This mechanism may also be the basis for the ability which allows patients to utilize "selective inattention" in regard to pain or discomfort.

Psychotherapy

The therapeutic aspects of biofeedback have been previously emphasized in Chapter 19. Results of research and clinical experience indicate the importance of combining biofeedback with psychotherapy to enhance the effectiveness of treatment. Although it may appear that biofeedback training and verbal psychotherapy represent opposite poles of a continuum, these two modalities have been combined successfully. Many biofeedback therapists employ both verbal therapy and biofeedback methods in the treatment of psychological as well as psychophysiological (psychosomatic) disorders. Several types of verbal therapy exist but the most commonly employed are those based on the psychoanalytic method originated by Sigmund Freud and the various cognitive behavior therapy methods developed in the last decade principally by Arnold Lazarus, Donald Meichenbaum, and Albert Bandura (Yates, 1970).

Psychoanalytic or psychodynamic therapy is concerned with the elucidation of unconscious factors determining behavior and the resolution of unconscious conflicts which originated in the psychosexual development of the individual. Although it would be difficult to combine biofeedback with psychoanalysis, (which is a specific, circumscribed, and time-consuming method), it appears that biofeedback techniques can be combined successfully with psychoanalytic therapy. The latter (psychoanalytically-oriented psychotherapy) differs from psychoanalysis in that treatment is usually of a much shorter duration and more flexible. Biofeedback procedures may enhance psychodynamic therapy (see Chap. 19).

On the other hand, it is interesting to speculate on psychodynamic therapy's role as an adjunct to biofeedback. During the initial phase of biofeedback treatment, resistance to change may occur. In some cases, this resistance may be related to underlying conflicts. Therefore, an exploration of the psychological factors that determine this resistance may be indicated. Dynamically-oriented psychotherapeutic techniques may thus be useful adjuncts to biofeedback. These techniques include the exploration of resistance, unconscious conflicts, dreams, and fantasy material (Klein and Davis, 1969; Freedman, Kaplan and Sadock, 1980).

Behavior Therapy

Because biofeedback and cognitive therapy methods both have similar origins within the learning tradition of psychology, these methods are viewed as compatible. In fact, many biofeedback therapists are trained in cognitive behavior therapy. Each of the major cognitive behavior techniques will be considered separately in what follows.

Systematic Desensitization

Systematic desensitization may be useful as an adjunct with biofeedback therapy when individuals suffer from specific fears or phobias in addition to other psychophysiological disorders. Frequently, it is necessary to employ a more systematic approach to counteract the anxiety or fear response. An example might be the application of systematic desensitization to treat an individual suffering from agoraphobia. In this case, the systematic desensitization might be applied concurrently with the biofeedback technique so that each may enhance the other in reducing the patient's fear responses both generally and specifically to certain social situations or in response to certain fear stimuli (see Chap. 17). Patients referred for biofeedback often have difficulty relaxing because of fears of being observed or performance anxiety. In such cases, systematic desensitization may be required prior to initiating biofeedback training.

Behavior Modification

Various mechanistic behavioral programs may enhance the effectiveness of biofeedback training. For example, some individuals may have difficulty practicing the relaxation exercises and other self-control procedures at home. A self-reinforcement behavioral modification program may be combined with biofeedback treatment. Behavior modification programs can also be useful in the application of biofeedback with certain institutionalized populations such as nursing home residents, the mentally retarded, or the severely mentally ill. Patients can choose rewards to earn by complying with the therapist's instructions through keeping careful records or maintaining home practice.

Aversive Conditioning

Aversive conditioning methods may be employed along with biofeedback treatment. Aversive conditioning may be useful in behavior disorders especially those involved in sexual deviancy. It appears to have its greatest application in the treatment of such sexual neuroses as voyeurism, pedophilia, exhibitionism, and sexual assaultive behavior (see Chap. 15). There is some evidence to suggest that feedback signals may have aversive properties for some patients. Nigl (1980) has indicated that using auditory feedback as an aversive stimulus increases the effectiveness of EMG biofeedback in treating chronic low back pain.

Assertive Therapy

A popular form of cognitive behavior therapy employed in both individual and group situations is assertion training. This may be used as an adjunct to biofeedback treatment in cases where patients lack many of the sufficient skills necessary to change environmental factors that may be producing stress. By becoming more confident in themselves through assertive training, some patients may be more able to learn self-regulation through biofeedback training than might otherwise be possible. However few studies have been reported where biofeedback and assertive training have been combined.

Cognitive Retraining

In addition to relaxation methods and other behavioral therapy techniques, cognitive restructuring, and "relabeling" may be useful in changing negative attitudes and enhancing the patient's preparation for learning self-control through biofeedback. Stress-related diseases and maladaptive behavior patterns may develop because of a patient's misinterpretation of life experiences or because of the inappropriate thoughts which accompany such symptoms. Certain cognitive techniques allow a patient to eliminate negative and maladaptive thoughts that interfere with biofeedback training.

Another cognitive technique is "thought stopping." This involves training the patient to stop consciously irrational or obsessive thoughts that trigger physiological symptoms and cause the patient to be depressed or anxious. Over time this results in an increase in positive self-statements and a decrease in negative self-statements or thoughts (Nigl, 1976).

Imagery Techniques

Imagery techniques such as covert positive reinforcement may be useful as adjuncts to biofeedback therapy when the therapist is confronted with a patient unable to eliminate stress (i.e., unable to relax) because of maladaptive behaviors or thoughts. Autogenic phrases also may be applied as an adjunct to biofeedback, the use of which has been discussed earlier (see Chaps. 1 and 3).

Physiological trend indicators are devices that can be useful adjuncts to imagery techniques to promote vasodilatation in thermal (skin temperature) biofeedback training. These devices are available in the form of an adhesive paper strip or a dot that contains film material treated with cholesterol derivatives. Numbers and colors corresponding to variations in skin temperature appear on the trend indicator and can be interpreted by the patient. An example of the clinical use of this device was presented in a case study of migraine (see Chap. 8).

Hypnosis

The use of hypnotic techniques can be an important adjunct to biofeedback for enhancement of relaxation and concentration (see Chap. 3 and Appendix).

In summary, biofeedback procedures are flexible and can be adapted to a number of parameters involving the patient's physical condition, personality, behavioral problems, or environmental factors. A biofeedback therapist should be encouraged to explore various combinations of techniques to determine which combinations may be the most suitable for a particular patient. In this way, biofeedback treatment can be matched to the individual's specific needs rather than approached in an overly mechanistic or dogmatic fashion. The more individualized the therapy is, the more likely it will produce desired changes in the patient's attitudes, behaviors, and physiological responses.

REFERENCES

Adler CS, Adler S: Strategies in general psychiatry, in Basmajian J (ed): *Biofeedback, Principles and Practice for Clinicians.* Baltimore, Williams and Wilkins, 1979.

Ayd FJ (ed): *Rational Psychopharmacotherapy and The Right To Treatment.* Baltimore, Ayd Medical Communications, 1975.

Baldessarini RJ: *Chemotherapy in Psychiatry.* Cambridge, Harvard University Press, 1977.

Freedman AM, Kaplan HI, Sadock BJ, in Freedman AM (ed): *Comprehensive Textbook of Psychiatry,* Vol II. Baltimore, Williams and Wilkins, 1980.

Hsiang-tung C: Acupuncture analgesia today. Chin Med J (Engl) 92 (1); 7, 1979.

Klein DF, Davis JM: *Diagnosis and Drug Treatment of Psychiatric Disorders.* Baltimore, Williams and Wilkins, 1969.

Lampe G: Transcutaneous Electrical Nerve Stimulation. Brochure. Minneapolis, Mn Med General, 1977.

Moore AJ, Byers JL: A miniaturized load cell for lower extremity amputees. Arch Phys Med Rehabil 57: 294, 1976.

Nigl A, Jackson B: Electromyograph biofeedback as an adjunct to standard psychiatric treatment. J Clin Psychiatr 40: 434–436, 1979.

Nigl, A: The use of thought-stopping and self reinforcement in the treatment of depression. Psychol Rep 38: 843, 1976.

Nigl A: EMG biofeedback as an adjunctive treatment of maladaptive sexual attitudes and behaviors. Beh Engin, in press, 1980.

Townsend RE, House JF, Addario DA: A comparison of biofeedback-mediated relaxation and group therapy in the treatment of chronic anxiety. Am J Psychiatr 132: 598, 1975.

Yates A: *Behavior Therapy.* New York, Wiley, 1970.

22

Research Methodology and Biofeedback

HISTORICALLY, biofeedback was first developed as a psychophysiological research technique. After many years of study by various researchers modifications were worked out in order for biofeedback to be applied to treat clinical disorders. The clinical application of biofeedback has been emphasized thus far, however, it is difficult to separate research aspects of biofeedback from the clinical methods. One of the characteristics of biofeedback is that it affords clinicians an excellent opportunity for collecting data, systematically, in order to determine the effectiveness of the treatment. Traditionally, it has been difficult for clinicians engaged in verbal psychotherapy to judge their own effectiveness because of the lack of controlled conditions. Due to limitations in time and funding resources, it is not easy for clinicians to conduct follow-up studies. Patients do not expect automatic review of the results of therapy. However, the essence of biofeedback is the collection of data which begins as soon as the patient is attached to the biofeedback unit. As has been noted in Chapter 20, the use of microcomputers and other data acquisition systems has increased the potential for applied research in biofeedback.

Schwartz (1979) recently presented his point of view regarding responsibility in biofeedback therapy. He stated that research must be an integral part of biofeedback in order to determine treatment efficacy. He acknowledged that many clinicians are disinclined to conduct research. However, he indicated that it does not require much additional effort to accumulate data regarding patients' progress. This might be aided by standardizing the biofeedback treatment for each type of disorder. He strongly emphasized that follow-up sessions must be a part of the responsible therapeutic application of biofeedback.

Each clinician-patient contact can serve as an opportunity for applied research (an "N = 1" experiment). Biofeedback therapists should recognize the potential for studying this natural history of psychosomatic disorders. Aubry Yates (1970) noted that behavior therapy could be considered in the context of an "N = 1" experiment because of the empirical perspective from which the behavior therapist operates. Since biofeedback can be considered in part an extension of behavior therapy, clinicians who regularly use biofeedback should collect data and analyze the results of their treatment as a regular part of their practice.

There are three primary issues in conducting applied biofeedback research: (1) issues involved in therapy outcome studies, (2) issues involved in single case experimental designs, and (3) issues involved in therapy analog research. Each of these will be discussed below.

Issues in Therapy Outcome Research

When engaging in applied psychological research, it is important to consider what treatment was effective in changing the disorder. Therapy outcome, therefore, is one of the main factors studied in clinical research and a very important variable. Based on his review of the psychotherapy literature, Frank (1979) suggested that information about the outcome of psychotherapy, in general, remains limited. Few significant relationships have been established between determinants* (which are a function of the treatment) and outcome variables.

The evaluation of psychotherapy has resulted in numerous published investigations, and several excellent reviews are available. Bergin (1971) indicated that psychotherapy is so complex that outcome must be measured in terms of specific factors rather than assessing generalities such as "was the treatment effective?" Criteria that should be considered when planning therapy outcome studies were listed by Paul (1969) as follows: "*what* treatment, by *whom,* is most effective for *this* individual with *that* specific problem, under *which* set of circumstances." Many of the research variables discussed in this chapter have been established for psychotherapy in general; however, they are relevant to research in biofeedback as well.

Bergin further states that therapy outcome studies must control for no treatment at all when attempting to measure the success of a particular form of psychotherapy. Some control is needed to contrast what happens to a group of untreated individuals with similar characteristics as those of the group receiving treatment during the same time period. A "true" no-treatment control group is impossible to achieve, however, since patients in control groups typically engage in a variety of help-seeking behaviors on their own even if put on a treatment waiting

*In this context, determinants are those elements of a therapist's style and method which may have a bearing on treatment outcome.

list. One way to eliminate this potentially confounding problem is to obtain samples of the types of therapeutic intervention given to individuals in the "no-treatment" control group. Although this procedure will not allow actual control of these events, knowledge of frequency and duration of various types of treatment-related activities can be compared statistically to that which is given the experimental groups. The following is an example of how this principle could be applied to biofeedback research. If one were studying the effectiveness of EMG treatment on a particular disorder, a similar group of patients could be designated as the no-treatment control group during the course of the experiment. They could then be contacted periodically to analyze systematic types of treatment-related activities. Such activities may include counseling from professionals, paraprofessionals, family, and friends as well as therapeutic recreational activities. These data could then be compared with the types of treatment given the experimental subjects or patients.

Another issue in outcome research is the control of placebo effects. Although "placebo" effects are more difficult to identify in psychological treatment than in pharmacological research, some agreement exists regarding what constitutes placebo effects in psychotherapy. Factors such as attention, mental set, or expectancy and social desirability are often considered important placebo factors affecting the course of treatment. These are often referred to as "nonspecific effects." Although they were once considered as merely artifacts to be controlled, Bergin indicates that placebo effects are an important part of the therapeutic relationship, no matter what type of therapy is being conducted including biofeedback. Placebo effects are present because of the social interaction between therapist and patient. As such, they must be considered an important part of the treatment process, rather than extraneous variables. Bergin believes that placebo effects should always be considered because they are valuable, in some ways, in alleviating human problems; the present authors concur. He does not believe that they are as potent as some authors have considered them to be in the past, however.

It is important to evaluate what factor(s) have played a primary role in producing positive or negative results. The question is, "Do specific biofeedback procedures produce any additional benefits beyond what would be produced by nonspecific effects of the therapeutic relationship?" Control of these factors may be accomplished by including one or more groups of patients in the experimental design who receive only attention and encouragement from a warm, supportive therapist.

In addition, control of expectancy and social desirability can be achieved by measuring the extent of these factors across all groups, including the experimental and control groups. Frequently this is done by including a pre- and posttreatment interview questionnaire and/or rating form to directly measure the influence of these factors on treatment outcome.

Frank (1979) stated that therapy outcome studies have been disappointing in their accumulation of relevant information about psychotherapy. However, certain generalizations can be made based on the research to date: psychotherapy appears to be somewhat more effective than informal or unstructured intervention; no one type of therapy has been demonstrated to be significantly more effective than another (with the possible exception of short-term behavior therapy of specific disorders such as phobias); most patients who show initial progress maintain it at the time of follow-up; and finally, determinants of therapeutic success depend heavily on personality factors of both the patient and therapist.

Frank established guidelines for future research on therapy outcome. These recommendations should be considered in evaluating existing research on biofeedback treatment, as well as in planning future biofeedback outcome studies. One area where problems exist in outcome research is the lack of homogeneity in the selected patients. According to Frank, it would be desirable to screen candidates from those available for treatment by eliminating all who would respond to any type of treatment. It appears that patients with certain personality characteristics and who are suffering from certain situational problems tend to improve no matter what treatment they receive.

The factors that cause these patients to get well no matter what the theoretical orientation of the therapist are

1. The patient's own recognition that there is "something wrong."
2. The patient's motivation to change.
3. A good working relationship (alliance) between the patient and the therapist.

Another factor to consider is the elimination of patients who suffer from low morale and poor self-esteem. Such patients improve merely because another individual takes the time and effort to interact with them and not primarily because of the specific effects of the treatment. It is also desirable to eliminate individuals suffering from "demoralization" caused by environmental factors of brief duration. Patients who are so completely demoralized that they probably would not improve, no matter what was done to them, should also be eliminated from a controlled study. Furthermore, Frank indicates that a method of classifying patients who respond to various types of therapy would enhance the results of the outcome studies. Certain types of patients may benefit more from EMG biofeedback than thermal training, even within a specific disorder such as tension headache or a chronic pain condition. The expectations of patients should also be considered and a method of assessing this should be included in the experimental design. The degree of congruence or the extent to which the personality of the therapist complements the personality of the patient should be assessed as part of the overall design. Locus of control* is an area which Frank sees as having great promise in increasing the specificity of the results. It appears that certain groups of patients could benefit from therapies which impose control upon them, whereas other patients would benefit more from therapies which allow them to develop their own internal control over events. Within the field of biofeedback, different procedures may benefit these types of patients differentially, and such information could be of great value in assessing the outcome of biofeedback treatment. Carlson and Feld (1978) indicated that changes in locus of control scores occurred after EMG biofeedback training. Those individuals who were found to be externally controlled shifted significantly in the internal direction as a result of the feedback training. Holliday and Munz (1978) report that effectiveness of EMG biofeedback was differentially related to locus of control of the subjects. A nonpsychosomatic group of subjects changed significantly more than a psychosomatic group in the direction of internal locus of control as measured by the Rotter scale. These authors concluded that the Rotter scale is a good predictor of locus of control for relatively normal subjects but not for those who suffer from psychosomatic illness. Although research on this point is meager, it is obvious that personality factors should be assessed carefully when evaluating the outcome of various forms of biofeedback.

Another area which Frank (1979) identified as posing problems to the interpretation of outcome research concerns the qualities of the therapist. Several studies have indicated that "active, personal participation" (a concept first identified by Whitehorn and Betz, 1975) and qualities such as warmth and empathy (as identified by Truax and Carkhuff, 1967) are important factors in determining the degree of success in any type of therapy. Thus, it appears that measurement of therapist qualities should be included as a variable in therapy outcome

---

*Locus of control (a concept developed by Rotter, 1975) is a psychological term which denotes whether an individual is more influenced by internal or external events.

research. The qualities of the biofeedback therapist have not been assessed adequately to date, and research is needed to determine whether or not various types of personality and behavioral characteristics enhance or impair the effectiveness of a therapist using biofeedback equipment.

Frank summarizes his review of therapy outcome research by stating that there are limitations that are difficult to control under any circumstances. One of these is the fact that psychotherapy, including biofeedback, does not occur in a vacuum. The patient's personal life and psychosocial existence constantly change during the course of treatment. These changes may significantly affect the result of the treatment either in a positive or negative manner. Many of these events are impossible to control and limit the power of analysis in therapy outcome.

Experimental Design

The researcher has several choices in experimental design to measure the outcome of biofeedback treatment. These designs can be either "within-subject" or "between-subjects." Within-subject (intracentric) designs occur when statistical comparisions are made on the same subjects over time, while between-subject (inter-centric) designs measure differences between different groups of individuals. As Mahoney (1979) points out, however, individual subjects can also be used in a between-subject design although this is not as common. Single case studies or a small number of individuals are usually employed in a within-subject design, however, such designs can also be used with large groups of subjects as well. There is no restriction in the number of subjects which can be employed with either of these two designs. The reader is referred to reviews by Campbell and Stanley (1966) and Paul (1969).

Mahoney (1979) presented 12 common experimental designs which are conducted in the area of therapy outcome evaluation. Three of these designs offer promise as methods of controlling extraneous variables and for allowing an adequate demonstration of the effectiveness of a given treatment. The first of these is called the "Solomon four group." In this particular design, subjects are assigned randomly to four treatment conditions. Two of these groups receive the treatment under consideration. In one group the dependent variable is measured before and after treatment, while in the other group, the dependent variable is only measured after treatment. The remaining two groups are control groups; one to control for the dependent variable both pre- and posttreatment (in other words, the dependent variable would be measured at the same time that it was measured for the experimental group); and one where the dependent variable is measured only after the treatment ends for the experimental groups. Although Mahoney considers this design to be useful and adequate for controlling the method of testing treatment success (i.e., measuring the dependent variable), it is limited in that it does not control for the effects of subject participation in an experiment.

Mahoney (1979) considers the "attention and control group design" to be valuable in therapy outcome research. There are six groups in this design, four of which are identical to the Solomon group design. The two new groups are exposed to an attentive and supportive therapist or "pseudotherapist"* controlling the effects of participation in the experiment. One group is tested both pre- and posttreatment, while the remaining group is tested only after the attention is given. The only limitation to this design according to Mahoney is that it does not adequately control for the expectancies of the subject.

The best design, which controls for many of the placebo effects in psychotherapy, is referred to by Mahoney as the "placebo and control group" design. In this design, there are again six conditions, but instead of two of the groups receiving some form of attention, they receive an experimental manipulation that is designed to have an equal degree of credibility as that of the therapeutic method under study. In addition, there is a measurement of subject's expectations regarding the effectiveness of this manipulation. In other words, an attempt is made to determine whether or not the subject actually believed in the pseudotreatment they were given. An example of an experiment on therapy outcome which used this type of design was conducted by Nigl (1975) to determine the effectiveness of covert positive reinforcement (a cognitive behavioral method developed by Cautela, 1971). In addition to the experimental group which received the covert positive reinforcement (CPR), there were two control groups that did not receive treatment at all but were given either a pre- or a posttest alone, and two groups that were given a treatment based on mental imagery that is very similar in format to the CPR treatment. This treatment was called imagery practice, and subjects were given a brief lecture regarding its development using fictitious names. They were also given results of various research studies which supposedly had taken place

*A pseudotherapist, usually a student, acts as a therapist in the study but has no professional experience or credentials.

verifying the effectiveness of this treatment. The results of this study indicated that the subjects who received the imagery practice condition believed very strongly that it was actually a therapeutic method and that it was effective based on the pre- and posttreatment questionnaires and rating forms that were administered to them.

Few, if any, studies on biofeedback techniques have utilized these experimental designs, and, therefore, many extraneous variables and placebo effects obviously have not been adequately controlled. Some of the weak designs which Mahoney (1979) included in his list of 12 commonly used designs include those which are frequently seen in reports on biofeedback. In one of these, a pretest and posttest is conducted following the application of biofeedback techniques and there is no control group. Although one may conclude that there was a change in the dependent variable measured (e.g., muscle tension or peripheral vasodilatation) there is no way of knowing whether or not this change occurred because of the biofeedback technique.

A design useful to biofeedback researchers is one which uses a "multiple baseline" technique. In this design, biofeedback techniques are administered at various times. Since time is an important factor in biofeedback training, such a design controls for the effects of the passage of time on changes in physiological symptoms. If one could combine this with controls for attention and other placebo effects, including subjects' expectancies, such a design would adequately measure the success of biofeedback treatment under most conditions.

Issues in Single Case Designs

One of the controversial aspects of applied clinical research, especially as it relates to the outcome of various forms of psychotherapy, is the validity of research involving case studies where a single patient (N = 1) or a few patients are studied rather than using a large sample "between groups" design. Much has been written about the inherent weakness of data collected from only one individual. It was noted in previous chapters that leaders in the field of biofeedback have criticized themselves and their colleagues for the preponderance of single case reports as well as lack of well-controlled, well-designed experimental methodology. The use of single case studies has a valid place in applied clinical research, however. Some experts feel that data collected objectively in a well-planned single case design can result in as much information as with a large group study, which is statistically more powerful (Hersen and Barlow, 1976).

For example, Kiesler (1971) reports that single case methodology has much to offer the clinical researcher and should not be quickly dismissed as being a "weak" design. He argued for the use of the single case approach especially when evaluating newer forms of treatment, such as biofeedback. Dukes (1955) reviewed over 200 single case studies published over a 25-year period. He offered the following reasons as to when N = 1 studies are desirable:

"(1) when between individual variability for the function under scrutiny is known to be negligible, hence results from the second subject may be considered redundant; (2) when one case reported in depth parsimoniously exemplifies many; (3) when one case provides negative results—one negative case is sufficient to demand revision of a traditionally accepted hypothesis; (4) when one has limited opportunity to observe an instance of a particular behavior, (rare behavior, such as multiple colorblindness and the like); (5) when the research situation is greatly extended in time, requires extensive or specialized training of the subject or entails intricate and difficult to administer controls; (6) when the researcher simply wants to focus on a problem by defining questions, defining variables and indicating approaches," p. 74.

Other supporters of single case designs include Chassan (1967) and Shontz (1965). Hersen and Barlow (1976) presented a comprehensive review of single case experimental design methodology for applied clinical research.

Lazarus and Davison (1971) believed that the use of single case methodology represents one of the most creative and challenging aspects of applied clinical research, for the following reasons: (1) A case study may provide new directions in treatment that would not ordinarily be obtained through group designs. (2) A case study may permit the investigation of rare, but important, phenomena which occur so infrequently that large group designs would be impractical or impossible.

Usually, clinical practitioners are unable to conduct complicated large group designs. The use of single case methodology allows them to quantify their treatment methods, however. New therapeutic techniques can develop only when clinicians take the time and effort to systematically apply such techniques under different circumstances with different types of patients, even though such research may not be tightly controlled.

Kazdin (1979) described common single case designs reported, which control for extraneous variables to obtain valid data regarding effectiveness of therapeutic techniques. Two designs will be described here because they are the most commonly used in single case studies, i.e., the "ABAB" or "reversal" design and the multiple baseline design. The ABAB* design measures treatment success by comparing dependent variables obtained during a baseline with those variables that exist following the application of the treatment. Baseline data are first measured until a stabilization occurs. In biofeedback research, the patient is first evaluated with a specific instrument, such as the EMG, and baseline measurements are taken until the patient achieves a stabilization or threshold regarding muscle potential. At that point, the biofeedback treatment takes place and the patient receives feedback about his performance. Following the stabilization in physiological measures, e.g., EMG values, the biofeedback is withdrawn (in ABAB terminology, this is the "second A" phase). Then, as the dependent variables change again, the intervention (biofeedback treatment) is reinstated (the "second B" phase).

The second design for single case studies involves the use of a multiple baseline. Baseline data are gathered on more than one response of a single subject or group of subjects. Following stabilization of each behavior measured, intervention is applied to one of the behaviors. While this occurs, baseline measurements are still obtained on the other behaviors which are not being tested. When all responses again show stabilization, the intervention is then applied to a second behavior or response and the remaining responses are monitored under the baseline procedures. If each response varies only when the intervention is introduced, then a cause-effect relationship has occurred between the treatment method and the response change. The statistical power of this technique is such that if it can be shown that a form of treatment causes measurable changes in different responses in the same individual, this type of treatment should be effective in producing behavioral change. Therefore, there is a relationship between multiple baselines and multimodal biofeedback. In biofeedback research, a particular biofeedback procedure, such as EMG, could be measured by simultaneously obtaining baselines on other physiological responses (e.g., galvanic skin response, heart-rate, EEG, and peripheral vasodilatation). If it can be shown that EMG training produces measurable changes in these responses using a multiple baseline procedure,

*The letters A and B refer to two different experimental conditions.

this would add credence to the hypothesis that EMG feedback is an effective method of producing behavioral change.

Methodologic Problems

Kazdin (1979) discussed common methodological problems in single case design, such as the effects of data trends when measuring baselines. Behavior may already be changing in the direction opposite from that which is desired as a goal with therapy. This condition is ideal because the treatment technique is designed to change such behavior in an opposite direction. Such a trend will likely cause weak or ineffective treatments to produce nonsignificant behavioral changes while powerful techniques will be validated because a behavioral change occurs even though an opposite trend exists during the baseline period. If the patient is deteriorating at the start of treatment when baselines are being measured, then improvement is easier to demonstrate. If the patient is beginning to improve at the time when biofeedback starts, then continued improvement is less easily documentable. It is more difficult, however, to show improvement if the baseline trend is already in the desired direction. For example, in biofeedback treatment an individual with chronic headaches may be beginning to relax the frontalis muscle through medication and admonishments from his physician to "slow down." Evaluating the effect of the intervention in these cases is difficult. When the baseline shows a positive trend, the intervention must be shown to produce beneficial changes in order to conclude that the treatment was effective. Although it might be desirable in these cases to withhold the treatment until the baseline condition stabilizes and no trends exist, this is not usually possible in clinical situations when an individual comes for treatment.

"Intrasubject" variability is also fraught with difficulty in interpretation. Excessive variability in a patient's response occurs when the patient demonstrates significant fluctuations in the target response, making it difficult to predict future levels of performance. This situation does not provide a stable base for evaluating the effectiveness of treatment. Although many researchers resolve this problem by averaging the data over a predetermined time period so that fluctuations appear less extreme, Kazdin points out that it is more valid to identify or to try and control the reasons for such variability.

Statistical Evaluation

The application of statistical tests in single case research is problematic, and the use of single case designs is controversial according to Kazdin (1979). In many cases, "nonparametric"* statistics must be employed that do not allow as powerful an evaluation of significance as commonly used univariate and multivariate statistics that are usually applied to large group designs. However, statistical tests are available for evaluating the effectiveness of treatment, and these are described by Jones, Vaught, and Reid (1975), Hersen and Barlow (1976), and Kazdin (1979). Recently, Hubbard and Resch (1980) developed a new analysis of variance design which eliminates methodological problems due to training effects in multi-session biofeedback studies.

Issues in Therapy Analogue Research

Although it would be desirable if clinical research studied the effectiveness of biofeedback therapy under conditions which replicate the clinical therapeutic situation, it is often impractical to carry out such research. Kazdin (1979) pointed out some of the problems in attempting to do controlled clinical research. There may not be a sufficient number of patients with the same problem within a certain time-span to meet the demands of an adequate experimental design. For this reason, clinical biofeedback research has often been conducted with few subjects or on a single case basis. Administrative problems in various clinics and institutions limit the possibility of applied research and may, in fact, discourage the researcher. It may be difficult to obtain sufficient therapists who are willing to perform procedures in accordance with the rigors of experimental design. Most important of all, there is the ethical consideration of placing patients who come in for help on a waiting list and withholding treatment.

A "therapy analogue research" study involves the application of therapeutic treatments that are applied to subjects (who are not actual patients) for problems that are similar to actual clinical situations that usually are not as severe or as complex. Such research allows the experimenter greater control than would be possible if conducting research in an actual clinical setting with real patients. For example, a greater number of subjects would be available for treatment. This would increase the validity of the findings obtained and increase the possibility of using powerful statistical techniques to analyze the data. In addition, well-controlled procedures are easier for other experimenters to replicate. Thus it is more likely that knowledge will advance because of the ease with which similar studies can be conducted.

There are certain problems, however, with analogue studies with

*Nonparametric statistics are used when the data are not normally (i.e., normal curve) distributed.

respect to the degree of generalization possible from laboratory results to clinical situations. Kazdin (1979) believed that analogue research can be a useful research technique that has much to offer, although it certainly would be desirable whenever possible to do research under actual clinical conditions. One of the issues in analogue studies discussed by Kazdin is the choice of the clinical problem by which therapeutic intervention is evaluated. Bernstein and Paul (1971) criticized the selection of certain problems (e.g., small animal phobias in college students) as a standard against which to judge the effectiveness of various therapies. The generalization of such mild fear or anxiety to actual clinical phobias is questionable. It appears that much of the previous research has failed to take into account the effects of social desirability and social approval which may have motivated subjects to exhibit behaviors markedly in contrast to their subjective reports.

Characteristics of the sample population are also an important factor. Much of the analogue research has been done with college students because of the convenience of using volunteers who obtain research credit for their participation. The fact that college students, as a population, may differ markedly from the individuals seen in clinical practice must be considered. The greater the degree of discrepancy, the less likely it is that results obtained with college students have any bearing on clinical situations.

Another important variable is the choice of therapist. Often therapy analogue research studies have employed less experienced therapists who may be graduate students with little or no previous clinical experience (pseudotherapists). It is desirable wherever possible to use experienced therapists who are knowledgeable in the technique in order to increase the generalizability* of the experimental results.

Although there are many weaknesses in analogue research, Kazdin makes the interesting point that college students are often less motivated than actual patients in obtaining positive results from the treatment. (College students are often less motivated than patients because they do not feel a need to change.) If a treatment technique can cause measurable change in behavior of college students (who are participating for credit and not personally invested in the resolution of a problem), then the likelihood is greater that patients, who may be more motivated, will show significant improvement. It may be that the use

---

*In psychological research, the term "generalizability" is used to refer to how well experimental findings can be used to explain clinical phenomena.

of college students (although they are unlike actual patients) may enhance the validity of positive results because of the low probability of success. As Kazdin points out, laboratory analogue research should not be ruled out as a method of assessing the effectiveness of various types of treatment.

In conclusion, there is a need for well-conducted, well-controlled, and well-designed research to evaluate the effectiveness of clinical biofeedback techniques. Much of the research undertaken to date has suffered from inadequacies, many of which have been outlined in this chapter. Although it is difficult to conduct adequate research in this area because of the complexities involved, therapists and students should not be discouraged from attempting such research. Clinicians should endeavor to collect data in a systematic manner in their particular settings. Only by being as *systematic* and as *objective* as possible will biofeedback therapists contribute to the growth, development and knowledge of biofeedback. Through such efforts, effective clinical application of biofeedback techniques will be enhanced greatly. Because of the unique factors involved in biofeedback treatment, the therapist has an excellent opportunity to provide effective treatment for a variety of human problems and also obtain and transmit data regarding the effectiveness of particular biofeedback techniques.

REFERENCES

Bergin A: The evaluation of therapeutic outcomes, in Bergin A, Garfield S (eds): *Handbook of Psychotherapy and Behavior Change.* New York, Wiley, 1971, p. 217.

Bernstein D, Paul G: Some comments on therapy analogue research with small animal phobias. J Behav Ther 2: 225, 1971.

Campbell D, Stanley J: *Experimental and Quasi-experimental Designs for Research.* Chicago, Rand-McNally, 1966.

Carlson J, Feld J: Incentives and locus of control in frontal EMG training. Proceedings of the Biofeedback Society of America 9th Annual Metting, 1978.

Cautela J: Covert conditioning, in Jacobs A, Sachs L (eds): *The Psychology of Private Events.* New York, Academic Press, 1971, p. 112.

Chassan J: *Research Design in Clinical Psychology and Psychiatry.* New York, Appleton, 1967.

Dukes W: N=1. Psychol Bull 64: 74, 1955.

Frank J: The present status of outcome studies. J Consult Clin Psychol 47: 310, 1979.

Hersen M, Barlow D: *Single Case Experimental Designs.* New York, Pergamon, 1976.

Holliday J, Munz D: EMG feedback training and changes in locus of control. Proceedings of the Biofeedback Society of America 9th Annual Meeting, 1978.

Hubbard D, Resch W: A new analysis of variance design with application to biofeedback studies. Proceedings of the 11th Meeting of Biofeedback Society of America, 1980.

Jones R, Vaught R, Reid J: Time series analysis as a substitute for single subject analysis of variance designs, in Patterson et al (eds): *Behavior Change, 1974.* Chicago, Aldine, 1975, p. 164.

Kazdin A: Methodological and interpretive problems of single case experimental designs. J Consult Clin Psychol 46: 629, 1979.

Kiesler D: Experimental designs in psychotherapy research, in Bergin A, Garfield S (eds): *Handbook of Psychotherapy and Behavior Change.* New York, Wiley, 1971, p. 36.

Lazarus A, Davison G: Clinical innovation in research and practice, in Bergin A, Garfield S (eds): *Handbook of Psychotherapy and Behavior Change.* New York, Wiley, 1971, p. 196.

Mahoney M: Experimental methods and outcome evaluation. J Consult Clin Psychol 46: 660, 1979.

Paul G: Behavior modification research: design and tactics, in Franks C (ed): *Behavior Therapy: Appraisal and Status.* New York, McGraw-Hill, 1969.

Rotter J: Some problems and misconceptions related to the construct of internal versus external control of reinforcement. J Consult Clin Psychol 43: 56, 1975.

Schwartz G: Research and feedback in clinical practice, in Basmajian J (ed): *Biofeedback-Principles and Practice for Clinicians.* Baltimore, Williams and Wilkins, 1979, p. 274.

Shontz F: *Research Methods in Personality.* New York, Appleton, 1965.

Truax C, Carkhuff R: *Toward Effective Counseling and Psychotherapy.* Chicago, Aldine, 1967.

Whitehorn J, Betz B: *Effective Psychotherapy with the Schizophrenic Patient.* New York, Aronson, 1975.

Yates A: *Behavior Therapy.* New York, Wiley, 1970.

23

The Clinical Application of Biofeedback

THIS CHAPTER is devoted to examination and illustration of issues concerning the clinical application of biofeedback techniques. Biofeedback therapy is currently utilized by individuals in a number of health service disciplines. An outline of clinical practice will be described which appears to be typical of the standardized therapeutic approach used by doctoral level practitioners, especially in the fields of psychology and behavioral medicine. The outline may not reflect other types of clinical application (including the use of biofeedback training by paraprofessionals and/or technicians under the supervision of a licensed professional). The clinical perspective adopted in this text is medical in nature and broader than is usually needed to function adequately in some situations where biofeedback has been applied. Therefore, although the following procedures may not be applicable to individuals utilizing feedback techniques for rehabilitation, as opposed to therapy, they may serve as a general model of acceptable clinical practice.

Outline of Clinical Procedures

Certain standardized procedures have been widely adopted by clinicians engaged primarily in therapy. Procedures at first were verbally transmitted at conferences and workshops across the country; however, recently attempts have been made to standardize them in texts concerning the clinical use of biofeedback (e.g., Basmajian, 1979). Fair (1979) concentrated on various therapeutic strategies when using biofeedback. He emphasized the importance of the initial biofeedback session. Because of the scanty knowledge in the professional and lay community regarding biofeedback, it is important that biofeedback therapists take the time to introduce the potential patient adequately to the theory and methodology of biofeedback. Many new biofeedback therapists have had difficulty with their first few patients because they have tried to engage immediately in feedback training without properly orienting the patient. There is a natural eagerness which appears to be part of learning how to use biofeedback effectively in a clinical setting. This eagerness may create impatience among inexperienced biofeedback therapists. The wish to demonstrate to patients the effectiveness of biofeedback can be compelling. Once one has learned to manipulate instrumentation appropriately, it may be difficult to remember that the emphasis should always be on the interaction between therapist and patient and not entirely on sophisticated equipment and methodology.

Many clinicians have found it useful to have brochures describing biofeedback treatment. Such information is useful to referral sources who can transmit necessary data to potential patients prior to their first session. This kind of literature helps to allay uncertainties or fears and reduce prejudices harbored by patients who have little knowledge of biofeedback or of what will be expected of them. It is also important that patients receive information regarding the extent to which psychophysiological factors contribute to the etiology of their symptom(s). Patients coming for treatment may know little about their bodily functioning. It is not unusual for biofeedback therapists to be confronted by anxious or frankly hostile patients who do not understand why they have been referred for psychological treatment. (This is especially true if the patient has a physiological problem and is being referred to a nonmedical professional, such as a psychologist.) Frequently, the referring physician has insufficient knowledge concerning biofeedback to explain thoroughly the reasons for the referral. The biofeedback therapist, therefore, has to be sensitive to the needs of the patient and carefully reassure those individuals who fear that referral for biofeedback indicates they are suffering from a "mental illness" or that they are "crazy" or that their symptoms are all in their head. Although detailed explanations are necessary for individuals suffering from complex psychophysiological disorders, a brief explanation of the autonomic nervous system often provides enough data to help the patient feel more comfortable with the prospect of biofeedback treatment. Such explanations in themselves have a therapeutic effect which is often not realized by therapists and is frequently taken for granted. Many patients are grateful for having their symptoms explained, and they then may be stimulated to find out more about how their body functions in order to understand themselves better and increase their independence in health areas.

Since the primary objective of biofeedback treatment is the development of self-regulation, the more the patient acquires self-knowledge,

the more positive he will feel about changing his behavior and attitudes. Thus, the patient gains knowledge about himself in order to
acquire greater self-control through biofeedback procedures.

There is a danger that the enthusiastic biofeedback therapist may
make exaggerated claims for the efficacy of the treatment. Caution
should be exercised especially in the initial stages of treatment. The
patient should be informed of the probability of success for his particular problem or symptom. It is not uncommon for biofeedback therapists to receive referrals on disorders they have not treated before. If
this occurs, patients should be informed of this fact before they are
allowed to begin therapy and be given the opportunity to select a
professional who has had experience in using biofeedback for their
particular symptom or problem. Biofeedback therapists, of course,
must eventually treat problems they have not encountered; however,
the patient should be informed of this fact.

Enthusiasm and a positive attitude towards one's professional en-
deavors increases the probability of success in all forms of psychological intervention; however, caution and restraint must be exercised.

Although therapists may begin the initial session with a thorough
assessment of the patient's history and an exploration of prior forms
of treatment, it appears that it is more important in biofeedback to give
an explanation of what will take place. The patient then will have the
opportunity to decline further treatment. Once this information has
been given and the patient appears to understand why he has been
referred for biofeedback and how biofeedback can help him, the next
important step is a thorough analysis of the patient's background.

Depending on the nature of the patient's initial response, an extended session or two initial sessions may be necessary before treatment actually begins. Standardized questionnaires are helpful in
allowing the patient to report information about his medical and/or
psychological background thus allowing more time for questions and
insuring that the patient understands the psychophysiological aspects
of his problem. Several questionnaires have been found to be useful
in providing necessary information prior to engaging in biofeedback
treatment. For example, for nonmedical practitioners the Life History
Questionnaire (Lazarus, 1971) offers a detailed format which provides
information regarding the patient's psychosocial background. Questionnaires developed by researchers to assess medical histories are
also generally available and provide useful information on past and
present physiological problems. The combination of a behavioral
questionnaire and a medically oriented questionnaire adequately sur-

vey the background information and should be employed regularly by biofeedback therapists. Specific questionnaires have also been developed by biofeedback clinicians to assess particular issues related to the presenting symptoms. These assessment devices are usually used throughout the treatment to evaluate progress, thus they are similar to the behavioral assessment that will be described later in this chapter.

Relaxation Training

As previously noted, biofeedback is rarely used in isolation from other techniques. One of the important adjuncts is progressive relaxation training. A review of deep muscle relaxation exercises has already been presented (see Chap. 3). Other examples are cited by Bernstein and Borcovec (1973), Goldfried and Davison (1976), and Fair (1979). In addition to relaxation techniques, autogenic training, hypnosis, and meditation have also been successfully combined with biofeedback.

Depending on the nature of the problem, the initial biofeedback session can be devoted to training the patient in relaxation skills. It is useful for the patient to have a method of following the relaxation procedure precisely as it has been presented in the clinic at least for the first few weeks of treatment. Therefore, individuals often are given a cassette tape of the standardized relaxation method used by their therapist. Individuals without access to a tape recorder are provided with a written transcript of the exercise. They are instructed to practice two or three times a day during the entire treatment program with each relaxation session lasting approximately 20 to 30 minutes. More frequent daily practice may be required for individuals suffering from severe states of tension or complicated psychophysiological stress-related disorders.

Behavioral Monitoring

In addition to relaxation methods, the patient should also be exposed to systematic self-monitoring procedures, and this should be explained to the patient. Self-monitoring is an important procedure which enables the therapist to gain an accurate understanding of the extent of the problem as well as noting the patient's progress throughout treatment. The subjective data obtained through self-monitoring are used by clinicians as one of the primary dependent variables with which to assess the effectiveness of treatment. Standardized self-monitoring forms are often used which improve the patient's compliance and increase the accuracy of the data obtained.

With self-monitoring, the patient is forced to take an active role in the course of his own treatment. The therapist must stress the fact that the patient is a prime agent in modifying the symptom. The therapist's main role is actually that of a facilitator or trainer. Since the patient has the responsibility of following through on the therapist's instructions, it must be understood that accurate record keeping is essential for treatment. The therapist has the responsibility of insisting that the patient keep careful records and follow through with home practice on the various methods demonstrated. If the therapist allows the patient to keep inaccurate records, the overall effectiveness of the program will be affected seriously. Some therapists have adopted procedures to insure that accurate record keeping is carried out by the patient. As noted in Chapter 19, resistant patients often fail to maintain adequate records of their symptoms between sessions, thereby thwarting treatment. If the resistance cannot be successully resolved through traditional therapeutic maneuvers, patients can be assessed a small fee for failure to provide adequate records or, in extreme cases, the treatment may be terminated for patients who do not follow through with the steps in the agreed upon therapy contract.

The therapist must be flexible and must exercise caution in utilizing such techniques, however. In certain cases, it might be more beneficial to provide therapy at a particular time than for the therapist to have accurate records about what occurred to the patient since the last session. This is especially true in cases where the therapeutic relationship is weak because of the patient's lack of trust or inability to form interpersonal relationships. It would also be highly unethical for a therapist to turn a patient away from treatment when the patient was displaying intense conflicts or an exacerbation of symptoms (e.g., depression). Overall, however, the importance of self-monitoring cannot be overemphasized. It is a key element of treatment and a skill which enables the patient to continue treating himself long after therapy has terminated. Self-monitoring is more than an assessment technique, it teaches self-control which enhances the patient's ability to regulate his responses to stress in the future.

Baseline Physiological Data

Before biofeedback treatment can actually begin, baseline physiological data must be obtained. At least two baseline sessions, and preferably three to five, are undertaken before beginning the actual treatment program. Such procedures insure that an accurate assessment of the patient's physiological status is obtained and appropriate controls for the influence of extraneous variables have been included. Thus, a patient who is suffering from a situational stress problem (e.g., work-related problem) may demonstrate significantly high levels of physiological stress as measured by the biofeedback instrument if the baseline session is held at that time. Therefore, the baseline data obtained would be an overestimate of his usual degree of physiological dysfunction. Subsequent treatment sessions would then appear to be more successful than they might otherwise be. Often baselines can be taken either before or after the relaxation training has begun. Usually the biofeedback treatment is not begun for several weeks until after the patient has learned to relax and to monitor his presenting symptoms and adequate baseline measurements have been obtained.

An important factor in obtaining baseline measurements involves the placement of the biofeedback sensors and the type of biofeedback measurement employed. Fair (1979) recommends using EMG baseline data from three areas of the body, electrothermal information from the nondominant hand, and skin conductance from the palmar surface of the dominant hand. His rationale for using three types of physiological measures instead of one or two is related to the fact that individuals differ in their expression of tension through the somatic system. It is important, therefore, to determine which physiological response is a symptomatic indicator of stress, i.e., the patient demonstrates poor physiological control. Usually EMG and skin temperature data are sufficient in the majority of cases. Even if the patient has a specific symptom, such as migraine, it is important to obtain data on more than one physiological variable. Often migraine patients do not demonstrate problems in terms of their peripheral vascular functioning; some patients may, in fact, present disturbances of frontalis muscle tension or of other physiological responses.

EMG Electrode Placement in Baseline Assessment

In obtaining EMG baselines, many authors state that EMG forehead or frontalis muscle data can be used as a general measure of the patient's overall level of muscular tension. Goldstein (1972) recommends it as one of the best areas for initial biofeedback training. Recent evidence, however, suggests that the frontalis muscle may not be an adequate measure of general anxiety, and therefore should not automatically be assumed to be the best muscle site for all patients (Alexander, 1975; Suarez, Kohlenberg, and Pagano, 1979). Many clinicians have employed feedback from the forearm extensor muscle, initially, to demonstrate biofeedback principles to the patient. In certain cases, the use of the forearm muscle may be desirable because placing electrodes on the patient's forehead is uncomfortable and causes undue anxiety or embarrassment for the new patient. Individuals with verbalized or unconscious anxiety regarding attachment to an electronic instrument may often display paniclike reactions to having their heads "wired up" in this fashion. In addition, many people are familiar with how tension feels in the arm but are not familiar with tension in the forehead muscle (except for individuals with muscle tension headaches). After individuals have become familiar with biofeedback treatment and are more comfortable with electrode placement, then frontalis muscle training may be more appropriate. It must be noted, however, that there is insufficient evidence at this time to indicate a preference of one muscle placement over another; especially in the initial phase of the biofeedback treatment.

Baseline Variability

The variability of baselines must be recognized by biofeedback therapists. This is especially important with certain physiologic variables such as skin temperature which is known to vary considerably even within the same patient over a short period of time. Sdorow et al. (1979) and Packer and Selekman (1977) believe that the subjects' hand temperatures show an upward drift from the initial reading obtained during a baseline session. Therefore, therapists and researchers who use relatively short baseline periods may be allowing a regression effect to take place so that their findings are biased in favor of temperature increasing. Therefore, it is important that therapists allow sufficient time for baseline measurements to be taken in skin temperature biofeedback, otherwise positive changes may be due solely to the fact that skin temperature increases in the majority of individuals, regardless of what is presented to them. Some authors recommend using certain criteria to establish a baseline for skin temperature. Taub and Emurian (1976) used a criteria of no temperature change greater than 0.25°F for four consecutive 65-second intervals. Surwit, Shapiro, and Feld (1976) used a criteria of no temperature change greater than 0.2°C in any 4 consecutive minutes, with a minimum of 10 minutes and a maximum of 30 minutes as a criteria for an adequate baseline in their studes. Therefore, it would appear that between 15 to 30 minutes is desirable for obtaining a baseline level of skin temperature in the initial biofeedback session as well as subsequent sessions. Kinsman and Staudenmayer (1978) advocate the use of the analysis of covariance to analyze clinical data in order to eliminate statistical bias. The analysis of covariance may help eliminate the effect of initial differences in baseline measurements between individuals. This is only a relevant procedure in terms of group experimentation, however, and such strenuous statistical procedures do not seem warranted for clinical situations, where treatment is applied to only one individual at a time.

There is evidence that skin temperature variability is independent of the type of disorder the patient may be suffering from, prior to treatment. For example, Trask and Gankel (1979) found that there was no difference between the baseline temperature responses in normal subjects compared with patients suffering from migraine. These authors concluded that the presence of migraine did not result in permanent changes in hand temperature. They also suggested, however, that perhaps changes which did occur were not detectable by the methods used in their study. They also noted that males tended to have higher hand temperatures, lower temperature variability and needed more time to increase their temperature than females. The authors took this to mean that there may be a ceiling effect with respect to males which has to be considered in skin temperature biofeedback. Male patients may seem to be more successful than female patients because of their tendency to obtain higher temperatures according to this one study. Further research is needed in this area before conclusions can be made and before firm recommendations can be given to therapists in regards to the appropriate method of baseline measurement.

Baseline variability is an important factor in EMG biofeedback as well. Malec, Phillips and Sipprelle (1977) concluded that the greater the variability in EMG baseline, the greater the reduction of EMG readings with biofeedback. In this study, the frontalis muscle was used and continuous auditory feedback was given to subjects after the baselines were obtained. Thus, it appears that biofeedback researchers should use baseline standard deviations as well as baseline mean as covariates to control for initial subject differences. Malec et al. warned that failure to control for such variability could result in a Type II error in the interpretation of results. (Type II error means that an erroneous conclusion is made; i.e., the experimental method had no significant effect on a dependent variable.) Kinsman and Staudenmayer (1978) have cautioned biofeedback therapists about the effect of the law of initial values (LIV) on decreases of EMG activity over time. Failure to consider the effects of LIV may bias the results of any experiment or therapy program. LIV refers to the fact that the higher the pretraining baseline level, the greater the decrease of EMG activity over time. This is also an important variable in clinical work as well as experimentation. Therapists should be well aware of the fact that individuals with high pretreatment levels of EMG activity, of necessity, show great reductions in such activities following relaxation procedures in biofeedback training. Such results should not be overinterpreted. Indeed the patient should be encouraged to continue to concentrate on reducing muscle tension to improve his functioning in real-life circumstances. Conversely, individuals with low EMG baselines should not be considered treatment failures if they reduce their EMG levels only slightly over the course of treatment. Treatment success should not be measured in terms of the magnitude of change between baseline and posttreatment EMG levels, but rather the degree of significance of the change when baseline variability is analyzed statistically. Kinsman and Staudenmayer (1978) suggest that baseline data should be used as a covariate and analysis of covariance should be used to assess the significance of treatment.

Psychological and Behavioral Assessment

Prior to beginning biofeedback treatment, it is important that an adequate assessment of physiologic and behavioral data be undertaken. Thus, patients can be screened for those personality and other factors which may affect the results of treatment. Each patient should have a complete psychological test battery consisting of an intelligence test, a neuropsychological screening test, a self-report, the Minnesota Multiphasic Personality Inventory (MMPI), and projective personality tests. In addition, behavioral instruments such as the Fear Survey Schedule (Wolpe, 1973) or the Reinforcement Survey Schedule (Tondo and Cautela, 1974) are used to measure the frequency and intensity of various behavioral symptoms. Furthermore, such questionnaires can be used to obtain data about reinforcing conditions which may be utilized in a behavior therapy program in conjunction with biofeedback. In addition to informing the therapist about potential complications such as resistance or lack of compliance, such evaluations provide information when used as a pretest and subsequently compared to data obtained following treatment (posttest). Thus, the pretest/posttest differences can be used as another measure of treatment success.

Psychological testing can be very useful in determining the efficacy of biofeedback procedures as opposed to other types of psychological or psychiatric intervention. If the patient were found to be suffering from a neurotic disorder, biofeedback treatment may be delayed or postponed until more intensive verbal psychotherapy and/or medication was used to treat this preexisting condition. Individuals referred for biofeedback treatment may be suffering from serious emotional or mental disturbances which should not be overlooked by the biofeedback therapist. Such conditions have to be treated either prior to beginning biofeedback treatment or concurrently with it. At times it may be necessary to refer the patient to another practitioner for traditional psychotherapy if the personality and emotional disturbance is serious. Furthermore, psychological tests can be helpful in cases where legal complications exist and the therapist may be asked to testify on his patient's behalf. Psychological testing can be useful to determine whether or not patients suffering from chronic pain are malingering or hysterical. Such information is useful in cases of chronic low back pain where litigation is involved, and the patient is attempting to receive compensation for psychophysiological damages arising from industrial or other trauma. Biofeedback therapists who are not psychologically trained or do not have an adequate background in psychological testing should work in consultation with a psychiatrist or psychologist (see Chap. 20).

Biofeedback Treatment

The choice of biofeedback instrumentation is usually dependent upon the type of symptom. For example, EMG feedback is indicated with muscle tension headaches while electrothermal or skin temperature feedback is indicated for migraine. If the patient suffers from generalized anxiety with no specific physiological complaint, however, the treatment of choice is often a combination of EMG and electrothermal feedback. There are indications that patients can learn to relax more quickly if given more than one type of physiological feedback. Many clinicians employ both EMG and electrothermal feedback as part of their routine practice. A recent study by Nigl (1978) indicated that bimodal feedback training resulted in greater reductions in both EMG and thermal feedback than feedback from either EMG or electrothermal alone.

Prior to beginning biofeedback treatment many clinicians conduct a stress profile analysis to determine specific psychophysiologic responses correlated with stress for a particular patient. Although stress profiles may vary in complexity, such an analysis basically consists of physiological measurement of various responses, e.g., EMG frontalis, EMG extensor, skin temperature from the digits and/or EDR. Once baselines have been obtained the patient is asked to engage in a stressful mental activity (e.g., serial 7's—counting backward from 700 by 7's). During this the patient's physiological responses are monitored and recorded. Then the patient is requested to relax and further measurements are made during this "recovery" phase. More complicated stress profile analyses have been developed involving measurement of several physiological responses and several types of stress inducement (Budzynski, 1980). Following the pretreatment assessment, actual biofeedback training can begin.

The focus of feedback training regardless of which type of instrument is used should be to teach the individual to develop greater control over his physiological responses. The current sophistication of biofeedback instrumentation affords the therapist an opportunity to effectively condition the patient in a short period of time. EMG and electrothermal units have different levels of sensitivity which can be manipulated progressively in order to teach the patient to develop an increasing control over a specific physiological response. Initially the patient is presented with feedback representing a particular gain setting on the instrument where the patient is functioning at a moderate level of activity. The meter indicates that the patient is at midrange for that particular gain setting. Over time the patient learns to reduce the physiological response so that the meter reading drops to near zero for that scale. At that point the next highest level of sensitivity is employed that will bring the meter reading back up to a moderate level. Therefore, the patient has to relax that much more in order to reduce it once again. This training is continued until either the lowest sensitivity level is reached or the patient reports a significant decrease in symptoms.

During biofeedback training, the goal is to teach the patient to develop an awareness of internal states correlated with deep levels of relaxation. Ultimately, such states will be correlated with physiological control. The biofeedback training is gradually reduced in emphasis as the patient progresses and learns physiological self-control. Near the end of treatment, the electronic feedback is not used at all, but rather the patient is encouraged to concentrate on his own physiological sensations (feedback) to reduce tension and arousal. At this stage, the instrument can still be attached to the patient so that the therapist can monitor the patient's activity; thus the therapist can determine whether the patient can reduce physiological arousal without receiving auditory or visual feedback. The patient thus is gradually weaned from the instrument and taught to rely solely on his physiological sensations to relax. In addition to developing a greater awareness of self, the patient is encouraged to practice the relaxation exercises at home and to begin to transfer the skills to real-life situations including his work setting.

It is helpful to include cognitive strategies such as the use of imagery techniques or positive self-statements which the patient can utilize in situations when it is not possible to engage in a concentrated relaxation procedure. Over time the patient relies more on his own psychophysiological mechanisms of control than becoming dependent on the therapist and the electronic instruments.

Following the successful completion of biofeedback treatment, the patient should arrange followup sessions. It is very important that followup sessions become part of the routine practice of biofeedback therapists, as it is important that the patients continue to monitor their symptoms. In this way the effectiveness of treatment can be measured over a specific time period. The first followup session should probably be scheduled 1 month after the end of treatment and the second, 4 to 6 months later. The same measures that were used at the pretreatment phase should be part of the posttreatment followup. Baseline measurements should be carried out under standardized conditions when treatment begins to insure that the pretest, posttest changes accurately reflect the effects of biofeedback training. The same type of psychological and/or behavioral assessment should be employed at pretest and posttests. Cahn and Cram (1979) reported that changing the method of subjective estimation of symptoms (in this case, headache pain symptoms) created significant differences in the measurement of change. This finding suggests that the use of different forms of assessment could bias the treatment results at followup. The type of assessment must remain constant from the pretreatment session to the followup session.

Illustrative Case

Representative case studies illustrate how biofeedback techniques can be applied to a variety of disorders.

Migraine

A 32-year-old woman, married with three children, was referred by her family physician for biofeedback and relaxation treatment for a 12-year history of migraine. She was taking Fiorinal and frequently needed injections of Prolixin (fluphenazine). She was a medical assistant but not working at the time of treatment. Psychological testing showed her to be an obsessive-compulsive individual with rigidity of thought and constricted emotions. She had great difficulty admitting responsibility for her symptom of pain. She was initially hostile and resistant to consulting a non-medical professional for treatment; she indicated that she did not believe that biofeedback would help her. Both EMG and electro-thermal biofeedback were employed because in addition to the migraine two to three times per week she also had daily tension headaches. Initial baseline EMG measurements from the frontalis muscle showed very high readings and the baseline distal temperature obtained from the middle finger of her nondominant hand averaged below 70°F. She was trained in deep muscle relaxation and autogenic phrases and provided with physiological trend indicators (small strips containing a crystalized cholestoric substance) to monitor her distal temperature several times a day. After the fifth treatment session, the EMG training was discontinued because her tension headaches had disappeared and she was able to relax in the session. Her self-confidence also increased and she began to talk more favorably about the biofeedback treatment. However, it was not until the 20th session that her distal temperature decreased significantly during the session. Subsequently she reported reductions in the severity and frequency of migraine attacks. After the 20th session her migraines had subsided to less than one attack every 3 to 4 weeks.

Treatment progress was enhanced at that point by an incident which occurred in the patient's personal life. She had experienced the death of an infant son several years before and had tried to use cardiopulminary resuscitation or CPR to save the child. She failed, however, and had felt guilty about this incident. Psychological testing and other information indicated that she had not adequately resolved her guilt and was still grieving for the deceased child. Because of her increased confidence following treatment, however, she was able to enroll in a CPR training course. Some weeks after she had successfully learned to control her muscle tension and distal temperature, she was to be tested for a certificate in CPR. The afternoon of the day she was to be tested, the patient developed intense migraine and noticed that the physiological trend indicator showed she was suffering significant vasoconstriction. She went to class without taking medication and was the only individual in her class to successfully pass the CPR test. When she returned home from the class, her headache had disappeared and she noted that the physiological trend indicator showed that her distal temperature had increased to 94.5°F. Thus, she became aware of the correlation between her headache and her anxiety. She became even more successful in subsequent biofeedback sessions, and therapy was terminated after the 25th session. At that point her migraines occurred less than once every 3 months and at a 1-year followup she was still practicing the relaxation exercises each day and reported having only three episodes of migraines in a 12-month period.

Posttreatment psychological testing revealed that this patient's obsessive-compulsive tendencies and her rigidity had decreased substantially. This was confirmed by reports from her husband that her daily routine had been modified significantly. Instead of cleaning and vacuuming the house every day, she only did major cleaning once a week. She was also less rigid in terms of the schedule she imposed on herself and family members. Therefore, it appears that the treatment she received resulted not only in greater physiological control but also in her ability to be more flexible and more open to new experiences and alternative behaviors.

Nigl and Fischer-Williams (1980) indicated that EMG biofeedback resulted in significant improvement of low back pain in several patients.

These individuals were able to control their muscle tension and also reduce their pain symptoms even though they were receiving significant secondary gains from their symptoms at the time they were intially referred. Biofeedback, therefore, may be an effective technique when secondary reinforcement (e.g., high workman's compensation payments, sympathy from relatives, etc.) makes it difficult for patients to be treated successfully with standard techniques.

Sexual Deviation

A 19-year-old male college student was referred for psychotherapy because of a tendency to become sexually aroused by males and an inability to achieve an erection with females. There was no history of homosexual behavior, however. He was the only male in a family of eight children and was the third youngest child. He reported that as a young boy his older sisters often dressed him up as a girl. Later he became sexually stimulated by wearing female clothing although he never allowed himself to continue this habit once he reached adolescence. He became extremely aroused by male classmates and had difficulty preventing an erection from occurring. He had been treated with verbal psychotherapy for approximately 1 year without success prior to the initiation of biofeedback treatment.

He reported masturbating several times a week to homosexual but not heterosexual fantasies. A decision was made to utilize physiologic training to promote changes in mental imagery as well as his attitudes and behavior. An EMG feedback instrument that recorded signals from his forearm extensor muscles was employed in this case. He was shown nude pictures of males and females and asked to fantasize about each individually for 3 to 5 minutes. During each fantasy period an average EMG rating was obtained. The pictures were presented to him in a predetermined random order. His muscle potential was significantly higher when shown pictures of nude females, but remained at the baseline level or below when he was shown nude males. The training, therefore, consisted of the patient's stimulation of an anxiety response in himself while viewing the pictures and fantasizing about nude males. However he attempted to relax and feel comfortable while fantasizing about nude females.

The patient was able to alter his level of physiologic arousal so that he was more relaxed in response to heterosexual fantasies at the end of treatment. The frequency of masturbatory activities involving homosexual fantasies was reduced from an average of five per week to less than one per week; the frequency of heterosexual masturbatory activities increased from an average of less than one to an average of three and a half per week at the end of treatment. Treatment sessions were terminated by the patient following a successful heterosexual experience in which he achieved orgasm during intercourse. At one year followup the patient continued his studies and was achieving satisfactory grades. He reported that he was romantically involved with a woman with whom he had achieved successful intercourse prior to the termination. He also reported his homosexual fantasies had been eliminated.

This treatment result was replicated in two other cases of sexual dysfunction (exhibitionism and transvestism). Laye (1979) presented evidence that the nonspecific effects of biofeedback training can successfully change an individual's sexual orientation. In his study, a patient was given false feedback about his alpha rhythm. He learned to control his sexual desires on that basis alone even though verbal psychotherapy had not been effective previously. Stroebel (1979) suggested that clinicians manipulate the expectancies which biofeedback patients bring with them into the sessions so that it correlates with the level of physiological control that the patient eventually achieves. This will maximize the learning which takes place. It appears that the nonspecific or placebo effects of biofeedback can be beneficial, but they also may create difficulties if these effects are not adequately monitored or assessed by the therapist.

These case studies are presented with the hope of providing an understanding of how biofeedback can be utilized to treat different types of disorders. The results should not be overinterpreted, but rather serve as a model for treatment with similar cases. Biofeedback training offers great potential as a treatment of physiological symptoms and/or disorders which are related to anxiety and tension. The potential misuse is also apparent, however. It is hoped that standards of practice, regulations, and certification of those who engage in biofeedback therapy will be further developed to protect patients who seek or are referred for biofeedback treatment. Thus, the judicious and appropriate use of biofeedback will be insured.

This book was written in part as an answer to the question of why students and practitioners of biofeedback should be familiar with the range of physiological functions and with some aspects of pathology. Various biofeedback techniques are generally carried on for research treatment or both. The two are intertwined. An essential part of modern physiological research is the use of theories, hypotheses, and concepts as tools to guide orderly experimentation. Results lead to modification of the tools and to the rewards of greater understanding. Research and treatment using concepts based on previous experimental and clinical studies have the greatest chance for genuine discovery and successful outcome. Without such preparation, it is frequently an unfocused repetition of previous efforts, or worse, a determined and purposeful course based on mistaken concepts. The more a researcher/clinician achieves a detailed awareness of human physiology and previous discoveries about that physiology (which are really the same thing), the more likely it is that his work will have useful results.

Nonmedical practitioners should be aware of relevant physiological variables in treating a patient's symptom complex. A simplistic or inflexible approach which views biofeedback as merely a matter of applying a specific technique to eliminate a specific symptom (ignoring the natural history of disease) may have grave consequences. This is a serious matter.

A prerequisite to responsible treatment of a human being is a responsible diagnosis. Such a diagnosis not only utilizes all of the reasonably discoverable facts about the present condition of the individual but also considers what is probable about variations in that condition which may occur with time and different treatments. Responsible treatment, in its turn, continuously uses such a diagnosis as a guide in deliberately planned initial and followup stages of action, and in watchfulness for unfavorable developments. Unexpected changes in the patient are reviewed with the diagnostician, whose previous analysis may need modification. None of this can proceed efficiently unless the treating practitioner is familiar with his patient as both a normally and abnormally functioning human being.

As therapists from many disciplines and diverse educational backgrounds adopt biofeedback techniques as a "routine" part of their practices, it is increasingly clear that both research and treatment require detailed physiological knowledge and are impoverished by the lack of it.

Returning to the metaphor of the mirror (see the historical review in the Appendix), those clinicians, unfamiliar with human physiology, may cause the reflection viewed by the patient of his own physiological functioning to be inaccurate. Thus, the patient may develop a distorted image of himself.

Realizing, however, the importance of skillful practice of the art as opposed to theory, the following quotation from the classical encyclopedist, Celsus (25 B.C.–50 A.D.) may be relevant: "Diseases are cured, not by eloquence, but by remedies well and duly applied of which, if any sage with discretion, though he have no tongue, know well the proper usage, he shall become a greater physician than if without practice he ornament well his language."

REFERENCES

Alexander A: An experimental test of assumptions relating to the use of electromyographic biofeedback as a general relaxation training technique. Psychophysiology 6: 656, 1975.

Basmajian J: *Biofeedback-Principles and Practice for Clinicians.* Baltimore, Williams and Wilkins, 1979.

Bernstein D, Borcovec T: *Progressive Muscle Relaxation Training: A Manual for the Helping Professions.* Champaign, Ill., Research Press, 1973.

Budzynski T: Stress profile analysis. Seminar at 11th Annual Meeting of Biofeedback Society of America, 1980.

Cahn T, Cram J: Changing measurement instrument at followup: a potential source of error. Proceedings of the Biofeedback Society of America 10th Annual Meeting, 1979.

Fair P: Biofeedback strategies in psychotherapy, in Basmajian J (ed): *Biofeedback-Principles and Practice for Clinicians.* Baltimore, Williams and Wilkins, 1979, p. 112.

Goldfried M, Davison G: *Clinical Behavior Therapy.* New York, Holt, 1976.

Goldstein I: Electromyography: a measure of skeletal muscle response, in Greenfield N, Steinbach A (eds): *Handbook of Psychophysiology.* New York, Holt, 1972.

Kinsman R, Staudenmayer H: Baseline levels in muscle relaxation training. Biofeedback Self-Regul 3: 97, 1978.

Laye R: Use of biofeedback training specifically for its nonspecific effects: a case study of sexual exhibition. Proceedings of the Biofeedback Society of America 10th Annual Meeting, 1979.

Lazarus A: *Behavior Therapy and Beyond.* New York, McGraw-Hill, 1971.

Malec J, Phillips A, Sipprelle C: Baseline variability as a predictor of EMG biofeedback performance. Unpublished manuscript, University of South Dakota, 1977.

Nigl A: Feedback complexity and its effects on reducing blood pressure and pulse rate. Proceedings of International Congress of Applied Psychology, Munich, Germany, 1978.

Nigl A, Fischer-Williams M: EMG treatment of chronic low back strain. Psychosomatics, in press, 1980.

Packer L, Selekman W: Within subjects controls in EMG and thermal biofeedback training: the baseline effect. Proceedings of the Biofeedback Society of America 8th Annual Meeting, 1977.

Sdorow L, Palladino J, Cook J, Lashinsky D, Mazzocco P, Williams C: Length of baseline and skin temperature training. Proceedings of the Biofeedback Society of America 10th Annual Meeting, 1979.

Stroebel C: The application of biofeedback techniques in psychiatry and behavioral medicine. Psychiatric Opin 16: 13, 1979.

Suarez A, Kohlenberg R, Pagano R: Is EMG activity from the frontalis site a good measure of general bodily tension in clinical populations. Proceedings of the Biofeedback Society of America 10th Annual Meeting, 1979.

Surwit R, Shapiro D, Feld J: Digital temperature autoregulation and associated cardiovascular changes. Psychophysiology 13: 242, 1976.

Taub E, Emurian C: Feedback-aided self-regulation of skin temperature with a single feedback locus. Biofeedback Self-Regul 1: 147, 1976.

Tondo T, Cautela J: Assessment of imagery in covert reinforcement. Psychol Rep 34: 131, 1974.

Trask T, Gankel W: Baseline response patterns of hand temperature in normal and migraine subjects. Proceedings of the Biofeedback Society of America, 10th Annual Meeting, 1979.

Wolpe J: *The Practice of Behavior Therapy.* New York, Pergamon, 1973.

Historical Appendix—Integration of Biofeedback and the Major Psychological Theories

THE METAPHOR of the mirror used in assisting patients to look at themselves through the art of psychotherapy is familiar to mental health professionals. What the patients "see" in this mirror is purported to be a picture of their "inner lives" with their underlying structures and conflicts.

In the physical examination and measurement of a patient's current physiological status tests such as electrocardiograms, x-rays, and computed axial tomography (CAT) scanning, provide a picture of their outer lives (the habitus). This information can be shared with them through the reflections of the clinician functioning as the metaphorical mirror.

Biofeedback is a technique which may serve to reflect both the inner and outer habitus simultaneously. The fusion of the mind and body (psyche and soma) in this way may be unique in its approach.

The basic premise that underlies this treatment is that biofeedback is a form of psychologic therapy and, as such, its origins are the same as those of other psychological, psychiatric, and medical approaches to the patient.

The concept of mind and body as a duality has run as a thread through the history of medicine up to the second half of the 20th century. Since an appreciation is required of what fusion between the mind and body entails, it is advisable to review the concept of this duality as it developed over the centuries, from the humanistic (psyche) and mechanistic (soma) schools of thought.

From Antiquity to the Time of Freud

Primitive tribes shared the belief that a supernatural agency which they did not understand was involved in the occurrence of natural events. In this belief system (animistic), these agencies were represented as either good or evil spirits. Associated with this was man's drive for understanding coupled with a desire to control his environment. Thus, belief in magic evolved which presumed to control events through supernatural means.

A connection between deviation from health and supernatural powers can be found in the *Bible* in the Book of Daniel with the case of psychosis in the story of Nebuchadnezzar (Nabu-kudurri-usur). The divinity's curse was visited upon an individual for punishment in the form of illness.

In the 5th century B.C., the first shift from this type of thought with belief in the supernatural occurred. Men sought control over mental illness and other diseases through a more rational and logical approach.

The ancient Greeks may be considered the first of those who espoused this "humanism" and thus are known as humanists. It was in the *Corpus Hippo-*

489

craticum, a collection of approximately 70 books, that this idea was initially developed. Hippocrates of Kos (460–377 B.C.), a contemporary of Plato and Aristotle, was a "healer" as opposed to a priest (shaman). His *Corpus* is a cornerstone of observation, for example, in his description of malaria. Hippocrates' theories are naturalistic and based on the physician Empedocles' four elements.

The macrocosm (external environment) according to Empedocles (490–430 B.C.) was thought to consist of four elements: fire, earth, air, and water, with a corresponding attribute for each: hot, dry, cold, and wet. In the microcosm (internal environment) of men, there existed four humors, where blood was associated with the first pairing (fire-hot), black bile the second, yellow bile the third, and mucus the fourth. A man's character was thought to be determined from these physical characteristics (perhaps the first expressed attempt at fusion of body and mind). It was believed that an excess of blood caused a man to be plethoric, excess black bile to be melancholic, yellow bile to be choleric or bilious, and mucus to be phlegmatic. Melancholy for example seemed to have its origin from the "black bile" (Greek: *melaina chole*) associated with malaria. Thus, health and character development were viewed as the result of this balance (The Golden Mean). Conversely, paucity, excess, or disequilibrium was seen to lead to ill health.

Claudius Galen of Pergamum (130–200 A.D.), a physician and researcher, is credited with formulating the first theory of characterology, or behavior of the body habitus. The plethoric individual was thought to be obese, robust, possessing increased "appetite" and sexual drive (the hypomanic constellation). The melancholic was regarded as being dark, hirsute, with a slow pulse, increased "appetite," compulsive, and exhibiting decreased interest in sex (the depressive constellation). The choleric or bilious individual was seen as flaccid, obese, glabrous, slow, with decreased interest in sexual activities and decreased intelligence but "good natured" (the retarded). Last, the phlegmatic character was seen as thin, dry, energetic, and with an increased interest in sexual drives (the compulsive).

The Greeks also described five disorders with psychologic bases for disturbed behavior. Epilepsia included all types of seizures; mania included the various states of excitation; melancholia, all retarded states including depression; paranoia was regarded as ignorance, thought disorder, and defect of logic; and phrenitis (inflammation of the brain) or obnubilation (Greek: *nubilos*, "cloud"), "clouded" consciousness.

Aesculapius (Ασκληπιος, or Asklepios), according to myth the son of Apollo and the mortal Coronis, was believed to have been instructed in the healing art by his sun-god father. He was, however, most likely an historical figure (similar to the physician, architect of pyramids, and prime minister of ancient Egypt, Imhotep), and the disciples ("sons") of Aesculapius became the military surgeons during that era, where a ritual sprang up around them which was practiced in a temple setting. The Greek temples therefore attracted a number of seriously ill patients among the suppliants. Dreams were important in the temple ritual and this may have constituted the first time that dreams were systematically used for therapy via an immediate transference cure (the "incubation sleep" of Osler 1921, p. 3). Votive tablets were left in the temples as testimonials of healing.

A dualism of humanism and naturalism emerged in the Greek thought. Plato propounded the philosophy of idealism, wherein an idea, for example the concept of truth, is promulgated as the ideal goal. His pupil, Aristotle, however, propounded elements consistent with naturalism, believing that it was foolish to observe the transient and imperfect phenomenon as a goal in itself. Hippocratic thinking was based on clinical observation and the four humors and was diametrically opposed to Aristotle's view.

Aurelius Cornelius Celsus (25 B.C.–50 A.D.), author of *De Re Medica,* was probably an encyclopedist rather than a physician. His methodology was Hippocratic, i.e., humoral, and in his classification of mental disease *insania* was noted to be both acute and chronic. In this classification, phrenitis became delirium, while epilepsy and melancholia remained unchanged. A fourth category, *lethargos,* is described which included such states as narcolepsy, cataplexy, the encephalitic condition, and apoplexia which described strokes. In his system, cephalalgia accounted for acute and chronic head pains, such as with tension headache and migraine. Another category involved thought content versus perceptual content and dealt with the emotional and affective elements seen in manic-depressive psychosis or hebephrenia. This description served to identify one who was "foolish in spirit." Also described is an acute disorder called "cardiacus" or an anxiety state which constitutes the first mention of a psychosomatic disorder.

Galen is said to have written over 500 medical works and was physician to the Roman emperor Marcus Aurelius. He dissected the 5th cranial nerve in the pig and discovered the innervation of the larynx. His system of medicine was based on teleology, the belief that anatomy was structured for a purpose. He believed that one must exert will power to behave appropriately, and that it was helpful to meet periodically with a trusted friend with whom one could bare one's soul and gain support. He was the first classical writer to describe a format for psychotherapy.

From the 3rd century to the 11th century (the early Middle Ages), there was much political instability and upheaval in Western Europe so that science regressed and beliefs reverted to superstition and magic. The eastern portion of the Roman Empire (Byzantine culture) survived and became custodian of classical learning, making, however, few original contributions.

The Byzantines, in their turn, passed on the scientific medical tradition to the Arabic speaking world. One of the great Arabic physicians was Al-Razi or, more commonly, Rhazes (865–925 A.D.), named from his birthplace Rai. Later, another Arabian physician, the Persian Ibn Sina, better known as Avicenna (980–1037 A.D.), wrote *al-Qanan* (*The Canon*). This was regarded throughout the Middle Ages as an infallible oracle. Avicenna also described a cause for melancholia in the frustrated love of a son for his mother, made familiar in the famous painting. He noted that "love sickness" tends to increase the pulse rate.

A third "Arabian," Moses ben Maimon (Maimonides, 1135–1204 A.D.), is known as the father of psychosomatic medicine. He was a Jew from Cordoba in Spain who became chief physician in Cairo. He postulated that a disturbance in the psyche could lead to disturbance in the body.

The continuation of superstition and the belief in demons (demonology) in the West can be traced from early times. The Romans fostered local superstition with the belief that ignorance among subject populations led to more facile rule. They also believed that stress fostered aggression and that illiteracy reawakened or maintained belief in animism. Demonology and cults of saints arose, dynamically perhaps, representing projections of good and evil parental images in a less sophisticated age.

The Church tried to control the rise in demonology. In 305 A.D., the second Synod stated that magicians were in collusion with the devil. In 429 A.D., Theodosius's *Codex* stated that practicing magic was a criminal act. These beliefs persisted, however.

In 1487, two Dominican monks, Johann Sprenger and Heinrich Kramer, wrote *Malleus Maleficarum (Witches' Hammer)*. The book included (1) a "proof" of the existence and activities of witches; (2) a collection of case histories; and (3) a legal and procedural manual to show that confession was important in ridding the soul of the demon but that first the body must be made uncomfortable for the demons. A person suspected of possession must first experience exorcism and then be made subject to torture. The monks believed that only the soul could be saved from the demon; the flesh was contaminated and must be burned. Since mental illness was regarded as a manifestation of the devil, it was to be punished.

In the 17th century, "witches," demonics, and the mentally ill were still being tortured and burned, and tens of thousands died. Humanism, however, had a resurgence with the coming of the Renaissance, and physicians began to bring psychiatry back into the fold of medicine, with leaders such as Agrippa (Cornelius Agrippa von Nettesheim, 1486–1535), Paracelsus (Theophrastus Bombastus von Hohenheim, 1493–1541), and Wier (Johann Weyer 1515–1588).

Weyer, who was protected from the Inquisitors by Duke William of Cleves, studied mental illness intensively and pioneered descriptive psychiatry. His book, *De Praestigiis Daemonum (Concerning the Power of Demons,* 1563), went through six editions in 20 years, and was considered a turning point in the treatment of insanity. James I of England tried unsuccessfully to refute this important book. Weyer stated that physicians should care for the mentally ill and that legal safeguards should be proposed.

Felix Platter (1536–1614), in his book *Praxis Medica.* (1625), proposed that the mind works through sensors. He suggested that there were both external and internal sensors; internal sensors included judgment, memory, and imagination and were controlled by consciousness. He proposed a theory of consciousness, noting that disturbances of consciousness lead to behavioral problems. Problems with external sensors were felt to be caused by intoxicants, such as poisons, and mental shock, for example grief, rage, or falling in love. Causes of internal problems of consciousness included head trauma, blood congestion, old age, and constitutional factors.

Juan Luis Vives (1492–1540), a humanist philosopher, wrote *De Anima et Vita* (*Life and the Spirit,* or, *Soul and Mind* in 1538). In this psychological treatise he proposed that the meaning of the soul was a theological question and the concern of the clergy, but that its functioning was in the province of the physician. Through introspection he arrived at the concept of linkage of thought through chains of word symbols; thus, the association of ideas (generally attributed to Hobbes, see below). His thoughts are similar to those which were proposed to explain preconscious ideation or subliminal perception. From his study of emotions he concluded that *Omnes affectus ex amore* ("all emotions are due to love"). This resembles some of the statements of the libido theory. He also felt that love was mixed with hate; a precursor to the modern narcissistic and egoistic theories.

The 17th century was a century of transition and heralded the age of mechanism, which carried on the tradition of the naturalists. The essentialist philosophers, Hobbes, Locke, Berkeley, and Hume, however, were opposed to the mechanists and it is from this school that vitalism developed. The vitalist school became the sounding board for the humanists, so that the humanism-mechanism psyche-soma duality was perpetuated. For the vitalists, mental events were thought to result from the senses. Although they acknowledged that man was a "machine," they felt that "there is something more." This "something more" was given the name *élan vital.* The vitalists (humanists) became "functionalists" and the mechanists (naturalists) became "somatists" with an organic approach.

A third school of thought, the clinical, dealt with anatomic observations, and this group is represented by Thomas Willis, who described the Circle of Willis, and Thomas Sydenham, the "Hippocrates of English medicine."

A fourth trend, that of medicolegal (forensic) psychiatry, was exemplified by Paolo Zachia, court physician to the popes. He pioneered formal inquiry into how to deal with those who commit crimes but are insane.

Thomas Willis was concerned with the care of the mentally ill. He himself had been imprisoned for debt but was able to leave debtor's prison by becoming a guard; he reported how admission to view those inmates of the Convent of Bethlehem (Bedlam) was sold to the curious so that they could see the madmen ("fools' party").

Several commissions in France were created to reform the hospitals during the 18th century. Phillippe Pinel (1745–1826), in Paris became chief physician of the Bicêtre and later of the Salpêtrière (originally a munitions or saltpeter factory). In 1793, Pinel "struck off the chains" of the patients in the Bicêtre and wrote a text concerning more humane methods of restraining the mentally ill. Although he was thought to be a counterrevolutionary, what came to be known as "Pinel's bequest" was based on his experiences in that hospital. This advocated humane surroundings for the mentally ill, "moral treatment," and the principle that the hospital rather than the prison should be the place for the treatment of these individuals. He advocated that the hospital was the proper place for research and study of mental diseases. Keeping progress notes, Pinel believed in observation, collection, and organization of descriptive psychiatry so as to improve diagnosis. His "bequest" also dealt with training and suggested that young physicians should come to the hospital to be attached to preceptors as the clinical model.

William Cullen (1712–1790), of the mechanist school proposed the organic theory of mental illness in his book *First Lives of the Practice of Physick* (1777). He felt that a central nervous system coordinates the body; this led to the neuronal theory. For him mental deviation was secondary to a disturbance in the central nervous system and he therefore termed these disturbances "neuroses." He believed nervous energy was similar to electrical energy and felt that the brain was governed by this.

George Ernst Stahl (1660–1734) proposed the first theory of combustion, the phlogistin theory. This developed directly from the theory of *élan vital,* i.e., that there was something "more" in a material which made it combustible, and he is viewed as the founder of the school of vitalism. He believed that physicians should examine the nature of the passions which he felt were causative of disease (psychosomatic orientation). Later, Esquirol (Jean Étienne Dominique Esquirol, 1772–1840), a student of Pinel's became interested in descriptive psychiatry, phenomenology, and nosology. He differentiated between hallucinations and delusions.

In the latter part of the 18th century, a Viennese physician, Franz Anton Mesmer (1734–1815), who belonged to no particular school of thought gained prominence with his theory concerning "animal magnetism." He believed that astrological influences affected health and disease and were governed by a magnetic fluid which existed as kind of a transmitter of planetary force. His graduation thesis *De Planetarum Influxu* (*On the Influence of Planets,* 1766) suggested that individuals with power could influence the balance of nature by manipulating this substance. In his work with trance-induction he used light or object fixation.

In Paris, Mesmer became successful doing group seminars using mass hypnosis and inducing hysterical convulsions. The Royal Commission of 1784, however, investigated Mesmer through the auspices of the French Academy of Science, and the report by Antoine Laurent Lavoisier, Joseph Ignace Guillotin, and Benjamin Franklin condemned the practice. In thereafter took hypnosis approximately 100 years to recover (see Chap. 3).

In the first half of the 19th century, Bertrand in France artificially induced sleep. Others such as James Braid (1795–1860), the Scottish surgeon, began to use anesthetics, although both of them disclaimed animal magnetism. Braid introduced the term *hypnosis* and medicine began to reconsider this subject with the French physician, Étienne Georget (1795–1828). Jean Martin Charcot (1825–1893), Chief of the Salpêtrière, began systematic studies on hypnosis and once Charcot became interested in it, the subject became legitimate. Other schools, such as the one at Nancy, where Ambrose-August Liebault (1823–1904) and Hippolyte-Marie Bernheim (1840–1919) practiced in the second half of the 19th century, also studied hypnosis and noted that, the suggestibility induced, develops from a psychological state.

In the 19th century in France, Pinel's bequest continued. Deterioration of behavior and habit patterns were seen to result from a deterioration in an organic structure and demonstrations with alcoholic degeneration were used as examples. This was an important concept for the mechanists who saw deterioration as being familiar, constitutional, and genetic. Deterioration was felt to account for patients' aberrant behaviors. It did not, however, take the concept of psychology into account, which was supported by the vitalists.

Humanists who traveled to England from France began to state that restraints should not be used on the insane. This was first appreciated by the Tuke(s) (William, Henry, Samuel) and later Robert Gardiner Hill (1811–1878) at the Lincoln Asylum, and John Conolly (1794–1866) at Hanwell who concurred in this.

Edward Parker Charlesworth (1782–1853) had first established the use of restraints only through a physician's order which must be documented (charted). Hill continued this practice and sought to abolish the "straight jacket." Conolly stated dramatically that restraints were not needed.

Next in the mechanist school, Wilhelm Griesinger (1817–1868), a Swiss-German physiologist, introduced the term *ego*. He was a somaticist who believed that brain function was secondary to brain anatomy.

Other important German thinkers included Ernst Brücke (1819–1892) of the Helmholtz School of Physiology who carried on with the mechanistic somatic tradition. It was in his laboratory that Freud worked on neurologic staining techniques as a medical student.

Gustav Theodor Fechner (1801–1887), a German romantic and mystic, first emphasized the importance of human cycles and rhythms. The Berlin otolaryngologist Wilhelm Fliess (1858–1928), and early confidant of Freud's, expanded this thought, and it is from his teachings that the pseudoscience of biorhythms developed. Biorhythms are not to be confused with the legitimate concerns of chronopsychophysiology.

Bachhofen, another of the fathers of psychosomatic medicine, developed psychiatric insights in the vitalist school. Richard von Krafft-Ebing (1840–1902), also in this group, wrote his textbook *Psychopathia Sexualis* (1886) dealing with dramatic case reports of criminal sexual psychopathology. He first described paralysis agitans as a result of syphilis. Pierre Janet (1859–1947), a contemporary of Freud, initiated controversy on the question of nonconscious thoughts being "subconscious" or "unconscious." Ewald Hecker (1843–1909) as an astute observer of symptoms first described catatonia and hebephrenia. Emil Kraepelin (1856–1926) of Munich, who coined the term *dementia praecox* (about 1896), initiated the classification system of mental disorders used up to the time of World War II.

From Freud to the Present

In his outlined paper "Project for a Scientific Psychology," Sigmund Freud (1856–1939), a Viennese physician, attempted to integrate behavior and physiology using mathematical and neurological notations. Although this had been the cherished endeavor of those interested in mental health research for hundreds of years, Freud was one of the first to approach the problem as a neurologist trying to understand human behavior (1966).

Because Freud's background contained elements of both the humanistic and the mechanistic schools, a paper directed towards this synthesis does not appear to be such an unusual project. Freud, however, lacked the information to begin to correlate parts of behavior to specific neuronal activity. His frustration with the elusiveness of his questions made him abandon this line of research, and thereafter he focused on dynamic and intrapsychic approaches to the understanding of behavior. He never waivered, however, in his belief that ultimately behavior would be understood in terms of neurophysiology and biochemistry.

Contemporaries of Freud, including Janet, Kraepelin, Viodler, Morton Prince, Poe, and others, perpetuated the long-standing concept of the duality of body and mind regarding behavior. Thus, the humanists looked "within" and attempted to understand things beyond explaining, with apperception of ways which lent themselves less easily to critical scrutiny. (This might be expressed in modern terminology as the nonverbal, right-hemisphere appreciation of reality.) The mechanists, on the other hand, noted precise observations and pondered the workings of an object or system so that they could express them in mathematical or chemicophysical formuli to avoid having "to do with" those less concretely known aspects of human life.

Although Freud evolved from a mechanistic beginning, his interests and literary background, as well as his observations of behavior, thrust him into a more humanistic application and frame of reference. Thus, the inheritance that comes from psychoanalysis follows along these lines and therefore has been open from its inception to the criticism of lack of "hard scientific data."

Mechanists such as Kraepelin and Bleuler treated patients with schizophrenia. Krafft-Ebing of the Allgemeine Krankenhaus in Vienna described his observations of sexual behavior in a very different form than Freud's. Certain followers of Freud, although founding their own schools of thought, still adhered to the humanistic approach. Alfred Adler emphasized the concept of "masculine protest" and the role of social service and community psychiatry, while Carl Jung developed the ideas of the collective unconscious and archetypes.

The mechanists, as exemplifed by the biologic school of behavior, emphasized the organicity of the disease process as evidenced objectively. Formal study of psychosomatic medicine dates from this time, as well as the constitutional theories of body habitus and behavior such as propounded by Sheldon, Kretschmer, and Lombroso.

One of the main thrusts of the mechanists was in the field of behaviorism. Behavior was observed and ways were sought to modify it through conscious choice utilizing a system of rewards and punishments while past history and underlying causes were considered less important. These behaviorists included Watson, Meyer, Weiss, Hunter, Lashley, Tollman, Hull, and Skinner (see Chap. 1). They were content to allow the alleged underpinnings of behavior to remain relatively unexplained in the so-called black box.

Analysts from the humanistic camp approached the workings of the black box with the tool of intuition, rather than with the electron microscope or the microelectrode. Desires and drives were subjected to analytic thought by the artist rather than by the scientist.

Mechanists in the past approached patients as "subjects" and a certain doctor-patient dependency resulted. To the humanists, however, the patient is an "individual with independent life," with whom they attempt to work in a mutual fashion, although exceptions to each category are well known. No one school of thought, however, is free standing nor did it originate from only one camp.

Diverse schools of thought are derived from humanistic or mechanistic philosophies which superficially reveal little of their origins from the parent school. Analytic thought in the humanist school, for example, has contributed to the development of Gestalt psychology through theorists such as Hartheimer, Koffka, Keller and Lewin as well as Fritz Perls. The Gestaltists flow rather loosely from the original 19th century German concept of Gestalt in which the human being was seen as being more than the sum of his parts. This is the "something extra" which was called the *élan vital* by the vitalists.

Another marker distinguishing the mechanists from the humanists lies in the phenomenon of measurement. In order that measurement of any given property be meaningful, a comparison is required between the measurement recorded "here and now" and the past state prior to the measurement. To the analytical schools of thought, this comparison is believed to be not merely intriguing but basically revealing. Thus, forays into a patient's past in order to understand the present, form an integral part of the structure of analysis.

Mechanistic trends were represented by organic and somatic considerations, and vitalistic trends by the psychological or functional concerns. A mechanistic trend can be observed in five fields. The first was the microbiological, with Fleming's discovery of penicillin in 1938 as an example. The second was the biochemical field with the discovery of the role of vitamins, the elucidation of phenylketonuria and enzyme deficiencies in mental diseases, and many endocrinologic studies. The third approach, the genetic, comprised studies of schizophrenic twins, constitutional factors, and the ideas involving bipolar depression. The fourth neuroanamatomical track emphasized the importance of the reticular activating system (RAS), basal ganglia, and limbic system for drives such as sexuality and aggression, the search for food, the level of consciousness, and sleep. Last, neurophysiology leads to functional measurements such as the electroencephalogram (EEG) developed by Berger in 1929, dream analysis, motivation, the expectancy wave, intentionality, and biofeedback.

Organic therapies followed from these, including Manfred Siegel's development of insulin coma, and later the use of metrazol by Von Minduna in 1933. Electroconvulsive therapy with Cerletti in 1935 and prefrontal lobotomy pioneered by Moniz (1932) and by Fulton and Jacobson (1936) continued this tradition. Psychopharmacology developed out of this school beginning first with opiates, halabor, bromides (1826), chloral hydrate (1870), barbiturates (1920s), rauwolfia compounds (1930), and the era with phenothiazine major tranquilizers introduced by Jean Delay in 1952. This was followed by the introduction of minor tranquilizers (anxiolytics) in the 1950s, antidepressants, and Lithium.

Psychological lines of development from the humanistic school are characterized by the development of ego psychology with such contributors as Anna Freud, Heintz Hartman, Erik Erikson, Renee Spitz, with cognitive studies in learning theory. Learning theory (stimulus-response) owes its inheritance to Descartes, passed down through Pavlov, Bekterev, and Thorndyke. Watson, Skinner, and Searles are also of this camp. Gestaltists, including Goldstein, Berner, Hagen, and Fritz Perls, come from this school as well. Personality theory as it has developed over the last 50 years is exemplified by Carl Rogers with "self-theory," George A. Kelly with "personal construct theory," and Dollard and Miller with "social learning theory."

One of the first serious efforts to combine these four threads is exampled by the work of the synchronists, such as Judd Marmor, Jules Masserman, Dollard (mentioned above), Lazarus, and Kurt Lewin. Communication theory and information theory combined in general systems theory as proposed by Sandler, Joffee, and Peter Freud, and feedback loops became quite important. Mathematical models, such as cybernetics of Weiner, and personal theories, including group therapies, milieu and family therapies, also developed here.

This led to intrapersonal theory; in other words, the understanding of man from the subjective point of view from which existential psychology evolved. Authors such as Carl Jospurs, Biswanger, Buper, Meechie, Hydiger, Sartre, and Lang have been important here. This moved the therapist into the patient/empathic-response encounter.

The first uniquely American development was that of preventive psychiatry. Here, Adolph Meyer at Johns Hopkins Hospital in Boston and Clifford Beers who wrote *The Mind That Found Itself*, in 1908, were important.

Much thought has been devoted to the controversy over the relative importance of "nurture versus nature." Does the innate or the genetic predisposition of the organism or individual have more influence on his ultimate behavior, than the environment which shapes the person? Humanists reflected the latter, while mechanists emphasized the former.

From the mid-19th century to the mid-20th century, humanistic thought tended to separate psychiatry from the rest of medicine, so that isolation and mutual misunderstanding developed. With the recent gains in knowledge from the mechanistic (biologic) school, however, psychiatry has again come closer to the rest of medicine. Recent discoveries in psychopharmacology, cerebral metabolism, and genetics have provided evidence for the biological basis of psychological events.

A vast array of psychotropic drugs proliferated during the 1950s and 1960s. Studies of identical twins have thrown light on the genetics of schizophrenia; the biogenic amine hypotheses emerged; and data regarding neurotransmitters and receptors sensitive to dopamine accumulated. One of the most far-reaching concepts now conceives of the brain as a "gland." The fact that the brain not only processes information, but also elaborates and secretes neurohormones, neurotransmitters, and neuromodulators has revolutionized concepts and captured the imagination of workers both in and outside the field of neuropsychiatry. The characterization of the endogenous opiate substances —the endorphins and enkephalins—and the discovery of benzodiazepine-like receptor sites has played a significant part in this. Many researchers coming from the mechanistic school believe that we may now begin to understand human behavior not only on a neuronal but on a molecular or submolecular basis, to a greater extent than Freud and others ever thought possible.

Much effort has been directed toward shortening the process in therapies derived from humanistic approaches or to broadening the base of possible application. Examples of this are group psychotherapy, focal psychotherapy, and brief psychotherapy, as well as direct analysis. Also treatment methods which have relied less on the speculative end of the unconscious and which dealt more with the "executive" or ego functions have developed in response to these problems. The emphasis on ego psychology and the work of Heinz Hartman and Eric Erickson are examples of these approaches. Recent extensions of analytic thought have resulted in increased interest and new discoveries in narcissism and borderline states especially by Otto Kernberg and Heinz Kohut.

Marmor (1980) encapsulates the past half century of psychologic thought through the concept of successive revolutions of which he describes four: the analytic, behavioristic, human potential and transpersonal. The number of "isms" is legion and each has contributed its own interpretation to the understanding of human behavior. It is beyond the scope of this book to do more than mention the better known of these. A testing out of their origins however, suggests that they may ultimately derive from one or other of the two camps. Thus, clinicians are faced with a question of whether the nurture/nature conflict, learned versus heredity, acquired or environmental, need ever be resolved. Must it be one or the other, or can a synthesis or fusion be a realistic goal to pursue? The authors of this volume believe that biofeedback should be examined as representing or contributing to "fusion" of these belief systems. As described in the chapter on the history of the development of biofeedback, the behaviorists of the mechanistic school are initially responsible and should be given the credit for its origin. No technique need remain the property of any one group, however, when it could usefully serve many schools.

If one combines, for example, the instrumentation and techniques of biofeedback, with an emphasis on understanding how the condition may have arisen psychologically, and second how the patient can alter his condition through learning and understanding, thereby becoming more independent as an entity or self, then one can see the possibility of this fusion. The individual is given the responsibility for his own healing through utilization of the "mirror" which is provided by the therapist.

The traditional approach often associated with the mechanists is modified in the biofeedback therapy view of the participant/consumer. Biofeedback "monitors" can include television screens, and the patient's own basic metabolic and biological functions can be represented through electronic interpretation and symbols for the patient to observe and utilize. The patient then makes use of this information by discovering that he can alter these findings through *conscious thought*. This is an important concept. Functions that were previously relegated to the "autonomic nervous system" and therefore to "limbo" as regards modification, are now known to be modifiable by the patient.

In the "age of anxiety," control of the self is sought after not only for interaction with others but also for self-gratification. If one understands that one can improve the quality of life while resolving unpleasant sensations or symptoms, then one is more motivated to put forth effort in that direction. If this is coupled with insight into the sources of these unpleasant elements, then truly a synthesis of the two schools of thought can be achieved. The pathology of the individual is described by the mechanistic method in terms of how it happens, while through the humanistic approach one attempts to understand why it arose. The origin of the mechanism takes no precedence over the mechanism itself, nor vice versa, for both are important.

It is unlikely and indeed undesirable, that biofeedback should represent the only means by which this fusion is possible. However, it is one way in which to think of this fusion, and one way in which to apply it for the benefit of both the patient and the clinician.

Biofeedback is a useful tool for clinicians by uniting, at least in part, energies traditionally devoted to separating the two main streams of thought in matters of health. To lose perspective of its limitations however, could generate yet another "cult" or school of thought. Biofeedback is not a panacea, but it does seem to have demonstrable usefulness in a variety of conditions and disorders.

Biofeedback techniques are not so complex as to mystify or frustrate those who wish to utilize them. However, its practice requires the degree of sophistication one would expect for dealing with serious problems and difficulties. Its usefulness is intriguing in terms of this postulated fusion while satisfying those pragmatic clinicians who have been displeased with theories and speculations in the past.

Much remains to be explored in biofeedback's potential use, and in ascertaining its limitations. It did not arise *de novo* but as a result of an evolutionary process which began more than a millennium ago. Though its full impact is as yet unknown, at least a beginning has been made.

REFERENCES

Arieti S (ed): *American Handbook of Psychiatry* I–VI. New York, Basic Books, 1974.

Bonaparte M: *Female Sexuality.* New York, International Universities Press, 1953.

Boring E: *A History of Experimental Psychology.* New York, Appleton, 1950.

Brenner C: *An Elementary Textbook of Psychoanalysis.* New York, International Universities Press, 1955.

Cameron N: *Personality Development and Psychopathology.* Boston, Houghton Mifflin, 1963.

Erickson E: *Childhood and Society.* New York, Norton, 1950.

Fenichel O: *The Psychoanalytic Theory of Neurosis.* New York, Norton, 1945.

Fordham F: *An Introduction to Jung's Psychology.* Harmondsworth, Penguin Books, 1953.

Frankl V: *Man's Search for Meaning.* New York, Simon & Schuster, 1963.

Freedman A, Kaplan H, Sadock B (eds): *Comprehensive Textbook of Psychiatry/III.* Baltimore, Williams & Wilkins, 1980.

Freud A: *The Writings of Anna Freud—The Ego and the Mechanisms of Defense.* New York, International Universities Press, 1966.

Freud S: *The Standard Edition of the Complete Psychological Works of Sigmund Freud, Vol I—Pre-psycho-analytic Publications and Unpublished Drafts*—"Project for a Scientific Psychology." London, The Hogarth Press, 1966.

Fromm E: *The Art of Loving.* New York, Harper & Row, 1956.

Gedo J, Goldberg A: *Models of the Mind.* Chicago, The University of Chicago Press, 1973.

Jones E: *The Life and Work of Sigmund Freud.* New York, Basic Books, 1961.

Jung C: *Abstracts of the Collected Works of C. G. Jones—A Guide to the Collected Works,* Rockville, Princeton University Press, Information Planning Associates, 1976.

Lidz T: *The Person.* New York, Basic Books, 1968.

Marmor J: Recent trends in psychotherapy. Am J Psychiatr 137:4, 1980.

May R: *Love and Will.* New York, Norton, 1969.

May R: *Man's Search for Himself.* New York, Norton, 1953.

Maltz M: *Psycho-Cybernetics.* New York, Simon & Schuster, 1960.

Menninger K: *The Human Mind.* New York, Alfred A. Knopf, 1961.

Osler W: *The Evolution of Modern Medicine.* New Haven, Yale University Press, 1921, pp. 3–15.

Paul I: *Letters to Simon.* New York, International Universities Press, 1973.

Roazen P: *Freud and His Followers.* New York, Alfred A. Knopf, 1971.

Schafer R: *A New Language for Psychoanalysis.* New Haven, Yale University Press, 1976.

Stekel W: *Interpretation of Dreams.* New York, Liveright, 1943.

Van der Post L: *Jung and the Story of Our Time.* New York, Vintage Books, 1975.

Waelder R: *Basic Theory of Psychoanalysis.* New York, International Universities Press, 1960.

Index